Lecture Notes in Business Information Processing   562

Series Editors

Wil van der Aalst , *RWTH Aachen University, Aachen, Germany*
Sudha Ram , *University of Arizona, Tucson, USA*
Michael Rosemann , *Queensland University of Technology, Brisbane, Australia*
Clemens Szyperski, *Microsoft Research, Redmond, USA*
Giancarlo Guizzardi , *University of Twente, Enschede, The Netherlands*

AF173764

LNBIP reports state-of-the-art results in areas related to business information systems and industrial application software development – timely, at a high level, and in both printed and electronic form.

The type of material published includes

- Proceedings (published in time for the respective event)
- Postproceedings (consisting of thoroughly revised and/or extended final papers)
- Other edited monographs (such as, for example, project reports or invited volumes)
- Tutorials (coherently integrated collections of lectures given at advanced courses, seminars, schools, etc.)
- Award-winning or exceptional theses

LNBIP is abstracted/indexed in DBLP, EI and Scopus. LNBIP volumes are also submitted for the inclusion in ISI Proceedings.

Rébecca Deneckère · Marite Kirikova ·
Janis Grabis

Editors

Perspectives in Business Informatics Research

24th International Conference, BIR 2025
Riga, Latvia, September 17–19, 2025
Proceedings

 Springer

Editors
Rébecca Deneckère 🆔
Université Paris 1 Panthéon-Sorbonne
Paris, France

Marite Kirikova 🆔
Riga Technical University
Riga, Latvia

Janis Grabis 🆔
Riga Technical University
Riga, Latvia

ISSN 1865-1348   ISSN 1865-1356 (electronic)
Lecture Notes in Business Information Processing
ISBN 978-3-032-04374-0   ISBN 978-3-032-04375-7 (eBook)
https://doi.org/10.1007/978-3-032-04375-7

© The Editor(s) (if applicable) and The Author(s), under exclusive license
to Springer Nature Switzerland AG 2026

This work is subject to copyright. All rights are solely and exclusively licensed by the Publisher, whether the whole or part of the material is concerned, specifically the rights of translation, reprinting, reuse of illustrations, recitation, broadcasting, reproduction on microfilms or in any other physical way, and transmission or information storage and retrieval, electronic adaptation, computer software, or by similar or dissimilar methodology now known or hereafter developed.
The use of general descriptive names, registered names, trademarks, service marks, etc. in this publication does not imply, even in the absence of a specific statement, that such names are exempt from the relevant protective laws and regulations and therefore free for general use.
The publisher, the authors and the editors are safe to assume that the advice and information in this book are believed to be true and accurate at the date of publication. Neither the publisher nor the authors or the editors give a warranty, expressed or implied, with respect to the material contained herein or for any errors or omissions that may have been made. The publisher remains neutral with regard to jurisdictional claims in published maps and institutional affiliations.

This Springer imprint is published by the registered company Springer Nature Switzerland AG
The registered company address is: Gewerbestrasse 11, 6330 Cham, Switzerland

If disposing of this product, please recycle the paper.

Preface

This book constitutes the proceedings of the 24th International Conference on Perspectives in Business Informatics Research, BIR 2025. The conference was held September 17–19, 2025, in Riga, Latvia.

The scope of BIR covers the thematic areas of business informatics and its research. The main theme of the BIR 2025 conference, "Bridging Knowledge, Process, and Systems for Responsible Digital Transformation", explores how the integration of knowledge management, process modeling, and information systems can drive responsible digital transformation in business environments. This theme highlights the need to create digital solutions that not only foster innovation and efficiency but also promote ethical, sustainable, and inclusive practices. By focusing on the convergence of business knowledge, process optimization, and emerging technologies such as AI and smart systems, the conference addressed how these elements could be harmonized to support organizations in navigating the challenges of digital transformation. It explored how responsible business practices, aligned with both technological advancements and societal needs, could shape the future of business informatics, ensuring that digital transformations are both innovative and ethically grounded.

The 18 full papers and 5 short papers presented in the book were carefully reviewed and selected from a total of 61 submissions to the main conference. Out of all the submissions, three were desk rejected. All the remaining submissions were single-blind reviewed by at least three Program Committee (PC) members. The acceptance rate for full papers was 29.5%. The authors received recommendations to be improve in the camera-ready versions.

The contributions in the volume have been organized in the following topical sections: Intelligent Decision-Making and Data Management, Human Factors and Well-Being in Digital Systems, Enterprise Architecture, Modeling and Governing Adaptive Organizations, Process Mining and Digital Twin Perspectives, LLM and Generative AI in Modeling & Engineering, Smart Life, and Structuring Security for Responsible Digital Systems.

The conference program started with the workshops. The main conference included sessions on keynotes and research papers. The three invited keynote presentations were: "*Modeling Business Systems and Processes with SysML v2*" by Gerd Wagner, Brandenburg University of Technology, Cottbus, Germany; "*Why Post-Merger IS Integration Often Fails and How To Fix It*", by Ksenija Lace, Riga Technical University, Latvia; and "*Responsible Business Innovation in the Age of Digital Transformation and Generative AI*" by Kurt Sandkuhl, University of Rostock, Germany.

We want to thank all authors who submitted their work to BIR 2025, and also the PC members for their hard work in reviewing the submitted papers. We thank Springer for the swift communication and support of the proceedings production process and EasyChair.org for providing an excellent conference management system. Finally, we want to thank all the Organization Committee members and the student volunteers for their valuable assistance.

September 2025

Rébecca Deneckère
Marite Kirikova
Janis Grabis

Organization

Steering Commitee

Robert Buchmann	Babeş-Bolyai University of Cluj-Napoca, Romania
Rimantas Butleris	Kaunas Technical University, Lithuania
Peter Forbrig	Rostock University, Germany
Björn Johansson	Linköping University, Sweden
Dimitris Karagiannis	University of Vienna, Austria
Mārite Kirikova	Riga Technical University, Latvia
Andrzej Kobylinski	Warsaw School of Economics, Poland
Raimundas Matulevicius	University of Tartu, Estonia
Lina Nemuraite	Kaunas Technical University, Lithuania
Jyrki Nummenmaa	University of Tampere, Finland
Malgorzata Pankowska	University of Economics in Katowice, Poland
Andrea Polini	University of Camerino, Italy
Václav Repa	Prague University of Economics and Business, Czech Republic
Kurt Sandkuhl	Rostock University, Germany
Janis Stirna	Stockholm University, Sweden
Benkt Wangler	University of Skövde, Sweden

General Chair

Jānis Grabis	Riga Technical University, Latvia

Program Chairs

Rébecca Deneckère	Université Paris 1 Panthéon-Sorbonne, France
Mārite Kirikova	Riga Technical University, Latvia

Workshop Chairs

Ruta Pirta	Riga Technical University, Latvia
Martin Henkel	Stockholm University, Sweden

DC Chairs

Tarmo Robal   Tallinn University of Technology, Estonia
Diana Kalibatiene   Vilnius Gediminas Technical University,
       Lithuania
Jānis Grundspeņkis   Riga Technical University, Latvia

Program Committee

Gundars Alksnis   Riga Technical University, Latvia
Said Asar   Institut Mines-Télécom Business School, France
Peter Bellstrom   Karlstad University, Sweden
Nourhene Ben Rabah   University of Paris 1 Panthéon-Sorbonne, France
Tomas Bruckner   Prague University of Economics and Business,
       Czech Republic
Robert Andrei Buchmann   Babeş-Bolyai University of Cluj-Napoca,
       Romania
Witold Chmielarz   University of Warsaw, Poland
Chiara Di Francescomarino   University of Trento, Italy
Hector Florez   Universidad Distrital Francisco José de Caldas,
       Colombia
Ana-Maria Ghiran   Babeş-Bolyai University of Cluj-Napoca,
       Romania
Mubashar Iqbal   University of Tartu, Estonia
Amin Jalali   Stockholm University, Sweden
Bjorn Johansson   Linköping University, Sweden
Michael Alexander Kaufmann   Lucerne University of Applied Sciences and Arts,
       Switzerland
Shahrzad Khayatbashi   Linköping University, Sweden
Janne J. Korhonen   Aalto University, Finland
John Krogstie   Norwegian University of Science and Technology,
       Norway
Michael Le Luc   Mälardalen University, Sweden
Moonkun Lee   Chonbuk National University, South Korea
Sotirios Liaskos   York University, Canada
Francisco J. Lopez-Pellicer   University of Zaragoza, Spain
Audrone   LupeikieneVilnius University, Lithuania
Bartosz Marcinkowski   University of Gdańsk, Poland
Raimundas Matulevicius   Tartu University, Estonia
Andreas Martin   FHNW, Switzerland
Andrea Morichetta   University of Camerino, Italy

Laila Niedrite	University of Latvia, Latvia
Jyrki Nummenmaa	Tampere University, Finland
Jacob Norbjerg	Copenhagen Business School, Denmark
Victoria Paulsson	Linköping University, Sweden
Małgorzata Pankowska	University of Economics in Katowice, Poland
Jens Myrup Pedersen	Aalborg University, Denmark
Pierluigi Plebani	Politecnico di Milano, Italy
Paul Pocatilu	Bucharest University of Economic Studies, Romania
Andrea Polini	University of Camerino, Italy
Henderik A. Proper	TU Wien, Austria
Barbara Re	University of Camerino, Italy
Vaclav Repa	Prague University of Economics and Business, Czechia
Ben Roelens	Open University, The Netherlands
Kurt Sandkuhl	University of Rostock, Germany
Manuel A. Serrano	UCLM, Spain
Hanlie Smuts	University of Pretoria, South Africa
Janis Stirna	Stockholm University, Sweden
Frantisek Sudzina	Aalborg University, Denmark
Ann Svensson	University West, Sweden
Torben Tambo	Aarhus University, Denmark
Pedro Valderas	Universitat Politècnica de València, Spain
Filip Vencovsky	Prague University of Economics and Business, Czech Republic
Gianluigi Viscusi	Linköping University, Sweden
Gatis Vitols	Latvia University of Life Sciences and Technologies, Latvia
Hans Weigand	Tilburg University, the Netherlands
Anna Wingkvist	Linnaeus University, Sweden
Hans Friedrich Witschel	FHNW, Switzerland
Jelena Zdravkovic	Stockholm University, Sweden
Alfred Zimmermann	Reutlingen University, Germany
Iryna Zolotaryova	Simon Kuznets Kharkiv National University of Economics, Ukraine

Sub-reviewers

Amirhossein Gharaie	Linköping University, Sweden
Ijeoma Ekeh	University of Tartu, Estonia
Faiz Ali Shah	University of Tartu, Estonia

Marcus Triller	University of Rostock, Germany
Aritha Kumarasinghe	Riga Technical University, Latvia
Theodore Kindong	Linköping University, Sweden
Ben Hellmanzik	University of Rostock, Germany
Vjatšeslav Antipenko	University of Tartu, Estonia
Benjamin Nast	University of Rostock, Germany
Morena Barboni	University of Camerino, Italy
Filippo Lampa	University of Camerino, Italy

Abstracts of Keynote Talks

Why Post-Merger IS Integration Often Fails and How To Fix It

Ksenija Lace ⓘ

Riga Technical University, Faculty of Computer Science and Information Technology,
6A Kipsalas Street, Riga, LV-1048 Latvia
ksenija.lace@rtu.lv

Abstract. Mergers and acquisitions (M&A) are powerful mechanisms for accelerating business transformation—but their true value is only realized after the deal, during post-merger integration. In this critical phase, information system (IS) integration becomes the backbone for unifying operations, enabling synergy, and driving organizational alignment.

Despite well-designed technical plans, IS integration efforts often fail. Why? Because integration isn't just technical—it's deeply human. Misalignment between business and IT, limited experience in M&A contexts, and a lack of engagement from key stakeholders are common barriers to success.

This keynote addresses how to design post-merger IS integration strategies that bridge these gaps. Drawing from over 20 years of experience and six real-world acquisitions, it will explore a structured approach to post-merger IS integration that goes beyond technology. It will consider how to accelerate integration timelines, reduce friction between teams, and ensure that strategic goals drive technical decisions.

The keynote presents a methodology designed to guide practitioners—especially those without prior M&A experience—on selecting systems to integrate and choosing optimal integration strategies. It combines system architecture thinking with human-centric design, incorporating motivation theory and gamification elements to improve engagement and cross-functional collaboration.

The talk will bring together practice and theory to offer a practical, actionable path forward for organizations undergoing M&A. Attendees will gain a deeper understanding of how to approach post-merger IS integration not just as a technical challenge, but as a transformational opportunity—where information systems serve as the nervous system of the newly formed enterprise.

In an era where the pace of acquisitions continues to rise, successful IS integration is no longer optional—it is a primary strategic objective.

Keywords. Mergers & Acquisitions · Post-merger integration · Information systems · Game-based learning · Instructional Design · Serious Games

Responsible Business Innovation in the Age of Digital Transformation and Generative AI

Kurt Sandkuhl

University of Rostock, Institute of Computer Science, Albert-Einstein-Str. 22, 18057 Rostock, Germany
kurt.sandkuhl@uni-rostock.de

Business innovation, and also organizational innovation, emerges in different shapes that are often enabled by new technologies, frequently involve changes in business models, and always affect some organizational stakeholders. These innovations can take the form of new products or services, redesigned processes, novel ways of engaging customers, or entirely new revenue models.

Responsible business innovation has to start from understanding the effects of the planned innovation - on the organization, on individuals, and on the business. This includes not only intended benefits, such as increased efficiency or new value propositions, but also unintended consequences, such as job displacement, privacy concerns, or ethical dilemmas. Designing the required organizational and technological implementation to prevent or at least minimize unwanted properties is a crucial step. Controlling the behavior of these innovations is necessary to avoid deviations that might lead to reputational damage or social harm. Thus, responsible business innovation is a multidimensional endeavor that integrates technological competence, stakeholder responsibility, and adaptive governance.

The talk focuses on responsible business innovation in the context of digital transformation and artificial intelligence (AI). Digital transformation refers to the profound rethinking of how organizations use technology, people, and processes to fundamentally change business performance. It typically includes digitalization—the use of digital technologies to change a business model and provide new revenue and value-producing opportunities. Digital transformation often demands the adoption of agile ways of working, the development of new skills among employees, and new approaches to customer engagement. Research on digital transformation has produced a rich set of insights into best practices, such as leadership commitment, cross-functional collaboration, continuous learning, and a clear digital strategy.

For artificial intelligence, and in particular generative AI, such best practice recommendations are still sparse. This is largely due to the short innovation cycles, the unpredictability of technological capabilities, and the rapid pace at which AI models evolve. Generative AI presents new opportunities and risks, particularly in areas such as content creation, decision automation, and human-computer interaction. As a result, organizations face challenges not only in adopting these technologies but also in ensuring they are used in a responsible and transparent manner.

Starting from different types of business innovation—such as product, process, service, and business model innovation—the talk investigates important features of responsible business innovation in the age of AI and explores the potential to learn from digital transformation to navigate the challenges posed by AI adoption.

Modeling Business Systems and Processes with SysML v2

Gerd Wagner 🆔

Brandenburg University of Technology, Cottbus, Germany
gwagner57@gmail.com

The *Systems Modeling Language* version 2 (SysML v2) is built upon 20 years of experience with using SysML v1 and 30 years of experience with using UML for (software) systems modeling, as well as 20 years of experience with using BPMN for process modeling. While SysML v1 is based on UML, SysML v2 is based on the *Kernel Modeling Language* (KerML), which improves UML and BPMN by (1) providing a new approach to behavior and process modeling that is integrated with state structure modeling, and (2) defining a formal semantics.

In UML and SysML v1, behavior/process modeling has been scattered among three different modeling languages (Activity Diagrams, State Machines, Sequence Diagrams), which overlap with each other without being conceptually and semantically integrated. SysML v2 allows modeling behavior and processes in a declarative integrated way based on the concepts of *actions* and *successions*. Actions can be atomic or composite, and they can be instantaneous or sustained.

In the same way as objects are *classified* by object types, actions are classified by *action types*. Both object types and action types may have attributes as well as various kinds of properties, including *action(-valued) properties*. For an object representing a system or a part of a system, the values of its action properties represent the actions performed by it. When an action type has action properties, the action type is composite and its action properties, also called *action steps*, represent its component actions. Action steps are sequenced with the help of *successions*, which are connection properties expressing temporal precedence.

Unlike the Petri-Net-style operational semantics of BPMN and Activity Diagrams, SysML v2 has a Tarski-style model-theoretic semantics where the elements of a (process) model are considered as predicates that are interpreted by mapping them to relations over a universe consisting of individuals representing data values, objects and actions.

With its logical approach, SysML v2 can be considered as a *declarative* process modeling language. We discuss this by comparing it to the logic-based workflow management approach DECLARE. While most declarative business process modeling languages are limited to control flow concepts and do not consider state structure modeling, SysML v2 is a full-fledged systems modeling language that integrates process modeling with state structure modeling.

However, one major deficiency of SysML v2 is its lack of an event modeling concept. In the talk, we consider possibilities how to add events and event flows to SysML v2.

Contents

Intelligent Decision-Making and Data Management

Storage Management in Short-Term Electricity Trading: An Experimental Analysis with Genetic Algorithms

Mathis Wilz[(⊠)] [iD] and Richard Lackes[iD]

Chair of Business Informatics, Technische Universität Dortmund, Dortmund, Germany
{mathis.wilz,richard.lackes}@tu-dortmund.de

Abstract. The integration of renewable energies into the electricity grid increases the importance of flexible storage systems and short-term trading. This study examines how intelligent storage management systems can be profitably integrated into short-term market and identifies suitable capacities for these operations. Using a genetic algorithm, we optimize buy and sell decisions of 15-min products in the German Continuous Intraday Market for different battery storages over the year 2021. Our results show that a storage management strategy generated by the genetic algorithm enables significant arbitrage revenues with increasing storage capacity. However, with an increasing battery size, decreasing marginal profits are to be expected. In addition, we were able to show that it is possible to generate positive revenues without the need of a storage system by utilizing intra-product price differences. The genetic algorithm we used provides an intelligent strategy for optimizing storage usage and is capable of integrating forecasts into its decision making process.

Keywords: Continuous Intraday Electricity Market · Genetic Algorithm · Arbitrage Trading · Battery Storage Optimization

1 Introduction

Steady expansion of renewable energy sources (RES) not only leads to increased participation in increasingly short-term markets but also requires a more flexible supply of electricity in periods when less electricity is generated. In Germany, as of 2024, a total of 1.497 gigawatts of battery energy storage systems (BESS) with a nominal capacity of over 1 MW have been installed [1]. The trend is likely to increase significantly over the next years, particularly for large storage systems, to be able to shift much larger quantities of electricity to periods with little sun and wind [2]. While participating on the balancing energy market (reserve) is initially obvious, trading on the spot markets will also become more attractive due to increased price levels, fast response times and falling storage prices [3, 4]. The intraday market (IDM), which offers market participants the last opportunity before delivery to optimize their portfolio and therefore has a high liquidity, particularly in the last few hours before delivery, is likely to be of considerable interest here [5]. The products are traded at hourly, half-hourly and quarter-hourly

© The Author(s), under exclusive license to Springer Nature Switzerland AG 2026
R. Deneckère et al. (Eds.): BIR 2025, LNBIP 562, pp. 3–19, 2026.
https://doi.org/10.1007/978-3-032-04375-7_1

intervals, enabling the optimization of the electricity portfolio on an individual basis. In certain instances, there is significant volatility in energy prices, rendering the utilization of battery storage a financially viable option (Fig. 1).

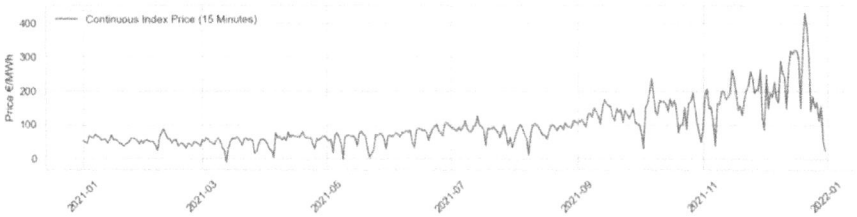

Fig. 1. Annual price view for 15-min products in Germany 2021 (aggregated to days)

In recent studies, various strategies have already been evaluated in research to generate profits on the IDM through pure trading without own production. This mostly risk-free or low-risk exploitation of price differences is also known as arbitrage trading. Basically, IDM threshold-oriented methods [6] or different approaches to so-called pair trading, e.g. using the greedy method [7, 8] can be mentioned. The latter are procedures designed to ensure that buy and sell decisions are matched in pairs, either in the same trading zone or across trading zones, so that price differences can be exploited profitably. An emerging branch in the field of arbitrage trading is the use of artificial intelligence using deep reinforcement learning [9–12]. Here, for example, Bertrand and Papavasiliou were able to show with their experimental setup that machine learning methods in conjunction with heuristics (Markov Decision Process) can outperform comparable benchmarks in terms of profitability on the German IDM [9]. It is important to note that here, as in [13, 14], trading was simulated on a contract level. This contract data from the limit order book is important for in-depth analyses, which can also be used to explain revenue losses of BESS, for example due to bid-ask spreads [15, 16].

Longer-standing literature has largely failed to identify profit opportunities for long-term arbitrage-only applications with storage [17, 18]. This was due to high investment costs for storage technologies or too few times when the price spread would be high enough for such trading options. However, more recent studies show that arbitrage transactions can now be one of the main sales drivers for battery storage in electricity markets [10, 19] and are likely to play an important role in the competitiveness of energy storage if storage prices continue to fall [20]. The choice of battery characteristics also plays a major role here, determining the charging and discharging speed and capacity and thus the intended use of the battery.

The aim of this article is to evaluate the extent to which battery size on real-time markets affect potential profitability. In an experiment, we consider different sizes of intraday-only battery storage systems on the German intraday market, which use a genetic algorithm (GA) to make buy and sell decisions over the course of a year. For this purpose, we use a simplified framework of real-time trading based on volume-weighted prices, which offers high flexibility and delivers fast and sufficiently good results with little effort. Actual costs, such as possible grid charges or trading fees, are not considered in this scenario. The scope of application will be limited to the German intraday market. For the most part, however, this approach should also be applicable to other European markets.

2 Characteristics of the Continuous Intraday Market

The EPEX Spot Continuous Intraday Market (IDM) is a central component of European electricity trading and is operated by EEX AG, one of the largest energy exchanges in Europe. This market enables market participants to trade electricity products for the current day in near real time and to react quickly to changes in the schedule or forecast deviations. The IDM therefore comes after the day-ahead market (DAM), on which trading takes place one day earlier. The main difference between the two markets is the way in which the trades are processed. While all bids for all hours of the following day must be submitted at 12 noon on the DAM and a unit price for each hour is announced shortly afterwards, trading on the IDM is continuous [21].

This means that a bid can be placed for any product at almost any time from the start of trading, provided it is not in the past. The bids of the trading participants are brought together in real time using a matching algorithm. The price determination procedure here is pay-as-bid. Traded products are hourly, half-hourly and quarter hourly. A special feature of the German IDM are the different trading phases. While most real-time markets, at least in Europe, close half an hour before delivery, in Germany trading can continue up to 5 min before delivery in the respective control area. There is a total of four of these control zones. [22] This study will focus exclusively on quarter-hourly products. For further information on the market, we recommend the article by Kiesel and Paraschiv, who have examined the characteristics of quarter-hourly products at IDM in detail [23].

As the intraday market is subject to significantly higher short-term fluctuations than the previous markets, it harbors both more risk and higher profits. The first companies (e.g. kyon energy) with intraday battery storage systems are already active on the market and are taking advantage of this high-risk, high-reward characteristic. In this paper we will deal exclusively with the intraday market. This means that our agent could theoretically submit a bid for a product at any time. A bid on the IDM has four basic characteristics: *1.* a delivery start and a delivery end, in which electricity is fed in or out evenly. *2.* An order type, i.e. whether the bid is a buy or a sell. *3.* The price for the product in €/MWh and *4.* The quantity to be traded (in MWh). Further properties are added for cross-border trading or transactions across control areas (delivery area). However, these are not considered in this analysis.

3 Decision Model

To estimate the revenue potential of arbitrage trading with and without a battery, we need to define the framework conditions that will apply in this experiment:

1. Since in continuous trading it is possible to trade almost any product at any time, the potential solution space is infinite. We therefore need fixed points in time at which trading is to take place. For this purpose, we have chosen a time window of 15 min. This means that the agent makes a decision every 15 min for all products that lie within its current decision range.
2. The first condition raises the question of the price at which a product should be traded. This is because pricing according to the pay-as-bid principle can quickly result in different prices, even at the same time. While similar contributions use real bids [9], we use the volume-weighted price of all bids in 15-min time periods for the respective product at the relevant time grid. Of course, this has the disadvantage that it is never certain that a trade could really be executed at exactly this price.
3. We only consider the 15-min products on the intraday market, as these are particularly susceptible to short-term changes in RES. We also assume that our participation in the market has no influence on prices and that every trading request made by the agent can be realized.
4. The trading strategy used should be balanced and feasible. This means that the agent should only ever make decisions that do not exceed the storage, in- and outfeed capacity. At no time should more trades be concluded than could be delivered. In a real scenario failure to comply with a contract would result in penalty costs (REBAP) and must be considered by the algorithm.
5. The test setup should be kept simple. For this reason, the agent always trades in fixed volumes. Loss of efficiency, as used in [10] is not considered. An implementation of these is possible in principle but would make the implementation of the experiment more difficult and would lead to unwieldy values in purchasing and sales. The same applies to operating costs such as grid fees, trading fees or acquisition costs.

The agent should now act in this environment by making decisions on a rolling basis. The time window considered in the experiment is the entire year 2021 from January 1 up to and including December 31. This year is characterized by the increased price level, which peaked in 2022 and continues to this day (as of the end of 2024).

The aim of the model is to illustrate the possible actions of a decision-maker on the IDM who has a limited battery capacity and wants to maximize his total revenue. In this experiment, the storage system can only ever be charged or discharged by a percentage of its maximum capacity *vlimit* within a partial period. The decision horizon considered at a point in time comprises $t = 1, 2, \ldots, T = 96$ periods per day (d). Within each period, action spaces (a) can be carried out or planned for associated products (s). $J^{d,t}$ forms an action matrix (Fig. 2) which represents all decisions during the planning horizon for the relevant part of the trading day and can take the following forms:

$$
J^{d,t}_{a,s} = \begin{cases} 1, & on\ purchase \\ -1, & on\ sale \\ 0, & do\ nothing \end{cases} \tag{1}
$$

Product

	$s = 0$	$s = 1$	$s = 2$	$s = 3$	$s = 4$	$s = 5$	$s = 6$	$s = 7$
$a = 0$	$J_{a,s}^{d,t}$	$J_{a,s=1}^{d,t}$	$J_{a,s=2}^{d,t}$	$J_{a,s=3}^{d,t}$	$J_{a,s=4}^{d,t}$	$J_{a,s=5}^{d,t}$	$J_{a,s=6}^{d,t}$	$J_{a,s=7}^{d,t}$
$a = 1$		$J_{a=1,s=1}^{d,t}$	$J_{a=1,s=2}^{d,t}$	$J_{a=1,s=3}^{d,t}$	$J_{a=1,s=4}^{d,t}$	$J_{a=1,s=5}^{d,t}$	$J_{a=1,s=6}^{d,t}$	$J_{a=1,s=7}^{d,t}$
$a = 2$			$J_{a=2,s=2}^{d,t}$	$J_{a=2,s=3}^{d,t}$	$J_{a=2,s=4}^{d,t}$	$J_{a=2,s=5}^{d,t}$	$J_{a=2,s=6}^{d,t}$	$J_{a=2,s=7}^{d,t}$
$a = 3$				$J_{a=3,s=3}^{d,t}$	$J_{a=3,s=4}^{d,t}$	$J_{a=3,s=5}^{d,t}$	$J_{a=3,s=6}^{d,t}$	$J_{a=3,s=7}^{d,t}$
$a = 4$					$J_{a=4,s=4}^{d,t}$	$J_{a=4,s=5}^{d,t}$	$J_{a=4,s=6}^{d,t}$	$J_{a=4,s=7}^{d,t}$
$a = 5$						$J_{a=5,s=5}^{d,t}$	$J_{a=5,s=6}^{d,t}$	$J_{a=5,s=7}^{d,t}$

Actionspace

Fig. 2. Formal representation of an action matrix

Greyed-out boxes represent actions that were in the past and are therefore infeasible. The action section a = 0 always represents the actual situation, and therefore the real prices are known exactly, whereas price data of products (s = 1, 2, .. S) for actions a > 0 has to be estimated. Real and estimated prices are shown in the analogue price matrix $P^{d,t}$ (Fig. 3).

In order to determine the related prices, we use volume-weighted prices for each product at quarter-hourly intervals. In calculating the prices and their notation, we follow the notation of the article by Narajewski and Ziel [24]. For example, a volume-weighted price $_xID_y^{d,s}$ can be calculated for a product s on day d using the EPEX SPOT data. Here, x and y delimit the period of the trades considered for this product - where $x \geq 0$ and $y > 0$. $\mathbb{T}_{x,y}^{d,s}$ forms the time window under consideration, which can be set to the last 15 min before delivery with x = 0 and y = 0.25 for example.

$$_xID_y^{d,s} := \frac{1}{\sum_{k\epsilon\mathbb{T}_{x,y}^{d,s}} V_k^{d,s}} \sum_{k\epsilon\mathbb{T}_{x,y}^{d,s}} V_k^{d,s} P_k^{d,s} \qquad (2)$$

The volume-weighted price *ID* is formed from the respective volumes (*V*) with the corresponding prices (*P*) of all contracts (*k*) that come into existence in this period. The prices can be also differentiated by every action space (*a*) The last 5 min, in which trading is no longer possible, are not excluded in this article, as no data is available for this timespan. Figure 3 shows a corresponding example of such a price matrix.

Product

	s = 0	s = 1	s = 2	s = 3	s = 4	s = 5	s = 6	s = 7
a = 0	${}_0^a ID_{0.25}^{d,s}$	${}_{0.25}^0 ID_{0.25}^{d,1}$	${}_{0.5}^0 ID_{0.25}^{d,2}$	${}_{0.75}^0 ID_{0.25}^{d,3}$	${}_1^0 ID_{0.25}^{d,4}$	${}_{1.25}^0 ID_{0.25}^{d,5}$	${}_{1.5}^0 ID_{0.25}^{d,6}$	${}_{1.75}^0 ID_{0.25}^{d,7}$
a = 1		${}_0^1 ID_{0.25}^{d,1}$	${}_{0.25}^1 ID_{0.25}^{d,2}$	${}_{0.5}^1 ID_{0.25}^{d,3}$	${}_{0.75}^1 ID_{0.25}^{d,4}$	${}_1^1 ID_{0.25}^{d,5}$	${}_{1.25}^1 ID_{0.25}^{d,6}$	${}_{1.5}^1 ID_{0.25}^{d,7}$
a = 2			${}_0^2 ID_{0.25}^{d,2}$	${}_{0.25}^2 ID_{0.25}^{d,3}$	${}_{0.5}^2 ID_{0.25}^{d,4}$	${}_{0.75}^2 ID_{0.25}^{d,5}$	${}_1^2 ID_{0.25}^{d,6}$	${}_{1.25}^2 ID_{0.25}^{d,7}$
a = 3				${}_0^3 ID_{0.25}^{d,3}$	${}_{0.26}^3 ID_{0.25}^{d,4}$	${}_{0.5}^3 ID_{0.25}^{d,5}$	${}_{0.75}^3 ID_{0.25}^{d,6}$	${}_1^3 ID_{0.25}^{d,7}$
a = 4					${}_0^4 ID_{0.25}^{d,4}$	${}_{0.25}^4 ID_{0.25}^{d,5}$	${}_{0.5}^4 ID_{0.25}^{d,6}$	${}_{0.75}^4 ID_{0.25}^{d,7}$
a = 5						${}_0^5 ID_{0.25}^{d,5}$	${}_{0.25}^5 ID_{0.25}^{d,6}$	${}_{0.5}^5 ID_{0.25}^{d,7}$

Actionspace

Fig. 3. Formal representation of a price matrix

The algorithm runs through the year 2021 on a rolling basis and considers a quarter-hourly window with possible trading options for the coming hours. (Example Fig. 2 & 3 with a 6 × 8 matrix) As only one decision can be made per product at any one time (every quarter of an hour), this creates a funnel of possible courses of action. According to these rules, the product that is about to be delivered can only be traded once, while the product that is to be delivered in two hours can be traded eight times (2 × 4 quarters). If a new decision vector is created with the next time step, the revenue ($revenue_t$) is recalculated as a continuous indicator (starting with $revenue_t = 0$):

$$revenue_t = \sum_{s=1}^{S} (J_{a=0,s}^{d,t} * P_{a=0,s}^{d,t} * v * (-1)) + revenue_{t-1} \tag{3}$$

The row of a = 0 is representing the trading activities and determine additional revenues, depending on the traded volume (v). Rows a = 1 to a = 5 are the planning horizon. In order to consider battery storage, the algorithm keeps an additional status vector of past decisions and the current battery status. This vector is continuously offset against the new decisions (1, −1, 0) so that it can be ensured that the storage and feed-in and feed-out capacity is not exceeded by a new decision combination (Fig. 4).

Whenever there is a change on storage (B), the new storage level is taken into account as the basis for the next decisions.

$$B_{t+1} = B_t + (J_{0,0}^{d,t} * v + J_{0,1}^{d,t-1} * v) \tag{4}$$

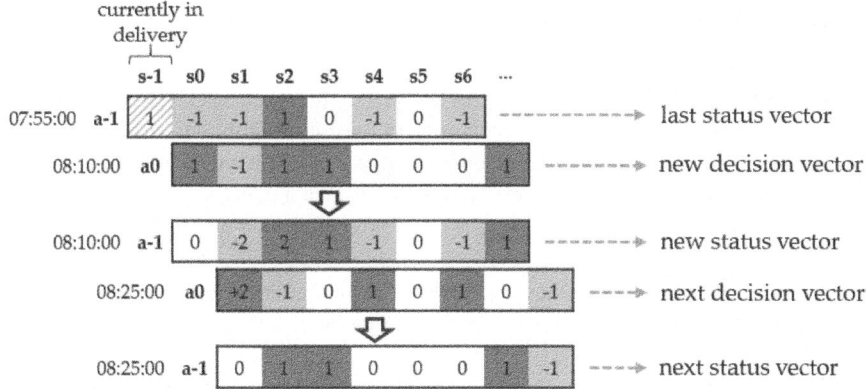

Fig. 4. Calculation of status vectors with new decisions to determine the storage status. Decisons are always made at the last possible trading time (5 Min. before delivery).

4 Model Solution by Genetic Algorithm

Although the original problem is simplified by assumptions and framework conditions, the autonomous search for an optimal solution proves to be difficult due to the large solution space. In the present study, however, a heuristic approach in the form of a genetic algorithm (GA) is pursued, as it can develop working solutions within a short period of time and covers a potentially larger solution space through random mutations. Although the GA is probably outperformed by other algorithms when it comes to determining the best possible result, we believe it is a good benchmark for comparable problems.

A GA is a population-based method whose individuals represent proposed solutions for a complex problem. The procedure is based on the theory of evolution and iteratively runs through a simple multi-phase process to determine a sufficiently good solution for the problem using heuristics. An iteration of a GA takes place after the initialization of the population and usually has the steps selection, crossover, mutation and fitness evaluation. This iterative procedure ensures that better decision combinations are improved generation by generation, while bad or invalid solutions die out.

While a classical GA makes binary decisions, in this study there are three decision options that lead to buy, sell or wait. A possible set of decisions is represented by an individual in the population.

Initialization. At the beginning of the run, the individuals are created and the associated prices are determined. For this purpose, every individual is represented as a matrix $J^{d,t}$ and is randomly filled with decisions. Each element in the matrix is an action option for a product (column) at a decision time (row) that is either imminent or still within the planning horizon. To create more feasible solutions, a weighting was applied so that do nothing occurs twice as often as *buy* or *sell*. A mask is used to fill in only those places with a decision that are still feasible at the selected start time. In this and the following runs, we decided on a population size of 25 individuals to form the starting population. To determine the prices, the volume-weighted prices are calculated for each product at quarter-hourly intervals. The historical trading data from EPEX SPOT was used for this purpose. How the prices are calculated can be seen in the article by Narajewski and Ziel [24].

Fitness Function. After initialization (or at the beginning of each iteration), the so-called fitness is determined for every individual of the current population. It is calculated using a fitness function that takes the decision matrix $J^{d,t}$ of an individual (i). Unwanted characteristics should lead to a reduction in its fitness via a penalty term. These include exceeding or falling short of:

- *Storage Volume:* This represents the capacity of the battery storage. If it is exceeded or below zero, a penalty term is used. This varies in size:

  - If a decision leads to an exceeded or undercut storage volume for the coming delivery, a very high penalty term is deducted from the fitness. This penalty is considered as extremely high, because it is a multiple of the charged or discharged volume multiplied with the corresponding price.
  - If a decision leads to an exceeded or undercut storage volume while the delivery is still at least one period (15 min) in the future, a moderate penalty term is deducted from the fitness. (rather uneconomical) This should reduce the tendency to accumulate commitments over time, leading to large trades just before delivery to meet battery storage limits.

- *Loading Volume*: A fixed amount of energy (v) that can be charged or discharged in one time step t. If more is stored or discharged than the loading volume allows, a moderate penalty term is deducted for the individual. If this happens directly for the next delivery, the penalty term is very high.

The general fitness of an individual (i) without penalty terms and can be calculated in the following way:

$$Fitness_i = \underbrace{\sum_{a=0}^{A}\sum_{s=0}^{S}(J_{a,s}^{d,t} * P_{a,s}^{d,t} * v * (-1)) +}_{\text{revenue of individual}} \underbrace{b_i * \frac{1}{S}\sum_{s=0}^{S}P_{0,s}^{d,t}}_{\text{residual value of individual}} ,$$

$$while\ b_i = B_t + \sum_{a=0}^{A}\sum_{s=0}^{S}(J_{a,s}^{d,t} * v) \tag{5}$$

The fitness calculation always evaluates the complete individual, including the forecast horizon. The remaining storage of the individual is also considered so that there is no incentive to sell off the storage in favour of a better valuation at the end of the planning horizon.

Selection and Recombination. In recombination, components of the individuals are exchanged with each other. The aim of this procedure is to open a larger search space and to reuse already established structures. To increase the performance generation by generation, a preselection is made for the individuals to be combined. For this purpose, the simple method of fitness-proportional selection is used, which is also known as the "roulette wheel" method [25, 26]. Here, the individuals of the current population are sorted in descending order according to their fitness and, depending on this, are given a probability with which they will be selected for the subsequent recombination. Random individuals are selected for the actual recombination.

The recombination is carried out by means of a submatrix crossover in which individuals exchange their partial solution at a random point. Invalid individuals can arise during the submatrix crossover, so a repair mechanism has to be used.

Mutation. Mutation is another random change process and serves to increase diversity within the population by randomly changing a component of an individual. In concrete terms, this means that after recombination, the decision is changed at a randomly chosen element in the individual decision matrix [27]. Here, too, a repair is subsequently required.

The repair of infeasible individuals is not necessary in a conventional GA, as all conditions can be mapped via the fitness function. However, this would mean that the algorithm would need more time to converge. Therefore, in our algorithm the individuals are repaired after recombination and mutation so that only feasable individuals are considered for the next generation. The repair uses the current storage status and the pending decisions to check whether the storage and loading capacity has been exceeded for each future delivery time. For this purpose, the column total of the respective individual with the status vector is formed product by product. If the schedule exceeds the loading volume or storage capacity, this is compensated for by additional trades for the corresponding product. In our experiment, we limit the number of genes mutated per individual to one. In e.g. a 6×8 matrix, this means that a gene has a 1:33 chance of mutating to another state. The mutation rate in this case reflects the rate at which an individual mutates at all (Mutation: yes/no). For larger individuals, two mutations were permitted. In special cases, the algorithm is also permitted to trade more than the permitted maximum volume to comply with the secondary conditions.

Survival Process. To ensure that fitness does not deteriorate again generation after generation, the best individuals are transferred to the next generation recombination. This process is often called elitism [27, 28] and, in our case, applies to the best two individuals of the current generation. The remaining individuals for the new generation consist of recombination of the current generation.

5   Results

With the framework conditions described, we would now like to evaluate the extent to which battery sizing affects potential profitability on real-time markets. To this end, we are considering different battery storage systems on the German IDM in several scenarios (Table 1).

Table 1. Settings for genetic algorithm.

Setting	Characteristic
Capacity (in MWh)	0.0, 0.25, 0.5, 1.0, 2.0
Load Volume (in MWh)	0.0 *, 0.25
Trade Volume (in MWh)	0.25
Considered Products per Individual	8, 16 **
Planning Horizon per Individual	6, 14 **

* The agent without storage may not load or unload
** The largest storage (2MWh) can trade more products at the same time and has a longer planning horizon

In the GA, the number of generations was set to 100 and the mutation probability of 0.9 was selected via grid search. By default, a 6x8 matrix was selected for the action matrix, so a product can be traded for the first time two hours before delivery. Although a longer planning horizon is used for the larger battery, it also means that prices are often not available at some trading or planning times.

The charging and discharging speed was set at 0.25 MWh for each time period. This is slightly below the average trading volumes per trade for the 15-min products in 2021, which are shown in Fig. 5.

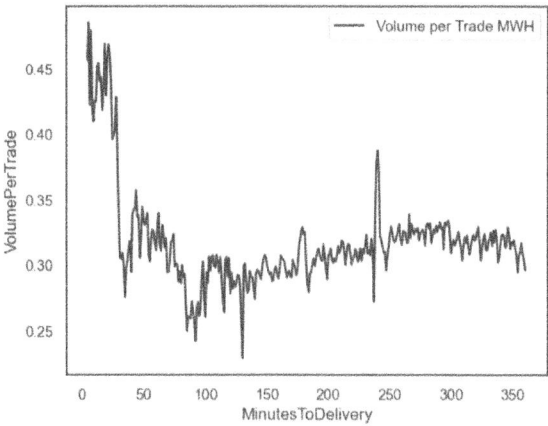

Fig. 5. Timeline of average volume per trade for 15-min products in 2021 from 360 min to delivery.

To find out whether the algorithm can generate positive revenues at all, a run with a perfect price forecast (no price variation) is performed for each storage size. While the curves for the algorithms with storage volume show very similar dynamics, the algorithm without a storage unit has a significantly lower revenue. This clearly shows that the revenue depends heavily on whether a battery is used for trading at all. It is noticeable here, that a significantly stronger increase can be seen from around September, which can be attributed to the higher electricity prices in the end of 2021.

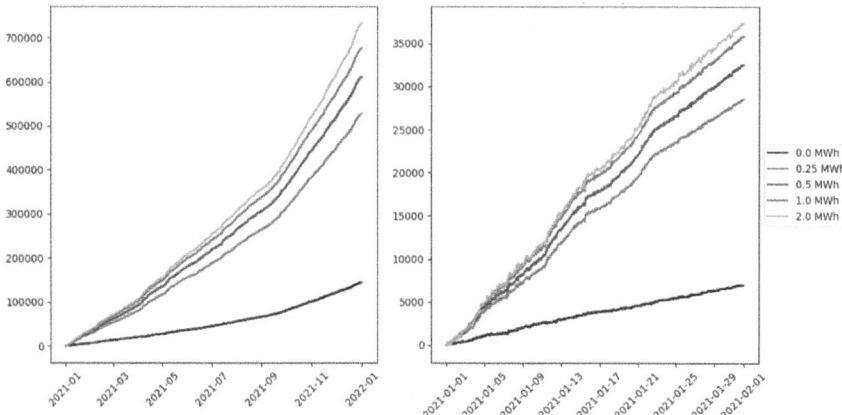

Fig. 6. Revenue of agents with perfect price forecast (left - full year view, right - January)

The curves also suggest that the marginal profits for the next largest storage unit decreases rapidly at the same charging/discharging speed. While the determined revenue for the agent without storage is €144,230, this rises to €528,169 as soon as a battery (0.25 MWh) is available for intermediate storage. The next largest battery (0.5 MWh), on the other hand, generates a relatively lower revenue of €610,855. The bottleneck here is the limited feed-in and feed-out quantity, which ensures that only one unit (0.25 MWh) can be delivered at a time.

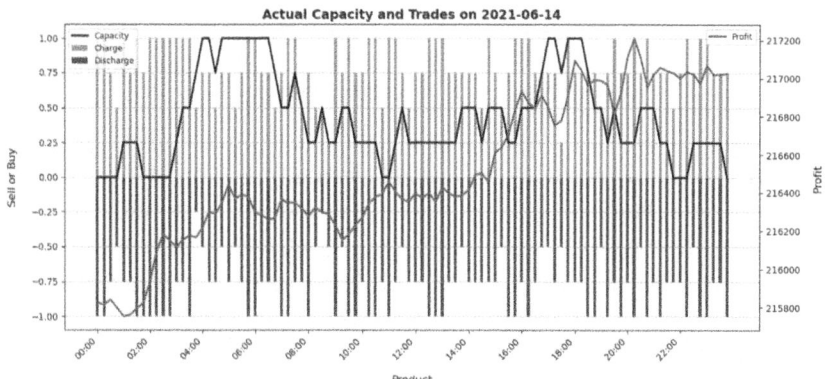

Fig. 7. A random trading day for a battery with storage (1 MWh)

5.1 Detail View

The decisions made by the agents can be seen graphically in Fig. 7. This shows the daily progression of an agent (1MWh) on a random day with its buy and sell decisions and its current state of charge. It can also be pointed out here that the storage system is fully charged shortly before peak times and then sold during periods when electricity is more expensive. This behavior can also be seen in the annual average in Fig. 8: Here, the storage is at its highest level before the price peaks.

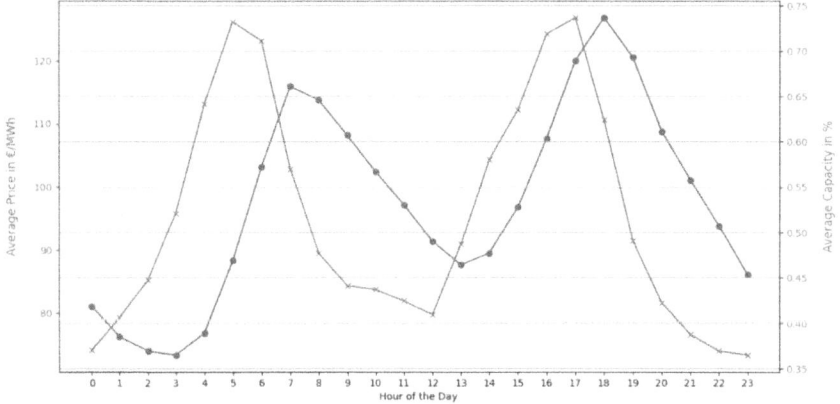

Fig. 8. Average price and capacity for each hour of the day

The following table contains the revenues and number of charging cycles for the runs carried out (Table 2):

Table 2. Results of the various runs under perfect price forecast.

Capacity	Charging Cycles	∅ Battery Level	Revenue
0 MWh	0	–	144.230 €
0.25 MWh	6573	49.6% (0.124)	528.169 €
0.5 MWh	3849	50.0% (0.250)	610.855 €
1.0 MWh	2163	51.7% (0.517)	676.445 €
2.0 MWh	1213	49,9% (0.997)	733.089 €

5.2 Benchmark

In order to compare the results of the agents, we have created a benchmark that operates according to simple rules: The benchmark agent makes its decision based on just two products. Always the first one, which is about to be delivered, and the next one, which

Table 3. Pseudocode for the Benchmark Algorithm

Benchmark Algorithm
Input: price_current, next_price (Price for the next product)   Variables: **decision** (actual decision), **storage** (actual Storage), **storage_min** and **storage_max** (fixed to capacity limit), **revenue, trade_volume**   **Output: decision** for current time, updated **storage, revenue**

1	*IF NEXT_PRICE > PRICE_CURRENT AND STORAGE < STORAGE_MAX THEN*
2	$\mid$ *decision ← 1*
3	*ELSE IF NEXT_PRICE < PRICE_CURRENT AND STORAGE > STORAGE_MIN THEN*
4	$\mid$ *decision ← - 1*
5	*ELSE THEN*
6	$\mid$ *decision ← 0*
7	*storage ← decision * trade_volume*
8	*revenue ← decision * trade_volume * price_current * -1*

would be delivered in the next time period. The assumptions made in Sect. 3, coding and revenue calculation remain the same in principle (Table 3).

This benchmark was carried out for the same period. The continuous revenue curve is very similar to that of the GA and can be seen in Fig. 6 (Fig. 9).

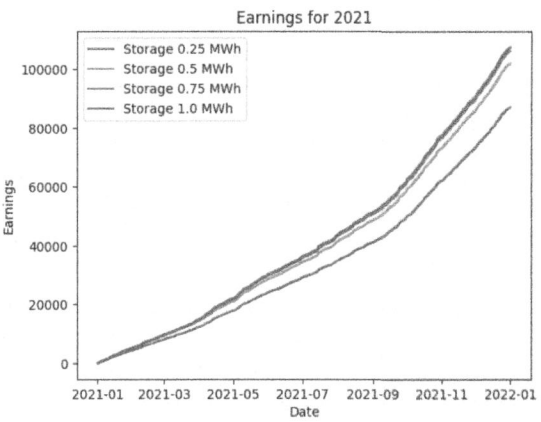

Fig. 9. Performance of the benchmark algorithm with different battery sizes

A comparison of the revenue curves show that the GA agents have very similar revenue dynamics, but the absolute revenue is significantly higher. This is due to the fact that the GA agents 1. can trade several products at the same time and 2. have a longer planning horizon, which makes it possible to optimize storage usage. Ultimately, it can be stated for the benchmarks that their revenues are roughly at the level of the GA agent without a storage.

6 Discussion

As can be deduced from the results of the experiment, the algorithm is able to obtain significant positive revenues by utilizing the Genetic Algorithm. By varying the battery size, we can draw conclusions about storage utilization and marginal revenues. The jump from no storage to a small storage (0.25 MWh) leads to a strong revenue increase of about 266% (with perfect price prediction), which underlines the fundamental importance of storage capacity for arbitrage trades. However, the results show decreasing marginal returns with increasing battery capacity. The increase in revenue to 0.50 MWh is around 16%, while the jump to 1 MWh only yields just under 7% more. Theoretically, the revenues could be increased by larger feed-in and feed-out sizes and a proportionally larger storage facility. However, a single player would quickly reach the natural limits of the market by simply stacking up the storage volume [15].

However, we had to limit our experiment to a number of restrictions, which we had to accept due to the data situation and complexity of the problem. These included the discretization of the problem and the associated formation of volume-weighted prices. To simplify the optimization problem, our experiment also assumes no cost structures for amortization, trading costs, efficiency losses or spreads. Instead, we assume a liquid market in which we can always buy and sell at the average price. Other papers, like Bertrand and Papavasiliou [9] or Schaurecker et al. [14] have a much more complex experimental setup here, but have not the implementation of a planning window considering future prices. In our opinion, the latter point also deserves more attention, as there has been significant progress in this area. Here, for example, Marcjasz, Unijewski et al. [29] were able to show that they were able to beat the naïve approach when forecasting intraday prices - in other words, they were able to provide significantly better price forecasts than the last known price.

Similar to the results of Schaurecker et al., we were able to determine that batteries with fast and small storage units appear to be more profitable in terms of dimensioning. It must also be said that Schaurecker et al. [14] used significantly larger batteries for their experiment. However, it remains to be seen whether intraday-only battery trading can really pay off in the long term. The ever falling prices for BESS currently speak in favour of battery trading [20, 30]. In addition, it can be expected that electricity prices in Europe will remain at a high level in the medium to long term. [31] Both trends could favour the use of BESS. Supplemental contributions about the extent to which price uncertainties, for example due to forecasting errors, could affect profitability would be interesting for future studies. It can be hypothesized that less accurate forecasts will have a substantial impact on profitability. However, how forecasts interact with the storage problem and to what extent traders can hedge against risks here is an interesting field of research.

7   Conclusion

The objective of this paper was to use an experimental approach to examine seizing of battery storages in the continuous German intraday market. For this purpose, a GA was implemented that trades at discrete time intervals and takes a planning horizon into account. This should allow identification of arbitrage options, taking into account a storage limit. The first finding here is that the size of the battery storage is an important driver of profitability, but that the marginal profit decreases rapidly. Additionally, we demonstrated that the algorithm could achieve positive intraday turnover without utilizing storage even once. However, this is only possible with accurate price forecasting techniques. We also demonstrated that small, fast charging and discharging storage units perform best on the intraday market. Using a battery can be associated with considerable revenues, but the marginal profit decreases rapidly for each next larger battery. In addition to these findings, our approach provides a framework that can handle price predictions to enable intra-product trading for higher profits.

Disclosure of Interests. The authors have no competing interests to declare that are relevant to the content of this article.

References

1. Reuther, T., Kost, C.: Photovoltaik- und Batteriespeicherzubau in Deutschland in Zahlen: Auswertung des Marktstammdatenregisters. Freiburg, Germany (2024). https://www.ise.fra unhofer.de/content/dam/ise/de/documents/publications/studies/2024-02-photovoltaik-und-batteriespeicherzubau-in-deutschland.pdf. Accessed 09 Dec 2024
2. Ullah, F., et al.: A comprehensive review of wind power integration and energy storage technologies for modern grid frequency regulation. Heliyon **10**(9) (2024). https://doi.org/10.1016/j.heliyon.2024.e30466
3. Killer, M., Farrokhseresht, M., Paterakis, N.G.: Implementation of large-scale Li-ion battery energy storage systems within the EMEA region. Appl. Energy **260**, 114166 (2020). https://doi.org/10.1016/j.apenergy.2019.114166
4. Naseri, N., Ghiassi-Farrokhfal, Y., Ketter, W., Collins, J.: Understanding and managing the participation of batteries in reserve electricity markets. Decis. Support. Syst. **165**, 113895 (2023). https://doi.org/10.1016/j.dss.2022.113895
5. Kremer, M., Kiesel, R., Paraschiv, F.: An econometric model for intraday electricity trading. Philos. Trans. Ser. A Math. Phys. Eng. Sci. **379**(2202), 20190624 (2021). https://doi.org/10.1098/rsta.2019.0624
6. Bertrand, G., Papavasiliou, A.: An analysis of threshold policies for trading in continuous intraday electricity markets. In: 2018 15th International Conference on the European Energy Market (EEM), Lodz, pp. 1–5 (2018)
7. Bowen, D., Hutchinson, M.C., O'Sullivan, N.: High-frequency equity pairs trading: transaction costs, speed of execution, and patterns in returns. JOT **5**(3), 31–38 (2010). https://doi.org/10.3905/jot.2010.5.3.031
8. Finhold, E., Heller, T., Leithäuser, N.: On the potential of arbitrage trading on the German intraday power market. JEM (2023). https://doi.org/10.21314/JEM.2023.027
9. Bertrand, G., Papavasiliou, A.: Adaptive trading in continuous intraday electricity markets for a storage unit. IEEE Trans. Power Syst. **35**(3), 2339–2350 (2020). https://doi.org/10.1109/TPWRS.2019.2957246

10. Cao, J., Harrold, D., Fan, Z., Morstyn, T., Healey, D., Li, K.: Deep reinforcement learning-based energy storage arbitrage with accurate lithium-ion battery degradation model. IEEE Trans. Smart Grid **11**(5), 4513–4521 (2020). https://doi.org/10.1109/TSG.2020.2986333

11. Harrold, D.J.B., Cao, J., Fan, Z.: Data-driven battery operation for energy arbitrage using rainbow deep reinforcement learning (2021). http://arxiv.org/pdf/2106.06061v1

12. Xu, H., Li, X., Zhang, X., Zhang, J.: Arbitrage of energy storage in electricity markets with deep reinforcement learning (2019). http://arxiv.org/pdf/1904.12232v2

13. Kuppelwieser, T., Wozabal, D.: Intraday power trading: toward an arms race in weather forecasting? OR Spectrum **45**(1), 57–83 (2023). https://doi.org/10.1007/s00291-022-00698-5

14. Schaurecker, D., Wozabal, D., Löhndorf, N., Staake, T.: Maximizing battery storage profits via high-frequency intraday trading (2025). http://arxiv.org/pdf/2504.06932v2

15. Cognéville, E., Deschatre, T., Warin, X.: Battery valuation on electricity intraday markets with liquidity costs (2024). http://arxiv.org/pdf/2412.15959v1

16. Kath, C., Ziel, F.: Optimal order execution in intraday markets: minimizing costs in trade trajectories (2020). http://arxiv.org/pdf/2009.07892v2

17. Kloess, M.: Electric storage technologies for the future power system—an economic assessment. In: 2012 9th International Conference on the European Energy Market, Florence, Italy, pp. 1–8 (2012)

18. Steffen, B.: Prospects for pumped-hydro storage in Germany. Energy Policy **45**, 420–429 (2012). https://doi.org/10.1016/j.enpol.2012.02.052

19. Krishnamurthy, D., Uckun, C., Zhou, Z., Thimmapuram, P.R., Botterud, A.: Energy storage arbitrage under day-ahead and real-time price uncertainty. IEEE Trans. Power Syst. **33**(1), 84–93 (2018). https://doi.org/10.1109/TPWRS.2017.2685347

20. Campana, P.E., et al.: Li-ion batteries for peak shaving, price arbitrage, and photovoltaic self-consumption in commercial buildings: a Monte Carlo analysis. Energy Convers. Manage. **234**, 113889 (2021). https://doi.org/10.1016/j.enconman.2021.113889

21. Linnemann, M.: Energiewirtschaft für (Quer-)Einsteiger. Springer, Wiesbaden (2024)

22. 50hertz, Amprion, Tennet, TransnetBW, Fahrplananmeldung in Deutschland: Prozessbeschreibung, https://www.50hertz.com/xspProxy/api/staticfiles/50hertz-client/dokumente/vertragspartner/bilanzkreiskunden/20230401fpmde.pdf, last accessed 2025/07/14

23. Kiesel, R., Paraschiv, F.: Econometric analysis of 15-minute intraday electricity prices. Energy Econ. **64**, 77–90 (2017). https://doi.org/10.1016/j.eneco.2017.03.002

24. Narajewski, M., Ziel, F.: Econometric modelling and forecasting of intraday electricity prices. J. Commod. Mark. **19**, 100107 (2020). https://doi.org/10.1016/j.jcomm.2019.100107

25. Holland, J.H.: Adaptation in Natural and Artificial Systems: An Introductory Analysis with Applications to Biology, Control, and Artificial Intelligence. MIT Press, Cambridge (1992)

26. Shukla, A., Pandey, H.M., Mehrotra, D.: Comparative review of selection techniques in genetic algorithm. In: 2015 International Conference on Futuristic Trends on Computational Analysis and Knowledge Management (ABLAZE), Greater Noida, India, pp. 515–519 (2015)

27. Man, K.F., Tang, K.S., Kwong, S.: Genetic algorithms: concepts and applications [in engineering design]. IEEE Trans. Ind. Electron. **43**(5), 519–534 (1996). https://doi.org/10.1109/41.538609

28. Wu, X., Jain, L., Graña, M., Duro, R.J., d'Anjou, A., Wang, P.P. (eds.): Information Processing with Evolutionary Algorithms. Springer, London (2005)

29. Marcjasz, G., Uniejewski, B., Weron, R.: Beating the naïve—combining lasso with naïve intraday electricity price forecasts. Energies **13**(7), 1667 (2020). https://doi.org/10.3390/en13071667

30. Cole, W., Karmakar, A.: Cost projections for utility-scale battery storage: 2023 Update. NREL/TP-6A40-85332. https://www.nrel.gov/docs/fy23osti/85332.pdf. Accessed 14 July 2025

31. Liebensteiner, M., Ocker, F., Abuzayed, A.: High electricity price despite expansion in renewables: how market trends shape Germany's power market in the coming years. Energy Policy **198**, 114448 (2025). https://doi.org/10.1016/j.enpol.2024.114448

Improving Group Decision-Making Through a Collaborative Serious Game

Corina Stampfli[(✉)] [ID], Sandra Schlick [ID], and Hans-Friedrich Witschel [ID]

FHNW University of Applied Sciences and Arts Northwestern Switzerland,
Riggenbachstrasse 16, 4600 Olten, Switzerland
corina.stampfli@hotmail.com

Abstract. The growing importance of collaborative or group decision-making in business projects is accompanied by several challenges, mainly cognitive biases. This paper focuses on identifying the key biases that affect group decision-making and explores the potential of serious games as a training method to address these issues. Using a design science research methodology, a game prototype was developed to improve group decision-making in corporate environments by increasing players' awareness of bias-influenced decisions. The findings indicate that there is a need to provide specifically designed games for team-based decision-making, and only a limited number of existing games are specifically designed for corporate decision-making contexts. Our contribution addresses the lack of integrated training tools that increase cognitive bias awareness for decision making in projects, demonstrating the potential of a collaborative serious game to mitigate biases such as groupthink bias, authority bias, and social loafing while providing actionable insights for enhancing its design and effectiveness. It shows that every bias requires specific game characteristics, such as storyline, feedback mechanisms, and role concepts.

Keywords: Group decision-making · cognitive bias · serious game · role-play · adventure · project management

1 Introduction

Group decision-making is crucial to the success of projects, especially in complex contexts where diverse stakeholders must be involved and various interests and factors must be considered. Although group decisions have become increasingly common for effective project implementation, they pose challenges, including the risk of poor or indecisive outcomes, often leading to project failures [1]. A primary cause of ineffective group decisions lies in cognitive biases, which usually stem from the inherent limitations described by Bounded Rationality, such as constraining people's processing capacity and incomplete information. Further theories, such as prospect theory, explain how individuals make decisions under risk and uncertainty, and demonstrate that risk behavior varies with the perceived certainty of outcomes. These theories highlight the complexity of decision-making and the impact of cognitive biases in group settings [2].

© The Author(s), under exclusive license to Springer Nature Switzerland AG 2026
R. Denec…re et al. (Eds.): BIR 2025, LNBIP 562, pp. 20–36, 2026.
https://doi.org/10.1007/978-3-032-04375-7_2

Using the example of a large enterprise in the transportation sector, the most common biases hindering project group decisions were identified with interviews. One frequently occurring bias in practice was groupthink, where team members withhold opposing opinions to maintain harmony and consensus. Hierarchical structures often reinforce these dynamics, where authority bias plays a role. This leads to adopting leadership opinions and suppressing critical thinking and alternative perspectives. Leaders who dominate decisions reduce motivation and engagement, leading to social loafing [3].

Awareness of these biases is crucial to improving group decision-making. Traditional training methods are often ineffective, whereas experimental methods promise better results [4]. They create interactive learning environments where participants can directly experience the dynamics and consequences of decision-making processes and learn to identify and overcome biases [3].

This paper aims to analyze the challenges posed by cognitive biases in group decision-making within project management and proposes a serious game as a training solution. The main research question is, "How does implementing a collaborative serious game as a training strategy improve group decision-making in project teams by addressing cognitive biases?".

The paper's relevance lies in its dual contribution: first, from a research perspective, it seeks to address a gap in the literature at the intersection of group decision-making, project management, and serious games; second, from a business perspective, it provides implications for organizations facing the limitations of traditional decision-making methods.

2 Literature Review

The literature review provides a comprehensive examination of the theoretical and practical foundations relevant to this research by connecting the challenges of group decision-making, the potential of serious games as an innovative training approach, and the existing research gap. The literature review followed a structured approach to identify relevant theories and practical studies on group decision-making, cognitive biases, and serious games. Scientific databases (Web of Science, Scopus, IEEE Xplore) were used to search for publications between 2000 and 2024. The following search queries and keywords were used: ("cognitive bias" AND "group decision*"), ("serious game*" AND "bias"), and ("project management" AND "group decision*" AND "bias").

Group decision-making, involving formally established groups of 3 to 20 individuals with specific tasks and shared goals, represents a challenge for collective decision-making [1]. As projects become increasingly complex, group decision-making is crucial for project management, which requires considering individuals' personalities, past experiences, and intentions. Despite the advantages of collaborative decision-making, it can sometimes lead to poorer outcomes than individual decision-making because it is influenced by biases [5]. These biases arise from individual perception of social reality, where subjective interpretation of information creates systematic deviations from rational decision-making [6, 7].

2.1 Biases in Group Decision-Making

The literature distinguishes between different individual and group biases, which can affect decision-making. One common individual bias is overconfidence, which occurs when decisions are made with excessive confidence and risks are underestimated. Another is the sunk cost bias, where people continue investing in a project based on previously committed resources, even if it no longer makes rational sense [4]. Additionally, individuals often over-rely on past experiences, misinterpret new evidence, and underestimate their abilities, resulting in poor decisions [6]. Individual biases are closely linked to information biases, demonstrating how personal predispositions and limited perception influence the processing and interpretation of information in decision-making [8]. Decisions in a group can help to overcome individual biases. For example, individuals may recognize biases in others more quickly than they recognize them in themselves, potentially leading to better decision-making outcomes [4]. However, it is essential to note that not all problems of individual biases are eliminated in groups. Sometimes, they may be amplified, or new group biases, such as the groupthink bias, arise [4, 6]. This psychological bias affects social dynamics by suppressing independent thought and reducing information diversity. Groupthink aims to minimize conflicts in favor of consensus, but this often leads to poorly informed decisions due to the undue influence of a dominant minority. Janis [9] identified eight key symptoms of groupthink that illustrate how it undermines decision-making: the illusion of invulnerability, collective rationalization, belief in inherent morality, stereotyped views of outgroups, direct pressure on dissenters, self-censorship, the illusion of unanimity, and the emergence of self-appointed "mind guards" who block alternative viewpoints. These symptoms contribute to a false sense of consensus and discourage critical evaluation, ultimately reducing the quality of decisions. Understanding and recognizing these symptoms is essential for developing strategies that foster open dialogue and mitigate groupthink in team-based decision-making contexts. Mitigating group biases requires promoting diverse viewpoints and critical evaluation of information to enhance decision quality [4, 6].

Furthermore, group decision-making dynamics are also influenced by cultural contexts, as reflected in Hofstede's cultural dimensions—power distance, uncertainty avoidance, and individualism vs. collectivism. For example, authority bias, a tendency to overly trust authority figures, often arises in hierarchical cultures, leading to conformity and suppressed dissent [10]. In addition to cultural factors, the roles of participants within a group also impact the occurrence of these biases. The composition and dynamics of project teams significantly influence the prevalence of biases. Projects often involve diverse participants representing different departments and opinions, but their temporary nature means that team members are generally unfamiliar with one another [11]. A mix of personalities and roles fosters creativity, counters biases, and improves decision quality [12]. Additionally, ensuring openness to diverse opinions and promoting awareness of bias among team members is essential for effective group decision-making [4].

2.2 Leveraging Biases with Games

Serious games, defined as all types of games used for more than just entertainment, offer several advantages over traditional training methods for group decision-making [13]. They can enhance critical thinking, simulate decision-making processes, or increase participant engagement, which provides benefits in addressing group decision-making challenges, particularly in dealing with complex issues such as reducing cognitive biases in project decisions [14]. Numerous studies confirm the effectiveness of these games in raising awareness and mitigating biases by creating controlled environments that allow participants to navigate scenarios and identify their cognitive errors [15]. Furthermore, games can be adapted to address cultural aspects, thereby increasing awareness of specific challenges faced by particular groups. Research highlights that game genres such as simulations, role-playing, and adventure games are particularly suited to improving group decision-making. These genres offer diverse opportunities to combine interactive scenarios with realistic or narrative approaches. However, there is a lack of clear classifications and guidelines to identify the optimal genre for specific training goals. Varying approaches and inconsistent taxonomies complicate the systematic integration of serious games into complex decision-making contexts, particularly in business projects [16].

Despite the potential of serious games, a significant research gap persists. While cognitive biases, such as overconfidence or groupthink, are well-documented (e.g., [3]), specific guidelines to help groups systematically reduce biases in decision-making are lacking. Moreover, most existing applications focus on specific biases or educational contexts, neglecting their combination with business requirements or complex group scenarios. The literature further reveals that integrating serious games into professional contexts is underexplored, and various examples are not designed to address bias reduction [17].

This research addresses the gap by connecting the three themes of group decision-making, cognitive biases, and project management. The aim is to develop a training solution that reduces group- and culture-specific biases in decision-making. Building on existing work (e.g., [17]), a structured approach to designing serious games is applied to close the gap.

3 Methodology

The research aims to close the gap in the interplay between group decision-making, biases, and project management, and to develop and evaluate a serious game that mitigates group biases in decision-making. This approach aligns with Design Science Research (DSR) [18], emphasizing iterative artifact development.

The study takes a pragmatic perspective, combining qualitative methods to explore the problem and design solutions. It employed multiple methods, integrating interviews, observations, and questionnaires to gather data across four distinct phases of the Design science research. The data collection was conducted from October 2023 to April 2024.

The selection focused on studies that provided conceptual clarity or practical insights related to the application of serious games in decision-making contexts. The insights from this review informed both the biased selection and the game design requirements.

During the **awareness phase**, cognitive biases were identified through semi-structured interviews conducted in two rounds with project managers and team members from a large transportation company. The first round explored practical decision-making challenges, while the second round focused on bias awareness and validation. These findings were validated through a thorough literature review described above. Sample interview questions included (see Tble 1):

Table 1. Interview questions for the awareness phase

Round	Question	Expected Outcome
1	Take an example of a recent project and try to answer the questions based on the example. From your perspective, what is the typical decision-making process in projects at your company?	The answers are specific and related to an example. The typical decision-making process involves group decision-making. Strategic, tactical, and operative decisions need to be made
1	What difficulties and challenges are encountered in group decision-making? Why? How does this become apparent?	Challenges related to biases are expected. The decision-making is prone to errors or takes a long time
1	How is knowledge shared and transferred in projects? What are the consequences?	Understand the mechanism of knowledge sharing and the challenges. Biases also influence knowledge sharing
2	Explanation of several biases and the concept of bias. What biases do you think are present in project decisions? Give an example	The most important biases are individual and group biases

Four interviews were conducted in two rounds. The first round explored whether group decision-making poses practical challenges and helped narrow the focus to cognitive biases. The second round aimed to raise awareness of these biases in practice and compare them with findings from the literature.

During the suggestion phase, the design requirements and characteristics of the game were formulated to address biases, with a focus on enhancing group decision-making. In the development phase, a serious game prototype was created using Microsoft Power-Apps, leveraging the Jaccard framework for collaborative game design [19]. The game progressed through several stages, where participants must collectively navigate scenarios designed to expose and mitigate biases. The game development process, guided by the Jaccard framework [19], was structured to create a tool for raising awareness of cognitive biases. The author designed the game as part of a master's thesis in Business Information Systems. While the author does not have a formal background in psychology or game design, the development was informed by established literature on cognitive and group decision-making biases (e.g. [4, 7] and serious game design. Interviews with subject matter experts provided critical feedback throughout the project's development and evaluation phases. The game was tested with participants from a corporate environment, focusing on perceived learning, engagement, and awareness of biases.

The game was tested in the evaluation phase with five groups of participants, each comprising 3 to 5 members (total n = 22). All participants were from the project environment of the same transport company, where the biases had previously been investigated. Participants were actively involved in group decision-making processes within their current projects, ensuring they possessed relevant practical experience with the decision-making challenges the game was designed to address.

Twenty-two individuals participated in the game, organized into five groups of three to five members. All participants were project team members or managers working in a large transportation company and were selected based on their active involvement in group decision-making processes. An additional control group of 18 non-players was selected simultaneously, with similar professional backgrounds and project experience, to assess the differences in bias awareness between players and non-players in a post-game questionnaire.

The study was conducted in moderated workshop sessions, including gameplay, observations, and post-game group discussions. Participation was voluntary, and all data were anonymized to ensure no personal information could be traced back to individuals.

All participants who had previously participated in the awareness phase interviews did not take part in the game; however, the game participants came from a similar professional background. To address potential concerns about overlap, this separation ensures that prior exposure to biased concepts during interviews did not influence the game evaluation results.

Feedback for evaluating the collaborative serious game was gathered through gameplay observations, group interviews, and post-game questionnaires, which were conducted two to three weeks after the game. Both players and non-players completed the post-game questionnaire to assess their knowledge of biases and analyze the differences. The following methods were used:

- Semi-structured group interviews with predefined questions covering bias recognition, game experience, and learning transfer
- Post-game questionnaires administered 2–3 weeks after gameplay, including Likert-scale questions on bias awareness and open-ended questions about real-world application
- Observation protocols during gameplay using structured coding sheets
- Bias awareness assessment questionnaire for both players and non-players, measuring pre- and post-game knowledge differences

The collaborative serious game session lasted approximately 90 min, including gameplay and debriefing phases.

The questionnaire was designed to ask participants to provide examples of biases implemented in the game, assessing their understanding and perception of these concepts.

For groupthink, for example, the following question was asked: *"Groupthink refers to a behaviour where individuals align with the group's position or judgment, regardless of their own opinion. The desire for unanimity within a group can suppress critical thinking and individual opinions, ultimately leading to poorer decisions. How would you rate your awareness of groupthink in group decision-making? Can you provide an example of a decision where you, in hindsight, think these biases might have played a role?"*.

The data analysis includes:

- Qualitative data analysis for semi-structured interviews, observations, and group debriefing (thematic analysis, content-structured qualitative content analysis)
- Qualitative analysis of questionnaire (selective coding, clustering).

The study was conducted according to the ethical guidelines of the University of Applied Sciences and Arts Northwestern Switzerland (FHNW). All participants were informed about the study's objectives, procedures, and content, and provided written informed consent prior to participation.

The methodology is limited by the small sample size and its focus on a single organizational and team context, which reduces generalizability. The short game duration may also limit its ability to simulate complex decision-making dynamics or measure long-term impacts. The methodology ensures a rigorous and iterative development process that balances practical relevance with theoretical contributions. Despite the limited sample size and organizational scope, the study offers practice-based insights that demonstrate the game's effectiveness in raising awareness of bias, providing a valuable foundation for future, broader applications.

4   Challenges in Group Decision-Making and Debiasing Methods

This section examines the challenges of group decision-making, strategies to mitigate cognitive biases, and game characteristics and genres that can effectively address the issues.

Various biases often influence effective project decision-making, as highlighted in the literature and reinforced through interviews. In total, five semi-structured interviews were conducted with project managers and team members from the participating organization. The interview process consisted of two rounds: the first explored whether group decision-making poses practical challenges and helped narrow the focus to cognitive biases; the second aimed to raise awareness of these biases in practice and compare them with findings from the literature.

In contrast to the literature, interviews highlighted the prominence of group biases and their connection to cultural factors. In the context of our study, biases identified through interviews were found to encompass both individual and group aspects, necessitating a further division into decision-making biases. Decision biases occur in decision-making processes and can be attributed to individual or group dynamics [20]. While individual biases are well-documented in the literature, interviews indicate that groupthink, sunflower bias, and authority bias are more critical to address in project environments due to their significant impact on group dynamics. Authority bias is commonly observed in group decisions and is particularly substantial in project decision-making. The litera-ture review indicates it is strongly linked to group biases and cultural factors. Authority bias is also closely related to sunflower bias. While authority bias pertains to individuals excessively deferring to authority figures, sunflower bias involves group members overly aligning with a dominant individual, typically a leader, thereby suppressing critical anal-ysis and diverse perspectives [6]. This interplay between the two biases underscores the impact of hierarchical and cultural factors on organizational decision-making. Further-more, authority bias can lead to decreased motivation and awareness of participation. This often results in social loafing, where some group members do not contribute, believing their input is irrelevant [6]. Groupthink and sunflower bias complicate decision-making by suppressing dissent and promoting uniformity, thereby increasing the risk of subop-timal outcomes. The interviews identified groupthink bias as relevant and emphasized the impact of group biases when decisions are overridden by the management board or aligned with management opinion. This indicates a combined occurrence of groupthink and sunflower bias. These dependencies of the different biases were not highlighted in the literature review; however, the interviews indicated a relationship between the various biases. Groupthink and sunflower bias frequently co-occur, and sunflower bias can exacerbate groupthink by discouraging dissenting views and promoting uniform decision-making processes [21].

To mitigate group and authority biases, research highlights various debiasing strate-gies for detecting and addressing these challenges. Fischhoff identifies core approaches, including educating individuals about specific biases, illustrating their influence, and providing feedback complemented by coaching and targeted interventions. Muntwiler [22] expands this framework by introducing strategies for strategic decision-making, highlighting the diversity of debiasing techniques. Games are particularly effective as training interventions, as they raise awareness of biases and mitigate their effects through experiential learning and integrated feedback mechanisms.

Interviews revealed a general lack of awareness regarding biases in decision-making. Consequently, the game's primary goal should be to increase awareness rather than attempt comprehensive cultural change. To achieve this, the game targets four key biases: authority bias, groupthink, sunflower bias, and social loafing. These requirements guide the exploration of specific game characteristics that can effectively address and mitigate these biases, thereby enhancing group decision-making.

5   Game Suggestions

Game characteristics are analyzed to meet the requirements. To create an effective edu-cational game, it is essential to include clear learning objectives and elements that demonstrate the intended learning outcomes [23]. The game should, in part, achieve the learning goal and, in part, implement a game mechanism to make learning activities fun and motivate the players [17]. The following factors should be incorporated to fulfill these requirements.

Table 2. Game and Learning Characteristics

Characteristic	Characteristic type	Reason
Incorporating clear learning objectives	Learning	Alignment of the goals
Demonstrating the effects of this bias	Learning	Bias awareness
Focusing on tactical and operational decisions	Learning	Transfer to practice
Incorporating experiential learning theory	Learning	Engagement and transfer
Providing a feedback and reflection system	Learning	Reflection and learning
Implementing a role-concept	Game	Simulating team decisions (dynamics)
Having a time limit	Game	Realistic pressure
Developing a digital game that engages motivation	Game	Learner motivation
Having engaging content and a compelling storyline	Game	Immersion
Providing collaborative elements	Game	Team Interaction

The analysis of game genres meeting the specified characteristics concludes that adventure, role-playing, and simulation games—or their combinations—offer substantial potential for mitigating cognitive and group biases. Incorporating role-based dynamics is particularly important, as players who identify with their assigned roles tend to behave more authentically.

Key design decisions were made based on the pre-analysis of potential game types. Given these characteristics, role-playing games emerge as the most suitable option due to their adaptability in addressing various biases. Role-playing games, combined with adventure games' features, provide various learning opportunities by allowing players to explore and experiment with different options at every stage [24]. The game's main idea is to introduce a team of players to a scenario where they must collaborate to make decisions and solve problems together. Each player has a role that may comprise hidden instructions. This makes it possible to create game situations that act as "traps" for cognitive and social biases, i.e., making it more likely that the team will make a biased decision. Then, the game simulates the adverse outcomes of those biased decisions and discusses the findings to allow participants to experience these consequences, thereby raising their awareness of the underlying biases. The game centers on role-play, with predefined roles tailored to simulate social dynamics such as authority and groupthink. These roles are designed to encourage perspective-taking and highlight biases during gameplay. An additional alternative involves participants creating a preferred avatar before the game to enhance identification and engagement with their roles or playing their real-life roles [24, 25].

The literature offers contrasting views regarding the use of storylines. Some studies emphasize the importance of an engaging and exciting narrative [24], while others argue that realistic scenarios are more effective in ensuring the transfer of learning [26]. For this game, a fantasy storyline was chosen to captivate participants and focus their attention on identifying biases rather than relying on prior knowledge. The game incorporates a feedback system, combining immediate feedback after key decisions with reflective debriefing sessions to reinforce understanding. Collaborative elements, such as information sharing and team-based challenges, replicate real-world group dynamics and promote interaction.

Different simulations are integrated into the game for each bias, summarized in Table 3.

Table 3. Bias and Simulations

Bias	Simulation (Trap)	Integration in the game
Groupthink Bias	Illusion of unanimity	Early feedback reinforces the group's consensus perception, even when it is inaccurate, unless it is actively questioned
	Self-Censorship	"One person is instructed to play the role of a 'reserved member' withholding important information"
	Direct pressure	Time pressure discourages dissent
	Collective rationalization	Contradictory evidence is introduced to question an initial decision (see the first row of the table), but at a stage when much effort has already been put into implementing it
Social Loafing	Non-participation	Distracted role simulates a lack of contribution
Sunflower Bias	Deference to authority	Non-player characters give misleading advice that influences decisions
Authority Bias	Over-reliance on leadership opinions	Implement a leadership role; a leadership role is instructed to give misleading advice

The bias simulations in Table 3 are theoretically grounded in perception and reaction patterns observed in organizational settings. Each bias trap exploits specific perception errors: groupthink leverages the human tendency to perceive false consensus through selective information processing, while authority bias exploits the automatic deference reaction to perceived expertise or hierarchy. Sunflower bias manipulates social perception by presenting dominant figures as credible sources, triggering conformity reactions even when information quality is questionable. Social loafing occurs when individuals perceive their contributions as less significant, resulting in reduced engagement and subsequent reactions. These perception-reaction cycles illustrate how cognitive shortcuts and social dynamics interact to create systematic decision-making errors in projects, which the game reveals through controlled scenarios that expose the gap between intended rational decision-making and actual biased behavior patterns.

6 Development of the Game

The first step in the development process was to define the context and objectives. The game was designed for individuals in project management roles at a large transportation company in Switzerland. It was played in groups of three to five players. Each participant needed a laptop, and the game was conducted on-site in a room. The game was built using PowerApps, part of the Office 365 suite, and is easily accessible. The game combines learning functions, such as rewards and scores for motivation, collaborative interpretation of information, structured analysis of bias-related scenarios, and timely feedback mechanisms that guide player reflection and enhance learning outcomes.

Derived from the game mechanism, the goals of a concrete game prototype were built. Set in a fictional environment, players took on the roles of an adventure team tasked with rebuilding a damaged region. The core objective was to foster effective collaboration, promote awareness and reflection on cognitive biases, and support the development of sound group decision-making skills. At the beginning of the game, participants were assigned to predefined roles, each representing distinct characteristics designed to stimulate specific cognitive biases, such as authority bias and the suppression of dissenting opinions. The game was structured into five decision-making rounds, each followed by a reflection or feedback phase to encourage learning and awareness of bias. The following Table 4 provides a brief overview of the goal and rules for each decision round. The game prototype is accessible via the provided link as a downloadable zip file. Additionally, a demonstration video of the artifact has been made available.

Table 4. Game description

Game Step	Description	Printscreen (only German)
Role choice	The roles in the game are divided (authority person, harmony-oriented person, reserved person, long-established person)	
Decision 1 and feedback	In the first round, all players received the same information and were asked to jointly select a planning tool for future tasks. This initial decision was intentionally kept simple to familiarize participants with the game mechanics.	
Reward	All participants were awarded ten points to build motivation regardless of their choice.	
Decision 2	In the second round, players had to choose a technology for rebuilding the fictional city. This scenario required active discussion and role-based argumentation, with asymmetric information distribution across players. Groupthink, self-censorship, and authority bias were actively triggered and subsequently reflected upon in a structured debrief, which included a theoretical explanation of these biases.	
Decision 3	The third scenario involved selecting a prototyping method. All participants had access to the same materials—images and videos—but were misled by a non-player character, the "queen," who suggested incorrect conclusions. With the help of embedded hints, players were encouraged to identify conflicting arguments. This round simulated the sunflower bias by illustrating the risks of over-reliance on a dominant perspective.	
Decision 4	In the following round, participants had to choose a strategy for city construction. The options available were directly influenced by the first decision, creating an opportunity to reflect on earlier choices. Although the group had received points for the initial decision, they were now asked to question its validity, thereby simulating groupthink under consistency pressure and the sunk cost effect. The team could restart or continue with a suboptimal strategy.	
Decision 5	The final decision required the group to determine how to support citizens moving into their new homes. Again, information was distributed unevenly: one player had all the necessary details but was distracted by a side activity embedded in the game. This scenario once simulated social loafing and tested the group's ability to mitigate information asymmetry.	

Throughout the game, players received points based on their ability to recognize and avoid bias-driven decisions.

Game mechanics such as point systems and rewards enhanced engagement and motivation. Players were required to interpret information, analyze scenarios, and provide structured feedback, ensuring a close alignment between game mechanics and learning objectives. The user interface featured interactive elements and a consistent layout to support intuitive use. Nevertheless, the prototype had limitations: moderator guidance replaced auditory feedback, and complex group dynamics such as groupthink could only be partially simulated. While the narrative provided sufficient structure for gameplay, it left room for more in-depth interactive storytelling. Future iterations will enhance interactivity, expand narrative elements, and integrate the game into a broader training framework for sustained learning impact.

7   Evaluation

In the evaluation, the characteristics from Table 2 are assessed first, followed by an evaluation of the biases (requirements).

Evaluating the game's characteristics, including role-playing, storyline, and feedback mechanisms, revealed significant discrepancies between theoretical expectations and practical outcomes. Although prior literature highlights the importance of on-site collaboration and competitive elements for engagement [27], the evaluation revealed that these aspects were less influential in practice. Participants responded positively to the game's simplicity and reported that hybrid or online formats were equally effective as in-person sessions. Collaborative elements, such as the distribution of asymmetric information among players, were more critical to engagement and learning, aligning closely with findings in the literature and frequently emphasized in participant feedback.

The role concept, widely regarded in the literature as crucial for enhancing social interaction and raising awareness of bias, was validated in the game but revealed notable deviations. Participants struggled to fully assume the predefined roles described during the short game duration, highlighting the importance of sufficient time for role adoption. Roles aligned with participants' personalities were more effective, while those that diverged posed challenges. Additionally, roles had varying impacts on biases; they effectively addressed social loafing and authority bias when paired with specific instructions, but had minimal influence on tackling sunflower bias. The absence of role-specific feedback in specific scenarios further limited their effectiveness. These findings suggest that while the role concept is valuable, its design must consider game duration, participant traits, and targeted biases to maximize its impact.

The feedback approach implemented in the game differed from the literature, advocating immediate feedback after each task. Instead, a staggered approach was employed, providing feedback after the initial decision and emphasizing reflection during the debriefing. By withholding explanations of biases until the debriefing, participants engaged in open discussions and independently identified biases, enhancing their critical thinking and awareness.

The fantasy storyline was more engaging than realistic scenarios, contrasting with some literature suggesting realistic settings might be more effective [26]. Unlike realistic scenarios, the fantasy setting eliminated reliance on project experience, forcing participants to focus solely on their roles and the provided information. This approach emphasized cognitive biases and effectively achieved the game's learning objectives.

The statements regarding the requirements and the implemented biases were compared to evaluate the effects and the importance of the biases. The game focused on groupthink bias, as the literature emphasized the most significant influence on group decisions and highlighted various symptoms of groupthink in the artifact [4, 6]. The feedback in the questionnaire shows that the authority bias is the most important. This finding was unexpected and contradicted the existing literature, which had anticipated a greater focus on groupthink bias. Since the authority bias was also built into the game, this difference is of little relevance for evaluating the game's impact.

Not all biases were addressed equally well in the game. Groupthink and authority biases were consistently acknowledged, with participants providing detailed, real-world examples of their effects and strategies for mitigation. In contrast, awareness of sunflower bias and social loafing varied among groups, with some participants failing to identify these biases or their consequences. This discrepancy suggests that not all biases are equally amenable to the same game design elements, indicating that each may require different debiasing methods. Participants frequently highlighted authority bias, citing examples such as repeated interference by authority figures in flat agile structures and unchallenged group decisions resulting from directive leadership. These scenarios align with the literature and reinforce the study's findings on the influence of authority bias in decision-making.

The game's evaluation indicated that participants could effectively recognize groupthink and authority bias during gameplay and in the post-game questionnaire. They offered detailed, real-world examples and demonstrated an understanding of how these biases influence group decision-making. For instance, one participant noted that they remained silent during a disagreement because a dominant team member had already expressed a strong opinion, mirroring real project situations where authority figures unintentionally suppress alternative views. Another group admitted to following the majority despite doubts, simply to avoid delaying the decision process. However, they struggled to identify the interplay between these biases or how one might reinforce another, as suggested by the literature. For instance, authority bias can aggravate social loafing when participants feel that their contributions are undervalued, and sunflower bias can promote groupthink by suppressing dissenting opinions. This gap highlights a potential area for improvement in the game's design.

Despite this limitation, participant feedback revealed that the game was well-received and effective as a training method. This finding is consistent with the existing literature, which suggests that collaborative games can help mitigate biases and improve group decision-making. This feedback contributed to the various characteristics implemented in the game. While the game has raised awareness of bias, its long-term effects on decision-making remain unknown. Participants who played the game provided more concrete and nuanced examples of biases than non-players, indicating a greater likelihood of recognizing and addressing biases in practice. Improving the game to highlight interdependencies among biases and tailoring elements to address specific biases could further enhance its effectiveness.

7.1 Discussion

The evaluation confirmed that the collaborative serious game effectively raised awareness of cognitive biases, particularly groupthink and authority bias, while engaging participants through a fantasy storyline and role-playing elements. Participants recognized symptoms of groupthink, such as self-censorship and the illusion of unanimity, and identified authority bias through real-world examples, demonstrating the game's relevance to decision-making processes. However, awareness of sunflower bias and social loafing varied, with some participants failing to identify these biases or their consequences, suggesting the need for more tailored game elements to address them.

While valuable, the game's role-playing feature revealed deviations from theoretical expectations. Participants found it challenging to fully adopt roles that diverged from their personalities, particularly within the game's short duration. Roles aligned with participants' traits proved more effective, contradicting literature assumptions that diverse role alignment improves bias recognition [24, 25]. The delayed reflective debriefing also proved more effective than immediate feedback, challenging established serious games principles [26]. Additionally, the fantasy storyline outperformed realistic scenarios, opposing findings that realistic settings ensure better learning transfer [26]. Although the game succeeded in raising awareness of bias, its long-term impact on decision-making remains unclear. Players demonstrated a deeper understanding of biases than non-players, offering more specific mitigation strategies. However, the game could benefit from improvements, such as highlighting interdependencies among biases and refining characteristics to address less-recognized biases, like sunflower bias and social loafing. These enhancements would further strengthen the game's potential as a tool for improving group decision-making.

8 Conclusion and Contribution

This study confirms that implementing a collaborative serious game as a training strategy enhances group decision-making by raising awareness of cognitive biases. The research contributes to the academic field by addressing a critical gap: the lack of specific training tools integrating cognitive biases, project management, and group decision-making.

The study contributes to the literature on bias mitigation and serious game design by demonstrating how a game can enhance awareness of cognitive biases in a project environment. The findings further challenged existing literature [26] by showing that debriefing and reflection, rather than immediate feedback, can enhance learning outcomes. It provides empirical insights into designing effective serious games, revealing the importance of aligning roles with participants' personalities and tailoring game elements to specific biases. Overall, this study provides evidence that a well-designed adventure role-playing game can significantly reduce biases, such as groupthink, authority bias, social loafing, and sunflower bias, among project teams. This offers valuable insights into designing and implementing serious games for bias mitigation in group decision-making contexts.

The paper has several limitations. The evaluation was based on a small sample from a single corporate context, which limits the generalizability of the results. Future work should focus on refining the role concepts for more flexible or personalized role adoption, integrating further biases to assess lasting behavior change. Conducting and expanding the application of the game to various organizational contexts and integrating it into broader training programs could further enhance its effectiveness. The study adhered to established quality criteria for qualitative research [28]. Credibility was ensured by involving participants from real-world project teams and designing the game around practical decision-making challenges. Dependability and confirmability were supported through the structured use of Jaccard's framework and systematic feedback analysis. Transferability was facilitated by detailed documentation of the game's design and evaluation, offering a foundation for further research and application in diverse organizational contexts.

References

1. Morelli, M., Casagrande, M., Forte, G.: Decision making: a theoretical review. Integr. Psychol. Behav. **56**, 609–629 (2022). https://doi.org/10.1007/s12124-021-09669-x
2. Buchanan, L., O'Connell, A.: A brief history of decision making. Harv. Bus. Rev. **84**, 32 (2006)
3. Rumeser, D., Emsley, M.: Can serious games improve project management decision making under complexity? Proj. Manag. J. **50**, 23–39 (2019). https://doi.org/10.1177/8756972818808982
4. Virine, L., Trumper, M.: Project Decisions: The Art and Science, 2nd edn. Berrett-Koehler Publishers, Oakland (2019)
5. Grünig, R., Kühn, R.: Successful Decision-Making: a Systematic Approach to Complex Problems. Springer, New York (2005)
6. Bang, D., Frith, C.D.: Making better decisions in groups. R Soc. Open Sci. **4**, 170193 (2017). https://doi.org/10.1098/rsos.170193
7. Kahneman, D.: Maps of bounded rationality: psychology for behavioral economics. Am. Econ. Rev. **93**, 1449–1475 (2003). https://doi.org/10.1257/000282803322655392
8. Acciarini, C., Brunetta, F., Boccardelli, P.: Cognitive biases and decision-making strategies in times of change: a systematic literature review. Manag. Decis. **59**, 638–652 (2020). https://doi.org/10.1108/MD-07-2019-1006
9. Janis, I.L.: Victims of groupthink: a psychological study of foreign-policy decisions and fiascoes (1972)
10. Gültekin, D.G.: Understanding and mitigating authority bias in business and beyond. In: Siniksaran, E. (ed.) Advances in Human Resources Management and Organizational Development, pp. 57–72. IGI Global (2024)
11. Ding, R.: Successful project decision-making. In: Ding, R. (ed.) Key Project Management Based on Effective Project Thinking, pp. 75–94. Springer, Heidelberg (2016)
12. Hällgren, M.: Groupthink in temporary organizations. Int. J. Manag. Proj. Bus. **3**, 94–110 (2010). https://doi.org/10.1108/17538371011014044
13. Susi, T., Johannesson, M., Backlund, P.: Serious games - an overview (2015)
14. Reynaldo, C., Christian, R., Hosea, H., Gunawan, A.A.S.: Using video games to improve capabilities in decision making and cognitive skill: a literature review. Procedia Comput. Sci. **179**, 211–221 (2021). https://doi.org/10.1016/j.procs.2020.12.027
15. Dunbar, N.E., Miller, C.H., Adame, B.J., et al.: Implicit and explicit training in the mitigation of cognitive bias through the use of a serious game. Comput. Hum. Behav. **37**, 307–318 (2014). https://doi.org/10.1016/j.chb.2014.04.053
16. Silva, F.G.M.: Practical methodology for the design of educational serious games. Information **11**, 14 (2020). https://doi.org/10.3390/info11010014

17. Hou, H.-T.: Diverse development and future challenges of game-based learning and gamified teaching research. Educ. Sci. **13**, 337 (2023). https://doi.org/10.3390/educsci13040337

18. Hevner, A.R., Chatterjee, S.: Design Research in Information Systems: Theory and Practice. Springer, New York (2010)

19. Jaccard, D., Suppan, L., Sanchez, E., et al.: The co.LAB generic framework for collaborative design of serious games: development study. JMIR Serious Games **9** (2021). https://doi.org/10.2196/28674

20. Vyas, V., Zweifel, T.: Gorilla in the cockpit: breaking the hidden patterns of project failure and the system for success (2022)

21. Sicina, R.: Learn from Failure: The Key to Successful Decision Making. AuthorHouse (2017)

22. Muntwiler, C.: Cognitive biases and debiasing in strategic decision making. Dissertation, University of St.Gallen (2024)

23. Cesario, J.: What can experimental studies of bias tell us about real-world group disparities? Behav. Brain Sci. **45**, e66 (2022). https://doi.org/10.1017/S0140525X21000017

24. Greco, M.: The use of role–playing in learning. games-based learning advancements for multi-sensory human computer interfaces: Tech. Effect. Pract. 157–173 (2009). https://doi.org/10.4018/978-1-60566-360-9.ch010

25. Harris, J.N., Swab, R.G., Mercer, I.S., Tomczyk, D.A.: Role-playing as experiential learning: using dungeons and dragons to teach management concepts. In: Developments in Business Simulation and Experiential Learning: Proceedings of the Annual ABSEL Conference, vol. 50 (2023)

26. Johnson, C., Bailey, S., Buskirk, W.: Designing effective feedback messages in serious games and simulations: a research review, pp. 119–140 (2017)

27. Wang, C., Huang, L.: A systematic review of serious games for collaborative learning: theoretical framework, game mechanic and efficiency assessment. Int. J. Emerg. Technol. Learn. (iJET) **16**, 88 (2021). https://doi.org/10.3991/ijet.v16i06.18495

28. Lincoln, Y.S., Guba, E.G., Pilotta, J.J.: Naturalistic inquiry. Int. J. Intercult. Relat.elat. **9**, 438–439 (1985). https://doi.org/10.1016/0147-1767(85)90062-8

From Data Quality for AI to AI for Data Quality: A Systematic Review of Tools for AI-Augmented Data Quality Management in Data Warehouses

Heidi Carolina Tamm[1,2] and Anastasija Nikiforova[2(✉)] ⓘ

[1] AS Swedbank, Tallinn, Estonia
[2] University of Tartu, Tartu, Estonia
Anastasija.Nikiforova@ut.ee

Abstract. High data quality (DQ) is essential for analytics, compliance, and AI performance, yet its management remains complex, often manual, and resource intensive. This study investigates the extent to which existing tools support AI-augmented data quality management (DQM) in data warehouse environments. To this end, we conduct a systematic review of 151 DQ tools to evaluate their automation capabilities, particularly in detecting and recommending DQ rules in data warehouse - a key component of data ecosystems. Using a multi-phase screening process based on functionality, trialability, regulatory compliance (e.g., GDPR), and architectural compatibility with data warehouses, only 10 tools met the criteria for AI-augmented DQM. Most tools emphasize data cleansing and preparation for AI, rather than leveraging AI to improve DQ itself. Although metadata- and ML-based rule detection techniques are present, features such as SQL-based rule specification, reconciliation logic, and explainability of AI-driven recommendations remain scarce. The study contributes practical guidance for tool selection and identifies critical design requirements for next-generation AI-driven DQ solutions, advocating a complementary shift in focus from "*data quality for AI*" to "*AI for data quality management.*"

Keywords: Artificial Intelligence · Data Quality · Data Quality Management · Data Quality Tool · Data Management · Data Warehouse · Explainable AI · Machine Learning · Rule Detection

1 Introduction

In today's data-driven era, data serves as a critical asset, enabling the transformation of raw facts into actionable insights for decision-making across industries. However, the utility of these insights depends on data quality (DQ), a concept gaining attention since the 1960s and becoming prominent in computer science by the 1990s [1, 2]. The projected growth of global data to 175 zettabytes by 2025 [3] amplifies the challenge of ensuring high-quality data while balancing storage and processing efficiency. Poor DQ carries significant costs - up to 19% of businesses report customer loss due to inaccurate or incomplete data [3]. The emergence of AI and Large Language Models (LLMs) further

© The Author(s), under exclusive license to Springer Nature Switzerland AG 2026
R. Deneckère et al. (Eds.): BIR 2025, LNBIP 562, pp. 37–53, 2026.
https://doi.org/10.1007/978-3-032-04375-7_3

raises the stakes, as these systems depend on high-quality inputs to function effectively. This has led to widespread emphasis on *"data quality for AI."* However, leveraging AI to enhance DQ management itself, i.e., reversing the focus, remains underexplored.

Despite the ongoing shifts to decentralized, domain-driven architectures, traditional data warehouses (DW) continue to serve as central infrastructures for integrating and analyzing organizational data [5]. These systems aggregate data from disparate sources across data ecosystem(s) (within and outside an organization's data ecosystems) but are often plagued by complex and time-consuming data quality management (DQM) tasks. Tracing data lineage and defining rules is particularly burdensome. Compliance obligations, such as General Data Protection Regulation (GDPR), add to the cost and complexity of maintaining DQ [6].

To address these challenges, automation -and particularly AI-driven automation-holds strong promise. Considering relative predictability of DQ requirements within DWs environment [7], we assume such solutions are already widely available in the market, seeking for the most appropriate for being adopted. This study, inspired by the challenges faced by a financial institution seeking to modernize its DQM (one of authors belongs to), investigates whether the market offers tools that support automated DQM, particularly rule detection and anomaly identification in DWs. From both a practitioner and research perspective, identifying such tools is a first step toward engineering more effective, AI-enhanced DQM systems.

We conduct a systematic review of 151 tools, assessing their functionality, integration with DWs, regulatory compliance, and support for rule discovery. Ultimately, only 10 tools met the defined criteria and were capable detecting DQ rules or anomalies automatically. Our findings suggest that while some tools offer ML or metadata-driven features, the landscape remains fragmented and lacks comprehensive AI augmentation, with current tools most often prioritizing data cleaning for AI applications, rather than using AI to improve DQ. As such, ML is rather seen as a "consumer" of DQ with the vast of research and developments on ensuring DQ for ML, with limited use of ML for DQM. Thus, we advocate a focus shift from the traditional focus on ensuring DQ for ML models to using AI and ML to improve data quality management, i.e., from *"Data Quality for AI"* to *"Data quality for AI and AI for Data Quality Management"*.

The paper is structured as follows: Sect. 2 provides the background, Sect. 3 presents the methodology, Sect. 4 presents results, Sect. 5 discusses findings, limitations, and future directions, and the final section concludes the study.

2   Background

This section provides a brief overview of foundational concepts and a review of related literature to contextualize the study.

2.1   Concepts

Data quality refers to the extent to which data meets specific requirements, commonly aligned with ISO 9000[1] standards. Definitions range from abstract notions of *"fitness for*

---

[1] https://www.iso.org/standard/62085.html.

use" [8, 9] to measurable dimensions such as *completeness, timeliness, accuracy*, and *consistency* [1]. These dimensions are context-dependent, varying by domain, data type, and use case and often evolving over time [2, 10]. Efforts have been made to standardize DQ dimensions for specific sectors [11, 12], e.g., the European Parliament and Council mandate seven dimensions for financial institutions, which include *completeness, accuracy, consistency, timeliness, uniqueness, validity*, and *traceability* [13]. However, these remain largely domain-specific and lack general applicability.

DQ assessment typically combines subjective -user evaluation- and objective - computational techniques- approaches [11, 14]. Objective methods include detecting incorrect values, constraint violations, and integrity issues, highlighting the interplay between technical tools and stakeholder needs [11, 14]. Effective DQM follows a top-down approach, translating business needs into enforceable rules categorized as *business DQ rules*, which describe quality expectations in business terms, and *data quality rule specifications*, which define physical-level requirements [15]. Profiling and validation tasks help quantify DQ and ensure adherence to such rules [16].

Data warehouses, integral to large organizations, consolidate historical and operational data across systems and act as a "*single source of truth*"[2], often, however, being issue prone. DQ issues may stem from poor input data (e.g., entry errors, database design flaws) or from integration and migration processes [17]. These include formatting issues, missing records, and duplicates, often addressed through reconciliation and conformance checks[3]. Metadata -physical, logical, and conceptual- plays a vital role in DQ, supporting traceability, integration, and rule generation [18]. As such, metadata is increasingly used as a foundation for automated DQ analysis methods.

2.2 Related Work

To inform this study, we conducted a systematic literature review (SLR) of existing literature on surveys of DQ tools, as well as the SLR on automated DQ rules detection. As this is not a central focus of this study, we do not provide methodological details about the conducted SLRs, which, however, are available on Zenodo[4].

Our *SLR of DQ tools surveys* revealed three relevant studies: [19, 20], and [21]. Neely et al. [21] evaluated tools in engineering asset management, and Houston et al. [20] explored tools for clinical trials. Both studies primarily focused on domain-specific tools rather than on automated DQ rule detection. Given the rapid evolution of technology they are also now somewhat outdated today. [19] reviewed 667 tools, identifying only 13 capable of automating routine tasks such as scheduling checks. However, none addressed automated DQ rule generation, central to this study's objectives.

Our *SLR on automated DQ rule generation* identified 10 relevant studies (available on Zenodo (see footnote 4)), with several more studies published in 2024 and 2025 (with SLR conducted in late 2023). Most studies focus on Integrity Constraints (ICs) rather than comprehensive DQ rules. These ICs include techniques for identifying data inconsistencies or constraints [22], with newer approaches extended to optimizing

---

[2] https://www.sap.com/insights/what-is-A-data-warehouse.html.

[3] https://www.experian.co.uk/business/glossary/data-reconciliation/.

[4] https://doi.org/10.5281/zenodo.15882759.

rule discovery for big data [23–25]. Advanced approaches, such [25], include entity-enhancing rules, which combine ML and rule-based methods to address both entity and conflict resolution, and Heine et al.'s [26] *RADAR* - a domain-specific language employing Autoregressive Integrated Moving Average (ARIMA) models for DQ rule specification. Recent advancements in automated DQ include *SAGED* - an error detection tool introduced in [27], which leverages few-shot meta-learning to detect errors in data being added to the system, generating feature vectors through meta-classifiers. Sartore et al. [28], in turn, presented an anomaly detection system using fuzzy logic for agricultural data editing developed for the United States Department of Agriculture's National Agricultural Statistics Service. Finally, [29] presented prototype called *DQ-MeeRKat* that offers automated monitoring through reference-data-profile-annotated knowledge graphs to verify that newly inserted or up-dated data continues to conform to the constraints stored in the reference-data-profiles, with the intent to come up in the future to achieve what the authors call "AI-based surveillance state", which would be capable of characterizing various kinds of data to detect drifts and anomalies in DQ at early stages.

Despite progress, most proposals emphasize specific dimensions such as uniqueness or domain-specific use cases, with the lack of solutions comprehensively detecting DQ rules, while specializing in data warehouses. Moreover, early stages of our SLR demonstrated that most DQM studies focus on ensuring DQ for ML tasks [30–32], neglecting AI and ML's potential in augmenting DQM itself. This underscores the need for a focus shift and motivates the present study.

3 Methodology

This study employs a systematic review methodology [33], adapted to examine DQ tools. The objective is to identify tools that leverage AI -ML or alternative methods-for automatically detecting DQ rules and anomalies, while also allowing users to define custom rules for DQ adjustments. To attain this objective, five key **research questions** were established.

Q1. What is the current landscape of DQ tools?
Q2. What functionalities do DQ tools offer?
Q3. Which data storage systems DQ tools support? and where does the processing of the organization's data occur?
Q4. What methods do DQ tools use for rule detection?
Q5. What are the advantages and disadvantages of existing solutions?

To address these questions, tools were identified through a combination of rankings from technology reviewers and academic sources. A Google search was conducted using keyword *("the best data quality tools" OR "the best data quality software" OR "top data quality tools" OR "top data quality software") AND "2023"* (search conducted in December 2023). Additionally, this list was complemented by DQ tools found in academic articles, identified with two queries in Scopus, namely *"data quality tool" OR "data quality software"* and *("information quality" OR "data quality") AND ("software" OR "tool" OR "application") AND "data quality rule"*.

For **selecting** DQ tools, several exclusion criteria were applied. Tools from sponsored, outdated (pre-2023), non-English, or non-technical sources were excluded. Academic papers were restricted to those published within the last ten years, focusing on the computer science field. This resulted in 16 ranking lists[5], and 35 academic papers, and 151 DQ tools. A list of sources and tools is provided on Zenodo (see footnote 4).

To structure the **review** process and facilitate answering the established questions (Q1−Q3), a review protocol was developed, consisting of three sections (protocol is available on Zenodo). The initial tool assessment was based on *availability, functionality*, and *trialability* (e.g., open-source, demo version, or free trial). Tools that were discontinued or lacked sufficient information were excluded. The second phase (and protocol section) focused on evaluating the functionalities of the identified tools. Initially, the core ***DQM functionalities*** were assessed, such as *data profiling, custom DQ rule creation, anomaly detection, data cleansing, report generation, rule detection, data enrichment*. Subsequently, *additional **data management functionalities*** such as *master data management, data lineage, data cataloging, semantic discovery*, and *integration* were considered. These parameters were selected based on the authors' experience with DQ tasks, discussions with DQ professionals, and previous research [10].

The final stage of the review examined the tools' *compatibility with data warehouses* and GDPR compliance. Tools that did not meet these criteria were excluded. As such, the 3rd section of the protocol evaluated the tool's environment and connectivity features, such as whether it operates in the *cloud, hybrid*, or *on-premises*, its *API support, input data types (.txt,.csv,.xlsx,.json)*, and its ability to connect to data sources including *relational* and *non-relational databases, data warehouses, cloud data storages, data lakes*. Additionally, it assessed whether the tool processes data *on-premises* or in the *vendor's cloud environment*. Tools were excluded based on criteria such as not supporting data warehouses or processing data externally.

As such, the review applied the following selection criteria: (1) Exclusion Criteria (EC): (1a) *EC1: Tool does not exist*; (1b) *EC2: Tool is outdated or has been discontinued*; (1c) *EC3: Tool does not qualifies as a DQ tool*; (1d) *EC4: Tool is part of another tool, integrated system or suite*; (1e) *EC5: Insufficient information available about the tool*; (1f) *EC6: Tool only checks only a single data attribute*; (1g) *EC7: Tool does not detect DQ rules or anomalies*; (1h) *EC8: Tool detects anomalies, but does not support the definition of DQ rules*; (1i) *EC9: Tool is not suitable for data warehouses*; (1j) *EC10: Data processing location is unclear*; (1k) *EC11: Tool processes data exclusively in the vendor's cloud environment*; (2) Inclusion Criteria (IC): (2a) *IC1: Tool supports automated DQ rule detection*; (2b) *IC2: Tool is capable of detecting anomalies and allows users to define custom DQ rules*.

Finally, DQ tools were reviewed, and data **synthesized.** Tools were reviewed based on testing of tools, information on official websites, demos, and documentation.

---

[5] Datamation, Simplilearn, TechTarget, Solutions Review, TechRepublic, Geekflare, TrustRadius, BIS (Grooper), G2, Slashdot, SourceForge, PeerSpot, SoftwareReviews, WebinarCare, HubSpot, Gartner.

4   Results and Analysis

4.1   The Data Quality Tools Landscape

RQ1 examined the availability and characteristics of DQ tools, focusing on their existence, functionality, and availability for testing or demos. Initially, tools were filtered using the EC1-EC5 exclusion criteria. We evaluated the availability of trials and documentation and assessed the level of detail in the information provided for each tool. A detailed summary of analysis results is available on Zenodo (see footnote 4).

The search identified 151 DQ tools, with 46 excluded during validation (Fig. 1, 2). Four tools were found to *no longer exist* (*Data Preparator, DataMentors, Synchronos*, and *matchIT DQ Solutions*), six were *discontinued or marked legacy* (e.g., *Datiris Profiler* and *Experian Pandora*), and nine tools were *"duplicates,"* or *"integrated into larger platforms"* (e.g., *Rapid Data Profiling* and *Self-Service Data Preparation* within *DataRobot AI Platform*). Additionally, 27 tools were found to be *irrelevant to DQ*, primarily focusing on functionalities such as data integration or customer management. After exclusions, 105 tools remained for further analysis.

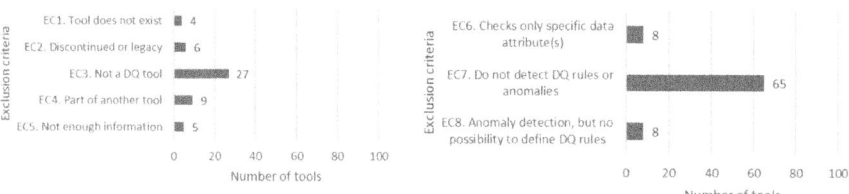

Fig. 1. Tools excluded at the 1st phase.

Fig. 2. Tools excluded at the 2nd phase.

Trial availability varied: 13 tools were *open-source*, 10 offered *free trials*, 5 provided *demos*. 12 tools had a trial request form, and 43 offered demo requests, though most received *no response*, with some resulted in *sales calls*, with 2 cases resulting in a *software provider call*, and one - *free license* for a trial. A total of 22 tools were *non-trialable*, requiring direct purchase. Despite these limitations, no tools were excluded based solely on trial availability. For non-trialable tools, reviews were based on available documentation, websites, and videos. Around half provided public documentation, while 45 (42.9%) did not. Some tools lacked sufficient details, providing heavily generic marketing content. To address this, we introduced a *"Level of Information"* attribute to assess the clarity and completeness of the provided materials. Of the reviewed tools, 72 were well-described, 28 had partial descriptions, and 5 were excluded due to insufficient information. Several tools lacked clear functional descriptions. For instance, the *Black Tiger Platform* provided vague details about its DQ features, and tools such as *DataStreams* and *OpenDQ* were unclear on their DQ capabilities beyond validation, reporting. *Deduplix Ixsight* mentioned fuzzy matching models, but their functionality was not explained in detail. In the first phase, 51 tools were excluded, leaving 100 tools for further analysis, as shown in Fig. 1, 2.

4.2   Features of Data Quality Tools

Next, we examined the features and functionality of DQ tools, particularly their ability to automatically detect DQ rules. Detailed results are available on Zenodo (see footnote 4). The 100 tools were mapped to the DQ functionalities (Fig. 3). The most popular DQ functionalities included *data cleansing* (75%) and *profiling* (67%) were the most common features, while only 12% of tools supported *DQ rule detection. SQL-based rule definition*, critical for data warehouse users, was the least common, present in 6% of tools.

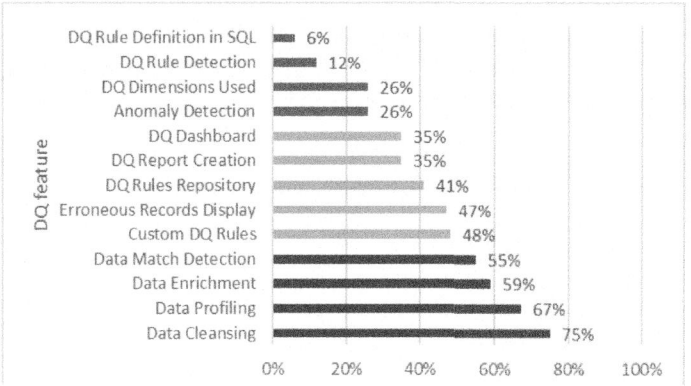

Fig. 3. Relative frequency of features

The tools were also evaluated for *additional functionalities* such as *master data management, data lineage, cataloguing, semantic discovery,* and *data integration,* with their relative frequencies presented in Fig. 4. Some tools appeared to be purely DQM-focused (e.g., *OpenRefine, Ataccama DQ Analyzer*), while others were multi-functional platforms (e.g., *SAP Information Steward, Syniti Knowledge Platform*).

Eight tools were narrowly focused on specific attributes (e.g., *email, address validation*) or anomaly detection but lacked custom rule definitions (incl. based on the discovered anomalies). Examples include *Experian Email Validation, Informatica Address Verification, Holodetect, Rapid Data Profiling,* and *Talend Data Fabric*. 65 tools lacked both *anomaly detection* and *DQ rule detection*, with 54 being cleansing-focused, with 31 of them lacking *custom rule definition* (e.g., *TIBCO Clarity, OpenRefine*). These tools are primarily suited for data preparation for ML tasks. After applying EC6-EC8 exclusion criteria, 19 tools remained - 12 that could detect DQ rules and 7 that detected anomalies and allowed custom rule definitions.

The final 19 tools were further analysed for their ability to detect DQ rules or anomalies, define custom DQ rules, and other functionalities (Table 1). Tools capable of detecting and recommending DQ rules (IC1) were more multifunctional than those under IC2[6],

---

[6] Data enrichment and cleansing are mapped for statistical purposes but are not in the scope of this study seeking for DQ tools for DW where data cleansing and enrichment are not used locally.

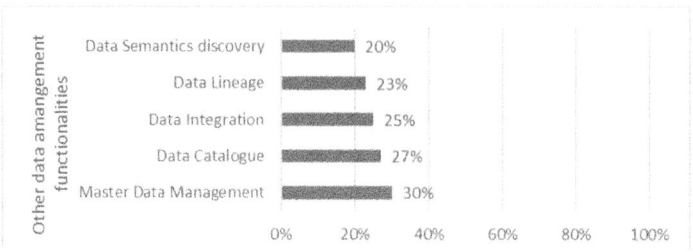

Fig. 4. Relative frequency of other data management functionalities.

i.e., were more likely to allow custom rule definitions. For IC1 tools, SQL rule definition was rare (8.3%). Data management functionalities (Table 2) were more frequent among IC1 tools, further supporting their multifunctional nature.

Table 1. Relative frequency of DQ features.

Functionality	IC1	IC2
Custom DQ Rules	100%	100%
DQ Rules Repository	91.7%	100%
Anomaly Detection	91.7%	100%
Data Profiling	100%	85.7%
Erroneous Records Display	100%	71.4%
DQ Report Creation	91.7%	71.4%
DQ Dashboard	75%	85.7%
DQ Dimensions Used	75%	57.1%
Data Match Detection	75%	42.9%
Data Cleansing	75%	42.9%
DQ Rule Detection	100%	0%
Data Enrichment	50%	28.6%
DQ Rule Definition in SQL	8.3%	57.1%
Custom DQ Rules	100%	100%

Table 2. Relative frequency of other data management functionalities.

Functionality	IC1	IC2
Data Semantics discovery	75%	57.1%
Data Catalogue	75%	57.1%
Data Lineage	75%	42.9%
Master Data Management	66.7%	14.3%
Data Integration	41.7%	28.6%

The included tools (IC1 and IC2) offered broader functionality than excluded tools (Fig. 5), which primarily focused on data cleansing and enrichment. This aligns with the study's aim to identify tools for DQ issue detection rather than issue fixing, as data warehouses rely on correcting issues at the source before loading data.

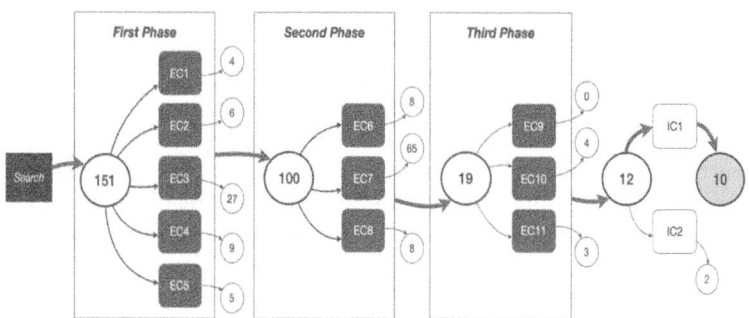

Fig. 5. Review process.

4.3   The Environment and Connectivity

This section evaluates the environment solutions and connectivity features (RQ3) of the 19 DQ tools. Detailed results are available on Zenodo (see footnote 4). All 19 tools supported *connections to data warehouses*, incl. Compatibility with relational and non-relational databases, cloud data storages, data lakes, and popular systems such as *Teradata Vantage, Snowflake, and Amazon Redshift*. As such, no tools were excluded. Then, tools were analyzed with relation to their *deployment environments*. 13 tools were *cloud-based*, two tools operated both *on-premises* and in the *cloud*, one - *on-premises*, one - *hybrid*, and one tool offered cloud or *hybrid deployment*.

Regarding *data processing location*, 7 tools supported processing on *the vendor's or organization's side*, 4 processed data in *private clouds*, one - *on-premises*, three - in the *vendor's cloud*, and four - *lacked information* on processing locations. To ensure GDPR compliance, tools with *unknown* processing locations or *vendor-cloud-only* processing were excluded, leaving 12 tools - 10 capable of detecting DQ rules, and 2 alternatives (IC2) that detected anomalies and allowed custom rules definition.

Overall, the review process involved three phases, narrowing down from 151 tools to 12 suitable candidates ((based on EC1-EC11), Fig. 6). Initial *validation* (EC1-EC5) excluded tools that did not exist, were discontinued, or lacked sufficient information. This reduced the list to 100 tools with DQ functionalities. Exclusions based on *inability to detect DQ rules or anomalies, along with the custom rule definition* (EC6-EC8) reduced the list to 19 tools - 12 DQ **rule detectors** (IC1) and 7 **anomaly detectors** with custom rule definition (IC2). Tools *failing to meet environmental and connectivity expectations* (EC9-EC11) were excluded, leaving 12 tools - 10 meeting the main goal (IC1) and 2 alternatives meeting IC2. These are *AbInitio Enterprise Data Platform, Anomalo, Ataccama ONE, Collibra Platform, DQLABS Platform, DvSum, Global IDs Data Quality Suites, Informatica Cloud Data Quality, Informatica Data Engineering Quality, Informatica Master Data Management, LiTech Data Quality Management.*

Among the non-trialable tools, some allowed demo requests or provided documentation. Open-source tools were significantly reduced, with 11 excluded as lacking DQ rule detection (EC7) or custom rule definitions (EC8). All tools with available free trials were also excluded for the same reason.

Some alternative DQ tools were identified as semi-automated DQ rule detection solutions being able to detect anomalies and enable users to define their own DQ rules. Among the 7 anomaly detection tools, for 4 tools, it was unclear where the data is processed, and one tool processed data on the vendor's cloud. Following the exclusion criteria, only 2 suitable solutions remained: (1) *Anomalo* that uses unsupervised ML to detect DQ issues without predefined rules or thresholds, allowing users to adjust monitoring without coding; (2) *LiTech DQ Management* that consolidates data validations into a single platform, encompassing a DQ rule repository and DQ reports. It leverages ML to autonomously generate DQ validations, including anomaly detection with an integrated alerting system. Other anomaly detectors (IC2) primarily focused on data preparation for ML or business analytics, offering functionalities such as *data cleansing* and *enrichment* but without using DQ rules, with examples including *Experian DataArc360, Rapid Data Profiling*. The heatmap in Fig. 6 visualizes tool selection based on defined criteria, emphasizing the challenges in identifying suitable tools for AI-augmented DQM in DW.

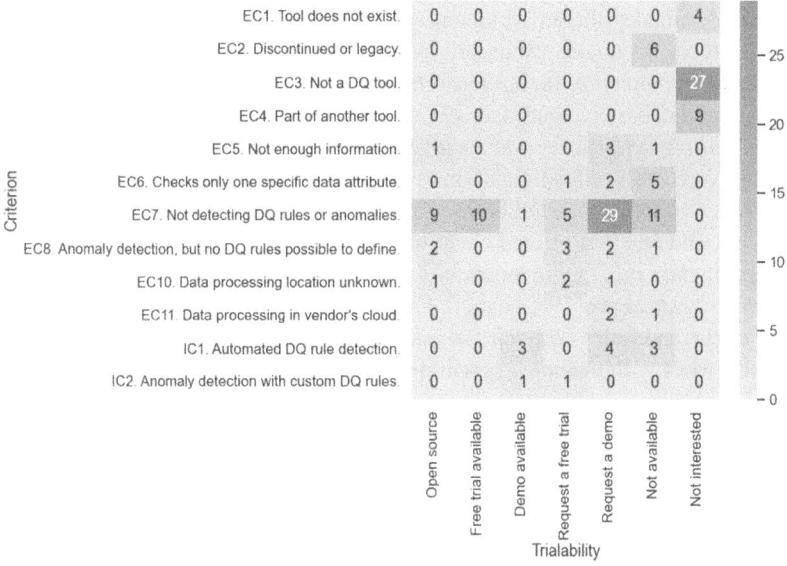

Fig. 6. Heatmap of tool counts by selection criteria and trialability.

4.4 Solutions Supporting the Data Quality Rule Detection

As a result, only ten DQ tools satisfied the defined criteria, being able to detect DQ rules and suited for use with data warehouses. Our analysis identified four primary methods (RQ4) employed by these tools for DQ rules discovery (detailed tool-by-tool description is available on Zenodo (see footnote 4)): (1) **metadata-based detection**

(*DQLabs Platform*); (2) **built-in rules and ML** (*Ataccama ONE Platform, DvSum*); (3) **metadata and ML** (*AbInitio Enterprise Data Platform, Informatica* products); (4) **ML-only detection** (*Collibra, Syniti Knowledge Platform*).

Five tools emphasize *metadata* as the foundation for rule discovery, while six incorporate ML. One tool, *Global IDs DEEP Platform*, provides limited details on its approach to DQ rule detection, however, emphasizes *metadata management* and *data lineage*. As such, it can be inferred that metadata serves as an essential foundation for (AI/)ML-driven DQ rules discovery. However, solutions tailored specifically to data warehouses and their complex ecosystems remain scarce.

Finally, all ten tools were cloud-based and connected to data sources via APIs, ensuring broad compatibility and flexibility across various data environments, including public, private, and virtual private clouds.

4.5 Advantages and Disadvantages of Current Solution

As part of RQ5, we examined the strengths and limitations of the DQ tools capable of detecting DQ rules, to derive insights for future advancements. Key features of these tools are summarized in Fig. 7, with detailed breakdown of features per tool available on Zenodo. Our analysis revealed that all the 10 DQ tools form the final pool possess the capability for *data profiling*, enabling users to define *custom rules, generate DQ reports, maintain and organize rules in DQ rule repository*, and *report erroneous records for their further investigation*, and the ability to connect to data warehouses via APIs. Some tools support management of *DQ rules* by allowing them to be *edited, accepted, and rejected*, along with *tagging DQ rules with relevant data elements and business terms*. As such, they have been categorized as advantages and "minimum requirements" for AI-augmented DQM.

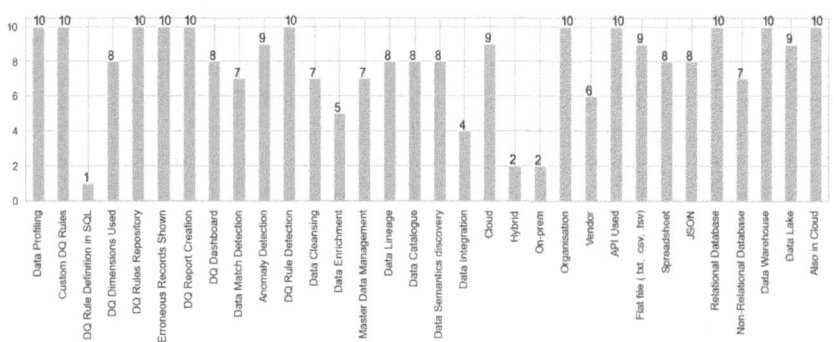

Fig. 7. Frequencies of DQ, other data management, environment, and connectivity features.

While these tools offered valuable functionality, several gaps were identified: (1) lack of support of the *detection of reconciliation rules*, critical for ensuring data consistency across systems; (2) *SQL-based rule definition* was rare, despite its relevance for data warehouse users; (3–4) many tools lacked *support for diverse data types* (e.g., integer, float, Boolean, string, date), with many tools rather focusing on selected data types, ignoring others, *and failing to cover a broad range of DQ dimensions* (e.g., referential integrity, external consistency) or tag detected rules with relevant dimensions; (5) analysed tools often lacked transparency in rule recommendation logic, hindering stakeholder involvement to *modify, accept, or reject suggested rules* before implementation; (6) while *cloud computing* offers benefits such as scalability and flexibility, for many tools it remained unclear if existing solutions were maximizing these advantages.

Although current DQ tools demonstrate strengths, they lack critical capabilities, preventing the identification of a "silver bullet" solution for comprehensive AI-augmented DQM in data warehouse environments.

5 Discussion

5.1 Discussion and Implications

This study aimed to assess the extent to which current DQ tools support AI-augmented DQM in DW environments. Through a systematic review of 151 tools, we identified only 10 that met key criteria, including support for rule detection, metadata utilization, DW integration, GDPR-compliant deployment, and user-driven configurability. Such a drastic reduction aligns with prior studies, such as [19], who found only 17 suitable tools out of 667, noting limitations such as proprietary focus or minimal DQ measurement features. The main barriers include discontinued products, limited functionality, and inadequate documentation or trial access, highlight the market's fragmentation, making tool selection difficult for organizations.

The findings reveal a significant gap in both commercial and academic tool offerings. While many tools support data profiling and cleansing, few implement automation capabilities that actively leverage AI or ML to improve DQ [30, 31]. I.e., AI is largely treated as a *consumer* of high-quality data rather than an *enabler* of DQ processes.

Only a small fraction of tools utilized ML-based techniques, and those that did often lack transparency and user control. Metadata-driven methods are common but remained underutilized in dynamic rule generation. Few tools offered hybrid approaches that combine metadata inference, ML-based anomaly detection, and rule-based logic, even though such combinations show high potential [25, 26].

Moreover, support for SQL-based rule definition essential in DW contexts was rare, despite being widely acknowledged as a critical feature [10, 15]. Most tools also lacked support for tagging rules with DQ dimensions [9], reconciliation logic, and collaborative rule validation between business and technical stakeholders.

As such, this study has several practical and theoretical implications. The findings reveal critical gaps in current tools for augmented DQM tailored to DW. This gap presents opportunities for the development and commercialization of advanced AI-augmented solutions that can detect and enforce DQ rules automatically, streamlining DQM processes, reducing human workload, and lowering operational costs while ensuring regulatory compliance with regulations such as GDPR. More specifically, our analysis, including of strengths and weaknesses of the analysed tools (Sect. 4.5), suggest key priorities for developing AI-augmented DQM tools: (1–2) **automated rule generation** enabling rule generation for diverse data types and domains, using metadata as the foundation for ML-driven rule discovery and anomaly detection, and leveraging

Natural Language Processing (NLP) and LLMs to create **rules in both SQL and natural language formats** for technical and business stakeholders and their collaboration; (3) **comprehensive data types coverage** and domains (finance, healthcare, education, etc.), automatically determining the type based on the data to cover all data elements of DW, (4) **broad DQ dimension coverage** addressing commonly used dimensions and integrating domain-specific requirements, such as financial reporting standards [13] to be followed by financial institutions to report DQ (by specific set of DQ dimensions); (5) **efficient processing using cloud computing** for scalability, while (6) ensuring **in-stack or private cloud data processing for GDPR (and other regulation) compliance**; (7) **enhanced governance and collaboration by linking rules to roles** (e.g., data (quality) stewards, business analysts, information owners) to streamline governance and reduce rule overload. To move the field forward, future tools must address both technical and organizational needs, bridging the gap between automation and explainability, and between AI engineers, DQ stewards and business users.

For practitioners, the study offers actionable guidance for evaluating and selecting appropriate DQ tools based on functionality, explainability, deployment flexibility, and integration with existing DW infrastructures. With only 10% of widely promoted tools meeting criteria for DQM in DW, organizations can use this study to filter irrelevant tools and focus on testing viable candidates, improving tool selection and adoption.

The study advances the dialogue on leveraging AI, and ML, in particular, for automating (or at least augmenting) DQM. It lays the groundwork for a theoretical framework for automated DQ rule detection (in DW), which so far has been limited to a very few studies, such as a ML-based solution for DQ controls as an essential instrument in DQM [34]. Moreover, this study challenges the dominant narrative of "*data quality for ML*" by advocating a complimentary shift to "***ML (or broader – AI) for data quality management***" advocating AI-driven tools that enhance DQ processes while ensuring high-quality data across ecosystems for analytics, ML, and informed decision-making.

The rise of LLMs presents a timely opportunity to initiate a broader dialogue on how emerging technologies, including LLMs and Explainable AI (XAI), can enhance DQM and data governance within complex data ecosystems [35]. LLMs offer potential to improve DQM by enabling natural language interaction, automating rule generation, summarizing anomalies and root causes, enhancing interpretability through context-aware explanations, enriching metadata, and supporting semantic discovery across heterogeneous or unstructured data sources [36–39]. These capabilities promise increased scalability, improved support for multimodal data, and reduced manual effort in routine quality tasks. Despite these advantages, LLM integration in DQM remains limited and underexplored in academic literature, with most advances occurring in proprietary settings. This aligns with [40] analysis –centred around DQ for ML though–identified 4 tools – *Winpure*, *Ataccama ONE*, *Soda Core*, and *Evidently*– that have begun integrating AI, with *Soda Core* incorporating generative pre-trained transformers (GPT) for rules suggestion and monitoring tasks to support non-technical users. Based on our own experience, tools like Ataccama ONE, Collibra Data Quality & Observability, Informatica Intelligent Data Management Cloud, and Soda have started incorporating generative models, though mostly in early-stage or narrowly scoped applications [41]. Nevertheless, several challenges remain, particularly in domain-specific and regulated contexts where general-purpose models may struggle with specialized vocabularies, logic, or compliance requirements. Key concerns include explainability, data privacy, trust in outputs, legal constraints (e.g., GDPR), and risks of overreliance or misinterpretation. Future research should prioritize responsible and transparent adoption of LLMs and XAI in DQM, especially through human-in-the-loop approaches, clear traceability, and interdisciplinary co-design. Open collaboration between academia, industry, and tool providers will be critical to realizing the transformative potential of LLMs for improving data quality across increasingly complex and federated data ecosystems.

5.2 Limitations

This study has several limitations. A primary limitation of this study is the reliance on secondary data for tools that were not available for testing, predominantly sourcing information from software providers' websites, videos, and documentation, which may introduce selection or interpretation bias. Documentation completeness, in turn, affected the analysis, e.g., for some tools, the data processing location remained unclear. Second, although the systematic search was broad, drawing from over 50 sources and over 150 tools, some tools may have been missed, and only 10 tools met the inclusion criteria for automated DQ rule detection. Third, the study focuses specifically on data warehouses; while justified, this limits generalizability to other architectures such as data lakes or operational databases. Finally, given the rapid pace of technological change, especially in generative AI, this study represents a snapshot in time. Still, it offers a relevant foundation for further development of AI-augmented DQM tailored to data ecosystems. While this study centers on traditional DQM in data warehouses, we acknowledge that ML-specific concerns, such as bias, imbalance, or high dimensionality, may diverge from conventional DQ metrics like completeness. Bridging these perspectives warrants further research, especially in ML-integrated data ecosystems.

6 Conclusion

This study systematically reviewed 151 DQ tools to evaluate their suitability for AI-augmented DQM in DW. Through a multi-phase evaluation process, only 10 tools were found to support automated rule detection and align with key organizational requirements, revealing a significant gap in both market and academic offerings. Core limitations include the lack of SQL-based rule definition, weak reconciliation support, limited transparency of AI-generated rules, and narrow data type or DQ dimension coverage. While metadata- and ML-based methods show promise, hybrid approaches combining metadata, ML, and rule-based logic, though considered most effective, remain rare.

The results reveal that most tools focus on ensuring *"data quality for AI"* rather leveraging AI for DQ management itself. AI is still largely treated as a consumer of data rather than an enabler of DQM. As AI and low-code technologies advance [35], we anticipate the rise of user-friendly, self-service DQ tools, empowering non-technical users to conduct DQM more independently and efficiently [42].

As such, this study advocates renewed focus on integrating AI/ML into DQM to enable dynamic, explainable rule detection across data types and business domains. Key design requirements for future tools include SQL-based and natural language rule definition, explainable AI for business-technical collaboration, GDPR-compliant deployment, and scalable cloud architectures vital to enabling robust and accessible DQM within data warehouse ecosystems. The findings will inform the next phase of our research - requirements engineering for the development of an AI-augmented DQM tool, grounded in the strengths and limitations identified among the final pool.

Practically, the study offers a roadmap for organizations to evaluate and select suitable DQ tools aligned with DW-specific needs. Theoretically, it enriches the theoretical foundation for AI-driven DQM solutions in DW and beyond. It underscores the need for interdisciplinary collaboration to address the shortcomings of current tools, making a call for both helixes to shift the dominant narrative of *"data quality for ML"* toward *"data quality for AI and AI for data quality management"*, highlighting the potential of emerging technologies such as LLMs to transform DQM and data governance. This shift can empower organizations to harness the full potential of AI, building robust data ecosystems and maintaining them, ensuring high-quality data for diverse applications, and fostering progress in data management practices.

Declaration of Generative AI and AI-Assisted Technologies in the Writing Process. The authors hereby discloses that ChtGPT-3.5 was used to improve the conciseness and clarity of selected sentences in this study. After using this tool/service, the authors reviewed and edited the content as needed and take full responsibility for the content of the published article.

Disclosure of Interests. The authors have no competing interests to declare that are relevant to the content of this article.

References

1. Scannapieco, M., Catarci, T.: Data quality under the computer science perspective, Rome, Italy (2002)
2. Nikiforova, A.: Definition and evaluation of data quality: user-oriented data object-driven approach to data quality assessment. Baltic J. Mod. Comput. **8**(3) (2020)
3. Coughlin, T.: 175 zettabytes by 2025. Forbes (2018). https://www.forbes.com/sites/tomcoughlin/2018/11/27/175-zettabytes-by-2025/
4. Dixon, M.: The cost of bad data: have you done the math? Global Marketing Alliance (2020). https://www.the-gma.com/the-cost-of-bad-data-have-you-done-the-math
5. Blohm, I., Wortmann, F., Legner, C., Köbler, F.: Data products, data mesh, and data fabric: new paradigm (s) for data and analytics?. Bus. Inf. Syst. Eng. 1–10 (2024)
6. Karkošková, S.: Data governance model to enhance data quality in financial institutions. Inf. Syst. Manage. (2022)
7. Fadler, M., Legner, C.: Who owns data in the enterprise? Rethinking data ownership in times of big data and analytics. In ECIS (2020)
8. Wang, R.Y., Strong, D.M.: Beyond accuracy: what data quality means to data consumers. J. Manag. Inf. Syst. **12**(2), 5–34 (1996)
9. Batini, C., Scannapieco, M.: Data and Information Quality, 1st edn. Springer, Cham (2016). https://doi.org/10.1007/978-3-319-24106-7
10. Cichy, C., Rass, S.: An overview of data quality frameworks. IEEE Access **7**, 24634–24648 (2019). https://ieeexplore.ieee.org/document/8642813, https://doi.org/10.1109/ACCESS.2019.2899751

11. Batini, C., Cappiello, C., Francalanci, C., Maurino, A.: Methodologies for data quality assessment and improvement. ACM Comput. Surv. (CSUR) **41**(3), 1–52 (2009)
12. Sidi, F., Panahy, P.H.S., Affendey, L.S., Jabar, M.A., Ibrahim, H., Mustapha, A.: Data quality: a survey of data quality dimensions. In: 2012 International Conference on Information Retrieval & Knowledge Management, pp. 300–304. IEEE (2012)
13. European Parliament Council. Regulation (EU) no 575/2013 of the European parliament and of the council of 26 June 2013 on prudential requirements for credit institutions and investment firms and amending regulation (EU) no 648/2012 (2013). https://eur-lex.europa.eu/legal-con tent/EN/TXT/?uri=CELEX:32022R0439
14. Lacagnina, C., et al.: Towards a data quality framework for EOSC. Technical report (2023)
15. Plotkin, D.: Data Stewardship, 2nd edn. Academic Press (2020). https://doi.org/10.1016/ C2019-0-03988-X
16. Loshin, D.: The Practitioner's Guide to Data Quality Improvement, 1st edn. Morgan Kaufmann (2010). https://doi.org/10.1016/C2009-0-17212-4
17. Liu, Q., Feng, G., Tayi, G.K., Tian, J.: Managing data quality of the data warehouse: a chance-constrained programming approach. Inf. Syst. Front. **23**, 375–389 (2019)
18. Hedden, H.: The Accidental Taxonomist, 2nd edn. Information Today, Inc. (2016)
19. Ehrlinger, L., Wöß, W.: A survey of data quality measurement and monitoring tools. Front. Big Data **5** (2022)
20. Houston, L., Probst, Y., Yu, P., Martin, A.: Exploring data quality management within clinical trials. Appl. Clin. Inform. **9**, 72–81 (2018)
21. Neely, M., Lin, S., Gao, J., Koronios, A.: The deficiencies of current data quality tools in the realm of engineering asset management. In: 12th Americas Conference on Information Systems, AMCIS 2006, vol. 1, pp. 430–438. Association for Information Systems (2006)
22. Ilyas, I.F., Chu, X.: Trends in cleaning relational data: consistency and deduplication. Found. Trends® Databases **5**(4), 281–393 (2015)
23. Li, M., Wang, H., Li, J.: Mining conditional functional dependency rules on big data. Big Data Min. Anal. **3**(1), 68–84 (2019)
24. Taleb, I., Serhani, M.: Big data pre-processing: closing the data quality enforcement loop. In: Proceedings - 2017 IEEE 6th International Congress on Big Data, pp. 498–501 (2017)
25. Fan, W., Han, S., Wang, Y., Xie, M.: Parallel rule discovery from large datasets by sampling. In: Proceedings of the ACM SIGMOD International Conference on Management of Data, SIGMOD 2022, pp. 384–398. (2022)
26. Heine, F., Kleiner, C., Oelsner, T.: Automated detection and monitoring of advanced data quality rules. In: Hartmann, S., Küng, J., Chakravarthy, S., Anderst-Kotsis, G., Tjoa, A., Khalil, I. (eds.) DEXA 2019, Part I. LNCS, vol. 11706, pp. 238–247. Springer, Cham (2019). https://doi.org/10.1007/978-3-030-27615-7_18
27. Abdelaal, M., Ktitarev, T., Städtler, D., Schöning, H.: SAGED: few-shot meta learning for tabular data error detection. In: EDBT, pp. 386–398 (2024)
28. Sartore, L., Chen, L., van Wart, J., Dau, A., Bejleri, V.: Identifying anomalous data entries in repeated surveys. J. Data Sci. **22**(3), 436–455 (2024)
29. Ehrlinger, L., Gindlhumer, A., Huber, L.-M., Wöß, W.: DQ-MeeRKat: automating data quality monitoring with a reference-data-profile-annotated knowledge graph. In: Proceedings of the 10th International Conference on Data Science, Technology and Applications (2021)
30. Byabazaire, J., O'Hare, G., Delaney, D.: Data quality and trust: a perception from shared data in IoT. In: 2020 IEEE International Conference on Communications Workshops (ICC Workshops), pp. 1–6. IEEE (2020)
31. Li, N., Qi, Y., Li, C., Zhao, Z.: Active learning for data quality control: a survey. ACM J. Data Inf. Qual. (2024)
32. Lu, Y., et al.: Machine learning for synthetic data generation: a review. arXiv preprint arXiv: 2302.04062 (2023)

33. Kitchenham, B., Brereton, P.: A systematic review of systematic review process research in software engineering. Inf. Softw. Technol. **55**(3), 2049–2075 (2013)
34. Walter, V., Gyoery, A., Legner, C.: Deploying machine learning based data quality controls–design principles and insights from the field (2022)
35. Pucci, E., Sancricca, C., Andolina, S., Cappiello, C., Matera, M., Barberio, A.: Improving understandability and control in data preparation: a human-centered approach. In: Guizzardi, G., Santoro, F., Mouratidis, H., Soffer, P. (eds.) CAiSE 2024. LNCS, vol. 14663, pp. 284–299. Springer, Cham (2024). https://doi.org/10.1007/978-3-031-61057-8_17
36. Fernandez, R.C., Elmore, A.J., Franklin, M.J., Krishnan, S., Tan, C.: How large language models will disrupt data management. Proc. VLDB Endow. **16**(11), 3302–3309 (2023)
37. Kliimask, K., Nikiforova, A.: TAGIFY: LLM-powered tagging interface for improved data findability on OGD portals. In: 2024 Fifth International Conference on Intelligent Data Science Technologies and Applications (IDSTA), Dubrovnik, Croatia, pp. 18–27 (2024). https://doi.org/10.1109/IDSTA62194.2024.10746941
38. Pernici, B., et al.: The future of sustainable data preparation. In: CEUR Workshop Proceedings, vol. 3741, pp. 486–497 (2024)
39. Varma, S., Shivam, S., Ray, B., Biswas, S.: Reimagining enterprise data management using generative artificial intelligence. In: 2024 11th IEEE Swiss Conference on Data Science (SDS), pp. 107–114. IEEE (2024)
40. Zhou, Y., Tu, F., Sha, K., Ding, J., Chen, H.: A survey on data quality dimensions and tools for machine learning invited paper. In: 2024 IEEE International Conference on Artificial Intelligence Testing (AITest), pp. 120–131. IEEE (2024)
41. Roht, K.: Generative AI in data quality management. UT Institute of Computer Science Graduation Theses (2025)
42. Sundberg, L., Holmström, J.: Democratizing artificial intelligence: How no-code AI can leverage machine learning operations. Bus. Horiz. **66**(6), 777–788 (2023)

Human Factors and Well-Being
in Digital Systems

Designing Human-Centric Digital Workplaces: A Bibliometric Analysis of Technology-Related Stressors in Flexible Working Arrangements

Hasan Koç[(✉)] [iD] and Jennifer Hynes [iD]

Berlin International University of Applied Sciences, Salzufer 6, 10587 Berlin, Germany
{koc,hynes}@berlin-international.de

Abstract. This study presents a bibliometric analysis of scholarly literature on technology-related stressors in flexible working arrangements (FWAs), with a focus on informing the human-centric design of digital workplaces. Using a systematic search across four major databases and forward snowballing, 32 articles indexed in Web of Science were analysed. The field has experienced rapid growth since 2020, with a notable increase in international collaboration, though research remains concentrated in the Global North. The analysis identified core journals, influential authors, and foundational works. Conceptual structure analysis revealed three main research clusters: the work-life technology interface, application of the Job Demands-Resources (JD-R) framework, and employee well-being in ICT-supported FWAs. Thematic analysis showed a post-pandemic shift toward well-being, work engagement, and coping, reflecting an increasing emphasis on human-centric outcomes. The findings underscore the importance of designing digital workplaces that balance technological efficiency with employee autonomy, psychosocial support, and well-being. Limitations include the small sample size, reliance on abstract-based conceptual analysis, exclusion of non-indexed literature, and the Eurocentric bias in the data set. The results provide a foundation for future research and practice in developing sustainable, human-centric digital work environments.

Keywords: Technostress · Flexible Working Arrangements · Human-Centric Digital Workplaces · Bibliometric Analysis

1 Introduction

The rapid digital transformation of organisations has fundamentally redefined the nature of work. Flexible working arrangements (FWAs), including remote [1, 2], hybrid [3, 4], and telework [5–7] models as well as digital workplaces [8, 9], are becoming increasingly prevalent across sectors [1, 10]. While FWAs offer notable advantages such as increased autonomy [11, 12] and work-life integration [11, 13, 14], they also introduce new challenges related to the pervasive use of digital technologies for work purposes [3, 15]. Among these challenges, technostress, the stress experienced due to the use of Information and Communication Technologies (ICTs) [16], emerge as a critical concern

© The Author(s), under exclusive license to Springer Nature Switzerland AG 2026
R. Deneckère et al. (Eds.): BIR 2025, LNBIP 562, pp. 57–75, 2026.
https://doi.org/10.1007/978-3-032-04375-7_4

for both employees [17–19] and organisations [20, 21]. Technostress can negatively impact well-being [22], job satisfaction [23, 24], and productivity [25], raising important questions about how digital transformation can be managed in a human-centric and sustainable manner.

Recent scholarly literature demonstrates that while digital transformation and FWAs offer increased autonomy and flexibility, they also intensify work demands and blur the boundaries between work and personal life, leading to heightened technostress and work-related stress [26]. Empirical studies show that factors such as excessive digital actions outside regular hours and frequent virtual meetings significantly increase stress levels in highly digitalized environments [27]. As digital transformation accelerates, organizations are increasingly recognizing that the success of flexible working arrangements depends not only on technological advancements but also on the ability to address human needs and experiences [28, 29]. Recent scholarship emphasizes that a huma-centric approach, prioritizing employee well-being, engagement, and autonomy, is not merely about technology adoption, but focuses on tailoring digital initiatives to meet the diverse needs of individuals within various contexts [30]. This shift towards a more human-centric approach recognizes that successful digital transformation depends largely on understanding and addressing the experiences and interactions that users have with technology [31]. While technology use offers significant productivity gains, it also introduces new job demands, such as blurred work-life boundaries and increased cognitive load, which can negatively impact well-being if not managed carefully [32]. A digital workplace is a holistic set of interconnected technologies that employees utilize daily to perform their tasks, supporting communication, collaboration, and productivity in remote, hybrid, or flexible settings [33]. Designing human-centric digital workplaces requires not only technological optimization but also a strategic focus on psychosocial support, flexible boundaries, and the empowerment of employees to ensure well-being and sustainable performance [29, 34].

As FWAs continue to evolve and digital tools become ever more embedded in organizational processes, the academic literature on technology-related stressors has expanded rapidly. The field is characterized by a diversity of disciplinary perspectives, methodologies, and theoretical approaches [16, 35]. This diversity, while enriching, also makes it challenging to obtain a clear, quantitative understanding of the intellectual structure, influential contributors, and emerging trends within the research domain. Bibliometric analysis offers a systematic and quantitative approach to mapping the development of a research field by examining publication patterns, citation networks, authorship, and thematic evolution [36, 37]. Unlike conceptual or narrative reviews, bibliometric methods focus on the dynamics of scholarly communication, the identification of core journals and authors, and the detection of research trends and knowledge gaps. Such analyses are increasingly important for supporting evidence-based decision-making by researchers, practitioners, and policymakers in the context of responsible, human-centric digital transformation.

This study applies bibliometric analysis to the scholarly literature on technology-related stressors in FWAs, with the aim of interpreting the field's intellectual landscape and supporting the development of human-centric digital work environments. The following research questions guide the analysis: 1. How has the scholarly literature on technology-related stressors in flexible working arrangements developed? 2. Which journals, authors, and countries have played central roles in advancing this field and what are the collaboration patterns? 3. What are the foundational works and theoretical underpinnings of technostress research in FWAs? 4. What are the main conceptual themes in the literature on technology-related stressors in flexible working arrangements? 5. How have research priorities and thematic foci in this field evolved over time?

Against this background, the study is structured as follows: Sect. 2 outlines the review methodology. Section 3 presents the analysis results, addressing the research questions in dedicated subsections. Section 4 discusses the findings from a human-centric design perspective. Section 5 summarises the sutdy, addressing its limitations.

2 Methodology

This study follows the bibliometric analysis procedure proposed by [38], which includes the following steps: research design, data collection, data analysis, visualization, and interpretation. We conducted a systematic search across EBSCOhost, Scopus, ProQuest, and Web of Science to identify empirical studies on technology-related stressors in flexible working arrangements (FWAs). The search string combined two main concepts: ("new way? of working" OR "digital workplace?" OR telework OR "remote work?" OR "telecommut?" OR "virtual work?") AND ("digital stress" OR "technology-related stress" OR "technological stress" OR technostress* OR techno-stress* OR "techno-overload" OR "techno-complexity" OR "techno-uncertainty" OR "techno-insecurity" OR "techno-invasion").

Table 1. Overview of the article selection process for the bibliometric analysis

Stage	Database search (n)	Forward snowballing (n)	Reason for exclusion
Records identified	214	294	
Removed before screening	140	–	Duplicates, non-English, not peer reviewed
Screened	74	294	
Excluded after screening	55	276	Irrelevant to technostress/FWAs, non-empirical
Total eligible articles	19	18	
Excluded (not indexed)	5	–	Not available in Web of Science for bibliometric analysis

Final pool for bibliometric analysis: 32

Inclusion criteria were: empirical studies (quantitative or qualitative) published in English, in peer-reviewed journals or conference proceedings, focusing on adults in organizational contexts (including freelancers), with outcomes related to technology-related stressors (e.g., technostress, digital stress, digital well-being) in the context of flexible working arrangements supported by ICTs. Exclusion criteria were: non-empirical articles (e.g., reviews, editorials, conceptual papers), studies not addressing technology-related stressors, those not involving FWAs or lacking employee autonomy, and articles not published in English or not peer-reviewed. The procedure was supplemented by forward snowballing to identify additional relevant studies that may not be captured by database searches alone [39].

The systematic search across four databases initially identified 214 records. After removing 140 duplicates, non-English, or non-peer-reviewed articles, 74 records underwent title/abstract screening, excluding 55 for irrelevance to technology-related stressors or flexible work contexts, leaving 19 eligible articles. Forward snowballing of these 19 articles yielded 294 additional records, of which 276 were excluded during screening, resulting in 18 further inclusions. This produced a total of 37 eligible articles. For the bibliometric analysis, only articles indexed in Web of Science were included for consistency and comparability of bibliometric data [40]. As a result, five articles were excluded, yielding a final sample of 32 articles (see Table 1). Two independent reviewers screened all titles, abstracts, and full texts for eligibility. Discrepancies were resolved through discussion. To assess the consistency of the selection process, we calculated the inter-rater reliability using Cohen's kappa, achieving substantial agreement ($\kappa = 0.68$), which indicates a high level of consistency between reviewers [41].

3   Bibliometric Analysis

For the bibliometric analysis, we used the bibliometrix package in R [42]. Of the 32 articles in the pool, the metadata completeness was excellent, except for the DOI, which was missing in one article.

The analysis reveals a rapidly evolving field of study spanning from 2014 to 2024, with a robust annual growth rate of 25.89%, indicating a significant increase in scholarly interest and output especially after 2020. The corpus comprises contributions from 102 authors, with 28.12% of the articles demonstrating international collaboration. On average, each document is authored by 3.47 researchers, suggesting a trend towards collaborative research efforts. The pool's richness is evidenced by 164 keywords, while the substantial number of 2,072 references underscores the depth and breadth of the theoretical foundations of this research area. Having received 14.53 citations on average, the relative recency of the field is highlighted by the average article age of 1.75 years, indicating a contemporary and rapidly developing body of knowledge.

3.1   Scientific Outlets

Of the 32 articles, Internet Research has published the most studies (n = 4), followed by Frontiers in Psychology (n = 3), Information Technology & People (n = 3), and Computers in Human Behaviour (n = 2). Collectively, these four journals account for

38% of the articles in the pool, indicating their significant role in shaping the discourse on this subject (see Table 2). According to Bradford's Law [43], these journals can be considered the core sources for research in this area, suggesting that they consistently publish high-quality, relevant studies on the topic.

Table 2. Most relevant and local cited sources

Most relevant sources (Nr. of articles)	Most local cited sources (Nr. of articles)
Internet Research (4)	MIS Quarterly (103)
Frontiers in Psychology (3)	Journal of Applied Psychology (94)
Information Technology and People (3)	Computers in Human Behavior (83)
Computers in Human Behavior (2)	Information Systems Journal (56)
Others (1)	Information Systems Research (48)

Within the same pool, MIS Quarterly is the most frequently cited journal (n = 103), followed by the Journal of Applied Psychology (n = 94), Computers in Human Behavior Journal (n = 83).

3.2 Authors and Country Collaborations

Jaeung Lee emerges as the most influential author, receiving 129 total citations, closely followed by Ayoung Suh with 124 citations. Louise Leung and Renwen Zhang share the third position with 73 citations each, while Pengzhen Yin accumulates 66 citations. In terms of longitudinal contribution, Christian Maier demonstrates the most extended research timeline, spanning from 2014 to 2024 with two publications [12, 18]. Jaeung Lee follows with three articles [6, 23, 44] across this period, and Pengzhen Yin contributes two [19, 24]. The publication pattern indicates a high degree of diversity in authorship, with 92% of authors contributing a single article, 7% publishing two, and only 1% producing three articles (see Table 3). Total citation (TC) per year refers to the average number of citations an article receives per year since its publication.

Table 3. Authors' impact metric (Top 5 Authors according to TC)

Author	h_index	g_index	m_index	TC	NP	PY_start
Jaeung Lee	2	3	0,25	129	3	2017
Ayoung Suh	1	1	0,125	124	1	2017
Louise Leung	1	1	0,125	73	1	2017
Renwen Zhang	1	1	0,125	73	1	2017
Pengzhen Yin	2	2	0,286	66	2	2018

We investigated the distribution and international collaboration of scientific publications across various countries which have two or more records (see Fig. 1). Judging by the corresponding authors' countries, German institutions lead by contributing to 18.8% of the articles, with a notable but low multiple country publication (MCP) rate of 16.7%. This indicates limited international collaboration among German researchers. In contrast, Chinese institutions account for 15.6% of the articles, with a higher MCP rate of 40.0%, the second highest among the analysed countries, reflecting a stronger inclination towards international partnerships. French and US institutions each contribute 9.4% of the articles; however, while French publications have an MCP rate of 33.3%, indicating moderate international collaboration, US publications exhibit no MCP activity, suggesting a focus on domestic research collaborations. Finnish, Indian, and Italian institutions each contribute 6.3% of the articles. Notably, Indian institutions demonstrate the highest MCP rate at 50%, highlighting their international research collaborations, whereas Finnish and Italian institutions show no MCP activity.

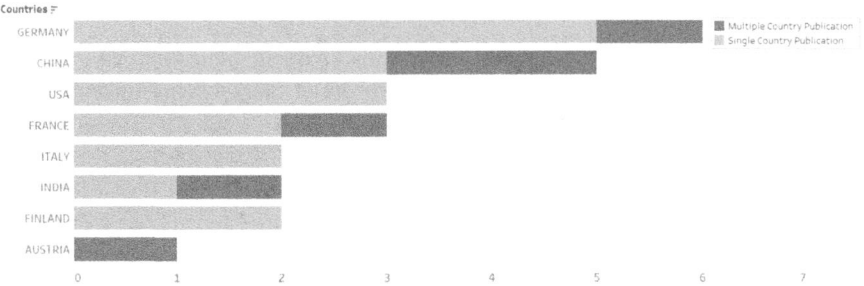

Fig. 1. Publishing countries and collaborations

Considering the nationality of all authors, Germany emerges as the most productive country with 19 authors, notably exhibiting a significant increase in 2022. China and the United States of America are tied for the second position, each contributing with 10 authors to the literature. Interestingly, the data suggests a shift in productivity for the U.S. American authors, who became more prolific after 2021. India and Italy have contributed with 6 and 5 authors respectively. Both countries only began contributing after 2022, suggesting a recent recognition of the importance of this field (see Fig. 2).

3.3 Influential and Seminal Articles

In the analysis, several articles within the pool emerged as particularly influential based on their citation metrics. The normalised TC score is calculated by dividing the actual count of citing items by the expected citation rate for documents published in the same year. [11] demonstrates strong impact with 53 total citations, translating to an average of 17.67 citations per year and a normalised total citation score of 3.53 (calculated by dividing the actual count of citing items by the expected citation rate for documents published in the same year). While [44] has received the highest absolute number of citations (124) over time, yielding an annual average of 15.50, its normalised total

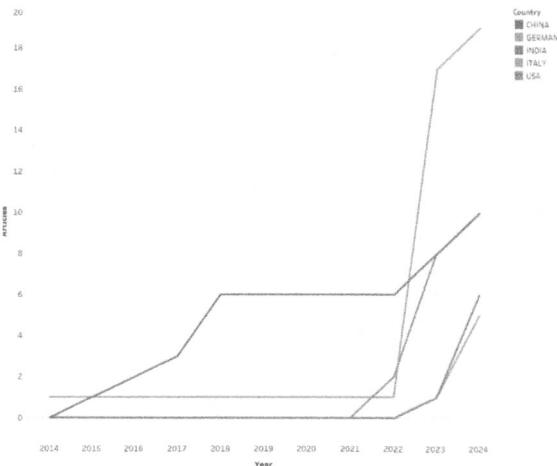

Fig. 2. Publication timeline of countries

citation score of 1.26 suggests a more moderate impact when adjusted for field and temporal factors. [9] exhibits robust citation performance with 47 total citations, an annual average of 11.75, and a normalised total citation score of 1.77. Importantly, [7] presents the highest normalised total citation score of 4.07, despite a lower absolute citation count of 11. Most global cited articles (with at least 10 total citations) are shown in Table 4.

Table 4. Most global cited documents

Article	TC	TC per year	Normalised TC	Year
[11]	53	17,67	3,53	2022
[44]	124	15,50	1,26	2017
[9]	47	11,75	1,77	2021
[7]	11	11,00	4,07	2024
[5]	73	9,13	0,74	2017
[24]	62	8,86	1,00	2018
[12]	26	2,36	1,00	2014

The Reference Publication Year Spectroscopy (RPYS) analysis of technology-related stressors in FWAs reveals a concentration of influential works in recent years, with notable historical roots. The most prominent peak occurs in 2020, accumulating 211 citations, with seminal contributions from [45–47] reflecting the surge in research interest coinciding with the global shift to remote work (see Fig. 3). This is closely followed by 2021 (206 citations), with [48–50]. The third highest peak is in 2017 with 144 citations. The most cited article is [44], two most influential authors as discussed earlier.

They are followed by [51] and [52]. Notably, 2007 stands out as a landmark year when examining the deviation from the 5-year median, marking the first instance of exceeding 100 citations and highlighting the foundational nature of publications from this period. [25] was cited 17 times within the analysed pool, and emerges as a particularly influential work. This is accompanied by significant contributions from [53] and [54]. References prior to 2007 refer to theoretical constructs (e.g., JD-R Theory, [55]), research methods (e.g., common method bias [56]), stress-related concepts (e.g., occupational stress [57] or work exhaustion [58]).

Table 5. Most frequently cited articles within the pool

Year	Article	First author	Local citations
2008	[59]	T.S. Ragu-Nathan	24
2011	[60]	Ramakrishna Ayyagari	21
2007	[25]	Monideepa Tarafdar	17
2015	[61]	Monideepa Tarafdar	16
2010	[62]	Joseph F. Hair	12
2010	[63]	Monideepa Tarafdar	12
2017	[44]	Ayoung Suh	11
2019	[16]	Didem Taşer	9
2007	[53]	Chudoba Ahuja	9
2007	[54]	Ravi S. Gajendran	9

The RPYS analysis, combined with an examination of the most frequently cited articles within our sample, reveals three significant patterns in the literature on technology-related stressors in FWAs. Firstly, five seminal works on technology-related stress emerge as foundational to the field: [25, 59–61, 63]. These studies collectively establish the theoretical underpinnings and conceptual framework for understanding technostress in organisational contexts. Secondly, [62] stands out as a primary methodological reference for quantitative studies in this domain, indicating its importance in guiding the analytical approaches employed by scholars. Lastly, [44] represents a pivotal contribution in contextualising technology-related stressors within FWAs, with a particular focus on teleworking. This study bridges the gap between broader technostress literature and the evolving landscape of FWAs, thereby setting a foundation for subsequent research in this area (see Table 5).

3.4   Conceptual Structure and Thematic Clusters

We conducted a conceptual structure analysis using Multiple Correspondence Analysis (MCA) on bigrams extracted from article abstracts, after removing generic methodological terms0F[1]. Examination of the resulting dendrogram indicated a three-cluster solution, as shown in Fig. 4. The next subsections detail the topics covered by the literature on technology-related stressors in FWAs.

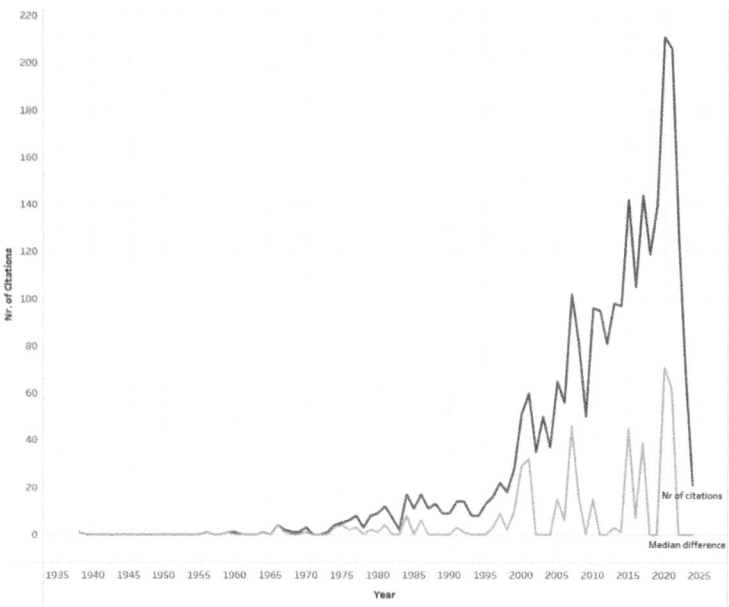

Fig. 3. Reference publication year spectroscopy analysis

Work-Life Technology Interface

Cluster 1 (red in Fig. 4) is characterized by terms such as work-family conflict, work-life balance, job resources, and technologies. This reflects a research focus on how digital technologies blur the boundaries between work and family domains, potentially exacerbating work-family conflict and challenging work-life balance. Prolonged remote working and the continuous use of technologies, especially during non work hours, can disrupt the work-life interface and cause work-family role conflict [2]. Blurred boundaries between work and family due to technology can trigger this conflict [13]. In this sense, techno-invasion, a dimension of technostress representing the intrusion of work-related demands into personal time due to technology, is shown to be directly associated with work-life balance issues [64] or work interference with private life

---

[1] The following terms were removed: study contributes, theoretical model, survey data, stress due, research model, online survey, case study, systematic review, quantitative analysis, qualitative study, empirical evidence, mediating role, moderating role, significant impact.

[65]. Related to technology use for work purposes, videoconferencing fatigue is found to significantly predict work-family conflict [66]. Increased permeability of borders between work and home is linked to higher levels of work-to-family conflict and, to some extent, family-to-work conflict [5].

Methodological terms such structural equation and serial mediation suggest that this cluster also encompasses studies employing advanced statistical models to investigate the relationships between technology use and work-life balance. Studies use Structural Equation Modelling (SEM) [67] to analyse their models, which include variables related to technology use (e.g., technostressors [12], technology characteristics [8], ICT demands [68]), resources (e.g., perceived organisational support [4], psychological capital [64], resilience [23], organisational trust [68]), and outcomes (e.g., technostrain [69], telework exhaustion [6], work-life balance [64], work engagement [70], job satisfaction [19], perceived effectiveness [2]). These concepts are not typically viewed as having simple, direct relationships. Researchers often hypothesize that effects are mediated (e.g., technology leads to stress, which in turn impacts work-life balance [64]) or moderated (e.g., segmentation preferences change the impact of technology-related stress on interruptions [71]).

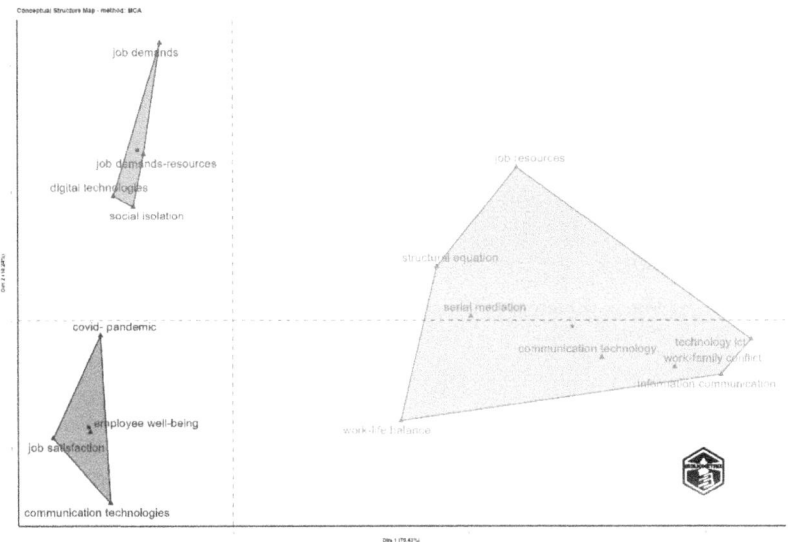

Fig. 4. Bigram-based multiple correspondence analysis with the abstracts (Color figure online)

Job Demands-Resources Framework

Cluster 2 (green in Fig. 4) represents theoretical conceptualizations of technostress through the Job Demands-Resources (JD-R) lens [55]. It focuses on how digital technologies create demands that must be balanced with appropriate resources. Numerous sources state they explicitly draw upon or extend the JD-R model that includes a broad range of job demands and resources. The model was developed to explain burnout and has been revised to include various factors [72]. The application of the JD-R model to the context of FWAs is highlighted as a contribution of these studies [21, 73, 74]. Some sources note that research on technology-related stress within the JD-R framework is still developing [11].

Within the JD-R framework, technology-related stressors, such as techno-overload, techno-invasion, techno-complexity, techno-insecurity, techno-uncertainty, and ICT demands are consistently conceptualized as job demands [4, 64, 68, 73]. Coping with these demands require sustained physical and/or psychological effort or skills and are associated with costs. An emerging concept, loneliness, is identified as a job demand in the FWA context within the JD-R framework [11]. [75] introduces Techno-Isolation (TIS) as a previously unreported technostressor arising from heavy dependence on ICTs for professional social interactions, particularly relevant in teleworking.

The JD-R framework includes the concept of job and personal resources that can buffer the negative effects of demands, or promote growth and goal achievement [55]. From this perspective, studies in this cluster focus on how resources balance or mitigate the demands due to technology use in FWAs. Resources can reduce the impact of perceived ICT demands [68], or buffer their negative effects [4, 21, 64]. Examples of resources discussed include remote e-working experience [11], organisational support [4, 21, 70], ICT support and training [4, 23], work-based learning [73], digital leadership capability [73], autonomy [5, 74], flexibility [4, 11, 68], organisational trust [68], psychological capital [64], self-efficacy [21], social support [21, 70, 75], digital mindset [18], and effective boundary management [7].

Employee Well-Being, Job Satisfaction and the Use of ICTs Within FWAs
The third cluster (blue in Fig. 4) centers on employee well-being, job satisfaction, and the use of ICTs within flexible work arrangements. A significant portion of the research focuses on understanding the consequences of using ICTs in FWAs. These studies examine how the interaction with or dependence on technology affects psychological outcomes, particularly employee well-being [6, 7, 9, 11, 19–21, 73] and job satisfaction [6, 7, 13, 18, 19, 68, 71, 75]. Technostress [18, 71], ICT demands [68], role ambiguity due to ICT [44] are among the factors explored for its negative consequences on the outcomes, such as stress [44], psychological challenges [17], mental health [74], strain [69], emotional responses, and overall well-being [73, 76]. These are presented as important outcomes for both individuals and organisations. While the term "covid-pandemic" appears among the cluster's keywords, its role is primarily to provide context and underscore the timeliness and relevance of these research topics, rather than serving as the main focus of the studies in this cluster. This suggests that the pandemic is frequently referenced to motivate or frame investigations into technostress and employee outcomes (e.g., [7, 68, 77]), but the substantive research emphasis remains on broader issues of technology use and personal experiences in flexible work environments.

3.5 Thematic Shifts in Research

We ran a words' frequency analysis over time, based on the author keywords. To account for the substantial increase in published research post-pandemic (only 12.5% of all articles in our pool were published in the pre-pandemic era), all term frequencies were normalized by the number of articles in each period. The decision to partition the analysis into pre-pandemic (2014–2019) and post-pandemic (2020–2024) phases is supported by the multi-correspondence analysis findings (Sect. 3.4), which revealed that while the COVID-19 pandemic frequently contextualizes studies, it serves as a temporal marker rather than a primary research focus. The results are shown in Table 6. Terms with zero frequency imply complete absence from the keywords. Nevertheless, these were included to highlight the emergence of new themes post-pandemic.

The keyword analysis reveals both continuity and transformation in the research focus on technology-related stressors in FWAs from the pre-pandemic to the post-pandemic period. Before the pandemic, technostress, job satisfaction, FWA (synonyms: telework, remote working, remote work), and work-life balance (synonyms: work-life conflict, work-family balance, family-work conflict, work-family conflict) were the most prominent keywords, indicating a strong emphasis on individual experiences and outcomes within flexible work contexts. In contrast, the post-pandemic era is characterized by a reordering of priorities: technostress remains central, but FWA rises in prominence, and new themes such as well-being (synonyms: mental health, psychological health), work engagement, performance, coping, and stress emerge as significant keywords, none of which appeared in the pre-pandemic period. Notably, job satisfaction drops sharply in rank, while well-being and work engagement become much more visible, reflecting a shift toward a human-centric perspective on employee experience and organizational health. The increased attention to well-being and stress underscores the field's adaptation to new realities and challenges introduced by the pandemic.

Table 6. Term frequency over time: Authors' keyword analysis

Pre-pandemic (2014–2020)		Post-pandemic (2021–2024)	
Top 10 Terms (Ordered by the normalised frequency)	Normalised Frequency	Top 10 Terms (Ordered by the normalised frequency)	Normalised Frequency
Technostress	0,50	Technostress	0,46
Job satisfaction	0,50	FWA	0,32
FWA	0,25	Well-being	0,21
Work-life balance	0,25	Work-life balance	0,18
Well-being	0,00	Work engagement	0,14
Work engagement	0,00	Performance	0,11
Performance	0,00	Stress	0,11
Stress	0,00	Coping	0,07
Coping	0,00	Covid-19	0,07
Covid-19	0,00	Job satisfaction	0,07

4   Discussion

Based on the evolution of technostress research in FWAs, this section provides actionable recommendations for designing human-centric digital workplaces and discuss the findings.

4.1   Themes, Shifts and Human-Centric Implications

The conceptual clusters identified in Sect. 3.4, work-life technology interface, JD-R framework, and employee well-being highlight three pillars for human centric digital workplace design.

The prominence of work-life balance and techno-invasion themes (Cluster 1) underscores the need for flexible boundary design. Unlike traditional offices, digital workplaces lack physical cues to separate work and personal life, exacerbating stress. This finding aligns with the thematic shifts in research (Sect. 3.5), where the post-pandemic rise of "coping" and "stress" keywords highlights the urgency of addressing boundary management in FWAs. Human-centric solutions should integrate adaptive technologies that automate digital detox periods [78], such as AI-driven notification silencing during non-work hours and support organisational policies that enable employees to define their own response windows for digital communication.

Cluster 2 shows that technology-related stress arises not only from technology itself, but from an imbalance between job demands and resources. Consistent with technostress research, various strategies can introduce resources to inhibit the negative impacts of demands. One effective approach is involvement facilitation [59], where employees participate in selecting and testing platforms to ensure usability and reduce technostress. Another key strategy is literacy facilitation [59], achieved through digital leadership that equips managers to understand and promote healthy technology use within their teams. Notably, these strategies align with the evolving role of Enterprise Architects, who are increasingly responsible for orchestrating the co-design of digital solutions and fostering digital literacy across the organization [79].

The surge in "well-being" and "work-engagement" in keywords (Sect. 3.5) signals a paradigm shift: organizations now recognize that employee well-being drives sustainable productivity. This aligns with Cluster 3's focus on employee well-being, job satisfaction, and ICT use in FWAs. To operationalize the human-centric shift, organizations should adopt evidence-based strategies informed by recent research. Embedding well-being analytics, they should regularly assess the impact of technology use adopting frameworks such as Digital Stressors Scale [50], and detect stress patterns that enable proactive interventions [80]. Informed by the data, organisations should leverage personalised well-being programs, and ensure that technology complements rather than disrupts health in the FWA context. One important aspect of "digital well-being" is the ethical responsibility to ensure that surveillance, data privacy, and security are rigorously protected [81]. Organisations must prioritize these ethical considerations as a fundamental part of any human-centric digital workplace strategy [82].

4.2 Collaboration Patterns and Inclusive Design

The bibliometric analysis reveals limited international collaboration (28.12% of articles) and a Eurocentric authorship bias, with German institutions contributing 18.8% of studies. The research from the Global South remains underrepresented. This geographic skew perpetuates a "socioeconomic sampling bias", where findings primarily reflect high-income, digitally mature contexts, limiting the generalizability of technostress frameworks [83]. To foster inclusive digital workplaces, future research should prioritize partnerships with Global South institutions to investigate localized stressors, such as infrastructure disparities, and informal labour dynamics.

5 Conclusion and Limitations

The bibliometric analysis documents the accelerated growth of research on technology-related stressors in flexible working arrangements and traces an accompanying shift toward human-centric outcomes. By isolating three conceptual clusters, work-life technology interface, Job Demands–Resources framing, and employee well-being, the study clarifies how technostress emerges in contemporary digital workplaces. The post-pandemic emphasis on well-being, engagement, and coping strategies signals a move beyond purely technological debates toward a richer understanding of employee experience. Future work should mitigate the current geographic bias by strengthening international collaboration and integrating perspectives from under-represented regions. As organisations steer their digital transformations, the findings show the importance of evidence-based measures that design technology as an enabler of sustainable, human-centric work rather than a source of strain.

This study has several limitations. First, the relatively small number of articles (n = 32) included in the bibliometric analysis may limit the generalizability of the findings. Second, the conceptual analysis relied on MCA of abstract bigrams rather than a full-text qualitative review, which may overlook important insights. Third, restricting the sample to articles indexed in Web of Science may have excluded relevant perspectives, particularly from industry reports and other non-indexed sources. Fourth, the observed conceptual clusters and thematic shifts may be influenced by the regional and institutional backgrounds of the contributing authors. The Eurocentric bias observed in the dataset could influence which topics are most prominent, potentially underrepresenting issues relevant to other regions.

Nevertheless, the analysis demonstrates that mitigating technostress in FWAs requires moving beyond technological efficiency to embrace human-centric design principles. By prioritizing boundary flexibility, resource empowerment, and well-being analytics, organizations can create digital workplaces where technology serves as an enabler of human potential rather than a source of strain. The post-pandemic thematic shifts toward coping and engagement suggest an emerging consensus: the future of work must be digitally advanced but fundamentally human.

References

1. de Menezes, L.M., Kelliher, C.: Flexible working, individual performance, and employee attitudes: comparing formal and informal arrangements. Hum. Resour. Manage. **56**, 1051–1070 (2017). https://doi.org/10.1002/hrm.21822
2. Banerjee, P., Gupta, R.: A mixed-method exploration of effects of technostress on remote/hybrid working professionals. Comput. Hum. Behav. **150**, 107974 (2024). https://doi.org/10.1016/j.chb.2023.107974
3. Mazzei, A., Ravazzani, S., Butera, A., Conti, S., Fisichella, C.: The affective commitment of newcomers in hybrid work contexts: a study on enhancing and inhibiting factors and the mediating role of newcomer adjustment. Front. Psychol. **13**, 987976 (2022). https://doi.org/10.3389/fpsyg.2022.987976
4. Harunavamwe, M., Kanengoni, H.: Hybrid and virtual work settings; the interaction between technostress, perceived organisational support, work-family conflict and the impact on work engagement. AJEMS **14**, 252–270 (2023). https://doi.org/10.1108/AJEMS-07-2022-0306
5. Leung, L., Zhang, R.: Mapping ICT use at home and telecommuting practices: a perspective from work/family border theory. Telem. Inform. **34**, 385–396 (2017). https://doi.org/10.1016/j.tele.2016.06.001
6. Duong, B., Lee, J., van Slyke, C., Ellis, T.S.: Distress coping responses among teleworkers. IEEE Trans. Profess. Commun. **66**, 259–283 (2023). https://doi.org/10.1109/TPC.2023.3290927
7. Jaiswal, A., et al.: Teleworking: role of psychological well-being and technostress in the relationship between trust in management and employee performance. IJM **45**, 49–71 (2024). https://doi.org/10.1108/IJM-04-2022-0149
8. Becker, J., Berger, M., Gimpel, H., Lanzl, J., Regal, C.: Considering characteristic profiles of technologies at the digital workplace: the influence on technostress. In: ICIS 2020 Proceedings (2020)
9. Selimović, J., Pilav-Velić, A., Krndžija, L.: Digital workplace transformation in the financial service sector: Investigating the relationship between employees' expectations and intentions. Technol. Soc. **66**, 101640 (2021). https://doi.org/10.1016/j.techsoc.2021.101640
10. Groen, B.A., van Triest, S.P., Coers, M., Wtenweerde, N.: Managing flexible work arrangements: teleworking and output controls. Eur. Manag. J. **36**, 727–735 (2018). https://doi.org/10.1016/j.emj.2018.01.007
11. Taser, D., Aydin, E., Torgaloz, A.O., Rofcanin, Y.: An examination of remote e-working and flow experience: the role of technostress and loneliness. Comput. Hum. Behav. **127** (2022). https://doi.org/10.1016/j.chb.2021.107020
12. Weinert, C., Maier, C., Laumer, S., Weitzel, T.: Does teleworking negatively influence IT professionals? In: Joseph, D. (ed.) Proceedings of the 52nd ACM conference on Computers and people research, pp. 139–147. ACM (2014). https://doi.org/10.1145/2599990.2600011
13. Ren, X., Hao, Y., Xu, J.: How do teleworkers relieve negative emotions to improve job performance through enterprise social media? The conservation of resources theory view. Soc. Sci. Comput. Rev. (2024). https://doi.org/10.1177/08944393241235183
14. Buomprisco, G., Ricci, S., Perri, R., de Sio, S.: Health and telework: new challenges after COVID-19 pandemic. Eur. J. Environ. Public Health **5** (2021). https://doi.org/10.21601/ejeph/9705
15. Ferrara, B., Pansini, M., de Vincenzi, C., Buonomo, I., Benevene, P.: Investigating the role of remote working on employees' performance and well-being: an evidence-based systematic review. Int. J. Environ. Res. Public Health **19** (2022). https://doi.org/10.3390/ijerph191912373
16. Tarafdar, M., Cooper, C.L., Stich, J.-F.: The technostress trifecta - techno eustress, techno distress and design: theoretical directions and an agenda for research. Inf. Syst. J. **29**, 6–42 (2019). https://doi.org/10.1111/isj.12169

17. Celuch, M., Oksa, R., Savela, N., Oksanen, A.: Longitudinal effects of cyberbullying at work on well-being and strain: a five-wave survey study. New Media Soc. **26**, 3410–3432 (2024). https://doi.org/10.1177/14614448221100782
18. Valta, M., Hildebrandt, Y., Maier, C.: Fostering the digital mindset to mitigate technostress: an empirical study of empowering individuals for using digital technologies. INTR (2024). https://doi.org/10.1108/INTR-09-2022-0766
19. Yin, P., Wang, C., Liang, L.: Consumer information technology use in the post-pandemic workplace: a post-acceptance adaptation perspective. ITP **36**, 1484–1508 (2023). https://doi.org/10.1108/ITP-09-2020-0657
20. Oksa, R., Pirkkalainen, H., Salo, M., Savela, N., Oksanen, A.: Professional social media-enabled productivity: a five-wave longitudinal study on the role of professional social media invasion, work engagement and work exhaustion. ITP **35**, 349–368 (2022). https://doi.org/10.1108/ITP-11-2021-0899
21. Capone, V., Schettino, G., Marino, L., Camerlingo, C., Smith, A., Depolo, M.: The new normal of remote work: exploring individual and organizational factors affecting work-related outcomes and well-being in academia. Front. Psychol. **15**, 1340094 (2024). https://doi.org/10.3389/fpsyg.2024.1340094
22. Wang, H., Ding, H., Kong, X.: Understanding technostress and employee well-being in digital work: the roles of work exhaustion and workplace knowledge diversity. IJM (2022). https://doi.org/10.1108/IJM-08-2021-0480
23. van Slyke, C., Lee, J., Duong, B.Q., Ellis, T.S.: Eustress and distress in the context of telework. Inf. Resour. Manag. J. **35**, 1–24 (2022). https://doi.org/10.4018/IRMJ.291526
24. Yin, P., Ou, C.X., Davison, R.M., Wu, J.: Coping with mobile technology overload in the workplace. INTR **28**, 1189–1212 (2018). https://doi.org/10.1108/IntR-01-2017-0016
25. Tarafdar, M., Tu, Q., Ragu-Nathan, B.S., Ragu-Nathan, T.S.: The impact of technostress on role stress and productivity. J. Manag. Inf. Syst. **24**, 301–328 (2007). https://doi.org/10.2753/MIS0742-1222240109
26. Brancati, M.C.U.: Digital technologies at work and psychosocial risks: evidence and implications for occupational safety and health. Luxembourg (2024)
27. Trenerry, B., et al.: Preparing workplaces for digital transformation: an integrative review and framework of multi-level factors. Front. Psychol. **12**, 620766 (2021). https://doi.org/10.3389/fpsyg.2021.620766
28. Cavicchioli, M., Demaria, F., Nannetti, F., Scapolan, A.C., Fabbri, T.: Employees' attitudes and work-related stress in the digital workplace: an empirical investigation. Front. Psychol. **16**, 1546832 (2025). https://doi.org/10.3389/fpsyg.2025.1546832
29. Kehrbusch, B., Engels, G.: Digital transformation—towards flexible human-centric enterprises. In: Vogel-Heuser, B., Wimmer, M. (eds.) Digital Transformation, pp. 497–526. Springer, Heidelberg (2023). https://doi.org/10.1007/978-3-662-65004-2_20
30. Soheil, H., Neumann, G., Alt, R.: A call for interdisciplinary research on applied human-centricity in a sustainable digital economy. In: Bui, T.X. (ed.) Proceedings of the 55th Annual Hawaii International Conference on System Sciences. 3–7 January 2022, pp. 4965–4696. Department of IT Management Shidler College of Business University of Hawaii at Manoa, Honolulu (2022)
31. Longo, F., Padovano, A., Umbrello, S.: Value-oriented and ethical technology engineering in industry 5.0: a human-centric perspective for the design of the factory of the future. Appl. Sci. **10**, 4182 (2020). https://doi.org/10.3390/app10124182
32. Pansini, M., Buonomo, I., Vincenzi, C. de, Ferrara, B., Benevene, P.: Positioning technostress in the JD-R model perspective: a systematic literature review. Healthc. (Basel Switz.) **11**, 446 (2023). https://doi.org/10.3390/healthcare11030446
33. Micic, L., Khamooshi, H., Raković, L., Matković, P.: Defining the digital workplace: a systematic literature review. SMJ **27** (2022)

34. Crnobrnja, J., Lalic, D.C., Romero, D., Softic, S., Marjanovic, U.: Digital transformation towards human-centricity: a systematic literature review. In: Thürer, M., Riedel, R., Cieminski, G. von, Romero, D. (eds.) Advances in Production Management Systems. Production Management Systems for Volatile, Uncertain, Complex, and Ambiguous Environments. IFIP Advances in Information and Communication Technology, vol. 731, pp. 89–102. Springer, Cham (2024). https://doi.org/10.1007/978-3-031-71633-1_7

35. Nastjuk, I., Trang, S., Grummeck-Braamt, J.-V., Adam, M.T.P., Tarafdar, M.: Integrating and synthesising technostress research: a meta-analysis on technostress creators, outcomes, and IS usage contexts. Eur. J. Inf. Syst. 1–22 (2023)

36. Ng, J.Y., Liu, H., Shah, A.Q., Wieland, L.S., Moher, D.: Characteristics of bibliometric analyses of the complementary, alternative, and integrative medicine literature: a scoping review protocol. F1000Res **12**, 164 (2023). https://doi.org/10.12688/f1000research.130326.2

37. van Raan, A.F.J.: Advanced bibliometric methods as quantitative core of peer review based evaluation and foresight exercises. Scientometrics **36**, 397–420 (1996). https://doi.org/10.1007/BF02129602

38. Zupic, I., Čater, T.: Bibliometric methods in management and organization. Organ. Res. Methods **18**, 429–472 (2015). https://doi.org/10.1177/1094428114562629

39. Wohlin, C.: Guidelines for snowballing in systematic literature studies and a replication in software engineering. In: Proceedings of the 18th International Conference on Evaluation and Assessment in Software Engineering, EASE 2014. Association for Computing Machinery, New York (2014). https://doi.org/10.1145/2601248.2601268

40. Paré, G., Kitsiou, S.: Chapter 9 methods for literature reviews. In: Paré, G., Kitsiou, S. (eds.) Handbook of eHealth Evaluation: An Evidence-based Approach [Internet]. University of Victoria (2017)

41. Landis, J.R., Koch, G.G.: The measurement of observer agreement for categorical data. Biometrics **33**, 159 (1977). https://doi.org/10.2307/2529310

42. Aria, M., Cuccurullo, C.: Bibliometrix : an R-tool for comprehensive science mapping analysis. J. Informet. **11**, 959–975 (2017). https://doi.org/10.1016/j.joi.2017.08.007

43. Black, P.E.: Bradford's law (2004). https://www.nist.gov/dads/HTML/bradfordsLaw.html

44. Suh, A., Lee, J.: Understanding teleworkers' technostress and its influence on job satisfaction. INTR **27**, 140–159 (2017). https://doi.org/10.1108/IntR-06-2015-0181

45. Califf, C.B., Sarker, S., Sarker, S.: The bright and dark sides of technostress: a mixed-methods study involving healthcare IT. MIS Q. **44**, 809–856 (2020). https://doi.org/10.25300/MISQ/2020/14818

46. Molino, M., et al.: Wellbeing costs of technology use during covid-19 remote working: an investigation using the Italian translation of the technostress creators scale. Sustainability **12** (2020). https://doi.org/10.3390/su12155911

47. Spagnoli, P., Molino, M., Molinaro, D., Giancaspro, M.L., Manuti, A., Ghislieri, C.: Workaholism and technostress during the COVID-19 emergency: the crucial role of the leaders on remote working. Front. Psychol. **11**, 620310 (2020). https://doi.org/10.3389/fpsyg.2020.620310

48. Ma, J., Ollier-Malaterre, A., Lu, C.: The impact of techno-stressors on work–life balance: the moderation of job self-efficacy and the mediation of emotional exhaustion. Comput. Hum. Behav. **122**, 106811 (2021). https://doi.org/10.1016/j.chb.2021.106811

49. Wang, B., Liu, Y., Qian, J., Parker, S.K.: Achieving effective remote working during the COVID-19 pandemic: a work design perspective. Appl. Psychol. **70**, 16–59 (2021). https://doi.org/10.1111/apps.12290

50. Fischer, T., Reuter, M., Riedl, R.: The digital stressors scale: development and validation of a new survey instrument to measure digital stress perceptions in the workplace context. Front. Psychol. **12** (2021)

51. Brooks, S., Califf, C.: Social media-induced technostress: its impact on the job performance of it professionals and the moderating role of job characteristics. Comput. Netw. **114**, 143–153 (2017). https://doi.org/10.1016/j.comnet.2016.08.020

52. Gaudioso, F., Turel, O., Galimberti, C.: The mediating roles of strain facets and coping strategies in translating techno-stressors into adverse job outcomes. Comput. Hum. Behav. **69**, 189–196 (2017). https://doi.org/10.1016/j.chb.2016.12.041

53. Ahuja, M.K., Chudoba, K.M., Kacmar, C.J., McKnight, D.H., George, J.F.: IT road warriors: balancing work-family conflict, job autonomy, and work overload to mitigate turnover intentions. MIS Q. **31**, 1 (2007). https://doi.org/10.2307/25148778

54. Gajendran, R.S., Harrison, D.A.: The good, the bad, and the unknown about telecommuting: meta-analysis of psychological mediators and individual consequences. J. Appl. Psychol. **92**, 1524–1541 (2007). https://doi.org/10.1037/0021-9010.92.6.1524

55. Demerouti, E., Bakker, A.B., Nachreiner, F., Schaufeli, W.B.: The job demands-resources model of burnout. J. Appl. Psychol. **86**, 499–512 (2001)

56. Podsakoff, P.M., MacKenzie, S.B., Lee, J.-Y., Podsakoff, N.P.: Common method biases in behavioral research: a critical review of the literature and recommended remedies. J. Appl. Psychol. **88**, 879–903 (2003). https://doi.org/10.1037/0021-9010.88.5.879

57. Clarke, S.G., Cooper, C.L.: The risk management of occupational stress. Health Risk Soc. **2**, 173–187 (2000). https://doi.org/10.1080/713670158

58. Moore, J.E.: One road to turnover: an examination of work exhaustion in technology professionals. MIS Q. **24**, 141 (2000). https://doi.org/10.2307/3250982

59. Ragu-Nathan, T.S., Tarafdar, M., Ragu-Nathan, B.S., Tu, Q.: The consequences of technostress for end users in organizations: conceptual development and empirical validation. Inf. Syst. Res. **19**, 417–433 (2008)

60. Ayyagari, R., Grover, V., Purvis, R.: Technostress: technological Antecedents and Implications. MIS Q. **35**, 831–858 (2011)

61. Tarafdar, M., Pullins, E.B., Ragu-Nathan, T.S.: Technostress: negative effect on performance and possible mitigations. Inf. Systems J **25**, 103–132 (2015). https://doi.org/10.1111/isj.12042

62. Hair, J.F., Black, W.C., Babin, B.J.: Multivariate Data Analysis. A Global Perspective. Pearson, Upper Saddle River (2010)

63. Tarafdar, M., Tu, Q., Ragu-Nathan, T.S.: Impact of technostress on end-user satisfaction and performance. J. Manag. Inf. Syst. **27**, 303–334 (2010)

64. Sharma, I., Tiwari, V.: Modeling the impact of techno-stress and burnout on employees' work-life balance and turnover intention: a job demands-resources theory perspective. Glob. Bus. Org. Exc. **43**, 121–134 (2023). https://doi.org/10.1002/joe.22206

65. Koç, H., Gasimov, C.: Exploring techno-invasion and work-life balance on digital platforms: a preliminary study with Amazon MTurk's gig workers. In: Hinkelmann, K., López-Pellicer, F.J., Polini, A. (eds.) BIR 2023. LNBIP, vol. 493, pp. 121–132. Springer, Cham (2023). https://doi.org/10.1007/978-3-031-43126-5_9

66. Li, B.J., Malviya, S., Tandoc, E.C.: Videoconferencing and work-family conflict: exploring the role of videoconference fatigue. Commun. Stud. **73**, 544–560 (2022). https://doi.org/10.1080/10510974.2022.2153894

67. Hair, J.F., Hult, G.T.M., Ringle, C.M., Sarstedt, M.: A primer on partial least squares structural equation modeling (PLS-SEM). SAGE, Los Angeles (2022)

68. Keeler, J.B., Scuderi, N.F., Brock Baskin, M.E., Jordan, P.C., Meade, L.M.: How job resources can shape perspectives that lead to better performance: a remote worker field study. JOEPP (2023). https://doi.org/10.1108/JOEPP-04-2023-0154

69. Shirish, A.: Cognitive-affective appraisal of technostressors by ICT-based mobile workers and their impacts on technostrain. HSM **40**, 265–285 (2021). https://doi.org/10.3233/HSM-200979

70. Berger, M., Schäfer, R., Schmidt, M., Regal, C., Gimpel, H.: How to prevent technostress at the digital workplace: a Delphi study. J. Bus. Econ. 1–63 (2023)

71. Becker, J., Lanzl, J.: Segmentation preference and technostress: Integrators' vs segmenters' experience of technology-induced demands and related spill-over effects. Inf. Manage. **60**, 103811 (2023). https://doi.org/10.1016/j.im.2023.103811

72. Bakker, A.B., Demerouti, E., Sanz-Vergel, A.: Job demands-resources theory: ten years later. Annu. Rev. Organ. Psychol. Organ. Behav. **10**, 25–53 (2023). https://doi.org/10.1146/ann urev-orgpsych-120920-053933

73. Alkhayyal, S., Bajaba, S.: Countering technostress in virtual work environments: the role of work-based learning and digital leadership in enhancing employee well-being. Acta Physiol (Oxf.) **248**, 104377 (2024). https://doi.org/10.1016/j.actpsy.2024.104377

74. Ruiner, C., Debbing, C.E., Hagemann, V., Schaper, M., Klumpp, M., Hesenius, M.: Job demands and resources when using technologies at work – development of a digital work typology. ER **45**, 190–208 (2023). https://doi.org/10.1108/ER-11-2021-0468

75. Mirowska, A., Bakici, T.: Working in a bubble: techno-isolation as an emerging techno-stressor in teleworkers. ITP **37**, 1403–1422 (2024). https://doi.org/10.1108/ITP-09-2022-0657

76. Derra, N., Regal, C., Rath, S., Kühlmann, T.: Examining technostress at different types of data scientists' workplaces. Scand. J. Inf. Syst. **34** (2022)

77. Wahl, I., Wolfgruber, D., Einwiller, S.: Mitigating teleworkers' perceived technological complexity and work strains through supportive team communication. CCIJ **29**, 329–345 (2024). https://doi.org/10.1108/CCIJ-05-2023-0061

78. Upendra, S., Kaur, J.: Break from digital screen using digital detox program in nursing students. Nurs. Health Sci. **26**, e13157 (2024). https://doi.org/10.1111/nhs.13157

79. Koç, H., Hynes, J.: Can enterprise architecture management professionals measure technostress levels and help implement coping strategies? In: AMCIS 2023 Proceedings. Association for Information Systems (2023)

80. Lathabhavan, R.: Mental well-being through HR analytics: investigating an employee supportive framework. PR **53**, 1110–1128 (2024). https://doi.org/10.1108/PR-11-2022-0836

81. Burr, C., Taddeo, M., Floridi, L.: The ethics of digital well-being: a thematic review. Sci. Eng. Ethics **26**, 2313–2343 (2020). https://doi.org/10.1007/s11948-020-00175-8

82. Roossien, C.C., de Jong, M., Bonvanie, A.M., Maeckelberghe, E.L.M.: Ethics in design and implementation of technologies for workplace health promotion: a call for discussion. Front. Digit. Health **3**, 644539 (2021). https://doi.org/10.3389/fdgth.2021.644539

83. Borle, P., Reichel, K., Niebuhr, F., Voelter-Mahlknecht, S.: How are techno-stressors associated with mental health and work outcomes? A systematic review of occupational exposure to information and communication technologies within the technostress model. Int. J. Environ. Res. ublic Health **18** (2021). https://doi.org/10.3390/ijerph18168673

Balancing Technical, Human and Environmental Perspectives: A Model-Driven Development Framework for Stakeholder Inclusion

Fatemeh Esmaeilnezhadtanha[1,2,3], Yves Wautelet[2(✉)], and Luca Spalazzi[3]

[1] University of Camerino, Camerino, Italy
fatemeh.esmaeilnezhadtahna@unicam.it
[2] KU Leuven, Brussels, Belgium
yves.wautelet@kuleuven.be
[3] Università Politecnica delle Marche, Ancona, Italy
l.spalazzi@univpm.it

Abstract. New and promising technologies constantly emerge. While they often show theoretical potential by defining high-value use cases, integrating them seamlessly into existing socio-technical ecosystems remains a significant challenge. This paper follows a Design Science Research approach to build a conceptual modeling-based framework to assesses how functional elements of new technologies align strategically with a set of technical, human, and environmental values. This approach is called the Model-Driven Framework for Security, Efficiency, Resiliency and Sustainability Value Alignment (MoDriSERSAl); it uses i* and Non-Functional Requirements (NFR) modeling tools to connect technical and human perspectives. The framework is materialized through a meta-model defining its concepts and a process fragment illustrating its application organization. We apply MoDriSERSAl to blockchain technology integration for Electronic Health Record (EHR) management to enable prioritization based on stakeholder inclusion (i.e. ensuring their needs and dependencies drive the integration process). MoDriSERSAl constitutes an effort towards stakeholder-based governance.

Keywords: Stakeholder integration · Strategic Alignment · MoDrIGo · Blockchain · i-star

1 Introduction

Conceptual modeling is a critical tool for building software systems and database architectures. Over the years, it has also been used to align technology developments with higher-level business, organizational, or individual strategies. Model-Driven Development (MDD) allows to bridge the gap between technical and human domains; models indeed provide a structured representation of processes, requirements, logical flows, and states, but also of abstract goals. Organizational models integrating such goals enable to identify potential synergies and dependencies among stakeholders. Goal-oriented frameworks like KAOS [1] or i-star [2] allow, through models, to translate high-level business objectives into technical implementation. In an era marked by increasing digitalization, traditional centralized models often struggle to meet the dynamic and multidimensional challenges posed by socio-technical systems. There is a clear and pressing need for a comprehensive evaluative framework capable of guiding the development and governance of such systems across sectors. Esmaeilnezhadtanha et al. [3]

© The Author(s), under exclusive license to Springer Nature Switzerland AG 2026
R. Deneckère et al. (Eds.): BIR 2025, LNBIP 562, pp. 76–87, 2026.
https://doi.org/10.1007/978-3-032-04375-7_5

have introduced the *Security, Efficiency, Resiliency,* and *Sustainability (SERS)* framework. This comprehensive framework responds to the growing complexity of modern technological infrastructures by evaluating and guiding the design of socio-technical systems. SERS provides a multidimensional structure that balances technical essentials with socio-technical aspects like stakeholder trust, cost-effectiveness, and ethical alignment. One could envisage adapting MDD to address the challenges of technology integration to ensure that stakeholder inclusion aligns with elements of the SERS framework. By structuring SERS dimensions as objectives with sub-objectives, it offers strategic guidance. The alignment (or misalignment) of functional elements provided by the new technology integration with SERS sub-objectives can then be studied.

This paper seeks to answer the research question: *how can conceptual modeling enhance stakeholder inclusion through integrating technical and human aspects of newly introduced technologies?* This question is tackled using a *Design Science Research (DSR)* approach. The latter drives the creation of a framework (or artifact) called *Model-Driven Framework for SERS Value Alignment (MoDriSERSAl).* It is materialized through a meta-model (i.e. a structuration of the theoretical constructs) and process fragment (i.e. how to apply MoDriSERSAl). MoDriSERSAl builds upon the Model-Driven IT Governance (MoDrIGo) framework [4] which was designed to align IT capabilities with business and IT strategies. MoDriSERSAl allows to study (i) the interests of individual stakeholders with respect to a new technological integration (i.e. stakeholder inclusion) and (ii) align the functional elements (features) furnished as services by the new technology (to meet stakeholders' needs) with the SERS sub-objectives. The new framework is applied in the field of blockchain integration for Electronic Health Record (EHR) management. This research is explorative.

2 Background

2.1 SERS Framework and Its Validity

The SERS framework defines a set of dimensions, i.e. security, efficiency, resiliency, and sustainability, along with their sub-elements in a hierarchical structure. Each dimension has its own objectives and sub-criteria to address the heterogeneity of challenges in technology. SERS is intended to serve as a decision-making tool, providing insights into the level of SERS achieved by technological developments or integrations. It thus acts as an evaluation framework for entire system performance, going beyond a narrow focus on functional performance alone. Being domain- and technology-independent, SERS is applicable to a wide variety of use cases.

Figure 1 summarizes the SERS framework. The four dimensions will be treated as objectives throughout this paper, and the sub-dimensions will be considered sub-objectives. The SERS framework was build out of a rigorous litterature review and validated with 14 experts, its full presentation is part of another scientific publication [3].

2.2 The *i** Framework

The *i** framework (short for "distributed intentionality") models stakeholders as actors who depend on one another to achieve goals, complete tasks, or provide resources [5];

Fig. 1. The SERS Framework: Objectives and Sub-Objectives.

i* comprises two primary models: (i) The **Strategic Dependency (SD) Model** captures the dependency relationships between actors in an organizational setting. Each actor is depicted as a node, while dependency links describe the relationship between a *Depender* (the actor requiring a task or resource) and a *Dependee* (the actor providing it). The SD model emphasizes external dependencies between actors, offering a high-level view of the organizational ecosystem; (ii) The **Strategic Rationale (SR) Model** complements the SD model by detailing the internal reasoning of actors. It provides an intentional description of processes through elements such as goals, tasks, and means-ends relationships. By visualizing why and how certain tasks are performed, the SR model facilitates exploration of process alternatives and helps actors identify designs that better align with their goals.

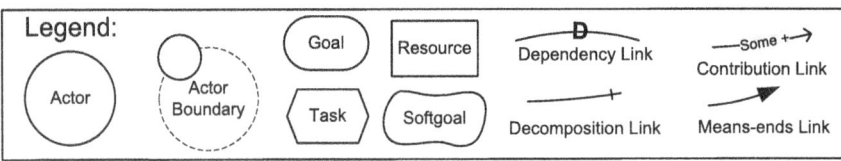

Fig. 2. *i** Elements and their Graphical Representation.

Figure 2 briefly summarizes the symbols used when instantiating these i* models into specific case diagrams.

2.3   The NFR Framework

The *Non-Functional Requirements* (*NFR*) framework is an approach designed for modeling and analyzing non-functional requirements. In a nutshell, NFR defines the qualities or constraints of a system, such as security, performance, scalability, and maintainability. Unlike functional requirements that specify what a system should do, NFRs focus on how the system should perform or behave under various conditions.

The framework enables stakeholders to represent and evaluate the trade-offs and interdependencies between NFRs using structured visual diagrams. These diagrams also enable to represent operationalizations (functional elements) or design choices support or hinder the fulfillment of non-functional requirements. NFR also facilitates reasoning about conflicts or synergies among different non-functional requirements, providing a systematic approach to balancing competing priorities.

By synthesizing the impact of design elements on strategic and quality objectives, NFR serves as a valuable tool for guiding decision-making in complex systems development, ensuring that both functional and non-functional goals are adequately addressed.

2.4   The MoDrIGo Framework

Wautelet [4] introduces MoDrIGo, a model-driven framework designed to align the development of business IT services with organizational strategies. The framework evaluates how specific internal tasks either support or hinder the achievement of strategic objectives. Unlike comprehensive methodologies that aim to encompass all organizational functionalities, MoDrIGo adopts a targeted approach. It dissects and evaluates organizational processes with a focus on strategic alignment at a granular level.

The framework leverages $i*$ to represent the organizational constructs of technology integration and their strategic alignment. Since it is more detailed and combines levels of abstraction, the i* SRD is considered here as a tactical view. The modeling approach explicitly captures how operational activities contribute, positively or negatively, to the realization of strategic objectives. These contributions can then be aggregated and analyzed using the NFR, which provides a higher-level, synthesized view of the impact on strategic objectives (it is here thus the strategic view). While there are conceptual overlaps between i* and NFR, their combined use in MoDrIGo allows for a richer analysis than either framework could achieve independently.

Wautelet et Rouget [6] also propose an extension to MoDrIGo to align sociotechnical systems with circular economy and sustainability frameworks values.

3   Research Approach

This research uses the DSR approach as described in Hevner et al. [7]. The rest of this section applies the three cycles of DSR to the implementation of MoDriSERSAl.

Relevance Cycle. The relevance cycle is about identifying a unique, relevant problem in a specific domain and addressing it with a design artifact tailored to meet those needs based on established principles [7]. Here, we aim to design an artifact that enhances stakeholder inclusion in the integration of new technologies, aligning with their broader needs and values. Such alignment fosters trust, shared benefits, and sustainable outcomes by balancing technical features with stakeholder-oriented priorities.

Rigor Cycle. The rigor cycle stresses the need to build on established theories and methods to ensure valid and credible science [7]. Here, we ground the development of MoDriSERSAl in MoDrIGo, which itself leverages i* and NFR. These have been validated across numerous case studies in the past, providing a robust foundation.

Design Cycle. The design cycle focuses on the detailed development of the artifact, which forms the primary contribution of the study [7]. To develop MoDriSERSAl, we started by analyzing the limitations of MoDrIGo, which lacks explicit support for stakeholder inclusion and broader socio-technical values. We then enriched its meta-model to incorporate SERS sub-objectives, enabling us to capture and evaluate stakeholder value alongside technical performance. Next, we defined a process approach that extends the combined use of i* for modeling stakeholder dependencies and NFR for assessing strategic alignment—already present in MoDrIGo—by prioritizing stakeholder inclusion and incorporating SERS sub-objectives. To demonstrate feasibility, we applied this theoretical model to an illustrative example in EHR management, refining it through iterative feedback from the application. This step-by-step evolution ensures MoDriSERSAl is a practical and well-founded tool.

4   The MoDriSERSAl Framework

4.1   MoDriSERSAl: Meta-model for Socio-Technical Systems Design

To formalize our approach, we created a meta-model using the syntax and semantics of the UML Class Diagram [8]; it is presented in Fig. 3. This meta-model provides a conceptual framework to integrate socio-technical systems design with SERS objectives and sub-objectives, emphasizing stakeholder inclusion.

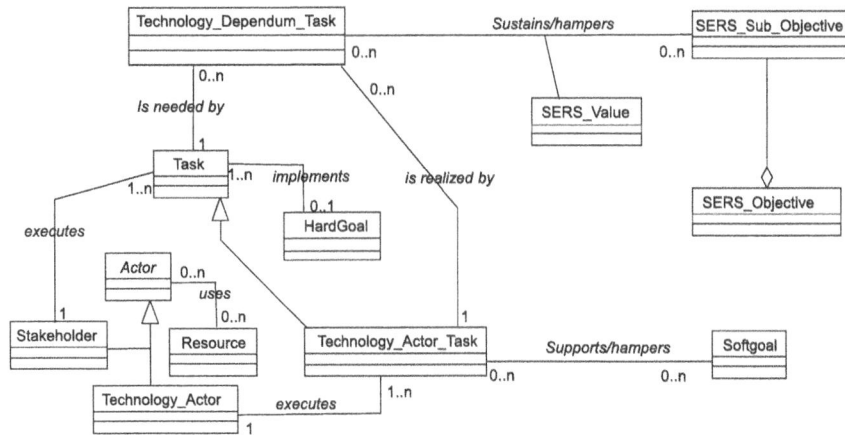

Fig. 3. Meta-Model.

Here are key elements and how they appear in the meta-model:

- *SERS Objectives* represent the high-level dimensions of the framework— *Security*, *Efficiency*, *Resiliency*, and *Sustainability*. These are broken down into *SERS_Sub_Objectives*, offering a detailed view aligned with the sub-dimensions in Fig. 1. The meta-model links these sub-objectives to *Technology_Dependum_Tasks*, which are tasks the new technology provides to other actors in the system;
- Stakeholders are modeled as *Actors*, acting as entities that perform or are affected by tasks within the socio-technical environment;

– *Technology_Dependum_Tasks*   support   *SERS_Sub_Objectives*   and   generate *SERS_Value*. Each task's contribution is assessed for its value to stakeholders and the system;
– *SERS Value* connects *Technology_Dependum_Tasks* to *SERS_Sub_Objectives*, providing a way to measure how these tasks contribute to overarching SERS Objectives. This enables a quantitative or qualitative evaluation of alignment.

Note that SERS objectives and sub-objectives operate at a strategic level, distinct from traditional softgoals, which are tactical because pursued by individual stakeholders. SERS objectives are aimed to align socio-technical systems with broader external norms.

4.2 MoDriSERSAI as a Development Process: Use of the Meta-model

The meta-model is designed to be instantiated on real-world cases with the support of i* and NFR. Figure 4 depicts, in the form of an i* SRD, the different roles of the development team involved in the MoDrISESAI application process. It shows how to apply the framework in a real life project through a set of tasks related to the creation of (i* and NFR) diagrams. It shows an example of how responsibilities might be assigned. It remains a "meta-level" guidance only that can be customized/tailored to specific cases in function of the needs. Different roles can be played by the same individual and vice-versa. It is important to note that the SRD presented in Fig. 4 is generic and represents the overall application process of MoDrISESAI; it should not be confused with subsequent domain-specific i* SRDs that emerge from the framework's application in particular domains.

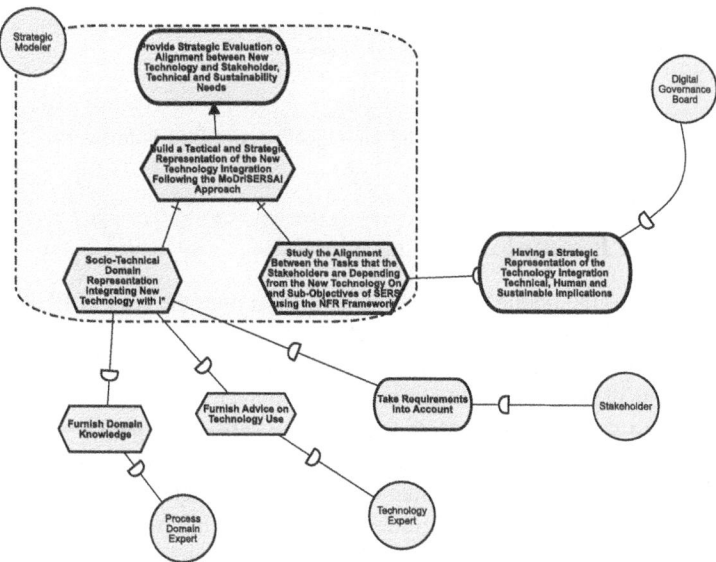

Fig. 4. The MoDriSERSAI Development Process as an i* Diagram.

Specifically, we highlight the development of:

(i) A domain-specific i* SRD, built by the Strategic Modeler role, to depict the future organizational setup, including the new technology. The domain SRD offers a tactical view, showing how technology-provided tasks meet stakeholder needs through explicit dependencies. In this domain SRD, technology is modeled as an actor, making clear how stakeholders (other actors) rely on it. This representation captures the impact of technology adoption on all stakeholders, promoting inclusivity by identifying value;

(ii) A domain-specific NFR diagram, including the SERS objectives and sub-objectives in a generic format. The latter are shown as NFRs (see Fig. 5) and the tasks that stakeholders depend upon from the newly integrated technology are represented as operationalizations (i.e. practical solutions that support or hinder the fulfillment of SERS sub-objectives).

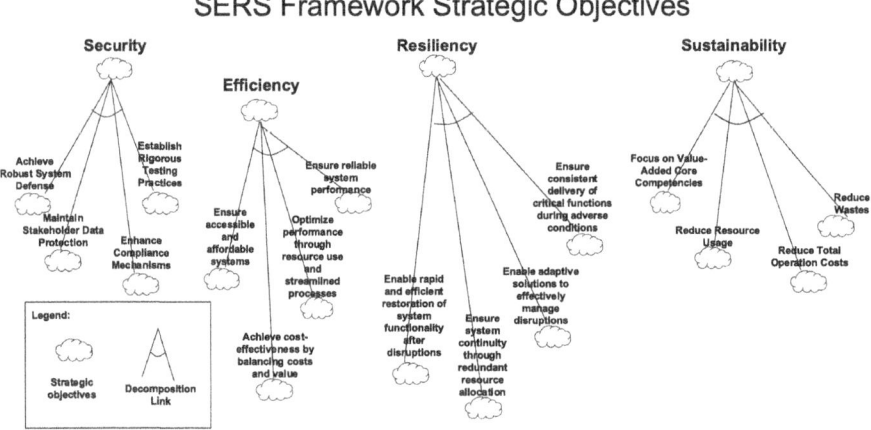

Fig. 5. Strategic objectives and sub-objectives of SERS Framework.

5 Illustrative Example

This section studies the application of MoDriSERSAl onto the case of EHR. The case focuses on the integration of blockchain technology into EHR management to address the stakeholder inclusion through this technology adoption and strategic SERS alignment. The system envisions blockchain as a foundational technology that provides functional services to various stakeholders (e.g. patients, hospitals, physicians, and insurance providers). These operational elements aim to enhance critical processes such as secure medical record storage, dynamic consent management, and automated claims processing. Blockchain can play a significant role in enabling trust, ensuring data security, and optimizing record management. Also, the use of blockchain technology allows to improve the governance of data and ensure that sensitive information remains protected and accessible.

5.1   The New Technology Serving and Including its Environmental Stakeholders: Tactical-View Represented with i*

As explained earlier, the MoDriSERSAl framework is applied by first constructing an i* SRD representing the application domain – i.e. here the integration of the new blockchain technology – into the organizational socio-technical environment (in this case EHR management). The process began with identifying the key actors—patients, hospitals, physicians, insurance providers, and the blockchain platform—as well as their interdependencies. Within the built i* diagram represented in Fig. 6, we can see that the new technology blockchain is included as an actor. Each other actor (i.e. stakeholder) is dependent on it for its internal goal and task realization. For instance *Patients* depend on *Blockchain* for *Patient Data Ownership and Control* which is ensured by the *Blockchain* by *Grant or Revoke Access to Personal Data*. Another example is that *Hospitals* depend on *Blockchain* for *patient consent management* which is ensured by the *Blockchain* by *Verifying and Logging Patient Consent*. Again, the Blockchain was introduced as an operational actor providing functionalities that align with the identified stakeholder dependencies. Tasks such as *Execute Automated Claims Validation* (through a smart contract) were explicitly modeled as capabilities offered by blockchain.

This tactical representation concretely supports stakeholder inclusion by ensuring that the technology serves as a direct response to stakeholders' diverse needs, rather than imposing a uniform technical solution. For example, *Grant or Revoke Access to Personal Data* empowers patients by giving them control over who accesses their records, addressing their need for autonomy and trust in the system—key inclusion indicators. Similarly, *Verifying and Logging Patient Consent* enables hospitals to meet regulatory and ethical obligations while streamlining consent processes, ensuring their operational priorities are met. Physicians benefit from *Execute Automated Claims Validation*, which reduces administrative burdens and speeds up reimbursements, directly addressing their efficiency needs. By modeling these dependencies explicitly, the i* SRD ensures that each stakeholder's perspective actively shapes the blockchain's functional design.

5.2   Depending Tasks Supporting SERS Sub-objectives: Strategic-View Represented with the NFR Framework

The *Technology_Dependum_Tasks* identified in the i* diagram (i.e., *Patient Consent Management, Immutable Medical Record Storage, Patient Data Ownership and Control, Smart Contract Automation for Claims Processing, Automated Billing and Payment Processing*, and *Fraud Prevention and Detection*) are represented as operationalizations in the NFR diagram. As discussed earlier, this diagram explicitly integrates the SERS objectives and their associated sub-objectives as NFRs.

Figure 7 demonstrates explicit linkages between each operationalization and various SERS sub-objectives, reflecting their strategic value. For example, *Patient Data Ownership and Control* aligns with the sub-objective *Optimize performance through resource use and streamlined processes* under the *Efficiency* dimension. Similarly, *Smart Contract Automation for Claims Processing* addresses the sub-objective *Maintain Stakeholder Data Protection*, directly contributing to the *Security* dimension. Additionally,

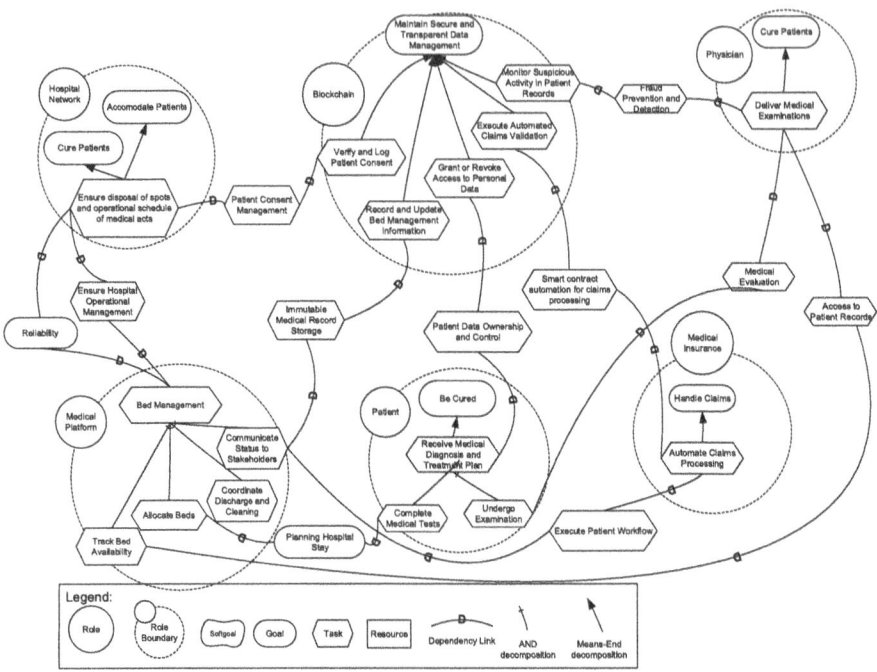

Fig. 6. Organizational Setting with Blockchain Integration.

the task *Fraud Prevention and Detection* aligns with *Enhance Compliance Mechanisms* within the *Security* dimension. Each operationalization, through these explicit connections, showcases how blockchain-enabled tasks effectively align with and support both tactical functionalities and broader strategic goals across technical and environmental priorities.

6 Discussion

From a governance perspective, MoDriSERSAl adopts a stakeholder-centric approach by systematically identifying gaps in alignment and suggesting refinements explicitly based on stakeholders' strategic goals. This governance perspective ensures stakeholders are active influencers in the technology integration process, transforming their roles from passive recipients into proactive decision-makers whose priorities directly inform technology adjustments.

Addressing the heterogeneity of stakeholder interests is a crucial strength of our framework. By explicitly modeling diverse dependencies and strategically aligning them, the framework balances varied and sometimes conflicting stakeholder needs. This represents a significant advancement to genuine stakeholder-orientation.

The scalability of the proposed approach is also an important consideration. The framework's application make sense in a governance context so within organizations that are sufficiently large to needing these kind of reflexions. As can be seen in the

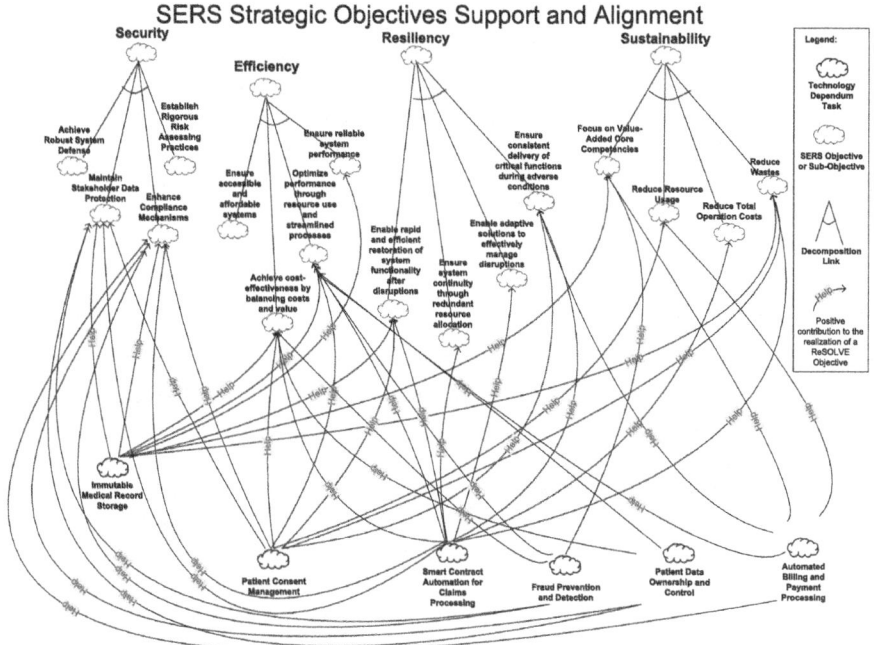

Fig. 7. Support of Inclusion Strategic Objectives.

strategic view, the complexity of the diagram can crow exponentionaly. This could be solved by integrating operationalizations in independent diagrams. Also the use of the Computer-Aided Software Engineering tool allows to help in the process of managing highly complex cases.

7   Comparison with Other Approaches and Related Work

ArchiMate [9, 10] provides an open standard language for modeling enterprise architecture across multiple layers (Strategy, Business, Application, Technology, Physical, and Implementation & Migration). Although ArchiMate's *goal* concept parallels MoDriSERSAl's strategic SERS objectives, it primarily seeks BITA through layered, detailed modeling of enterprise outcomes and capabilities. Unlike ArchiMate, MoDriS-ERSAl explicitly foregrounds stakeholder dependencies and values within a simpler, stakeholder-oriented hierarchy. ArchiMate evaluates technology primarily as an enabler for organizational processes, whereas MoDriSERSAl positions stakeholder interests explicitly as the primary driver for technology integration.

The Strategic Alignment Model (SAM) proposed by Avison et al. [11] highlights aligning business and IT strategies to achieve competitive advantage, leveraging case studies to diagnose and maintain alignment. SAM provides broad strategic alignment but does not incorporate a model-driven approach explicitly capturing stakeholder-specific dependencies or socio-technical SERS dimensions, critical aspects central to MoDriSERSAl.

Shah and Guild [12] examine stakeholder engagement models at different life cycle stages, linking stakeholder involvement explicitly to strategic ICT objectives. Their work provides valuable insights into stakeholder prioritization, complementing MoDriSERSAl's integration of Technology Dependum Tasks with strategic SERS sub-objectives.

8 Conclusion

This research has presented the MoDriSERSAl framework, a model-driven approach designed to align stakeholder inclusion and strategic value with the integration of new technologies, exemplified through blockchain adoption in EHR management. The study shows how functional dependencies of stakeholders wrt new technology can be evaluated and refined to maximize their alignment with both technical and sustainability-centric goals.

MoDriSERSAl effectively supports stakeholder inclusion through explicit stakeholder representation, tailored technology functionalities, strategic alignment with stakeholder values, identifiable stakeholder benefits, a robust governance approach, and a sophisticated handling of stakeholder diversity. Collectively, these characteristics position MoDriSERSAl as a fundamentally inclusive framework, ensuring stakeholders' interests and values remain central to socio-technical system integration processes.

Acknowledgments and Declaration of Gen AI in the Writing Process. The first author is enrolled on the National Ph.D Program in Blockchain and Distributed Ledger Technology, funded by the Italian Minister of University and Research.

During the preparation of this work the authors used ChatGPT 4o for copy-editing. The authors reviewed and edited the content and takes full responsibility for the content.

References

1. Van Lamsweerde, A.: Requirements Engineering: From System Goals to UML Models to Software Specifications. Wiley, Hoboken (2009)
2. Yu, E., Giorgini, P., Maiden, N., Mylopoulos, J.: Social Modeling for Requirements Engineering. MIT Press, Cambridge (2011)
3. Esmaeilnezhadtanha, F., Hasani, A., Spalazzi, L., Wautelet, Y., Del Bene, L.: Designing a healthcare data management system based on IoT-blockchain technology and system resiliency evaluation model. J. Inf. Telecommun. (2026)
4. Wautelet, Y.: A model-driven IT governance process based on the strategic impact evaluation of services. J. Syst. Softw. **149**, 462–475 (2019)
5. Yu, E.: Modeling Strategic Relationships for Process Reengineering, chap. 1–2, pp. 1–153. MIT Press, Cambridge (2011)
6. Wautelet, Y., Rouget, X.: Circulise, a model-driven framework to build and align socio-technical systems for the twin transition: Fanyatu's case of sustainability in reforestation. Expert Syst. Appl. **262**, 125664 (2025)

7. Hevner, A.R., March, S.T., Park, J., Ram, S.: Design science in information systems research. MIS Q. 75–105 (2004)
8. OMG. Unified modeling language. Version 2.5. Technical report (2015)
9. The Open Group. Archimate® 3.0.1 specification (2017)
10. Josey, A.: ArchiMate® 3.0.1 - A Pocket Guide. Van Haren, Zaltbommel (2017)
11. Avison, D., Jones, J., Powell, P., Wilson, D.: Using and validating the strategic alignment model. J. Strateg. Inf. Syst. **13**(3), 223–246 (2004)
12. Shah, M.U., Guild, P.D.: Stakeholder engagement strategy of technology firms: a review and applied view of stakeholder theory. Technovation **114**, 102460 (2022)

Requirements and Design Options for Adaptive Step Goals in Health Recommender Systems

Michael Fellmann[✉] 🆔 and Angelina Clara Schmidt 🆔

Institute of Business Informatics, University of Rostock, Rostock, Germany
{michael.fellmann,angelina.schmidt}@uni-rostock.de

Abstract. Sedentary behavior is a global threat to health. Increasing physical activity (PA), e.g., by walking more steps per day, can interrupt physical inactivity and is associated with a lot of positive health effects. However, individuals often struggle to integrate more steps into their daily lives. Therefore, motivating goals could serve as a remedy. They need to be challenging to nudge the individual towards more steps, yet at the same time, they should be attainable to prevent frustration. Up to now, commercial and research-based fitness devices and health recommender systems predominantly use static goals or provide rather simplistic adaptive approaches. Against this gap, we provide requirements and derive design options for adaptive step goal features in health recommender systems. We demonstrate the application of our requirements and design options to a concrete smartwatch-based recommender system that we are currently building, and finally provide a summary of our insights in the form of a checklist for designing adaptive step goal features.

Keywords: Adaptive Step Goal · Recommender System · Physical Activity

1 Introduction

Sedentary work environments contribute significantly to a decline in physical activity (PA). As physical movement becomes less integrated into daily routines, the importance of intentional physical activity increases. It is estimated that nearly a third of adults globally were insufficiently physically active in 2022, with this trend continuing to rise [1]. Physical inactivity is a concern of modern life, leading to non-communicable diseases and mortality. Higher levels of total physical activity, regardless of intensity level, and lower amounts of sedentary time, are associated with a lower risk of premature mortality [2]. Walking, which can be measured by step count, has been linked to positive physical and mental health benefits [3]. Because walking can be easily incorporated into everyday life, increasing step count is a practical and effective way to improve overall health. Customized goals and frequent goal adjustments lead to more steps, by supporting aligning ambitions with acutal capabilites, leading to improved step counts [4]. Wearable devices support this goal by tracking activity and providing feedback.

The three most popular suppliers of current commercial wearables are Apple, Samsung, and Fitbit. The Apple Watch does not set a direct step target. Instead, users can

© The Author(s), under exclusive license to Springer Nature Switzerland AG 2026
R. Deneckère et al. (Eds.): BIR 2025, LNBIP 562, pp. 88–104, 2026.
https://doi.org/10.1007/978-3-032-04375-7_6

customize three activity rings to represent their goals for movement (calories), training minutes, and standing up every hour. In this case, the daily number of steps influences the movement ring. Goals can be adjusted at any time. Every Monday, users receive a notification about their successes from the previous week, which also includes possible suggestions for goals based on previous performance. However, these require manual confirmation by the user [5].

Fitbit uses a default step goal of 10,000 steps per day, but users can customize this step goal. The Fitbit app also provides weekly summaries, enabling users to manually review and adjust their goals based on the previous week's activity [6].

Samsung uses a default value of 6,000 steps per day. After a week, Samsung also from time to time asks if the user wants to increase or reduce the goal.

Hence, current commercial tools rely on manual adjustments with supporting weekly summaries. More advanced and adaptive approaches are still limited in both research and application. Addressing this gap, we (i) identify fundamental requirements for automated step goal setting, (ii) derive design options to meet these requirements, and (iii) demonstrate the selection and application of these options in a real-world system.

We organize the paper as follows: Sect. 2 presents existing approaches to step goal setting and step count prediction. Section 3 outlines the requirements needed for adaptive step goal setting. Section 4 discusses design options to address these requirements. Section 5 explains how the design options are selected and applied to the Wearable Lifestyle Recommender system. Section 6 describes the ongoing implementation of the adaptive step goal feature.

2 Related Work on Adaptive Step Goal Setting

2.1 Approaches for Step Goal Setting

Recent studies have explored approaches to personalize step goals. Park et al. propose to recalculate dynamic step goals in their *JustWalk JITAI* project. Notifications are delivered up to 4 times per day to increase a person's steps and suggest daily step goals. Each user is provided with a suggested daily step goal notification in the morning. Step goals were adapted by using each participant's median daily steps: in cycle 1 from a 10-day baseline period and in subsequent cycles from the previous 26-day cycles, always excluding nonwear days. Goals varied between this reference up to that reference + 4000 steps, using a multisine signal design, and including 2000 steps as lower limit and 12000 steps as upper limit. For example, if the median steps are 5000, goals varied between 5000 and 9000 steps/day [7].

Similarly, Sze and Nangaku present *StepApp*, a personalized mobile health intervention designed to increase PA among Type 2 diabetes patients. A drastically increase in the daily step count was observed in the 12-week study ($n = 33$), nearly doubling the step count. In the context of user-specific goal calculation, the rule-based approach algorithm is designed to modify the suggested step goal for the upcoming week. This modification is based on the number of days in the current week in which the user achieved their goal. Thus, the algorithm functions to either increase, maintain, or decrease the step goal, in accordance with the user's prior performance [8].

Moving beyond rule-based methods, Zhou et al. introduce the fitness app *CalFit*, designed to enhance PA through personalized goal setting. Step goals are calculated and adapted using reinforcement learning (RL), rather than using fixed increments. The algorithm is adjusting the step goal daily based on recent step history and user response. The study highlights that the intervention group, which received personalized step goals based on RL algorithms, experienced an average increase of 700 steps per day. In contrast, the control group, with the fixed goal of 10,000 steps per day, experienced a decrease in daily step count of 1,520 over 10 weeks [9]. Non-personalized fixed step goals may lack the right level of challenge, being either too difficult or too easy, potentially hindering user progress [9].

Mintz et al. propose a behavioral analytics framework to design adaptive, personalized incentives for myopic agents. The approach involves modeling each agent's decision making. This is done by estimating their behavioral parameters from data. Then the incentives (like step goals) are optimized accordingly. Three variants were used for adaptive step goal calculation. In Variant 1, step goals were set to be a 10% increase over the individual's linear moving average step count from the previous week, allowing for gradual personalized progression. Variant 2 was a do-nothing plan, where the step goals were a constant 10,000 steps each day. In Variant 3, participant had no step goals for the first two weeks (initialization period), after which their goals increased by 20% each week, starting from a 20% increase over their average steps during the initial two weeks. The exercise goals were capped at a maximum of 12,000 steps a day [10].

2.2 Step Count Prediction

While effective goal setting strategies help tailor targets to user behavior, their effectiveness can be further enhanced through accurate step count prediction. Predictive models allow for anticipatory adjustments.

Vasedekis et al. propose *WeMoD*, a Machine Learning (ML) approach designed to predict a user's future daily step count using multimodal, real-world data. The model combines activity-related, personal, and contextual features, all of which contribute positively to prediction performance [11]. The Gradient Boosting Regressor yielded the best results for step prediction in this case [11]. Also, outlier detection and removal improve the prediction models, and days with less than 500 steps were excluded as no-wear days. While the generalized WeMoD model can detect patterns without prior knowledge of a specific user, the personalized model yields better accuracy [11].

Belitsky presents a personalized step count prediction model based on Recurrent Neural Networks architectures. Furthermore, an approach of using steps by hour data was proposed, which outperformed models trained on daily step counts. The data for this model was obtained from one individual collected over a period of five years. In this case, Long Short-Term Memory architecture and the Gated Recurrent Unit models demonstrated the best performance for forecasting step counts. The lowest step count threshold was set to 300, while extremely high values were not considered as outliers, as such behavior can occur occasionally. The dataset was augmented with information about months, years, holidays and weekends was added to the dataset. However, these features did not lead to improvements in the performance of the models [12].

Chatterjee et al. proposes a conceptualization of using statistical forecast models to forecast daily future steps with a ruleset to generate recommendations based on the forecasting outcome. Among the models they tested on step count data from 16 participants using the PMData dataset, ARIMA achieved the best accuracy. The system aims to forecast step data for the next 7 days based on the temporal pattern in the data. Those forecasted steps are classified into activity levels (e.g., sedentary, low active) based on rules. Based on the predicted weekly performance, tailored recommendations are generated [13].

3   Requirements for Adaptive Step Goal Setting

In the following, high-level functional requirements for the adaptive step goal feature will be derived and justified. They are derived for a healthy population in mind; goal setting for patients with special needs is out of scope.

Users differ in their ambition and ability to walk. Also, age and current health status influence the capacity to walk. Hence, the first and most fundamental requirement is that the goal is *adaptive to the actual steps* (R1) a user achieves *in reality*. These, in turn, may be heavily influenced by weekly patterns. For example, someone might perform long workouts on weekends, whereas someone else prefers to relax on weekends. Therefore, the goal has to *adapt to weekly patterns* (R2).

However, in case the user performs almost no steps and is generally physically inactive, then adaptation to this inactive lifestyle would result in very low step goals, posing a threat to health. There is an overwhelming amount of research, e.g., in the context of sedentary behavior (www.sedentarybehaviour.org), suggesting a wide range of adverse health effects of inactive lifestyles. Consequently, there has to be a lower limit of the daily step goal. In the opposite direction, and due to possible adverse effects of excessive walking, an upper limit seems reasonable. Therefore, *limiting goals* (R3) is required. When goals are within reasonable ranges and adapt to the users' real behavior, the user however needs to be "pushed" or "nudged" towards more ambitious goals since the lack of physical activity is considered as a global health risk leading to adverse outcomes such as all-cause mortality, cardiovascular disease mortality, cancer mortality, incidence of cardiovascular disease, cancer, and type-2 diabetes [14]. Therefore, not only adapting to the user, but also slightly increasing goals to *nudge the user* is beneficial (R4). However, the user should still be in control and be able to customize the automatic goal setting. For example, the user might want to adapt upper or lower limits and the strength of nudging. This resonates with numerous empirical studies suggesting that customization is one of the most important system features (R5). Finally, the adaptive step goal feature must also work when the user has not yet collected step count data, i.e., upon a "cold start" of the system (R6), and also ethical considerations when nudging the user have to be taken into consideration (R7). The following Table 1 gives a summary of all the requirements.

Table 1. Requirements for Adaptive Step Goal Setting.

ID	Requirement	Description
R1	Adapt to the actual steps	Consider how many steps the user really walks
R2	Adapt to weekly patterns	Consider variation such as more/fewer steps on weekends
R3	Limit goals	Do not suggest step counts near zero or excessive goals
R4	Provide nudging	Increase the step goal to encourage striving for more steps
R5	Allow customization	Give control to the user if they want to adapt settings
R6	Handle missing data	Make the system work independently of data quality
R7	Consider ethics	Apply principles such as transparency or autonomy

4   Design Options for Adaptive Step Goal Setting

Based on the requirements in the previous chapter that provide an abstract specification of *what* should be achieved, the options for doing so are elaborated in this chapter. It hence sheds light on *how* (in principle) the requirements can be translated to the design of an IT-based system by deriving Design Options (DO).

R1 (adapt to the actual steps) requires either capturing step data via a sensor ($R1_{DO1}$) as part of the health recommender system, or that the user self-reports daily steps ($R1_{DO2}$) or self-reported step goal attainment ($R1_{DO3}$) to gather data about real walking behavior. Alternatively, an automated approach could allow *step count prediction* ($R1_{DO4}$) (cf. Also Sect. 2.2) to estimate the current steps. To adapt to weekly patterns such as more/or less walking on weekends or certain weekdays (R2), either a *fixed time window* ($R2_{DO1}$) for pattern identification or an *adaptable time window* ($R2_{DO2}$) might be used. In regard to the limits of goals (R3), setting a *lower limit* ($R3_{DO1}$) as well as an *upper limit* ($R3_{DO2}$) are relevant options.

When it comes to nudging, a *fixed step goal increase* ($R4_{DO1}$), e.g., 500 steps, could be used, a *relative increase* ($R4_{DO2}$) such as x percent or a complex *adaptive goal increase* ($R4_{DO3}$) such as starting with more ambitious goals and then "fade out" the step increase upon approaching the upper limit value. Further, to not infinitely nudge the user towards reaching ever higher goals, an *upper limit for nudging* ($R4_{DO4}$) definitely should be considered as well as a *recovery period* ($R4_{DO5}$) after extensive training to prevent adverse effects of over-training.

In terms of customization (R4), providing the possibility to *customize limits* ($R5_{DO1}$) for lower and upper goal values would enable a more personalized adjusted corridor of values. Further, some individuals may prefer no nudging while others might opt for an even more "aggressive" nudging, so that the *strength of the nudging* ($R5_{DO2}$) might also be subject to personalization. These mentioned options, furthermore, could be combined into *different modes* ($R5_{DO1}$), serving as an umbrella for parameters. For example, modes could be *healthy, ambitious,* or *sportive* and provide different settings and defaults. In such a way, individuals who use the adaptive step goal for staying healthy have other defaults than athletes or runners.

When the adaptive step goal is used for the first time and no data has been collected yet, or if the user does not consistently use the system, then no data or missing data is the result. To prevent this situation, an option is to *require the availability of data* ($R6_{DO1}$). If this requirement is not fulfilled, the user cannot switch on the system, or the system automatically switches off in case of missing data. To avoid such restrictions, the system needs a mechanism to *substitute missing data with other "next best data"* ($R6_{DO2}$) from the user. For example, if the user just recently stopped using the system, then some older data might still serve as a proxy for more recent data. If this is also not possible, then *missing data might be substituted with reasonable default values* ($R6_{DO3}$).

Finally, according to ethical guidelines for assistance system development [15], relevant aspects are *transparency about the current goal* ($R7_{DO1}$), freedom to *switch off the system* ($R7_{DO2}$), being able to *provide feedback* about the system ($R7_{DO3}$) and also *reflection about the goals* ($R7_{DO4}$). These design options may contribute to a more responsible system use. The following Table 2 summarizes all design options.

Table 2. Design Options for Adaptive Step Goal Setting.

	Requirement	Design Options (DO1 … DOn)
R1	Adapt to the actual steps	$R1_{DO1}$: Capture step data via sensor $R1_{DO2}$: Use self-reported steps $R1_{DO3}$: Use self-reported goal attainment $R1_{DO4}$: Use step count prediction
R2	Adapt to weekly patterns	$R2_{DO1}$: Use a fixed time window for patterns $R2_{DO2}$: Use an adaptable time window for patterns
R3	Limit goals	$R3_{DO1}$: Set lower limit $R3_{DO2}$: Set upper limit
R4	Provide nudging	$R4_{DO1}$: Provide a fixed step goal increase $R4_{DO2}$: Provide a relative step goal increase $R4_{DO3}$: Provide adaptive step goal increase $R4_{DO4}$: Set upper limit for nudging $R4_{DO5}$: Offer recovery after extensive training
R5	Allow customization	$R5_{DO1}$: Allow customizable limits $R5_{DO2}$: Allow customizable nudging strength $R5_{DO3}$: Provide modes with presets
R6	Handle missing data	$R6_{DO1}$: Require availability of data $R6_{DO2}$: Substitute missing data with "next best data" $R6_{DO3}$: Substitute missing data with default values
R7	Consider ethics	$R7_{DO1}$: Provide transparency about the current goal $R7_{DO2}$: Enable the switch-off of the system $R7_{DO3}$: Consider user feedback about the system $R7_{DO4}$: Foster reflection about the goals

5 Scientifically Informed Selection and Application of the Design Options for the Wearable Lifestyle Recommender

5.1 Introduction to the WLR and Procedure

When crafting the adaptive step goal feature, a research group of four researchers carefully applied the design options (cf. Table 2) in a joint effort to create the WLR adaptive step goal feature (or *ASG*, for brevity). The research team consists of two undergraduate students (m), one graduate student (m), one doctoral researcher (f), and one professor (m), the latter two being the authors of the paper. Discussions were led in two phases. After a brainstorming phase where requirements and design options were collected, there was a consolidation phase where scientific literature was also consulted, and decisions were finally taken in a workshop. In the following, we step through the requirements and describe which options we selected for specifying our ASG feature to be implemented in the WLR.

The target system for which the ASG feature was designed is the Wearable Lifestyle Recommender (WLR). This is a smartwatch, smartphone, and server-side system that sends personalized, context-sensitive messages for micro-coaching. The system is being developed as part of an ongoing research effort at the University of Rostock. Personalization is possible with an extensive server profile allowing the specification of personal preferences regarding the timing, the amount, and the content of messages. Regarding the context, the system currently considers time, weekday, step count, and heart rate. It can easily be extended to consider further parameters such as sleep quality or Heart Rate Variability (HRV), amongst others. The architecture of the system has already been described here [16]. Part of the micro-coaching system are messages being reminders to own goals (which can be set for each of the four timeslots per day), reminders for physical activities, and educational messages containing briefly summarized science-backed advice on favorable lifestyles for work and private life.

In the current revision of the system, the reminder for physical activity is based on static step goals that can be set individually for each day, or for multiple days of a week (with pre-defined options Mon-Sun, Weekend, Workdays). However, setting manual goals can be a cumbersome and tedious task, so users are inclined to take a shortcut and set just one goal for all weekdays. Such a setting does not reflect individual life patterns, such as walking more/less on weekends, and consequently, daily step goals are inappropriate. While they are easy or almost trivially met on some days, on others, they are very hard to achieve, e.g., due to professional or family duties. Another difficulty with manual step goal setting is that it can be hard to determine an appropriate step count that is both favorable in terms of health and realistic given the personal motivation, time, and effort. An adaptive step goal feature can solve these problems and remove the burden of specifying and constantly revising personal step goals. In the following, the design options introduced so far are selected and applied to design the ASG feature.

5.2 Adaptation to Actual Steps, Weekly Patterns, and Limits (R1–R3)

Regarding the adaptation to actual steps (R1), the system already has an InfluxDB time series database where current steps and HR measured by a smartwatch (Samsung Galaxy

Watch 4) are stored. Therefore, we opt for *capturing steps via sensor* ($R1_{DO1}$). For the adaptation of the step goal to weekly patterns (R2), it was decided to use a *fixed time window of seven days* ($R2_{DO1}$). In more detail, it was decided to look back at the last seven *matching* weekdays. This means, for calculating the step goal of a Monday, the step count of the seven previous Mondays will be analyzed, if available. Otherwise, the system will consider data from the previous days or default values (cf. also options taken for R6).

To limit goals (R3), *both lower and upper limits* will be implemented ($R3_{DO1}$, $R3_{DO2}$). For a minimum lower limit, studies differ, but numbers between 2,300 [17] and 4,000 steps [18] seem to be the lower limit in terms of health effectiveness. Therefore, a lower limit of 2,000 steps seems to be justified. In the opposite direction regarding upper limits for step goals, the picture is less clear. However, there seem to be plateau effects regarding the contribution of steps to health around 6.000–8.000 steps (for adults) and 8,000 to 10,000 for younger adults [19]. Similarly, another study found that after the nudging study, most participants reached 10,500 steps, but not more [20]. Hence, there seems to be a "ceiling effect", i.e., people do not walk more, even if goals are higher. Moreover, few reviews include studies above 20,000 steps, so that possible adverse outcomes of excessive walking are less researched in comparison to the positive effects of moderate doses of walking. Therefore, an upper limit of 14,000 steps seems reasonable and is in line with other goal setting systems that have upper limits of 15,000 steps [21]. According to Tudor-Locke et al., adults should aim to accumulate at least 3,000 additional steps per day above their habitual activity or 7,000 to 8,000 total steps per day to meet minimum physical activity recommendations [22].

5.3 Nudging and Customization (R4, R5)

Concerning the nudging (R4), that is, a slight increase of the step goal above the average value the user achieved so far, an *adaptive step goal* was decided ($R4_{DO3}$). In more detail, since empirical research suggests a negative correlation between baseline step count and increase due to nudging interventions [21] (cf. Fig. 1, right), there seems to be a saturation effect. Owing to this slowdown in step count increase, we calculate the step goal addition based on the difference between the average and the upper goal limit (cf. Table 3). Further, it was decided to *stop the automatic increase (nudging) above the upper limit goal value* ($R4_{DO4}$), but not use this value as a strict cut-off value. In this way, if users walk a lot of steps, they still can receive their step goal based on their averages, but will not be nudged to walk even more. In regard to recovery, we make no assumptions since we do not want to patronize the user. Rather, they should decide for themselves if they strive to reach the daily goal or if it is wise to have a day off for recovery. However, in future versions of the ASG, we might consider additional sensor data such as HRV values that have a "significant positive correlation with reactivity and recovery from mental and physical stress" [23] to decide whether a step goal will be recommended. As an alternative to this, also extreme step counts such as 300% of the step goal might serve as an indicator for a day off.

Regarding customization (R5), we opted to allow the user to *customize the limits freely* ($R5_{DO1}$), but within the restriction of 2,000 steps for the lower limit and 14,000 steps for the upper limit. We decided to implicitly let the user *customize the nudging strength* (R5$_{DO2}$) via selection of a mode. Regarding the modes, consensus was to offer three modes named *healthy, ambitious,* and *sportive* (R5$_{DO3}$). The healthy mode is for individuals who perform steps to stay healthy. The ambitious mode is for individuals who perceive physical activity as an important aspect of their daily life. The sportive mode is intended for very ambitious individuals, up to semi-professional athletes. The difference between the modes is both the default values for lower and upper goal limits and the nudging strength, ranging from 10% more steps (healthy) to 20% (ambitious) to 30% (sportive). Due to the freedom to adjust the lower and upper goal values, users are free to configure the system such that it combines a very low goal limit with a strong nudging and a high upper goal limit. The following Table 3 provides a summary of the three modes and their parameters.

Table 3. Design Options for Adaptive Step Goal Setting.

Mode	Lower limit default value (min. 2,000)	Upper limit default value (max. 14,000)	Formula for the step goal increase to nudge users when they have average step counts between the lower and upper limit
Healthy	4,000	6,000	*Average + (GoalValue - Average) * 0,1*
Ambitious	6,000	8,000	*Average + (GoalValue - Average) * 0,2*
Sportive	8,000	12,000	*Average + (GoalValue - Average) * 0,3*

Healthy mode is intended for casual users who nevertheless want to walk a decent number of steps to achieve positive health effects. In line with this, the lower limit has a default value of 4,000 steps since values in this range or below are suggested in empirical studies on the minimum number of steps required for health improvement (cf. Sect. 5.2). Also, when looking at empirical data (cf. Fig. 1, left), this seems to be a viable lower limit. The upper limit default is 6,000, a number which is also a default value in commercial products such as Samsung Galaxy Watch, which target "standard" users, i.e., not only health enthusiasts. Nudging is low with max. 10% step goal increase.

Ambitious mode is intended for users who perceive physical activity as an important part of their daily life. In line with this, the lower limit has a default value of 6,000 steps. Since these users may want to consistently perform a notable level of physical activity but do not necessarily strive to reach higher and higher step counts, the upper limit default is set to 8,000, which is also a very attainable goal since the majority in an empirical study on nudging reached even 10,500 steps (cf. Fig. 1, left). Of course, users are free to set more ambitious upper limits for nudging. Nudging is moderate with max. 20% step goal increase.

Sportive mode is intended for enthusiasts striving to reach high standards and continuously improve. In line with this, the lower limit has a default value of 8,000 steps, which is above the default value of some commercial devices. The upper limit default is set to 12,000, which is also slightly above the default value of commercial fitness track-ers such as Fitbit devices. Of course, users are free to set even more ambitious upper limits up to 14,000 steps. Since users in this mode may want to continuously challenge themselves and improve, nudging is more "aggressive" with max. 30% goal increase.

The default settings of all modes are similar to step goals of another study suggesting four goals of 6,000, 8,000, 10,000, and 12,000 steps [21]. Moreover, independent of the mode setting, users are free to modify the lower limit and lower it to 2,000 steps as the lowest value. In the opposite direction, users are free to modify the upper limit to 14,000 steps. This is also in line with empirical data that shows that only a small fraction of individuals reach more than 13,500 steps (cf. Fig. 1, left). Moreover, studies that investigate the long-term effects of excessive step counts are rare, so there might be risks associated with excessive step counts.

Finally, a restriction for all modes will be that the difference between the lower and upper limit should be at least 2,000 steps. This minimum required "corridor" for nudging is in line with an empirical study suggesting that most participants improved 3,750 steps per day [20] (cf. Fig. 1, middle). Hence, improving 2,000 steps should be even more feasible.

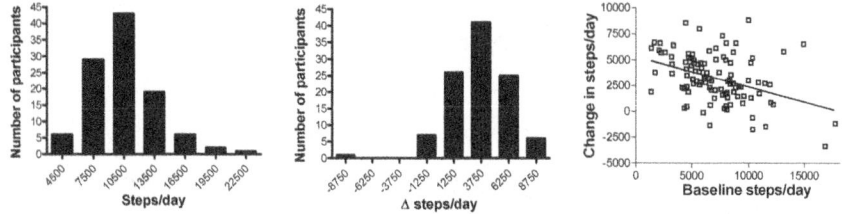

Fig. 1. Empirical data of the study from Chan, Ryan, and Tudor-Locke [20] on the health benefits of a pedometer-based physical activity intervention in sedentary workers. The **left** part shows the steps walked during the plateau phase of the study, the **middle** part shows the increase in steps during the 12-week study, and the **right** part shows the increase in steps per day in relation to the baseline physical activity (negative correlation at $P < 0.05$).

5.4 Compensation for Missing Data, Ethics (R6, R7)

In regard to missing data (R6), the *possibility to use the system despite missing data* (cold start problem) or incomplete data capturing is prioritized over requiring complete and consistent data. The need to compensate for missing data is even more pronounced due to the design decision to look back at seven matching days of the week (cf. Sect. 5.2). That is, we calculate the step goal of a Monday taking into consideration seven preceding Mondays. Based on this, the "cold start phase" of the system would be seven weeks and one day. So, a mechanism to *substitute missing data with "next best data"* ($R6_{DO2}$) is required. We implement this by using the step counts of non-matching weekdays as "next best data", in reverse chronological order. For example, consider that the daily step goal has to be calculated on a Monday. If the system was in use for exactly three weeks, then data from the two preceding Mondays is available as well as data from five preceding days, i.e., from Sunday backwards until the preceding Wednesday. Hence seven values are available to calculate the average step count. If, however also recordings from preceding days are missing, then *using default data values* is an alternative ($R6_{DO2}$). As default values, we use the lower limit value of the step goal, which depends on the selected mode (*healthy, ambitious, sportive*).

Finally, concerning ethical aspects, *the user will see the currently active step goal* at any time by accessing their server-side user profile ($R7_{DO1}$). Moreover, the ASG feature will have an *on/off switch* ($R7_{DO2}$). Regarding the possibility for users to *give feedback about the system* ($R7_{DO3}$) and its effects, no feature directly addressing this is planned. However, an indirect limited form of feedback or reaction to system use lies in the possibility to switch off the system, customize its limits, and adjust the mode. In future versions of the ASG feature, an automated checking procedure might be implemented that checks how often goals have been met (e.g., on a weekly basis) and, based on this, suggests adaptations of the parameters or switching between modes.

5.5 Summary of Selected Options

The following Table 4 shows a summary of the selected design options. Options that have been selected for full implementation are marked with "✓". Options that have been selected for partial or indirect implementation are marked with "(✓)".

Table 4. Final list of design options.

Design Options (DO)			
✓	$R1_{DO1}$: Capture step data via sensor	✓	$R5_{DO1}$: Allow customizable limits
✓		(✓)	$R5_{DO2}$: Allow customizable nudging strength
✓	$R2_{DO1}$: Use a fixed time window for patterns	✓	
✓		✓	$R5_{DO3}$: Provide modes with presets
✓	$R3_{DO1}$: Set lower limit	✓	$R6_{DO2}$: Substitute missing data with "next best data"
✓	$R3_{DO2}$: Set upper limit	✓	
	$R4_{DO3}$: Provide adaptive step goal increase	✓	$R6_{DO3}$: Substitute missing data with default values
		(✓)	
	$R4_{DO4}$: Set upper limit for nudging		$R7_{DO1}$: Provide transparency about the current goal
			$R7_{DO2}$: Enable the switch-off of the system
			$R7_{DO3}$: Consider feedback about the system

6 Demonstration, Ongoing Implementation and Critical Reflection of the Adaptive Step Goal Feature

6.1 Sample Calculations of Adaptive Step Goals

To demonstrate our adaptive step goal algorithm, Table 5 introduces three sample personas who have started to use the ASG feature. Bob is a casual user who recently switched on the ASG; Alice is ambitious and has already tracked her step data for 10 days, and

Jane is very enthusiastic about running and has used the ASG feature for 60 days. In rows 1–6, the current situation, including the activated mode of the ASG, the current day for which the step goal is to be calculated, and the input data, is specified. In row 7, a fictitious average step count value from the average calculation is shown. In row 8, the result of checking whether the nudging limit (i.e., the upper limit) is exceeded is shown. Whereas for Bob and Alice, the limit is not exceeded and hence an increased step goal is calculated (rows 9 and 10), Jane has exceeded the nudging limit and hence no further calculation is performed. In line 11, the final new adaptive step goal value is given.

What can be observed by looking at the table with sample calculations is that the closer a user's average steps are to the lower limit of the selected mode, the higher the goal increase will be. Whereas Bob's goal is increased by just 20 steps because he has almost reached the upper limit of the healthy mode, Alice has an increase of 380 steps because her average steps are close to the lower limit of the *ambitious* mode. This in line with empirical research suggesting a negative correlation between the number of baseline steps and the gain of steps induced by nudging Locke [20]. Furthermore, Jane receives no step goal increase because she has already overachieved the upper limit with her average step count of 13,500 steps. Jane may decide to customize her upper limit up to 14,000 steps and then again receive a slight nudging. Regarding the selected modes, Bob might consider switching to the ambitious mode since he has already reached the upper goal limit of the *health* mode. This could also be suggested by the system.

Table 5. Sample calculation for three Personas.

		Bob	Alice	Jane
1	Mode	Healthy	Ambitious	Sportive
2	Lower limit	4,000	6,000	8,0000
3	Upper limit	6,000	8,000	12,000
4	Current weekday	Monday	Monday	Monday
5	Input data	Step count for 4 previous days	Step count for 10 previous days	Step count for 60 previous days
6	Data used for avg steps calculation	Values from 4 previous days + 3*4,000 (default)	Step count of Monday last week + step count from 6 previous days	Step count of 7 previous Mondays
7	**Sample avg. Value**	**5,800**	**6,100**	**13,500**
8	Nudging limit exceeded?	No	No	Yes
9	Step goal formula	Avg + (GoalValue − Avg) * 0,1	Avg + (GoalValue − Avg) * 0,2	- not applicable -
10	Step goal calculation	5,800 + (6,000 − 5,800) * 0,1	6,100 + (8,000 − 6,100) * 0,2	- not applicable -
11	**New step goal**	**5,820**	**6,480**	**13,500**

6.2 Ongoing Implementation

In our ongoing implementation, we have already designed a graphical user interface for switching between the modes and setting the lower and upper limits (cf. Fig. 2). This UI is shown on the server-side backend of the WLR, and the implementation is ongoing.

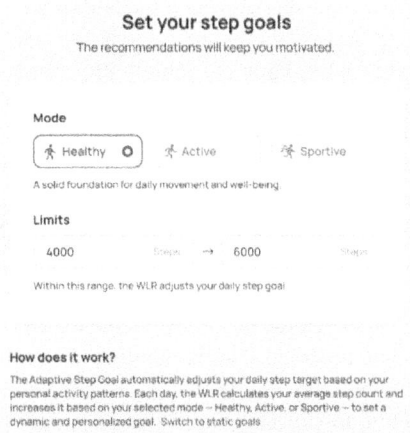

Set your step goals
The recommendations will keep you motivated.

Mode

🏃 Healthy   O   🏃 Active   🏃 Sportive

A solid foundation for daily movement and well-being

Limits

4000   Steps   →   6000   Steps

Within this range, the WLR adjusts your daily step goal

How does it work?
The Adaptive Step Goal automatically adjusts your daily step target based on your personal activity patterns. Each day, the WLR calculates your average step count and increases it based on your selected mode – Healthy, Active, or Sportive – to set a dynamic and personalized goal. Switch to static goals

Fig. 2. GUI component for the adaptive step goal feature.

6.3 Critical Reflection

According to the influential *Memorandum on Design-Oriented Business Informatics*, the principles that should be followed when conducting research are *abstraction, originality, justification* and *utility* [24]. The memorandum has been signed by major renowned researchers from the discipline. These principles can serve as a criterion to judge whether the research has been conducted properly and if the results create value. We therefore step through each of the principles in our critical reflection.

Abstraction. An artifact must be applicable to a class of problems. The class of problem is clearly described in the introduction. The problem is missing comprehensive approaches for adaptive step goal calculation. Since our ASG calculation scheme is not tailored to specific use cases or scenarios, it is widely applicable, and hence our approach provides a good level of abstraction.

Originality. An artifact must make an innovative contribution to the state of the art. The innovative aspect of the proposed ASG calculation scheme lies in the novel combination of numerous parameters and a comprehensive list of design options not known before at this level of detail.

Justification. This principle is essential for all scientific works since they should be comprehensibly justified and valid. We justified the selection and concrete application of design options either with literature or our own logical thinking and deductions. Moreover, default values of the calculation scheme have been grounded in empirical studies from the health domain.

Utility. An artifact must be able to generate a benefit for stakeholders today or in the future. The question about utility can be answered up to now by a line of argumentation implying that the tool has been built according to justified requirements that state favorable or necessary features, hence it can be deduced that an actual implementation of these features leads to the desired results. Furthermore, the elicitation of requirements, derivation of design options, and justified defaults for an ASG feature create value for engineers who design similar features. The real-world outcomes of the ASG feature on real step counts have to be explored in the second step. The conception of the ASG feature is like research on a new medicine in the preclinical phase, where it is agreed that the later impact on a living organism is not already part of the preclinical phase. This understanding has also been adopted in Information Systems [25].

7 Conclusion and Future Research Opportunities

Inactive lifestyles and sedentary behaviors are a global health problem leading to many health problems and even reduced life expectancy [14]. Though many commercial tools, such as fitness trackers, try to nudge the user towards a more active lifestyle and also provide step goals, the adaptation of the step goal often remains the task of the user. Despite some simplistic approaches, such as increasing or decreasing the daily step goal upon detecting constant overachievement or failure, research on more comprehensive approaches is still scarce. Against this gap, we (i) identified fundamental requirements for automated step goal calculation, (ii) derived design options, and (iii) showcased a scientifically informed selection and application of the design options for a real-world system, the Wearable Lifestyle Recommender (WLR). With these contributions and example instantiation of the requirements and design options, we hope to inspire and ease the future development of adaptive step goal features. As a takeaway, we complement this conclusion with a compact checklist of important design aspects for ASG features, shown in Table 6.

Table 6. Important design aspects for adaptive step goal features.

	Checklist
1	Capture step data via passive sensing to reduce the burden of data entry
2	Consider weekly patterns, such as more/fewer steps on weekends
2	Set reasonable upper and lower limits. Literature suggests 2,300–4,000 steps as the lower limit for positive health effects; plateau effects have been observed around 8,000–10,000 steps
4	Increase the step goal to nudge the user, but fade out the nudging when the user already walks a lot of steps. Also, consider different motivations of your users (e.g., staying healthy vs. winning a competition)
5	Set reasonable default values for standard users, but provide customization options for expert users (e.g., limit values and nudging strength)
6	Substitute missing current data with data from history or defaults
7	Consider ethical aspects such as transparency, and let the user switch off

As part of our ongoing work, we are currently implementing the ASG feature in our WLR system. Future research opportunities are studying the effect that different parameter settings have on the daily steps walked, and how to seamlessly combine machine learning-based step count prediction with more rule-based step goal calculations. While the former offers the promise to integrate multimodal data, such as e.g., the weather or calendar data, they need a lot of data, which is not available upon system start (cold start problem). The latter, however, can be used with smaller or no data recorded at all, and hence the system works "out of the box". Also, from a conceptual point of view, ML approaches can be used to forecast step counts and hence are *predictive*. In contrast, rule-based approaches calculate goals based on scientifically grounded values from medical research and hence are *normative*. Finding a balance between predictive and normative goal recommendations may be another future research opportunity. Finally, when calculating step goals, the aspect of recovery has to be taken into account to avoid overtraining. However, from the sheer volume of steps, the physical strain may not be accurately determined. Consequently, another research opportunity is the integration of biomarkers such as blood lactate as a proxy for strain and exhaustion might be incorporated in the adaptive step goal calculation.

Acknowledgement. We would like to thank Franz Großmann and Darius Marzisch for drafting the graphical user interface of the adaptive step goal feature of our Wearable Lifestyle Recommender system, as well as for the inspiring discussions.

References

1. Strain, T., Flaxman, S., Guthold, R., et al.: National, regional, and global trends in insufficient physical activity among adults from 2000 to 2022: a pooled analysis of 507 population-based surveys with 5·7 million participants. Lancet Glob. Health **12**, e1232–e1243 (2024). https://doi.org/10.1016/S2214-109X(24)00150-5
2. Ekelund, U., Tarp, J., Steene-Johannessen, J., et al.: Dose-response associations between accelerometry measured physical activity and sedentary time and all cause mortality: systematic review and harmonised meta-analysis. BMJ **366**, l4570 (2019). https://doi.org/10.1136/bmj.l4570
3. Kelly, P., Murphy, M., Mutrie, N.: The health benefits of walking. In: Mulley, C., Gebel, K., Ding, D. (eds.) Walking, pp. 61–79. Emerald Group Publishing, Bingley (2017). https://doi.org/10.1108/S2044-994120170000009004
4. Alqahtani, D., Jay, C., Vigo, M.: The effect of goal moderation on the achievement and satisfaction of physical activity goals. Proc. ACM Interact Mob. Wearable Ubiquit. Technol. **4**, 1–18 (2020). https://doi.org/10.1145/3432209
5. Apple Support. Ziele für deine Aktivitätsringe auf der Apple Watch anpassen. https://support.apple.com/de-de/guide/watch/apd29b30023c/watchos. Accessed 16 May 2025
6. Fitbit Help Center. How do I track my health and fitness goals with Fitbit? https://support.google.com/fitbit/answer/14236914?hl=en#zippy=. Accessed 16 May 2025
7. Park, J., Kim, M., El Mistiri, M., et al.: Advancing understanding of just-in-time states for supporting physical activity (Project JustWalk JITAI): protocol for a system ID study of just-in-time adaptive interventions. JMIR Res Protoc **12**, e52161 (2023). https://doi.org/10.2196/52161

8. Sze, W.T., Waki, K., Enomoto, S., et al.: StepAdd: a personalized mHealth intervention based on social cognitive theory to increase physical activity among type 2 diabetes patients. J. Biomed. Inform. **145**, 104481 (2023). https://doi.org/10.1016/j.jbi.2023.104481

9. Zhou, M., Mintz, Y., Fukuoka, Y., et al.: Personalizing mobile fitness apps using reinforcement learning. In: CEUR Workshop Proceedings, vol. 2068 (2018). http://ceur-ws.org/Vol-2068/humanize7.pdf

10. Mintz, Y., Aswani, A., Kaminsky, P., et al.: Behavioral analytics for myopic agents. Eur. J. Oper. Res. **310**, 793–811 (2023). https://doi.org/10.1016/j.ejor.2023.03.034

11. Vasdekis, D., Yfantidou, S., Efstathiou, S., et al.: WeMoD: a machine learning approach for wearable and mobile physical activity prediction. In: 2022 IEEE International Conference on Pervasive Computing and Communications Workshops and other affiliated events (PerCom workshops), pp. 385–390. IEEE, Piscataway (2022). https://doi.org/10.1109/PerComWorkshops53856.2022.9767541

12. Belitsky, M.: Deep Learning for personalized physical activity prediction based on step counts. Dissertation, Tilburg University (2021)

13. Chatterjee, A., Prinz, A., Riegler, M.: Prediction modeling in activity eCoaching for tailored recommendation generation: a conceptualization. In: IEEE Medical Measurements & Applications, Giardini Naxos - Taormina, Messina, Italy, pp. 1–6 (2022). https://doi.org/10.1109/MeMeA54994.2022.9856556

14. World Health Organization. WHO guidelines on physical activity and sedentary behaviour. World Health Organization, Geneva (2020)

15. Cap, C.H., Fellmann, M., Põder, J.-C.: Muster für ein ethisches design von assistenzsystemen. conexus **4**, 131–154 (2021). https://doi.org/10.24445/conexus.2021.04.009

16. Richter, H., Fellmann, M., Lambusch, F., et al.: Towards an architectural concept for a wearable recommendation system to support workplace productivity and well-being. In: Kurosu, M. (ed.) HCII 2022. LNCS, vol. 13304, Springer, Cham, pp. 416–429 (2022). https://doi.org/10.1007/978-3-031-05412-9_29

17. Harvard Health. Large study finds the sweet spot for daily step goals. https://www.health.harvard.edu/staying-healthy/large-study-finds-the-sweet-spot-for-daily-step-goals. Accessed 19 May 2025

18. ESC Press Office. World's largest study shows the more you walk, the lower your risk of death, even if you walk fewer than 5,000 steps. https://www.escardio.org/The-ESC/Press-Office/Press-releases/World-s-largest-study-shows-the-more-you-walk-the-lower-your-risk-of-death-even-if-you-walk-fewer-than-5-000-steps. Accessed 19 May 2025

19. Whole Health. How many steps a day do you need for health? Updating the research, a closer look at the science. https://www.thewholehealthpractice.com/post/how-many-steps-a-day-do-you-need-for-health-updating-the-research-a-closer-look-at-the-science. Accessed 19 May 2025

20. Chan, C.B., Ryan, D.A.J., Tudor-Locke, C.: Health benefits of a pedometer-based physical activity intervention in sedentary workers. Prev. Med. **39**, 1215–1222 (2004). https://doi.org/10.1016/j.ypmed.2004.04.053

21. Shibuta, T., Waki, K., Miyake, K., et al.: Preliminary efficacy, feasibility, and perceived usefulness of a smartphone-based self-management system with personalized goal setting and feedback to increase step count among workers with high blood pressure: before-and-after Study. JMIR Cardio **7**, e43940 (2023). https://doi.org/10.2196/43940

22. Tudor-Locke, C., Craig, C.L., Brown, W.J., et al.: How many steps/day are enough? For adults. Int. J. Behav. Nutr. Phys. Act. **8**, 79 (2011). https://doi.org/10.1186/1479-5868-8-79

23. Dong, S.-Y., Lee, M., Park, H., et al.: Stress resilience measurement with heart-rate variability during mental and physical stress. In: Annual International Conference of the IEEE Engineering in Medicine and Biology, pp. 5290–5293 (2018). https://doi.org/10.1109/EMBC.2018.8513531

24. Österle, H., Becker, J., Frank, U., et al.: Memorandum zur gestaltungsorientierten Wirtschaftsinformatik. Schmalenbachs Z betriebswirtsch Forsch **62**, 664–672 (2010). https://doi.org/10.1007/BF03372838
25. Karagiannis, D.: Welche Rolle kann bzw. soll die IT bei der Umsetzung und Unterstützung gestaltungsorientierter WI-Forschung spielen? Wirtschaftsinformatik: Ein Plädoyer für Rigor und Relevanz, pp. 45–47 (2010)

Enterprise Architecture

Advancing Enterprise Architecture Debt: Insights from Work System Theory

Simon Hacks[1]([✉])[iD] and Ada Slupczynski[2][iD]

[1] Stockholm University, Stockholm, Sweden
`simon.hacks@dsv.su.se`
[2] RWTH Aachen University, Aachen, Germany
`ada.slupczynski@swc.rwth-aachen.de`

Abstract. Enterprise Architecture (EA) debt emerges when short-term decisions lead to structural inefficiencies that hinder organizational agility and strategic alignment. This paper applies Work System Theory (WST) to categorize and analyze EA debt, offering a structured approach to identifying and managing it. We highlight key challenges, research gaps, and future directions by mapping EA debt to WST components. The findings emphasize the need for adaptive frameworks, improved stakeholder engagement, and systematic debt management strategies.

Keywords: Enterprise Architecture Debt · Foundational Theory · Work System Theory

1   Introduction

Enterprise Architecture (EA) debt has been defined as *"the deviation of the currently present state of an enterprise from a hypothetical ideal state"* [1]. It arises when decisions in EA are delayed, or shortcuts are taken, leading to problems. These problems can reduce an organization's ability to adapt, perform well, or achieve its goals. However, EA debt is not founded in any theory but adapted from the concept of technical debt [1], making it hard to study or manage effectively. A strong theoretical foundation can help by identifying EA debt, making it easier to measure and analyze. It also ensures that decisions about managing EA debt are based on evidence and not just intuition.

A theoretical foundation also improves how we study EA debt [2]. It allows researchers to look at its causes and effects in a structured way and identify patterns across different organizations. This makes it possible to develop better strategies for managing EA debt and to learn from the experiences of others. Additionally, having a theory allows EA debt to be connected to other fields, like IT management and organizational strategy, for a more complete understanding.

Work System Theory (WST) [3] is an excellent fit for studying EA debt because it looks at an organization's relationships between people, processes, technologies, and information. EA debt often arises when these elements are not aligned [4,5], and WST can help explain how these misalignments occur and

© The Author(s), under exclusive license to Springer Nature Switzerland AG 2026
R. Deneckère et al. (Eds.): BIR 2025, LNBIP 562, pp. 107–123, 2026.
https://doi.org/10.1007/978-3-032-04375-7_7

how they can be fixed. Another reason WST is a good choice is that it focuses on how systems change over time. EA debt is not static; it grows or evolves as organizations adapt to new challenges [6]. WST's focus on change makes it well-suited to study the dynamic nature of EA debt. Finally, WST emphasizes the role of stakeholders—people and groups affected by or involved in a system. EA debt often involves trade-offs between stakeholders, such as balancing short-term cost savings against long-term system performance [7]. WST provides a way to examine these trade-offs and their impact on the organization.

This paper explores how WST can provide a theoretical foundation for understanding EA debt. Using WST, we can better define, analyze, and manage EA debt, helping organizations improve their EA. The rest of this work is structured as follows: Sect. 2 provides an overview of EA debt and WST. Section 4 applies WST to real-world examples, illustrating how EA debt manifests across different system components. Section 5 identifies key research gaps in the existing literature, followed by the related work. Finally, Sect. 6 concludes the paper.

2   Foundations

2.1   Enterprise Architecture Debt

The increasing pace of digitalization and the widespread adoption of agile methods have significantly impacted how organizations manage their EA. One of the core challenges lies in the time available to define robust target architectures, as product owners tend to favor short-term business value over long-term architectural sustainability [8]. Simultaneously, there remains a scarcity of approaches that effectively support long-term architectural planning [9,10].

Therefore, Hacks et al. [1] introduced the concept of Enterprise Architecture Debt (EAD) by extending the idea of Technical Debt, formulated initially to describe technical shortcuts that hinder future IT development [11,12], to the enterprise level. While Technical Debt has proven valuable in identifying software deficits, guiding decision-making, and raising awareness [13,14], its focus remains mainly on isolated systems. This narrow scope often neglects the broader architectural concerns that span entire organizations [15–17].

EAD is "the deviation of the currently present state of an enterprise from a hypothetical ideal state" [1]. This deviation may result from short-term decisions that increase the future cost of change or from shifts in strategic direction that render previous architectural decisions suboptimal. In both cases, EAD acts as a hindrance to achieving an updated, strategically aligned EA. To support a shared understanding of the terminology in this emerging field, Slupczynski and Hacks [18] have developed a domain ontology that captures and structures key concepts in EAD. Research on EAD has evolved along two principal streams [6]: (1) technical aspects, which focus on architectural artifacts and tooling, and (2) socio-technical aspects, which consider stakeholder dynamics, organizational processes, and human decision-making.

In the technical stream, Salentin and Hacks [19] introduced the concept of EA Smells, a set of indicators for architectural inefficiencies. These were operationalized through a prototype capable of identifying such smells in ArchiMate models. Smajevic et al. [20] further advanced this work by developing an automated tool to support EA Smell detection.

Regarding managing EADs, Yeong et al. [21] proposed a prioritization method based on portfolio theory and utility functions, enabling organizations to evaluate and sequence their debt remediation activities. Building on this, Liss et al. [22] introduced refactoring strategies to eliminate identified debts. Complementing these approaches, Slupczynski et al. [23] proposed a process model for evaluating the prudence or recklessness of architectural debts, thus offering a decision-support perspective.

The socio-technical dimension of EAD is addressed in studies focusing on process integration and stakeholder engagement. Alexander et al. [6] proposed a management framework for EAD that includes identifying, collecting, assessing, prioritizing, and resolving debts. Jung et al. [4] contributed a workshop format designed to identify EADs and EA Smells not easily captured by models alone. This format was later refined by Daoudi et al. [5] for improved time efficiency and impact assessment.

To empirically assess the utility of the EAD concept, Hacks and Jung [24] conducted a controlled experiment with students tasked with modeling a fictitious organization. While the experiment did not yield a measurable improvement in EA outcomes, it represents an important first step in evaluating the practical impact of EAD as a conceptual tool.

There are also similar works to be considered: Chis et al. [25] explain how WST concepts can be lifted into an RDF knowledge graph that is continuously fed with run-time data from operational systems. By representing participants, information, and technologies as semantically linked nodes, the graph becomes a living digital twin of the enterprise work systems. Such a twin lets architects query cross-layer dependencies (e.g., "Which customer-facing capabilities still rely on an unsupported database engine?") and reason over them with off-the-shelf SPARQL and inference engines. In an EA Debt context, this offers two benefits: (1) fine-grained visibility of "hidden" debts that span several work systems, and (2) the ability to monitor debt interest automatically as the graph evolves with every change to the underlying landscape.

Flórez et al. [26] survey and re-implement more than 50 automated analyses for enterprise models, ranging from cost optimization to change-impact estimation. Expressed in an extended ArchiMate metamodel, the catalog highlights which additional metadata a model must contain for a given analysis to run correctly. From an EA Debt standpoint, the contribution is two-fold. First, several analyses (e.g., redundancy detection, technology obsolescence, workload bottlenecks) map directly onto known "EA smells" that signal debt. Second, the catalog clarifies input and output requirements, paving the way for repeatable, tool-supported debt dashboards rather than ad-hoc spreadsheet calculations.

Flórez et al. [27] present an approach that turns ArchiMate models into a living laboratory for automated enterprise analysis. Each "analysis method" is packaged as a plug-in that declares the extra attributes it needs (e.g., age, MTTR, license cost) and can be hot-deployed into their iArchiMate tooling.

Because the metamodel itself is extensible, the architecture repository evolves in lock-step with the battery of analyses a team wants to run. For EA Debt this matters on three levels: (1) Detection—plug-ins such as technology-obsolescence or redundancy-finder act as debt sniffers the moment the required metadata exist; (2) Quantification—the plug-ins return counts of affected elements (principal) plus impact-propagation graphs that approximate interest; and (3) Prioritization, architects can chain several plug-ins to compute composite risk scores, ensuring that remediation budgets attack the highest-yield debts first. The architecture, therefore, shifts EA Debt management from ad-hoc, spreadsheet-based exercises to a repeatable, continuously extensible pipeline.

2.2 A Theory for Enterprise Architecture Debt

In his work on work systems theory, Alter [3] refers to other IS theories, such as general systems theory, socio-technical theory, actor network theory, organizational routines, soft systems methodology, and activity theory. Alter also argues that one can view UML as a theory. In the context of IS, other theories, not considered by Alter, have been studied, including grounded theory, institutional theory, affordance theory, contingency theory, and chaos theory. To identify the theory most suitable for the representation of EA Debts, the presented theories have been analyzed based on their characteristics, such as the consideration of architectural elements, support for debt management, and consideration of decision making, including the long-term consequences.

Least Applicable Theories. As presented by McBride [28], *chaos theory* can be used to observe change and understand organizational behavior. It is applicable for complex systems with high unpredictability, which might make it interesting for EA consideration. However, it may struggle with the more measurable and manageable aspects of EA Debts. EA Debts can be systematic, traceable, and result from technical or enterprise decisions, but chaos theory might fail to capture such debts.

An increase of interest can be observed in using *affordance theory* for IS [29]. It focuses on the improvement of the perceived affordances of systems, making it a good choice for user involvement and UX consideration. However, it does not represent the strategy, technical dependencies, and system complexity related to EA Debts.

Another theory is the *contingency theory*, Reinking [30] presents the primary constructs of the theory applied in the context of IS. Contingency Theory may support decision-making by considering the context of the enterprise, but it does not have a formal way of representing EA artifacts, such as systems, components, and their dependencies. It is unsuitable to represent the architectural decision and its impact on the EA Debt.

Tatnall [31] advocates for the usage of *actor network theory*, especially in the context of the implementation of IS. Like Tatnall [32], Iyamu and Sekgweleo [33] focus on the applicability of actor network theory in the context of the social aspects of IS. Despite its usability for IS, it lacks the clear structures much needed in the EA Debt consideration. It typically does not consider the hierarchical structure, making it difficult to model the debt across various EA layers. Especially when considering the debt consequences and their propagation.

Vial and Rivard [34] argue that using *organizational routines* may improve the shared understanding of the stakeholders involved in IS Development. Organizational Routines focus on the representation of stakeholders and processes, which are recurring in nature. Organizational Routines do not model the decisions made, failing to consider debt propagation or long-term consequences. EA Debt not only focuses on the processes but also includes the consideration of technical, financial, and organizational aspects.

Moderately Applicable Theories. Currie [35] advocates using *institutional theory* in the context of change management in IS. It can represent the organizational context, including the consideration of how the organization shapes the decisions, allowing for the analysis of the dependency of the accumulated debts and the reasons behind them. But it does not model the technical facets of EA Debts, such as component dependencies or architecture, well. Those, however, are relevant for understanding and managing EA Debts.

Winter et al. [36] present the application of *soft systems methodology* for understanding the organization behind the IS, thanks to its explicit, well-established ways of modeling organizational activity. It might emphasize the stakeholder perspective on EA and underline conflicting stakeholder views. However, it might prove inefficient when considering more components, data flow, or technical dependencies of EA Debts. EA Debts need the representation of the impact that short-term decisions have on the long-term existence of the enterprise.

Mursu et al. use the *activity theory* to propose a model to help bridge the gap between the present and goal states. Activity theory focuses on activity and context, which might help identify some of the root causes, but may prove to be ineffective with the representation of the technical aspects, like architecture or infrastructure. This may hinder the monitoring of the technical decisions long-term influence.

Grounded theory has been widely used in the context of IS. Matavire and Brown [37] analyze its use and application, focusing on four approaches used in the IS context. Wiesche et al. [38] also studied how grounded theory is applied in the context of IS. Verdecchia et al. [39] applied grounded theory to architectural technical debts (ATD) to present the factors most relevant to stakeholders working with ATD. It can help represent the consequences and patterns of the EA Debts, but may be difficult to apply directly to EA artifacts due to its lack of representation of the architecture or risk related to technical decisions. Its strength lies in interpretation, rather than representation.

UML as a theory is well suited for the representation of the AS-IS state of the system, allowing for the documentation of the EA structures. Yet, it might be difficult to use to represent the consequences or the changes in EA

Debt over time, such as growing interest, decreasing system quality, or rationale for accepting certain debts. EA Debt is dynamic in its nature, which is not represented by the static UML.

Most Applicable Theories. Both Alter and Gregor [2] argue that *general systems theory* allows considering systems of interest on a high enough abstraction level to be applied to various systems. It considers input, throughput, output, feedback, boundary, and environment, but may fail to represent services, data flows, or architecture layers' interaction. Although quite general and applicable in many scenarios, it may have difficulties modeling EA artifacts or debts. Especially considering the management of EA Debts, it may fail to capture the technical granularity or to analyze the propagation of the debt through various architecture layers.

Luna-Reyes et al. [40] use *socio-technical theory* to represent the dualism in IS, focusing on social and technical challenges. Palvia et al. [41] propose a framework based on socio-technical theory to evaluate the quality of the newly implemented information system (IS). Rinta et al. [42] used socio-technical analysis to propose a two-level system-dynamics model to help predict the challenges of modernizing legacy systems with high technical debt and suggest suitable strategies. Socio-technical theory focuses on the interaction between stakeholders and systems, possibly helping to analyze how stakeholder involvement influences the debt. However, it may have problems considering the architecture and application layer due to the lack of a formal structure to represent software components, interfaces, and the various dependencies between them. Here, debt propagation is also difficult to model.

Work Systems Theory is well suited for EA Debts consideration as it provides a well-balanced model, focusing on the representation of processes, people, technologies, information structures, and their interaction. Its biggest flaw is that it might oversimplify the EA landscape by the use of the work system metaphor, oversimplifying the logic or glossing over the dependencies, which might lead to incomplete information.

Summary. From the theories, Work Systems Theory, General Systems Theory, and Socio-Technical Theory seem to show the most promising fit. WST is characterized as a structured and flexible framework, providing concepts relevant to EA Debt. While it would benefit from certain adaptation, it seems to require the least among the candidates. The other theories tend to focus on singular aspects of EA Debts, failing to capture EA Debt in its entire complexity. This analysis reveals that while several theories contribute valuable perspectives, only WST offers a sufficiently comprehensive and adaptable framework for capturing the multifaceted nature of EA Debts.

2.3 Work System Theory

Work System Theory was proposed by Steven Alter as a means to bridge the gap between business and IT stakeholders working on IS by proposing a method to describe the systems without the often complex IT concepts. Defined based on Gregor's [2] categories of theories, it is defined as *an integrated body of theory that includes a Type 1 analytical theory (the work system framework) and a Type 2 explanatory theory (the work system life cycle model), which in combination give the basis of a Type 5 design theory (WSM)* (Fig. 1).

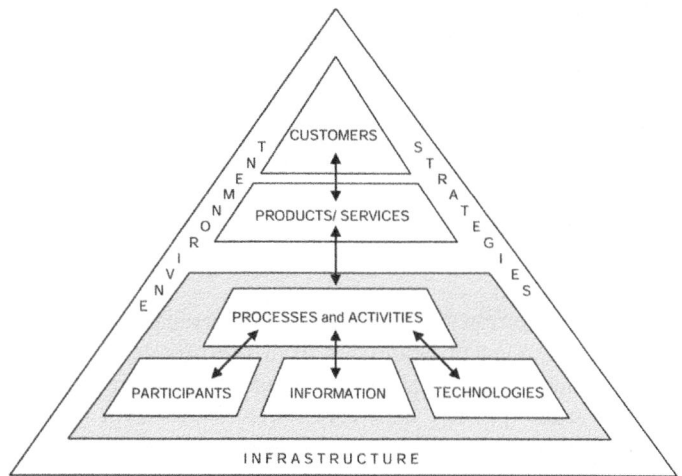

Fig. 1. The work system theory framework as proposed by Alter [3].

In 2013, Alter [3] presented an overview of the core concepts, extensions, and challenges related to WST. The core idea of the WST is to consider the systems in organizations using Work Systems as a base unit. A Work System is a socio-technological system where humans and machines perform work to provide specific products/services to their customers. To accomplish that, they use information, technology, and other resources.

Nine elements comprise a system [3]: Four of the elements are viewed as inside the work system, defining the system's core functionality: (1) **Processes and activities** are meant to produce products/services for the customers. The processes and activities of a work system define how work is performed (the as-is), not the ideal to-be state of the work system. (2) **Participants** perform the work within the work systems. They are not limited to IT users but also focus on participants who do not use IT systems directly. (3) **Information** entities in the context of work systems are *used, created, captured, transmitted, stored, retrieved, manipulated, updated, displayed, and/or deleted by processes and activities*. There is no distinction between data and information. (4) **Technologies** include both tools used by the participants and automated agents, allowing work systems to be decomposed into fully automated sub-systems.

Two elements are viewed as partially inside the work system, defining entities that interact with the core components of the work system: (1) **Products/Services** consist of information, physical things, and/or actions created for the customers. They should provide benefits to customers using them. (2) **Customers** receive the products/services and use them for purpose different than work activities inside the work system itself.

Three of the elements are viewed as outside the work system, despite directly influencing the work system: (1) **Environment** describes the *organizational, cultural, competitive, technical, regulatory, and demographic* context in which the work system operates. Factors of the environment might directly or indirectly affect the work system. (2) **Infrastructure** includes *relevant human, information, and technical resources* used by the work system or multiple work systems, which are managed outside of it. (3) **Strategies** *include enterprise strategy, department strategy, and work system strategy.*

3   Mapping Enterprise Architecture Debt to Work System Theory

EA debt is the accumulation of compromises, deferred decisions, or shortcuts in managing EA. This concept originates from the broader notion of technical debt as "the deviation of the currently present state of an enterprise from a hypothetical ideal state" [1]. EA debt arises when short-term fixes or decisions to address immediate challenges lead to structural weaknesses or architectural misalignments, creating long-term costs and reducing organizational agility.

EA debt is a multidimensional concept that impacts key aspects of an organization's systems, processes, technologies, and information flows. Its effects can be observed across various levels, from operational inefficiencies to strategic misalignment [4,5]. In the following, we illustrate the connection between EAD concepts and WST:

Participants and Customers: EA debt often originates from decisions prioritizing short-term productivity or immediate usability for specific teams [4]. Over time, these decisions can create gaps in skills, collaboration, and communication. For example, reliance on a small group of experts to maintain legacy systems may lead to knowledge silos, reducing the organization's flexibility and resilience.

Processes and Activities: Compromises in the design or implementation of processes can lead to inefficiencies or rigid workflows that fail to adapt to changing needs. For instance, quick fixes to streamline one part of a process may cause bottlenecks elsewhere, embedding inefficiencies into the system [43]. These process-related debts can make it harder for organizations to scale or innovate.

Technologies and Products: Using outdated, fragmented, or incompatible technologies is a major source of EA debt. Quick decisions to implement short-term solutions can lead to systems that are difficult to integrate, maintain, or scale. Over time, the cost of maintaining these technologies grows, and their limitations restrict the organization's ability to adopt innovations [44].

Information: Poorly designed IS or inconsistent data standards can contribute significantly to EA debt. Issues such as duplicate or incomplete data repositories, lack of integration between systems, or misaligned data structures [4,5] can reduce the quality and reliability of information. These issues often lead to errors, inefficiencies, and lost opportunities for leveraging data-driven decision-making.

Evolution: EA debt is not static; it evolves as the organization and its architecture respond to internal and external pressures. New business demands, emerging technologies, and shifting market conditions often require organizations to adjust their architecture rapidly [45]. While these adjustments may address immediate needs, they frequently create new forms of debt that must be managed in the future [6]. Understanding how EA debt accumulates, changes, and impacts the organization over time is essential for developing effective management strategies.

Alignment: EA primarily aims to align IT systems, processes, and capabilities with the organization's strategic objectives [46]. However, EA debt often undermines this alignment, reducing the architecture's ability to support the business effectively. Misaligned priorities among stakeholders [7], such as balancing cost savings, speed to market, and long-term architectural integrity, can create trade-offs that result in architectural compromises. Addressing EA debt requires careful consideration of these trade-offs to ensure the architecture continues to deliver value to the organization.

Interdependencies: EA is inherently interconnected [47], with changes in one area often affecting others. For example, implementing new technology may disrupt established workflows, while shifts in business strategy may render specific architectural components obsolete. The systemic nature of EA debt means that small decisions or compromises can have far-reaching consequences. A comprehensive understanding of these interdependencies is crucial for identifying the root causes of EA debt and mitigating its effects.

4   Work System Theory to Categorize Enterprise Architecture Debt

We illustrate the application of WST to categorize EA debts by two examples (cf. Fig. 2) from the original publication [1]: The first example centers on an automotive supplier specializing in high-end engine manufacturing. Over time, the company has undergone several mergers, resulting in a highly complex organizational structure. This complexity is mirrored in the company's internal processes, which have become inefficient and difficult to optimize. Although management is aware of these inefficiencies, its ability to improve the processes is constrained by collective bargaining agreements that protect employee positions for a set duration. This legal obligation restricts the organization's flexibility to reassign roles, consolidate responsibilities, or automate certain functions—measures that would otherwise improve efficiency and responsiveness.

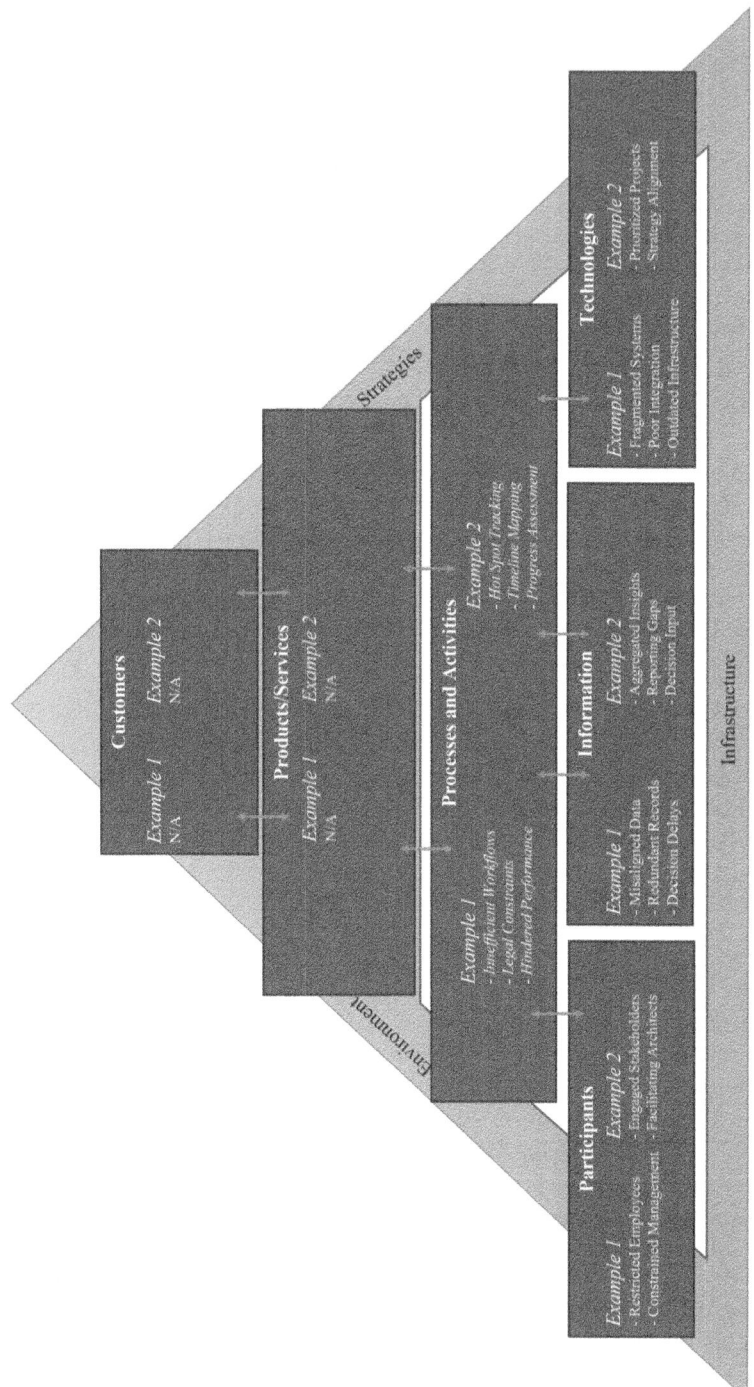

Fig. 2. Exemplary Illustration of Two EA Debts in the WST Framework.

This situation constitutes a clear instance of EAD. It results from a trade-off between economic efficiency (the desire to streamline operations) and legal obligations (employment protections). Because the organization consciously operates under suboptimal conditions that diverge from an ideal or intended architecture, these trade-offs accumulate as EAD. Explicitly categorizing this situation as EAD allows the organization to track and manage the resulting misalignments more deliberately, rather than treating them as static, unavoidable constraints.

Using the WST lens, this case reveals debt across multiple components:

- *Processes and Activities*: The core operational workflows are fragmented and suboptimal due to legacy practices inherited from merging organizations. These inefficiencies represent process-related EAD, where operational behavior deviates from the ideal streamlined state.
- *Participants*: Employees are locked into legacy roles and structures due to contractual agreements. This inhibits the evolution of participant roles to better align with current business needs or technological capabilities, contributing to participant-related debt.
- *Technologies*: Each merged entity likely introduced its own IT systems and tools. These may not be fully integrated, leading to technological fragmentation. The result is increased maintenance costs and limited scalability—hallmarks of technology-related EAD.
- *Information*: Misaligned or redundant data repositories across legacy systems degrade the quality and availability of information. This information-related debt impacts decision-making and slows response times.
- *Environment*: The most prominent external factor is the legal environment, namely, labor agreements, that shape and constrain the organization's architectural flexibility. These environmental constraints are outside the immediate control of the work system but heavily influence it.
- *Infrastructure*: Supporting systems and resources, such as shared IT platforms or HR systems, may still be segmented according to the pre-merger structure, impeding efforts toward consolidation and standardization.
- *Strategy*: The organization's strategic objectives may prioritize efficiency and agility, yet the current EA is misaligned with these goals due to legacy constraints and legal frameworks. This results in strategic misalignment debt.

This case exemplifies how multiple, interdependent forms of EA Debt can accumulate in a large, complex organization. By situating these issues within the WST framework, the organization can more effectively identify where debts reside, understand their causes and impacts, and develop a more structured approach to addressing them in future architectural planning.

The second example demonstrates how EAD can manifest as a misalignment between an organization's architecture and strategic target state. While the organization does not explicitly label this gap as "EA Debt", the underlying issue, an ongoing discrepancy between intended and current architectural realities, fits squarely within the EAD concept. Importantly, this case does not involve technical flaws or system degradation, but rather the challenges of steering enterprise-wide transformation toward strategic objectives, making the term technical debt inapplicable.

The organization has structured its EA into a set of focal areas called hot spots to operationalize its architectural strategy. Each hot spot corresponds to a key domain within the IT strategy, ranging from infrastructure and application modernization to data governance or process redesign. For each hot spot, enterprise architects define and map specific actions onto a timeline, creating a forward-looking roadmap of intended changes.

Progress is monitored through a structured, quarterly feedback mechanism. Architects conduct interviews with stakeholders who are accountable for each hot spot. These interviews yield qualitative insights and quantitative indicators, capturing how far each domain has progressed toward its target state. The collected data is then aggregated into reports that inform senior management, offering a high-level overview of architectural alignment and surfacing areas where goals are not being met.

This process represents a deliberate attempt to manage strategic alignment debt, a form of EA Debt characterized by persistent divergence between the designed trajectory of the EA and its practical implementation. When examined through the lens of Work System Theory, this case reveals EAD across several components:

- *Processes and Activities*: The architecture transformation is operationalized through recurring activities, such as roadmap planning, stakeholder engagement, and quarterly assessments. While these activities are structured, the presence of gaps and delays indicates that some processes are not performing as intended, creating process-related debt.
- *Participants*: Stakeholders from across the organization are central to the transformation effort. Their engagement in interviews and their roles in executing change initiatives reflect their importance and influence. Inconsistent ownership or uneven commitment across hot spots could result in participant-related EAD if human factors undermine progress.
- *Information*: Aggregating qualitative and quantitative feedback into executive reports is crucial for tracking architectural alignment. Any inaccuracies, inconsistencies, or delays in collecting or interpreting this information contribute to information-related debt.
- *Technologies*: The actions taken within each hot spot likely involve updates or replacements of legacy systems, data platforms, or infrastructure. Misalignment between architectural goals and technological implementation's actual pace or scope may result in technology-related debt.
- *Environment*: This initiative operates in a dynamic context of business demands, strategic shifts, and possibly regulatory or market pressures. External factors such as shifting priorities or budget constraints may contribute to deviations from the planned architectural path.
- *Infrastructure*: Shared resources, such as enterprise-wide data repositories, integration platforms, or workflow tools, may be impacted by or impact the architectural changes in each hot spot. Delays in upgrading infrastructure can ripple through the transformation process.

– *Strategy*: This case is fundamentally about alignment with strategic objectives. When planned architectural initiatives fall out of sync with execution, strategy-related EAD emerges. The entire initiative aims to identify, make visible, and reduce this type of debt.

Through the structured use of interviews, timelines, and progress reporting, the organization attempts to bridge the gap between "as-is" and "to-be" states, thereby mitigating alignment debt. However, this process also highlights how EAD can evolve as misalignments persist, priorities shift, or execution lags behind intention. Framing this challenge as EA Debt within the WST framework empowers the organization to manage it not as a vague strategic drift but as a specific, observable, and actionable deviation from architectural intent.

5 Future Directions

Existing research on identifying EA debt covers several elements that align with the categories of WST, offering a holistic perspective on how organizations can understand and manage their architectural shortcomings. This research can be differentiated into works identifying potential symptoms of EA debt, so-called EA Smells [19,43,48], and works trying to find efficient ways for the identification of EA debt that produce potential EA debts as a byproduct [4,5].

The *people* element is addressed through the roles and perspectives of EA stakeholders. Research [4] highlights the importance of involving stakeholders in identifying and prioritizing EA debt through workshops and interviews. This collaboration is essential for bridging the gap between technical and business perspectives, ensuring that EA debt is addressed with a shared understanding.

Processes are another focus [43]. This research examines inefficiencies and anti-patterns, such as redundant workflows and poorly integrated systems, which hinder operational performance and innovation. Methods and tools have been developed to identify these process-related issues. These efforts aim to enhance enterprise processes' overall quality and reduce the long-term impact of inefficiencies.

The *technologies* aspect of EA debt has received significant attention, particularly in terms of legacy systems and poorly integrated IT infrastructure. Studies [19,48] have adapted concepts like software architecture smells to the EA domain, identifying technical flaws that contribute to debt. Tools for detecting these "EA smells" in models have been proposed, providing a systematic way to assess and quantify the quality of an enterprise's technological architecture.

Information quality and flow within EA are recognized as important contributors to debt. Issues such as incomplete documentation, outdated data, and misaligned information repositories often exacerbate architectural challenges. Research [5] highlights the need for aggregated reporting mechanisms to track progress in aligning the actual EA state with the desired target state, emphasizing the role of reliable information in decision-making.

External constraints, such as legal, regulatory, and organizational factors, form another dimension of EA debt. Studies [4] have shown how factors like bargaining agreements or compliance requirements can limit an organization's flexibility to make necessary architectural changes. These constraints underscore the need for careful planning to navigate the trade-offs between operational needs and external obligations.

At the heart of EA debt research is the alignment of purpose, which reflects the deviation between an organization's current EA state and its ideal or target state. This misalignment is seen as the core definition of EA debt [1]. Frameworks and metrics are being developed to measure and address this misalignment, with catalogs of EA debts and smells providing tools to help organizations manage these gaps and ensure that their architecture remains aligned with strategic objectives.

While significant progress has been made in understanding EA debt, several gaps remain in its exploration through the lens of WST. For the people dimension, research often highlights stakeholder involvement in workshops and interviews. Yet, little attention is given to how differing roles, organizational cultures, and stakeholder incentives influence the prioritization and resolution of EA debt. Similarly, while anti-patterns and inefficiencies have been identified in the processes category, there is a lack of focus on the dynamic evolution of processes and their relationship with architectural changes over time.

Other dimensions of WST are similarly underexplored. In the information domain, gaps exist in understanding how robust data governance and integration practices can help manage information-related EA debt. For external constraints, while regulatory and legal obligations are recognized as contributors to EA debt, there is insufficient research on frameworks for balancing these constraints with architectural flexibility. Finally, in the alignment of purpose, the lack of standardized metrics to define and evaluate the "ideal state" of an EA poses a challenge, as does understanding how shifts in organizational strategy influence this alignment. Future research should address these gaps by developing adaptive frameworks, leveraging emerging technologies, and exploring stakeholder engagement strategies. Doing so will enable organizations to manage EA debt more effectively while aligning with dynamic business needs and external pressures.

6   Conclusion

Within this work, we explored the concept of EA debt through the lens of WST. While EA debt has traditionally been understood as an extension of technical debt, its broader implications across processes, technologies, information, and stakeholder engagement necessitate a more structured theoretical foundation. By categorizing EA debt within the WST framework, this study provides a structured approach to identifying, assessing, and addressing these inefficiencies, ensuring that organizations can make informed decisions about their EA.

Our findings highlight that EA debt manifests across multiple dimensions, including process inefficiencies, technological fragmentation, misaligned information flows, and stakeholder constraints. The case examples demonstrated how trade-offs between economic efficiency and legal obligations and misalignment between an organization's actual and target architecture contribute to the accumulation of debt. We also identified gaps in existing research, particularly regarding the role of stakeholder incentives, real-time data governance, and adaptive frameworks for managing EA debt in dynamic environments.

Key takeaways from this research include the importance of systematically identifying EA debt to improve architectural decision-making, the need for tools and methodologies to monitor and mitigate its effects, and the necessity of integrating stakeholder perspectives to align EA with strategic goals. Future research should focus on developing adaptive frameworks, leveraging emerging technologies, and refining methodologies for effectively quantifying and managing EA debt. Organizations can adopt a more structured and proactive approach to ensuring sustainable and agile enterprise architecture by advancing our understanding of EA debt through WST.

Disclosure of Interests. The authors have no competing interests to declare that are relevant to the content of this article.

References

1. Hacks, S., Höfert, H., Salentin, J., Yeong, Y.C., Lichter, H.: Towards the definition of enterprise architecture debts. In: 23rd EDOCW, pp. 9–16 (2019)
2. Gregor, S.: The nature of theory in information systems. MIS Q. **30**(3), 611–642 (2006)
3. Alter, S.: Work system theory: overview of core concepts, extensions, and challenges for the future. JAIS **14**, 72–121 (2013)
4. Jung, J., Hacks, S., de Gooijer, T., Kinnunen, M., Rehring, K.: Revealing common enterprise architecture debts: conceptualization and critical reflection on a workshop format industry experience report. In: 25th EDOCW, pp. 271–278 (2021)
5. Daoudi, S., Larsson, M., Hacks, S., Jung, J.: Discovering and assessing enterprise architecture debts. CSIMQ **35**, 1–29 (2023)
6. Alexander, P., Hacks, S., Jung, J., Steffens, U., Uludag, Ö., Lichter, H.: A framework for managing enterprise architecture debts - outline and research directions. In: 10th EMISA, vol. 2628, pp. 5–10. CEUR-WS.org (2020)
7. Hacks, S., Brosius, M., Aier, S.: A case study of stakeholder concerns on EAM. In: 21st EDOCW, pp. 50–56 (2017)
8. Uludağ, Ö., Kleehaus, M., Xu, X., Matthes, F.: Investigating the role of architects in scaling agile frameworks. In: 2017 IEEE 21st International Enterprise Distributed Object Computing Conference (EDOC), pp. 123–132. IEEE (2017)
9. Uludag, Ö., Reiter, N., Matthes, F.: What to expect from enterprise architects in large-scale agile development? A multiple-case study. In: 25th AMCIS (2019)
10. Gampfer, F., Jürgens, A., Müller, M., Buchkremer, R.: Past, current and future trends in enterprise architecture–a view beyond the horizon. Comput. Ind. **100**, 70–84 (2018)
11. Cunningham, W.: The WyCash portfolio management system. ACM SIGPLAN OOPS Messenger **4**(2), 29–30 (1993)
12. Li, Z., Avgeriou, P., Liang, P.: A systematic mapping study on technical debt and its management. J. Syst. Softw. **101**, 193–220 (2015)

13. Kruchten, P., Nord, R.L., Ozkaya, I.: Technical debt: from metaphor to theory and practice. IEEE Softw. **29**(6), 18–21 (2012)
14. Seaman, C., Guo, Y.: Measuring and monitoring technical debt. Adv. Comput. **82**, 25–46 (2011)
15. Addicks, J.S., Appelrath, H.J.: A method for application evaluations in context of enterprise architecture. In: Proceedings of the 2010 ACM Symposium on Applied Computing, SAC 2010, pp. 131–136. ACM, New York (2010)
16. Curtis, B., Sappidi, J., Szynkarski, A.: Estimating the principal of an application's technical debt. IEEE Softw. **29**(6), 34–42 (2012)
17. Nord, R.L., Ozkaya, I., Kruchten, P., Gonzalez-Rojas, M.: In search of a metric for managing architectural technical debt. In: 2012 Joint Working IEEE/IFIP Conference on Software Architecture and European Conference on Software Architecture, pp. 91–100 (2012)
18. Slupczynski, A., Hacks, S.: Towards a knowledge base of terms on enterprise architecture debt. In: Sales, T.P., de Kinderen, S., Proper, H.A., Pufahl, L., Karastoyanova, D., van Sinderen, M. (eds.) EDOC 2023. LNBIP, vol. 498, pp. 194–210. Springer, Cham (2023). https://doi.org/10.1007/978-3-031-54712-6_12
19. Salentin, J., Hacks, S.: Towards a catalog of enterprise architecture smells. In: 15. Internationalen Tagung Wirtschaftsinformatik, pp. 276–290. GITO Verlag (2020)
20. Smajevic, M., Hacks, S., Bork, D.: Using knowledge graphs to detect enterprise architecture smells. In: Serral, E., Stirna, J., Ralyté, J., Grabis, J. (eds.) PoEM 2021. LNBIP, vol. 432, pp. 48–63. Springer, Cham (2021). https://doi.org/10.1007/978-3-030-91279-6_4
21. Yeong, Y.C., Hacks, S., Lichter, H.: Prioritization of EA debts facilitating portfolio theory. In: Lichter, H., Fögen, K., Sunetnanta, T., Anwar, T. (eds.) 7th QUASOQ. CEUR Workshop Proceedings, vol. 2511, pp. 45–52. CEUR-WS.org (2019)
22. Liss, L., Kämmerling, H., Alexander, P., Lichter, H.: Towards a catalog of refactoring solutions for enterprise architecture smells. In: Gan, B., et al. (eds.) Joint Proceedings of SEED 2021 & QuASoQ 2021 co-located with 28th Asia Pacific Software Engineering Conference 2021, Taipei [Virtual], 6 December 2021. CEUR Workshop Proceedings, vol. 3062, pp. 60–69. CEUR-WS.org (2021)
23. Slupczynski., A., Alexander., P., Lichter., H.: A process for evaluating the prudence of enterprise architecture debts. In: 25th ICEIS, pp. 623–630. SciTePress (2023)
24. Hacks, S., Jung, J.: A first validation of the enterprise architecture debts concept. In: van der Aa, H., Bork, D., Proper, H.A., Schmidt, R. (eds.) BPMDS EMMSAD 2023. LNBIP, vol. 479. Springer, Cham (2023). https://doi.org/10.1007/978-3-031-34241-7_15
25. Chis, A., Ghiran, A.M., Alter, S.: Informing enterprise knowledge graphs with a work system perspective. Enterp. Modell. Inf. Syst. Archit. (EMISAJ) **19** (2024)
26. Florez, H., Sánchez, M., Villalobos, J.: A catalog of automated analysis methods for enterprise models. Springerplus **5**(1), 1–24 (2016). https://doi.org/10.1186/s40064-016-2032-9
27. Florez, H., Sánchez, M., Villalobos, J.: Extensible model-based approach for supporting automatic enterprise analysis. In: 2014 IEEE 18th International Enterprise Distributed Object Computing Conference, pp. 32–41 (2014)
28. McBride, N.: Chaos theory as a model for interpreting information systems in organizations. Inf. Syst. J. **15**(3), 233–254 (2005)
29. Volkoff, O., Strong, D.M.: Affordance theory and how to use it in is research. In: The Routledge Companion to MIS, pp. 232–245. Routledge (2017)
30. Reinking, J.: Contingency theory in information systems research. Inf. Syst. Theory 247–263 (2012)

31. Tatnall, A.: Actor-network theory in information systems research. In: Encyclopedia of Information Science and Technology, pp. 42–46. IGI Global (2005)
32. Tatnall, A.: Actor-network theory as a socio-technical approach to information systems research. In: Socio-Technical and Human Cognition Elements of Information Systems, pp. 266–283. IGI Global (2003)
33. Iyamu, T., Sekgweleo, T.: Information systems and actor-network theory analysis. IJANTT **5**(3), 1–11 (2013)
34. Vial, G., Rivard, S.: Conceptualizing information systems development as an organizational routine: implications and avenues for research. SIGMIS Database **53**(3), 91–107 (2022)
35. Currie, W.: Contextualising the it artefact: towards a wider research agenda for is using institutional theory. Inf. Technol. People **22**(1), 63–77 (2009)
36. Winter, M., Brown, D., Checkland, P.: A role for soft systems methodology in information systems development. EJIS **4**(3), 130–142 (1995)
37. Matavire, R., Brown, I.: Investigating the use of "grounded theory" in information systems research. In: SAICSIT 2008, pp. 139–147. ACM, New York (2008)
38. Wiesche, M., Jurisch, M.C., Yetton, P.W., Krcmar, H.: Grounded theory methodology in information systems research. MIS Q. **41**(3), 685-A9 (2017)
39. Verdecchia, R., Kruchten, P., Lago, P.: Architectural technical debt: a grounded theory. In: Jansen, A., Malavolta, I., Muccini, H., Ozkaya, I., Zimmermann, O. (eds.) ECSA 2020. LNCS, vol. 12292, pp. 202–219. Springer, Cham (2020). https://doi.org/10.1007/978-3-030-58923-3_14
40. Luna-Reyes, L.F., Zhang, J., Ramón Gil-García, J., Cresswell, A.M.: Information systems development as emergent socio-technical change: a practice approach. Eur. J. Inf. Syst. **14**(1), 93–105 (2005)
41. Palvia, S.C., Sharma, R.S., Conrath, D.W.: A socio-technical framework for quality assessment of computer information systems. IMDS **101**(5), 237–251 (2001)
42. Rinta-Kahila, T., Penttinen, E., Lyytinen, K.: Getting trapped in technical debt: sociotechnical analysis of a legacy system's replacement. MIS Q. **47**(1) (2023)
43. Lehmann, B., Alexander, P., Lichter, H., Hacks, S.: Towards the identification of process anti-patterns in enterprise architecture models. In: 8th QUASOQ. CEUR Workshop Proceedings, vol. 2767, pp. 47–54. CEUR-WS.org (2020)
44. Ampatzoglou, A., Ampatzoglou, A., Chatzigeorgiou, A., Avgeriou, P.: The financial aspect of managing technical debt: a systematic literature review. Inf. Softw. Technol. **64**, 52–73 (2015)
45. Day, G.S., Schoemaker, P.J.: Adapting to fast-changing markets and technologies. Calif. Manage. Rev. **58**(4), 59–77 (2016)
46. Boh, W.F., Yellin, D.: Using enterprise architecture standards in managing information technology. J. Manag. Inf. Syst. **23**(3), 163–207 (2006)
47. Winter, R., Fischer, R.: Essential layers, artifacts, and dependencies of enterprise architecture. In: 2006 10th IEEE International Enterprise Distributed Object Computing Conference Workshops (EDOCW 2006), p. 30 (2006)
48. Tieu, B., Hacks, S.: Determining enterprise architecture smells from software architecture smells. In: 23rd CBI, vol. 02, pp. 134–142 (2021)

LLM Support for Domain Experts in Enterprise Modeling: Experiences and Implications

Eric Müller[1]([⊠])(ID), Benjamin Nast[1](ID), and Kurt Sandkuhl[1,2](ID)

[1] University of Rostock, Rostock, Germany
{e.mueller,benjamin.nast,kurt.sandkuhl}@uni-rostock.de
[2] Jönköping University, Jönköping, Sweden

Abstract. Large language models (LLMs) have been found to be a support for modeling tasks in various application areas, including enterprise modeling (EM). In EM, LLMs can be applied to help domain experts create models efficiently that adhere to the correct syntax of the modeling language. In this context, how to organize the interplay of the domain expert and LLM is an important topic. Should the domain expert get an LLM-generated model and improve it (LLM-first) or should LLMs be used to improve models developed by domain experts (domain expert-first)? The paper investigates the interplay between domain expert and LLM by investigating three different application examples and conducting quasi-experiments. The results also contribute to determining the potential and limits of LLMs in EM.

Keywords: Enterprise Modeling · Modeling Method · Large Language Model · ChatGPT · Generative AI

1 Introduction

Generative artificial intelligence (GenAI) and, in particular, large language models (LLMs) have been found to be a valuable support for modeling tasks in various application areas. LLMs, such as OpenAI's ChatGPT, are attributed the capability to perform cognitive functions in a way that resembles a human-like manner and the ability to learn and self-correct [1]. Experience reports on the use of Co-Pilot in software engineering [2], ChatGPT in information system design for UML modeling [3], or the use of LLM in design and manufacturing [4] confirm this technology's potential for supporting modeling tasks. LLMs have also been used with promising results for tasks in enterprise modeling (EM) (see Sect. 3.3), which forms the motivation for this paper.

One of the perspectives of LLM use in EM that attracted research work is how to support domain experts. These are involved in modeling projects as representatives of enterprises who provide knowledge about the current situation in an enterprise, but they often do not have solid modeling knowledge. LLMs are

© The Author(s), under exclusive license to Springer Nature Switzerland AG 2026
R. Deneckère et al. (Eds.): BIR 2025, LNBIP 562, pp. 124–141, 2026.
https://doi.org/10.1007/978-3-032-04375-7_8

supposed to help them create models efficiently that adhere to the correct syntax of the modeling language. In this context, how to organize the interplay of the domain expert and LLM is an important topic. To start with, an LLM-generated model that the expert can check and improve would probably save more time than starting with the domain expert developing a model that the LLM checks for correct use of the modeling language. But does a generated model affect the perception of the domain expert on what is essential for the enterprise? Is domain expert-first preferable over LLM-first to achieve a higher model quality? And is there a difference between modeling the current situation and designing the "to be" of an enterprise when it comes to the domain expert-LLM interplay?

The intention of this paper is to contribute to the above topics by considering three different application examples and conducting quasi-experiments to address the following research questions (RQs):

– RQ1: What are the potentials and limitations of using LLMs in EM?
– RQ2: Which tasks can be best supported in which phases?
– RQ3: Does the order in which information is obtained (LLM-first or domain expert-first) have an influence on the quality of the results?

The paper is structured as follows: Sect. 2 briefly introduces the research method applied. Section 3 contains a summary of relevant background and related work. Section 4 contains the experiments of LLM use for EM in different application cases. Section 5 draws conclusions from the experiments and contains the findings regarding the RQs.

2   Research Method

Work presented in this paper is part of a research program aiming at developing methodical and technical support for domain experts in enterprise modeling. In this context, LLMs form an interesting option that we investigated in previous work with respect to the feasibility of using LLMs as a substitute for domain experts [5], the necessity to make changes in modeling methods [6], and the potential of generating multi-perspective models [7]. This paper explores the use of LLM for assisting domain experts and focuses on the three RQs defined in the introduction. The research method used to answer the RQs is a combination of literature review and quasi-experiments.

The literature search aimed at identifying related work and results from other scholars to be taken into account when investigating the potential of LLM. For this purpose, we extended the systematic literature review performed in one of our previous works [7] by reviewing scientific publications published in the last 12 months. The results are summarized in Sect. 3.3.

From the results of the literature analysis, we identified tasks of domain experts in modeling projects with significant potential for LLM support. To further investigate these tasks, we designed quasi-experiments. A controlled experiment in software engineering and information systems development is "a randomised or quasi-experiment in which individuals or teams (the study units) conduct one or more [. . .] tasks for the sake of comparing different populations, processes, methods, techniques, languages or tools (the treatments)" [8]. In our work, we perform a quasi-experiment; the study units are ChatGPT and domain experts, and the treatments are different modeling tasks. A quasi-experiment is "an experiment in which units are not assigned to conditions randomly" [9]. The experiments do not aim at testing a specific hypothesis but are exploratory research to answer the RQs defined. The experiment design is described in detail in Sect. 4.

3   Background and Related Work

3.1   Enterprise Modeling

EM is addressing the "systematic analysis and modeling of processes, organization structures, product structures, IT-systems or any other perspective relevant for the modeling purpose" [10]. The primary function of EM is to offer methods, tools, and techniques for representing and analyzing both the current ("as-is") state of an organization and envisioning the desired ("to-be") future state. One widely recognized application of EM is its use as a problem-solving instrument (see [11] and [12]). In this context, EM also serves as support for domain experts when analyzing and resolving a particular issue. An overview of EM methods, languages, and tools is visible in publications from the information systems community (see, e.g., [13]) and from industrial organizations (e.g., [14]).

For the experiments discussed in Sect. 4, we selected 4EM [15], a multi-perspective EM language. The 4EM language consists of different submodels, each of which focuses on a specific aspect or perspective of the enterprise: Goals Model, Business Rules Model, Concepts Model, Process Model, Actors and Resources Model, Products and Services Model, as well as Technical Components and Requirements Model. 4EM distinguishes relationships with which the modeling components are related within the submodel and relationships with components of other submodels. The latter relationship type is called inter-model relationship. They are used to trace decisions, components, and other aspects throughout the enterprise model. E.g., the motivation for why a certain business process exists in an enterprise is established with an inter-model relationship to a motivating goal.

3.2   Large Language Models

The release of ChatGPT by OpenAI marked a significant moment in integrating artificial intelligence (AI) into mainstream applications and problem-solving tasks. The model behind ChatGPT operates with 175 billion parameters and utilizes datasets that include nearly a trillion words sourced from various corpora [16]. Its training involves predicting the next sequence of tokens based on given contexts, which enables it to generate realistic and novel word sequences. LLMs like GPT-4 are pre-trained in a task-agnostic manner [17], which allows for flexible customization through in-context learning during runtime via natural language prompts. This advancement facilitates experimentation and prototyping in AI without the need for initial model training. LLMs can perform tasks like summarization, translation, grammar correction, and more, providing accessible AI tools across various fields.

3.3 LLMs in Enterprise Modeling

In our research context, the use of LLM has to be tailored to the domain experts' needs. Stirna and Persson [18] characterize the role of domain experts as providing essential domain-specific knowledge and insights about organizational units. This includes reviewing and validating EM outcomes and ensuring the integration of results from various teams into a coherent model. Krogstie [19] identifies the key phases of EM as: defining the scope of the project ("scoping"), documenting the current state ("as-is"), analyzing the existing situation and modeling potential solutions ("change alternatives"), and finally, modeling the desired future state ("to-be"). During the scoping phase, domain experts contribute by offering contextual knowledge about the domain. In the "as-is" phase, their primary input involves detailed knowledge of the current enterprise. During the analysis and exploration of alternatives, their creative input helps in designing viable and acceptable change options. Finally, in the "to-be" modeling phase, domain experts play a critical role in ensuring that all perspectives are integrated into a consistent and unified model.

A literature analysis was conducted to identify relevant research publications addressing the above-mentioned tasks of domain experts. This analysis used Scopus, IEEE Xplore, and AISeL as literature databases, with the result of some related work but no publications directly addressing our RQs:

The work by Klievtsova et al. [20] focuses on process modeling and takes the perspective of conversational modeling. The paper offers practical recommendations for LLM application in process modeling that might be relevant for the business processes perspective of enterprise models. Fill et al. [21] present the results of a series of experiments that investigate the engineering of prompts for generating and interpreting ER, BPMN, UML, and Heraklit models. One of the results of the paper is that the potential of LLMs for supporting modeling tasks is substantial if a textual problem description of the domain to be modeled exists. In [22], a framework for the automated generation and iterative refinement of process models is proposed. The framework starts from textual descriptions and includes a prompting strategy, the generation of Partially Ordered Workflow Language (POWL) models, model refinement, and error correction. Vidgof et al. [23] investigate typical tasks of the business process management (BPM) lifecycle, and discuss LLM application opportunities and future research directions. The paper does not contain any experiments or in-depth studies. Buchmann et al. [24] collect and structure what is expected from LLMs as support for semantics-driven systems engineering, like the support of multiple perspectives in EM or the importance of semantics. However, the paper does not present solutions and takes a wider scope of systems engineering. In [25], the focus is on the use of LLMs in the context of the Legal Goal-oriented Requirements Language.

In our previous work, we investigated whether domain experts in EM projects could be partly substituted by LLMs [5] when preparing EM projects, modeling the "as-is" situation, or developing alternatives for change. We conducted experiments showing that ChatGPT produced good results, but it cannot substitute domain experts. In an additional study [26], we extended this experiment into larger modeling tasks that confirmed the results of the experiments. Furthermore, we proposed a meta-model for integrating enterprise models, reusable prompts, and domain terminology [6].

4   Experiments on LLM Support for Domain Experts

This section describes the three quasi-experiments. All prompts and models created are available in a repository [27]. Based on previous research in this area (see Sect. 3) and the requirements of our use cases, we decided to use ChatGPT (GPT-4o) as the LLM to be investigated. We chose 4EM, a method primarily used in university teaching with a stakeholder-oriented approach, as the modeling language to be able to consider different perspectives of the enterprises. This allows us to evaluate the understanding of the relations between the different parts of the enterprises. For each experiment, the Process Model, Products and Services Model, and Actors and Resources Model are considered, as these cover the essential information that is relevant for the use cases. The procedure for each experiment was as follows:

1. Preparation of the Modeling Session: Based on our experience from previous work [26, 28], we exploratively carried out the iterative development of a prompting technique (see Fig. 1) to obtain the most precise and meaningful results possible. Some established prompt patterns are applied in this technique [29]. Since GPT-4o is not familiar with the individual objects in the submodels

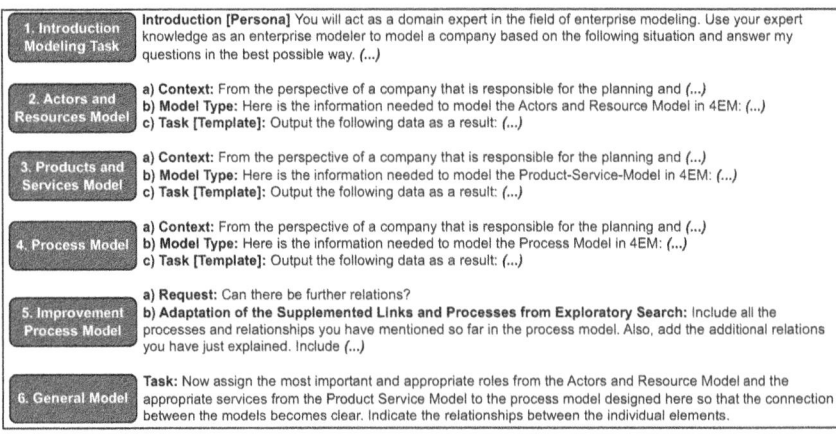

Fig. 1. Prompting technique

of the 4EM method, this information was also provided via the prompts. The prompting technique is therefore structured as follows: (1) introduction into the modeling task, (2) creation of the Actors and Resources Model, (3) Products and Services Model, (4) Process Model, (5) improvement of the Process Model and (6) General Model that combines the elements of the individual models.

The structure facilitates straightforward reuse and adaptation to the different domains. To adapt the context of the respective tasks, 2a), 3a), and 4a) are changed. The Request in 5a) was added after experiment 1 in order to obtain more possible connectors in the process model. This is discussed in more detail in Sect. 4.2. In 5b), information obtained through previous exploratory communication with the chatbot or from a domain expert can be supplemented.

2. Assessment of LLM Output Through Domain Expert: Domain expert 1 assesses the models created with ChatGPT with pre-defined criteria and discusses possible improvements or additions to the models:

- **Accuracy** indicates how correct the information provided is (e.g., correct, optional, out of scope, or wrong/hallucination). It is an important indicator of the reliability of the models.
- **Completeness** indicates the extent to which the answers given cover all the necessary information. If any missing information is found, it should be checked to see whether it is required or optional. A high degree of completeness ensures that all relevant aspects are included in the model.
- **Comprehensibility** assesses the ease with which the answers/results can be interpreted and understood by those who carry out the experiment or use the models. This is crucial to ensure that the models are clear and understandable for all participants.
- **Time** measures the duration to deliver the desired information. This is an important indicator for the efficiency of the model creation and can have an impact on the practicality of the approach.

3. Domain Expert Creates Model and Comparison with LLM Output: Domain expert 2 creates the four models to be examined without viewing the results of ChatGPT. It is then asked to compare its own models with those created with ChatGPT. The focus is on the following questions: *Would the expert add elements from ChatGPT to his own models? Is the additional information provided helpful, optional, out of scope, or false/hallucinations? How relevant are the missing elements in ChatGPT models?*

4. Quality Assessment with Both Domain Experts: Both domain experts are asked to make a qualitative evaluation of the models created in comparison (models completed by domain expert 1 vs. those created by domain expert 2). The main questions here are: *Do the models have the same content/meaning despite different terminology? Is there any information missing/to be added in both models? Are the results accurate enough or are elements out of scope?*

5. Create Model of to-be Situation: The potential improvements identified by domain expert 2 in terms of resource reduction (e.g., time savings, less material

wastage) and quality improvement are compared with the improvements identified by ChatGPT. ChatGPT is provided with an XML file of the General Model
created by a domain expert, so both the domain expert and ChatGPT have the
same model to derive improvements. To validate the chatbot's understanding
of the transmitted model, ChatGPT was first asked comprehension questions.
Finally, questions were asked about the optimization potential for the model.

4.1   Experiment 1: Event Planning

The first experiment conducted was in the event planning domain: *Planning,
implementation, and follow-up of a conference from the perspective of a hotel.*

Actors and Resources Model: Regarding the accuracy, domain expert 1 classified all elements included as relevant and correct. No elements are out of scope or
wrong. However, a few missing elements and relations were identified. The House
Technician was identified as a mandatory element in the role for Set-up and Dismantling. In some cases, the relations were not complete, e.g., IT not only supports
the Receptionist but also other areas or roles. The role of Assistance was identified as an optional element to be added to support the Event Manager (depending
on the hotel and size of the event). Figure 2 shows a model example created with
ChatGPT and improved by the expert, in which the added elements are marked
(*NEW*).

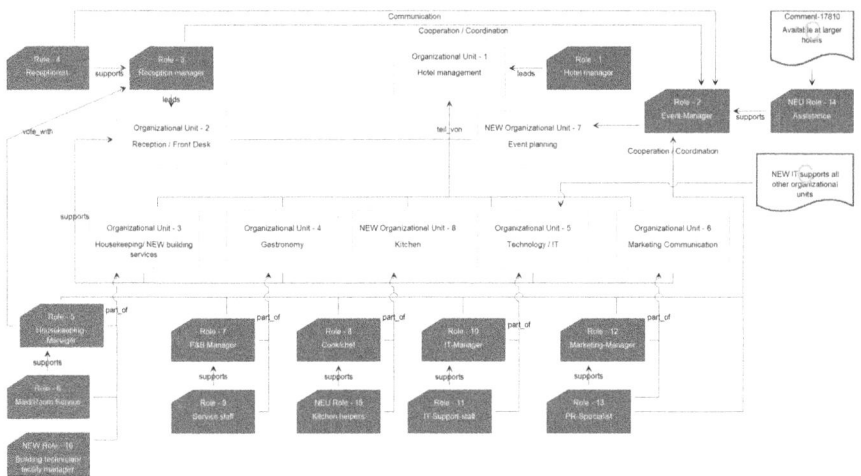

Fig. 2. Actors and Resources Model created with ChatGPT and improved by the expert

Products and Services Model: No elements were identified as being out of
scope or wrong. Budget Planning, Dismantling, and Route Planning (e.g.) were
identified as services that must be added (see Fig. 3).

Process Model: The relations between the processes are not sufficient as they usually run directly one after the other, which is unrealistic for event planning. In practice, most of the processes are interdependent and therefore run in parallel or also lead to previous processes, e.g., due to the lack of free capacity. However, the most important elements of the model were present. Only elements such as Agenda and Planning, which had already been identified as missing in the previous submodels, still needed to be added.

Comparison of Models: The comparison confirmed the main findings of domain expert 1. Domain expert 2 assessed some elements as out of scope (e.g., Hotel Director and IT Support Staff), and WLAN Access and Safety Concept as not necessary, as these are assumed anyway. It would also adjust the following elements: Process Request Receipt as a starting point, Logistical Participant Support as a sub-service of Kitchen, as well as invoicing as a sub-service. However, domain expert 2 also identified the relations as the main problem. This is mainly expressed in the Process Model, as many possible scenarios (e.g., cancellation from the hotel if there is no availability) are not shown at all.

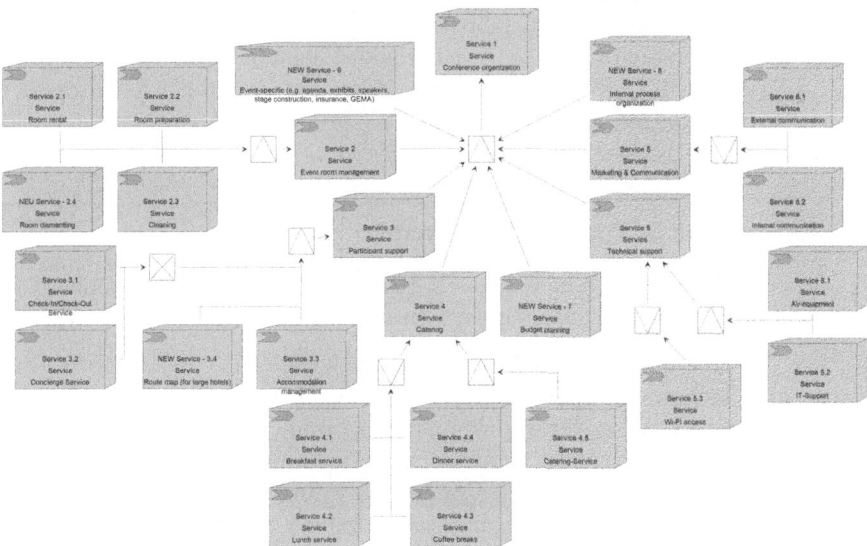

Fig. 3. Products and Services Model created with ChatGPT and improved by the expert

Quality Assessment: The basic meaning of the elements was found to be the same despite the different terminology. Also, the structure is quite similar. Nevertheless, a partially divergent view of all the elements to be modeled was identified (e.g., Marketing). For domain expert 2, the task for this does not lie with the hotel, unlike the opinion of domain expert 1. Another example is the optionally available topics, such as Agenda and Program Planning or Speakers. In principle, however, these considerations are not decisive, but can be attributed to the different approaches of the domain experts.

Overall, it was agreed that the models that were designed by the expert better represent the context to be modeled. This is largely due to the more extensive relations in the Process Model. The always correct relations in the other submodels, whereby all possible scenarios are mapped, also play a role. Nevertheless, according to the experts, most of the elements provided by ChatGPT can be used, even if they usually only represent the main elements. In particular, the experts rate the Actors and Resources Model created by ChatGPT as really good. It is easy to add your own elements or make individual changes, as the basic structure is already in place.

To-be Situation: Some optimization suggestions are almost identical, such as the use of an ERP system or information system. Nevertheless, the suggestions for some areas of application also differ. While the domain expert would like to automate the entire ordering system as much as possible, ChatGPT suggests setting up a demand-oriented forecast without specifically using digitization. The other optimization options show that both the chatbot and the expert would be able to identify more potential the more they question the processes. Nevertheless, the chatbot's understanding of the model provided must be positively emphasized here, especially for this sub-experiment. The suggestion of parallelizing processes, which is based on the identification of sequential processes, illustrates this considerably.

4.2   Experiment 2: Ventilation Systems

The second experiment conducted was in the ventilation systems domain: *Planning, implementation, and follow-up for retrofit ventilation systems from the enterprise's perspective.*

Actors and Resources Model: Domain expert 1 rated the accuracy of the model as very good. A few deviations were recognized (at least for the enterprise in which he works). As essential elements, the Site Manager was named as a supporting role for the Project Manager, and the Measurement and System Control Technician should be added. According to the expert, the Sales and Marketing, with the associated roles, is not necessarily relevant for the process at this level of detail.

Products and Services Model: The model is described as very generalized but quite useful. The reason for the relatively detailed presentation is that the chatbot does not depict all services typical for ventilation systems as a starting point, but has started directly with the service for retrofit ventilation systems. In this area, the expert rated the specified service elements as complete. However, he would not necessarily include the entire Maintenance and Support, as he considers this to be outside the scope, although this is definitely part of the service portfolio for ventilation systems in general.

Process Model: In terms of accuracy, the model contains many relevant elements for a retrofit ventilation system process. Many of the relations were considered useful. However, the main point of criticism identified was the absence of a short process sequence at the beginning of the entire process, which is absolutely essential for a retrofit process. This includes the preliminary assessment of the system with the associated measurements, which means that the actual retrofit offer can only be written if the potential is evident from the measured values. This is partially continued, as many processes are related to an *AND* connector. However, since, according to the expert, retrofit measures sometimes only involve replacing individual components of the ventilation system, it is advisable to set an *OR* connector there. Nevertheless, more possible scenarios could be identified by ChatGPT in the second experiment compared to the first experiment. The reason for this is the additional question about further relations shown in 5a) in Fig. 1. Figure 4 illustrates the effect of improving the prompting technique using an excerpt from the model. Domain expert 1 also rated Examination of Funding Opportunities and the Negative Feasibility Analysis as optional, as these processes are at least not practiced in his company. The last process should have a relation back to a previous process if the customer is dissatisfied, so that the error can be rectified, and the satisfied customer can be offered to create a Maintenance Plan or provide Customer Care and Support.

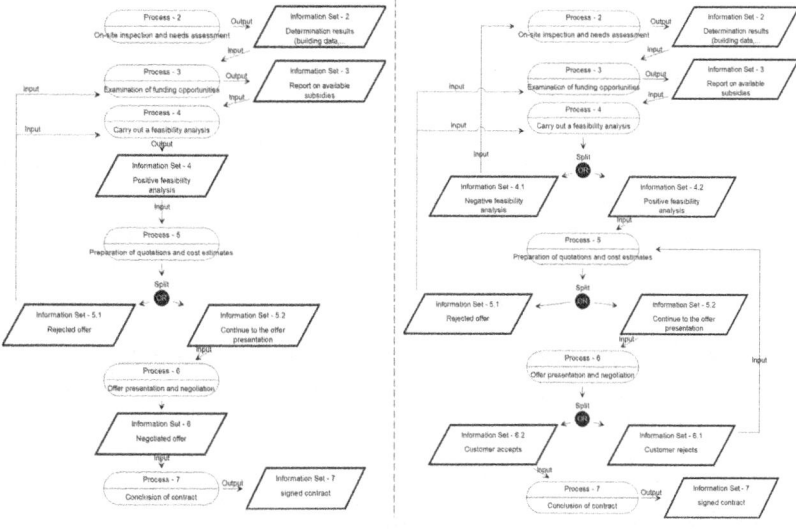

Fig. 4. Process Model created with ChatGPT (excerpt) before (left) and after (right) improvement with the additional prompt

Comparison of Models: The main criticism was once again that the models created with ChatGPT could not be used with very detailed knowledge. The process model of the chatbot does not include the upstream recording of measured values before the retrofit measures are carried out, and on the other hand, it involves the complete dismantling of the entire system (see Dismantling the Existing System and Dismantling the Old Ventilation System). In the case of retrofit measures, however, only individual parts of the ventilation system are replaced. In addition, the Calibration of the Ventilation System is technically incorrect. According to the expert, it is a calibration, and this takes place during commissioning and test run. Like expert 1, the expert also rated the arrangement and linking of Creating a Maintenance Plan as incorrect, as the maintenance plan is part of the process after the customer is satisfied. Otherwise, the defects must be eliminated with a loop leading back to Troubleshooting. Regarding the Actors and Resources Model in particular, the expert commented: "It looks more like the structure of a company that manufactures ventilation systems". This was mainly due to the modeling of the Sales and Marketing, which the expert considered to be out of scope for the modeling context of retrofit ventilation systems. Overall, however, the expert rated the models created by ChatGPT as very informative. Especially for people who are not familiar with the domain, these models can provide a good introduction. In addition, this sub-experiment showed that the expert also forgot to model some elements when creating his models. By comparing the models, the expert would therefore add Training of Customer Staff and Quality Inspection to his model. This illustrates the potential of using chatbots downstream of the model creation by a domain expert to identify missing or forgotten elements in the model.

Quality Assessment: Both experts rate the majority of the elements provided by ChatGPT as usable for the models. However, they explain more specifically: "Every company has its own fundamental approach to all models, which is why it is difficult to actually obtain these models from ChatGPT as they are practiced in the company". The main problem with the use of ChatGPT in modeling is that it is not yet possible to produce a correctly structured, graphical representation of the ChatGPT models as output. Since a lot of work still has to be done on the graphical implementation after the results have been output as modeling instructions in order to improve them afterwards, as experts themselves, the experts would tend to model the models on their own from the outset, given the current state of the art. However, the largely correct results of ChatGPT certainly show the experts that they would choose ChatGPT as a support in order to get an overview before the modeling carried out on their own. As an overview, they would use the modeling instructions (text/ID of the elements), which is the result of the prompt on which this experiment is based. Based on the modeling instructions, they would then develop a model with the help of their own knowledge, whereby they have both their own relevant, comprehensive domain-specific knowledge base and are guided by the general processes based on the instructions. In addition, ChatGPT can also reveal processes that the expert might not have considered, as was shown in the sub-experiments.

To-be Situation: Many of the proposed optimization measures were suggested by both the expert and the chatbot, such as the automation of quotation and report generation, as well as the use of an information management and CRM system. Nevertheless, ChatGPT also suggested approaches that are already used in practice in the experts' company. These include the use of IoT sensors, the creation of a cost-benefit analysis and the use of digitized test protocols and automatic test equipment. As a unique selling point, the domain expert also proposed a tool for employee deployment planning based on the relevant skills of the respective employees for the projects. This approach was not mentioned by the chatbot, at least not in the initial query. Overall, these results show high potential for Chat-GPT in the development of a future "target model".

4.3   Experiment 3: Management Consultancy

The third experiment conducted was in the management consultancy domain: *Company sales process from the perspective of the consulting enterprise.*

Actors and Resources Model: Domain expert 1 rated the model as quite extensive. Although all of the roles and organizational units shown there are basically represented in a management consultancy, the tasks of Sales and Project Management are performed by roles from the other organizational units in the expert's office. The reason for this may certainly be the size of the expert's office, which has around 15 people. Nevertheless, the expert generally considers it rather unusual that there are extra roles for both Sales and Project Management, as this is usually handled by either the Management or the highest position in the Consulting Department. HR & Administration and IT & Infrastructure and the roles within them were assessed as being outside the scope for this context, as the roles and associated tasks also exist, but are usually performed by external law firms or service providers, unless it is a secondary activity of a role. The expert would also include the Finance & Controlling in this context. One role that is missing in this model, according to the expert, is that of the Assistant/Secretary. In most cases, at least the Managing Directors have an Assistant, who in certain cases even supports the employees in the Advisory Department. The expert rated the basic naming of the organizational units and roles as very appropriate, although he also pointed out that there are often different names and levels for the employees in the Advisory Department.

Products and Services Model: Many elements were classified as correct by domain expert 1. However, the Project Management was classified as incorrect. Although it is an elementary component of Management Consultancy, according to the expert, it is not regarded as an extra service, but is a component of every service. Training & Workshops was judged to be out of scope because of the very infrequent implementation of individual training courses. In addition, the expert sees the Training Courses & Workshops as part of other services. For example, Service Management consulting and the sub-services always include corresponding workshops. As connectors to the sub-services, the expert would use the *OR* connector instead of the *AND* connector, as the model created by ChatGPT assumes that all sub-services are always executed as soon as the main service is selected. However, this is not the case, as, for example, only one IT Security Consultation can be carried out in the area of IT Consulting. In addition to the above adjustments, according to the expert, elementary services such as Subsidy Consulting, Reorganization & Restructuring, and Support for Business Start-ups must also be added for a Management Consultancy.

Process Model: ChatGPT's Process Model contains many relevant elements of a corporate sales process from the consulting firm's perspective in terms of accuracy. However, the expert particularly emphasized the many logical links and connectors between the elements. According to the expert, the Company Sale process includes a large number of steps backward and, in general, many scenarios that can occur during the process. This is illustrated in great detail in the model. In this context, the expert only criticizes that negative outcomes should also be depicted in the model, such as failure of the negotiations (can occur at any time) or rejection of the offer by the customer. Another point of criticism of the model created by ChatGPT for the expert is the lack of domain-specific knowledge. The model is supposed to be quite general, which it definitely is in the expert's opinion. Nevertheless, the expert is missing individual fundamental process steps, some of which were mapped to more irrelevant process steps. Here, the expert cites Target Group Analysis and Create Marketing Plan as examples. According to the expert, these are secondary processes. Instead, the expert would add more essential process steps, such as Requesting Required Documents, Carrying out an Actual Analysis, and Drawing up a Planning Calculation at the appropriate points in the model.

Model Comparison: The result of the evaluation was almost identical to that of domain expert 1 from the first sub-experiment. In the Actors and Resources Model and Products and Services Model, the same elements were rated as incorrect or out of scope (e.g., Project Management). In addition, in the ChatGPT models, the elements that were both added by domain expert 1 and modeled by domain expert 2 in their own models were labeled as missing (e.g., Funding Advice). In the Process Model and the General Model, the relevant relations were described as very detailed, although negative outcomes, such as the rejection of an interested party, are not depicted. In conclusion, the expert formulated his assessment of the models created by ChatGPT as follows: "The models provide you with a very good structure for modeling, which you can use as a guide and modify and enrich with domain-specific knowledge so that you end up with a comprehensive model in the shortest possible time".

Quality Assessment: As the expert's opinions were already almost identical in the previous sub-experiments, the previous results were only reinforced in this third part of the experiment. Both experts rated the models created by the domain expert as more meaningful than the ChatGPT models. The basis for this is the more extensive domain knowledge that is recognizable in the models. However, there were differences between the two experts with regard to their personal preferences for using ChatGPT in the modeling. While domain expert 1 would initially tend to model independently without the aid of ChatGPT and would only check whether he had forgotten or added elements using the chatbot once the models had been completed, domain expert 2 was more inclined to use the chatbot's predefined structure as a basis. The expert would then use these modeling instructions to create his modified models. Both approaches are certainly effective, but mainly show that the use of ChatGPT, albeit in different forms, makes sense in EM and would be practiced by experts.

To-be Situation: Most of the optimization potentials suggested by the chatbot have already been implemented in practice (e.g., the digitization of documents or the integration of regular quality controls). The only measure suggested by both the chatbot and the domain expert is the standardization of processes to save time and keep a constant quality level. The domain expert also mentions the optimization measures of setting up a database of interested parties, using chatbots for consultation reports, and using largely automated tools.

5   Discussion and Conclusions

5.1   Revisiting the Research Questions

RQ1: What are the potentials and limitations of using LLMs in EM?
The potential of ChatGPT in EM lies primarily in its ability to quickly and efficiently create a basic structure for models. This makes it possible to develop an initial model version in a short time to be used as a basis for further discussions or adjustments. This approach is particularly useful in time-critical projects. The study has also shown that it is possible to incorporate existing knowledge, which is gained from an expert or from explorative search with LLMs, at the appropriate points in the model. Based on the knowledge gained, the following modeling procedure using LLMs is therefore recommended: (1) Get model elements from ChatGPT, (2) Domain expert reviews output and names missing or wrong elements, (3) Named elements are transferred to ChatGPT to improve output, (4) ChatGPT provides elements for the improved model.

The experiments showed that ChatGPT was able to independently develop suggestions for automating and improving processes. The optimization suggestions created by ChatGPT on the basis of process descriptions support the further development of existing structures and reveal potential for automation and saving resources. ChatGPT proves to be a valuable tool, especially for standardized optimizations or regular adjustments to processes.

However, the results of the study also show clear limitations in the use of ChatGPT in EM. As ChatGPT was trained on generalized data, it is often unable to comprehensively access detailed specialist knowledge of specific industries. As a result, the models generated by ChatGPT are often generalized in specialized areas and require detailed post-processing by the domain experts. This shows that ChatGPT, at its current stage of development, is only a support and no alternative to domain experts. Another challenge is the limited ability of ChatGPT to create meaningful graphical representations of models. The modeling instructions generated by the model are purely text-based, which therefore requires additional work steps in order to implement them visually in modeling software. The work presented in [7] contains a promising approach.

RQ2: Which tasks can be best supported in which phases? In the "As-is" modeling phase, ChatGPT was able to provide useful support, particularly in structuring the individual elements of the models. It proved useful for outlining standard cross-domain processes and providing an initial structure that can then be further specified by experts. In the "Required changes and alternatives" phase, a differentiated picture emerged with regard to the performance of the model. In the experiments conducted, the models created by ChatGPT served as a solid basis, but were often adapted by experts before being accepted as complete or optimally suitable. The experts all stated that the Actors and Resources Model and the Products and Services Model were easier to adapt than the process model due to their lower complexity. The experts' modifications mostly concerned specific details that were either omitted from the initial ChatGPT models or only presented in general terms. In particular, the mapping of process details that are relevant to achieving certain business objectives or internal company standards often had to be revised or supplemented by the experts. In the phase of "Modeling the future situation", ChatGPT proved to be a creative source of inspiration thanks to its ability to generate various suggestions quickly and efficiently. On this basis, experts can define an initial direction and then work in greater depth on a precisely tailored design of the models.

RQ3: Does the order in which information is obtained (LLM-first or domain expert-first) have an influence on the quality of the results? In the case of very complex models, the experts stated that they would prefer to develop the model themselves, as it would not be worthwhile due to the time required to create the ChatGPT model in advance. The scenario in which the expert first creates a model and then uses the models created by ChatGPT to improve their models has resulted in a few elements being forgotten by the expert, but it is not preferred by the experts. The reason for this is, on the one hand, the enormous amount of time required to create the models, as the expert first creates his own models and then has to create the models using the modeling instructions from ChatGPT in order to compare the models with each other. On the other hand, the few elements forgotten by the expert during modeling are not elementary components and were probably only forgotten because the expert created the models in a very short time.

In summary, this shows that it makes sense to consult ChatGPT first to provide the expert with a solid basis that allows to make specific additions and clarifications. The procedure explained in the answer to RQ1 is recommended, whereby a modeling guide is developed in an interaction between the chatbot and the expert, which is then modeled by a third party to save the domain expert's time. The resulting model can then be optimized by the domain expert. Based on the experience gained, this seems the most efficient approach.

5.2   Limitations

As there is no established method for evaluating prompts [30], we developed them in an explorative way, so it is possible that better results could be achieved with exhaustive prompt engineering. While the use of a specific LLM (GPT-4o) is based on its current availability and performance, it limits the transferability to other models or future versions. Due to the rapid development in this area, it is possible that newer models may achieve significantly better results (especially by increasing the output tokens), reflecting the time-limited nature of the results.

Another limitation of the results is the experimental design of the study set-up (quasi-experiments). It is possible that differences in the interpretations and methodological approaches of the experts involved cannot be fully standardized, which can potentially lead to variations in the results. Possible differences in the interpretation of the modeling instructions between the user and the chatbot can occur, which can lead to deviations in the final modeling.

Subsequently, the experiments are also based on a limited number of application fields and processes. Although the selection of domains examined - event planning, ventilation systems, and management consultancy - provides an insight into different areas, generalizability is not proven. Furthermore, additional perspectives in enterprises should be considered (e.g., Concepts Model).

The choice of method for EM itself represents a limitation. The study is based exclusively on the 4EM framework, which supports specific modeling perspectives and structures. Since different EM methodologies vary in terms of scope, levels of abstraction, and stakeholder focus, the applicability and effectiveness of LLM support can vary significantly depending on the modeling language chosen. Therefore, it cannot be assumed that the results are transferable to other EM frameworks such as ArchiMate.

References

1. Russell, S.J., Norvig, P.: Artificial Intelligence: A Modern Approach. Pearson (2016)
2. Ziegler, A., et al.: Measuring github copilot's impact on productivity. Commun. ACM **67**(3), 54–63 (2024)
3. Cámara, J., Troya, J., Burgueño, L., Vallecillo, A.: On the assessment of generative AI in modeling tasks: an experience report with chatGPT and UML. Softw. Syst. Model. **22**(3), 781–793 (2023)
4. Wang, X., Anwer, N., Dai, Y., Liu, A.: ChatGPT for design, manufacturing, and education. Procedia CIRP **119**, 7–14 (2023)
5. Sandkuhl, K., Barn, B.S., Barat, S.: Neural text generators in enterprise modeling: can chatGPT be used as proxy domain expert? In: ISD 2023 (2023)
6. Barn, B.S., Barat, S., Sandkuhl, K.: Adaptation of enterprise modeling methods for large language models. In: Almeida, J.P.A., Kaczmarek-Heß, M., Koschmider, A., Proper, H.A. (eds.) PoEM 2023. LNBIP, vol. 497, pp. 3–18. Springer, Cham (2024). https://doi.org/10.1007/978-3-031-48583-1_1
7. Kolev, P.A., Pruss, H.H., Wilken, J.R., Sandkuhl, K.: Grass-root enterprise modelling: how large language models can help. In: Paja, E., Zdravkovic, J., Kavakli, E., Stirna, J. (eds.) PoEM 2024. LNBIP, vol. 538, pp. 123–139. Springer, Cham (2025). https://doi.org/10.1007/978-3-031-77908-4_8
8. Cook, T.D., Campbell, D.T., Shadish, W.: Experimental and Quasi-experimental Designs for Generalized Causal Inference. Houghton Mifflin, Boston (2002)

9. Sjøberg, D.I.K., et al.: A survey of controlled experiments in software engineering. IEEE Trans. Softw. Eng. **31**(9), 733–753 (2005)
10. Vernadat, F.B.: Enterprise modelling and integration: from fact modelling to enterprise interoperability. In: Enterprise Inter-and Intra-organizational Integration: Building International Consensus, pp. 25–33 (2003)
11. Bubenko Jr, J., Persson, A., Stirna, J.: An intentional perspective on enterprise modeling. In: Intentional Perspectives on Information Systems Engineering, pp. 215–237 (2010)
12. Persson, A., Stirna, J.: An explorative study into the influence of business goals on the practical use of enterprise modelling methods and tools. In: New Perspectives on Information Systems Development: Theory, Methods, and Practice, pp. 275–287 (2002)
13. Sandkuhl, K., et al.: From expert discipline to common practice: a vision and research agenda for extending the reach of enterprise modeling. Bus. Inf. Syst. Eng. **60**, 69–80 (2018)
14. Vernadat, F.: Enterprise modelling: Research review and outlook. Comput. Ind. **122**, 103265 (2020)
15. Sandkuhl, K., Stirna, J., Persson, A., Wißotzki, M.: Enterprise Modeling. Springer, Heidelberg (2014)
16. Brown, T., et al.: Language models are few-shot learners. Advances in Neural Information Processing Systems, vol. 33, pp. 1877–1901 (2020)
17. Huang, W., Abbeel, P., Pathak, D., Mordatch, I.: Language models as zero-shot planners: extracting actionable knowledge for embodied agents. In: Chaudhuri, K., Jegelka, S., Song, L., Szepesvari, C., Niu, G., Sabato, S. (eds.) Proceedings of the 39th International Conference on Machine Learning. Proceedings of Machine Learning Research, vol. 162, pp. 9118–9147. PMLR (2022)
18. Stirna, J., Persson, A.: Enterprise Modeling. Springer, Cham (2018)
19. Krogstie, J.: Quality of Business Process Models. Springer, Heidelberg (2016)
20. Klievtsova, N., Benzin, J.-V., Kampik, I., Mangler, J., Rinderle-Ma, S.: Conversational process modelling: state of the art, applications, and implications in practice. In: Di Francescomarino, C., Burattin, A., Janiesch, C., Sadiq, S. (eds.) BPM 2023. LNBIP, vol. 490, pp. 319–336. Springer, Cham (2023). https://doi.org/10.1007/978-3-031-41623-1_19
21. Fill, H.-G., Fettke, P., Köpke, J.: Conceptual modeling and large language models: impressions from first experiments with chatGPT. Enterp. Modell. Inf. Syst. Archit. (EMISAJ) **18**, 1–15 (2023)
22. Kourani, H., Berti, A., Schuster, D., van der Aalst, W.M.P.: Process modeling with large language models. In: van der Aa, H., Bork, D., Schmidt, R., Sturm, A. (eds.) BPMDS EMMSAD 2024. LNBIP, vol. 511, pp. 229–244. Springer, Cham (2024)
23. Vidgof, M., Bachhofner, S., Mendling, J.: Large language models for business process management: opportunities and challenges. In: Di Francescomarino, C., Burattin, A., Janiesch, C., Sadiq, S. (eds.) BPM 2023. LNBIP, vol. 490, pp. 107–123. Springer, Cham (2023). https://doi.org/10.1007/978-3-031-41623-1_7
24. Buchmann, R., et al.: Large language models: expectations for semantics-driven systems engineering. Data Knowl. Eng. **152**, 102324 (2024)
25. de Kinderen, S., Winter, K.: Towards taming large language models with prompt templates for legal GRL modeling. In: van der Aa, H., Bork, D., Schmidt, R., Sturm, A. (eds.) BPMDS EMMSAD 2024. LNBIP, vol. 511, pp. 213–228. Springer, Cham (2024). https://doi.org/10.1007/978-3-031-61007-3_17

26. Görgen, L., Müller, E., Triller, M., Nast, B., Sandkuhl, K.: Large language models in enterprise modeling: case study and experiences. In: Proceedings of the 12th International Conference on Model-Based Software and Systems Engineering, pp. 74–85. SCITEPRESS - Science and Technology Publications (2024)
27. Müller, E., Nast, B., Sandkuhl, K.: Dataset for "LLM support for domain experts in enterprise modeling: Experiences and implications" (2025). https://doi.org/10.5281/zenodo.15768586
28. Gutschmidt, A., Nast, B.: Assessing model quality using large language models. In: Paja, E., Zdravkovic, J., Kavakli, E., Stirna, J. (eds.) PoEM 2024. LNBIP, vol. 538, pp. 105–122. Springer, Cham (2025). https://doi.org/10.1007/978-3-031-77908-4_7
29. White, J., et al.: A prompt pattern catalog to enhance prompt engineering with ChatGPT (2023)
30. Ajith, A., Pan, C., Xia, M., Deshpande, A., Narasimhan, K.: InstructEval: systematic evaluation of instruction selection methods. arXiv preprint arXiv:2307.00259 (2023)

Modeling and Governing Adaptive Organizations

Variability of Changing Organizational Capabilities

Georgios Koutsopoulos$^{(\boxtimes)}$ (iD)

DSV, Stockholm University, Borgarfjordsgatan 12, 164 55 Kista, Stockholm, Sweden
georgios@dsv.su.se

Abstract. In the modern rapidly evolving business environments, organizations must continuously adapt their capabilities to remain competitive. The constant need for changing capabilities results in a plethora, not only of capabilities, but also of their variations. Several approaches for capability analysis exist, yet, the variability aspect of organizational capabilities has not been explored in depth. The aim of this paper is to gain insight into capability variability, by exploring integration potentials between capability modeling and variability modeling. In particular, the KYKLOS method, which is specialized for modeling changing capabilities, is utilized in combination with the Orthogonal Variability Model, which is specialized for capturing the variability aspect in software engineering. The study explores the theoretical foundations of each component, outlines the potentials of integrating them into a unified approach, and demonstrates its application using a case study. This integration is explored as a means to improve understanding and framing of capability variability and its boundaries.

Keywords: Capability · Conceptual Modeling · Variability · Software Product Lines · Orthogonal Variability Model · Change management · Boundaries

1 Introduction

Modern organizations are operating in consistently and rapidly changing environments. The concept of capability is gaining interest as a construct [1] that critically enables organizations not only to deliver value to their stakeholders, but also gain and sustain competitive advantages, especially when digital organizations are concerned [2]. The organizational environment's pace of change has surpassed the one of the actual organizations [3], and for this reason, modern organizations are experiencing a constant need to change and evolve, not only for achieving their goals and realizing their vision [4], but sometimes simply for ensuring survival in highly competitive contexts [5].

Organizational capabilities are increasingly recognized as critical assets that enable companies to deliver value and sustain competitive advantage. Capabilities, associated to aspects such as supply chain management, customer service, or manufacturing processes, evolve and adapt to shifting market conditions, customer demands, legal context, and technological advancements. As organizations grow and respond to external pressures, variability within these capabilities becomes necessary. However, this introduces

© The Author(s), under exclusive license to Springer Nature Switzerland AG 2026
R. Deneckère et al. (Eds.): BIR 2025, LNBIP 562, pp. 145–158, 2026.
https://doi.org/10.1007/978-3-032-04375-7_9

complex questions; How much can a capability variate while still being the same capability? And at what point does a capability transform into something different, no longer being the same capability or serving its original purpose?

This paper examines these questions by exploring capability variability on an operational level, adopting the theoretical perspective of capability variability that has been suggested earlier in [6]. Theoretically, the paper adopts an approach introduced in [6] about how much a capability can change before it ceases to be the same capability or even stops being a capability altogether. This is the KYKLOS approach [6], a capability modeling method designed to manage organizational capabilities which are dynamically changing over time. Its application involves and requires the identification of variations of a capability. Operationally, the paper explores how variations of capabilities can be managed within set boundaries using Software Product Lines (SPL) [7]. The motivation comes from a challenge that has been identified during the application of the KYKLOS method. This challenging aspect of KYKLOS is associated to its modeling procedure and concerns the lack of a systematic elicitation of variations. SPL, and the Orthogonal Variability Model (OVM) [7] in particular, is used as means to improve that variation elicitation aspect of KYKLOS's modeling procedure. This is demonstrated using a case study in the public Greek arts and culture sector to show how variability of organizational capabilities can be managed in practice.

The goal of this paper is *to explore the concept of organizational capability, with a focus on its variability aspect.* Identifying ways to improve the modeling procedure of KYKLOS can be considered a sub-goal for this paper. The potentials for an integration of the KYKLOS method and SPL are explored using a case study.

The rest of the paper is structured as follows. Section 2 briefly describes the relevant background, including the modeling approaches used in the paper. Section 3 explains the involved methodological decisions. Section 4 introduces the case study. Section 5 presents the analysis of the case with the combined modeling methods. Sections 6 and 7 provide a discussion and concluding remarks, respectively.

2 Background

This section provides a comprehensive summary of capabilities, as a concept, capability modeling, and variability modeling.

2.1 Organizational Capabilities

Capability, as a conceptual construct, and capability thinking, as a practice, are gradually gaining ground as enablers and facilitators for the documentation, planning, design, and analysis of businesses [2].

A noteworthy fact about organizational capabilities is the lack of a consistent and unanimous definition in the literature, despite the diversity of capability modeling approaches that exist in the literature [8]. This situation is further amplified by the fact that the theory of dynamic capabilities [9] provides a wider spectrum of definitions, that raise significantly the degree of ambiguity regarding the definition of capability. In this study the concept of organizational capability is defined as "*a potential to produce outcome(s) to fulfill an organization's intention(s) within a context, using a configured set of resources and behaviors*" [6].

2.2 Capability Modeling

The concept of organizational capability has gained ground as construct that adds value to organizational research and practice, and as a result, it has been part or core element of several modeling approaches with the aim to address organizational issues.

A few examples among the popular modeling approaches include the Capability-Driven Development (CDD) [2] and the Value Delivery Modeling Language (VDML) [10], which are stand-alone approaches that utilize the concept of capability, or the NATO Architecture Framework (NAF) [11], the Department of Defense Architecture Framework (DoDAF) [12], the Ministry of Defence Architecture Framework (MODAF) [13], and Archimate [14], which are Enterprise Architecture frameworks. Additionally, there are approaches that extend existing modeling approaches, like Capability Maps [15, 16] and i* [17], or independent approaches with new notations, like Capability-Oriented Designs with Enterprise Knowledge (CODEK) [18], and the domain-specific ones, like Digital Business Ecosystem Map (DBEmap) [19] and KYKLOS [6], which is described in detail in the following section.

The KYKLOS Modeling Method

KYKLOS is a domain-specific capability modeling method [6], developed to address the phenomenon of capability change. Its purpose is to support organizations in managing their changing capabilities, particularly as they evolve in response to internal and external triggers. The method is designed to facilitate continuous adaptation, which is crucial for survival and success in highly dynamic environments.

The method helps capturing, analyzing and depicting various aspects of the phenomenon of capability change, from their design and/or discovery to the actual change. KYKLOS splits this procedure into four key phases:

- Foundation Phase: Establishes the base for the analysis of the capability, identifying its value, scope, and ownership.
- Observation Phase: Focuses on identifying external and internal factors that drive the need for change, including Context factors and Key Performance Indicators along with organizational Intentions.
- Decision Alternatives Phase: Explores possible new configurations based on identified needs for change, analyzing different options utilizing existing and available capability components.
- Delivery of Change Phase: Implements the selected change and manages the capability's transformation, taking into consideration various attributes of change like intention, scope, and frequency.

KYKLOS provides a structured modeling language and notation (Table 1), implemented in a tool [20] using the ADOxx [21] meta-modeling platform.

Table 1. The KYKLOS graphical notation, from [22].

2.3 Variability Modeling

Variability modeling has its roots in software engineering, in particular in domains like SPL [7], the scope of which is the development of system "families" and customizable modularized software systems. Variability modeling provides the necessary tools and methods for capturing and analyzing the commonalities and differences among systems that belong to the same family. Its emphasis is on the varying components of these systems, along with the constraints among the variants, that is, which and how many variations may co-exist within the "family".

Variability modeling has an essential role in Software Product Line Engineering (SPLE) [23], enabling the development of a diverse, yet, related software products using a shared set of core components, while addressing variations in specific product features [7]. Variability refers to the ability to customize, adapt, or extend software systems to meet different customer needs or market demands. One of the most prominent approaches to variability modeling is the OVM.

The Orthogonal Variability Model

The OVM's focal point is the representation of variability separately from the system architecture and other core models. It introduces variation points, which represent aspects of the product where variability occurs, and variants, which are the possible configurations at those points [7, 23].

In OVM, variability is treated as the main modeling perspective, separate from functional modeling. This orthogonal separation provides clarity and modularity, allowing for variability to be modeled and analyzed independently. This model is particularly useful in managing complex dependencies and constraints between different variations [23]. The graphical notation of OVM is shown in Fig. 1. The main concepts of OVM and their definitions [7] are:

- Variation point: Describes something that can vary, without any information about how it can vary.
- Variant: A complete variation, always connected to a variation point. Describes how the variation point can vary.
- Variability constraint: Describes the permitted combinations of variants and the requirements and/or exclusions among them.

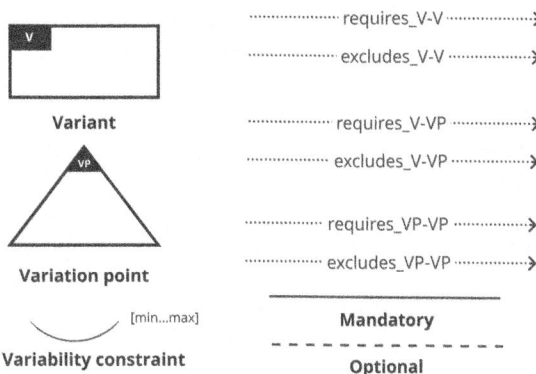

Fig. 1. The OVM graphical notation [23].

2.4   Theoretical Variability of Capabilities

The theoretical view on the topic of variability in organizational capabilities has been addressed in [6]. In particular, the definition provided in Sect. 2.1 of this paper establishes the necessary concepts for describing a capability, so that any missing associations result in a way to distinguish between capability and non-capability objects in an analysis or model. In other words, the definition sets the criteria for classifying capabilities as such and other relevant organizational concepts such as processes, resources, goals, etc. [2], as non-capabilities.

Regarding the question of how much a capability can vary while being the same capability, the answer requires employing a criterion of identity, which is "a principle specifying, in a non-circular way, the identity conditions of objects of a given kind" [24], and also provides logically sufficient condition(s) for the identity to be true [25]. When it comes to capabilities, the same capability may potentially fulfill varying organizational intentions, and may exist within various contexts. In addition, variating sets of resources may fulfill its operational realization. Yet, the delivered value cannot be variating, therefore, the produced value is identified as the criterion of identity for a capability.

3 Methodology

The aim of this paper is to explore the variability aspect of organizational capabilities. For this reason, capability thinking [2] is combined with variability analysis, both employing modeling perspectives. For the modeling part of this study, two modeling approaches have been utilized. The KYKLOS method [6], via the KYKLOS tool [20], and the Orthogonal Variability Model (OVM) [7, 23], which is optimized for modeling variability in SPLs. KYKLOS was chosen because of its domain-specificity, which is changing capabilities. It requires the identification of variating capability configurations, a fact that makes it an appropriate choice for this study. OVM is also optimal, since it is one of the prominent approaches for variability modeling.

To demonstrate the combination and integration of the two approaches, a case study has been used. Case study is an appropriate strategy for this research, since it facilitates acquiring deep insight on a specific phenomenon [26]. This is valuable for this study, because changing organizational capabilities is a complex phenomenon and in-depth investigation is required. The case has been described in detail in [27], since it has been used during the development of KYKLOS. It is now revisited to explore whether the combination with OVM will improve the procedure, and described in the next section. In other words, this is a secondary analysis of the case study using the two modeling approaches combined.

Regarding the data collection, the initially collected data were sufficient. The process is described in detail in [27]. In particular, one group and six individual semi-structured face-to-face interviews were conducted with all the managers and unit heads of the case study organization. The average duration of each interview was about one hour. After the interviews, two two-hour long participatory modeling [28] sessions took place. A few preliminary models were created, for example, a 4EM Goals model [29], and an e3value model [30]. These preliminary models were used as input for the KYKLOS model that is presented in Sect. 5. The models are also available in [27].

4 The Case Study

The Veria Arts Center is a public organization in the municipality of Veria, Greece, operating in the arts and culture sector. Its core mission is to organize and host arts and cultural festivals that engage the local community and contribute to the region's cultural development. Over the years, the Veria Art Center faced significant challenges that required it to adapt its operations and capabilities. Two major external pressures shaped its strategic decisions: (i) The Greek Government-Debt Crisis: This financial crisis led to reduced public funding and limited the center's financial resources, forcing it to operate with constrained budgets, and (ii) The COVID-19 Pandemic: Social distancing measures and restrictions on public gatherings prevented physical events, compelling the center to explore alternative ways to continue its activities.

In response to these challenges, the Veria Art Center implemented various operational configurations of its festival organization capability. These included:

- Normal Configuration: Traditional, full-scale physical events utilizing all available resources.

- Lean Configuration: A scaled-down version of operations with cost-saving measures and reduced resources.
- Digital Configuration: Fully online festivals using digital platforms to engage audiences remotely during the COVID-19 pandemic.
- New Normal Configuration: A hybrid approach combining physical and digital elements to adapt to post-pandemic conditions.

Throughout these changes, the Veria Art Center collaborated with local, national, and international partners, utilized various funding models (ticket sales, grants, sponsorships), and engaged with the audience through on-site interactions, live streaming, and social media campaigns. This case study demonstrates the center's efforts to remain resilient and continue delivering cultural value despite economic and public health crises. The case has been described in full detail in an earlier publication of the KYKLOS project [27], yet, in this paper, only a brief summary is provided, since the focal point lies in the analysis of variations.

4.1 Challenges in Application

The elicitation of capability variations, which is performed during the Decision phase of KYKLOS, has been considered successful and effective, however, it relies exclusively on domain expertise. The fact that there is no systematic support provided by the method for this step, apart from documenting the results, indicates room for improvement. For this reason, the integration of an improved variation elicitation is attempted in this paper. In particular, KYKLOS is re-applied in combination with OVM to the Veria Arts Center case, so that potentials for the evolution of KYKLOS are identified.

5   Integration of Capability and Variability Modeling

The initial application of KYKLOS to the Veria Arts Center case resulted in a complete model. In this section, the results of that task are presented, along with the OVM that has been created for this paper, along with their integration. The following sections provide a detailed report of the two models and their integration.

5.1 The Veria Arts Center Case KYKLOS Model

The initial application of KYKLOS to the case resulted in a model that sufficiently facilitated not only capturing the essential elements of the changing capability, but also the change attributes, as the scope of the method indicates. The model has been previously published in [31], so, a full report of this model is not within the scope of this paper. For this reason, a brief summary follows, reporting on the main aspects that were captured:

- The context factors that affected the Art Festival organization capability where social, economic and legal, like the budget reduction and the COVID-19 legislation. These were associated to specific KPIs that enabled assessing the capability. Examples of KPIs were the Expert employee replacement rate and the Percentage of Sold digital tickets. These were satisfied by the Digital operation configuration of the capability.

- The internal context of the capability, in other words, the organizational intentions that it aimed to satisfy were, as aligned with the Art Center's strategy, to provide educational and popular content to the citizens, via the organized festivals, to be operationally flexible, and to exploit the advantages of the crises, once their direct impact has been overcome.
- The active operational configuration during the time of the study was the digital one, yet, the analysis resulted in the design of a future configuration of the capability namely "New normal", which would exploit the lessons learned during the crises. This configuration would combine the lean operationalization with digital aspects, resulting in the potential to deliver hybrid art festivals, for example an event that was conducted on a physical site would be also streamed online for interested participants that were not in proximity with the municipality of Veria (Fig. 2).

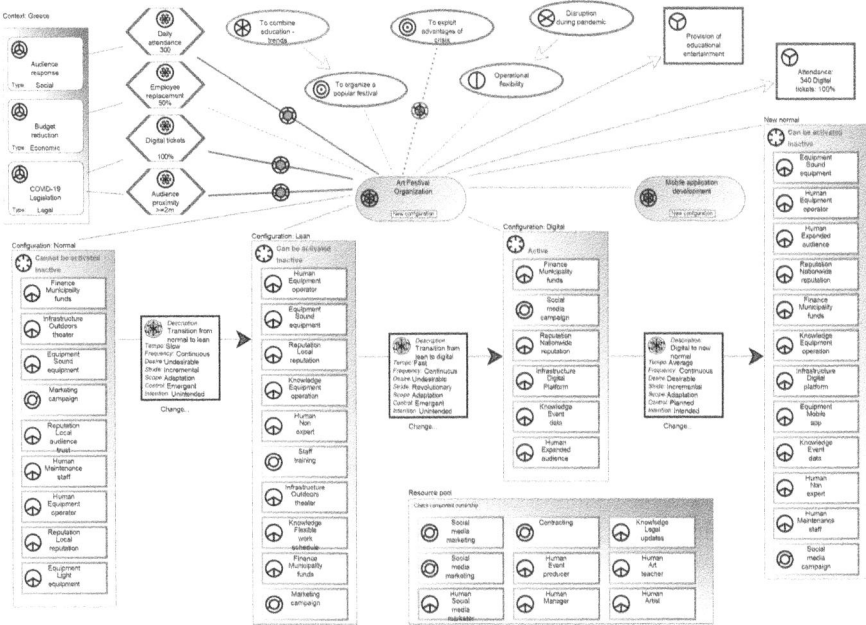

Fig. 2. The KYKLOS model for the Veria Arts Center case, from [31]

5.2   The Veria Arts Center Case OVM

The OVM of the case focused on identifying the variations points and variants that drove the elicitation of the different configurations at first place. In practice, the event organization capability, which, from a variability modeling perspective is a variation point, required the inclusion of four main variation points. These were the (i) Revenue generation model, (ii) Expertise procurement approach, (iii) Event delivery format, and (iv) Audience engagement approach. Each variation point is associated to its own variants.

For example, Revenue generation model has Sponsorships, Governmental financing, and Ticket Sales. Based on the variability constraint, at least one of these variants need to exist in our designed capability. Co-existing variants are allowed, up to three of them, and any combination is allowed. In a similar way, the OVM captures the variability aspect of the event organization capability. The OVM, with all the variation points, variants, and variability constraints is shown in Fig. 3.

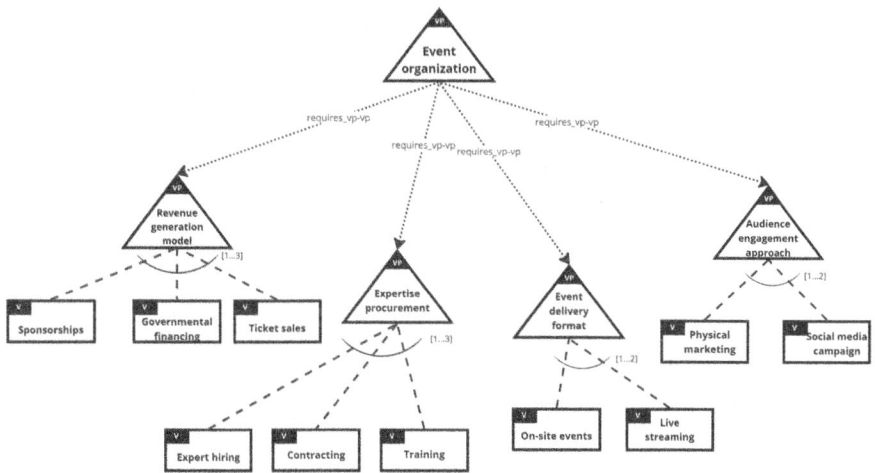

Fig. 3. The OVM for the Veria Arts Center case.

5.3 The Integrated Model

Modeling the various operational configurations of the event organization capability in the KYKLOS model has not been guided or supported by the method. It was a result of the domain experts' involvement. Regarding the OVM, it captures the variation points and variants of the capability without the potential to capture any of the other aspects of a changing capability, like the context, intentions, and change attributes. The key point of the integration is the concept of configuration in the KYKLOS method. It is defined as "the set of resources that are used by the capability along with the behavior elements that deliver it." [6]. KYKLOS also clarifies that a capability can have several configurations, yet, only one may be active at a given moment in time. In OVM, combinations of variants result in the development of various products in an SPL family. Every product has its own unique combination, even if the OVM does not capture the products themselves as combinations of variants. In this way, we can assume a degree of semantic consistency and a high degree of practicality in the integration. KYKLOS is gaining a path towards facilitating the identification of potential operational configurations. The integration is complementing OVM too, in terms of modeling the feasible capability "products". Therefore, the integration happens as follows. A KYKLOS capability gets associated to an OVM variation point, which, in returns is connected to the actual variation points, the variating aspects of the capability. Every variation gets associated to its variants. These can be combined into separate configurations, defined as sets of specific components/variants.

Figure 4 demonstrates these connections. The model can potentially become heavily cluttered, therefore in the current initial exploration, color-coding is used on a preliminary level for distinguishing the variant sets. No effort has been put in creating new notation elements for this integration, because the aim is to convert this to an automated module in the KYKLOS tool.

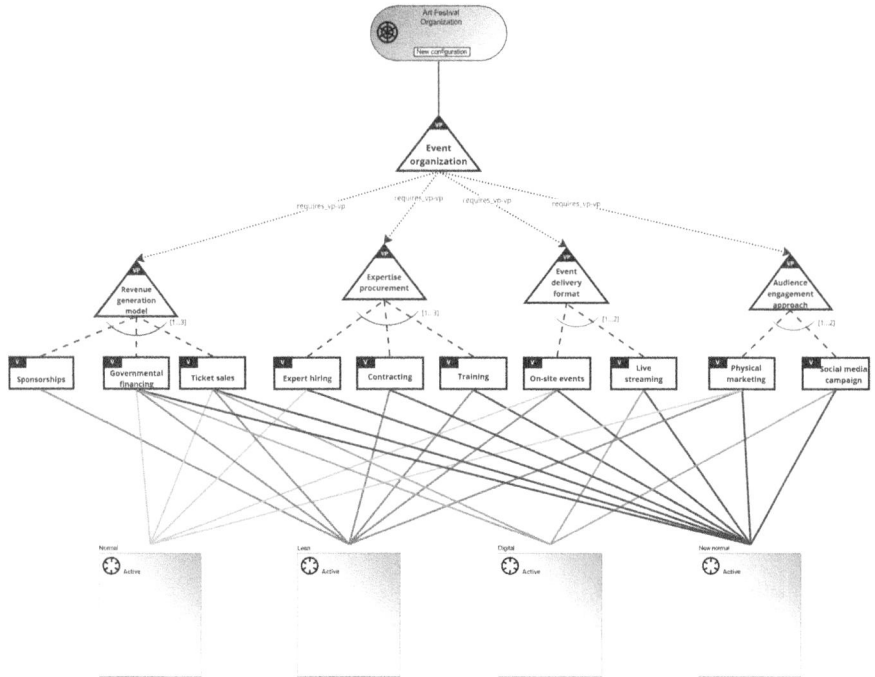

Fig. 4. The integration of KYKLOS and OVM for the Veria Arts Center case.

6 Discussion

In this paper, the variability aspect of organizational capabilities has been explored. This aspect has received limited attention in capability research. The combination of KYKLOS with OVM has provided valuable insights.

KYKLOS is a method that is efficiently capturing the multi-faceted phenomenon of changing capabilities, with the necessary context factors, intentions, KPIs, and change attributes. Yet, it provides limited guidance when it comes to identifying variating operational configurations of a capability. OVM, conversely, is designed to capture variation points and to frame the permitted variant combinations. However, the situational triggers and strategic intents that motivate the existence of those variants remains out of its scope.

The integration indicates that the two approaches can be considered complementary when it comes to the variability of changing capabilities.

Once the KYKLOS capability is mapped to OVM's variation points and variants, the elicitation of candidate configurations becomes an issue of systematic selection of sets of variants. Thus, the combination supports both the traceability of the capability to its motivating factors, and the operational design choice, a feature that could not be provided by any modeling method in isolation.

The initial questions concerned the boundaries or variability. Keeping the delivered value as the criterion of identity and treating KYKLOS configurations as OVM-compliant product instances, a clear distinction could be introduced between the elements that could vary and those that could not. This distinction is valuable while collaborating with stakeholders. In the Veria Arts Center case, options like "outsourcing experts" or "hybrid audience engagement" are regarded as valid variants of the same capability, where proposals like switching to purely commercial events are regarded as transformations that exceed the variability boundaries and violate the criterion of identity of the event organization capability.

Essentially, the variability constraints in the OVM part set the boundaries of the capability that is being designed. In case the variations are not known, producing all the potential combinations that the OVM allows provide the opportunity for identifying new capability variations. This is an efficient way to reduce significantly the dependency on domain experts, and even if this is not regarded as an issue, it can support the experts' task.

From a modeling perspective, the main contribution of this paper can be identified in the decomposition of the variability of organizational capabilities to the variability of capability components. The combined application of capability modeling and variability modeling on the Veria Arts Center case demonstrated not only an improved and more structured way to document existing variations, but also, and most importantly, a systematic way to design new variations of capabilities.

From a managerial perspective, the contribution can be considered twofold. The OVM variability constraints can provide an ex-ante analysis during capability design and planning. Instead of testing the applicability of capability variations holistically, the analysis can be simplified, in terms of testing the co-existence of single variants/components. The KYKLOS elements can provide an ex-post perspective to monitor the efficiency of specific variations/configurations. The combined activities can facilitate a flexible and structured analysis procedure.

Several future research paths exist. Initially, the integration needs to be solidified and implemented in a tool. The KYKLOS tool already uses all of the method's aspects, so it will serve as a convenient platform for adding a variability module. Algorithms can serve towards the automation of the analysis, and new notation elements will facilitate the users' interaction with the method. The modeling procedure will also have to be updated. Additionally, automating the translation between OVM variants and KYKLOS configurations can optimize the alignment of the analysis steps, and enable simulations using "what if" scenarios. This translation can potentially be achieved using organizational resources as the intermediate elements.

Additionally, this new version of KYKLOS with a variability extension will require verification, validation, and evaluation [32], to address the generalizability limits of the case study strategy employed in this study.

Overall, this study can be the starting point towards a "Capability Product Lines" or "Capability Lines" methodology, establishing a structured way to support organizations in identifying alternative ways to achieve the outcomes and produce the value that they are capable of.

7 Conclusions

The paper explored the potentials of integrating capability and variability modeling, as a means to improve the necessary steps of eliciting capability variations. In practice, KYKLOS, a capability change modeling method, and OVM, a variability modeling method, have been applied in combination on a case study. Initially, variability is introduced and established as one of the essential aspects of capability modeling. Second, the integration between KYKLOS and OVM was proven to improve the systematic elicitation of capability variants. The results indicate a promising starting point for the development of a structured modeling method and tool support, that will help organizations improve their capability management, in terms of robustness and resilience to change.

Disclosure of Interests. The author has no competing interests to declare that are relevant to the content of this article.

References

1. Wißotzki, M.: Capability Management Guide. Springer Fachmedien Wiesbaden, Wiesbaden (2018). https://doi.org/10.1007/978-3-658-19233-4
2. Sandkuhl, K., Stirna, J. (eds.): Capability Management in Digital Enterprises. Springer, Cham (2018). https://doi.org/10.1007/978-3-319-90424-5
3. Burke, W.W.: Organization Change: Theory and Practice. Sage Publications (2017)
4. Burnes, B.: Managing Change. Pearson, Harlow (2014)
5. Zimmermann, N.: Dynamics of Drivers of Organizational Change. Gabler, Wiesbaden (2011). https://doi.org/10.1007/978-3-8349-6811-1
6. Koutsopoulos, G.: KYKLOS - a modeling method and tool for managing changing capabilities in organizations (2024). http://urn.kb.se/resolve?urn=urn:nbn:se:su:diva-226282
7. Pohl, K., Metzger, A.: Software product lines. In: Gruhn, V., Striemer, R. (eds.) The Essence of Software Engineering, pp. 185–201. Springer, Cham (2018). https://doi.org/10.1007/978-3-319-73897-0_11
8. Koutsopoulos, G., Henkel, M., Stirna, J.: Dynamic adaptation of capabilities: exploring meta-model diversity. In: Reinhartz-Berger, I., Zdravkovic, J., Gulden, J., Schmidt, R. (eds.) Enterprise, Business-Process and Information Systems Modeling, pp. 181–195. Springer, Cham (2019). https://doi.org/10.1007/978-3-030-20618-5_13
9. Teece, D.J.: Explicating dynamic capabilities: the nature and microfoundations of (sustainable) enterprise performance. Strateg. Manag. J. **28**, 1319–1350 (2007). https://doi.org/10.1002/smj.640

10. Object Management Group (OMG): Value Delivery Modeling Language v.1.1 (2018). https://www.omg.org/spec/VDML/1.1
11. NATO: NATO Architecture Framework v.4 (2018). https://www.nato.int/nato_static_fl2014/assets/pdf/pdf_2018_08/20180801_180801-ac322-d_2018_0002_naf_final.pdf
12. USA Department of Defense: Department of Defense Architecture Framework 2.02 (2009). https://dodcio.defense.gov/Library/DoD-Architecture-Framework/
13. UK Ministry of Defence: Ministry of Defence Architecture Framework V1.2.004 (2010). https://www.gov.uk/guidance/mod-architecture-framework
14. The Open Group: Archimate 3.0.1. Specification (2017). https://publications.opengroup.org/i162
15. Beimborn, D., Martin, S.F., Homann, U.: Capability-oriented modeling of the firm. Presented at the IPSI Conference, Amalfi, Italy (2005)
16. Van Riel, J., Poels, G.: A method for developing generic capability maps: a design science study in the professional sport industry. Bus. Inf. Syst. Eng. **65**, 403–424 (2023). https://doi.org/10.1007/s12599-023-00793-z
17. Danesh, M.H., Yu, E.: Modeling enterprise capabilities with i*: reasoning on alternatives. In: Iliadis, L., Papazoglou, M., Pohl, K. (eds.) Advanced Information Systems Engineering Workshops, pp. 112–123. Springer, Cham (2014). https://doi.org/10.1007/978-3-319-07869-4_10
18. Loucopoulos, P., Kavakli, E.: Capability oriented enterprise knowledge modeling: the CODEK approach. In: Karagiannis, D., Mayr, H.C., Mylopoulos, J. (eds.) Domain-Specific Conceptual Modeling, pp. 197–215. Springer, Cham (2016). https://doi.org/10.1007/978-3-319-39417-6_9
19. Tsai, C.H.: DBEmap - A Modular Method for Designing Digital Business Ecosystems (2024). https://urn.kb.se/resolve?urn=urn:nbn:se:su:diva-234538
20. Koutsopoulos, G., Henkel, M., Stirna, J.: The KYKLOS tool for modeling changing capabilities. In: Cabanillas, C., Pérez, F. (eds.) Intelligent Information Systems, pp. 146–155. Springer, Cham (2023). https://doi.org/10.1007/978-3-031-34674-3_18
21. OMiLAB: The ADOxx Metamodelling Platform. https://www.adoxx.org/live/home. Accessed 26 June 2018
22. Koutsopoulos, G., Henkel, M.: An experience report on the implementation of the KYKLOS modeling method. In: Serral, E., Stirna, J., Ralyté, J., Grabis, J. (eds.) The Practice of Enterprise Modeling, pp. 103–118. Springer, Cham (2021). https://doi.org/10.1007/978-3-030-91279-6_8
23. Pohl, K., Böckle, G., van der Linden, F.: Software Product Line Engineering: Foundations, Principles, and Techniques. Springer, New York (2005)
24. Honderich, T. (ed.): The Oxford Companion to Philosophy. Oxford University Press, Oxford (2005)
25. Lowe, E.J.: What is a criterion of identity? Philos. Q. **39**, 1 (1989). https://doi.org/10.2307/2220347
26. Mills, A., Durepos, G., Wiebe, E.: Encyclopedia of Case Study Research (2020). https://doi.org/10.4135/9781412957397
27. Koutsopoulos, G.: Capabilities in crisis: a case study using enterprise modeling for change analysis. In: Buchmann, R.A., Polini, A., Johansson, B., Karagiannis, D. (eds.) Perspectives in Business Informatics Research, pp. 100–114. Springer, Cham (2021). https://doi.org/10.1007/978-3-030-87205-2_7
28. Stirna, J., Persson, A.: Enterprise Modeling: Facilitating the Process and the People. Springer, Cham (2018). https://doi.org/10.1007/978-3-319-94857-7
29. Sandkuhl, K., Stirna, J., Persson, A., Wißotzki, M.: Enterprise Modeling: Tackling Business Challenges with the 4EM Method. Springer, Heidelberg (2014). https://doi.org/10.1007/978-3-662-43725-4

30. Gordijn, J., Wieringa, R.: E3value User Guide - Designing Your Ecosystem in a Digital World. The Value Engineers B.V., Soest, The Netherlands (2021)
31. Koutsopoulos, G., Henkel, M., Stirna, J.: Modeling the phenomenon of capability change: the KYKLOS method. In: Karagiannis, D., Lee, M., Hinkelmann, K., Utz, W. (eds.) Domain-Specific Conceptual Modeling, pp. 265–288. Springer, Cham (2022). https://doi.org/10.1007/978-3-030-93547-4_12
32. Ralyté, J., Koutsopoulos, G., Stirna, J.: Verification, validation, and evaluation of modeling methods: experiences and recommendations. Softw. Syst. Model. (2025). https://doi.org/10.1007/s10270-025-01304-2

Importance of Business Ownership in a Data Programme Implementation

Bohdan Haidabrus[1,2,4](✉) , Vitalii Ivanov[3] , and Kateryna Kolesnikova[4]

[1] Riga Technical University, Riga, Latvia
haidabrus@gmail.com
[2] Accenture Baltics, Riga, Latvia
[3] Sumy State University, Sumy, Ukraine
[4] International IT University, Almaty, Kazakhstan

Abstract. Business Owners play a critical role in large-scale data programmes, serving as key decision-makers who ensure strategic alignment, prioritize value delivery, and maintain business accountability across Agile Release Trains. This paper explores the significance of Business Ownership in complex data programmes, where cross-functional collaboration, regulatory constraints, and interdependent data products present unique delivery challenges. It examines how Business Owners influence incremental and iterative development, from shaping PI objectives and prioritizing features to resolving blockers, coordinating dependencies, and validating value through system demos and Inspect & Adapt events. Drawing on a real-world case study within a leading fund and corporate services financial institution, this paper presents a practical implementation of Business Ownership in a large-scale data programme. It highlights how Business Owners were structured across business areas, integrated into delivery workflows, and empowered to drive scope, release planning, and risk-based decision-making. The findings underscore the importance of embedding Business Owners not only at the strategic layer but also in day-to-day agile execution to support adaptive planning and ensure business value realization. This study contributes to the growing body of knowledge on Lean-Agile governance in enterprise data initiatives, emphasizing Business Ownership as a cornerstone of sustainable and value-driven agility at scale.

Keywords: SAFe · Gen AI · Agile · Data Programme

1 Introduction

As organizations increasingly pursue data-driven strategies, large-scale data programmes have emerged as critical enablers of business agility and innovation. These initiatives often span multiple teams, systems, and domains—demanding structured coordination and alignment between business strategy and technical execution [4, 5]. The Scaled Agile Framework (SAFe) has become a widely adopted approach to manage such complexity, offering a robust structure for synchronizing work across Agile Release Trains (ARTs) while ensuring delivery of business value [27].

© The Author(s), under exclusive license to Springer Nature Switzerland AG 2026
R. Deneckère et al. (Eds.): BIR 2025, LNBIP 562, pp. 159–171, 2026.
https://doi.org/10.1007/978-3-032-04375-7_10

Within SAFe, several key roles collaborate to ensure the success of a programme, such as: Release Train Engineer, System Architect, Product Management, System Team and Business Owners (Fig. 1). Product Management guides the vision and roadmap, System Architects provide the technical direction, and Release Train Engineers (RTEs) facilitate execution and flow. However, among these, the role of Business Owners (BOs) remains uniquely vital yet often underutilized—especially in data programmes where strategic alignment is both essential and challenging.

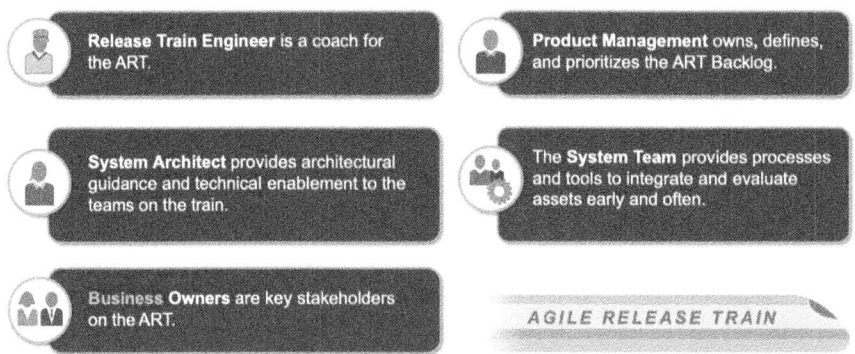

Fig. 1. Key roles on the ART.

BOs are accountable for maximizing the return on investment (ROI) by actively steering priorities, participating in critical ceremonies such as PI Planning and Inspect & Adapt, and evaluating value delivery [7]. In data programmes, they play a crucial role in clarifying ownership of data domains, resolving cross-functional dependencies, and ensuring that development efforts support broader business objectives. Their consistent engagement not only enhances governance and transparency but also reinforces a culture of shared accountability across the enterprise [26].

This paper explores the importance of Business Ownership in data programmes operating under SAFe, examining their interactions with other roles and their contribution to programme-level success. Through practical insights and case-based observations, we highlight the conditions under which BOs can effectively champion data initiatives and accelerate business value realization [24, 25].

Despite SAFe's emphasis on BOs as key stakeholders, their role is often treated as symbolic or limited to periodic involvement rather than continuous engagement. In practice, many data programmes fail to operationalize Business Ownership effectively due to organizational silos, lack of clear accountability, or insufficient Agile maturity. Data-specific challenges—such as regulatory compliance, opaque data lineage, and the distributed nature of data ownership—further complicate BOs' ability to steer and validate outcomes meaningfully. Moreover, existing SAFe literature tends to underrepresent how BOs operate within data-centric environments, where value is intangible, cumulative, and often only realized long after delivery. This gap creates a risk that BOs become disconnected from execution, undermining both alignment and value realization. Therefore, a more nuanced understanding is needed—one that critically examines not just the intended responsibilities of BOs but the actual constraints and enablers shaping their influence in data programmes.

2 Literature Review

Large-scale data programmes operate at the intersection of business strategy, technological capability, and organizational change. As organizations shift toward data-centric operations, effective governance, leadership, and role clarity become essential for delivering sustainable value [1]. The Scaled Agile Framework (SAFe), one of the most widely adopted approaches for scaling Agile practices, provides structured guidance on how to coordinate multiple Agile teams and roles across portfolios, programs, and teams [6]. Within SAFe, the roles of Product Management, System Architects, Release Train Engineers, and particularly BOs are foundational to strategic alignment and value delivery [17].

2.1 Value Definition and Delivery in Agile Programmes

The role of BOs in SAFe is defined as a small group of key stakeholders who are accountable for business outcomes and who participate actively in events such as Program Increment (PI) Planning and Inspect and Adapt workshops [17]. Despite this formal definition, academic literature on the practical and strategic functions of Business Owners remains scarce. While product-centric roles such as Product Owners have received considerable attention in Agile literature [2], BOs have been relatively under-researched, particularly in the context of data programmes, where business alignment is often complicated by fragmented data ownership, regulatory challenges, and unclear value attribution [3].

2.2 Data Ownership and Governance

Studies in data governance emphasize that business ownership of data assets is critical for ensuring data quality, compliance, and usability [1]. However, there is a persistent disconnect between technical execution and business strategy in large-scale data initiatives, often stemming from insufficient or unclear business leadership [6]. The importance of cross-role collaboration—between BOs, Product Managers, Architects, and Agile teams—has been recognized as essential for enterprise agility [20], yet few empirical studies focus on how these dynamics unfold in data-heavy environments.

Recent research suggests that aligning data programmes with business objectives requires more than product-level ownership; it requires executive-level engagement and continuous participation from those who understand the strategic imperatives and constraints of the business [9]. The BO role, when executed effectively, bridges the gap between data governance and product delivery, supporting decisions around prioritization, risk mitigation, and business value realization. Nevertheless, the current literature lacks detailed case-based insights into the BO role within Agile data programmes—an area this study aims to address. By bridging literature on agile governance, data management, and scaled delivery, the study seeks to offer both conceptual clarity and practical insights into how business ownership can be leveraged to maximize value from enterprise data initiatives.

2.3 Strategic Alignment and Portfolio Governance

The role of business stakeholders in ensuring alignment between IT initiatives and corporate strategy is well-established [12].

In SAFe, BOs are accountable for connecting the program backlog with business outcomes [6, 23]. In fintech industry, BOs from senior leadership ensure data programmes align with fund administration and fiduciary responsibilities. They act as investment gatekeepers, guiding technology spend based on regulatory and client impact [10].

2.4 Regulatory and Risk Oversight

Business ownership is critical in risk management, especially in regulated sectors like finance [10, 11]. Agile methods must adapt to ensure compliance doesn't become an afterthought in iterative delivery [14, 22]. Compliance Leads or Legal stakeholders at fintech companies often act as BOs for features with legal implications (e.g., audit trails, KYC automation). Their early engagement in SAFe ceremonies ensures regulatory constraints are built into features—not patched later.

2.5 Cross-Functional Leadership and Transformation Sponsorship

Leadership is a cornerstone of successful Agile transformations, especially when roles are clearly defined and actively engaged [20]. BOs play a central role in enabling Lean Portfolio Management [17, 19]. Data programme sponsors (e.g., Heads of Digital or Directors of Business Change) embody this role by championing cross-functional initiatives like the Data Governance or Enablement. Their involvement is crucial in breaking silos between IT, compliance, and business teams.

3 Research Methodology

This study adopts a qualitative case study approach to explore the role and impact of Business Ownership within a Scaled Agile data programme. The objective is to examine how BOs operate within the Scaled Agile Framework (SAFe) in a regulated financial services environment, with a focus on cross-functional leadership, strategic alignment, and value realization. The research employs a qualitative, exploratory case study design to investigate the multifaceted role of Business Ownership in a data programme operating within a Scaled Agile Framework (SAFe) environment. This design choice is underpinned by the nature of the research question, which seeks to understand how and why BOs contribute to value delivery, strategic alignment, and cross-functional leadership in complex, regulated domains such as financial services. Drawing from the methodological principles [11], the case study approach was selected to allow for an in-depth, contextualized examination of organizational behaviors, decisions, and social interactions. It facilitates exploration of both formal structures—such as defined SAFe roles and events—and emergent phenomena, including informal leadership dynamics, decision-making cultures, and cross-domain collaboration practices.

The study focuses on a single embedded case within the company, wherein the data programme serves as the core unit of analysis, and multiple sub-units (e.g., specific Agile Release Trains, Business Owner roles, product domains) are examined to provide a rich, nuanced understanding of business ownership in practice. This design supports both vertical analysis (within each role or function) and horizontal analysis (across stakeholder groups and events), enabling comprehensive interpretation of how BOs contribute to programme-level agility [26].

Moreover, the research adopts an interpretivist epistemology, acknowledging that knowledge about agile roles and organizational change is socially constructed and best understood through the experiences and perceptions of those directly involved. This philosophical stance supports the use of qualitative techniques, such as interviews and observations, which are sensitive to context, language, and meaning-making processes. To strengthen construct validity, multiple sources of evidence were triangulated, including direct observation of SAFe events, internal programme documentation, and interviews with stakeholders holding various vantage points within the value stream. The single-case study is not intended to offer statistical generalizability but rather to generate analytical generalization—insights that can inform similar contexts or programmes, particularly those involving data transformation initiatives in regulatory-driven sectors.

This design aligns with prior studies on agile governance and enterprise agility [22], which have emphasized the importance of understanding organisational roles and behaviours in situ. It also responds to calls within the agile literature for more practice-based, context-sensitive research that explores the real-world application of frameworks such as SAFe beyond prescriptive theory.

4   Results and Discussion

In SAFe ways of working, the BOs play a pivotal role in ensuring that agile delivery efforts remain aligned with organizational strategy and customer value. These individuals bring essential business context and actively participate in decision-making, particularly in areas involving risk assessment and trade-off analysis. Their engagement ensures that products and features are not only technically sound but also meet strategic objectives and stakeholder expectations.

Identifying appropriate Business Owners begins with evaluating the current leadership landscape—a collaborative effort typically led by the Release Train Engineer, SAFe Program Consultants, and senior business or portfolio leaders. These stakeholders should ask questions such as:

- Who holds accountability for business performance?
- Who has the authority and insight to guide ART toward delivering optimal solutions?
- Who possesses the expertise to assess both present and future technical capabilities?
- Who can represent customer interests, assist with removing delivery barriers, and validate program increments from a business perspective? (Fig. 2).

Fig. 2. Business Owners responsibility areas

There is no universally fixed profile for BOs, but they typically include senior leaders such as line-of-business managers, enterprise architects, heads of product or operations, and occasionally external customers in bespoke solution contexts. It is generally advisable to begin with a compact, cross-functional group—often four to six individuals—who bring both business and technical insights. As programme priorities evolve, so too may the composition of the BOs group to reflect shifting responsibilities and areas of focus.

In a Data Programme BOs responsibilities spans multiple layers of the agile delivery hierarchy, ensuring that what is built not only delivers customer value but also aligns with the broader goals of the enterprise. Figure 3 represents formalized BOs involvement across different layers, such as Business Areas, Programme/Product Management, Agile Teams.

4.1 Business Ownership Level in a Data Programme

Business Owners typically originate from diverse business areas such as operations, product management, client services, finance, or compliance. In large-scale transformation programmes—such as data platforms—this cross-functional representation is essential to aligning the work of ARTs with enterprise-wide objectives. BOs act as authoritative voices from their respective domains, enabling negotiation, alignment, and prioritization across competing functional interests.

By serving as strategic stakeholders on the ART, BOs ensure that their business areas' perspectives are represented during critical decision-making forums, including PI Planning, backlog prioritization, and Inspect & Adapt workshops. Their cross-domain visibility also enables the resolution of dependencies and systemic blockers that span organizational boundaries.

4.2 Programme and Product Management Level

During Program Increment (PI) Planning, BOs collaborate with Product Management, Release Train Engineers, and teams to define and refine PI objectives. They contribute by:

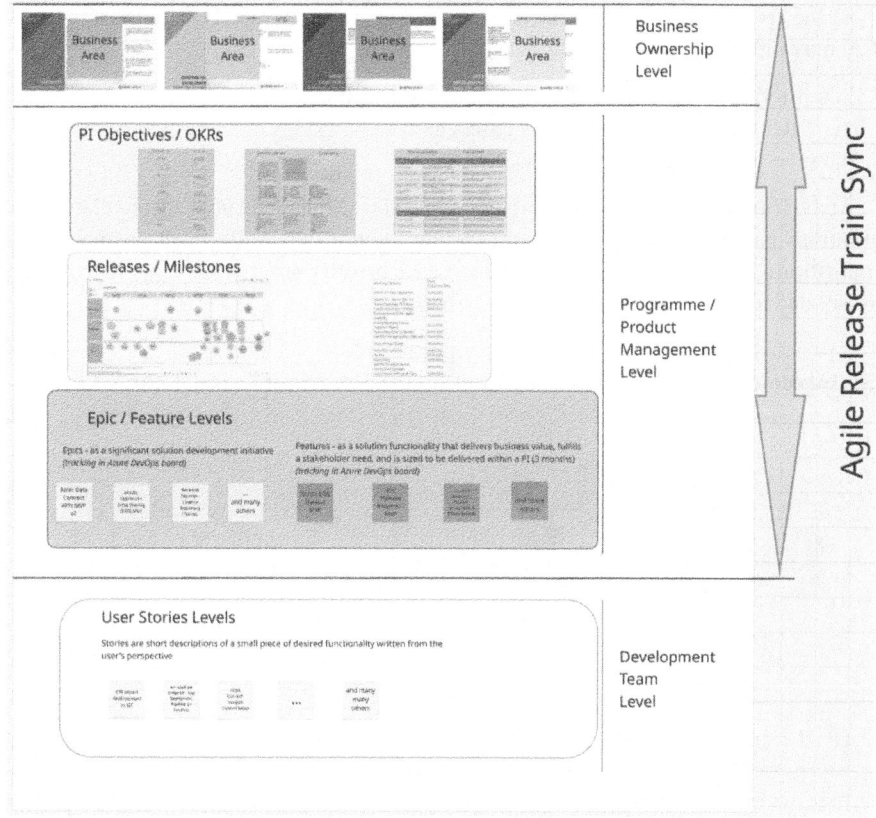

Fig. 3. Business Owners responsibility areas

- Providing business context for features under consideration.
- Clarifying value hypotheses and risk profiles.
- Ensuring objectives align with quarterly or programme-level strategies.

BOs are also responsible for assigning business value scores to team PI objectives, a key mechanism for driving prioritization and evaluating outcome alignment. This process ensures that delivery teams focus not merely on completing work, but on achieving outcomes that matter to the business. BOs play a role in shaping the release strategy by validating that feature groupings and release cadences reflect business priorities and external dependencies (e.g., client deadlines, regulatory milestones). Their presence helps align the system's release governance with delivery reality, especially when balancing compliance, technical readiness, and market timing.

At the epic level, BOs often act as Epic Owners or work closely with those who do. They may influence:

- Epic prioritization through participation in Portfolio Kanban,
- The articulation of Lean business cases, and
- The investment approval process.

At the feature level, BOs collaborate with Product Management to ensure that feature definitions include not only technical acceptance criteria but also clear business value propositions. Their insight ensures features serve broader programme objectives and are not isolated technical deliverables.

4.3   Incremental-Iterative Development on the Programme and Team's Level

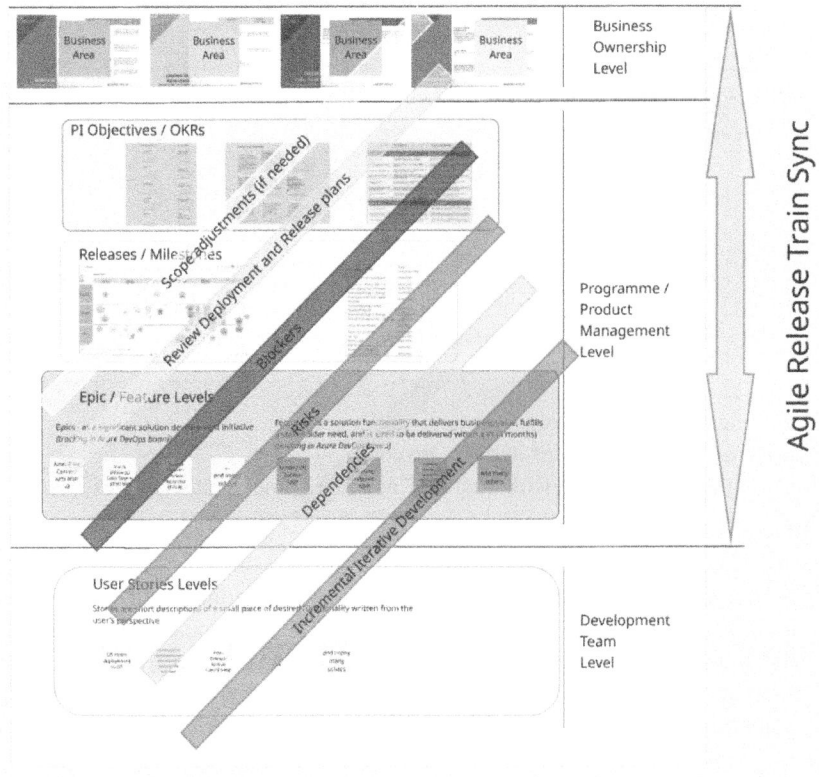

Fig. 4. Business Owners responsibility areas within incremental-iterative development

Incremental and iterative development is a cornerstone of agile delivery [16], enabling frequent value delivery, adaptation to change, and continuous learning. However, this approach is subject to a range of influencing factors that shape how effectively increments are planned, executed, and validated. In the context of a complex, cross-functional data programme, these factors become especially pronounced. Understanding them is critical for BOs and other stakeholders to navigate delivery uncertainty and ensure alignment with strategic goals (Fig. 4).

1. *Scope Adjustments and Re-Prioritization.* The iterative nature of agile development allows for scope to be continuously refined based on evolving business needs, user feedback, and technical insights [18]. However, frequent scope adjustments—while beneficial for agility—introduce variability in planning and resource allocation. Changes in regulatory requirements, stakeholder expectations, or technical feasibility may trigger mid-PI scope redefinition. BOs play a key role in negotiating trade-offs, ensuring that changes do not compromise overall value delivery or the program's strategic integrity.

2. *Review of Deployment and Release Plans.* Incremental delivery is often dependent on well-structured deployment and release strategies, especially in enterprise settings where multiple systems and environments must be synchronized (Fig. 5). BOs contribute by aligning business readiness with release timing, helping define go/no-go criteria, and ensuring that each release meets business value expectations. In data programmes, where dependencies across pipelines and environments are common, even minor release delays can cascade into significant delivery disruptions [29].

Fig. 5. Releases and Milestones plan after PI planning

3. *Blockers and Impediments.* Unresolved blockers—such as environment issues, missing data sources, unclear requirements, or organizational silos—can severely impact the flow of incremental development. Agile teams surface these blockers during daily stand-ups or PI execution, but BOs often have the authority or organizational influence to escalate and resolve systemic impediments. Their ability to engage with leadership, secure resources, or broker cross-departmental collaboration is vital to restoring flow and avoiding delivery stagnation.

4. *Risk Management.* Incremental development reduces delivery risk by enabling early validation and feedback. However, risks still persist and must be actively managed. Common risks include misalignment between features and business needs, scope

creep, inadequate testing, and data quality issues. BOs are instrumental in participating in risk-based prioritization (Fig. 6), shaping mitigation plans, and ensuring that risk tolerance [21] is aligned with business goals.

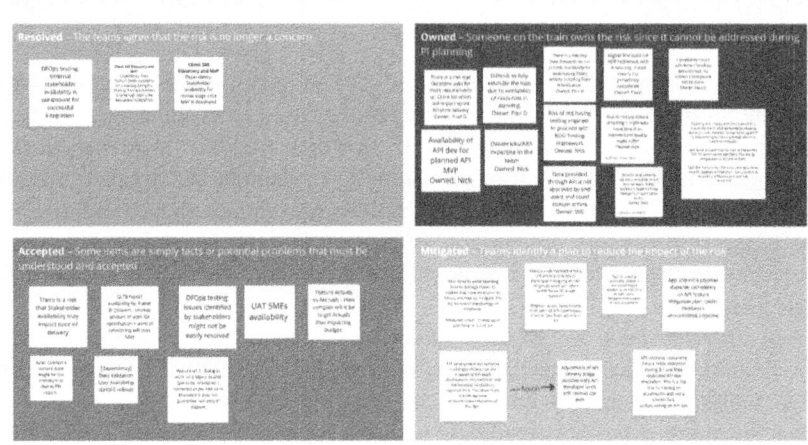

Fig. 6. Releases and Milestones plan after PI planning

5. *Cross-Team and Cross-Programme Dependencies.* In large-scale agile environments, especially data programmes, features and capabilities often span multiple teams and ARTs. Dependencies—whether technical, architectural, or organizational—must be identified and managed proactively. Failure to coordinate dependencies can lead to delays, rework, and quality issues [23]. BOs facilitate dependency resolution through ART syncs, coordination with external stakeholders, and participation in Solution Trains or Value Stream-level ceremonies.
6. *Technical and Business Feedback Loops.* The value of iterative development is maximized when feedback loops are short and actionable. These include: *System demos* (where increments are reviewed for functional and business acceptance and *Inspect & Adapt events* (where performance is retrospectively analyzed, Fig. 7). BOs participate in these feedback mechanisms to validate value, suggest course corrections, and help teams pivot when outcomes diverge from strategic goals.

The effectiveness of incremental and iterative development is not determined by process alone but by the surrounding ecosystem of scope governance, release coordination, risk awareness, and dependency management. Business Owners play a pivotal role in influencing these factors, not only through decision-making but also through their leadership in aligning business needs with delivery dynamics. Their active involvement ensures that each increment is not merely a technical output, but a validated step toward organizational value realization.

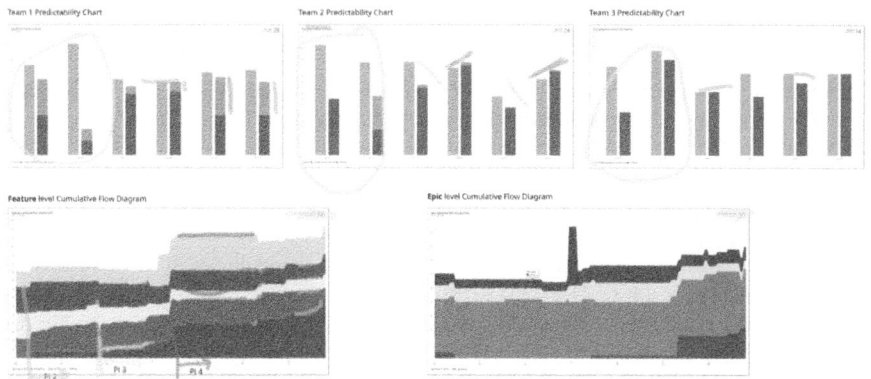

Fig. 7. Releases and Milestones plan after PI planning

5 Conclusion

The role of Business Owners within the SAFe is pivotal to ensuring strategic alignment, value realization, and operational cohesion in complex programme environments such as data platforms. Acting as accountable stakeholders and value stewards, BOs bridge the gap between business intent and agile execution. Their cross-functional representation across diverse business areas enables them to drive prioritization, resolve dependencies, and mitigate risks that span organizational boundaries.

Throughout the incremental and iterative delivery lifecycle, Business Owners influence critical activities—from shaping PI objectives and feature prioritization to validating system increments and refining product strategies. Their engagement fosters a culture of adaptive planning, continuous learning, and rapid feedback, ensuring that development efforts remain aligned with evolving business goals. Furthermore, they play a crucial role in managing scope adjustments, navigating delivery blockers, coordinating release plans, and ensuring that product increments meet both business and technical acceptance criteria.

This paper has examined these theoretical constructs in the context of a real-world application within a data programme at a leading fund and corporate services financial institution. It described how Business Ownership was structured and operationalized across business areas to support the delivery of data-driven capabilities. The implementation involved aligning Business Owners with strategic themes, empowering them to drive prioritization decisions, and embedding them throughout PI planning, system demos, and Inspect & Adapt events. Their involvement was essential for coordinating dependencies across teams, securing stakeholder engagement, and ensuring that each increment delivered measurable business value.

In data programmes, where complexity, compliance, and interdependencies are high, the active involvement of BOs is not optional—it is essential. Their sustained presence throughout planning and execution cycles enables the enterprise to deliver not just functioning solutions, but solutions that matter. As agile transformation deepens, investing in the clarity, empowerment, and integration of Business Owners will be key to scaling agility with purpose and measurable impact.

References

1. Wende, K.: A model for data governance—organising accountabilities for data quality management. In: 18th Australasian Conference on Information Systems (2007)
2. Zimmermann, A., Schmidt, R., Möhring, M., Sandkuhl, K.: Managing digital transformation through enterprise architecture. Bus. Inf. Syst. Eng. (2020)
3. Nguyen, D.: Success factors that influence agile software development project success. Am. Sci. Res. J. Eng. Technol. Sci. **17**(1), 172–222 (2016)
4. Mishra, D., Mishra, A., Ostrovska, S.: Impact of Agile methodologies in software development. J. Softw. Eng. **14**(3), 215–230 (2019)
5. Hasnain, M., Javed, M.Y., Akhtar, N.: Agile methodologies and their impact on big data analytics. Int. J. Data Sci. **7**(2), 112–128 (2022)
6. Leffingwell, D.: SAFe 5.0: The World's Leading Framework for Business Agility. Pearson, Boston (2021)
7. Denning, S.: The Age of Agile: How Smart Companies are Transforming the Way Work Gets Done. HarperBusiness, New York (2020)
8. Ertel, M.: DataOps: Implementing Agile Data Management. Springer, Berlin (2021)
9. Kersten, M.: Project to Product: How to Survive and Thrive in the Age of Digital Disruption. IT Revolution Press, Portland (2018)
10. Redman, T.C.: The impact of data governance on agile development. J. Data Manag. **11**(4), 88–102 (2018)
11. Hoelbeche, L.: Designing sustainably agile and resilient organizations. Syst. Res. Behav. Sci. **36**(5), 668–677 (2019). https://doi.org/10.1002/sres.2624
12. Jasiulewicz-Kaczmarek, M., Antosz, K., Zhang, C., Ivanov, V.: Industry 4.0 technologies for sustainable asset life cycle management. Sustainability **15**(7), 5833 (2023). https://doi.org/10.3390/su15075833
13. Gren, L., Torkar, R., Feldt, R.: The prospects of a quantitative measurement of agility: a validation study on an agile maturity model. J. Syst. Softw. **107**, 38–49 (2015). https://doi.org/10.1016/j.jss.2015.05.008
14. Conforto, E.C., Salum, F., Amaral, D.C., Da Silva, S.L., De Almeida, L.F.M.: Can agile project management be adopted by industries other than software development? Proj. Manag. J. **45**(3), 21–34 (2014). https://doi.org/10.1002/pmj.21410
15. Laney, D.: Infonomics: How to Monetize, Manage, and Measure Information as an Asset. Taylor & Francis, London (2018)
16. Schwaber, K., Sutherland, J.: The Scrum Guide (2020). Scrum.org, https://scrumguides.org. Accessed 31 Mar 2025
17. Scaled Agile Framework. https://framework.scaledagile.com/. Accessed 15 Feb 2025
18. Grabis, J., Haidabrus, B., Protsenko, S., Protsenko, I., Rovna, A.: Data science approach for it project management. Vide. Tehnologija. Resursi – Environ. Technol. Resour. **2**, 51–55 (2019). https://doi.org/10.17770/etr2019vol2.4163
19. Vedal, H., Stray, V., Berntzen, M., Moe, N.B.: Managing dependencies in large-scale agile. Lecture Notes in Business Information Processing, vol. 426, pp. 52–61 (2021). https://doi.org/10.1007/978-3-030-88583-0_6
20. Kniberg, H., Ivarsson, A.: Scaling agile in large organizations: lessons from spotify. In: Agile Conference 2019, pp. 20–34. IEEE Press, New York (2019)
21. Grabis, J., Minkevica, V., Haidabrus, B., Popovs, R.: Is team always right: producing risk aware effort estimates in agile development. In: International Conference on Business Informatics Research, Perspectives in Business Informatics Research, vol. 398, pp. 101–110 (2020). https://doi.org/10.1007/978-3-030-61140-8_7

22. Sato, K., Roberts, D., Johnson, P.: Overcoming challenges in Agile data projects. In: 12th International Conference on Data Science and Analytics, pp. 45–59. Elsevier, Amsterdam (2021)
23. Barton, D., Court, D.: Making advanced analytics work for you. Harv. Bus. Rev. **98**(3), 65–77 (2020)
24. Zhou, Y., Lin, H., Wang, J.: Technical debt in data-driven software systems. ACM Trans. Softw. Eng. **19**(5), 1–22 (2022)
25. Denysenko, Y., Ivanov, V., Luscinski, S., Zaloga, V.: An integrated approach for improving tool provisioning efficiency. Manag. Prod. Eng. Rev. **11**(4), 4–12 (2020). https://doi.org/10.24425/mper.2020.136115
26. CMMI Institute: Data Management Maturity (DMM) Model. Carnegie Mellon University, Pittsburgh (2014)
27. McKinsey & Company: The State of AI in 2021: The Data Leaders vs. the Data Laggers. https://www.mckinsey.com/capabilities/quantumblack/our-insights/global-survey-the-state-of-ai-in-2021. Accessed 31 Mar 2025
28. Ivanov, V., Vashchenko, S., Rong, Y.: Information support of the computer-aided fixture design system. In: CEUR Workshop Proceedings, vol. 1614, pp. 73–86 (2016)
29. Grabis, J., Haidabrus, B., Druzhinin, E., Kolesnikova, K.: Deployment and release management process in agile digital projects. In: Lecture Notes in Mechanical Engineering, pp. 124–136 (2024). https://doi.org/10.1007/978-3-031-61797-3_11

Modeling a Business Ecosystem from the Point of View of a Particular Participant

Ilia Bider[1,2](✉) ⓘ, Martin Henkel[1] ⓘ, and Erik Perjons[1] ⓘ

[1] Stockholm University, Borgarfjordsgatan 12, 164 55 Kista, Stockholm, Sweden
{ilia,martinh,perjons}@dsv.su.se
[2] University of Tartu, Ülikooli 18, 50090 Tartu, Estonia

Abstract. The scientific literature related to business ecosystems is growing. However, the major part of this literature is devoted to so-called Digital Business Ecosystems (DBE) that are largely related to only the networking part of the business ecosystems, i.e., exchange of values among their participants. Other parts related to the work of a participating enterprise, as well as its suppliers and regulators, are often left outside. In this work, we take a different approach, namely, to model an ecosystem that exists around a specific enterprise. The work is based on the concepts transferred to business from biological cybernetics, such as structural coupling and autopoiesis. In this work, the Fractal Enterprise Model (FEM) is used for modeling business ecosystems. The goal is to suggest some patterns expressed in the modeling language that can help an enterprise build a model of the ecosystem of which the enterprise is in focus.

Keywords: business ecosystems · modeling · structural coupling · autopoiesis · Fractal Enterprise Model · FEM

1 Introduction

The concept of business ecosystems was introduced by Moore; see, for example, [1]. This was done, at least partly, by transferring the concept of ecosystem from biology to business. According to [1], the ecosystem is built around a company's core business by adding elements that constitute the full environment in which the company operates. Though the concept of business ecosystem was introduced about 30 years ago, it became important for research in Information Systems (IS) relatively recently, when the IT platforms started to be considered as a backbone for so-called Digital Business Ecosystems (DBE) [2].

Most of the works related to business ecosystems, and DBE in particular, try to analyze and present ecosystems from an outside perspective by introducing different roles and investigating how the companies with these roles cooperate, e.g., using digital technology. However, this view may or may not correspond to the view of the company that participates in a DBE. The company may consider the DBE as one of the channels for getting orders (and, possibly, customers), which may not be the most important one.

© The Author(s), under exclusive license to Springer Nature Switzerland AG 2026
R. Deneckère et al. (Eds.): BIR 2025, LNBIP 562, pp. 172–182, 2026.
https://doi.org/10.1007/978-3-032-04375-7_11

For such a company or organization, it makes sense to consider the ecosystem in which it operates, as it may or may not coincide with the ecosystems of other DBE participants.

This difference in perspective means that a DBE in many research papers may capture only part of a company's broader business environment, as different actors define its boundaries based on their roles and objectives. For example, a company may engage in multiple ecosystems for procurement, innovation, or other purposes. As a result, what is labeled as a DBE in academic studies or strategic models often represents just a subset of the company's actual business landscape.

This paper has the practical goal of giving an organization a number of guidelines on **how to build a model of the ecosystem of which it is a part**. We achieve this goal by adopting a systems-theoretical perspective, viewing an organization as a system that operates within and constantly interacts with its environment. We will also use some essential concepts besides the concept of ecosystems, some of which were transferred from biology or biological cybernetics, such as structural coupling or autopoiesis.

The concept of *structural coupling*, which is related to ecosystems, was transferred from biological cybernetic [3] to social systems; see the works of Luhman [4, 5]. The idea of structural coupling is relatively simple; it suggests that a complex system adjusts its structure to the structure of the environment in which it operates, i.e., its ecosystem. The adjustment comes from the constant interaction between the system and its environment. Moreover, during the system evolution in the environment, some elements of the environment and interaction with them become more critical than others. The latter leads to the system adjusting to a limited number of environmental elements with which it becomes structurally coupled. According to Luhmann [5], a system deliberately limits its couplings to a few elements as a strategy for dealing with complexity.

An additional concept from biological cybernetics is *autopoiesis* [6]. Autopoiesis refers to a process within a system that continuously rebuilds and maintains itself by incorporating elements from its environment to ensure its ongoing function and stability. In biological systems, this means that living organisms constantly regenerate their components, such as cells and tissues, to sustain life. In organizational systems, this translates to processes that maintain the workforce, infrastructure, and resources necessary for operations. For example, an organization should substitute workers who leave, whether due to retirement or relocation. It should also substitute its equipment when it no longer satisfies production.

An organization's ecosystem includes various external actors that help replace its elements when they are lost or become unusable. Some of these replacements come from closely connected organizations with strong ties to the company, while others come from commodity vendors that provide easily replaceable supplies.

If the supply of materials to rebuild itself is limited, there can be competition for the resources. In such a case, competitors are part of the organization's ecosystem and must be represented in its model. Competition can be, for example, for customers or workers.

Lastly, any business operates under a system of laws, such as bookkeeping regulations. Unlike in nature, where rules are dictated by biological and physical laws, business laws are created by regulators, making them an integral part of the business ecosystem. Another key difference is that organizations, especially large ones, can influence these laws through lobbying, whereas in the natural world, living organisms cannot alter the fundamental laws of biology or physics.

As a result, the model of a business ecosystem around a given organization should represent markets, customers, vendors, and regulators, as well as relations between them, including relations to the organization itself. These relations should include the organization scanning the relevant part of the environment, which constitutes part of the so-called System 4 of the Viable System Model [7].

To build a model of the ecosystem in which a given organization operates, we need to use a modeling language. This language should have enough expressive power to represent ecosystem elements and relations. In this paper, we will use the Fractal Enterprise Model (FEM) [8, 9] for this purpose. There are two reasons for this. Firstly, FEM is our invention, and we have enough experience of using it for different purposes. Secondly, FEM has already been successfully used for finding structurally coupled elements of an organization. The results are published in [10], and they show that FEM can represent an essential part of an ecosystem that exists around a given organization.

FEM has a form of a directed graph with two types of nodes, *Processes,* and *Assets,* where the arrows (edges) from assets to processes show which assets are utilized by which processes and arrows from processes to assets show which processes help to have specific assets in "healthy" and working order. The arrows are labeled with meta-tags that show in what way a given asset is utilized, e.g., as *workforce, reputation, infrastructure,* etc., or in what way a given process helps to have the given assets "in order", for example, *acquire* new elements to fill an asset.

A FEM is built recursively by using a so-called unfolding procedure and two types of archetypes: process-assets archetypes that show which kind of assets might be needed for running a process, and an asset-processes archetype that shows which processes are required to maintain an asset in order. Unfolding starts with a primary process - the process that delivers value to a customer/beneficiary - by applying process-assets archetypes and alternating them with the asset-processes archetype.

The aim of this research is to create a set of patterns expressed in FEM that could be used for building a model of the ecosystem in which a given organization operates. The patterns are quite abstract, so they can be used for various organizations operating in various industries. Each pattern concerns a specific part of the business ecosystem, e.g., customers or suppliers. To connect the pattern to an enterprise, we need to represent not only the "external" elements – environment – but also some internal elements of the enterprise to which they are connected. Therefore, each pattern contains both external and related internal elements of an organization. As there is a limit on the length of the article, we present and discuss only one of the patterns here.

The rest of the paper is structured according to the following plan. In Sect. 2, we present our knowledge base used for creating a set of patterns. To this belong a set of concepts, like structural coupling, that were used in our research, and an introduction to FEM. We consider **this part essential**, as we do not anticipate that all readers are familiar with it. Section 3 presents one example of patterns from which one can create a model of an ecosystem in which a given organization operates. Section 4 is devoted to demonstrating how this pattern could be applied to create a model of an ecosystem. In Sect. 5, we discuss the results of our investigation and present plans for the future.

2 Knowledge Base

2.1 Structural Coupling

The concept of structural coupling comes from biological cybernetics, more specifically, from the works of Maturana and Varela; see, for instance, [6, 11]. When a system becomes structurally coupled to an element in its environment, that element—being a system itself—may also adapt its structure in response, creating a mutual interdependency between them. As a result of mutual interdependency, the structurally coupled systems change together, one changing itself as a reaction to changes in the other. The coupling might not be symmetrical, i.e., one system may dominate the other, making it more likely that the latter would change as a reaction to changes in the former.

The concept of structural coupling was adopted by other fields that use the systems theoretical approach. However, in the domain of organizational systems, which are socio-technical systems, the usage of the concept of structural coupling is not widely spread; see, however, [12]. In this work, we will consider the structural coupling between an *enterprise* and its *environment.*

2.2 Autopoiesis

According to Zeleny [13], there are three general types of processes in an autopoietic system: (1) Degradation, (2) Production, and (3) Bonding. Production is a process of creating new components. Bonding is a process of introducing new components into the system structure. Degradation is a natural process of components aging and falling out of the system structure, which requires the production of new components to be bound into the structure. The specific meaning of these generic processes depends on the system in question. In a post-review by Zeleny [14], there are several examples of the instantiation of the generic process.

2.3 Scanning the Environment – The Viable System Model

The Viable System Model (VSM) was developed by Stafford Beer [7] and his colleagues and followers [15, 16]. It represents an organization as a system functioning within its environment and consisting of two parts: *Operation* and *Management*. In its turn, *Operation* is split into several semi-autonomous operational units, denoted as *System 1*, that have some communication mechanism to ensure their coordination - *System 2*. Management, in turn, is split into three parts, denoted as *System 3*, *System 4*, and *System 5*. For the current paper, the most interesting part of VSM is *System 4*, which is responsible for *scanning the environment* to investigate *current trends and adjust the organization's offerings* to them.

2.4 Introduction to FEM and the IbisSoft Case

An example of a FEM diagram is represented in Fig. 1. This example is a partial model of the company called *IbisSoft*, which was co-started by the first author in 1989. The model reflects the company in its first years when it functioned as a distributor of the high-level software development tool called JAM from the US-based company called JYACC. The main business was selling JAM licenses and helping customers with software development projects that used JAM.

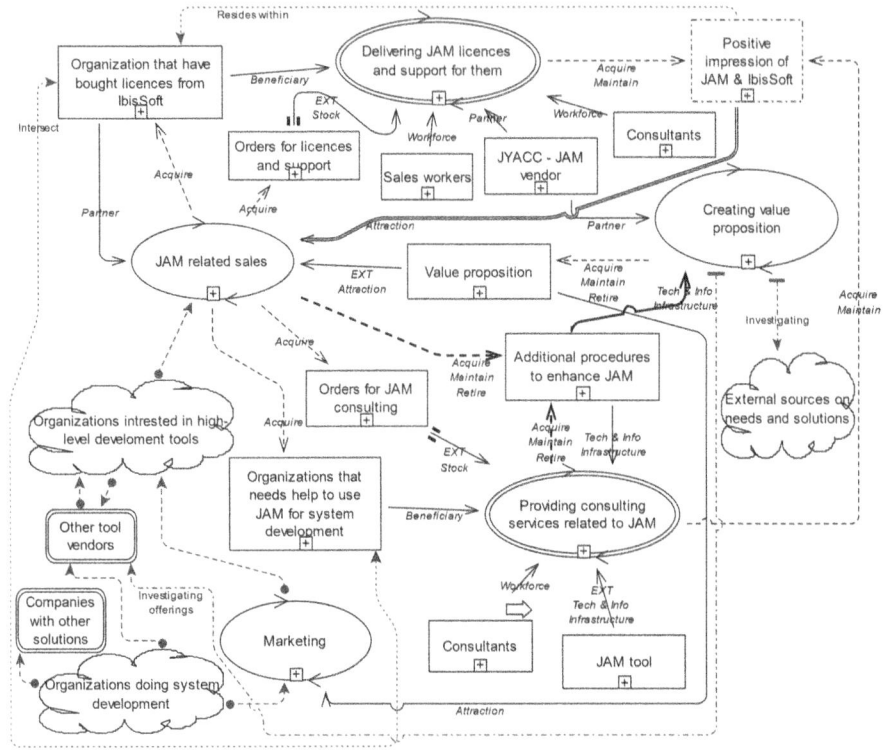

Fig. 1. An example of a FEM diagram

FEM has four concepts represented by shapes, two of which are used to present internal elements of the enterprise, and two are used to represent the environment. The shapes used for representing internal elements are *process* and *asset*, and there could be two types of relations between them: *used in* and *managed by*.

A process, depicted as an oval, represents a repetitive behavior (see Fig. 1). A process can be marked as a primary process – a behavior that produces some value for external stakeholders and for which the organization gets paid in one way or another. Such a process is visually represented with a double line border (see Fig. 1). An asset, depicted as a rectangle, represents a set of things that are engaged in the behavior and play a specific role in it, thus ensuring that the behavior continues to be repetitive (see Fig. 1). An asset can be marked as tacit – something that resides in the heads of people related to the given process. Such an asset is visually represented as having a dashed border (see Fig. 1). A process or an asset has a label attached to it that explains the kind of behavior that the process represents or the kind of elements the asset has. The labels are not standardized and are set by the modeler. Visually, the label is placed inside the shape that represents a process or asset.

A *used in* relation between a process and an asset means that the asset plays a certain role in the process. The relation is visually represented by an arrow with a solid line that goes from the asset to the process (see Fig. 1). A *managed by* relation between an asset and a process means that the process changes the set, i.e., adds or removes elements or changes their properties (see Fig. 1). The relation is visually represented by an arrow with a dashed line that goes from the process to the asset. To identify which role the asset plays in the process or how the process changes the asset, a label is added to the relation. The set of labels is standardized; more exactly, there are eight labels that can be added to a *used in* relation and three labels that can be added to a *managed by* relation. The latter are *Acquire*, *Maintain*, and *Retire*.

If a *used in* relation has a label *Stock*, the arrow's tail gets two additional vertical lines, see Fig. 1. This label means that for each process run, the run consumes one or several elements of the assets. Thus, this asset requires constant filling up. Label *EXT* (EXecutable template) means that the asset is a control element for the process, i.e., it has some instructions on completing the process runs. Other labels are self-explanatory.

A straightforward way of building a FEM that represents the internal structure of an organization is to start from a primary process, find all assets engaged in it, find processes that manage these assets, and repeat the search for assets for the management processes. Thus, building the model can be viewed as alternatively applying two types of archetypes (or patterns): a process-assets archetype and an asset-processes archetype [9]. In the end, we will get a recursively built graph that represents the operational activities of the organization in question.

The two concepts that are introduced to represent the environments are:

- External pool – a set of the same type of elements as in assets, which is represented by a cloud shape, see Fig. 1. The label inside the external pool describes its content.
- External actor, which is represented by a rectangle with rounded corners. An external actor is an agent, like a company or person, acting outside the boundary of the organization in question. It can be a competitor or collaborator. The label inside the external actor describes its nature. If the shape represents a set of external actors, the box has a double line, see Fig. 1.

To connect environmental concepts to other elements of a model, a new relation *drawing/adding* has been introduced. It can connect a process to a pool, an external actor to a pool, or connect two pools. The visual representation is an arrow with a dashed blue line and a rounded tail; see Fig. 1. If the arrow points to a pool, the arrow tail shows who adds elements to the pool. In the opposite direction, it shows who draws elements from the pool to convert them to their assets. The labels on these relations are not standardized; a modeler can set any text to explain what it represents.

Besides the *drawing/adding* relation, advanced FEM introduces two other relations: *Inspects/Monitors* and *Association*, see Fig. 1. The first relation connects a process with any other elements of the model, i.e., process, asset, pool, or external actor. In this case, the process exhibits an observing (*scanning*) behavior, i.e., gathering information from the observed with no or minimum intervention with it. Visually, this relation is represented by an arrow with a dash-dotted blue line and a small rectangular tail. The tail points to the observing process, and the arrow points to what it observes. A label in the form of free text can be added to specify the nature of the relation.

The relation *Association* has no definite meaning; it is used whenever there is a need to express something that is impossible to express with other relations. Visually, it is represented by an arrow with a blue dotted line. This relation can be symmetrical – an arrowhead on both ends or asymmetrical – an arrowhead only on one end. The meaning of the relation is explained using a free text label.

With this, we are finishing our short introduction to FEM; some new elements, like double lines, will be introduced in the following sections when they are needed. The readers interested to know more about FEM are referred to [8, 9, 17].

2.5   Using FEM to Represent an Ecosystem

For a modeling technique to be adequate for our task, it should be able to represent the main concepts related to ecosystems briefly discussed in the previous subsections, namely *structural coupling* (Sect. 2.2), *autopoiesis* (Sect. 2.3), and *scanning of the environment* (Sect. 2.4).

Regarding *structural coupling*, let us consider the model of IbisSoft presented in Fig. 1. IbisSoft has a limited possibility to influence how the company JYACC developed the software development tool JAM. However, JAM, being a flexible tool, allowed the creation of a library of additional generic routines that could enhance JAM and could be reused in new development projects. These generic routines are represented in the model of Fig. 1 as the asset *Additional procedures to enhance JAM*. This asset is acquired in the processes *JAM related sales* and *Providing consulting services related to JAM*. These reusable routines (procedures) were used in the consulting process directly (Providing consulting services related to *JAM*) and in the sales process indirectly (see *Creating value proposition*). Creating and using these routines constitutes how IbisSoft adjusts its offering to meet customer needs. This was a way to *adjust* IbisSoft to the market demands, i.e., to its *environment*.

The marketing efforts of IbisSoft and other companies selling high-level development tools influenced how organizations perceived system development. As a result, some organizations stopped developing systems using low-level programming languages and became interested in using high-level development tools. This shift, driven by marketing, is shown in Fig. 1, where organizations move from the pool of *Organizations doing system development* to *Organizations interested in high-level development tools*. This is a shift in the opposite direction to the own adjustment, i.e., activities of IbisSoft and other vendors of high-level tools *changed the environment*.

Regarding *Autopoiesis*, IbisSoft needed to constantly increase its customer base, firstly, to expand the business, and secondly, to compensate for the customers that no longer use JAM (this process is not shown in Fig. 1). The process related to sales encompasses in Fig. 1 both production and bonding of customers based on the *pool Organizations interested in high-level development tools*.

Regarding *scanning of the environment*, in Fig. 1, the process of creating a value proposition is linked by the *Inspects/Monitors* relation to *Other tool vendors* (external agent) and to *External sources on needs and solutions* (external pool). These relations show that IbisSoft did scanning of the environment to formulate its value proposition.

IbisSoft gathers information both from its direct competitors and from broader industry trends. In the first place, scanning concerns direct competitors, and in the second place, it concerns literature on the trends in system development.

3   An Example of Patterns

This chapter presents one example of patterns for modeling an ecosystem using FEM. To make the patterns clearer, elements belonging to the organization have green borders (or thicker borders in black-and-white prints), and processes that scan the environment have a blue background. Some arrows in the models in this section have a double line, which indicates a transitive relation. A transitive relation means that an indirect connection exists through one or more intermediate steps. For example, if process A influences process B, and process B influences process C, then A has a transitive influence on C. When making the model more detailed, the double-line arrow should be replaced with the actual steps that connect the elements. Instead of using a shortcut, one should show the specific processes and assets that make the connection.

The pattern presented in Fig. 2 is related to acquiring and maintaining (keeping) the customer base. It applies to any process or service that offers something people are willing to pay for. In Fig. 2, this process or service is the starting point of the graph. The main process for acquiring and maintaining customers is Sales.

The main attraction to become a customer is the value proposition. It is created based on several sources, like an investigation of competitors' offerings, as well as literature (reports) on the demands, both of which are examples of *environment scanning*.

Scanning is not the only source for adjusting value proposition; other sources include the sales process and the main process that delivers value to the customers. These sources influence the value proposition indirectly and are represented as transitive relations. How these transitive relations are expanded depends on the specific enterprise. These sources help the enterprise adapt to customers' and market (via *scanning*) needs, which are parts of *its structural coupling*. Customers, in turn, are influenced by the enterprise because they use its products or services. As long as they see a unique value in these offerings, they remain connected to the enterprise. However, if they perceive the products or services as commodities, they are more likely to switch to another provider.

The value proposition serves as an *EXT* to the primary process but in a transitive way. When building a complete model, this relation should be substituted by a chain, for example, creating a product specification, which is used as an *EXT* to the primary process. The process of creating a specification can be connected to external sources of information related to the process, which will expand the connection of the enterprise with its environment via *environmental scanning*.

An enterprise can be structurally coupled in more degree to its customers if it serves only a few permanent customers (a case taken in [18]). Note that, depending on the business, customers might be considered as a part of the company. Then, the sales process is responsible for autopoiesis related to customers.

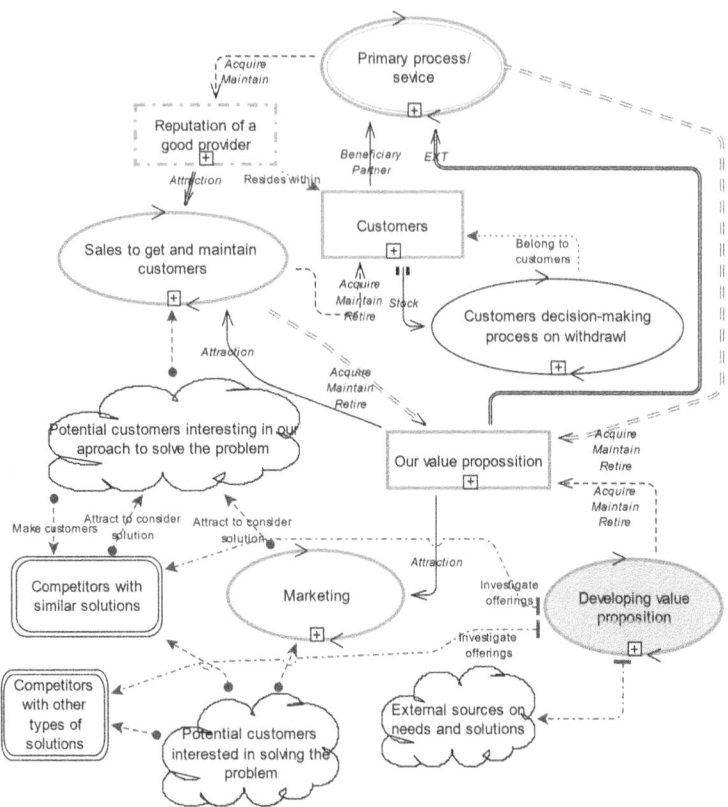

Fig. 2. Acquiring and maintaining customer base

4 An Example of Pattern Application

The model of Fig. 1 can be considered an application of the pattern in Fig. 2 to the activities of IbisSoft at the beginning of its existence. The model in Fig. 1 is a partial model of IbisSoft activities. It contains more components than in the pattern; for example, it has an asset that represents orders received from the customers. The labels inside the shapes are more concrete as they represent the actual activities of IbiSoft. Also, there are two primary processes in the IbisSoft model. Thus, the pattern from Fig. 2, applies to each of them. However, the sales process in Fig. 1 is common for the two primary processes.

The model in Fig. 1 also expands the transitive relations of Fig. 2. For example, the transitive relation that connects *Sales* to *Value proposition* in the pattern is realized by *Sales* is connected to *Additional procedures to enhance JAM*, and the latter is connected to *Create value proposition* by the *Tech & info infrastructure* relation. The relations that are included in the transitive link are highlighted by thicker arrows. In the same way, the transitive relation between the *Primary process* and the *Value proposition* in the pattern is realized by *Providing consultancy services* is connected to *Additional procedures to enhance JAM*, and the latter is connected to *Create value proposition* by the *Tech and info infrastructure* relation. Note that we have not expanded the transitive relation between *Positive impression* and *JAM-related sales* in Fig. 1, as this expansion is more complicated; see how it can be presented in [19].

Regarding structural couplings, IbisSoft was structurally coupled to the marketplace depicted in the model as *Organizations interested in high-level development tools*. This coupling means that all new customers were obtained from this pool. By the end of 1990, this pool almost disappeared in connection to moving to the Web, which was accompanied by programming using low-level programming languages. The market appeared once more, much later (about 10 years later), when Web applications became more complex, and they were too costly to develop without high-level tools. By the time the market disappeared, IbisSoft had changed its strategy and was uncoupled from this market, as seen in [20]. Another structural coupling of IbisSoft was to the partner, JYACC, as IbisSoft did not use or sell any other high-level development tool. This was explicitly revealed when JYACC had a problem moving its tool from the character-based environment to the graphical one. The first graphical version of the tool was of relatively poor quality, which negatively affected IbisSoft's business.

5   Conclusion and Plans for the Future

As mentioned, our goal is to help build a model of an ecosystem in which a particular enterprise participates. Such a model could be used for strategic decision-making. For example, consider that we have built and then analyzed the model related to the workforce. Suppose that the analysis has shown that the specialists that we have employed in a particular process are no longer prepared by any educational institution, and there is a high demand for them. The management needs to take some action in this situation. One alternative can be changing the process/service in which such specialists are employed, so that they need specialists who are easy to find in the labor market. Another alternative for a big enterprise is to create an educational department that prepares specialists or make an agreement with a local educational institution so that they can start such an educational program.

We are continuing our work to create patterns that help build a model of an ecosystem. We have presented one of the important patterns, but **due to the size limitation**, we cannot present other patterns, for example, related to employees, suppliers, or regulators. Also, we have not presented patterns related to a company being part of a DBE.

Our future activities include developing additional patterns and applying them to build an ecosystem of one of several enterprises. Another direction concerns the question of how to decide whether a certain element of a model represents a structural coupling rather than a commodity or commodity vendor. This can be formed as a set of questions for the stakeholders and rules for coloring the model according to the answers, e.g., using a red background color to identify structural couplings.

So far, we have found that FEM is adequate for creating the patterns. This does not exclude that a different modeling technique can be as good, or even better.

Acknowledgment. The work of the first author was partly supported by the Estonian Research Council (grant PRG1226).

References

1. Moore, J.: The Death of Competition. Leadership & Strategy in the Age of Business Ecosystems. HarperCollins (1996)
2. Nachira, F., Dini, P., Nicolai, A.: A network of digital business ecosystems for Europe: roots, processes and perspectives. In: Digital Business Ecosystems. European Commission, Bruxelles, pp. 1–20 (2007)
3. Maturana, H.: Autopoiesis, structural coupling & cognition. Cybern. Hum. Knowing **9**(3–4), 5–34 (2002)
4. Luhmann, N.: The autopoiesis of social systems. In: Geyer, F., van der Zouwen, J. (eds.) Sociocybernetic Paradoxes. Sage, London (1986)
5. Luhmann, N.: Introduction to Systems Theory. Polity Press (2013)
6. Maturana, H.R., Varela, F.J.: Autopoiesis and Congnition: The Realization of the Living, Reidel, Dordrecht. Holland (1980)
7. Beer, S.: The Heart of Enterprise. Wiley, Chichester (1979)
8. Bider, I., Perjons, E., Elias, M., Johannesson, P.: A fractal enterprise model and its application for business development. SoSyM **16**(3), 663–689 (2017)
9. Bider, I., Perjons, E., Klyukina, V.: Tool support for fractal enterprise modeling. In: Domain-Specific Conceptual Modeling, pp. 205–229. Springer, Cham (2022)
10. Bider, I., Perjons, E.: Identity management in an institution of higher education: a case study using structural coupling and fractal enterprise model. CSIMQ (27), 60–86 (2021)
11. Varela, F., Maturana, H.R., Uribe, R.: Autopoiesis: the organization of living systems, its characterization and a model. BioSystems **5**(4), 187–196 (1974)
12. Hoverstadt, P.: Defining identity by structural coupling in VSM practice. In: UK Systems Society, Oxford (2010)
13. Zeleny, M.: On social nature of autopoietic system. In: Boulding, K., Khalil, E. (eds.) Evolution, Order and Complexity, pp. 122–145. Taylor & Francis Group (1996)
14. Cadenas, H., Arnold, M.: The autopoiesis of social systems and its criticisms. Constructivist Foundations **10**(2) (2015)
15. Hoverstadt, P.: The viable system model. In: Systems Approaches to Managing Change: A Practical Guide, pp. 87–133. Springer, London (2010)
16. Espejo, R., Reyes, A.: Organizational Systems: Managing Complexity with the Viable System Model. Springer, Cham (2011)
17. Fractalmodel.org: Fractal Enterprise Model (2023). https://www.fractalmodel.org/
18. Hoverstadt, P.: The Fractal Organization: Creating Sustainable Oragnizations with the Viable System Model. Wiley, Hoboken (2008)
19. Bider, I., Perjons, E.: Discovery rules for depicting tacit knowledge usage and management in fractal enterprise models. In: Perspectives in Business Informatics Research, BIR 2024. LNBIP, vol. 529, pp. 209–224. Springer, Cham (2024)
20. Bider, I.: Structural coupling, strategy and fractal enterprise modeling. In: Research Challenges in Information Science, RCIS 2020. LNBIP, vol. 385, pp. 95–111. Springer, Cham (2020)

The Added Value of Data Science in Organizations – A Value Network Model Approach

Matthias Pohl[1]([⊠])(iD), Christian Haertel[2](iD), Daniel Staegemann[2](iD), and Klaus Turowski[2](iD)

[1] German Aerospace Center - Institute of Data Science, Jena, Germany
matthias.pohl@dlr.de
[2] Otto von Guericke University, Magdeburg, Germany
{christian.haertel,daniel.staegemann,klaus.turowski}@ovgu.de

Abstract. This paper investigates the complex dynamics of value creation through data science applications in manufacturing organizations, addressing the persistent challenge of quantifying and articulating the business value of data science initiatives. Through the application of a Value Network Model framework, this research examines how data science applications in Smart Manufacturing contexts contribute to organizational value creation, with a specific focus on the aerospace and aviation sectors. By analyzing various Smart Manufacturing use cases, the research demonstrates how value is exchanged and enhanced within complex intra-organizational networks. The findings provide insights into the strategic advantages of integrating data science into manufacturing practices and offer a methodology for examining value flows across business units. Future research directions include conducting comprehensive case studies across multiple Smart Manufacturing use cases and developing a more refined modeling concept to enhance the clarity of interdependencies and value exchanges.

Keywords: Value Creation · Value Network Model · Data Science · Aerospace Industry · Smart Manufacturing

1 Introduction

The effects and value creation associated with data science remain subjects of ongoing inquiry, underscoring the complexities involved in quantifying the advantages of such initiatives within organizations [1]. Data science experts frequently encounter challenges in establishing a compelling business case for data science in organizational contexts. While the costs related to personnel and infrastructure are readily apparent and can be easily quantified, the value generated by data science initiatives often lacks visibility and can be challenging to articulate. Numerous use cases for data science applications exist within organizational environments. In the manufacturing sector, it is commonplace to implement

© The Author(s), under exclusive license to Springer Nature Switzerland AG 2026
R. Deneckère et al. (Eds.): BIR 2025, LNBIP 562, pp. 183–198, 2026.
https://doi.org/10.1007/978-3-032-04375-7_12

solutions such as predictive maintenance, production schedule optimization, and demand forecasting as integral components of business processes. The influence of discrete data science applications, both at the organizational level and across various business units, presents a complex research challenge. Understanding these dynamics necessitates an examination of the interactions and interdependencies among different data-driven initiatives within the organizational ecosystem. Although the beneficial impact of a specific data science application in specialized domains (e.g., Supply Chain Management) upon another business unit (e.g., Production) appears conceptually compelling, empirical evidence to substantiate these claims is often limited. The investigation into value creation processes holds significant interest for both researchers and practitioners. The literature discusses various concepts and models pertaining to value creation. One of the most widely recognized frameworks is the value chain model [2], which categorizes value-adding activities into primary activities, such as procurement, production, sales, and customer service, and supporting activities, including human resources, technology, and facilities management. This model focuses on the transformation of inputs into outputs that deliver value to customers. Conversely, the value shop concept pertains to organizations that emphasize the provision of high-quality, customized services [3,4]. Unlike traditional manufacturing firms that adhere to a linear value chain approach, value shops operate based on specific customer requests, prioritizing the delivery of tailored solutions. An alternative framework, known as the value network model, considers both intra- and inter-organizational connections [3–6]. This model promotes collaboration among diverse stakeholders within the enterprise context, facilitating synergistic effects that can enhance overall value creation. By leveraging collaborative networks, organizations can uncover new opportunities for innovation and operational efficiency that extend beyond the scope of individual efforts.

Previous investigations into the complex structure of value realization in data science [7] led to the conceptualization of a Value Network Model [5]. The focus of this research is on the aerospace and aviation sectors, where the structural dynamics of manufacturing companies are carefully analyzed. In this study, an identified variety of pertinent use cases related to Smart Manufacturing, which illustrate the effective application of data science within the manufacturing industry, are taken into account [8]. By utilizing the Value Network Model, we aim to clarify how these Smart Manufacturing use cases are woven into organizational structures and contribute to overall value creation. This analysis not only emphasizes the transformative potential of data science in enhancing manufacturing operations but also highlights the strategic significance of value networks in optimizing organizational performance. In general, the study addresses the following research question: *How to apply a value creation network model approach to data science applications in manufacturing organizations?*

In the following, this paper provides an introduction to the essential concepts of the value network model, particularly focusing on its applications within Smart Manufacturing. Additionally, the paper will demonstrate this value network model through various Smart Manufacturing use cases, specifically designed to align with the typical business structures and operational frameworks found in aerospace industry companies. In conclusion, the paper will present a perspective on future research, underscoring the potential advancements in value network modeling.

2 Prerequisites

2.1 Value Creation Model

The value network model serves as a comprehensive framework that incorporates both intra- and inter-organizational connections. Widely recognized in scientific research, this model provides a systematic approach for identifying and analyzing value creation processes within network structures [5]. A significant feature of the value network model is the establishment of specific roles that act as central components within the network. These roles facilitate the exchange of value through both internal connections and broader external relationships among various organizations. By engaging in these exchanges, these roles enhance the overall value network, fostering a dynamic and interconnected system that prioritizes collaboration and mutual benefit among its participants.

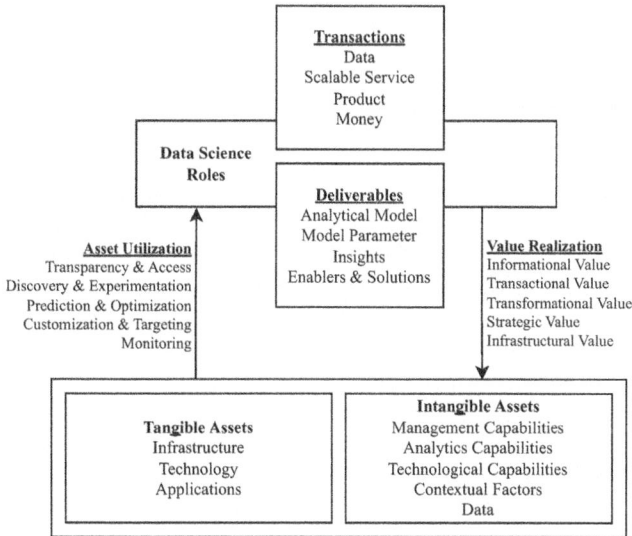

Fig. 1. Value Conversion Model of Data Science Roles according to [7]

In previous research, a structured literature review enabled the identification of typical role definitions within data science, specifically concerning their integration into a value network model [7]. The value creation process is defined as the utilization of both tangible and intangible organizational assets to generate transferable deliverables. Further value is achieved through the consumption of these transferred deliverables, which then translate into new assets. Tangible assets in this context include physical components such as IT infrastructure, technology, and software applications. In contrast, intangible assets manifest as data, along with essential analytical skills, effective technical handling, and a strong data-oriented culture, all of which are vital for utilization in data science roles. The deliverables produced from data science initiatives function as potential transaction forms with other stakeholders. These deliverables may include models, parameter sets, decision insights, and various proposed solutions. Conversely, transactions can take the shape of products, services, physical media, or monetary exchanges, representing different avenues for value transfer. The value derived from data science outputs can be classified into distinct categories. Informational value focuses on decision support and knowledge discovery, enabling organizations to make informed choices based on data insights. Transactional value centers on achieving business objectives, such as cost savings, revenue growth, and enhanced productivity. Moreover, general organizational benefits are categorized as transformational value, which includes the development of employee skills, increased customer loyalty, and improved market positioning. Lastly, infrastructural targets can be grouped into their own category, highlighting the foundational elements necessary for sustaining broader data-driven initiatives. An overview of the definition of a Data Science role according to the value conversion model is presented in Fig. 1.

2.2 Smart Manufacturing Use Cases

To effectively pinpoint an optimal starting point and leverage the potential benefits of data science initiatives, a comprehensive review of data analytics within the Smart Manufacturing context was conducted. The formulation of Smart Manufacturing use cases was crafted based on a structured literature review and organized according to the SCOR (Supply Chain Operations Reference) model [8]. This study provides an in-depth overview of the identified clusters of use cases, featuring detailed descriptions of each specific case, which highlight their relevance and importance within the Smart Manufacturing sector. Additionally, a clear articulation of the relationships between these use cases and overarching business objectives, along with the targeted aims of data analytics, ensures that each initiative is strategically aligned with operational efficiencies and data-driven decision-making. An overview of the elaborated use case groups in Smart Manufacturing is presented in Table 1.

The identification of use cases for value creation analysis will be addressed in subsequent phases of research. Among the typical use cases explored are demand forecasting (Supply Chain Planning), predictive maintenance (Maintenance Management), and the optimization of production schedules (Production Schedule & Control). Each of these applications holds significant promise for enhancing operational efficacy and contributing to overall profitability within contemporary manufacturing and service environments.

Table 1. Overview of Use Case Groups in Smart Manufacturing according to [8].

Production Phase	Use Case Group	Subgroup
Plan	Product Development	
	Requirement Analysis	
Source	Supply chain planning	Demand Planning
	Distribution Planning	
	Inventory Planning	
	Procurement	Purchase planning
		Master Production Scheduling
Make	Production Schedule & Control	Operations Management
		Machine Allocation Management
		Monitoring
	Energy Management	Resource Control
	Quality Management	Product Quality
		Process Quality
	Maintenance Management	Predictive Maintenance
	Internal Logistics	Warehouse Management
Deliver	Outbound Logistics	Distribution
		Transportation
	Customer Relationship Management	
	Customer Service Management	
Return	After-sales Management	Re-Manufacturing & Re-Cycle
		Spare-parts Management
		Technical Assistance
		Product Maintenance
Enable	Supply Chain Configuration	Factory Layout Management
		Supplier Management
		Material Flow Management
		Facility Management

2.3   Organizational Structure in Aerospace Industry Sector

In order to enhance our research framework, it is essential to establish the structural foundations of manufacturing organizations, as this is key to understanding the internal connections involved in the value conversion process. As a vital component of our preparatory work, we will conduct a thorough analysis of a business social network. In this investigation, we will gather and classify the various roles within companies operating in the *Aerospace Components Manufacturing* industry sector. This approach will allow us to identify and categorize typical functions and responsibilities found within these business units. For our analysis, we have selected a diverse sample of 14 companies, varying in size and geographic location, to ensure a comprehensive representation of the industry landscape (see Table 2).

The acquired dataset contains detailed information about the job positions of employees across the designated companies, providing a thorough insight into their organizational structures. The hierarchy within these organizations is primarily established through leadership and managerial roles, which define their

Table 2. Overview of Analyzed Companies in Aerospace Components Manufacturing.

Company	Size	Country	Location
I	1.001 to 5.000	DE	Bremen
II	10.001+	US	Arlington, VA
III	201 to 500	DE	Ottobrunn
IV	1.001 to 5.000	US	Hawthorne
V	10.001+	DE	Hamburg
VI	10.001+	FR	Toulouse
VII	10.001+	US	Cincinnati
VIII	10.001+	FR	Paris
IX	10.001+	CA	Dorval
X	10.001+	US	East Hartford
XI	10.001+	DE	München
XII	10.001+	US	Kent
XIII	1.001 to 5.000	VAE	Abu Dhabi
XIV	10.001+	UK	London

various functional business units. Additionally, employing named entity recognition enhances this analysis by pinpointing key roles and relationships within the data. When combined with data clustering techniques, this approach facilitates the identification of further business units.

The results of the organizational structure by the identified business units are presented in Table 3. These are divided into management processes, supporting processes, and core processes of a manufacturing company structure according to the value creation process [2]. In the analysis results, a full circle indicates a clearly identifiable leadership role within a specific business unit based on the data collected. In contrast, a half circle represents a grouping of similar positions that can be synthesized and categorized as a single business unit through clustering. In instances where a business unit cannot be assigned specific roles, an empty circle will be marked.

The achieved framework enables us to emphasize the internal organizational structure of a manufacturing enterprise, highlighting the applicability of Smart Manufacturing use cases across various units.

3   The Value Network Model Approach

The value network analysis is an advanced approach derived from established methodologies in scientific literature [5]. This analytical framework is divided into three distinct sub-analysis processes to comprehensively understand value creation and distribution within a network. In the following sections, we will outline the core concepts of this analysis and demonstrate its application through an in-depth examination of the value of data science applications.

Table 3. Overview of Management, Supporting, and Core Processes as Business Units in the Analyzed Companies.

Business Unit	Sub-Unit	I	II	III	IV	V	VI	VII	VIII	IX	X	XI	XII	XIII	XIV
Executive Management & Leadership		●	◐	◐	●	●	●	●		●	●	●	●	◐	●
Business Development & Strategy		●	●	◐	◐	●	●	◐		●	●	●	●	○	◐
	Product Management	○	◐	○	○	◐	○	○	●		●	◐	○	○	○
Legal & Compliance		○	○	●	◐	●	◐	◐		●	◐	◐	◐	●	●
	Contract Management	○	○	○	○	◐	○	◐	○		◐	◐	◐	○	○
	Export & Customs	○	○	◐	○	◐	◐	○	◐		○	◐	◐	○	◐
Program Management		●	◐	◐	○	◐	●	●		●	◐	●	●	●	●
	Aviation Program Management	○	○	◐	○	◐	◐	○	○		○	○	○	○	◐
	Space Program Management	●	○	○	○	◐	◐	○	○		○	○	○	○	○
	Dual-Use Program Management	○	○	○	○	◐	◐	○	○		○	○	○	○	●
Project Management		◐	◐	◐	◐	○	●	●		◐	◐	◐	◐	○	●
Marketing & Communications		●	◐	●	◐	◐	◐	◐	●		●	●	●	●	●
Finance		●	◐	◐	●	◐	●	◐		●	◐	●	◐	●	●
	Accounting	◐	◐	○	◐	◐	◐	◐	◐		◐	◐	●	○	○
	Controlling	◐	◐	◐	○	◐	◐	◐	◐		◐	◐	◐	○	◐
	Administration	◐	○	○	○	○	○	○	◐		◐	◐	◐	◐	◐
	Investors Relationship Management	○	◐	●	○	○	○	○	○		○	○	○	○	○
Human Resources		◐	●	◐	◐	●	●	●		●	●	●	●	●	◐
	Recruitment & Talent Acquisition	◐	◐	◐	◐	●	●	●	◐		◐	◐	◐	◐	◐
	HR Operations	◐	◐	◐	◐	●	◐	●	◐		◐	◐	●	◐	◐
	People Development	◐	○	◐	◐	●	◐	○	◐		○	◐	○	◐	●
	Employee Relationship Management	○	○	○	○	◐	○	○	○		◐	●	◐	○	○
IT & Digital Services		◐	◐	◐	◐	●	◐	●		◐	●	●	●	◐	◐
	Data Analytics & Business Intelligence	○	◐	○	◐	●	◐	◐	◐		◐	●	◐	○	◐
	Artificial Intelligence	○	◐	○	○	◐	◐	○	○		◐	○	○	○	○
Facility Management		○	○	◐	●	◐	●	○	○		○	◐	●	○	◐
Engineering / R&D		●	●	◐	◐	●	●	●		●	●	●	◐	◐	●
	Satellite Systems Engineering	◐	○	○	●	○	○	○	○		○	○	○	○	○
	Navigation System Engineering	○	○	◐	◐	○	○	○	○		○	○	◐	○	○
	Systems Engineering	○	○	○	◐	○	○	●	○		○	○	◐	○	●
	Aerospace Engineering	○	◐	◐	●	◐	◐	○	○		◐	○	○	○	○
	Launch System & Combustion Engineering	○	○	◐	○	◐	○	◐	○		○	○	○	○	●
	Electrical Engineering	◐	◐	◐	◐	○	◐	◐	◐		○	◐	◐	○	◐
	Avionics Engineering	◐	◐	◐	○	◐	◐	○	○		●	◐	◐	◐	○
	Mechanical & Structural Engineering	◐	◐	●	●	○	◐	○	◐		○	◐	●	○	●
	Propulsion & Thermal Engineering	◐	◐	●	○	◐	◐	○	○		◐	◐	●	○	◐
	Material & Process Engineering	◐	◐	◐	◐	●	◐	○	○		◐	◐	◐	○	◐
	Optical Engineering	●	○	○	○	○	◐	○	○		○	○	○	○	○
	Product Development	○	◐	◐	◐	◐	●	◐	◐		◐	◐	◐	○	○
	Scientific Research	●	◐	◐	○	◐	●	◐	◐		◐	◐	◐	○	◐
	Software Engineering	◐	◐	◐	●	◐	●	◐	●		○	◐	●	○	◐
Manufacturing & Production		◐	◐	◐	●	◐	○	●	●		●	●	◐	○	●
	Assembly, Integration & Testing	◐	◐	●	○	◐	○	◐	○		◐	○	○	○	●
	Quality Management	○	◐	◐	○	◐	○	◐	●		●	◐	◐	●	●
	Safety & Certification	○	○	◐	○	○	○	○	○		○	○	○	○	○
	Manufacturing Engineering	○	○	◐	○	○	○	○	○		○	○	◐	○	○
	Machining & Fabrication	○	○	◐	○	○	○	○	○		○	○	○	○	○
	Composite Manufacturing	○	○	◐	◐	○	○	○	○		○	○	○	○	○
	Welding	○	○	◐	◐	○	○	○	○		○	○	○	○	○
Supply-Chain & Procurement		●	●	◐	●	●	◐	●		●	●	●	●	●	◐
Mission Operations		○	○	◐	○	◐	○	○	○		●	●	◐	○	○
	Space Operations	●	○	○	◐	○	○	○	○		◐	●	○	○	○
	Flight Operations	◐	○	○	◐	○	○	○	○		●	◐	●	○	○
Maintenance & Operations		○	○	◐	◐	●	◐	◐		●	●	◐	●	●	◐
Customer Service		○	◐	○	◐	●	●	●		◐	●	◐	●	◐	◐
	Field Service	○	◐	◐	○	◐	○	◐	◐		◐	◐	◐	○	○
	Service Engineering	○	○	◐	○	◐	○	○	○		○	◐	○	○	◐
Sales		●	●	●	○	◐	●	◐	●		●	●	◐	○	●	◐

3.1   Value Creation Analysis

The identification of **roles** within the context of a value network is an essential foundational step for understanding how value is generated and exchanged. This process involves mapping out the various participants and their specific responsibilities, thereby clarifying how each contributes to the overall network. Subsequently, it is critical to identify the organizational **assets** that play a key part in the value creation process. These assets encompass both tangible resources, such as technology and infrastructure, and intangible elements, such as data and employee expertise. Additionally, establishing **effective methods** for leveraging these assets is vital for generating **deliverables** that can be exchanged for value. The activities involved in the value exchange process typically begin with one participant and culminate with another, creating **transactions** that characterize the operational framework of the exchange. Ultimately, the **realization of value** occurs when another party engages with the output generated by the value creation process. The thorough identification and analysis of these critical elements in the value creation process is collectively referred to as **value creation analysis**.

In the realm of value analysis for data science applications, previous research has already outlined the key roles of the various stakeholders involved in the data science ecosystem [7]. To understand the intricacies of value creation as described in this framework, it is crucial to further identify and define the roles of value exchange partners. This examination not only addresses external collaborations but also considers specific positions within internal organizational business units.

3.2   Impact Analysis

Impact analysis constitutes a methodological approach aimed at assessing the extent to which a designated role effectively converts received inputs into measurable value outcomes. This process involves a comprehensive evaluation of specific value inputs and their respective contributions to the overall benefits attributable to each role within the organizational framework. The primary objective of this analysis is to identify potential avenues for enhanced value realization, thereby enabling organizations to strategically optimize the utilization of their received resources. By systematically identifying these opportunities for value creation, organizations can improve overall performance, augment productivity, and achieve more favorable outcomes within each role, thereby contributing to organizational effectiveness and sustainability.

In the context of data science applications, it is imperative to undertake a comprehensive examination of the value realization pertaining to identified exchange partners (roles) that emerge from value creation analysis. This inquiry seeks to elucidate the effects of the outcomes generated by data science initiatives on these roles across diverse business units. By systematically assessing these interactions, organizations can gain a nuanced understanding of the broader implications of their data-driven strategies.

3.3   Exchange Analysis

Exchange analysis forms an examination of the overarching patterns and dynamics inherent in the processes of value exchange within complex systems. This analysis necessitates a systematic identification of the underlying logic and structured flow that dictate the generation, distribution, and eventual realization of value among various stakeholders. Additionally, it is imperative to assess whether the optimization of the system benefits all participants equitably or if specific roles or entities are disproportionately advantaged to the detriment of others.

In the context of value analysis for data science applications, it is crucial to closely examine the interconnections among valuable assets within the value network. These interconnections become apparent when realized value can be leveraged to generate additional value for other business units. By evaluating how these assets interact and exploring opportunities for value redistribution, organizations can uncover pathways for optimization and innovation.

4   Demonstration

In the following, we provide a detailed demonstration of the value network model approach as it applies to data science within manufacturing organizations. To illustrate this application, we have selected a series of use cases from Smart Manufacturing, each highlighting the practical implementation of data science in various manufacturing scenarios. Our focus will be on a specifically chosen use case that exemplifies the transformative potential of data science in enhancing manufacturing processes. In this analysis, we will identify and elaborate on the value creation assets linked to the use case, the methods utilized to leverage these assets, the anticipated deliverables, and the transactional relationships that play a role in the broader value creation framework. Following this examination, we will assess how different business units within the organization can realize value from the identified use case. Finally, through a careful analysis of the direct and indirect value realization, we aim to highlight a network of exchanges that underscores the interconnected benefits experienced by various stakeholders involved in the manufacturing process. This comprehensive approach will not only illustrate the value derived from data science initiatives but could also offer insights into fostering collaboration among different business units for optimized outcomes.

4.1   Value Creation Analysis

In the present analysis, we concentrate on demand forecasting as a pivotal component of *Demand Planning* and *Supply Chain Planning* (see Table 1). This use case is thoroughly documented in the academic literature, underscoring its critical role in enhancing operational efficiencies within supply chains. Demand forecasting employs sophisticated statistical methodologies and machine learning techniques to predict customer demand with elevated precision [9–16].

To enhance operational efficiency and strategic decision-making, a robust infrastructure is essential. This includes advanced data storage systems for secure, scalable information management and powerful computing resources for executing forecasting models. A reliable network infrastructure also enables seamless data sharing across the supply chain for timely information retrieval. In a technology-driven landscape, crucial tools include statistical analysis software to identify trends, machine learning platforms for predictive modeling, and big data processing tools that manage extensive datasets to extract valuable insights. Applications extend beyond data analysis to include specialized demand planning software for optimizing inventory and improving forecasting accuracy. Integrated ERP systems with forecasting modules offer a comprehensive view of operations, while business intelligence dashboards provide intuitive visualizations that support informed decision-making [14].

For this use case, several key components are vital for maximizing effectiveness, particularly in Analytics Capabilities. Statistical forecasting expertise is necessary for predicting future sales trends based on historical data, while data mining skills help uncover hidden patterns. Scenario planning abilities further enable teams to simulate future conditions and make informed decisions. Robust technological capabilities are also essential for executing value-generating transactions. This includes developing advanced algorithms for predictive analytics and deploying models effectively within business processes. Seamless integration of forecasting outputs with planning systems enhances organizational efficiency. Without data, the foundation for value creation is lacking. Organizations should leverage critical information such as historical sales data, promotional calendars, competitor insights, macroeconomic indicators, and market research data to better understand consumer preferences. Lastly, contextual factors and effective management capabilities are crucial for success [14, 16]. An overview of the tangible and intangible assets for the use case of demand forecasting are presented in Table 4.

In data science applications, creating an effective forecasting model is crucial, utilizing methods such as statistical analysis, machine learning, or causal modeling. It is important to define the types of deliverables produced throughout this process. These may include a comprehensive analytic model that reveals data patterns, specific model parameter sets for forecasting, actionable insights that enhance decision-making, and an integrated solution compatible with existing information systems [9, 13]. The transaction modality is largely influenced by the characteristics of the deliverable (see Table 5). Typically, this may appear as an additional data asset or as a comprehensive solution offered through a service or product [10]. The development of predictive models for demand forecasting represents a core function of data science. However, methods of asset utilization also extend to various business units, each contributing distinct insights. Different forms of value realization can be linked to both strategic and infrastructural business units. Strategic units focus on long-term value creation aligned with organizational goals, while infrastructural units optimize operational processes and maintain essential frameworks [12, 14] (see Table 6).

4.2   Value Network Analysis

Through an in-depth analysis of value creation metrics, particularly asset utilization and value realization (see Table 7), we can clarify the connections between various business units via the concept of value exchange. For instance, within the *Supply Chain & Procurement* unit, various forms of value can be identified through the optimization of material procurement. This is accomplished by integrating multiple data sources to enhance demand forecasting, which supports proactive Supplier Relationship Management driven by forecast-based purchasing needs. Additionally, logistics planning is refined through accurate volume and timing forecasts, ensuring efficient resource allocation that aligns with actual demand [12,14].

Table 4. Overview of the Tangible and Intangible Assets for Demand Forecasting.

Tangible Assets	
Infrastructure	Data storage systems
	Computing resources for running forecasting models
	Network infrastructure for data sharing across the supply chain
Technology	Statistical analysis software
	Machine learning platforms
	Big data processing tools
Applications	Specialized demand planning software
	ERP systems with forecasting modules
	Business intelligence dashboards for visualization
Intangible Assets	
Management Capabilities	Cross-functional collaboration skills
	Change management processes
	Performance measurement frameworks
Analytics Capabilities	Statistical forecasting expertise
	Data mining skills
	Scenario planning abilities
Technological Capabilities	Algorithm development
	Model deployment
	Integration of forecasting outputs with planning systems
Data	Historical sales data
	Promotional calendars
	Competitor information
	Macroeconomic indicators
	Market research
Contextual Factors	Industry seasonality patterns
	Market volatility understanding
	Supply chain network knowledge

In the *Manufacturing & Production* unit, a focus on Quality Management enables the realization of transactional value. This can be achieved through strategic quality resource allocation that addresses production needs influenced by precise demand forecasts. Moreover, inspection prioritization is guided by volume forecasts, enhancing the quality assurance process, while defect prevention strategies are specifically targeted at high-demand products, thereby reducing waste and improving customer satisfaction.

The *Sales* department is another pivotal area where value is generated. Here, both transactional and informational value can be realized through comprehensive sales planning that relies on accurate product demand forecasts. These forecasts also account for product characteristics and industry-specific attributes, further refining the planning process. Opportunity prioritization is informed by these demand forecasts, allowing sales teams to direct their efforts toward high-potential leads [10].

Table 5. Overview of the Deliverables and Transactions for Demand Forecasting.

Deliverables	
Analytical Models	Time-series forecasting models
	Machine learning algorithms for demand prediction
	Causal models incorporating external factors
Model Parameters	Seasonality indices
	Trend coefficients
	Promotional lift factors calibrated to your specific business context
Insights	Demand patterns
	Promotion effectiveness
	Demand drivers
	Anomaly detection
Enablers & Solutions	Automated forecasting pipelines
	Collaborative forecasting platforms
	Exception management tools
Transactions	
Data	Enriched demand data sets that can be shared with suppliers/partners
Scalable Service	Demand forecasting as a service for different business units or external partners
Product	Packaged forecasting solution with your organization's specific demand patterns encoded
Money	Cost savings from improved inventory management
	Increased revenue from better product availability

Table 6. Overview of the Asset Utilization and Value Realization for Demand Forecasting.

Asset Utilization	
Transparency & Access	Making historical demand data and forecasts available across the organization
Discovery & Experimentation	Testing different forecasting methods and parameters to improve accuracy
Prediction & Optimization	Developing predictive models for demand forecasting and optimizing inventory levels
Monitoring	Tracking forecast accuracy and implementing continuous improvement processes
Value Realization	
Informational Value	Better understanding of demand patterns and drivers across your product portfolio
Transactional Value	Reduced stockouts
	Lower safety stock requirements
	Improved order fulfillment
Transformational Value	Shift from reactive to proactive planning
	enabling more agile supply chain operations
Strategic Value	Enhanced ability to launch new products with more accurate demand estimates
Infrastructural Value	Foundation for advanced capabilities like automated replenishment or collaborative planning

By understanding and leveraging these interconnections, we can integrate business units through enhanced value creation and value exchange.

Table 7. Value Realization in related Business Units and Sub-Units (IF - Informational Value, TA - Transactional Value, TF - Transformational Value, S - Strategic Value, IS - Infrastructural Value).

Business Unit	Sub-Unit	IF	TA	TF	S	IS	Order
Executive Management & Leadership	–				●	●	Indirect
Business Development & Strategy	–			●	●		Indirect
Business Development & Strategy	Product Management	●			●		Direct
Program Management	–			●		●	Indirect
Project Management	–		●	●			Indirect
Marketing & Communications	–		●			●	Indirect
Finance	Controlling	●	●				Indirect
IT & Digital Services	Data Analytics & BI	●				●	Direct
IT & Digital Services	Artificial Intelligence			●		●	Direct
Engineering/R&D	Systems Engineering				●	●	Indirect
Manufacturing & Production	Quality Management		●				Direct
Supply-Chain & Procurement	–	●	●	●	●	●	Direct
Sales	–		●	●			Direct

4.3   Exchange Analysis

Based on our analysis of the value network, which illustrates the various forms of value realization and the distinctions between direct and indirect relationships (see Table 7), we can develop a comprehensive value exchange network. This network highlights the intricate interconnections between different business units through their value exchange dynamics.

In this illustration (see Fig. 2), the green arrows represent the flow of value originating from the data science business unit, which may be integrated within the IT department. Notably, the thick arrows denote direct value exchanges, indicating a clear and immediate transfer of benefits between units, while the thin arrows signify indirect value exchanges. These indirect exchanges correspond to various types of value and demonstrate how benefits can be realized even when the relationship is not immediately visible. This nuanced understanding of value exchange is essential for optimizing collaboration and ensuring that all units are aligned in their strategic objectives.

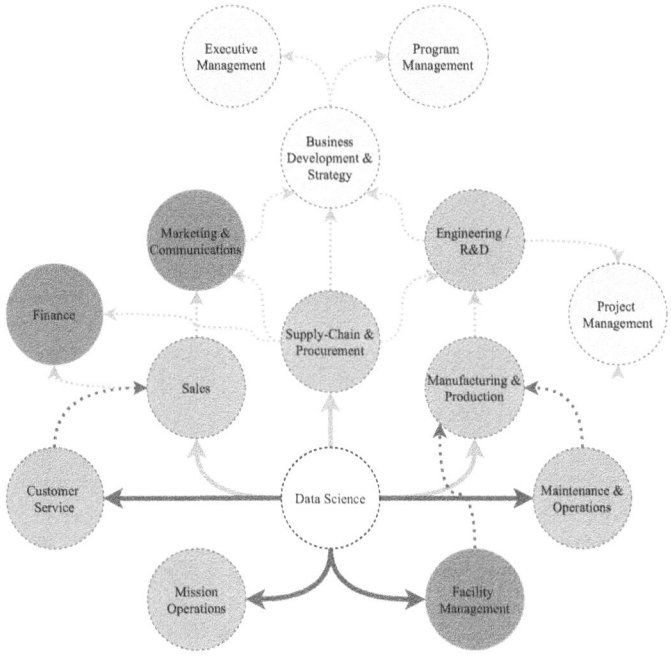

Fig. 2. Demonstration of Value Exchange Network

The green value flow emphasizes the connection between business units corresponding to the use case of demand forecasting. In parallel, we examined the predictive maintenance use case, illustrated by the blue value flow. This analysis highlights the incremental evaluation process, showing that a comprehensive value exchange network must account for multiple use cases to effectively harness data insights. Moreover, this approach illustrates the proactive involvement of various business units, whether through their contributions to data science initiatives or their broader role in value creation. By examining these interconnected use cases, organizations can refine their operational strategies, ultimately leading to improved performance and a stronger value proposition in the marketplace.

5   Conclusion

The paper presents an application of the value network model approach, focusing on the value analysis of data science applications within manufacturing organizations. This study emphasizes the significance of understanding how data science can foster value creation in a multifaceted industrial environment. To elucidate the organizational structure of manufacturing entities, we employed social network analysis. This method provides a solid framework for identifying key relationships and interactions among various stakeholders, forming the foundation for effectively mapping the value network within the organization. Additionally, we examined a range of data science use cases emerging from advancements in Smart Manufacturing. These examples serve as compelling demonstrations of how value can be generated and enhanced in this context. Through the application of the value network model, we illustrate how value is exchanged within the intricate inner-organizational network. This analysis offers valuable insights into the dynamics of value flow and collaboration among different business units, ultimately highlighting the strategic advantages of integrating data science into manufacturing practices.

In future, we intend to conduct a comprehensive case study that will encompass multiple use cases from the domain of Smart Manufacturing. Moreover, given that the modeling approach is semi-structured, we acknowledge the necessity of developing a more refined modeling concept. This concept will enhance the clarity of the interdependencies and value exchanges, thereby improving the applicability and effectiveness of the value network model in diverse scenarios.

References

1. Pohl, M., Staegemann, D.G., Turowski, K.: The performance benefit of data analytics applications. Procedia Comput. Sci. **201**, 679–683 (2022)
2. Porter, M.: Competitive advantage: creating and sustaining superior performance. Simon and Schuster (1998)
3. Thompson, J.: Organizations in Action: Social Science Bases of Administrative Theory. McGraw-Hill, New York (1967)
4. Stabell, C.B., Fjeldstad, D.: Configuring value for competitive advantage: on chains, shops, and networks. Strateg. Manag. J. **19**(5), 413–437 (1998)
5. Allee, V.: Value network analysis and value conversion of tangible and intangible assets. J. Intellect. Cap. **9**(1), 5–24 (2008)
6. Biem, A., Caswell, N.: A value network model for strategic analysis (2008)

7. Pohl, M., Haertel, C., Turowski, K.: Value creation from data science applications - a literature review. In: Hinkelmann, K., López-Pellicer, F.J., Polini, A. (eds.) Perspectives in Business Informatics Research, pp. 327–338. Springer, Cham (2023). https://doi.org/10.1007/978-3-031-43126-5_23

8. Pohl, M., Haertel, C., Staegemann, D., Turowski, K.: Categorization of data analytics projects in smart manufacturing. In: 2024 IEEE International Conference on Big Data (BigData), pp. 3153–3157 (2024)

9. Douaioui, K., Oucheikh, R., Benmoussa, O., Mabrouki, C.: Machine learning and deep learning models for demand forecasting in supply chain management: a critical review. Appl. Syst. Innov. **7**(5), 93 (2024)

10. Feizabadi, J.: Machine learning demand forecasting and supply chain performance. Int. J. Log. Res. Appl. **25**(2), 119–142 (2022)

11. Goel, L., et al.: Revealing the dynamics of demand forecasting in supply chain management: a holistic investigation. Cogent Eng. **11**(1), 2368104 (2024)

12. Hofmann, E., Rutschmann, E.: Big data analytics and demand forecasting in supply chains: a conceptual analysis. Int. J. Logist. Manag. **29**(2), 739–766 (2018)

13. Mediavilla, M.A., Dietrich, F., Palm, D.: Review and analysis of artificial intelligence methods for demand forecasting in supply chain management. Procedia CIRP **107**, 1126–1131 (2022)

14. Seyedan, M., Mafakheri, F.: Predictive big data analytics for supply chain demand forecasting: methods, applications, and research opportunities. J. Big Data **7**(1), 53 (2020)

15. Vandeput, N.: Data Science for Supply Chain Forecasting. De Gruyter (2021)

16. Walter, A., Ahsan, K., Rahman, S.: Application of artificial intelligence in demand planning for supply chains: a systematic literature review. Int. J. Logist. Manag. **36**(3), 672–719 (2025)

Process Mining and Digital Twin Perspectives

Discovering Object-Centric Causal Nets with Edge-Coarse-Graining in Process Mining

Ednira de Moura Figueiredo🆔 and Amin Jalali$^{(\boxtimes)}$🆔

Stockholm University, Stockholm, Sweden
edfi6431@student.su.se, aj@dsv.su.se

Abstract. Process mining enables organizations to discover, monitor, and improve processes using event data. Traditional process mining methods focus on one object type (a.k.a. case notion) when analyzing a process, such as 'orders' in the Order-to-Cash process. This narrow case notion selection can lead to incomplete insights and misleading results. Object-Centric Process Mining (OCPM) addresses this by analyzing the process from multiple object types perspectives, such as 'orders' and 'deliveries.' However, current OCPM algorithms often create complex models. These models are hard to comprehend for stakeholders as they are either not good at dealing with noise or lack the power to identify important workflow patterns like parallel and exclusive choices and merges. Thus, this paper introduces a new method to discover Object-centric Causal Nets (OCCN). This method builds on Causal nets, which show the causal links between activities. It supports object-centric analysis and handles concurrency and choices better. In this method, we merge redundant process flows using an edge-coarse-graining technique, which makes the models easier to interpret by removing unnecessary visual clutter. We implemented the method in Python. In a user study, we compared OCCN with Object-Centric Petri Nets, and the result shows that OCCN models are easier to understand and help users recognize patterns more effectively.

Keywords: Object-Centric Process Mining · Process Discovery · Causal Nets

1 Introduction

Process mining is an emerging research area that supports data-driven process analysis, enabling the discovery of process models from event logs. These models reveal the actual behavior of processes, which helps organizations detect problems, check compliance, and improve operations based on facts rather than assumptions [1].

Most existing process mining techniques analyze processes from a single-case perspective. They focus on the order of activities linked to one object type (e.g.,

© The Author(s), under exclusive license to Springer Nature Switzerland AG 2026
R. Deneckère et al. (Eds.): BIR 2025, LNBIP 562, pp. 201–218, 2026.
https://doi.org/10.1007/978-3-032-04375-7_13

an 'order') to discover the workflow. When multiple object types are involved, this approach can produce misleading or incorrect results. For instance, if an order includes several items, the activity "create order" may appear several times from the 'item' perspective, although it was performed only once. This issue is a known limitation in classical process mining methods due to projecting the data into one specific object type (a.k.a flattening) rather than recording relations between occurred events with all object types [2].

Object-Centric Process Mining (OCPM) was introduced to solve this problem. It considers all relevant object types for each event and avoids event log flattening. OCPM also captures object interaction over time, creating a more accurate yet complete event log. The introduction of the Object-Centric Event Log standard [3] has further supported this development. It defines how events, objects, and their relationships should be logged in a standard way.

Despite these advances, current object-centric discovery methods still produce complex models. These models are difficult for business stakeholders to understand [4], which contradicts the original goal of process mining, i.e., to help organizations gain clear insights into their processes. Examples of such methods include Object-Centric Petri Nets (OCPN) [5] and Object-Centric Directly-Follows Graphs (OC-DFG) [6].

To overcome these limitations, this paper contributes to the current body of knowledge by i) proposing a novel method for discovering Object-centric Causal Nets (OCCN), enabling process discovery with native support for concurrency, choice, and object-centric semantics, ii) applying an edge-coarse-graining technique for process model simplification, reducing redundancy and improving the interpretability of discovered models, iii) providing the tool support as a Python-based implementation to enable discovery of OCCN models, allowing reproducibility and adoption, and iv) conducting a comparative user study using the Technology Acceptance Model (TAM) [7], showing that OCCN models are perceived as significantly more intuitive and useful than existing Object-Centric Petri Nets. The results demonstrate that OCCN models are considered more intuitive, understandable, and better suited for pattern recognition tasks.

The remainder of this paper is organized as follows. Section 2 gives related work on Causal nets. Section 3 elaborates on the methodology. Section 4 defines how OCCN models can be discovered and visualized. Section 5 gives the result of the user study, and Sect. 6 discusses the limitations and future directions. Section 7 concludes the paper.

2   Background

This section provides a background on Causal nets (C-nets) [8], the foundation for defining our method to discover object-centric Causal nets.

C-nets were specifically designed for process discovery to overcome limitations inherent in traditional process modeling languages, such as internal inconsistencies and rigid execution semantics. Unlike languages that prescribe fixed execution paths, C-nets focus on capturing the causality between activities, resulting in models that are inherently more flexible and simple [8]. These characteristics make Causal nets particularly suitable for settings where processes are to be discovered directly from event data.

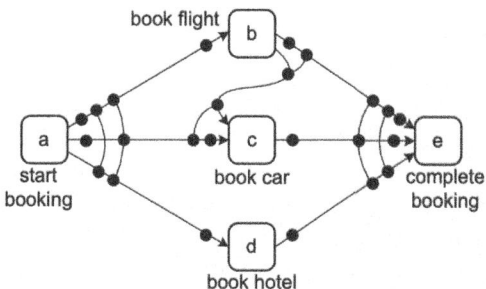

Fig. 1. A C-net model showing a trip booking process (taken from [8])

Figure 1 is an example of a C-net modeling a trip booking process [8]. The model consists of activities where the flow of the process is defined using arcs. On each arc, black dots appear before and after activities. A set of connected dots represents bindings associated with each activity. Bindings specify combinations of activities that either precede (input bindings) or succeed (output bindings) a given activity.

For instance, in the example, activity a has four possible output bindings: b, c, bd, and bcd. Notably, cd is not a valid output binding for a, indicating that booking a car and a hotel without booking a flight is not allowed. Bindings with more than one dot represent an AND-split (parallel execution), such as bd, while bindings with a single dot represent one possible outcome, such as b or c. The existence of multiple bindings expresses an XOR-split (exclusive choice) among these bindings—e.g., activity a can be followed by one of the available outgoing bindings.

Causal nets can also incorporate additional annotations, such as activity frequencies, binding frequencies, and dependency measures. Activity frequencies show the number of times an activity has occurred. Binding frequencies indicate how often a particular binding was followed. Dependency measures quantify the strength of causal relationships between activities and help filter out spurious correlations that are frequent but not causally significant [8,9].

Due to their simplicity and expressiveness, Causal nets are used both internally within discovery algorithms and as final representations to produce readable process models. They form the foundation of several widely-used process mining algorithms, including heuristics mining algorithms, the Genetic Miner, and the Fuzzy Miner [1,8]. Furthermore, Causal nets can be converted into other modeling notations, such as Petri nets, when needed, providing additional flexibility for analysis and system integration [8].

Given these properties, Causal nets provide a natural starting point for extending process discovery techniques to object-centric settings, where simplicity, flexibility, and the ability to represent concurrency and choice behavior are critical.

3 Method

In this study, we followed the Design Science Research (DSR) framework [10] with five activities, namely: explicate the problem, define requirements, design and develop the artifact, demonstrate the artifact, and evaluate the artifact.

In *Problem explication* and *Requirements Definition*, we conducted a document analysis through a literature review to identify research gaps and requirements. The literature review encompassed a document examination to unveil features of existing discovery algorithms and analyze their applicability in this study [5,9,11–16]. We also performed tool analysis to understand and define requirements from previously developed artifacts in the domain. The tool analysis helped us understand existing tools' capabilities and limitations.

In *Artifact Design and Development*, we designed and implemented the discovery and visualization algorithms iteratively, continuously evaluating design choices and refining the implementation. This approach produced both prescriptive knowledge (embedded in the artifact) and descriptive knowledge (rationales behind design decisions) [10]. The resulting artifact is an instantiation: a Python program developed to mine and visualize Object-centric Causal Nets (OCCN) models from an Object-centric event log (OCEL).

In *Artifact Demonstration*, we compared Object-Centric Petri Net models and the OCCN discovered by our algorithm. In *Artifact Evaluation*, we employed the Technology Acceptance Model (TAM) [7] to assess perceived usefulness and perceived ease of use. Also, we evaluated participants' ability to identify different workflow patterns in two given models. We also collected and analyzed qualitative feedback to showcase how users perceived the artifact.

4 Approach

4.1 Discovering Object-Centric Causal Nets

We define a method for discovering Object-Centric Causal Nets (OCCNs) in three steps: (1) discovering individual Causal nets for each object type using flattened logs, (2) merging and visually refining the nets to distinguish bindings and object types, and (3) aggregating redundant edges to enhance model clarity and interpretability.

1. Discovering Individual C-Nets: To discover an object-centric Causal net, we flatten the event log for each object type and apply the Causal net discovery algorithm separately to obtain one model per object type. Flattening means projecting an object-centric event log based on one object type and converting it to a traditional single-case notion log. This approach is similar to previous studies [5,6], which prioritize simplicity and reuse existing discovery techniques using flattened event logs.

For instance, object types could include 'orders', 'items', 'products', 'packages', and 'customers' in an order management process. A 'customer' object may 'place' multiple 'order' objects. By flattening the log per object type, we can apply heuristics discovery techniques to discover Causal nets for each type.

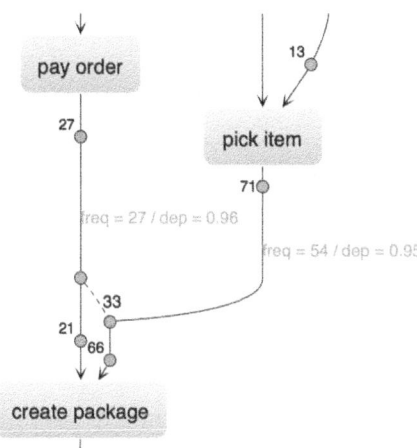

Fig. 2. An excerpt from a sample C-net illustrating both single and compound bindings identified during the initial discovery step of the algorithm.

The Causal net for each object type is heuristically mined by identifying bindings that represent AND, XOR, and OR splits and joins, using replay techniques described in [15] and the Flexible Heuristics Miner [13]. The C-net features two types of bindings: single bindings and compound bindings, as shown in Fig. 2, where single bindings capture XOR splits/joins, while compound bindings capture AND splits/joins.

For example, the input binding before "create package" with a frequency of 21 is a single binding, showing that this activity followed the "pay order" without the occurrence of "pick item" (an XOR join) in 21 cases. In contrast, another input binding with a frequency of 33 is a compound binding showing that "create package" was performed after both "pay order" and "pick item" had occurred (an AND-join).

2. Merging C-Nets and Refining the Model: To discover an Object-Centric C-net, we follow three steps, i.e., 1) merging all discovered C-nets for different object types, ii) distinguishing between input and output bindings using different graphical notions to enhance readability, and iii) using different colors to distinguish between different object types in the model.

First, our algorithm merges all discovered C-nets into a new model. However, the model can become very complex due to many bindings. Such a complex model can hinder the readability and understandability of the end models, so we followed two more steps after the first merge to simplify the model.

To distinguish between input and output bindings, our algorithm visualizes output bindings using circles and input bindings using diamonds. In Fig. 3, the activity "reorder item" has an input binding (diamond) connecting from "item out of stock," indicating that "item out of stock" precedes "reorder item." The output binding of "item out of stock" (circle) similarly shows that it is succeeded by "reorder item."

Fig. 3. An excerpt from the discovered C-net after applying modified visual encoding for input and output bindings in the second step of the algorithm.

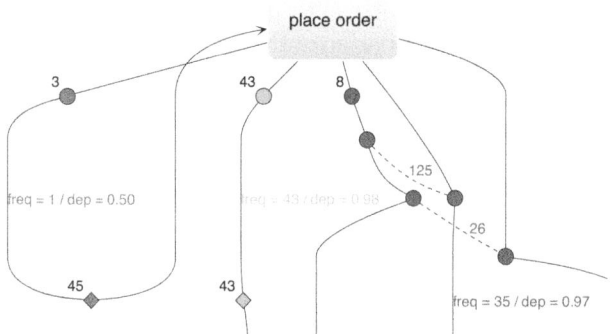

Fig. 4. An excerpt from a sample Object-Centric C-net illustrating the structure resulting from the second step of the discovery algorithm. (Color figure online)

To distinguish between different object types, our algorithm assigns different colors to bindings based on their corresponding object types. Figure 4 shows the single binding of object types 'customers' in red, 'orders' in yellow, and both single and compound bindings of 'items' in purple. Here, we can see two AND-split patterns (with frequencies of 125 and 26) for the 'items' object type after placing an order.

3. Aggregating Single Bindings: Current object-centric discovery algorithms generate complex models that are difficult to interpret for business stakeholders [4,17]. One reason for such difficulty is the number of redundant flows showing the same order between activities for different object types. One approach to simplifying such complex models is called Edge-Coarse-Graining, which is a subset of Coarse-Graining techniques used to simplify complex graphs [18,19]. In general, adjusting the granularity of the model for the target analysis can improve its capability to reveal more patterns [20–23].

Our algorithm followed the Edge-Coarse-Graining technique by merging edges with single bindings with the same source and target nodes. Thus, this approach can remove extra unnecessary edges. Figure 5 illustrates this type of morphism, called λ, where we can map edges with the same source and target nodes into the new edges, thus aggregating edges into a more coarse level edge (a.k.a. Edge-Coarse-Graining). In this figure, such a mapping shall define h_1 for e_1 and e_2 as well as defining h_2 for e_3 and e_4. This means that the $\lambda(e_1) = \lambda(e_2) = h_1$ and $\lambda(e_3) = \lambda(e_4) = h_2$. Aggregating edges can reduce the graph size while representing the flow of work.

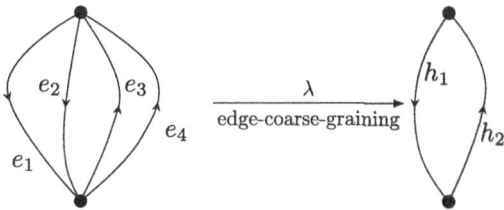

Fig. 5. Edge-coarse-graining technique to merge flows (adopted from [24])

Figures 6a and 6b show the edges between activities 'create package' and 'send package' before and after merging the edges, respectively. After merging edges, the algorithm defines an aggregated object type, recording the attributes of the merged edges. In this example, the frequency and dependency attributes for two merged edges are assigned to the newly mapped one, enabling users to investigate the underlying edges for each object type.

Finally, the algorithm enriches the model with statistical information like mean, median, minimum, and maximum occurrence of each activity for different object types. Instead of depicting this information in the model, we add it as a tooltip, which will be shown if a user hovers the mouse over the activity node. Thus, OCCN compromises information load and simplicity in a user-centered visualization approach. Simplicity enhances understandability and is a target feature in process mining models [1], especially in the object-centric approach [6]. Figure 7 shows the number of objects related to the activity 'place order' for each object type. Details of the approach are provided in [25].

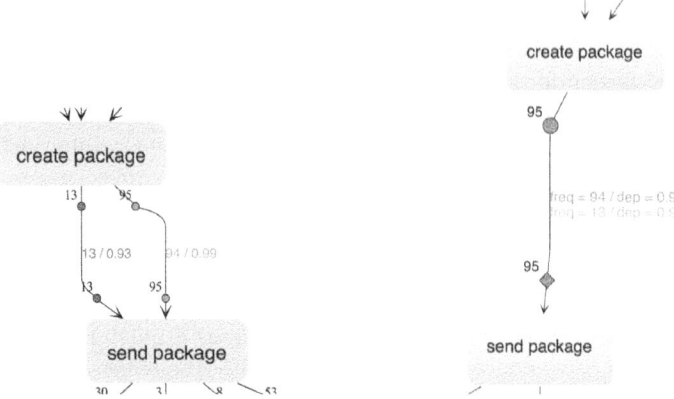

(a) An excerpt from the discovered C-net before applying the Edge-coarse-graining technique.

(b) An excerpt from the discovered C-net after applying the Edge-coarse-graining technique.

Fig. 6. Illustration of a discovered object-centric C-net before and after applying the Edge-coarse-graining technique.

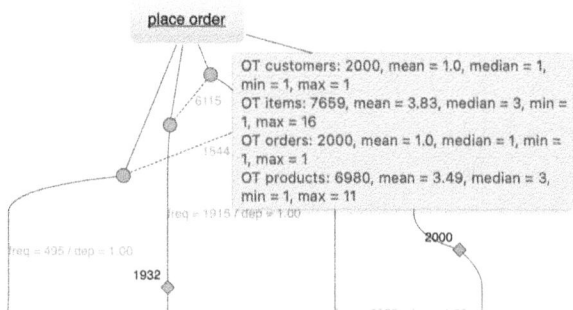

Fig. 7. An excerpt from the discovered C-net illustrating the use of tooltips to provide additional detail on demand.

4.2   Implementation

We implemented two algorithms in Python for the discovery and visualization of Object-Centric Causal Nets (OCCNs). The implementation, along with illustrative examples, is publicly available via GitHub[1]. The user interface is provided through a Jupyter Notebook environment, which facilitates guided interaction with the code. Users are only required to specify the path to the event log file; the selection of object types and dependency measures is optional and can be customized as needed. The discovered process model is rendered as an interactive SVG within a notebook cell, supporting user engagement through mouse-hover tooltips that display activity-related statistics. Accordingly, the intended user profile includes familiarity with Jupyter Notebooks, which offers usability advantages over command-line interfaces for exploratory and visual analysis.

---

[1] https://github.com/ednira/cnets_project.

5   Demonstration and Evaluation

There are currently two main approaches to object-centric process discovery: Object-Centric Petri Nets (OCPN) [5] and Object-Centric Directly-Follows Graphs (OC-DFG) [6]. OCPN can discover control-flow patterns such as parallel join/split or exclusion join/split. Therefore, we use OCPN as a baseline for comparison with our approach. This section first demonstrates how discovered OCPN process models and OCCN model (using our method) look side by side. Then, it presents the results of a user acceptance evaluation.

5.1   Demonstration

Figure 8 presents the OCPN model discovered using OC-PM (Fig. 8a), the OCPN model discovered using PM4Py (Fig. 8b), and the OCCN model discovered using our approach (Fig. 8c), all based on the same publicly available log file, Procurement-to-Pay OCEL 2.0 [26]. We intentionally provide a zoomed-out version of the models here, as it allows observing the general structure and flow of the process. As can be seen, the flow of work is recognizable in the model discovered using our approach, while it is very difficult in the one discovered using OC-PM. The model discovered using PM4Py is also difficult to follow due to many silent activities (the ones filled with color and without any activity names). For those interested in exploring the models in more detail, the full process models can be accessed in the GitHub repository and in [25].

The complexity of process models can be measured using different techniques that mainly consider the number of different control-flow elements within the model. As none of the metrics are adapted for object-centric process models, we counted the number of different elements and compared the total numbers, indicating estimates on the complexity of each discovered model. Table 1 shows the number of different types of visual elements, like object type, activity, arc, place, binding, and silent transition, for each model. As can be seen, OCCN models incorporate less number of total visual elements, indicating these models might be less complex for users to comprehend. We have evaluated how users perceived these models as follows.

5.2   Evaluation Design

We evaluated our method using both quantitative and qualitative approaches. The evaluation focused on two main aspects: (1) user comprehension, which was assessed through pattern recognition tasks, and (2) user acceptance, based on the Technology Acceptance Model (TAM) [7]. Additionally, open-ended feedback was collected to inform potential improvements.

Table 1. Number of visual elements exists in discovered object-centric process models.

	Object Types	Activities	Arcs	Places	Bindings	Silent Transitions	Total
OCPN (OC-PM)	7	10	104	37	0	30	188
OCPN (PM4PY)	7	10	78	16	0	17	128
OCCN (our approach)	7	10	20	0	40	0	77

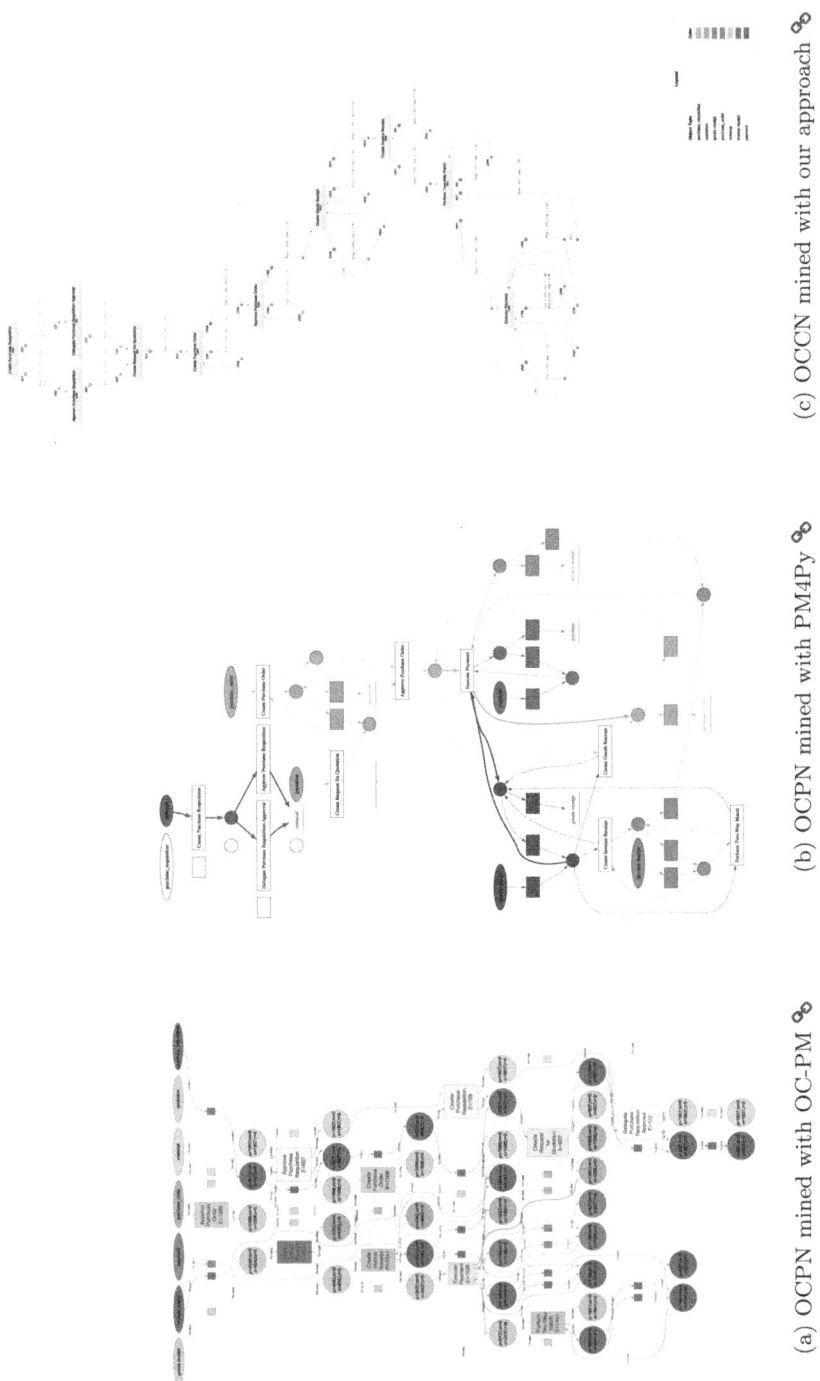

(a) OCPN mined with OC-PM   (b) OCPN mined with PM4Py   (c) OCCN mined with our approach

Fig. 8. Demonstrating OC-Petri nets and OCCN models discovered from Procurement-to-Pay OCEL 2.0 (contains colors – perception will be limited when converted to grayscale - full versions are available in provided GitHub links.)

We employed a comparative survey-based approach, where participants analyzed an OCCN model (discovered using our method) and an OCPN model (discovered using the OC-PM tool). Both models were based on the same log file, i.e., the Order Management Object-centric Event Log [27]. We selected this log file because many participants, regardless of their background, would likely have experience with online ordering, making the process familiar to them.

The participants were students from the Department of Computer Science at Stockholm University (DSV/SU). The questionnaire was designed to measure pattern recognition abilities, perceived usefulness (PU), and perceived ease of use (PEU) and to gather qualitative feedback. To minimize bias, participants were divided into two groups: one started with the OCCN model, and the other began with the OCPN model.

The questionnaire consisted of three sections:

– Pattern recognition task – Participants were asked to identify control flow patterns in the models through both open-ended and multiple-choice questions.
– Perceived usefulness (PU) and perceived ease of use (PEU) – These were measured for each model using the Technology Acceptance Model (TAM).
– Open-ended feedback – Participants were invited to reflect on the strengths and challenges of both models.

5.3 Pattern Recognition

Participants answered open-ended questions for the pattern recognition task, which helped us assess their understanding of the model after the first author explained the patterns with diagrams in the questionnaire. Respondents stated that this was the most challenging part of the questionnaire. The second set comprised multiple-choice questions showing parts of the model for pattern identification.

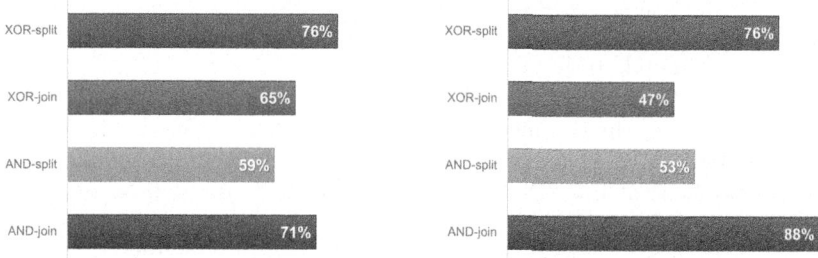

(a) Using Open-ended Questions   (b) Using Multiple-choice Questions

Fig. 9. The ratio of correctly identified workflow patterns using discovered OCCN model by participants

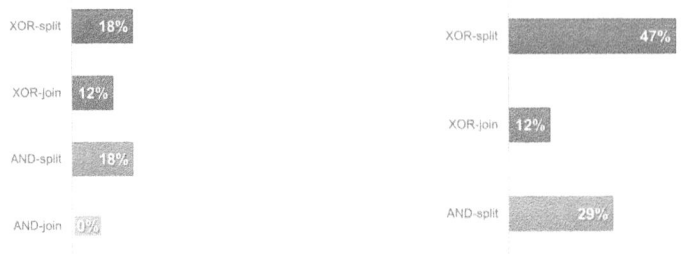

(a) Using Open-ended Questions   (b) Using Multiple-choice Questions

Fig. 10. The ratio of correctly identified workflow patterns using discovered OCPN model by participants

As shown in Fig. 9, most respondents correctly identified all four patterns in the OCCN model, and there is a balance between the results of both question types. 76% of the respondents correctly recognized XOR-split in the model, used in open-ended questions, and 88% correctly identified AND-join in multiple-choice questions about the model. Figure 10 shows the object-centric Petri net model results, where participants could not recognize the patterns satisfactorily.

5.4   User Acceptance

We used the Technology Acceptance Model [7] to evaluate the user acceptance, which is one widely used method in evaluating information systems artifacts in general and business process-related artifacts in particular [28–31]. We collected responses from 17 participants using a structured questionnaire. Among the participants, 70.59% were bachelor's students, while 29.41% were master's students. Regarding professional experience, 41.18% had at least two years of industry experience, and 23.53% had prior knowledge of process modeling languages. Additionally, participants were asked about their online shopping frequency, as the models examined in the study refer to an order management process. A large majority (94.12%) reported that they shop online, with 70.59% doing so approximately once per month.

Figure 11 displays the aggregated distribution of responses regarding participants' perceptions of the two modeling languages—OCCN (denoted as M1) and OCPN (denoted as M2). The results reveal that both Perceived Usefulness (PU) and Perceived Ease of Use (PEU) medians for OCCN are at least two points higher than those for OCPN. Specifically, the median PU and PEU scores for OCCN are 5.17 and 4.5, respectively, while both scores for OCPN are 2.5.

Figure 12 presents a more detailed comparison of these perceptions. The results indicate a clear preference for OCCN, with higher scores across both dimensions (PU and PEU). However, further analysis was conducted to assess whether these differences are statistically significant.

Normality testing was performed on the responses for PU in the OCCN group, which revealed that the data followed a normal distribution except for the Perceived Usefulness of OCCN. As a result, the non-parametric Mann–Whitney U test was employed to determine whether the perceived usefulness of OCCN and OCPN differed significantly. The test yielded a p-value of 0.00178, indicating a statistically significant difference in perceived usefulness between the two models.

To evaluate the Perceived Ease of Use, the independent samples t-test and the paired samples t-test were applied. Both tests resulted in a p-value of approximately 0.0001, confirming that the observed differences in perceived ease of use between the two models were statistically significant.

Cronbach's alpha was calculated to assess the internal consistency of the Perceived Usefulness (PU) and Perceived Ease of Use (PEU) constructs. As shown in Table 2, the values for both PU and PEU exceeded 0.9, which is considered excellent and well above the generally accepted threshold of 0.7.

Table 2. Cronbach's Alpha for PU and PEU of both models

Language	PU	PEU
OCCN	0.95	0.90
OCPN	0.94	0.92

5.5   User Feedback Evaluation Result

The last question asked for feedback about the used models. The feedback was analyzed by splitting it into sentences and finally reducing them to words that best summarize the feedback, keeping users' words as much as possible. The list of words was loaded into an online word cloud generator [32]. The word cloud visually demonstrates the users' sentiments about object-centric modeling languages. The size of each word indicates how frequently users mentioned it. They declared a poor understanding of the Object-centric Petri net model (OCPN) and deemed it cluttered and unintuitive. Conversely, the OCCN model was considered easy, understandable, clear, and intuitive. Figures 13a and 13b show users' sentiments visually.

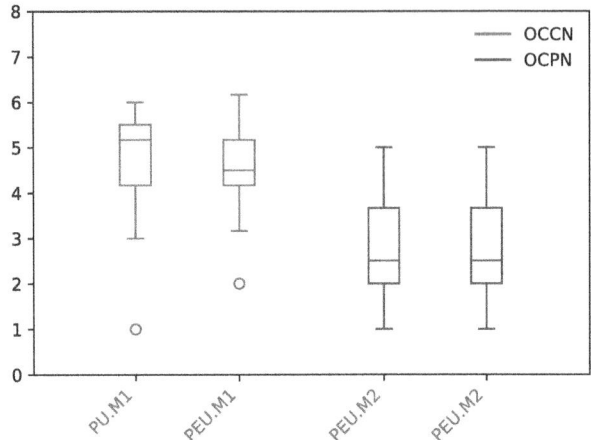

Fig. 11. Aggregated Perceived Usefulness (PU) and Aggregated Perceived Ease of Use (PEU) for OCPN and OCCN (contains colors – perception will be limited when printed/converted to grayscale)

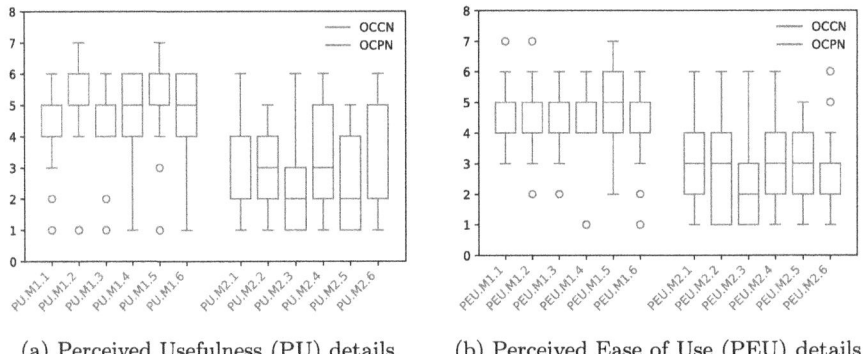

(a) Perceived Usefulness (PU) details   (b) Perceived Ease of Use (PEU) details

Fig. 12. Detailed comparison of PU and PEU between OCPN and OCCN models (contains colors – perception will be limited when printed/converted to grayscale)

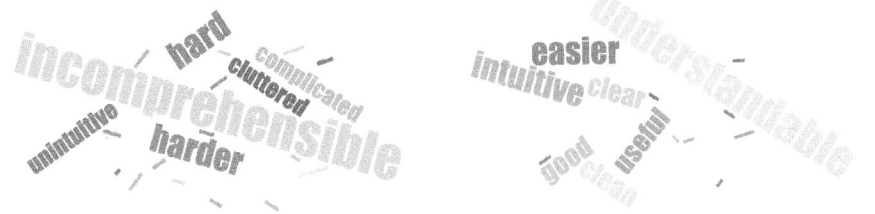

(a) Object-centric Petri net sentiment   (b) Object-centric Causal nets sentiment

Fig. 13. Word clouds showing participant sentiment for each model

6   Discussion

The implemented artefact is developed to discover OCCN from OCEL, making it compatible to be used along with other process mining libraries like PM4Py. It is particularly important as one can filter logs based on functionality provided by other libraries and discover relevant OCCN using our developed artefact.

Despite the promising results and positive user evaluations, several limitations and potential threats to validity should be acknowledged to provide appropriate context for the findings of this study.

Lack of Inter-object Type Binding Analysis: Although the proposed method effectively discovers object-centric causal nets (OCCN) for individual object types, it does not account for inter-object type bindings, which are causal relationships that span across different object types. Consequently, patterns involving complex interactions between related objects, such as between 'orders' and 'items,' are not explicitly represented in the resulting OCCN models - even though users can implicitly follow them. This limits the method's ability to capture cross-object process dynamics fully. Addressing this limitation is a key direction for future work.

Evaluation Population and External Validity: The user study was conducted with student participants. While many had relevant educational backgrounds, the generalizability of the results is limited. To strengthen external validity, future evaluations should include a larger and more diverse participant pool, particularly involving professionals from industry settings.

Future Directions: There is a need to extend the discovery algorithm to identify and model patterns that span across different object types. Currently, OCCN captures intra-object type behavior effectively; however, uncovering causal relationships that involve interactions between multiple object types could provide an even richer and more holistic understanding of complex processes. Exploring these inter-object type patterns remains an important step toward advancing the capabilities and applicability of object-centric process mining.

Another promising direction is to explore how graph-based process mining [33] methods can apply graph simplification techniques to improve visualizations. While OCEL can be converted into event knowledge graphs [34] and vice versa [35], these graphs often become too complex for practical use. This challenge is especially evident with OCEL-based approaches, as related tools continue to evolve. As demonstrated in this paper, graph simplification can enhance the user experience. Therefore, further research is needed to determine how these techniques can help end users interact more effectively with graph-based process mining.

7 Conclusion

In this paper, we introduced a novel approach for discovering object-centric causal nets (OCCN), addressing the limitations of existing object-centric process discovery methods regarding complexity, interpretability, and support for concurrency and choice. By extending traditional Causal nets and incorporating an edge-coarse-graining technique, our method enables the generation of simplified yet expressive models that are more comprehensible for stakeholders. We implemented the approach in Python and conducted a comparative evaluation with Object-Centric Petri Nets, revealing that OCCN offers higher user acceptance and better support for pattern recognition tasks. Our findings underscore the potential of OCCN as a user-centered alternative for object-centric process analysis.

Acknowledgements. We would like to thank Shahrzad Khayatbashi from Linköping University for her valuable feedback and for reviewing the implementation.

References

1. Aalst, W.: .Process Mining: Data Science in Action, 2nd edn., pp. 3–23. Springer, Heidelberg (2016). https://doi.org/10.1007/978-3-662-49851-4_1
2. van der Aalst, W.M.: Object-centric process mining: unraveling the fabric of real processes. Mathematics **11**(12), 2691 (2023)
3. Berti, A., et al.: OCEL 2.0 specification (2024)
4. Khayatbashi, S., Sjölind, V., Granåker, A., Jalali, A.: AI-enhanced business process automation: A case study in the insurance domain using object-centric process mining. In: International Conference on Business Process Modeling, Development and Support, International Conference on Evaluation and Modeling Methods for Systems Analysis and Development, pp. 3–18. Springer, Heidelberg (2025). https://doi.org/10.1007/978-3-031-95397-2_1
5. van der Aalst, W.M., Berti, A.: Discovering object-centric petri nets. Fund. Inform. **175**(1–4), 1–40 (2020)
6. Aalst, W.M.P.: Object-centric process mining: dealing with divergence and convergence in event data. In: Ölveczky, P.C., Salaün, G. (eds.) SEFM 2019. LNCS, vol. 11724, pp. 3–25. Springer, Cham (2019). https://doi.org/10.1007/978-3-030-30446-1_1
7. Davis, F.D.: Perceived usefulness, perceived ease of use, and user acceptance of information technology. MIS Q. **13**(3), 319 (1989)
8. van der Aalst, W., Adriansyah, A., van Dongen, B.: Causal nets: a modeling language tailored towards process discovery. In: Katoen, J.-P., König, B. (eds.) CONCUR 2011. LNCS, vol. 6901, pp. 28–42. Springer, Heidelberg (2011). https://doi.org/10.1007/978-3-642-23217-6_3
9. Weijters, A.J.M.M., van der Aalst, W.M.P., De Medeiros, A.K.A.: Process mining with the HeuristicsMiner algorithm. BETA publicatie: working papers. Technische Universiteit Eindhoven (2006)
10. vom Brocke, J., Hevner, A., Maedche, A.: Introduction to design science research. In: vom Brocke, J., Hevner, A., Maedche, A. (eds.) Design Science Research. Cases. PI, pp. 1–13. Springer, Cham (2020). https://doi.org/10.1007/978-3-030-46781-4_1

11. Van der Aalst, W., Weijters, T., Maruster, L.: Workflow mining: discovering process models from event logs. IEEE Trans. Knowl. Data Eng. **16**(9), 1128–1142 (2004)
12. Weijters, A.J., Van der Aalst, W.M.: Rediscovering workflow models from event-based data using little thumb. Integrat. Comput.-Aided Eng. **10**(2), 151–162 (2003)
13. Weijters, A.J.M.M., Ribeiro, J.T.S.: Flexible heuristics miner (FHM). In: 2011 IEEE Symposium on Computational Intelligence and Data Mining (CIDM), pp. 310–317. IEEE (2011)
14. Mannhardt, F., de Leoni, M., Reijers, H.A.: Heuristic mining revamped: an interactive, data-aware, and conformance-aware miner. In: 15th International Conference on Business Process Management (BPM 2017), pp. 1–5. CEUR-WS.org (2017)
15. Vanden Broucke, S.K., De Weerdt, J.: Fodina: a robust and flexible heuristic process discovery technique. Decis. Supp. Syst. **100**, 109–118 (2017)
16. Günther, C.W., van der Aalst, W.M.P.: Fuzzy mining – adaptive process simplification based on multi-perspective metrics. In: Alonso, G., Dadam, P., Rosemann, M. (eds.) BPM 2007. LNCS, vol. 4714, pp. 328–343. Springer, Heidelberg (2007). https://doi.org/10.1007/978-3-540-75183-0_24
17. Jalali, A.: Object type clustering using markov directly-follow multigraph in object-centric process mining. IEEE Access **10**, 126569–126579 (2022)
18. Song, C., Havlin, S., Makse, H.A.: Self-similarity of complex networks. Nature **433**(7024), 392–395 (2005)
19. Gfeller, D., De Los Rios, P.: Spectral coarse graining of complex networks. Phys. Rev. Lett. **99**(3), 038701 (2007)
20. Khayatbashi, S., Miri, N., Jalali, A.: OLAP operations for object-centric process mining. In: International Conference on Advanced Information Systems Engineering, pp. 111–118. Springer, Heidelberg (2025). https://doi.org/10.1007/978-3-031-94590-8_14
21. Khayatbashi, S., Miri, N., Jalali, A.: Advancing object-centric process mining with multi-dimensional data operations. Springer, Heidelberg (2025)
22. Miri, N., Jalali, A.: Uncovering patterns in object-centric process mining: An approach using drill-down and roll-up techniques. In: Haghighi, P.D., Greguš, M., Kotsis, G., Khalil, I. (eds.) Information Integration and Web Intelligence, pp. 49–54. Springer, Cham (2025)
23. Miri, N., Khayatbashi, S., Zdravkovic, J., Jalali, A.: OCPM^2: extending the process mining methodology for object-centric event data extraction. In: International Conference on Business Process Modeling, Development and Support, International Conference on Evaluation and Modeling Methods for Systems Analysis and Development, pp. 123–140. Springer, Heidelberg (2025). https://doi.org/10.1007/978-3-031-95397-2_8
24. Lu, X.: Causal-net category. Version Number: 5 (2022)
25. De Moura Figueiredo, E.: Discovering object-centric causal nets by merging causal nets from independent object type analyses (2024). https://su.diva-portal.org/smash/record.jsf?pid=diva2%3A1955576&dswid=-246. Accessed 20 Sept 2024
26. Park, G., Unterberg, L.T.G.: Procure-to-payment (p2p) object-centric event log in ocel 2.0 standard (2023). https://doi.org/10.5281/zenodo.8412920
27. Knopp, B., van der Aalst, W.M.P.: Order management object-centric event log in ocel 2.0 standard (2023). https://doi.org/10.5281/zenodo.8337463
28. Jalali, A.: Evaluating user acceptance of knowledge-intensive business process modeling languages. Softw. Syst. Model. **22**(6), 1803–1826 (2023)
29. Jalali, A.: Evaluating perceived usefulness and ease of use of CMMN and DCR. In: Augusto, A., Gill, A., Nurcan, S., Reinhartz-Berger, I., Schmidt, R., Zdravkovic,

J. (eds.) BPMDS/EMMSAD -2021. LNBIP, vol. 421, pp. 147–162. Springer, Cham (2021). https://doi.org/10.1007/978-3-030-79186-5_10

30. Jalali, A., Maggi, F.M., Reijers, H.A.: A hybrid approach for aspect-oriented business process modeling. J. Softw. Evol. Process **30**(8), e1931 (2018)

31. Jalali, A.: Weaving of aspects in business process management. Complex Syst. Inf. Model. Q. **15**, 24–44 (2018)

32. Davies, J.: Word cloud generator. https://www.jasondavies.com/wordcloud. Accessed 01 May 2025

33. Jalali, A.: Graph-based process mining. In: Leemans, S., Leopold, H. (eds.) ICPM 2020. LNBIP, vol. 406, pp. 273–285. Springer, Cham (2021). https://doi.org/10.1007/978-3-030-72693-5_21

34. Khayatbashi, S., Hartig, O., Jalali, A.: Transforming event knowledge graph to object-centric event logs: a comparative study for multi-dimensional process analysis. In: International Conference on Conceptual Modeling, pp. 220–238. Springer, Heidelberg (2023). https://doi.org/10.1007/978-3-031-47262-6_12

35. Khayatbashi, S., Hartig, O., Jalali, A.: Transforming object-centric event logs to temporal event knowledge graphs. In: International Conference on Business Process Management, pp. 300–313. Springer, Heidelberg (2024). https://doi.org/10.1007/978-3-031-78666-2_23

ReACMe: Repetition Aware Clustering Methodology for Business Process Log Collections

Caterina Luciani[1]([envelope]) [iD], Luigi Bucchicchio[1] [iD], Andrea Morichetta[1] [iD], Marco Piangerelli[1,2] [iD], and Andrea Polini[1] [iD]

[1] University of Camerino, Via Madonna delle Carceri 7, 62032 Camerino, Italy
{caterina.luciani,luigi.bucchicchio,andrea.morichetta,
marco.Piangerelli,andrea.polini}@unicam.it
[2] Vici & C. S.p.A., Via J. Gutenberg, 5, 47822 Santarcangelo di Romagna, Italy

Abstract. Process-Aware Information Systems (PAIS) are extensively employed to support organizational workflows, with configurations that often differ across various usage contexts. Analyzing the event logs they generate is essential for understanding this variability; however, traditional process mining techniques often face scalability challenges, particularly when dealing with loops and a large number of process instances. This paper introduces *ReACMe*, a parametric, unsupervised clustering methodology that bypasses model generation by leveraging n-gram-based features and a repetition-aware dissimilarity measure. Using the k-medoids algorithm, ReACMe effectively groups similar logs and allows to identify representative medoids. The approach is validated on both public datasets and a real-world e-government scenario, demonstrating its efficiency and practical applicability.

Keywords: Clustering · Event Logs · E-Government · n-grams · Visualization

1 Introduction

Process-Aware Information Systems (PAIS) support the execution and logging of business processes based on predefined models [1–3]. These logs can be analyzed using process mining techniques [4] to identify deviations from expected behavior, aiding in alignment with organizational goals and process improvement [5,6]. However, managing variability in large-scale, distributed environments remains a major challenge [7], especially when processes are adapted to local contexts [8–10]. Variability arises due to contextual differences and requires understanding both common and distinct behaviors [11]. While configurable models can support this by capturing shared structure and differences [11], their adoption is limited due to the lack of full lifecycle support [12]. Mining and merging models from individual logs [13] is computationally costly and ineffective with high variability.

To overcome these limitations, we propose the *Repetition Aware Clustering Methodology (ReACMe)*, which clusters event logs from multiple PAIS

© The Author(s), under exclusive license to Springer Nature Switzerland AG 2026
R. Deneckère et al. (Eds.): BIR 2025, LNBIP 562, pp. 219–237, 2026.
https://doi.org/10.1007/978-3-032-04375-7_14

installations into homogeneous groups, reducing analysis complexity. ReACMe simplify variability analysis using a representative log per cluster (e.g., the medoid), and supports identifying deployment-specific factors influencing process execution.

Unlike previous work [14], ReACMe introduces a parametric n-gram-based dissimilarity measure that accounts for repeated behaviors, then computes a distance matrix from XES logs, and applies the k-medoids algorithm [15] for clustering in non-Euclidean spaces. With ReACMe is possible to focus on activity differences, control-flow patterns, or a balance of both.

ReACMe was implemented within a framework and validated on 192 benchmark logs provided by the 2020 process mining conference and a real-world e-government case study, following design science research principles.

In summary, the main contributions of this paper are:

– A log clustering methodology designed to handle repeating behaviours
– A new parametric dissimilarity measure based on different lengths of n-grams
– An efficient algorithm for analysing large log datasets
– An ad hoc visualization to highlight patterns in datasets
– An open source software that implements the described functionality
– A validation on an external dataset and an e-government use case

The structure of the paper is as follows: Sect. 2 reviews the related work; Sect. 3 describes the proposed methodology; Sect. 4 illustrates a practical example and validates the approach using two datasets—one composed of synthetic data and the other derived from e-government sources; finally, Sect. 5 draws the conclusions.

2   Related Works

Variability in PA. Business processes are coordinated activities aimed at specific goals [16]. Process-Aware Information Systems (PAIS) embed these processes into software, enabling automation and control while generating event logs for process mining [16]. These logs—structured by the XES standard into logs, traces, and events—capture case and activity IDs with timestamps [17]. Process executions often vary by context (e.g., municipalities), forming process families with variants defined by predicates [18]. Managing these variants is key but challenging if done manually.

CoSeLoG is a project aimed at creating a cloud infrastructure for Dutch municipalities to manage services like permits, fees, and licenses. While processes share common structures, they vary locally due to demographic, legal, and territorial differences [19–23]. Municipalities, unlike companies, are not in competition, which encourages knowledge sharing and collaboration in process management. In the Coselog project, this led to harmonized processes and the development of a common, flexible information system within a shared framework [19, 20]. The common information system stores data as event logs and analyzes them using Process Mining techniques, enabling a better understanding of process execution, identification of inefficiencies, and opportunities to improve efficiency and productivity. Additionally, the standardization of processes simplifies their configuration across different municipalities, which can choose from a limited set of predefined options [24]. In the case of municipalities, managing variability through the use of configurable models offers great advantages: in the case of a law change, it will be possible to update a single process instead of an entire collection, saving time, resources, and also the likelihood of avoiding errors that may occur when changing individual processes [24]. The authors in [25] present an application of feature models to facilitate the exchange of information and the reuse of models in the Brazilian public sector. The authors in [26–28] present an extension of feature models to handle the Variability in PA, creating a mapping with the elements of the BPMN notation.

Trace Clustering. Clustering groups data by similarity without needing predefined group counts [29,30], but results depend on analyst choices [31]. Key steps include feature selection, algorithm choice, validation, and interpretation [31]. Features can be diverse, redundant, or noisy [32], and high dimensionality complicates analysis [33,34], often requiring dimensionality reduction [31,35]. Algorithms like k-medoids handle non-Euclidean distances well [15,36]. Clustering must be validated and interpreted to yield actionable insights [31,37]. One of the most relevant areas in event log clustering is trace clustering, which assumes the presence of tacit variants within logs [38]. Its goal is to group traces into homogeneous subgroups to enhance model quality and comprehensibility [39].

Trace clustering approaches fall into three main categories: feature-vector-based, trace-sequence-based, and model-based clustering [40,41]. In [42], logs are transformed into context-aware feature sets using maximal repeats, capturing common process regions. Clustering is performed hierarchically using Euclidean distance and evaluated through metrics such as average events and arcs per cluster. A similar strategy is enriched with timing in [43] to detect concept drift, while [44,45] adopt a divisive clustering method based on significant substrings. In [38], profiles such as activity, 2-grams, originators, and performance are used, with distances like Euclidean, Hamming, and Jaccard. Algorithms like k-means and Self-Organising Map are applied; [46] further introduces dimensionality reduction techniques. Model-based approaches include [47,48], which compare weighted dependency graphs using activity and transition frequencies. Expert-driven clustering is explored in [40], where experts define clusters based on frequent patterns, and in [49], through semi-supervised learning combining expert input with clustering constraints. Lastly, [50] propose an object-centric method using a Directly-Follows Graph, distinguishing object types and applying various distance measures like Levenshtein and Euclidean.

N-Grams. Event logs are encoded into feature spaces for analysis [51] with methods like trace replay, graph embedding, and word embedding. In particuar N-grams, extracted as substrings of length n from traces (e.g., 2-grams from abcd yield {ab, bc, cd}), are effective for capturing local patterns while mitigating exponential feature growth. Using 1-grams isolates individual activities, and incorporating n-grams helps uncover patterns and dependencies in event logs, enhancing process understanding [52].

3   ReACMe Methodology

ReACMe (Repetition Aware Clustering Methodology) is a parametric methodology that allows the clustering of business process log collections according to different relevant parameters. The proposed methodology is sensitive to repetitions in the log, possibly generated either by erroneous operations performed by the user, or failures of the system, or simply repeating behaviour resulting from the implemented logic of the system. The methodology can be applied to any data-set of XES event logs, with traces identified by a case id. The methodology extracts features from the logs and generates a distance matrix according to a defined dissimilarity measure. The distance matrix will be taken as input by a clustering algorithm to identify clusters of logs

The dissimilarity measure is calculated considering different parameters, identified by the tuple $< \gamma, \Delta, \Phi, \Xi, \delta, \phi, \xi >$ where the first parameter, $\gamma \in [0, 1]$, allows the analyst to choose whether to consider activities ($\gamma{=}1$) or n-grams ($\gamma{=}0$) or a balance between the two ($\gamma \in \,]0, 1[$).

Table 1. Methodology parameters

γ—Activities vs Grams: $[0, 1]$					
Δ	Equal Activity	$\{0, 1\}$	δ	Equal Grams	$\{0, 1\}$
Φ	Not Equal Activity	$\{-1, 0\}$	ϕ	Not Equal Grams	$\{-1, 0\}$
Ξ	Semi-Equal Activity	$\{0, 1\}$	ξ	Semi-Equal Grams	$\{0, 1\}$

The six remaining parameters form two triplets: uppercase (Δ, Φ, Ξ) for activities and lowercase (δ, ϕ, ξ) for n-grams. Each pair encodes analogous semantics: In particular, Δ and δ refer to the weight assigned to similar activities or n-grams; Φ and ϕ represent the negative weight to assign to different activities or n-grams and, finally, Ξ and ξ are the weights for semi-equal activities or n-grams, i.e. those that exist in both logs, but in one is repeating, in the other is not repeating. These parameters allow analysts to modulate sensitivity based on analytical priorities.

Definition 1 (Trace). *Given a finite nonempty set A of activities a, a trace σ, of length l, is a finite sequence of activities corresponding to an execution of a process P*

$$\sigma = a_1, ..., a_l \quad a_i \in A \tag{1}$$

A trace permits to precisely identify sequences of actions that are related as they represent the execution of a case within a log. The collection of all the considered traces will result in a log as defined in the next definition.

Definition 2 (Log). *A generic log is a nonempty finite set of traces σ.*

$$\mathcal{L} = \{\sigma_1, ..., \sigma_m\} \tag{2}$$

From each trace we extract subtraces of specific length n called n-grams.

Definition 3 (n-gram). *Given a trace σ, of length l, a generic n-gram is defined as a subtrace of n consecutive activities*

$$ng = a_k, a_{k+1}, a_{k+2}, ..., a_{k+n-1} \quad 1 \leq k \leq l - n + 1 \tag{3}$$

Definition 4 (Multiset of n-grams).
For a positive integer n and trace σ, the Multiset of n-grams $\mathcal{M}_n(\sigma)$ is the pair $(\mathbb{M}_n(\sigma), \mu)$, where:
$\mathbb{M}_n(\sigma)$ *is the set of distinct n-grams in σ*
$\mu : \mathbb{M}_n(\sigma) \to \mathbb{Z}^+$ *assigns the multiplicity of each n-gram in σ*

$$\mathcal{M}_n(\sigma) = \{ng_1^{\mu(ng_1)}, \ldots, ng_t^{\mu(ng_t)}\} \tag{4}$$

Then, in order to have a global view of the n-grams in a Log, we provide the union of the multiset of each trace in the Log.

Definition 5 (Multiset of a Log).
Given a positive number n and a log $\mathcal{L} = \{\sigma_1, ..., \sigma_m\}$, the multiset of n-grams for $\mathcal{L}$ is defined as the union of the multiset of the traces in the log:

$$\mathcal{M}_n(\mathcal{L}) = \bigcup_{i=1}^{m} \mathcal{M}_n(\sigma_i) \tag{5}$$

where the union of the multiset for the traces σ_1 and σ_2, given n-grams of length n, is defined as the following multiset:

$$\mathcal{M}_n(\sigma_1) \cup \mathcal{M}_n(\sigma_2) = (\mathbb{M}_n(\sigma_1) \cup \mathbb{M}_n(\sigma_2), max(\mu_{\mathbb{M}_n(\sigma_1)}, \mu_{\mathbb{M}_n(\sigma_2)}))$$

This facilitates the comparison of logs with a similar number of distinct traces but differing total numbers of traces—a common scenario in contexts such as public administration processes.

Once the Multiset of a Log is created, we map the n-grams multiplicity into labels. Hence, we defined the following:

Definition 6 (Labeled Log). *Given a Log multiset $\mathcal{M}_n(\mathcal{L})$ we define the corresponding labelled log $\mathcal{K}$ that is derived as follow*

$$\mathcal{K}_n(\mathcal{L}) = \left\{ (ng, l) : ng \in \mathbb{M}_n(\mathcal{L}) \wedge l = \begin{cases} R & if \ \mu(ng) > 1 \\ NR & if \ \mu(ng) = 1 \end{cases} \right\} \tag{6}$$

with R indicating Repeated n-gram and NR indicating Not Repeated n-gram

Finally, in order to compute the dissimilarity matrix required by the clustering algorithm we defined the dissimilarity measure between pairs of Logs as:

Definition 7 (Dissimilarity Measure). *The dissimilarity between two logs is calculated according to the parametrization $\gamma\_ \Delta\Phi\Xi\_ \delta\phi\xi$ and according to the dimension of the gram n:*

$$diss^n(\mathcal{L}_i, \mathcal{L}_j) = 1 - sim^n(\mathcal{L}_i, \mathcal{L}_j)$$

$$= 1 - \left\{ \gamma \frac{|\Lambda_1|\Delta + |U_1/I_1|\Phi + |I_1|\Xi}{U_1} + (1 - \gamma) \frac{|\Lambda_n|\delta + |U_n/I_n|\phi + |I_n|\xi}{U_n} \right\}$$
(7)

where, for $m \in \{1, n\}$:

$$I_m = \mathbb{M}_m(\mathcal{L}_i) \cap \mathbb{M}_m(\mathcal{L}_j) \tag{8}$$

$$U_m = \mathbb{M}_m(\mathcal{L}_i) \cup \mathbb{M}_m(\mathcal{L}_j) \tag{9}$$

$$\Lambda_m = \mathcal{K}_m(\mathcal{L}_i) \cap \mathcal{K}_m(\mathcal{L}_j) \tag{10}$$

I_m and U_m are, respectively, the intersection and union of the underlying sets of n-grams for $\mathcal{L}_i$ and $\mathcal{L}_j$. While Λ_m is the intersection between two sets of labeled logs.

From the above definitions, we can derive the distance matrix using the pairwise dissimilarity measure defined in Eq. 7 for all logs, as reported in Table 2. The computed distance matrix can be then passed as input to any clustering algorithm. In this work, clustering is performed using the *k-medoids* algorithm, suitable for non-Euclidean spaces.

Table 2. Dissimilarity Matrix

	$\mathcal{L}_1$	...	$\mathcal{L}_i$	...	$\mathcal{L}_j$
$\mathcal{L}_1$	0.0	...	$diss(\mathcal{L}_1, \mathcal{L}_i)$	...	$diss(\mathcal{L}_1, \mathcal{L}_j)$
...		0.0	...		...	...
$\mathcal{L}_i$			0.0	...	$diss(\mathcal{L}_i, \mathcal{L}_j)$
...				0.0	...
$\mathcal{L}_j$					0.0

Since the optimal number of clusters is unknown, the *silhouette method* is used [53]. It assesses clustering quality by comparing cohesion within clusters and separation between them. For each point, a silhouette score (ranging from -1 to 1) is computed based on average intra and inter cluster distances, with higher scores indicating better defined clusters (see Definition 11).

$$s_i = \frac{b_i - a_i}{max\{a_i, b_i\}} \quad i = 1, 2, ..., N \tag{11}$$

where $a(i)$ = average dissimilarity of i to all other objects of cluster A, $d(i, C)$ = average dissimilarity of i to all objects of cluster C and $b(i)$ = $min\{d(i, C)\}$ and N is the total number of data points.

To select the optimal number of clusters, the silhouette score is computed for values from 2 to $m - 1$, where $m = \log N$. The number of clusters that yields the highest silhouette score is selected as optimal.

4   Validation

In this section, ReACMe is applied to a hands-on example and then tested on two datasets, one external synthetic dataset[1] provided in the International Conference of Process Mining (ICPM) of 2020[2], the other one coming from the Public Administration.

The methodology is equipped with an efficient algorithm implemented in an ad hoc tool[3] composed of two main components, the Java-based application for generating the dissimilarity matrices after taking in input the XES event logs folder and the Python-based clustering component, responsible for calculating clusters using the previously generated matrices.

As soon as it is run, the ReACMe tool asks for a configuration of parameters and, starting from the XES files in the input folder, it will generate the results in the output folder: between many overview files, as its main result the tool generates a text file listing the log names alongside their corresponding classifications. To visually validate the clustering quality, results can be displayed through an ad hoc heatmap[4] designed to highlight recurring behavior and shared activities within clusters.

4.1   ReACMe Hands-on Example

To illustrate our methodology, we apply it to a simple use case. Although the approach is designed for scenarios where models are not known a priori and operates directly on logs, for demonstration purposes, we consider three logs (Log_1, Log_2, and Log_3) and their generating models (see Fig. 1), analyzing them using 2-grams (see Table 3).

Each log is composed of a different number of traces, as shown in Table 3 (column σ). Each trace is then mapped in a multiset of traces (column $\mathcal{M}_2(\sigma)$) according to the first step of ReACMe (see Definition 4).

For example, Log_1 contains only one trace, and the multiset of 2-grams contains three elements (AB, BC, CD) with multiplicity 1. In the case of Log_2 instead, two traces exist. The former case does not present any repetition while the latter contains the repetition of different activities, potentially generated by a repeating behaviour, on the assumption that activities are univocally identified. The multiset of Log_2 is composed by (AB, BC, CD) in the first trace, and (AB, BC, CE, EF, FB, CD) with different multiplicities in the second trace (multiplicity greater than 1 for a single 2-gram indicates the presence of a cycle in the model). Once $\mathcal{M}_2(\sigma)$ is computed, its underlying set, $(\mathbb{M}_2(\sigma))$, can be immediately calculated.

In the second step of the methodology, we compute the multiset for each log, consisting in the union of the individual multiset of each trace. The results are shown in Table 3 (column $\mathcal{M}_2(\mathcal{L})$).

---

[1] https://data.4tu.nl/articles/__/14626020/1.

[2] https://icpmconference.org/2020/process-discovery-contest/downloads/.

[3] https://github.com/LuigiBucchicchio/Reacme.

[4] https://github.com/vq1lpvoq6n/heatmap-source.git.

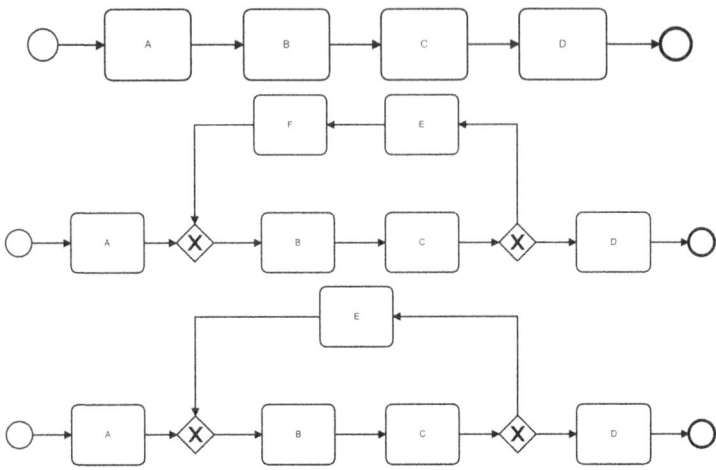

Fig. 1. Representing models for Log_1, Log_2, and Log_3

In the third step, each log multiset is mapped to a set of tuples considering the 2-grams and the corresponding label $\mathcal{K}_2(\mathcal{L})$ according to Definition 6. In particular, the 2-grams are labeled as repeating (R) if there is at least one trace of the log in which the 2-gram element has multiplicity greater than one, not repeating (NR) otherwise. For example, in Log_1 all elements are labeled as not repeating. In Log_2, on the other hand, some 2-grams are labeled as repeating (BC CE, EF, FB) and some not (AB, CD). Note that the element BC, which has multiplicity 1 in the first trace and multiplicity 3 in the second, is labeled as repeating because the cardinality greater than 1 indicates the possibilities of a repeating behavior in the logic of the underlined system/model.

Table 3. Application of the first three steps of ReACMe to example logs

	σ	$\mathcal{M}_2(\sigma)$	$\mathcal{M}_2(\mathcal{L})$	$\mathcal{K}_2(\mathcal{L})$
Log_1	ABCD	AB^1, BC^1, CD^1	AB^1, BC^1, CD^1	(AB, NR), (BC, NR), (CD, NR)
Log_2	ABCD	AB^1, BC^1, CD^1	AB^1, BC^3, CE^2, EF^2, FB^2, CD^1	(AB, NR), (BC, R) (CE, R), (EF, R), (FB, R), (CD, NR)
	ABCEFBCEFBCD	AB^1, BC^3, CE^2, EF^2, FB^2, CD^1		
Log_3	ABCD	AB^1, BC^1, CD^1	AB^1, BC^3, CD^1, CE^2, EB^2	(AB, NR), (BC, R) (CD, NR), (CE, R), (EB, R)
	ABCEBCEBCD	AB^1, BC^3, CE^2, EB^2, CD^1		

In the fourth step, the dissimilarity matrices are calculated between pairs of logs according to Definition 7. The resulting matrices are generated according to two different parametrizations, 0_100_101 and 0_100_100, and are reported in Tables 2a and 2b respectively. The distance matrices differ mainly for the parameter ξ. For example, the dissimilarity between Log_1 and Log_2 in the case of the former parametrization is 0.5 as shown in Eq. 12; while for the latter it is 0.67 as shown in Eq. 13.

$$
\begin{aligned}
diss^2(Log_1, Log_2) &= 1 - sim^2(Log_1, Log_2) \\
&= 1 - \left\{ 0\frac{|\mathcal{I}_1|1 + |U_1/I_1|0 + |I_1|0}{U_1} + (1-0)\frac{|\mathcal{I}_2|1 + |U_2/I_2|0 + |I_2|1}{U_2} \right\} \\
&= 1 - \frac{|\mathcal{I}_2|1 + |I_2|1}{U_2} = 1 - \frac{2+1}{6} = 0.50
\end{aligned}
\tag{12}
$$

$$
\begin{aligned}
diss^2(Log_1, Log_2) &= 1 - sim^2(Log_1, Log_2) \\
&= 1 - \left\{ 0\frac{|\mathcal{I}_1|1 + |U_1/I_1|0 + |I_1|0}{U_1} + (1-0)\frac{|\mathcal{I}_2|1 + |U_2/I_2|0 + |I_2|0}{U_2} \right\} \\
&= 1 - \frac{|\mathcal{I}_2|1}{U_2} = 1 - \frac{2}{6} = 0.67
\end{aligned}
\tag{13}
$$

Finally, the fifth step of the methodology consists in running the clustering algorithm using the dissimilarity matrix as input. In our work we used the k-medoid algorithm, but it is worth mentioning that any clustering algorithm can be adopted. Considering the previous two parameterizations, 0_100_101 and 0_100_100, that differs only for the ξ parameter, the logs corresponding to models that have loops are clustered together (see Fig. 2) since the repeating activities are considered relevant for the analysis $\xi = 0$, while in case $\xi = 1$ logs 1 and 3 are clustered together since we do not consider cycles to be relevant for our analysis, and then the control flows of the two logs are indeed closer.

(a)

	Log_1	Log_2	Log_3
Log_1	0.0	0.50	0.4
Log_2		0.0	0.43
Log_3			0.0

(b)

	Log_1	Log_2	Log_3
Log_1	0.0	0.67	0.6
Log_2		0.0	0.43
Log_3			0.0

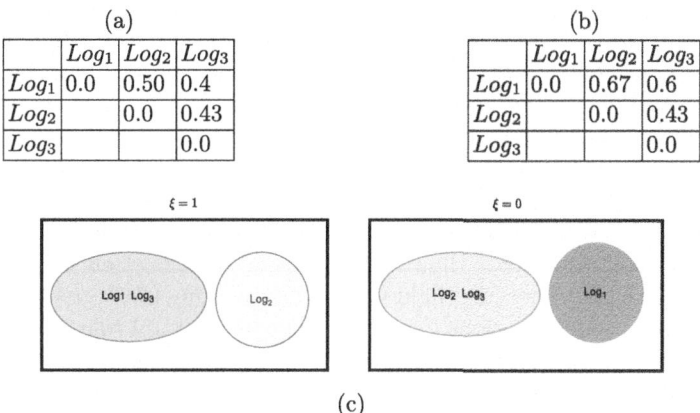

(c)

Fig. 2. Dissimilarity matrices (a), (b) and clustering of logs (c) from the running example

4.2   Validation on Synthetic Dataset

In order to test the ReACMe methodology, the data-set provided in the International Conference of Process Mining (ICPM) held in 2020 [54] was used. The conference provides different data-sets to promote a contest consisting in the evaluation of discovery algorithms. In this validation the *training data-set* of the challenge was used. The training data-set contains 192 XES files of 1000 traces each, where each log represents a variation of the basic model "pdc_2020_0000000.xes". The logs were generated starting from the basic model and applying 7 possible types of perturbations A, B, C, D, E, F, G where their meaning is summarised in Table 4.

Table 4. Dataset variations: each combination of the A–F mutations defines a distinct model, while the G mutation is applied only at the event log level

Digit	Variation	Values	Description
A	Dependent tasks	0, 1	If 1, it is impossible to bypass dependent tasks
B	Loops	0, 1, 2	If 0, the model has no loops. If 1, all transitions that are a shortcut between the loop and the main flow are disabled
C	OR constructs	0, 1	If 0, OR constructs are disabled
D	Invisible tasks	0, 1	If 1, some transitions are made invisible
E	Optional tasks	0, 1	If 1, it is possible to skip some transitions
F	Duplicate tasks	0, 1	If 1, some transitions are relabeled to existing labels
G	Noise	0, 1	If 1, 20% of traces are made noisy by deleting an event, moving one event in the trace, or copying one event in the trace

The methodology includes seven parameters (Table 1). In this validation, we use 2-grams ($\gamma = 0$) to capture control flow while avoiding the exponential growth of features with higher n-grams [52]. Two parameterizations are tested (Table 5 (a), (c)): P_1 treats repeated behavior as identical to non-repeated ($\xi = 1$), P_2 treats it as distinct ($\xi = 0$). In Table 1 (b), (d) the results of the clusterization are shown and mutations driving each cluster are highlighted, excluding A, C, and E, which appear in all combinations in the clusters but do not produce detectable patterns with ReACMe. In Table 5 (e) the mapping between the classification is shown.

For both parameterizations, the heatmap supports visual cluster validation (see Fig. 3 (a) and (b)). The heatmap displays activity patterns, with activities on the X-axis (ordered by frequency) and logs on the Y-axis (grouped by cluster, from Cluster 0 downwards). Blue lines separate clusters. Cell colors indicate absence (white), non-repeating (light green), or repeating (dark green) activities.

Across all parameterizations, mutation B plays a central role, distinguishing logs with no loops (B = 0), simple loops (B = 1), and complex loops (B = 2). This results in a clear separation of logs based on loop structure of the models underling them. For both parameterizations execution time is less than 2 min on a i7-11800H processor (78.4 s for P1 and 76.7 s for P2).

Table 5. Parametrization and clusters for P_1 (a,b) and P_2 (c,d), and mapping between the cluster elements (e)

(a)

Param.	γ	Δ	Φ	Ξ	δ	ϕ	ξ
P_1	0	1	0	0	1	0	1

(b)

Cluster ID	B	D	F	G
	B	D	F	G
0		0	0	0
5		0	0	1
2		0	1	0
7	0	0	1	1
8		1	0	0
9		1	0	1
10		1	1	0/1
1	1	0	0	0/1
12		0	1	0/1
3	2	0	0	0/1
11		0	1	0/1
6	1/2	1	0	0/1
4		1	1	0/1

(c)

Param.	γ	Δ	Φ	Ξ	δ	ϕ	ξ
P_2	0	1	0	0	1	0	0

(d)

Cluster ID	B	D	F	G
	B	D	F	G
3	0	0/1	1	0/1
4	0	0/1	0	0/1
0	1/2	1	0	0/1
1	1/2	0	1	0/1
2	1/2	0	0	0/1
5	1/2	1	1	0/1

(e)

Cluster ID P_2	Cluster ID P_1
0	6
1	11, 12
2	1, 3
3	0, 5, 8, 9
4	2, 7, 10
5	4

Parametrization P_1. This parametrization identified 13 clusters, shown in Table 5 (b). When B = 0, the logs are from models without loops. These clusters generally contain fewer activities, even when repetition (F) or noise (G) is introduced. The baseline cluster includes unperturbed logs, while others reflect the impact of F, G, or D (invisible transitions), either alone or in combination. Cluster 10 mixes perturbed and unperturbed logs. By artificially separating the perturbed logs within the cluster from the unperturbed ones, it can be seen that the noise introduces 30% of new behavior, while in the already discussed clusters the new behavior generated by the noise is greater than 45%, leading to separate clusters.

In the case of B = 1, the logs come from models with simple loops. Here, both perturbed and unperturbed logs are grouped together, with differences mainly driven by the presence of repetitions (F).

For B = 2, logs are generated from models with complex loops. Again, unperturbed and noisy logs may appear in the same cluster, depending on the presence of mutations F and G. When invisible transitions are active (D = 1), they further affect cluster composition and mix single and complex loops, for a similar mechanism that led to mix perturbed and unperturbed logs in Cluster 10.

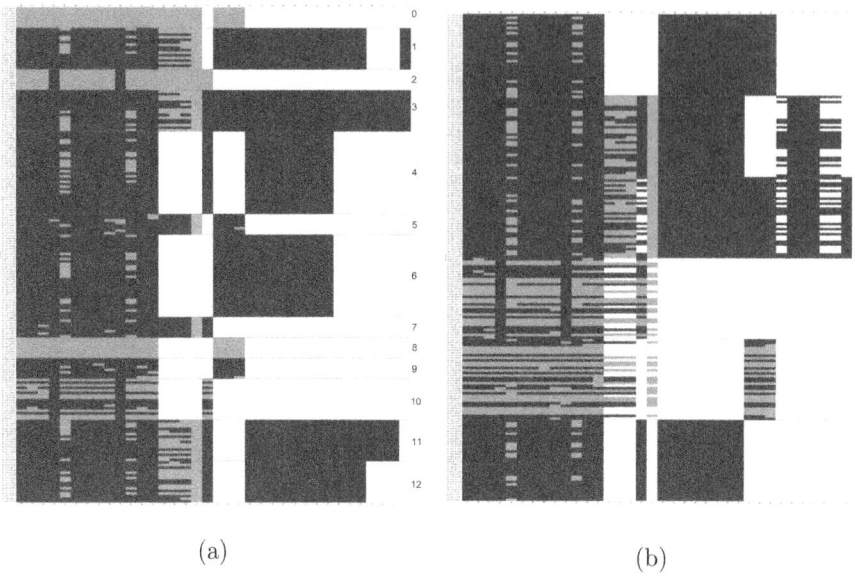

(a)   (b)

Fig. 3. Cluster heatmap for P_1 (a) and P_2 (b)

Parametrization P_2. This parametrization identified 6 clusters, shown in Table 5 (d). In this clusterization it is possible to identify two macrocategories of clusters by observing the value of parameter B. The visualization of the patterns is shown in the Heatmap in Fig. 3 (b). The macrocategory where B equals 0 includes Cluster 3 and Cluster 4. In both clusters, there is no distinction made between noise (G) and invisible tasks (D). However, Cluster 3 is characterized by repeated behavior (F = 1), which is visible through the dark green columns on the heatmap. In contrast, when B is equal to 1 or 2, the macrocategory consists of four clusters: Cluster 0, Cluster 1, Cluster 2, and Cluster 5. Each of these clusters reflects a different combination of the D and F mutations.

Although P1 does not explicitly consider repeating behavior, it separates logs by each one of B values. This apparent paradox is due to how other mutations influence the structure. In models without loops (B=0), some paths cannot be fully traversed, leading to inherently repeated or non-repeated patterns—visible in the heatmap of the log collection. Notably, only one activity ("t11") appears exclusively without repetition. If the non-repeating behavior is considered totally different from the repeating behavior, the logs that have repeating behavior are nevertheless more similar to each other, than to the ones generated from models without loops.

From the application of ReACMe to this external dataset, which exhibits variability phenomena, it was possible to highlight the effectiveness of the methodology in distinguishing patterns within the data and in supporting the analyst in reducing the dataset's complexity.

4.3 Validation on a Real Dataset: Apr Fin 2012 Process

PA serves as an ideal case study for variability, as local administrations offer similar services adapted to regulations and local factors, while also complying with national and international laws [55,56]. In this experiment, the event logs of 22 municipalities for a simple process were considered, using 4 parametrizations shown in Fig. 4 (a) and (c). $P1$ and $P2$ are activity-based parameterizations (1-grams) while $P3$ and $P4$ are based on 2-grams. Since the results for $P3$ and $P4$ are identical to $P2$ only the latter is shown on the cluster heatmap.

Through the $P1$ heatmap (b), it's possible to observe the presence of a large cluster consisting of 19 municipalities exhibiting the simplest behavior found in the collection, while the logs with the repeated activities are clustered alone. This experiment demonstrates the flexibility of ReACMee and its adaptability to real-world settings.

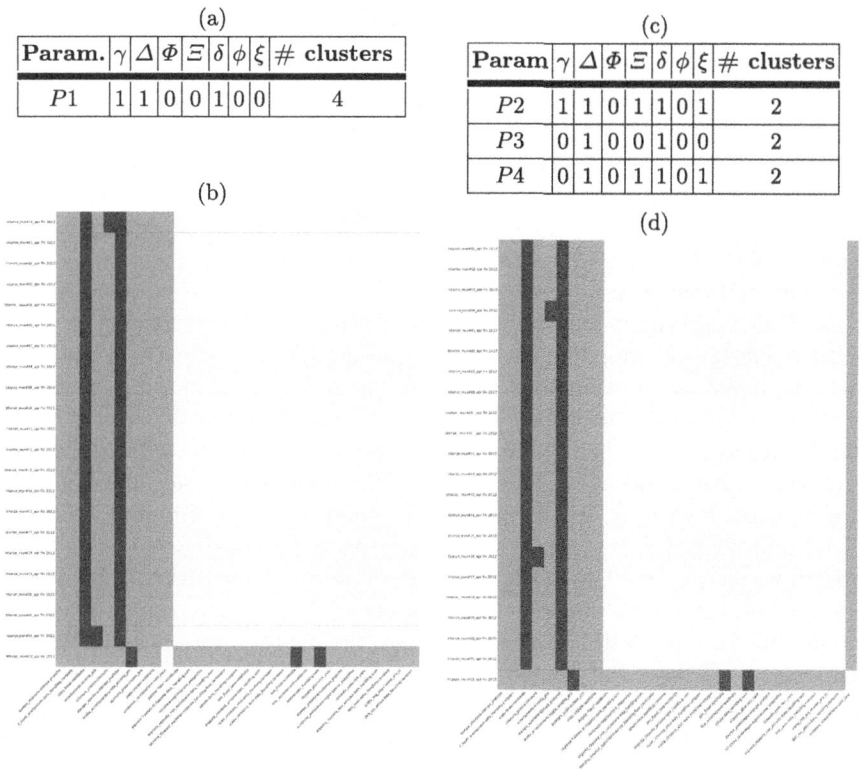

(a)

Param.	γ	Δ	Φ	Ξ	δ	ϕ	ξ	# clusters
$P1$	1	1	0	0	1	0	0	4

(c)

Param	γ	Δ	Φ	Ξ	δ	ϕ	ξ	# clusters
$P2$	1	1	0	1	1	0	1	2
$P3$	0	1	0	0	1	0	0	2
$P4$	0	1	0	1	1	0	1	2

(b)

(d)

Fig. 4. Parametrization settings and corresponding cluster heatmaps. $P1$ is shown on the left as baseline, other variants on the right

5 Conclusions

Variability is an inherent phenomenon that arises when processes designed to achieve the same goal are carried out in slightly different ways. Effectively managing collections of event logs that exhibit such variability offers several advantages, including the ability to implement changes more efficiently, facilitate reuse of process knowledge, and streamline the analysis of complex process behavior.

When dealing with large collections of event logs, a pre-processing phase often becomes necessary to reduce complexity and improve the interpretability of the data. One common approach involves clustering logs that represent similar variants of a process and then selecting a representative from each cluster for modeling and further analysis. Additionally, these logs may contain traces in which certain transitions or sequences of activities are repeated. Such repetitions—reflected as loops in the corresponding process models—may either indicate noise or errors, or conversely, they may represent meaningful behavior, such as users repeatedly visiting the same web pages, which could signal particular interest or intent.

To address the challenges posed by repeated behavior in process logs, this work introduces ReACMe—a Repetition-Aware Clustering Methodology. ReACMe enables the flexible clustering of event logs by taking into account different interpretations of repetitive behavior. Unlike traditional trace-level clustering approaches, which tend to perform best within a single organizational context, ReACMe is specifically designed to handle cross-context variability, making it suitable for identifying and analyzing process differences across diverse organizational environments.

ReACMe builds upon and extends methodologies such as TLV-diss [14], introducing a clustering approach that distinguishes between repetitive and non-repetitive behavior in event logs. The method relies on an n-gram-based representation of traces to capture both structural and behavioral patterns, which are then aggregated at the log level. Each n-gram is labeled to indicate whether it reflects repeated behavior, enabling the methodology to account for loops or recurrences that may be either noise or semantically meaningful. From this labeled representation, a custom dissimilarity matrix is constructed using a dedicated function designed to reflect both structure and repetition. This matrix serves as input for the k-medoid clustering algorithm, which groups similar logs and identifies a representative exemplar (i.e., the medoid) for each cluster. The entire process reduces the number of logs to analyze while preserving key variability across process executions. Notably, ReACMe is parametric: for example, when the parameter is set to 1, two logs sharing the same 2-gram structure but differing in repetition labels are treated as equivalent, allowing users to adjust the sensitivity of the clustering to repeated behavior.

This approach is particularly valuable for practitioners who need to simplify complex datasets without losing critical information. For example, in the case study involving public administration processes presented in Sect. 4.3, ReACMe successfully reduced a collection of 22 logs to just 4 representative clusters. This made it significantly easier to identify key process variants and enabled more focused, efficient analysis.

The methodology has been rigorously evaluated on two datasets: one provided during the 2020 Process Mining Conference that explicitly highlights the variability phenomenon, and another real-world dataset obtained from a major European public administration IT provider. These evaluations demonstrate the effectiveness and practical relevance of ReACMe in both synthetic and real-world scenarios.

Public Administration (PA) processes serve as an ideal testing ground for studying variability. These processes must conform simultaneously to broad national regulations and to localized, region-specific rules, naturally giving rise to variations. The proposed methodology is particularly well-suited to PA environments because of its minimal assumptions and strong respect for data sensitivity—two crucial features when working with highly regulated and privacy-sensitive data. Given the strict compliance and data handling requirements in the public sector, methodologies like ReACMe that operate with minimal prerequisites are especially advantageous for improving and managing process performance in such contexts.

Moreover, the performance observed on both the synthetic and real-world collections highlights the efficiency of ReACMe in simplifying log collections during the preprocessing phase. This is particularly valuable for tasks such as variability analysis or the construction of configurable models—activities that are traditionally known to be computationally expensive [55,57,58].

In future work, we intend to extend the proposed approach by incorporating the frequency of n-grams, which may provide additional insights into recurring patterns and their significance within event logs. Another planned direction is to integrate the methodology with concept drift analysis, as introduced in [59], in order to better handle evolving processes over time. Furthermore, a possible avenue for development involves leveraging AI techniques to compare n-gram patterns across logs that contain activities with different labels. This would allow us to evaluate the effectiveness of our approach in scenarios where semantic variation is present, and to benchmark it against label-agnostic methods such as the one proposed in [60].

Declaration and Acknowledgements

- Funded by the European Union – NextGenerationEU - Piano Nazionale di Ripresa e Resilienza, Missione 4 Istruzione e Ricerca - Componente 2 Dalla ricerca all'impresa - Investimento 1.5, ECS_00000041 VITALITY - Innovation, digitalisation and sustainability for the diffused economy in Central Italy
- Caterina Luciani's work is partially funded by Maggioli S.p.A.
- The authors gratefully acknowledge the support of Claudia Raffaelli and Lorenzo Spina
- AI was used for text translation, sentences polishing and rephrasing
- All authors declare no conflicts of interest

References

1. Günther, C.W., van der Aalst, W.M.: A generic import framework for process event logs. In: International Conference on Business Process Management, pp. 81–92. Springer (2006)
2. Dumas, M., Van der Aalst, W.M., Ter Hofstede, A.H.: Process-Aware Information Systems: Bridging People and Software through Process Technology. Wiley (2005)
3. Perez-Castillo, R., Weber, B., Pinggera, J., Zugal, S., de Guzmán, I.G.R., Piattini, M.: Generating event logs from non-process-aware systems enabling business process mining. Enterp. Inf. Syst. **5**(3), 301–335 (20a11)
4. Van der Aalst, W.M.: Process-aware information systems: lessons to be learned from process mining. In: Transactions on Petri Nets and other Models of Concurrency II, pp. 1–26. Springer (2009)
5. Aguilar-Saven, R.S.: Business process modelling: review and framework. Int. J. Prod. Econ. **90**(2), 129–149 (2004)
6. Rubin, V., Lomazova, I., Aalst, W.M.V.D.: Agile development with software process mining. In: Proceedings of the 2014 International Conference on Software and System Process, pp. 70–74 (2014)
7. Dijkman, R., La Rosa, M., Reijers, H.: Managing large collections of business process models-current techniques and challenges. Comput. Ind. **63**(2), 91–97 (2012)
8. Cecconi, A., Augusto, A., Di Ciccio, C.: Detection of statistically significant differences between process variants through declarative rules. In: International Conference on Business Process Management, pp. 73–91. Springer (2021)
9. Taymouri, F., La Rosa, M., Dumas, M., Maggi, F.M.: Business process variant analysis: survey and classification. Knowl.-Based Syst. **211**, 106557 (2021)
10. Taymouri, F., Rosa, M.L., Carmona, J.: Business process variant analysis based on mutual fingerprints of event logs. In: International Conference on Advanced Information Systems Engineering, pp. 299–318. Springer (2020)
11. Arriagada-Benítez, M., Sepúlveda, M., Munoz-Gama, J., Buijs, J.C.: Strategies to automatically derive a process model from a configurable process model based on event data. Appl. Sci. **7**(10), 1023 (2017)
12. Rosa, M.L., Aalst, W.M.V.D., Dumas, M., Milani, F.P.: Business process variability modeling: a survey. ACM Comput. Surv. (CSUR) **50**(1), 1–45 (2017)
13. Buijs, J.C., van Dongen, B.F., van der Aalst, W.M.: Mining configurable process models from collections of event logs. In: Business Process Management, pp. 33–48. Springer (2013)
14. Corradini, F., Luciani, C., Morichetta, A., Piangerelli, M., Polini, A.: $TLV-diss_\gamma$: a dissimilarity measure for public administration process logs. In: International Conference on Electronic Government, pp. 301–314. Springer (2021)
15. Schubert, E., Rousseeuw, P.J.: Faster k-medoids clustering: improving the pam, clara, and clarans algorithms. In: International Conference on Similarity Search and Applications, pp. 171–187. Springer (2019)
16. Dumas, M., La Rosa, M., Mendling, J., Reijers, H.A., et al.: Fundamentals of business process management, vol. 1. Springer (2013)
17. Van Der Aalst, W.: Data science in action. In: Process Mining, pp. 3–23. Springer (2016)
18. Stańczyk, U., Jain, L.C.: Feature selection for data and pattern recognition: an introduction. In: Feature Selection for Data and Pattern Recognition, pp. 1–7. Springer (2015)

19. Vogelaar, J., Verbeek, H., Luka, B., van der Aalst, W.M.: Comparing business processes to determine the feasibility of configurable models: a case study. In: Business Process Management Workshops: BPM 2011 International Workshops, Clermont-Ferrand, France, 29 August 2011, Revised Selected Papers, Part II 9, pp. 50–61. Springer (2012)

20. Van Der Aalst, W.M.: Configurable services in the cloud: supporting variability while enabling cross-organizational process mining. In: OTM Confederated International Conferences On the Move to Meaningful Internet Systems, pp. 8–25. Springer (2010)

21. Schunselaar, D.M., Verbeek, H., Van Der Aalst, W.M., Reijers, H.A.: Petra: a tool for analysing a process family. In: International Workshop on Petri Nets and Software Engineering 2014 (PNSE'14), 23–24 June 2014, Tunis, Tunesia, pp. 269–288. CEUR-WS. org (2014)

22. Schunselaar, D.M., Verbeek, H., Reijers, H.A., van der Aalst, W.M.: Yawl in the cloud: supporting process sharing and variability. In: Business Process Management Workshops: BPM 2014 International Workshops, Eindhoven, The Netherlands, 7–8 September 2014, Revised Papers 12, pp. 367–379. Springer (2015)

23. Schunselaar, D.M.M., Verbeek, E., van der Aalst, W.M.P., Raijers, H.A.: Creating sound and reversible configurable process models using CoSeNets. In: Abramowicz, W., Kriksciuniene, D., Sakalauskas, V. (eds.) BIS 2012. LNBIP, vol. 117, pp. 24–35. Springer, Heidelberg (2012). https://doi.org/10.1007/978-3-642-30359-3_3

24. Buijs, J.C.: Flexible evolutionary algorithms for mining structured process models. Ph.D. thesis, Technische Universiteit Eindhoven (2014)

25. Loiola, E.M., da Silveira, D.S., Araújo, J., Moreira, A.: Business process families: a case study in the brazilian public sector. In: CAiSE Industry Track. Citeseer (2016)

26. Cognini, R., Corradini, F., Polini, A., Re, B.: Extending feature models to express variability in business process models. In: Advanced Information Systems Engineering Workshops: CAiSE 2015 International Workshops, Stockholm, Sweden, 8–9 June 2015, Proceedings 27, pp. 245–256. Springer (2015)

27. Cognini, R., Corradini, F., Polini, A., Re, B.: Business process feature model: an approach to deal with variability of business processes. In: Domain-Specific Conceptual Modeling: Concepts, Methods and Tools, pp. 171–194 (2016)

28. Cognini, R., Polini, A., Polzonetti, A., Re, B.: Bpfm: a notation and an approach to homogenize variable business processes for public services. In: 2015 IIAI 4th International Congress on Advanced Applied Informatics, pp. 34–39. IEEE (2015)

29. Fraley, C., Raftery, A.E.: How many clusters? which clustering method? answers via model-based cluster analysis. Comput. J. **41**(8), 578–588 (1998)

30. Saxena, A., et al.: A review of clustering techniques and developments. Neurocomputing **267**, 664–681 (2017)

31. Xu, R., Wunsch, D.: Survey of clustering algorithms. IEEE Trans. Neural Networks **16**(3), 645–678 (2005)

32. Alelyani, S., Tang, J., Liu, H.: Feature selection for clustering: a review. Data Clustering: Algorithms Appl. **29**(1) (2013)

33. Verleysen, M., François, D.: The curse of dimensionality in data mining and time series prediction. In: International Work-Conference on Artificial Neural Networks, pp. 758–770. Springer (2005)

34. Khalid, S., Khalil, T., Nasreen, S.: A survey of feature selection and feature extraction techniques in machine learning. In: 2014 Science and Information Conference, pp. 372–378. IEEE (2014)

35. Jain, A.K., Murty, M.N., Flynn, P.J.: Data clustering: a review. ACM Comput. Surv. (CSUR) **31**(3), 264–323 (1999)
36. Hastie, T., Tibshirani, R., Friedman, J.H., Friedman, J.H.: The Elements of Statistical Learning: Data Mining, Inference, and Prediction, vol. 2. Springer (2009)
37. Halkidi, M., Batistakis, Y., Vazirgiannis, M.: On clustering validation techniques. J. Intell. Inf. Syst. **17**(2), 107–145 (2001)
38. Song, M., Günther, C.W., Van der Aalst, W.M.: Trace clustering in process mining. In: International Conference on Business Process Management, pp. 109–120. Springer (2008)
39. Zandkarimi, F., Rehse, J.R., Soudmand, P., Hoehle, H.: A generic framework for trace clustering in process mining. In: 2020 2nd International Conference on Process Mining (ICPM), pp. 177–184. IEEE (2020)
40. Lu, X., Tabatabaei, S.A., Hoogendoorn, M., Reijers, H.A.: Trace clustering on very large event data in healthcare using frequent sequence patterns. In: International Conference on Business Process Management, pp. 198–215. Springer (2019)
41. Zelst, S.J.v., Cao, Y.: A generic framework for attribute-driven hierarchical trace clustering. In: International Conference on Business Process Management, pp. 308–320. Springer (2020)
42. Bose, R., van der Aalst, W.M.: Trace clustering based on conserved patterns: towards achieving better process models. In: International Conference on Business Process Management, pp. 170–181. Springer (2009)
43. Luengo, D., Sepúlveda, M.: Applying clustering in process mining to find different versions of a business process that changes over time. In: International Conference on Business Process Management, pp. 153–158. Springer (2011)
44. Greco, G., Guzzo, A., Pontieri, L., Sacca, D.: Discovering expressive process models by clustering log traces. IEEE Trans. Knowl. Data Eng. **18**(8), 1010–1027 (2006)
45. Medeiros, A.K.A.D., et al.: Process mining based on clustering: a quest for precision. In: International Conference on Business Process Management, pp. 17–29. Springer (2007)
46. Song, M., Yang, H., Siadat, S.H., Pechenizkiy, M.: A comparative study of dimensionality reduction techniques to enhance trace clustering performances. Expert Syst. Appl. **40**(9), 3722–3737 (2013)
47. Jung, J.Y., Bae, J.: Workflow clustering method based on process similarity. In: International Conference on Computational Science and Its Applications, pp. 379–389. Springer (2006)
48. Jung, J.Y., Bae, J., Liu, L.: Hierarchical clustering of business process models. Int. J. of Innov. Comput. Inf. Control **5**(12), 1349–4198 (2009)
49. Koninck, P.D., Nelissen, K., Baesens, B., Snoeck, M., Weerdt, J.D., et al.: An approach for incorporating expert knowledge in trace clustering. In: International Conference on Advanced Information Systems Engineering, pp. 561–576. Springer (2017)
50. Ghahfarokhi, A.F., Akoochekian, F., Zandkarimi, F., van der Aalst, W.M.: Clustering object-centric event logs. arXiv preprint arXiv:2207.12764 (2022)
51. Barbon Jr., S., Ceravolo, P., Damiani, E., Marques Tavares, G.: Evaluating trace encoding methods in process mining. In: International Symposium: From Data to Models and Back, pp. 174–189. Springer (2020)
52. Bose, R.J.C., Van der Aalst, W.M.: Context aware trace clustering: Towards improving process mining results. In: proceedings of the 2009 SIAM International Conference on Data Mining, pp. 401–412. SIAM (2009)
53. Rousseeuw, P.J.: Silhouettes: a graphical aid to the interpretation and validation of cluster analysis. J. Comput. Appl. Math. **20**, 53–65 (1987)

54. Verbeek, E.: Process discovery contest 2020 (2021). https://doi.org/10.4121/14626020.v1, https://data.4tu.nl/articles/dataset/Process_Discovery_Contest_2020/14626020/1

55. Van Oirschot, Y., van Dongen, B., Buijs, J., Dijkman, R.: Using trace clustering for configurable process discovery explained by event log data. university of technology, master of business information systems, department of mathematics and computer science (2014)

56. Buijs, J.C., van Dongen, B.F., van der Aalst, W.M.: Towards cross-organizational process mining in collections of process models and their executions. In: Business Process Management Workshops: BPM 2011 International Workshops, Clermont-Ferrand, France, 29 August 2011, Revised Selected Papers, Part II 9, pp. 2–13. Springer (2012)

57. Döhring, M., Reijers, H.A., Smirnov, S.: Configuration vs. adaptation for business process variant maintenance: an empirical study. Inf. Syst. **39**, 108–133 (2014)

58. Leemans, S.J.: Robust process mining with guarantees. In: BPM (Dissertation/Demos/Industry), pp. 46–50. Springer (2018)

59. Corradini, F., Luciani, C., Morichetta, A., Piangerelli, M.: Managing variability of large public administration event log collections: Dealing with concept drift. In: International Conference on Business Informatics Research, pp. 31–44. Springer (2023)

60. Corradini, F., Luciani, C., Morichetta, A., Piangerelli, M., Polini, A.: Label-independent feature engineering-based clustering in public administration event logs. EGOV-CeDEM-ePart **222**, 2022 (2022)

A Research Roadmap for Digital Twins of an Organization

Arianna Fedeli[1(✉)] ⓘ, Ghina Kassem[2], Khaled Sherif[2] ⓘ,
Emanuele Laurenzi[2] ⓘ, and Andrea Polini[3] ⓘ

[1] Gran Sasso Science Institute, L'Aquila, Italy
`arianna.fedeli@gssi.it`
[2] University of Applied Sciences and Arts Northwestern Switzerland, Olten,
Switzerland
`{ghina.kassem,khaled.sherif}@students.fhnw.ch, emanuele.laurenzi@fhnw.ch`
[3] University of Camerino, Camerino, Italy
`andrea.polini@unicam.it`

Abstract. The Digital Twin of an Organization (DTO) rapidly changes
how businesses operate. A DTO is a dynamic, virtual replica of an organization's processes, systems, and assets with immense potential to gain
real-time visibility into its operations, optimize processes, and make data-
driven decisions. However, realizing a DTO presents several obstacles,
including accurately reflecting the organization and addressing technical
implementation issues. This work presents a twofold contribution: a systematic analysis of existing academic literature to identify key obstacles
hindering DTO adoption, and a validation workshop involving 40 working students with professional experience in the Information and Communication Technology sector. The workshop served to validate the identified challenges and elicit potential solutions. The outcome is a roadmap
outlining a core set of challenges essential to the development of DTOs,
along with actionable guidelines to support their implementation in organizational settings.

Keywords: Digital Twin · Digital Twin of an Organization · DTO
Challenges · DTO Roadmap

1 Introduction

The increasing complexity of organizational systems, coupled with the growing
availability of real-time digital data, has highlighted the need for advanced methods to model, monitor, and adapt organizations in a dynamic and data-driven
way. In this context, the concept of the Digital Twin of an Organization (DTO)
is emerging as a promising paradigm. A DTO extends the concept of a classical
Digital Twin (DT) and Process Digital Twin (PDT) [16] with a dynamic, virtual representation of an entire enterprise, encompassing its processes, systems,
people, and assets. Distinct from the physical or product-centric DT, the DTO

© The Author(s), under exclusive license to Springer Nature Switzerland AG 2026
R. Deneckère et al. (Eds.): BIR 2025, LNBIP 562, pp. 238–254, 2026.
https://doi.org/10.1007/978-3-032-04375-7_15

provides a view of the organization, enabling real-time insights, optimization, and data-driven decision-making [2] with virtual replicas. Enhancing the current enterprise activities, which often operate in silos, focusing on specific business processes or functions [5], with a DTO representation offers the potential for a unified platform to capture a complete vision of the organization and focusing on the different stakeholders involved, the organization's structure, processes, resources, data, and goals [36]. When creating DTOs, executives can experiment with different and new strategies, identify bottlenecks, and simulate the impact of changes before implementing them in the real world. Despite its potential, the development and practical adoption of DTOs remain at an early stage [2]. Only a few studies currently exist [1,14] on the practical aspects and implementation of DTOs within companies, leading to preliminary findings that focus more on simulating specific business processes rather than the comprehensive representation of DTOs in their entirety.

To address these gaps, this paper presents a **research roadmap** that identifies key challenges and outlines strategic directions for future investigation. The roadmap is developed by a dual-method approach: (i) a structured review of the scientific literature, where we identified the state-of-the-art and proposed 12 open challenges; and (ii) a practitioner-oriented workshop, conducted with 40 industry professionals currently involved in the Master of Science program in Business Information Systems (BIS) at the University of Applied Sciences Northwestern Switzerland (FHNW), to capture practical insights and barriers to DTO implementation in real-world organizational settings. The workshop candidates, which will be comprised of individuals with both technical and business expertise, offered a hands-on approach, and practical skills and knowledge from various industries. Integrating with the literature, the workshop participants aimed to gather qualitative data through focused and structured discussions, allowing for a deeper exploration of the issues identified in the literature. Therefore, participants rated these challenges with high, medium, and low priorities, and practical guidelines were suggested [20]. Finally, we proposed the DTO roadmap, designed to serve as a strategic guide for researchers, combining academic and practitioners' findings with guidelines to start implementing a DTO.

2   Background

The DT technology, which involves creating a virtual representation of a physical entity, has paved the way for a new concept: the DTO. The concept of the DTO is not entirely new, as it builds on the already established practices of extending and digitalizing processes within an organization [2], where they have progressively adopted digital tools to model business operations, facilitating process monitoring, control, and transformation. The DTO extends these functionalities to encompass entire organizational processes, systems, and operations, permitting real-time simulation and analysis of organizations' behavior and performance [3].

According to Negri et al. [27], the DTO can be understood as a progressive model that mirrors an organization's digital maturity degree, with three key integration levels between the physical and virtual worlds: the model, shadow, and twin [35]. At its core, the *DTO model* provides a static organizational representation, diagrams, process maps, and conceptual models, manually maintained and disconnected from real-time data. This level aligns with established practices like BPMN [37] and TOGAF [21], which aid documentation but lack integration or responsiveness. The *DTO Shadow* enhances this by introducing real-time data capture from enterprise systems, IoT devices, and APIs, creating a dynamic digital reflection of the organization. Supported by real-time integration and event-driven architectures [6,8,17], this layer improves situational awareness and decision-making, though it still depends on human interpretation. At its most advanced stage, the *DTO Twin*, or simply DTO, is a fully synchronized, autonomous digital replica of the organization. Beyond real-time mirroring, it integrates predictive models, optimization techniques, and intelligent agents capable of interacting with and influencing operations [9,24,35]. This enables scenario-based simulations, automated decision-making, and continuous optimization. Supporting technologies include machine learning, digital simulation, AI-driven decision support systems, and cyber-physical feedback mechanisms.

However, as Caporuscio et al. [14] emphasize, at the current stage, DTOs represent a significant technological challenge, yet they expose a multitude of engineering challenges. Indeed, as also discussed by Parmar et al. [29], building a DTO is a collective effort required by the entire organization to consider several interconnected aspects. Indeed, different from a DT of a physical object, which, once modeled, can be reused for different DTs, a DTO is strictly unique to each organization. This uniqueness is given by the specific business processes that the organization decided to follow, as well as the various stakeholders involved in it [10]. This uniqueness cannot be replicated or transferred to another organization, as it encompasses the specific processes, structures, culture, and dynamics of the organization it represents. This involves the collaboration of various stakeholders, each bringing unique expertise to ensure its success.

Consequently, according to Agrawal et al. [1], evaluating and selecting the most suitable technological capabilities for DTO implementation proves difficult, potentially resulting in biased choices and overlooked opportunities. In general, there is a lack of conceptual and methodological maturity at the current stage, which is essential to transform DTO from an emerging technological vision to a stable and strategic component for the governance of future organizations [19,23].

3   Literature Analysis and Workshop Protocol

We conducted a literature analysis to identify key challenges and opportunities related to DTOs. While not exhaustive or systematic, it provided a targeted overview. To validate and expand on these findings, we held a workshop with 40 students from the Master of Science in Business Information Systems at FHNW, who are also professionals in various industries. This workshop offered practitioner insights, further refining the identified challenges.

Research Strategy. We conducted a literature analysis to identify key challenges and barriers to DTO implementation. Relevant keywords included "Digital Twin of an Organization", "DTO", "DTO Stakeholders", "DTO Components", "DTO Challenges", and "DTO Barriers". We reviewed papers from major scientific databases, Web of Science [33], Science Direct [11], IEEE Xplore [15], and ACM Digital Library [25], commonly used in Information Systems and Computer Science research. We considered publications from 1960, marking the conceptual origin of DTs, through 2024 to ensure stable data. Articles were selected based on relevance to DTOs, focusing on real-world applications, architectures, challenges, and benefits. Inclusion criteria required studies to propose or apply digital twins in organizational contexts. We excluded non-English works, studies without DTO design or application strategies, and non-scientific or inaccessible texts (e.g., posters, abstracts). The initial search yielded 282 publications. After applying the exclusion criteria, 120 documents remained. We then conducted backward snowballing [18], identifying 3 additional articles. All 123 documents were reviewed in full, and 17 were found to align fully with the main scope. Further details on the protocol and results are available in the repository[1].

Workshop Organization. To further analyze the potential of DTOs, a workshop was organized with 40 Master of Science students from FHNW, specializing in Business Information Systems. This diverse group, composed of working professionals with backgrounds in both technical and business domains, brought valuable expertise to the discussion. These students were selected for their academic foundation in information systems and their practical experience in various ICT-related industries. Participants reported an average of 7+ years of professional experience, and their roles ranged from business managers to software developers, consultants, and business analysts. The workshop aims to provide a dual perspective, from the literature and practitioners, to derive unique insights into the challenges and opportunities associated with DTOs. The workshop aimed to build a shared understanding of DTOs and stimulate critical reflection. It began with a theoretical session by experts, covering DTO principles, motivations, and benefits, followed by practical activities to deepen engagement. Participants were divided into two groups, with parallel sessions led by facilitators. After the first round, facilitators switched rooms to ensure consistency. Group outcomes were not shared to preserve independent insights. The groups conducted brainstorming sessions to explore DTO applications across diverse sectors, encouraging creative thinking beyond textbook definitions. Moderators facilitated discussions, linking academic knowledge with professional experience. After brainstorming, participants anonymously rated the urgency of literature-based challenges via a questionnaire. Moderators then guided group discussions to compare ratings, identify patterns, and explore discrepancies. These insights informed the roadmap in Sect. 5.

---

[1] https://github.com/AriannaFedeli/DTO-roadmap.

4   Challenges and Barriers in DTO Adoption

Transforming your organization's paradigm is more than applying a new technology; it is about changing how an organization perceives and manages itself. However, this complex activity brings several challenges. Literature analysis results expose several challenges that would cause a setback in adopting DTOs inside organizations. Those challenges are reported in Table 1. For each Challenge (CH), it is also highlighted how it slows down the DTO adoption.

Table 1. Challenges and Barriers affecting DTO Adoption

ID	Challenge	Description
CH1	**Lack of devices capacity** [5, 28, 29]	Insufficient device capabilities hinder data collection and system performance, especially in heterogeneous environments
CH2	**No clear strategy** [2, 4, 5, 12–14, 28, 30, 38]	Unclear roadmaps and expertise gaps delay DTO deployment and create strategic paralysis and uncertainties
CH3	**High investment** [12, 14, 34]	Substantial upfront costs for modeling and infrastructure deter organizations, particularly those with limited digital maturity
CH4	**SME financial barriers** [4, 12]	Ongoing lifecycle costs (updates, integrations) strain budgets, making DTOs unsustainable for SMEs
CH5	**Costs of infrastructure** [28, 30]	Fragmented, expensive tech stacks with interoperability issues escalate total ownership costs
CH6	**Lack of expertise** [2, 26, 38]	Scarcity of interdisciplinary skills (e.g., modeling + analytics) slows development and maintenance
CH7	**Access to data streams** [4, 12, 14, 19, 26, 31]	Scalable, low-latency infrastructure is critical but challenging for real-time data synchronization
CH8	**Varying data quality** [2, 32, 38]	Inconsistent, incomplete data from disparate sources undermines model accuracy and trust
CH9	**Long-term sustainability** [4, 5, 12]	Dependency on third-party APIs and unclear ROI threaten DTO longevity
CH10	**Cultural barriers** [12, 13, 32]	Employee pushback against data-driven workflows necessitates change management
CH11	**Capture complex dynamics** [5, 12, 13, 28, 30, 38]	Modeling intangible human interactions (e.g., teamwork, decisions) remains elusive
CH12	**Ethical concerns** [19, 26, 29, 38]	Granular monitoring risks privacy violations and algorithmic bias without transparent governance

The lack of devices with sufficient capacity (CH1) hinders the ability to collect necessary data for the DTO, creates uncertainty, and inhibits organizations from taking the first steps. Indeed, the system's complexity is directly tied to the number and capacity of devices, with insufficient capacity decreasing performance and provoking problems on data integration, on capturing tacit knowledge, and on maintaining the DTO's accuracy over time [28]. As noted in existing research [29], the complexity of systems, especially those handling large datasets in real-time, is influenced by the availability and quality of devices needed to collect data across diverse, heterogeneous systems that must collaborate. Up to now, many organizations lack the infrastructure, such as sensors or IoT devices, necessary to collect and process real-time data for the DTO [5].

The **absence of clear implementation strategies (CH2)**, which encompasses a lack of expertise in communication framework development, uncertainties around data handling, and insufficient knowledge of digitization and data visualization, is a present challenge. These gaps hinder the organization's ability to effectively deploy a DTO system. Determining the point to start with digitization is a major issue for many organizations [12,13]. There is often uncertainty about which parts of the organization to model first, which technologies should be prioritized, or how to assess the initial value of the DTO. This lack of a clear starting point can result in strategic paralysis [14], where organizations struggle to make decisions, delaying the process and diminishing the potential benefits of a DTO. As the literature suggests, organizations often face difficulties when attempting to bring together these varied data sources into a cohesive DTO. The literature further highlights the importance of having a well-defined strategy for the implementation process to ensure that organizations can navigate the complexities of digital transformation [5,30]. Without a clear strategy, organizations are likely to encounter difficulties, starting with ensuring that the DTO accurately reflects their operations and delivers measurable value in its execution.

Closely related to this, the **High Initial Investment (CH3)** challenge requires developing and maintaining accurate virtual and simulation models for a DTO. These models must be capable of representing complex processes, which often necessitates advanced computational resources and specialized expertise. Several studies [12,14,34] emphasize this challenge, as starting a DTO initiative often involves substantial up-front costs, both for the necessary infrastructure and for the modeling efforts. For organizations with limited digital maturity or those under pressure to demonstrate short-term returns, this initial investment can be daunting. The development of a DTO requires sophisticated modeling techniques to capture the intricate dynamics and interactions within an organization's operations [7]. Moreover, the need to continuously update and maintain the virtual system adds to the ongoing costs of the DTO system.

Financial barriers (CH4) in DTO development extend throughout the entire lifecycle of the system, provoking concerns for many organizations, particularly small and medium-sized enterprises (**SMEs**), as they navigate the ongoing costs associated with a DTO. Literature suggests that the costs involved in continuously updating models, integrating new systems, and ensuring consistent data flow require sustained investment over time [12]. For instance, as highlighted in [4], as organizations evolve, their systems and processes could change, and the DTO needs to adapt to these shifts. Keeping the virtual model up-to-date requires ongoing technical support, software upgrades, and hardware enhancements, each of which comes with additional costs. This becomes especially difficult to manage when organizations are uncertain about the long-term value of the DTO.

A key challenge in implementing DTOs is the **High Infrastructure Cost (CH5)** due to the fragmented and complex technology stack required [28,30]. DTOs rely on multiple tools, as data integration platforms, simulation software, AI models, often from different vendors, increasing both acquisition and integration costs. Organizations must invest substantial effort into ensuring these disparate tools can interoperate, leading to higher integration costs and an ongoing need for specialized expertise. Additionally, maintaining interoperability between various systems requires continuous effort, driving up both operational and maintenance costs. This challenge becomes particularly difficult for SMEs, which often lack the financial resources to deploy and sustain a comprehensive DTO infrastructure.

Furthermore, the **Lack of a Necessary Skill (CH6)** and an expertise workforce with the necessary knowledge to design, integrate, and maintain a DTO is a significant barrier to adoption [2,26,38]. This challenge arises from the multifaceted nature of DTOs, which require a combination of skills spanning business knowledge, systems modeling, data analytics, and specialized technical expertise. Finding professionals who can bridge the gap between these different areas of expertise, even in interdisciplinary sectors where technical and strategic knowledge is necessary, is pivotal [2]. Also, the cost required to upskill the existing staff or hire new experts must be considered.

Even if a DTO is successfully implemented, maintaining and scaling it presents further obstacles. Literature shared the struggle of dealing with massive volumes of live data, where experts need to have a **continuous access and storage of live-streamed data (CH7)** [4,12,14,19,26,31]. The volume, velocity, and variety of real-time data generated by sensors, user interactions, and digital systems in an organization demand a robust infrastructure capable of handling high-throughput data ingestion and storage at scale. In this context, the difficulty of ensuring continuous access to real-time data while also maintaining the integrity of that data is exponential, especially when DTOs are applied to dynamic environments where data needs to be updated rapidly to reflect changes in the physical system.

Accordingly, the challenge of **processing of data of varying quality (CH8)** was highlighted [2,32,38]. Literature [2] mentioned how data from different sources, especially legacy systems, may be incomplete, inconsistently formatted, or less reliable than data from modern technologies like IoT devices. These discrepancies complicate integration, reduce confidence in DTO outputs, and require significant effort to clean and standardize data. Ensuring that data streams between these layers of the DTO remain consistent and are processed efficiently requires implementing common data standards, protocols, and governance frameworks.

A critical challenge in maintaining and scaling DTO is in the difficulty of **guaranteeing long-term sustainability (CH9)** of them [4,5,12]. For example, DTOs could rely on third-party software APIs for data exchange, but when these are deprecated or discontinued, the system risks becoming obsolete unless it undergoes constant updates and maintenance. Even though these aspects can be handled, the long-term impact and the return of investment and value proposition of DTOs remain unclear in this context, mainly because is an emerging concept that has not yet seen real developments in organizations [5].

Beyond technology and cost, DTO implementation faces significant organizational and **Cultural barriers (CH10)**. In particular, fostering a data-driven culture to support organizational change remains underexplored [12,13,32]. DTOs demand a shift in mindset across all levels [13], requiring employees to adopt data-centric practices that often contradict established routines. Resistance to change, especially without strong leadership and communication, can hinder adoption. The literature alerts that many DTO initiatives could neglect this cultural dimension, focusing mainly on technical aspects.

Developing a DTO requires addressing the challenge of **capturing intricate dynamics (CH11)** within organizational operations. As highlighted in the literature [5,13,30], DTOs must go beyond representing processes and systems to also reflect complex, often intangible elements such as human behavior and organizational interactions. For example, modeling informal decision-making or interdepartmental collaboration, like between sales and marketing, is critical as they are rarely formalized. Informal workflows, interpersonal dynamics, and non-linear decisions complicate the creation of comprehensive digital models [12,28,38]. While sensors can capture quantifiable data, DTO could miss the human factors that significantly influence performance [5,28]. Thus, effective DTOs must integrate both hard data (e.g., production metrics) and soft data (e.g., team dynamics, leadership styles).

DTOs must address **Ethical Concerns (CH12)** related to data transparency and employee monitoring. The literature highlights the risks that DTOs pose in organizational settings [19,29], building on existing debates around digital surveillance tools. While it is possible to track discrete metrics, DTOs aggregate data from diverse sources, behavioral analytics, IoT sensors, and AI models to form dynamic, detailed representations of workplace activities. This raises concerns about how such monitoring is perceived and experienced, especially as DTOs centralize data across platforms, including HR systems and wearable devices. As DTOs inherently enable feedback loops that can adjust roles or tasks, governance mechanisms are needed to safeguard transparency, mitigate bias, and protect employee autonomy [26,38].

5   Roadmap for DTO

This section outlines a research and implementation roadmap for DTO adoption, integrating literature-derived challenges with empirical evidence from practition-

Table 2. Urgency heatmap of DTO challenges based on urgency scores

Challenge	Urgency Point	Urgency Level
CH1: Lack of devices	2.40	Low
CH2: No clear strategy	5.40	High
CH3: High investments	5.25	High
CH4: SME financial barriers	2.06	Low
CH5: Cost of infrastructure	1.90	Low
CH6: Lack of expertise	3.50	Moderate
CH7: Access to data streams	1.87	Low
CH8: Varying data quality	2.44	Low
CH9: Long-term sustainability	3.94	Moderate
CH10: Cultural barriers	3.88	Moderate
CH11: Capture complex dynamics	4.50	High
CH12: Ethical Concerns	5.00	High

ers. Indeed, workshop participants rated each challenge on a scale from 1 (not urgent) to 6 (highly urgent), enabling prioritization for strategic planning. We then categorized the urgency scores as Low (1.00–2.50), requiring minimal concern, Moderate (2.51–4.00) requiring attention, or High (4.01–6.00) perceived as an immediate concern, as shown in Table 2. This data permits us to build the roadmap, structuring the challenges around the four EA layers: Business, Application, Information, and Technology, providing a strategic view of DTO implementation. While each challenge is mapped to a primary layer, many span multiple domains, reflecting their interdependence, as illustrated in Fig. 1. These findings help identify where to focus early efforts and how to plan long-term strategies, and can evolve alongside DTO maturity. Detailed results are available in the repository[2].

Business Layer. The business layer includes the organizational strategies, goals, processes, and structures that DTOs aim to support and transform.

Among the various issues surfaced during the study, participants consistently emphasized the lack of a clear strategic direction **(CH2)** as the most urgent concern, assigning it a mean urgency score of 5.40. This underscores the need for organizations to articulate coherent, long-term strategies for DTO development. As several participants pointed out, the lack of a defined vision often results in fragmented initiatives with limited business value. While digital transformation is a widely known concept, the concrete articulation of DTOs, scope, goals, and alignment with business processes remains ambiguous. One participant remarked, "Without a clear north star, you can digitize parts of the organization but remain directionless," capturing the strategic drift experienced in many cases. This signals the need for structured frameworks and adaptable tem-

---

[2] https://github.com/AriannaFedeli/DTO-roadmap.

plates to support DTO planning and implementation, in line with the iterative, maturity-driven approach described by [5].

The challenge of high investment **(CH3)** requirements was rated with an urgency score of 5.25, particularly salient in traditional sectors such as manufacturing, where the technological baseline is often outdated. Participants noted that organizations tend to underestimate the cumulative nature of DTO costs, which include not only technological infrastructure (e.g., IoT devices, simulation models, interoperability layers) but also specialized personnel and long-term operational expenses. Even in cases where strategic intent exists, the burden of initial and ongoing investment acts as a major inhibitor to adoption. This challenge, also to its implications for budgeting and strategic resource allocation, affects technological decisions across other layers of the DTO stack.

Concerns about the long-term sustainability **(CH9)** of DTOs were also recurrent, with this issue receiving a moderate urgency score of 3.94. Participants reflected on the need for sustained organizational commitment, funding continuity, and architectural choices that support system evolution over time. As DTOs are not short-term projects but rather dynamic infrastructures, there is a risk of them being initiated as pilot experiments that lack follow-through. Some participants expressed concern that DTOs might "become short-term pilots without long-term support or funding, particularly when organizational priorities shift". Sustainability was discussed not only in technical terms (e.g., modularity and decoupling to enable incremental updates) but also from a broader strategic and societal perspective, including the need for alignment with Environmental, Social, and Governance indicators.

Cultural aspects further complicate the business layer. The issue of cultural barriers **(CH10)** and internal resistance to change, captured under the theme of cultural barriers, received an urgency score of 3.88. Participants described a variety of challenges: reluctance to embrace new technologies, limited understanding of DTO benefits, and heterogeneous levels of digital maturity across departments. These issues were particularly pronounced in traditional or hierarchical organizations, where DTOs are often perceived as disruptive. One participant stated, "It is not just about knowing the technology, it is about making people feel safe about the changes that come with it", emphasizing the emotional and behavioral dimensions of this transformation. To overcome such resistance, participants recommended participatory design practices, co-creation workshops, and experiential learning initiatives aimed at building trust, reducing uncertainty, and fostering shared ownership.

Although the issue of financial constraints for SMEs **(CH4)** was perceived as less urgent, it still represents a considerable barrier to entry for many organizations. Participants assigned this concern a relatively low urgency with a score of 2.06, but stressed its importance for ensuring inclusive access to DTO innovation. SMEs often lack the resources to experiment with DTOs, unlike larger firms. Therefore, participants suggested that DTO strategies for smaller organizations should focus on lightweight, modular, and scalable solutions that offer immediate, tangible value. Leveraging open-source technologies, shared data platforms, and regional innovation ecosystems was proposed as a viable path forward.

Proposed Guidelines. Participants propose that Model-Driven Engineering practices [22] could support the **lack of strategies (CH2)**, defining an approach for developing DTO, with goals and requirements at different abstraction levels, ensuring traceability and consistency across implementations. In this domain, EA frameworks (e.g., TOGAF, ArchiMate) could be extended to include DTO-specific elements [32] (e.g., dedicated viewpoints, links DTO and business capabilities, and models of interactions between digital and physical processes). This could support addressing the **high investment challenge (CH3)**, shifting in mindset to see the DTOs as long-term strategic assets. Integrating DTO planning into EA, through capability maps, cost-benefit analyses, and risk assessments, can help align investments with business value and make DTO benefits visible to decision-makers. Ensuring **long-term sustainability (CH9)** requires modular, loosely coupled DTO architectures that enable continuous evolution. Participants suggest embedding DTOs in ESG-oriented strategies to ensure both technical and organizational resilience. To address **financial barriers for SMEs (CH4)**, participants propose lightweight, incremental DTO implementations using open-source tools, modular components, and shared platforms. Public–private partnerships and targeted funding mechanisms were also suggested. Overcoming **cultural barriers (CH10)** requires participatory design, user engagement, and change management practices. Internal champions, co-creation workshops, and hands-on training can build trust and reduce resistance.

Application Layer. This layer focuses on the software systems and services that operationalize DTOs. The challenge of capturing complex dynamics **(CH11)** scored 4.50, revealing the difficulty in faithfully modeling real-world processes and interactions within an DTO. The emphasis on ethics reflected growing sensitivity to issues such as employee monitoring, algorithmic decision-making, and data sovereignty. Several participants noted that "DTOs have the potential to become intrusive if not designed with ethical guardrails in place," underscoring that trust and transparency must be integral to any DTO strategy.

Also, Ethical concerns **(CH12)** were rated highly (5.00), which reflects growing awareness among practitioners about issues such as privacy, surveillance, and data transparency. Ethical concerns were rated highly (5.00), reflecting growing awareness among practitioners about issues such as privacy, surveillance, and data transparency. Participants emphasized that DTOs need to represent not only structural aspects of organizations but also dynamic processes and interactions that evolve. Addressing this requires advances in simulation capabilities and real-time decision support. AI in DTOs raises ethical questions about bias, accountability, and explainability. Several participants pointed out the risks of using DTOs as black-box decision systems, especially when simulating or predicting human behavior. The lack of expertise **(CH6)** was scored 3.50, highlighting the need for upskilling and training to support DTO initiatives. Participants noted a significant gap in the necessary skills and knowledge to develop and implement DTOs, highlighting the importance of investing in education and training programs for existing teams.

> **Proposed Guidelines.** It is essential to embed **ethical considerations (CH12)** in designing DTOs through frameworks that ensure transparency, privacy, explainability, and data sovereignty. Bias and black-box decision-making should be mitigated, especially with AI intersects with human behavior. Enhancing simulation capabilities to **capture complex dynamics (CH11)**, adopting multi-agent modeling, and developing real-time decision support systems capable of catching the evolving and complex dynamics of organizations is crucial. The **lack of expertise (CH6)** calls for dedicated upskilling initiatives through cross-disciplinary training programs that integrate technical, organizational, and ethical dimensions of DTOs. Continuous learning opportunities and the establishment of validation and certification procedures should be set to ensure that DTO applications meet both functional and ethical standards.

Information Layer. The Information layer includes the availability, structure, and management of data that fuels DTOs. Here, the data quality (**CH8**) and cost of infrastructure (**CH5**) reflect the infrastructural and financial constraints tied to data acquisition. Although these challenges received relatively low urgency scores, 2.40 and 1.90 respectively, they were not considered irrelevant. Some participants noted that Some participants stated that in sectors such as healthcare and manufacturing, high-quality data remains difficult to obtain due to legacy systems, lack of standardization, or insufficient sensors coverage. However, the perceived low urgency of these challenges may stem from a growing reliance on mature cloud infrastructures and affordable IoT solutions, which are progressively reducing the technical and financial barriers to data collection and management. While these challenges are cataloged in the Information layer, they also contaminate the Technology Layer, where their implications are more directly connected to the implementation, scalability, and integration of enabling technologies.

> *Proposed Guidelines.***Data Quality (CH8)** is essential to establish robust data governance frameworks that ensure consistency, accuracy, and reliability across data sources. This includes defining clear roles and responsibilities, adopting conceptual data models, and developing semantic assets as ontologies [14]. Designing the data flows and integration pipelines is key to enabling access and exchange across distributed systems [5]. In parallel, to mitigate the **Cost of Infrastructure (CH5)**, organizations should exploit mature cloud-based and hybrid architectures that offer flexible storage and compute capabilities while minimizing capital expenditure. The design of efficient data flows and integration mechanisms is also critical to enable connectivity among distributed systems, supporting both real-time and batch data processing.

Technology Layer. The lower urgency given to the lack of devices and access to data streams challenges (**CH1** scored 2.40, **CH7** scored 1.87) was often justified by the participants' current work environments. Many of them already operate in companies that have adopted IoT platforms, ERP systems, or other data-generating infrastructure. As one participant worker in the manufacturing sector shared, "Getting data is not the problem, we are drowning in it. The challenge is knowing what to do with it." This shift in focus, from data availability to data interpretation and usage, suggests that some technological barriers are gradually being overcome, allowing attention to shift to more strategic and organizational issues.

> ***Proposed Guidelines.*** To address the **lack of devices (CH1)**, organizations should adopt cost-effective and scalable strategies for data acquisition by leveraging the increasing affordability of IoT and edge technologies. This enables incremental deployment of sensing infrastructure, particularly in sectors where full digitization is still in progress (SMEs). To ensure that the **data stream** collected is **accessible** and meaningful across the organization **(CH7)**, cloud-based data platforms could be exploited. Also, it could be useful to introduce automated data validation and anomaly detection mechanisms to ensure that ingested data is accurate and reliable.

6   Observation and Conclusion

Several challenges need to be overcome to fully reach DTO's potential. In this research paper, we highlighted 12 main challenges that could drive the development and easier application of DTOs inside organizations. The workshop participants evaluate these challenges in terms of urgency perceived and propose solutions to overcome those. One limitation of this study lies in the composition of the workshop participants, who were primarily working students. Indeed, the working students may not represent the full spectrum of stakeholders involved in the implementation of DTOs. This may have influenced the perceived urgency of certain challenges, potentially underestimating their criticality compared to views from senior professionals or executives. The analysis of these data results in the *DTO Research Roadmap* presented and guidelines for starting to enable a DTO. By addressing these areas, future research can contribute to the maturation of DTO technology and its widespread adoption. Future studies could include a broader range of stakeholders through interviews, focus groups, or co-design workshops, ensuring representation from various sectors, organizational roles, and experience levels. Nevertheless, since the identified challenges were derived from a structured literature review and systematically categorized according to the Enterprise Architecture layers, we argue that the resulting roadmap retains its general validity and applicability. Also, future research needs to focus on industry-specific DTO elements, novel methodologies, and emerging technologies, and consider diverse organizational contexts. Indeed, the unique requirements of organizations based on their nature must be carefully examined.

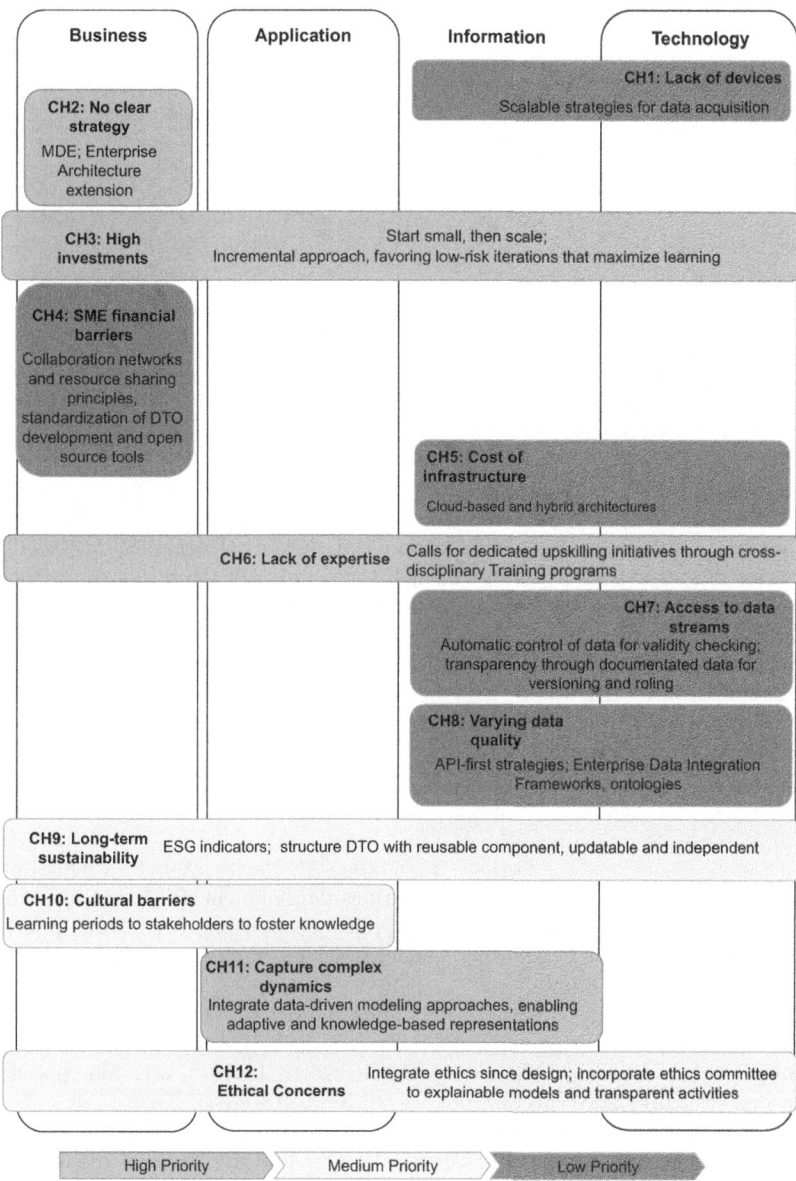

Fig. 1. DTO challenges categorized into levels of impact and proposed guidelines.

Acknowledgements. The work for this paper has been carried out within the module "Emerging Topics in Business Information Systems", an elective course of the Master of Science in Business Information Systems from the FHNW University of Applied Sciences and Arts Northwestern Switzerland. This work is also supported by Project PE 0000020 CHANGES, PNRR Mission 4 Component 2 Investment 1.3" funded by EU - NextGenerationEU.

References

1. Agrawal, A., Fischer, M., Singh, V.: Digital twin: from concept to practice. J. Manag. Eng. **38**(3), 06022001 (2022)

2. Becker, M.C., Pentland, B.T.: Digital twin of an organization: are you serious? In: Marrella, A., Weber, B. (eds.) BPM 2021. LNBIP, vol. 436, pp. 243–254. Springer, Cham (2022). https://doi.org/10.1007/978-3-030-94343-1_19

3. Bizzdesign: Building a digital twin of your organization (2023). https://bizzdesign.com/blog/building-a-digital-twin-of-your-organization/

4. Caccamo, C., Pedrazzoli, P., Eleftheriadis, R., Chiara Magnanini, M.: Using the process digital twin as a tool for companies to evaluate the return on investment of manufacturing automation. Procedia CIRP **107**, 724–728 (2022). https://doi.org/10.1016/j.procir.2022.05.052. https://www.sciencedirect.com/science/article/pii/S2212827122003365, leading manufacturing systems transformation - Proceedings of the 55th CIRP Conference on Manufacturing Systems 2022

5. Caporuscio, M., Edrisi, F., Hallberg, M., Johannesson, A., Kopf, C., Perez-Palacin, D.: Architectural concerns for digital twin of the organization. In: Jansen, A., Malavolta, I., Muccini, H., Ozkaya, I., Zimmermann, O. (eds.) ECSA 2020. LNCS, vol. 12292, pp. 265–280. Springer, Cham (2020). https://doi.org/10.1007/978-3-030-58923-3_18

6. Corradini, F., Fedeli, A., Fornari, F., Polini, A., Re, B.: X-IoT: a model-driven approach for cross-platform IoT applications development. In: Proceedings of the 37th ACM/SIGAPP Symposium on Applied Computing, SAC 2022, pp. 1448–1451. Association for Computing Machinery, New York (2022). https://doi.org/10.1145/3477314.3507164

7. Corradini, F., Fedeli, A., Fornari, F., Polini, A., Re, B.: DTMN a modelling notation for digital twins. In: Sales, T.P., Proper, H.A., Guizzardi, G., Montali, M., Maggi, F.M., Fonseca, C.M. (eds.) EDOC 2022. LNBIP, vol. 466, pp. 63–78. Springer, Cham (2023). https://doi.org/10.1007/978-3-031-26886-1_4

8. Corradini, F., Fedeli, A., Fornari, F., Polini, A., Re, B.: Floware: a model-driven approach fostering reuse and customisation in IoT applications modelling and development. Softw. Syst. Model. **22**(1), 131–158 (2023)

9. Corradini, F., Fedeli, A., Polini, A., Re, B.: Towards a digital twin modelling notation. In: 2022 IEEE International Conference on Dependable, Autonomic and Secure Computing, International Conference on Pervasive Intelligence and Computing, International Conference on Cloud and Big Data Computing, International Conference on Cyber Science and Technology Congress (DASC/PiCom/CBDCom/CyberSciTech), pp. 1–6 (2022). https://doi.org/10.1109/DASC/PiCom/CBDCom/Cy55231.2022.9927827

10. Di Salle, A., et al.: Waste management through digital twins and business process modeling. In: Proceedings of the ACM/IEEE 27th International Conference on

Model Driven Engineering Languages and Systems, MODELS Companion 2024, pp. 513–517. Association for Computing Machinery, New York (2024). https://doi.org/10.1145/3652620.3687796

11. Direct, S.: Research articles. www.sciencedirect.com
12. Dorofeev, A., Kurganov, V., Filippova, N., Petrov, A., Zakharov, D., Iarkov, S.: Improving transportation management systems (TMSs) based on the concept of digital twins of an organization. Appl. Sci. **14**(4) (2024). https://doi.org/10.3390/app14041330. https://www.mdpi.com/2076-3417/14/4/1330
13. Dumas, M.: Constructing digital twins for accurate and reliable what-if business process analysis. Problems@ BPM **2938**, 23–27 (2021)
14. Edrisi, F., Perez-Palacin, D., Caporuscio, M., Giussani, S.: Developing and evolving a digital twin of the organization. IEEE Access **12**, 45475–45494 (2024). https://doi.org/10.1109/ACCESS.2024.3381778
15. Explore, I.: Research articles. http://www.ieeexplore.ieee.org/Xplore/home.jsp
16. Fedeli, A., et al.: How low-code platforms support digital twins of processes. Softw. Syst. Model. (2025). https://doi.org/10.1007/s10270-025-01310-4
17. Fedeli, A., Fornari, F., Polini, A., Re, B., Torres, V., Valderas, P.: FloBP: a model-driven approach for developing and executing IoT-enhanced business processes. Softw. Syst. Model. **23**(5), 1217–1246 (2024)
18. Felizardo, K.R., Mendes, E., Kalinowski, M., Souza, É.F., Vijaykumar, N.L.: Using forward snowballing to update systematic reviews in software engineering. In: Proceedings of the 10th ACM/IEEE International Symposium on Empirical Software Engineering and Measurement, pp. 1–6 (2016)
19. Frerichs, M., Nüttgens, M.: Modeling the enterprise digital twin: towards an open platform for analytics & compliance operations. In: Modellierung 2022, pp. 65–75. Gesellschaft für Informatik eV (2022)
20. Greefhorst, D., Proper, E., Greefhorst, D., Proper, E.: The Role of Enterprise Architecture. Springer, Cham (2011)
21. Josey, A.: TOGAF® version 9.1-A pocket guide. Van Haren (2016)
22. Kent, S.: Model driven engineering. In: Butler, M., Petre, L., Sere, K. (eds.) IFM 2002. LNCS, vol. 2335, pp. 286–298. Springer, Heidelberg (2002). https://doi.org/10.1007/3-540-47884-1_16
23. Kunin, V.A., Ryskov, I.E.: Application of digital twin of an enterprise in the context of implementation of the sustainable development concept in financial management. In: Rumyantseva, A., Anyigba, H., Sintsova, E., Vasilenko, N.V. (eds.) Finance, Economics, and Industry for Sustainable Development, pp. 79–92. Springer, Cham (2024). https://doi.org/10.1007/978-3-031-56380-5_7
24. Lehto, T.: A new game changer for business operations: digital twin of an organization (DTO) (2024). https://www.qpr.com/blog/www.qpr.com/blog/digital-twin-of-an-organization
25. Library, A.D.: Research articles. http://www.dl.acm.org
26. Lyytinen, K., Weber, B., Becker, M.C., Pentland, B.T.: Digital twins of organization: implications for organization design. J. Organ. Des. (2023). https://doi.org/10.1007/s41469-023-00151-z
27. Negri, E., Fumagalli, L., Macchi, M.: A review of the roles of digital twin in cps-based production systems. Procedia Manuf. **11**, 939–948 (2017). https://doi.org/10.1016/j.promfg.2017.07.198. https://www.sciencedirect.com/science/article/pii/S2351978917304067, 27th International Conference on Flexible Automation and Intelligent Manufacturing, FAIM2017, Modena, Italy, 27–30 June 2017

28. Park, G., Van Der Aalst, W.M.: Realizing a digital twin of an organization using action-oriented process mining. In: 2021 3rd International Conference on Process Mining (ICPM), pp. 104–111 (2021). https://doi.org/10.1109/ICPM53251.2021.9576846

29. Parmar, R., Leiponen, A., Thomas, L.D.: Building an organizational digital twin. Bus. Horiz. **63**(6), 725–736 (2020). https://doi.org/10.1016/j.bushor.2020.08.001. https://www.sciencedirect.com/science/article/pii/S0007681320301014

30. Rabe, M., Kilic, E.: Concept of a business-process-related digital twin based on systems theory and operational excellence. In: 2022 IEEE 28th International Conference on Engineering, Technology and Innovation (ICE/ITMC) & 31st International Association For Management of Technology (IAMOT) Joint Conference, pp. 1–9 (2022). https://doi.org/10.1109/ICE/ITMC-IAMOT55089.2022.10033175

31. Riss, U., Groher, W.: Digital twin of the organization - new requirements in business process management and beyond (2022)

32. Riss, U.V., Maus, H., Javaid, S., Jilek, C.: Digital twins of an organization for enterprise modeling. In: Grabis, J., Bork, D. (eds.) PoEM 2020. LNBIP, vol. 400, pp. 25–40. Springer, Cham (2020). https://doi.org/10.1007/978-3-030-63479-7_3

33. Web of Science: Research articles. www.webofscience.com

34. Shen, B., et al.: A cloud-edge collaboration framework for generating process digital twin. IEEE Trans. Cloud Comput. **12**(2), 388–404 (2024). https://doi.org/10.1109/TCC.2024.3362989

35. Tao, F., et al.: Digital twin and its potential application exploration. Comput. Integr. Manuf. Syst. **24**(1), 1–18 (2018)

36. Uhlemann, T., Lehmann, C., Steinhilper, R.: The digital twin: realizing the cyber-physical production system for industry 4.0. Procedia CIRP **61**, 335–340 (2017). https://doi.org/10.1016/j.procir.2016.11.152

37. White, S.A.: Introduction to BPMN. IBM Cooperation **2** (2004)

38. Wurm, B., et al.: Digital twins of organizations: a socio-technical view on challenges and opportunities for future research. Commun. Assoc. Inf. Syst. **52**, 552–565 (2023). https://doi.org/10.17705/1CAIS.05223

LLM and Generative AI in Modeling and Engineering

Empirical Insights into the Usage of Generative AI in Software Engineering

Kevin Stutz[1], Kurt Sandkuhl[2], and Michael Möhring[1](✉)

[1] Reutlingen University, Alteburg Str. 150, Reutlingen, Germany
Michael.moehring@reutlingen-university.de
[2] Chair of Business Information Systems, University of Rostock, 18051 Rostock, Germany
Kurt.sandkuhl@uni-rostock.de

Abstract. The usage of generative AI in the software engineering domain could be a beneficial tool. All phases of the software development can be supported. However, there are also different challenges that can occur. Based on empirical studies we examined and validated the usage of Generative AI in software engineering. We derived possible use cases, limitations and future research opportunities.

Keywords: Generative AI · Software Engineering · Expert Study

1 Introduction

Generative AI is an upcoming new technology [1] used in many business applications, such as in marketing for customer communication or ad generation [2]. It can improve operational processes in many ways. In particular, it offers the potential to increase productivity and efficiency across various domains while simultaneously contributing to cost reduction [3]. Reflecting this potential, the adoption of generative AI in business contexts rose markedly in 2024 compared to the previous year, with particularly strong growth observed in the IT division [3].

Despite this increase, a 2024 survey conducted by the Capgemini Research Institute revealed that only 11% of senior executives reported using generative AI in software engineering [4]. This is noteworthy given that among organizations utilizing generative AI in software development, approximately half reported improvements in the implementation activities and software quality [4]. Nonetheless, despite the promising potential of generative AI in software engineering, the current state of research in this area remains in its early stages [5]. Due to the importance in software engineering and the sparse research in this field, we have chosen a qualitative research method to answer the following research question: *How can generative AI be used in software engineering and what are the possible challenges using them?*

As the existing research in the field does not cover all aspects of AI use, our research focuses on the usage of Generative AI within the software engineering process [6] and the occurring challenges (see Sect. 2). The paper is structured as follows: first a research background of related research papers is given. Afterwards, a qualitative study

© The Author(s), under exclusive license to Springer Nature Switzerland AG 2026
R. Deneckère et al. (Eds.): BIR 2025, LNBIP 562, pp. 257–271, 2026.
https://doi.org/10.1007/978-3-032-04375-7_16

is designed in the method and data collection section. The empirical results of our study are described in the research section followed by a further validation round. Afterwards a conclusion and discussion is presented including implications, limitations and future research opportunities.

2 Related Research and Research Background

In recent years, the integration of generative AI into software engineering has emerged as a transformative trend [2]. This development builds upon foundational concepts in both traditional software engineering [6] and machine learning [2].

Software engineering is defined as the technical aspect of software development [6]. Traditionally, it involves several phases—conceptualization, design, implementation, deployment, and testing [6]—each presenting distinct challenges such as managing complexity, ensuring high quality, and meeting time and budget constraints [7]. Within these phases, various roles—ranging from domain experts and architects to developers and testers—collaborate to meet project goals [6]. However, due to the complexity and error-proneness of programming, identifying and fixing defects remains a persistent challenge [8], often requiring significant time and effort [9].

Generative AI, as a subfield of AI enabled through machine learning [2], offers new capabilities that are highly relevant for software engineering [10]. These generative models are trained on vast datasets [11] and demonstrate the ability to generate human-like text [2] and even source code [12]. With generative AI tools such as OpenAI's ChatGPT [2] and Microsoft's Copilot [13], developers can now interact with AI systems using natural language prompts to generate or analyze code [12], accelerating implementation and debugging processes [2]. The ability of generative AI to understand the structure and semantics of programming languages in a manner like natural language processing [12] has opened up new avenues for AI-assisted software development [2].

This convergence of AI and software engineering is not without its challenges [14]. The use of generative AI introduces concerns regarding output reliability [15], bias, and explainability which is particularly relevant in critical areas of application [12]. Additionally, there is an ongoing debate over intellectual property [12] and accountability for decisions made with the use of generative AI tools [16].

Despite these challenges, early research suggests that generative AI can have a significant impact in software engineering [10]. It holds promise in supporting software engineers during conceptual design [2], automating parts of implementation [12], facilitating testing, and even understanding documentation [2].

While prior studies have explored the role of generative AI in software engineering, they have predominantly focused on specific areas such as its implications for software engineering education [17, 18] or the roles most affected by generative AI [19]. Other publications only focus on individual phases of the development process, like requirements engineering [20].

However, there is a sparse research of empirically grounded theories on how generative AI can be used in the entire software engineering process and what challenges arise using it. This study seeks to address this research gap by systematically investigating the application of generative AI throughout the full software engineering process.

3 Method, Data Collection and Data Analysis

To explore the current use of generative AI in software engineering, this study applied a qualitative research approach by analyzing the empirical data in relation to the Straussian variant of Grounded Theory (GT) [21, 22]. This qualitative research methodology is particularly well-suited for emerging research areas [21–23], as it facilitates the development of theory grounded in empirical data rather than relying solely on theoretical considerations [24].

3.1 Methodology of Qualitative Data Analysis

The analysis followed the structured coding process outlined by Strauss and Corbin, consisting of three main steps: open coding, axial coding, and selective coding [21–23]. During open coding, phenomena present in the text are identified, named, categorized, and described with the assistance of codes [21–23]. Generative questions, such as "Where is this happening?" [25] and "What are your motives and goals, what do you want to achieve?" [25], supported deeper insights and help to grasp the complexity and multi-layered nature of the phenomenon [25]. One example of applying open coding [21, 22] is described in the following. The part of the expert's response stating "[…] rapid generation of Python and PowerShell scripts" to the question of how generative AI is currently being used in software engineering was labeled with the code *code generation.*

Axial coding involved organizing the codes into categories using the coding paradigm, which links them through their conditions, context, underlying strategies, and consequences [21, 23]. Finally, selective coding focused on relating these categories to a selected core category [23], leading to the construction of a theoretical model [26] that explains and predicts the usage of generative AI in software engineering.

Memos were written throughout the coding process to capture ideas, identified categories, their properties and generative questions, thus facilitating the oversight of the research process [22]. The analysis was conducted with the understanding that theory construction is a creative, yet disciplined process [27, 28], in which the researcher's interpretive role is acknowledged and incorporated [22, 29]. Furthermore, different human coders analyzed the data and reflected on the results to avoid biases [30].

3.2 Data Collection

Qualitative data was collected through an online expert study supported by the tool LimeSurvey. This method was chosen over interviews to mitigate certain biases and practical limitations of verbal interviews, such as time constraints, the artificial nature of the interview situation [31], and the influence of the interviewer [32]. The online study provided respondents with flexibility in completing the questionnaire and allowed for a rapid and efficient data collection process [33].

The questionnaire was designed to include both open and closed questions. Open-ended questions offer differentiated and extensive material and are particularly useful when not all potential answers are known, or new aspects are expected to be discovered [34], which is inherent to the nature of GT [23].

The expert study was distributed to individuals with at least one year of professional experience in software engineering, ensuring that participants had sufficient domain expertise to provide informed perspectives on the application of generative AI in software engineering.

A pretest with two domain experts was conducted to evaluate clarity, resolve potential problems, and estimated completion time [35]. The final study was distributed to approximately n = 50 experts in the second quarter of the year 2024.

3.3 Sample Description

In total, n = 40 experts accessed the survey, with n = 34 valid responses retained after data cleaning. Of these, n = 27 responses were fully completed, while n = 7 were partially completed. Data cleaning involved removing duplicate entries (identified via IP address) and excluding respondents who only viewed the first page of the survey. This was done to ensure a high quality of the dataset.

The final sample included experts with diverse backgrounds in software engineering in terms of age, experience, job role, company size, and industry sector. Nearly half of the experts had more than ten years of experience in software engineering. The gender distribution was predominantly male (26 out of 27 fully completed responses). Participants represented a range of roles, from junior software engineers to C-level executives, and were employed in organizations of varying sizes, from small companies to large enterprises. Industries represented included IT, consulting, automotive, finance, and education, among others.

Of the n = 27 fully completed responses, n = 25 experts reported having used generative AI in their work. Most commonly, usage occurred during the implementation phase of software development (100% of those involved in that phase), followed by the conception phase (54.55%), testing (54.17%), design (39.13%), and deployment (27.27%). This underlines also the importance of this topic in practice.

4 Results

This section presents the results of the data analysis (Sect. 3.1) done based on the collected empirical expert data of the usage of generative AI in software engineering. The findings are synthesized into a theory developed through the Straussian GT approach [21, 22], described in the previous chapter and visualized in the result model (Fig. 1). The model explains how generative AI is currently used in software engineering and where the use cases and potentials lie. The model also highlights the challenges of using generative AI and sets out where the use of generative AI can be expanded to increase the use cases and potentials. The argumentation in the following is also underlined by excerpts from the qualitative expert data.

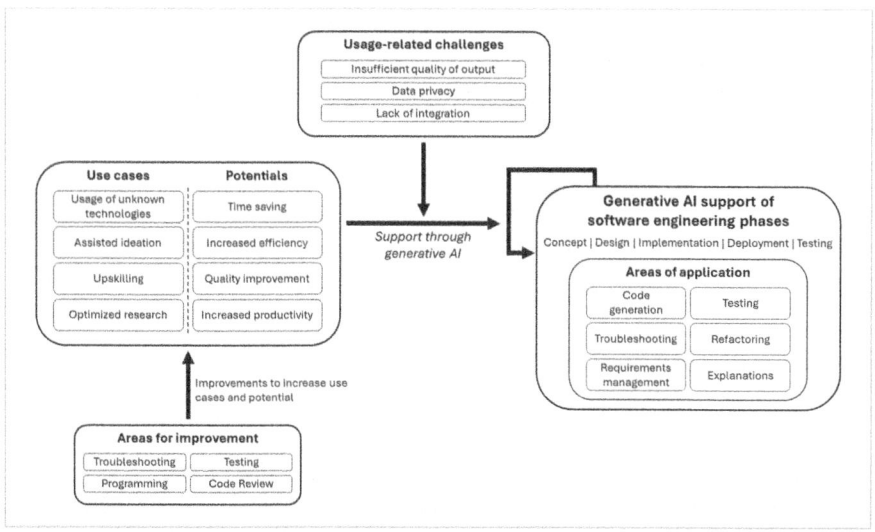

Fig. 1. Final model of the usage of Generative AI in Software Engineering

4.1   Generative AI Support of Software Engineering Phases

The category *Generative AI of software engineering phases* outlines the stages of the software engineering lifecycle [6] in which generative AI is currently being applied. As revealed by the analysis of quantitative data, generative AI is already utilized across all phases of software engineering—from concept and design, to implementation, deployment, and testing. Expert responses to how they have used generative AI in software engineering revealed six primary application areas within these phases: requirements management, code generation, refactoring, troubleshooting, testing, and explanations. In the following a comprehensive description of the experts view of this application area is given.

Requirements management encompasses activities from the conception phase [6], including "Writing of requirements", "Sharpening requirements", and "Requirements management". *Code generation*, situated in the implementation phase [6], involves tasks such as "Source code generation" and "Completion of code". *Refactoring* refers to restructuring existing code without altering its functionality, aiming to clean up the code and improving its design [36]. Refactoring combines the answers from participants such as "Improve code", "Write code sections more efficiently" or "Refactoring".

During *testing*, generative AI supports various activities, such as the "Design of automated end-to-end tests (e2e), code generation for e2e tests", the "creation or suggestion of test cases based on program code", and the "generation of unit tests". End-to-End tests are used to test entire user workflows [37], while unit tests examine isolated code components and compare outcomes to expected results [38].

Troubleshooting, another significant area of generative AI application in the testing phase, involves identifying and resolving issues uncovered during testing [39]. The asked experts reported using generative AI to "Fix program errors using existing code", "Have errors analyzed […] and rectified" or "Troubleshooting".

The final area—*explanations*—is characterized by the use of generative AI to enhance understanding of technologies, code, and errors. Our experts are using generative AI to "Have technology explained", "Explain code", "Have existing code explained", "Have code sections explained" and "Have errors […] explained". Due to its cross-cutting nature, this activity cannot be assigned to a specific software engineering phase and is thus considered phase-transcending.

The core category *Generative AI of software engineering phases* is self-referential. This reflects the non-linear nature of software engineering processes, where iteration and regression between phases are common [6].

4.2   Use Cases and Potentials

The category *Use cases and potentials* is closely linked to the core category (Sect. 4.1) and describes the specific use cases and potentials enabled by the integration of generative AI in software engineering. Four key use cases and four potential benefits were identified during the theory creation based on the experts's answers, which are described in detail below.

4.3   Potentials

The first potential of generative AI in software engineering is *time savings*, as tasks can be completed more quickly. The experts indicated that generative AI enables "faster […] development" or "quicker goal achievement through code generation".

The second identified potential is *increased efficiency*. The experts described that generative AI supports more effective work and leads to "increased […] efficiency". Increased efficiency, defined as the ratio of useful output to input resources such as time and energy [40], implies that generative AI allows users to accomplish tasks more effectively with minimal resource expenditure.

Other experts reported a potential is *quality improvement*. Participants mentioned outcomes such as "better code quality" and "fewer errors", which highlights how generative AI can enhance the quality of work performed during software engineering.

The fourth identified potential is *increased productivity*. As noted by Hall [41], productivity increases when the same output is achieved with fewer resources or when more output is produced with the same resources. By implication, generative AI can enable software engineers to complete the same tasks with reduced resources or to accomplish more within the same resource constraints. Our experts referred to this with responses such as "increased productivity" or "productivity gain".

4.4   Use Cases

The first identified use case of generative AI in software engineering is the *usage of unknown technologies*. According to the experts, generative AI enables "fast and effective work even with limited familiarity with certain technologies or programming languages". That means that new technologies can be faster e.g., integrated into first Proof-of-Concepts or MVPs.

The second use case is *assisted ideation*. The experts reported that generative AI tools support brainstorming and offer suggestions during the design process. These tools also aid in solution finding, providing as one expert noted "More diverse ideas (more solution variants faster than with Google)".

Beyond direct support for software engineering tasks, generative AI also contributes to the *upskilling* of individuals. Participants indicated that exposure to diverse AI-generated solutions supports learning, and that generative AI assists "when familiarizing with new technologies, as it can explain concepts and generate tutorials".

The final identified use case involves *optimized research*/search. One expert for example stated that using generative AI was "better than Googling, because it applies directly to my question/problem. I didn't have to make the mental leap myself". Another participant emphasized that generative AI reduces the time spent searching for specific solutions.

Besides use cases, we identified several challenges in the following.

4.5 Usage-Related Challenges

As shown in Fig. 1, the category *Usage-related challenges* functions as a moderating factor. This category encompasses the challenges encountered when employing generative AI in software engineering and influences the strength of the relationship between the identified *use cases and potentials* and the core category *Generative AI support of software engineering phases* [42]. In the course of theory development, three primary challenges were identified that impact the effectiveness of generative AI support in software engineering based on our experts' data.

The first challenge concerns the *insufficient quality of output* when using generative AI, aligning with issues previously discussed in Sect. 2. The experts reported "hallucinations" as an issue, with one respondent explicitly noting, "The code is sometimes just wrong" thereby emphasizing the potential for incorrect outputs. This might also influence the code quality and the possibility of using it.

The second challenge relates to *data privacy*, also previously addressed as a general concern in Sect. 2. Several experts identified "data privacy" as a critical issue. The "mistrust of a third party when it is an external tool" was also mentioned as a challenge in this context. Many see the use of generative AI in software engineering as a challenge.

The third and final challenge is the *lack of integration* of generative AI. Software engineers describe this challenge, for example, as "copy paste necessary, not in the same tool", "availability (within the IDEs)" or "integration into the workflow is not yet barrier-free enough". IDEs, or Integrated Development Environments, are software applications used for coding [43]. As evidenced by the responses, the integration of generative AI into the workflow or the tools utilized for development activities is currently inadequate.

4.6 Areas for Improvement

The fourth category identified in the developed theory concerns *areas for improvement* and encompasses activities where enhanced support from generative AI could amplify existing use cases and potentials. Given this interrelation, this category is conceptually linked to the category *use cases and potentials*. Four specific areas for improvement were identified, each of them is examined in detail in the following.

This first area—*troubleshooting*—is an area in which generative AI is already being used, as previously discussed in Sect. 4.1. Although generative AI is already employed in this domain, the experts expressed a desire for "better troubleshooting" and increased assistance in "debugging and error resolution". One expert noted, "When troubleshooting, it is sometimes exhausting to work with AI" reflecting limitations in the current capabilities of generative AI tools.

The second area for improvement is *testing*, another domain in which generative AI is already in use. However, experts expressed a desire for further enhancement. When asked where they would like to see increased support through generative AI, participants cited needs such as "generation of unit tests/E2E" or "test generation".

Programming is the third identified area. This code includes tasks such as "concrete coding", "code generation and suggestions", and "setting up new modules [...] based on the current project's pattern".

The final area for improvement is *code review*. Code reviews involve the examination of written code by a person other than its author to ensure quality, correctness, and robustness [44]. Experts expressed interest in greater generative AI assistance in this process, citing needs such as "reviewing large codebases", "code analysis" and "suggestions for improving existing code".

5 Theory Validation

Different approaches would be possible to validate the newly developed theory presented in Sect. 4. Grounded theory (GT) is exploratory and inductive, so the validation process should align with the interpretative and constructivist nature of GT [45]. One general validation approach aiming at the constructivist perspective would be revisiting or extending the GT process's data foundation. Here, re-evaluating the theoretical saturation would be possible, i.e., to ensure that theoretical saturation has truly been reached and, if required, conduct follow-up or additional surveys to confirm or refine the theory. From our perspective, this approach would only be adequate if there are reasons to believe the theory does not hold. Several ways would be possible to validate the latter, such as peer review, expert evaluation, triangulation, or comparative surveys or case studies. We selected two approaches to be presented in this section:

- Triangulation (Sect. 5.1): We use data from another method (qualitative content analysis of expert interviews) and compare the findings to the grounded theory to test convergence or divergence.
- Comparative survey analysis (Sect. 5.2): We apply the theory to data from a different survey (i.e., from a different organizational context) and analyze whether the theory holds across contexts or needs adaptation.

Sections 5.1 and 5.2 present the two studies, and Sect. 5.3 contains the comparison with the theory.

5.1 Study on LLM in IT Consultancy

In the autumn of 2024, we conducted a study in IT consultancy companies focusing on using LLMs in IT project management and software or IT systems development (see [46]). Two series of interviews were conducted based on different guidelines. In the first series, IT consultants were asked about the extent to which generative AI is already used. The aim was to determine the experiences and expectations, focusing on LLM to make consultancy work easier. The second series is conducted with AI experts and focuses on the technical capabilities of LLM to assess which expectations are justified and which are unrealistic. All expert interviews were conducted as semi-structured interviews via online video calls, recorded, transcribed, and the key statements summarized.

For the first round, a total of n = 14 IT consultants working for five different IT companies were recruited. As a result of the interviews, process models were developed that show typical activities of the consultants (such as requirements engineering, release planning, IT system documentation, user stories, or user manuals) and highlight the individual steps in these activities with high potential for LLM use. These steps were more thoroughly investigated in the second interview series.

A key application of generative AI in IT consulting lies in organizing and summarizing customer data. These systems can swiftly process extensive datasets and identify pertinent information, making them particularly useful for drafting formal proposals and offer documents. Moreover, generative AI can support the creation of these materials by generating templates that consultants can personalize and enhance, thereby minimizing manual work and accelerating the documentation process.

Another significant use case is in project planning and oversight. Generative AI can contribute to the creation of milestone schedules and the monitoring of project progress. By analyzing past project data, AI tools can produce initial drafts of planning documents, which human experts then refine. In addition, AI's ability to detect trends and patterns allows it to flag potential risks or deviations early on, enabling a more proactive approach to project management.

In the realm of requirements engineering, generative AI also offers substantial benefits, especially in gathering and structuring requirements and formulating user stories—tasks traditionally seen as time-consuming. AI can extract and organize requirements from various documents, identify gaps or inconsistencies, and assist in converting them into user stories for integration into project management systems. While this enhances the clarity and detail of requirement specifications, the outputs still require careful human review to ensure accuracy. Looking ahead, the automation of this process could become increasingly feasible.

Generative AI is also valuable in generating and refining text, particularly for producing release notes and technical documentation. According to several AI experts, fully automating the generation of release notes from user stories could be achievable in the near future. Furthermore, AI can help produce and summarize content, simplifying the creation and maintenance of documentation.

In conclusion, insights from expert interviews underscore the wide-ranging potential of generative AI in IT consulting. It can boost efficiency and reduce the burden of routine tasks by structuring complex information and automating content creation. However, human oversight remains indispensable to ensure outcomes' quality and reliability.

Generative AI is best viewed as a powerful enabler that enhances, rather than replaces, the work of IT consultants—ultimately saving time and increasing productivity.

5.2 Study on LLM Use in Software Engineering

The study was conducted in early 2023 as an online survey in-house within a single enterprise [47]. The enterprise is one of the largest German IT service providers with more than 10,000 employees and 6,000 staff in software development. The study's objective was to collect information about the expectations of software developers, how LLMs could support their future work in the software development process, and experiences from past use of LLMs. Within the time frame of one month, the survey resulted in n = 273 responses. The resulting dataset contained n = 142 completed questionnaires.

The study aimed to explore the expectations and experiences of software developers regarding the use of large language models (LLMs), particularly focusing on those with and without prior experience. Developers without experience expressed optimism about LLMs, expecting improvements in speed and productivity for the overall development process. They even saw LMs as essential for future software development, though they did not anticipate using them for team communication.

Developers who had used LMs confirmed many of these expectations. They reported increased productivity and considered LMs indispensable for future work. However, they raised concerns about the quality of work when using LMs and doubted their suitability for team communication.

Regarding specific development phases, both groups saw LLMs as valuable during implementation and unit testing, mainly as coding assistants. Developers also hoped LLMs would aid documentation and knowledge sharing during maintenance. Experienced users confirmed positive support from LMs in these phases but noted challenges with maintaining coding standards and best practices. No improvements were reported for integration or system testing tasks.

Overall, opinions on LMs varied across other development phases, with both advantages and disadvantages mentioned. The feedback was balanced, showing no clear consensus except in the area of implementation and unit testing, where LMs were viewed favorably.

The study concludes that LMs could take over some software development tasks in the future, especially in coding and unit testing. Developers also see them as increasingly important for productivity, knowledge management, and early research. LMs are already widely used for code generation and as alternatives to search engines. However, doubts remain about their ability to enhance code quality and their role in team communication.

5.3 Comparing Study Results and Theory

The study presented in Sect. 5.1 [46] also addresses the use of generative AI in software engineering (SE), but from the perspective of IT consultancy, which is much wider and includes activities beyond SE. Nevertheless, most of the potential areas for LLM use included in the theory were also identified in the study. This supports the findings in the theory development.

The study discussed in Sect. 5.2 [47] had an intention very similar to the survey underlying the theory development, but was conducted in a completely different context (focus on only one company) and significantly earlier. Even in this study, the results achieved are very close to the theory, as the expectations found in the study are now visible as use cases in the theory.

The following Table 1 summarizes the validation results by showing the comparison of theory, triangulation results, and comparative survey.

Table 1. Validation results: comparison of theory, triangulation results, and comparative survey

Theory Element	Comparison	
	to Expert Interviews (5.1) [46]	to SE Survey (5.2) [47]
Primary application areas		
Requirements management	Confirmed and broken down into activities	expected
Code generation	Identified as potential area, but not considered in detail	confirmed
Refactoring	Not considered	expected
Troubleshooting	Identified as potential area with focus on helpdesk	expected
Testing	Identified as potential area with focus on user stories	confirmed
Explanations	Identified as potential area with focus on documentation	expected
Potential		
Time saving, increased efficiency, quality improvement, increased productivity	Time saving and increased efficiency were explicitly stated by the experts	All aspects mentioned as expected potential
Use Cases		
Usage of unknown technologies, assisted ideation, upskilling, optimized research	This aspect was not subject of the investigation, but upskilling was mentioned in the interviews	This aspect was not subject of the investigation
Usage-related Challenges		
Insufficient quality of output, data privacy, lack of integration	Experts confirmed the need to control output quality and to observe data privacy	The survey confirmed the need to control output quality and to observe data privacy. Upskilling was seen as a challenge
Areas for Improvement		
Troubleshooting	Confirmed	Confirmed
Testing	Confirmed	Confirmed
Programming	Confirmed	Confirmed
Code review	Confirmed	Confirmed

6 Conclusion, Discussion and Future Research

Generative AI is an important topic in general as well as specifically in software engineering [2, 5]. Based on our empirical research we followed the research question how generative AI can be used in software engineering and what possible challenges can be found on the way implementing it in practice. We found different use cases and potentials how enterprises can use generative AI in this area and use case related challenges. Without addressing them, the potentials of using generative AI in the phases of software engineering can be reduced or even not be valuable. The developed theory demonstrates that generative AI can be employed throughout the entire software engineering lifecycle [6]—from concept and design, to implementation, deployment, and concurrent testing. Within these phases, several areas of application were identified where generative AI is particularly prominent, including code generation, testing, troubleshooting, refactoring, requirements management, and explanations. It enables the usage of unknown technologies, assists with ideation, facilitates upskilling, and optimizes the research. The potentials derived from its use include time savings, increased efficiency, quality improvement, and increased productivity. Furthermore, the realized use cases and potentials contribute to achieving the goals of software development. The realization of these use cases and potentials aids in meeting the core objectives of software development—namely high quality, high productivity, timeliness, and adherence to budget constraints [7]. For example, time savings directly contribute to timely delivery, while increased productivity and quality improvements align with the goals of high productivity and quality. Increased efficiency additionally supports cost reduction, time optimization, and quality enhancement [9], which collectively facilitate goal attainment. Generative AI also helps mitigate common challenges that hinder these goals. As described in Sect. 2, programming requires extensive expertise and know-how [8]. Generative AI can reduce this by assisting less experienced developers in working with unknown technologies and by supporting upskilling. Furthermore, it facilitates the ideation of simpler solutions, helping to overcome the challenge of identifying the most efficient implementation strategy, with the goal of reducing complexity, error rates, development duration, and associated costs [8, 9]. Optimized research / search helps uncover relevant information about customers, dependencies, or application domains which is a challenge especially during the early project phases [8]. Through increased use of GenAI within the areas of improvement troubleshooting, testing, programming and code review, the use cases and potential can be amplified. Comparing these areas to the goals of software development and common engineering challenges further supports this implication.

Programming, as discussed in Sects. 2, 4, is a complex and resource-intensive activity requiring strategic thinking and domain expertise [8]. Therefore, broader use of generative AI in this area opens up additional potentials and use cases. Achieving high software quality requires not only the identification of errors but also their resolution [8, 9]. These processes consume time, incur costs, and affect productivity. Consequently, deploying generative AI more extensively in testing and code review (for identifying issues), and in troubleshooting (for resolving them), can better support development goals and further unlock the value of this technology.

Like other research, also our research has limitations. A limitation can be found e.g., in the collected expert sample and the chosen qualitative research method. We reduced the limitations by validating our findings with two further studies [46, 47] and used different coders and reflections to avoid biases [30]. However, studies gaining insights from experts outside Europe (e.g., North America, Asia, etc.) and comparing it with our results would enlarge the body of knowledge. Furthermore, other research methods such as case studies or quantitative studies [23] could also provide more insights into the application of generative AI over time in the future, exploring the different improvements and future advances of this technology as well as regulatory and ethical implications.

References

1. Bloomberg: Generative artificial intelligence (AI) revenue worldwide from 2020 with forecast until 2032 (in billion U.S. dollars). https://www.statista.com/statistics/1417151/generative-ai-revenue-worldwide/. Accessed 9 May 2025
2. Kulkarni, A., Shivananda, A., Kulkarni, A., Gudivada, D.: Applied Generative AI for Beginners: Practical Knowledge on Diffusion Models, ChatGPT, and Other LLMs. Apress, Berkeley (2023)
3. Capgemini Research Institute: Harnessing the Value of Generative AI, 2nd edn. Top Use Cases Across Sectors. Capgemini (2024). https://www.capgemini.com/insights/research-library/generative-ai-in-organizations/. Accessed 14 May 2025
4. Capgemini Research Institute: Turbocharging software with Gen AI: How organizations can realize the full potential of generative AI for software engineering. Capgemini (2024). https://www.capgemini.com/de-de/wp-content/uploads/sites/8/2024/07/Capgemini_Research_Institute_Report-Gen-AI-in-Software-Engineering.pdf. Accessed 9 May 2025
5. Nguyen-Duc, A., et al.: Generative artificial intelligence for software engineering – a research agenda. arXiv preprint arXiv:2310.18648 (2023)
6. Brandt-Pook, H., Kollmeier, R.: Softwareentwicklung kompakt und verständlich: Wie Softwaresysteme entstehen. Vieweg+Teubner, Wiesbaden (2008)
7. Abts, D., Mülder, W.: Grundkurs Wirtschaftsinformatik: Eine kompakte und praxisorientierte Einführung, 9th edn. Springer Fachmedien Wiesbaden, Wiesbaden (2017)
8. Dooley, J., Kazakova, V.A.: Software Development, Design, and Coding: With Patterns, Debugging, Unit Testing, and Refactoring, 3rd edn. Apress, New York (2024)
9. Gerlich, R., Gerlich, R.: 111 Thesen zur erfolgreichen Softwareentwicklung: Argumente und Entscheidungshilfen für Manager, Konzepte und Anleitungen für Praktiker. Springer, Heidelberg (2005)
10. McKinsey & Company: Potential impact of generative artificial intelligence (AI) on productivity worldwide in 2023, by business functions (in billion U.S. dollars). In: Statista (2023). https://www.statista.com/statistics/1446250/worldwide-artificial-intelligence-impact-by-business-function/. Accessed 14 June 2024
11. Feuerriegel, S., Hartmann, J., Janiesch, C., et al.: Generative AI. Bus. Inf. Syst. Eng. **66**, 111–126 (2024). https://doi.org/10.1007/s12599-023-00834-7
12. Huang, K., Xie, A.: Overview of ChatGPT, Web3, and new business landscape. In: Huang, K., Wang, Y., Zhu, F., Chen, X., Xing, C. (eds.) Beyond AI: ChatGPT, Web3, and the Business Landscape of Tomorrow, pp. 3–36. Springer, Cham (2023)
13. Microsoft (ed.): Microsoft Copilot for Microsoft 365 overview (2024). https://learn.microsoft.com/en-us/copilot/microsoft-365/microsoft-365-copilot-overview. Accessed 26 July 2024
14. Banh, L., Strobel, G.: Generative artificial intelligence. Electron. Mark. **33**(1), 1–17 (2023)
15. Perov, V., Perova, N.: AI hallucinations: is "artificial evil" possible? In: 2024 IEEE Conference on Biomedical Engineering, Radioelectronics and Information Technology (USBEREIT), pp. 114–117. IEEE (2024)

16. Huang, K., Ponnapalli, J., Tantsura, J., Shin, K.T.: Navigating the GenAI security landscape. In: Huang, K., Wang, Y., Goertzel, B., Li, Y., Wright, S., Ponnapalli, J. (eds.) Generative AI Security: Theories and Practices, pp. 31–58. Springer, Cham (2024)

17. Daun, M., Brings, J.: How ChatGPT will change software engineering education. In: Proceedings of the 2023 Conference on Innovation and Technology in Computer Science Education, vol. 1, pp. 110–116 (2023)

18. Petrovska, O., Clift, L., Moller, F., Pearsall, R.: Incorporating generative AI into software development education. In: Proceedings of the 8th Conference on Computing Education Practice, pp. 37–40 (2024)

19. Şimşek, T., Gülşeni, Ç., Olcay, G.A.: The future of software development with GenAI: evolving roles of software personas. IEEE Eng. Manag. Rev. (2024)

20. Arora, C., Grundy, J., Abdelrazek, M.: Advancing requirements engineering through generative AI: assessing the role of LLMs. In: Generative AI for Effective Software Development, pp. 129–148. Springer, Cham (2024)

21. Strauss, A., Corbin, J.: Grounded theory methodology: an overview. In: Denzin, N.K., Lincoln, Y.S. (eds.) Handbook of Qualitative Research, pp. 273–285. SAGE Publications, Thousand Oaks (1994)

22. Strauss, A., Corbin, J.: Basics of Qualitative Research: Grounded Theory Procedures and Techniques. SAGE, Newbury Park (1990)

23. Recker, J.: Scientific research in information systems: a beginner's guide. In: Progress in IS, 2nd edn. Springer, Cham (2021)

24. Eisend, M., Kuß, A.: Grundlagen empirischer Forschung: Zur Methodologie in der Betriebswirtschaftslehre, 3rd edn. Springer Fachmedien Wiesbaden, Wiesbaden (2023)

25. Breuer, F., Muckel, P., Dieris, B.: Reflexive Grounded Theory: Eine Einführung für die Forschungspraxis, 4th edn. Springer Fachmedien Wiesbaden, Wiesbaden (2019)

26. Vollstedt, M., Rezat, S.: An introduction to grounded theory with a special focus on axial coding and the coding paradigm. In: Kaiser, G., Presmeg, N. (eds.) Compendium for Early Career Researchers in Mathematics Education, pp. 81–100. Springer, Cham (2019)

27. Strübing, J.: Grounded theory und theoretical sampling. In: Baur, N., Blasius, J. (eds.) Handbuch Methoden der empirischen Sozialforschung, pp. 457–472. Springer Fachmedien Wiesbaden, Wiesbaden (2014)

28. Strauss, A.L., Corbin, J.: Grounded Theory. Beltz/Psychologie Verlagsunion, Weinheim (1996)

29. Locke, K.: Rewriting the discovery of grounded theory after 25 years? J. Manag. Inq. **5**(3), 239–245 (1996)

30. Baran, M.L., Jones, J.E.: Mixed Methods Research for Improved Scientific Study. IGI Global, Hershey (2016)

31. Myers, M.D., Newman, M.: The qualitative interview in IS research: examining the craft. Inf. Organ. **17**(1), 2–26 (2007). https://www.sciencedirect.com/science/article/pii/s1471772706000352

32. West, B.T., Blom, A.G.: Explaining interviewer effects: a research synthesis. J. Survey Stat. Methodol. **5**(2), 175–211 (2017). https://doi.org/10.1093/jssam/smw024

33. Evans, J.R., Mathur, A.: The value of online surveys: a look back and a look ahead. Internet Res. **28**(4), 854–887 (2018). https://doi.org/10.1108/IntR-03-2018-0089

34. Krosnick, J.A.: Questionnaire design. In: Vannette, D., Krosnick, J. (eds.) The Palgrave Handbook of Survey Research, pp. 439–455. Palgrave Macmillan, Cham (2018). https://doi.org/10.1007/978-3-319-54395-6_53

35. Weichbold, M.: Pretest. In: Baur, N., Blasius, J. (eds.) Handbuch Methoden der empirischen Sozialforschung, pp. 349–356. Springer, Wiesbaden (2019). https://doi.org/10.1007/978-3-658-21308-4_23

36. Fowler, M.: Refactoring: Improving the Design of Existing Code. Addison-Wesley Professional, Boston (2018)
37. Mollah, H., van den Bos, P.: From user stories to end-to-end web testing. In: 2023 IEEE International Conference on Software Testing, Verification and Validation Workshops (ICSTW), pp. 140–148. IEEE (2023)
38. Olan, M.: Unit testing: test early, test often. J. Comput. Sci. Coll. **19**(2), 319–328 (2003). https://www.researchgate.net/profile/michael-olan/publication/255673967_unit_testing_test_early_test_often
39. Elmishali, A., Stern, R., Kalech, M.: An artificial intelligence paradigm for troubleshooting software bugs. Eng. Appl. Artif. Intell. **69**, 147–156 (2018)
40. Vanhoucke, M.: The Illusion of Control: Project Data, Computer Algorithms and Human Intuition for Project Management and Control. Springer, Cham (2023)
41. Hall, B.H.: Innovation and productivity. NBER Working Paper No. 17178, National Bureau of Economic Research, Cambridge, MA (2011). http://www.nber.org/papers/w17178
42. Aguinis, H., Edwards, J.R., Bradley, K.J.: Improving our understanding of moderation and mediation in strategic management research. Organ. Res. Methods **20**(4), 665–685 (2017). https://doi.org/10.1177/1094428115627498
43. Murphy, G.C.: Beyond integrated development environments: adding context to software development. In: 2019 IEEE/ACM 41st International Conference on Software Engineering: New Ideas and Emerging Results (ICSE-NIER), pp. 73–76. IEEE (2019)
44. Tufano, R., Pascarella, L., Tufano, M., Poshyvanyk, D., Bavota, G.: Towards automating code review activities. In: 2021 IEEE/ACM 43rd International Conference on Software Engineering (ICSE), pp. 163–174. IEEE (2021)
45. Goldkuhl, G., Cronholm, S.: Adding theoretical grounding to grounded theory: toward multi-grounded theory. Int J Qual Methods **9**(2), 187–205 (2010). https://doi.org/10.1177/160940691000900205
46. Jehnert, M., Meyer, C., Sandkuhl, K.: Interview study to determine the potential of large language model usage in IT-consultancy. In: 25th International Conference on Business Information Systems, BIS 2025, Poznan, Poland, 25–27 June 2025. LNBIP, vol. 554. Springer, Cham (2025)
47. Pruss, H.: Untersuchung der Auswirkungen von autoregressiven Sprachmodellen auf die Arbeitsweise von Software-Entwicklern. Bachelor-Thesis, Wirtschaftsinformatik (2023)

Conceptual Modeling and AI in the Service of Legal Analysis: A Design Science Project

Georgios Koutsopoulos[1]([✉]) [iD], Noran Kniby[1] [iD], Pauline Wiman[1] [iD],
Ingrida Karina-Berzina[2] [iD], and Janis Stirna[1] [iD]

[1] Department of Computer and Systems Sciences, Stockholm University, Borgarfjordsgatan 12,
Kista, 16407 Stockholm, Sweden
{georgios,pauline.wiman,js}@dsv.su.se, nkniby@proton.me
[2] Department of Law, Stockholm University, Universitetsvägen 10 C,
10691 Stockholm, Sweden
ingrida.karina-berzina@juridicum.su.se

Abstract. As digitalization increases its pace, the legal field produces far more text than manual analysis can keep up with. Parsing large bodies of material such as Intellectual Property rulings by hand is both slow and labor-intensive, to the point where it is considered unfeasible. In this paper, the CLAIM tool, developed to tackle this challenge by blending conceptual modeling with a large language model, is presented and evaluated. Conceived as a Design Science artifact, the tool was motivated by stakeholder requirements gathered through participatory modeling workshops. The prototype runs in two consecutive stages: automated information extraction followed by semantic querying. Its capabilities are illustrated on a corpus of EU trademark-cancellation decisions brought on grounds of bad-faith filing. CLAIM's evaluation was based on user-testing and interviews, resulting in a set of highly positive responses.

Keywords: Conceptual modeling · Intellectual Property · Legal analysis · Large Language Model · ChatGPT · Design Science Research · Requirements Engineering · Evaluation

1 Introduction

The ongoing digital transformation that has affected all areas of modern society during the last decades has led to a major increase in the production of textual data, and that includes the legal domain [1]. Modern legal professionals encounter an ever-growing volume of legal documents such as case law, statutes, contracts and regulations [2]. Historically, legal analysis has been entirely manual, relying on the expertise of legal professionals to identify and analyze important information from the existing legal documents. The rise of digital tools did not mitigate the need for human involvement, in particular, the dependence on human judgment when identifying, interpreting, and converting legal content to machine-readable formats [2]. In addition, barriers derived from technical aspects, for example programming skills, have limited the accessibility of

© The Author(s), under exclusive license to Springer Nature Switzerland AG 2026
R. Deneckère et al. (Eds.): BIR 2025, LNBIP 562, pp. 272–285, 2026.
https://doi.org/10.1007/978-3-032-04375-7_17

legal computational methods for the majority of legal scholars and practitioners. Consequently, large-scale empirical research that involves legal texts has been rare, focusing mostly on doctrinal analysis of small sets of specific influential cases [3].

Intellectual Property (IP) [4] is a subdomain of Law that is characterized by vast repositories of judicial decisions on cases concerning trademarks, patents, and copyrights. Although analyzing such corpora could bring to light valuable patterns and trends that are not evident through the traditional manual approaches, the scale of handling manually extensive corpora often deters such initiatives. Thus, valuable insight may remain covered. This challenge also represents the opportunity to develop more efficient scalable solutions.

Recently, advancements in Artificial Intelligence (AI) in the area of Large Language Models (LLMs) have resulted in promising solutions. State-of-the-art LLMs have evolved into efficient task performers with minimal task-specific tuning [5]. Regarding their performance in legal tasks, they have even demonstrated levels of performance that can be comparable and sometimes, even superior than human experts [6]. Harnessing the strengths of AI to automate parts of legal analysis can reduce the required time and effort. In parallel, the use of Conceptual Modeling (CM) and Enterprise Modeling (EM) [7] can ease the process of analysis by providing a structured foundation for establishing associations among legal concepts and designing supportive systems.

This paper reports on such a supportive tool, namely CLAIM (Case-based Legal Analysis of IntellectualProperty Matters), developed as a Design Science Research (DSR) [8] project. It is a domain-specific tool, designed to enable and facilitate the analysis of IP decisions. The aim of the paper is to *report on the development of the CLAIM tool,* including the elicited requirements, the conceptual and technical foundation, the demonstration, and evaluation of the tool.

The rest of the paper is structured as follows. Section 2 briefly outlines the theoretical foundation of this paper, and Sect. 3 explains the methodological decisions. Section 4 presents the tool, including the requirements elicitation, development, and evaluation. Sections 5 and 6 discuss the overall project and provide concluding remarks, respectively.

2   Background

2.1   Legal Analysis in Intellectual Property Law

A broad range of legal protections over intangible creations, for example patterns, trade secrets, trademarks, and creative works, is provided by IP law [9]. Across various judicial levels, legal decisions are produced constantly and globally, resulting in the formation of substantial repositories of legal cases. Despite the jurisdictional differences in legal systems, local context and terminology, these repositories consist of decisions that often share a common pattern, which consists of factual narratives, legal reasoning, and final rulings [4, 9].

The increasingly higher rate of digitization of legal documents has equally increased the availability of such decisions, and this fact enables and facilitates opportunities for empirical legal research on extensive legal corpora in order to identify IP trends or similar patterns [2]. However, this wealth of data often renders the task challenging. Legal corpora have the tendency to be heterogeneous, using specialized jargon, complex and unclear reasoning, and context-specific citations [10]. Moreover, the outcomes are not explicitly stated in case documents, requiring extensive interpretation. Taking these into consideration, it is safe to assume that manual analysis is necessary, making the task resource- and labor-intensive, and also susceptible to errors [11]. This is the main reason for which legal researchers are increasingly turning to computational methods that automate the analysis tasks such as information extraction and document classification [2]. This shift is usually associated with and relies on Natural language Processing (NLP) and AI-based approaches.

2.2 Model-Driven and Semantics-Based Approaches

One path to the efficient handling of the complexity of the analysis of legal documents is Model-Driven Development (MDD), which uses CM to guide the software development process [12]. These models are usually not dependent of specific platforms, and they provide a structured way to define system behavior and domain knowledge without the need for extensive low-level coding. In the context of legal analytics, MDD is particularly valuable due to the need for adaptable and maintainable systems that facilitate managing variations in legal processes and documents [13]. EM, which is a special case of EM, is particularly well-suited for capturing the abstract information structures and workflows that exist within legal procedures. Participatory modeling techniques [14] help bridge the gap between domain experts like legal practitioners and scholars, and system designers. It enables the collaborative development of models that reflect recurring patterns in legal reasoning and documentation. Such efforts provide a means for scaling up high-quality, reusable solutions for analyzing legal texts [15].

2.3 Large Language Models in Legal Applications

In parallel, LLMs like ChatGPT have demonstrated substantial promise in the domain of legal analysis. Trained on extensive and varied sets of documents and structured corpora, LLMs seems to be adept at interpreting inconsistent legal language and extracting semantic meaning from complex texts [5, 10]. This is particularly valid when the tasks involved concern annotation, classification and summarization of the given legal documents [6].

However, despite their advantages, LLMs raise valid concerns regarding the transparency and reliability of their outcomes. The legal domain in particular has strict requirements on these aspects, since potential errors in interpretation may result in critical consequences. Integrating LLMs with structured model-driven approaches has the potential to mitigate these concerns by introducing transparency in the structure of logic and domain-specific constraints that are applied during legal analysis. More specifically, the abilities of LLMs, for example, performing semantic parsing, can benefit, in terms of consistency and interpretability, from the existence of underlying conceptual models in the software architecture [16].

3   Methodology

The CLAIM project and tool has been elaborated under the lens of the DSR framework suggested in [17]. It emphasizes the development of artifacts that solve real-world problems, while in parallel contributing to academic knowledge [17]. This section presents the methodological decisions that have driven the project, structured around the essential DSR stages, (i) Problem explication, (ii) Requirements elicitation, (iii) Artifact design and development, (iv) Demonstration, and (v) Evaluation of the artifact [17].

3.1   Problem Explication and Requirements Elicitation

The initial phases of the project focused on eliciting the main challenges in analyzing large volumes of legal documents, specifically in the domain of IP law. For this, we relied on domain experts, in particular, we collaborated with the IP Law research group, which belongs to the Department of Law (Juridicum) of Stockholm University. As our direct stakeholders, a representative of the research group took part in four 3-h workshops with the research team that were conducted in the Department of Computer and Systems Sciences. The workshops were conducted in order to gain a deeper understanding of the challenge, and elicit requirements for the planned solution. To collect data, the think-aloud protocol [18] was employed. Half of these workshops involved participatory modeling [14], during which the legal expertise was combined with modeling experience to produce conceptual models capturing domain knowledge and procedural logic. Apart from the models, a set of requirements was elicited to document CLAIM's main functionalities and attributes, classified as Functional Requirements (FRs) and Non-Functional Requirements (NFRs), according to the instructions and semi-formal format suggested in [19].

3.2   Artifact Design and Development

The tool was developed drawing on the two approaches mentioned earlier; CM and LLMs. Combining the structure and robustness provided by CM and the adaptability and semantic depth of LLMs can result in a valid response to the given challenge. From the modeling perspective, the Unified Modeling Language (UML) [20] was used for two purposes. Initially, a Domain model was created to capture the essential of the IP legal domain, like trademarks and proceedings stages, as a platform-independent construct. Afterwards, a StateMachine diagram was created to capture the procedural dynamics of IP law cases, like appeals and decision outcomes.

Technically, CLAIM has been build using Node.js [21] as the backend engine, using HTML/CSS/Javascript protocols, interfacing with a MariaDB database [22], the architecture of which was based on the domain model. These were used in conjunction with OpenAI's ChatGPT-4o through their APIs. The application's core logic is built in Node.js, while OpenAI's ChatGPT-4o is integrated via API calls to provide semantic analysis. Within the Semantics-driven Engineering framework, ChatGPT fulfils two key functions in the CLAIM project: (i) knowledge capturing, and (ii) end-user facing [16]. To showcase CLAIM, we applied it to a case study examining EUIPO decisions that annulled trademarks on the grounds of bad-faith filing; details are presented in later sections.

3.3 Demonstration and Evaluation

For the demonstration and evaluation of the tool, the selected strategy is the "Quick & Simple", one of the four strategies suggested in the Framework for Evaluation of Design Science (FEDS) [23]. The strategy has been selected because it is optimal for naturalistic summative evaluations, and a limited number of design and development iterations is involved. Its suitability fits small and low-risk artifacts, like CLAIM. Its low cost is an additional motivator.

Regarding the practical application of the strategy, a combination of two approaches was selected. User testing [24] was combined with a semi-structured interview [25]. As mentioned before, the stakeholder of this project is the IP Law research group of Juridicum, therefore, a representative of the group participated as domain expert, both in the user testing and interview part of the evaluation. The interview question set consisted of 16 questions and was based on the Technology Acceptance Model (TAM) [26], with a focus on Perceived Ease of Use, Usefulness, and Intention to Use. In particular:

- Perceived Ease of Use (Q1–Q5) captures first impressions, interaction flow, technical hiccups, clarity of outputs and the respondent's confidence in using the tool unaided.
- Perceived Usefulness (Q6–Q12) – explores how well the tool supports trademark-cancellation research: relevance to typical queries, time-savings, depth and accuracy of extracted reasoning (e.g., bad-faith factors), and the clarity of statistical summaries.
- Intention to Use (Q13–Q16) – gauges future adoption, willingness to recommend, specific high-value use cases, and the improvements required for regular use.

Overall, the 16 questions provide a rounded view of usability, practical utility and adoption potential, while also eliciting concrete feedback on shortcomings and desired enhancements.

4   Tool Requirements

The requirements for CLAIM were elicited during four workshops with a representative of the IP Law research group and the development team. The group converted stakeholder frustrations that were expressed during the workshops into a complete set of system requirements. The requirements were classified as FRs and NFRs [19], expressing what the tool is expected to do, and how to do it, respectively. Each requirement was assigned a priority 1 to 3, with one being the essential ones, and 3 the optional enhancing ones. Table 1 shows the elicited requirement specification.

Table 1. The requirement specification for CLAIM.

ID	The system shall:	Priority
FR1	Capture core trademark metadata (name, number, NICE classes, registration data)	1
FR2	Extract structured facts from cancellation decisions (dates, legal grounds, bad-faith factors)	1
FR3	Accept natural-language or structured prompts over the full dataset	1
FR4	Pull complementary data for every mark from the EUIPO API	1
FR5	Provide basic descriptive and comparative statistics on extracted data	1
FR6	Support follow-up questions within the same chat session	2
FR7	Offer in-app guidance and prompt examples to lower the learning curve	3
FR8	Link directly to EUIPO eSearch for any queried mark number	3
FR9	Return results as bar/pie/line charts and/or structured text lists	2
NFR1	Respond to typical analytic queries in a few seconds	1
NFR2	Be usable by non-technical jurists (minimal set-up, plain-language UI)	1
NFR3	Minimize factual error in extracted fields and numeric summaries	1
NFR4	Handle $\geq 2\,000$ cancellation decisions without performance loss	2
NFR5	Present output with clear structure and consistent formatting	2
NFR6	Default to structured output before free-text prose	2
NFR7	Sort graphical elements in descending order when that aids reading	3

5 The Tool

5.1 Tool Architecture

Insights from the workshops enabled the creation of a domain model for IP claims, as shown in the UML diagram of Fig. 1. A Case, which is a cancellation action brought against a registered mark, exists as a Document and can involve one or many Trademarks. A Trademark is applied for at least one time, and may be registered one or more times. Every Application is for one Registration. From one or more Documents, the system derives assessment Factors; these Factors, after being Confirmed, feed into Assessments of Case Documents, and any Factor or Assessment may be reused across multiple cases. This structure enables a case-based analysis approach, letting past decisions inform the appraisal of new disputes, via the extracted factors, hence the tool's name.

Each Case must pass through at least one Proceedings stage (and up to four). Every Proceedings stage is handled by exactly one Institution and may result in a single Outcome (the decision). An Outcome can, in turn, attract at most one Appeal. Outcome is an abstract superclass with four mutually exclusive specializations: Cancelled (affecting the trademark registration), Rejected (referring to the case), and Partially annulled (also about the trademark), and Suspended (also about the case).

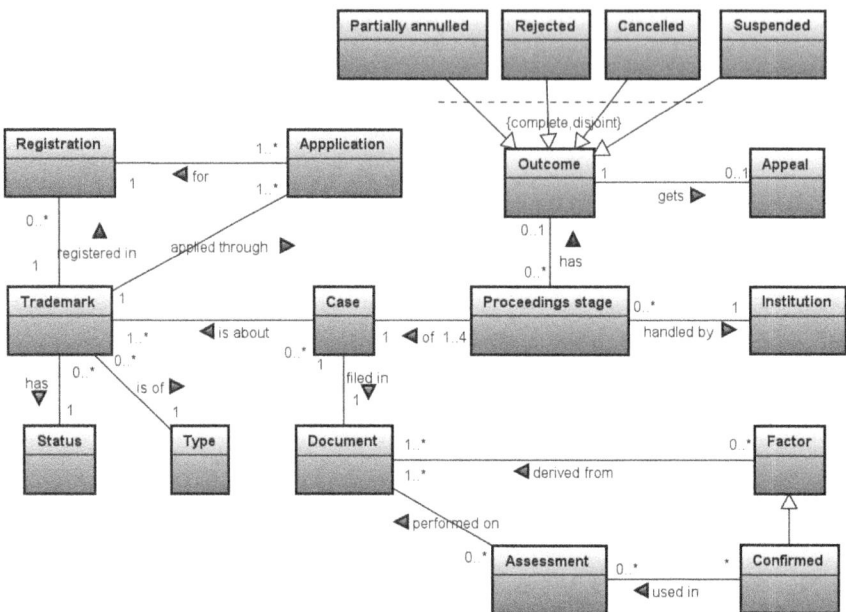

Fig. 1. The domain model for IP cases.

The domain model has been implemented as a MariaDB data schema, capturing all essential concepts and their relationships so that every possible case, its relevant information, and the links among information objects can be stored and queried.

5.2 States of Legal Cases

One of the most important aspects of the IP domain is the procedure that a case goes through before a final decision is made. The states of a case object have been modeled as a UML StateMachine diagram [20], which shows not only the possible states, but also the triggers for state transitions, and the conditions affecting variating state outcomes.

In particular, as shown in Fig. 2, a case is initiated by being Filed, and this initiates the procedure. Once forwarded, the case is Being evaluated for its validity. The event of the finalization of the evaluation triggers two potential states. If the case is evaluated as invalid, the case's filing is Rejected and it gets finalized. If the filing is valid, it transitions to the accepted state. Sending it for processing is the event that triggers the transition to the state where the case Being processed. This is a composite state that includes four exclusive and distinct sub-states. These are the states where the case is Processed, by the Cancellation division unit, the Court of Appeals, the General Court, and the Court of Justice of the EU. This transition to a specific sub-state depends on the number of appeals at the current moment, that is, 0–3 appeals, respectively.

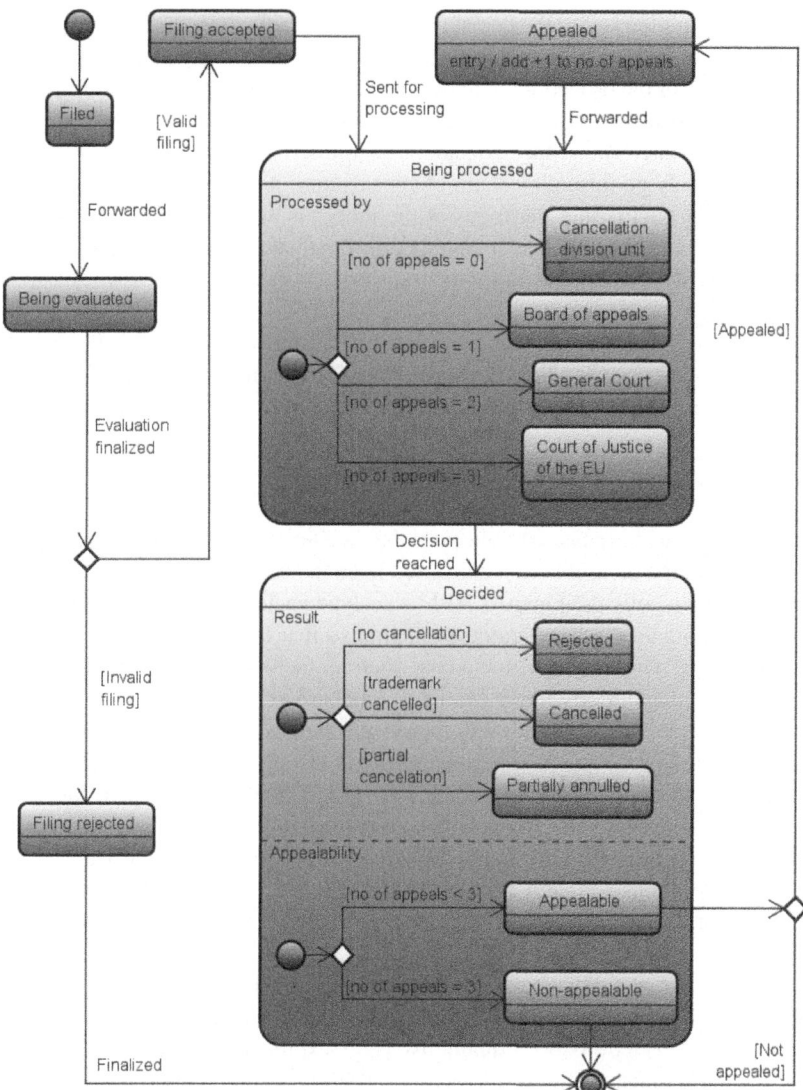

Fig. 2. The StateMachine diagram for the case states.

Reaching a decision is the event that triggers the transition to the Decided state. This is another composite state that consists of two regions, the Result region, and the Appealability. The result region, consists of three possible sub-states, in a way that has also been captured in the Domain model in an earlier sub-section of this paper. In other words, the decision will transition to one of the three sub-states: (i) Rejected, (ii) Cancelled, or (iii) Partially annulled. In the second region of the composite state, the appealability of the decision is captured. Regarding the appealability of the decision, it depends on the number of appeals so far in the process. In practice, if less than three appeals have been filed so far, the decision is still appealable, if the appeals have reached the number three, the decision is no longer appealable. A Non-appealable decision leads to the finalization of the procedure, while an Appealable decision can go through another round of appeal. If it does not, the procedure is finalized, if it does, the state transitions to the Appealed state. The Appealed state is forwarded to Being processed again. The case may iteratively go through a chain of appeals until it reaches its finalization.

A noteworthy fact is that the focus of the model is on a conceptual level, in other words, even if a state can only lead to one specific other state, the differentiation between the states, along with the trigger(s) for the transition, have been deemed worth capturing in the model.

The StateMachine diagram has been used as complementary structure for documenting the IP cases in CLAIM, due to the high complexity of case states in the legal procedure, which was not possible to capture in the Domain model.

5.3 Process of Analysis

CLAIM works in two successive processing phases. During the corpus-processing phase, every decision in the dataset is first converted from its original format into plain text. A Python script then calls the OpenAI API to analyze each file, using the factor classes defined in the domain model to guide extraction so that the resulting data stay semantically consistent. The extracted metadata, such as factors, dates, grounds, and other attributes are written directly into a MariaDB database via the same script.

Once the corpus has been indexed, the system moves to prompt processing, which enables querying. When a user submits a question through the interface, the front-end passes it to the back-end service, where it is logged and forwarded to the OpenAI API. ChatGPT translates the natural-language request into SQL, and the back-end runs that query against the MariaDB store. The raw results are returned to ChatGPT with formatting instructions so that it can turn them into readable text and, when requested, graph specifications. The formatted answer returns back to the front-end, which renders it as text, charts, or both.

By relying on ChatGPT's built-in understanding of semantics and code-generation abilities, CLAIM avoids building a retrieval engine. In its present form the tool performs content analysis [27] it transforms qualitative legal text into quantitative insights, chiefly by counting the frequency of relevant factors and summarizing those counts for the user.

5.4 Interface

The CLAIM interface is organized around a pale-green header that carries the logo and subtitle, beneath which the main workspace is split into a wide chat panel and a narrower sidebar (Fig. 3). The chat panel shows the dialogue between the user and ClaimBot, offers a single-line prompt box with a send button, and lets the user choose whether replies appear as text, graphs or a combination of both. The sidebar provides a search field for entering an EU trademark number, a direct link to the EUIPO Case-Law portal, and a button that opens a separate help page containing prompt instructions and a glossary (Fig. 4.)

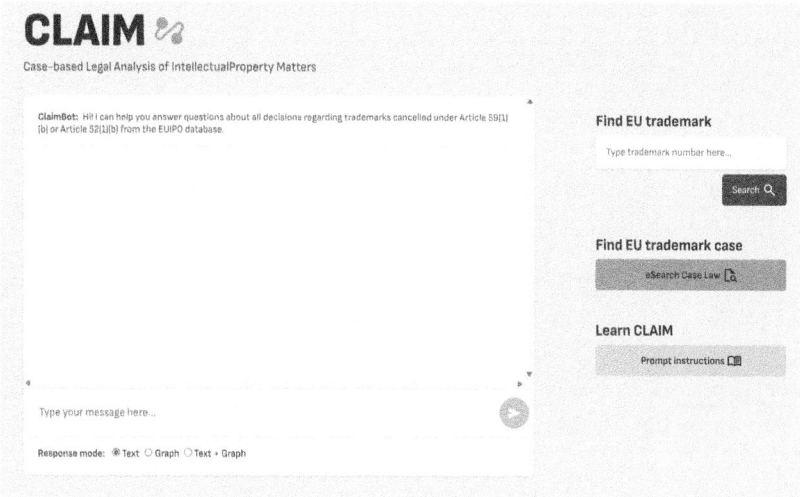

Fig. 3. CLAIM's landing screen.

Fig. 4. Instructions and guidelines to use CLAIM.

6 Evaluation Results

The evaluation results indicate a highly positive reception of CLAIM by the IP Law research group. More specifically, during the ~90 min user testing, the tool was asked to generate graphs (Fig. 5) or answers questions, often in a sequential manner (Fig. 6).

The analysis of the answers, along with comments provided during the testing session can be summarized in Table 2.

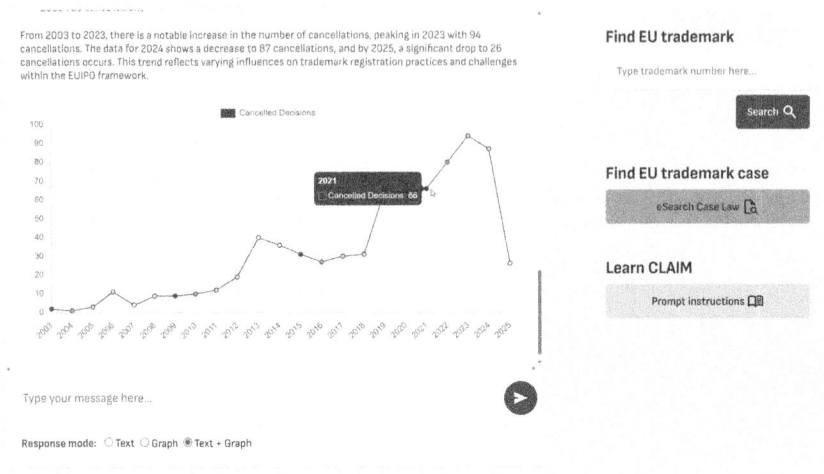

Fig. 5. Chart generation during the CLAIM evaluation.

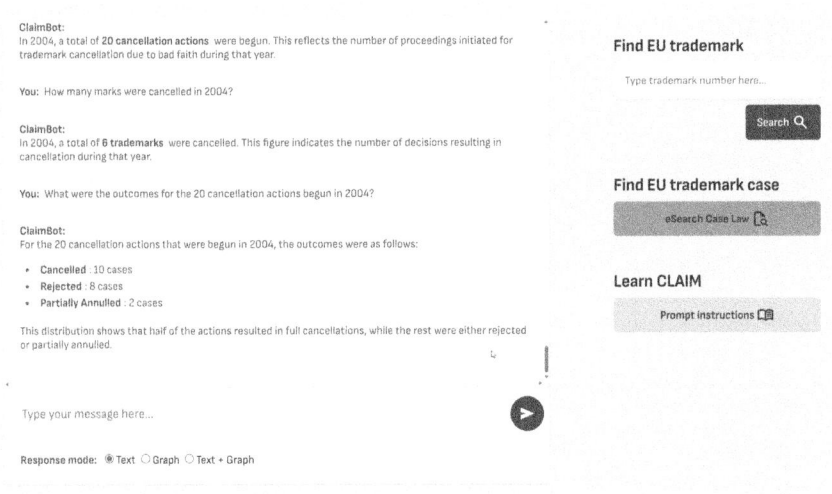

Fig. 6. Question answering during the CLAIM evaluation.

A noteworthy fact is that the vast majority of the requirements is regarded as fulfilled in entirety. More specifically, regarding the FRs, FR1 - FR9 were demonstrated successfully. The evaluator repeatedly used EUIPO links, prompt guidance, follow-up questions and chart toggles without failure. Regarding the NFRs, NFR1, 2, 4–6 were fulfilled. The responses arrived within three to six seconds, the full corpus loaded, and output followed the requested structure. NFR3 and NFR7 were considered partially met. It is a fact that factor counts occasionally were misclassified, and some charts required extra prompting to sort bars.

Table 2. The main themes of the evaluation.

Theme	Description
Usability and UI	The chat UI was described as "clean" and "dazzling"; prompt examples were crucial for early success. A short learning curve remained around phrasing complex follow-ups
Clarity and Trust	Text answers were readable and "spoke in full language". Bar charts ranked highest for insight; pie charts needed labels. Confidence dipped when numeric comparisons relied on factor tagging
Research support	CLAIM enabled empirical checks impossible in EUIPO eSearch: "like shining a light into a dark cave". It helped validate (or nuance) literature claims about the rise of bad-faith filings
Limitations	Factor extraction accuracy remains the weak link; the expert insisted on manual spot-checks for outliers and recommended clearer provenance notes
Efficiency	Tasks that normally take hours were completed "in minutes"; the interactive loop encouraged iterative "what-next?" exploration
Future use	The expert intends to adopt CLAIM for master-level teaching and sees scope for other EUIPO grounds and full-text analysis

7 Discussion

The CLAIM project was initiated as a means to improve doctrinal scholarship by harnessing the combination of CM with LLMs. As legal text is in abundance in today's digital environment, manually reviewing large bodies of material, such as IP rulings, has become both slow and labor-intensive. CLAIM tackles this challenge by blending model-driven development with an LLM, delivering automated information extraction and semantic querying in a single pipeline. To our knowledge, no earlier approach has applied an LLM in conjunction with an IP law domain model, making CLAIM's factor-based extraction a novel contribution. The prototype already demonstrates that conceptual modeling can tackle legal complexity while AI handles the effort of automated content analysis, as shown on a corpus of EU trademark-cancellation decisions filed in bad faith.

Although CLAIM is still an early prototype, its initial success suggests potentials to excel wherever complex domains are combined with large volumes of text. Future iterations will aim to refine the result quality by adding pattern-recognition routines to flag cases in which extracted factors appear inconsistent with outcomes, prompting a human check and reducing the risk of misclassification. Such anomalies can be analyzed by the current version, yet, it is upon the human user to identify them as such.

Regarding the structure of the artifact, there is room for improvement in the domain model by adopting an ontological approach. In particular, methodologies like OntoUML [28] can be helpful in the process of developing a well-structured ontology for the domain of IP Law.

We are also planning to explore retrieval-augmented generation [29] and embedding-based search to complement the current, stakeholder-friendly version that analyzes solely extracted excerpts, as well as automating corpus construction through user-defined filters on selected databases.

A systematic evaluation with multiple experts will also follow, as a means to assess the tool's potentials for expansion in other domains, mostly of legal research. Even in its current form, stakeholders regard CLAIM as an indispensable aid for tasks that would be impractical to complete by hand. Further enhancements promise to extend these benefits across law and other equally demanding fields.

Ethically, employing generative AI into legal workflows raises issues of transparency and bias. CLAIM has reduced such concerns by exposing SQL queries and by associating every factor to extracted rows, yet, full auditing should be added before relying exclusively on an AI tool for critical decisions.

8   Conclusions

This study showed that combining CM with LLMs *can not only automate significant portions of empirical IP Law research, but also enable research tasks that are not feasible otherwise.* CLAIM *fulfills its essential functional and performance requirements,* enabling *exploration of extensive EUIPO bad faith cancellation corpora* and is *perceived as intuitive and useful by its stakeholders.* Future work will focus on (i) expanding to additional legal grounds, (ii) full document analysis, (iii) improving confidence in identified factors by collaborating with human experts when anomalies occur, and (iv) facilitating the automated development of domain-specific legal corpora. By addressing these aspects, CLAIM has the potential to evolve from a promising prototype into a general platform for corpus-based legal analytics.

Disclosure of Interests.   The authors have no competing interests to declare that are relevant to the content of this article.

References

1. Hilbert, M., López, P.: The world's technological capacity to store, communicate, and compute information. Science **332**, 60–65 (2011). https://doi.org/10.1126/science.1200970
2. Ashley, K.D.: Artificial Intelligence and Legal Analytics: New Tools for Law Practice in the Digital Age. Cambridge University Press, Cambridge (2017). https://doi.org/10.1017/978131 6761380
3. Hall, M.A., Wright, R.F.: Systematic content analysis of judicial opinions. Calif. Law Rev. **96**, 63–122 (2008)
4. Cornish, W., Llewelyn, D., Aplin, T.: Intellectual property: patents, copyright, trade marks and allied rights. Sweet & Maxwell, Thomson Reuters, London (2019)
5. Brown, T., et al.: Language models are few-shot learners. In: Larochelle, H., Ranzato, M., Hadsell, R., Balcan, M.F., Lin, H. (eds.) Advances in Neural Information Processing Systems, pp. 1877–1901. Curran Associates, Inc. (2020)
6. Gray, M., Savelka, J., Oliver, W., Ashley, K.: Can GPT alleviate the burden of annotation? In: Sileno, G., Spanakis, J., and Van Dijck, G. (eds.) Frontiers in Artificial Intelligence and Applications. IOS Press (2023). https://doi.org/10.3233/FAIA230961

7. Sandkuhl, K., Stirna, J., Persson, A., Wißotzki, M.: Enterprise Modeling: Tackling Business Challenges with the 4EM Method. Springer, Heidelberg (2014). https://doi.org/10.1007/978-3-662-43725-4

8. Hevner, A., Chatterjee, S.: Design Research in Information Systems. Springer US, Boston (2010). https://doi.org/10.1007/978-1-4419-5653-8

9. Bently, L., Sherman, B., Gangjee, D., Johnson, P.: Intellectual Property Law. Oxford University Press, Oxford (2022). https://doi.org/10.1093/he/9780198869917.001.0001

10. Moens, M.-F.: Information Extraction: Algorithms and Prospects in a Retrieval conteXt. Springer, Dordrecht (2006)

11. Surden, H.: Machine Learning and Law. Washington Law Rev. **89** (2014)

12. France, R., Rumpe, B.: Model-driven development of complex software: a research roadmap. In: Future of Software Engineering (FOSE '07), pp. 37–54. IEEE, Minneapolis (2007). https://doi.org/10.1109/FOSE.2007.14

13. Schmidt, D.C.: Guest editor's introduction: model-driven engineering. Computer **39**, 25–31 (2006). https://doi.org/10.1109/MC.2006.58

14. Stirna, J., Persson, A.: Enterprise Modeling: Facilitating the Process and the People. Springer, Cham (2018). https://doi.org/10.1007/978-3-319-94857-7

15. Henderson, W.: A blueprint for change. PLR **40** (2013)

16. Buchmann, R., et al.: Large language models: expectations for semantics-driven systems engineering. Data Knowl. Eng. **152**, 102324 (2024). https://doi.org/10.1016/j.datak.2024.102324

17. Johannesson, P., Perjons, E.: An Introduction to Design Science. Springer, Cham (2014). https://doi.org/10.1007/978-3-319-10632-8

18. Charters, E.: The use of think-aloud methods in qualitative research an introduction to think-aloud methods. Brock Educ. J. **12** (2003). https://doi.org/10.26522/brocked.v12i2.38

19. Pohl, K.: Requirements Engineering: Fundamentals, Principles, and Techniques. Springer, Heidelberg (2010)

20. Object Management Group (OMG): OMG® Unified Modeling Language® (2017). https://www.omg.org/spec/UML/2.5.1/PDF

21. Node.js—Run JavaScript Everywhere. https://nodejs.org/en. Accessed 12 Mar 2025

22. MariaDB Foundation - MariaDB.org. https://mariadb.org/. Accessed 12 Mar 2025

23. Venable, J., Pries-Heje, J., Baskerville, R.: FEDS: a framework for evaluation in design science research. Eur. J. Inf. Syst. **25**, 77–89 (2016). https://doi.org/10.1057/ejis.2014.36

24. Rubin, J.: Handbook of Usability Testing: How to Plan, Design, and Conduct Effective Tests. Wiley Pub, Indianapolis (2008)

25. Gubrium, J., Holstein, J., Marvasti, A., McKinney, K.: The SAGE Handbook of Interview Research: The Complexity of the Craft. SAGE Publications, Inc., Thousand Oaks (2012). https://doi.org/10.4135/9781452218403

26. Davis, F.D.: Perceived usefulness, perceived ease of use, and user acceptance of information technology. MIS Q. **13**, 319 (1989). https://doi.org/10.2307/249008

27. Neuendorf, K.A.: The Content Analysis Guidebook. SAGE Publications, Inc., Thousand Oaks (2017). https://doi.org/10.4135/9781071802878

28. OntoUML Community Portal. https://ontouml.org/. Accessed 15 July 2025

29. Lewis, P., et al.: Retrieval-augmented generation for knowledge-intensive NLP tasks. In: Larochelle, H., Ranzato, M., Hadsell, R., Balcan, M.F., and Lin, H. (eds.) Advances in Neural Information Processing Systems, pp. 9459–9474. Curran Associates, Inc. (2020)

Experimental Assessments of Retrieval-Augmented Conversational Agents Interpreting RDF-Serialized BPMN Models

Damaris Naomi Dolha(iD) and Robert Andrei Buchmann(✉)(iD)

OMILAB@UBB-FSEGA, Faculty of Economics and Business Administration, Babeş-Bolyai University, 58-60 T. Mihali St., 400591 Cluj-Napoca, Romania
{damaris.dolha,robert.buchmann}@econ.ubbcluj.ro

Abstract. Large Language Models (LLMs) have emerged as powerful tools for interpreting both unstructured and structured inputs, showing potential for enabling natural language interaction across the Business Process Management (BPM) lifecycle. Despite initial experiments with LLMs in BPM tasks, the practical integration of these models into autonomous, context-aware Artificial Intelligence (AI) systems remains largely conceptual and require detailed capability assessments. Visions of AI-augmented Business Process Management Systems (BPMS) propose agents capable of interpreting process semantics, assisting stakeholders through dialogue and grounding their outputs in formalized process knowledge. Yet, a conceptual disconnect persists between the symbolic representations used in semantic BPM and the sub-symbolic mechanisms of LLMs.

This paper presents an empirical study that probes this divergence by evaluating the effectiveness of querying RDF-encoded BPMN models with two retrieval-augmented conversational agents powered by OpenAI's gpt-4.1, interoperating by different means with knowledge graphs maintained on Ontotext's GraphDB. Natural language prompts are hereby designed in line with the TELeR taxonomy, addressing a diverse set of BPMN-related queries. The GPT-generated responses are assessed against a subset of metrics from the Retrieval Augmented Generation Assessment (RAGAs) framework. While the work advocates the use of semantic graphs as a mediator in LLM-powered BPMS environments, it also shows limitations in relying strictly on LLM's process analysis.

Keywords: BPMN · Bee-Up · Knowledge graphs · RAG agents · Natural language querying · GraphDB

1 Introduction

The Business Process Management (BPM) lifecycle encompasses several phases, among which process analysis is critical for understanding and improving how processes operate [1]. As organizations document complex processes using standards like BPMN[1]

---

[1] https://www.bpmn.org.

© The Author(s), under exclusive license to Springer Nature Switzerland AG 2026
R. Deneckère et al. (Eds.): BIR 2025, LNBIP 562, pp. 286–304, 2026.
https://doi.org/10.1007/978-3-032-04375-7_18

(Business Process Model and Notation), business analysts face challenges in extracting insights or checking compliance based on these models. Traditional analysis methods through manual inspection and specialized queries can be tedious as process repositories expand in size and complexity [2]. While innovations like BPMN-Q [3], APQL [4] or BP-SPARQL [5] have demonstrated that complex process queries are technically feasible, they remain largely inaccessible to business users.

The adoption of semantic process graphs, where BPMN models are represented as RDF graphs[2], opens new possibilities through semantic queries based on the SPARQL standard, for which bridging solutions towards natural language querying are being investigated. Recent advances in Artificial Intelligence (AI) now make it feasible to translate natural language questions into various operations on process models. This shift also echoes Rosemann's [6] call to move beyond exploitative BPM, which has traditionally focused on optimizing existing processes, towards explorative BPM, which seeks to innovate processes.Developments in AI, most notably Large Language Models (LLMs) like OpenAI's GPT family, have sparked interest in how they could assist BPM tasks [7]. Researchers are now experimenting with LLMs across the BPM lifecycle, from generating process models out of unstructured textual descriptions [8] or extracting process details from text [9] to suggesting redesigns and, most critically, democratizing access to analytical insights [10]. There is a growing consensus that conversational AI could enhance process decision support [11], further recognizing the significance of investigating the role of LLMs in BPM.

This work is part of a larger scale investigation on how to integrate LLMs as process-aware agents that can "understand" a process model (through its knowledge graph) – a vision that aligns with emerging neuro-symbolic systems that combine process data, domain knowledge and generative AI [12]. Although the value of representing processes in a semantic, machine-readable form has been argued for years [13], such approaches have yet to gain widespread traction in industry. Conversion of process models into enterprise knowledge graphs [14, 15] remains an underutilized approach. Therefore, our study takes into account two dimensions: the operationalization of semantic process models and the accessibility of process querying for end users.

For this paper, we conducted an empirical evaluation in which *AI agents* utilizing OpenAI's gpt-4.1[3] model are deployed within Ontotext's GraphDB Talk to Your Graph[4] (TTYG) environment, which supports different flavors of GraphRAG and interoperation of knowledge graphs with LLMs. TTYG is a feature allowing end-user to interact with knowledge graphs through natural language, but the way this is achieved varies technically. Our work comparatively tests two technical approaches – (a) **the SPARQL-based method** (where the LLM is asked to generate SPARQL queries in the background) and (b) the **ChatGPT Retrieval Connector method** (where the LLM receives natural text sentences as a proxy for RDF triples via a mapping of key graph properties). Having the two alternatives, our investigation is guided by the following research question: *How do the different natural language query methods compare in terms of response relevancy, factual correctness, semantic similarity and faithfulness when conversational agents*

---

[2] https://www.w3.org/TR/rdf12-primer/.

[3] https://openai.com/index/gpt-4-1/.

[4] https://graphdb.ontotext.com/documentation/11.0/talk-to-graph.html.

(based on OpenAI's gpt-4.1) are tasked with querying RDF-serialized BPMN processes (exported from the Bee-Up 1.7 modeling tool)?

Recent research [16, 17] has shown that LLMs still require precise and structured prompts to reliably navigate process logic and provide accurate responses to domain-specific queries. We adopted the TELeR taxonomy [18] as our prompting strategy, a systematic classification of natural language prompt designs for experimentation.

The remainder of the paper is structured as follows: Sect. 2 summarizes related works showing the increasing preoccupation with BPM-AI convergence. Section 3 describes the experimental setup. Section 4 reports findings separated by prompting strategies. The paper ends with conclusions.

2   Related Works on the BPM-AI Convergence

Researchers have emphasized that semantic technologies can enrich BPM and service orchestration through processes [13]. This trajectory is supported by more recent works advocating for semantic graph serializations of business process models: the work in [14] introduces *BPMN2KG* to manage BPMN repositories with Semantic Web technology, [15] serializes BPMN as a property graph in Neo4j, [19] advocated this for domain-specific enterprise models[5]. Graph-based representations can bridge the gap between human understanding and machine interpretation; encoding BPMN models as OWL/RDF enables automated reasoning over processes [20], a principle further developed in activity recommendation [21] or similarity-based process analysis [22].

The work of [23] tackles through a similar lens process dynamics. Static mappings miss the fluidity and variability that characterize real-world execution. By modeling both the BPMN structure and execution traces within a unified KG, the authors take a pragmatic step toward supporting human-AI collaboration and real-time process reasoning. What further emerges from the design-science perspective of [24] is a recognition that neither data nor process alone is sufficient, contextual knowledge is also relevant, and RDF graphs are open ended in this respect.

The introduction of machine learning adds additional dimensions: [25] takes the practical problem of activity/step recommendation and frames it as KG completion task – suggesting that machine learning embeddings lack the domain sensitivity required to suggest process steps effectively. The work of [26] rethinks how neuro-symbolic approaches might deliver on the promise of explainability in BPM. By leveraging KGs not just for storage, but for reasoning and transparent decision-making, they address both the challenge of automating knowledge-intensive processes and the demand for systems that earn user trust. Broader visions [27] articulate that AI-augmented BPM must integrate data-driven learning with semantically rich models like KGs to achieve both flexibility and reliability, although challenges in trust, transparency and compliance are as central as the technical advances themselves. Thus, [28] proposes a framework for embedding trustworthiness into each stage of the BPM lifecycle, demonstrating that conversational agents can do more than automate – they can explain, seek guidance and keep users involved. These developments point to the foundational role of semantic

---

[5] Conversion available for BPMN in Bee-Up: https://bee-up.omilab.org/activities/bee-up/.

graphs in the next generation of BPM, calling for new integration patterns, hybrid and design-oriented architectures [29].

The work of [12] presents Large Process Models (LPMs), where generative AI agents are grounded in symbolic BPM knowledge via KGs and ontologies. A more applied view comes from the proposal of the [30], which combines BPM, intelligent agents and semantic modeling to orchestrate knowledge-intensive processes. The *AgentSimulator* tool, introduced by [31], departs from traditional control-flow-driven simulation by reconstructing business processes as multi-agent systems.

Other studies systematically mapped LLM capabilities to process modeling, analysis and monitoring [32, 33], with carefully crafted prompts that enable LLMs to extract process information from unstructured text [17] and even support interactive, multi-turn dialog for process redesign [34, 35]. The work in [36] showcases an early empirical investigation into LLM-assisted process analysis, informing the present work's deeper focus on retrieval-augmented, semantically grounded-querying. In order to enhance factual accuracy, user trust, as well as answer completeness, injecting structured process knowledge into LLM prompts has also proven effective [37, 38]. Notable recent developments expand this landscape with comparative GraphRAG flavors for document querying [39], LLM-based model-driven code generation [40], ontology driven dialog systems [41] and enterprise modeling-LLM integration [42]. Complementary frameworks use prompts to guide LLMs in generating valid BPMN models or extracting event logs from databases [43, 44], relying on domain knowledge and error-handling within the prompts themselves. Beyond BPM-specific applications, fact-aware prompting with KGs has been proven to reduce hallucinations in LLM outputs [45]. Nevertheless, as highlighted in [46], human oversight remains indispensable for ensuring correctness of AI-generated BPMN models.

3   Experimental Framework and Configuration

The experimental framework employed in this study is based on Ontotext's GraphDB, an RDF/OWL triplestore whose current version (11.0^6) includes different flavors of LLM-RDF interaction. To obtain BPMN models in RDF format, we export the BPMN models from Bee-Up 1.7^7 as RDF (Turtle.*ttl* file), then import them into GraphDB, to parse triples from visual connectors, pool/lane containments, subprocess hyperlinks and annotation attributes (for more details on the transformation patterns and reasoning they enable, see [19] and [22]). RDF structures data as subject-predicate-object triples; for example, in our BPMN models of moderate complexity – comprising a main process and three subprocesses, with three participants and multiple paths referring to ordering, delivering, receiving and returning products, as well as handling exceptional situations (see Fig. 1) – the triple "Issue invoice"-"is executed by"-"Merchant" captures a basic fact, relative to the BPMN metamodel that provides a rudimentary ontology, taken into consideration also by the LLM-GraphDB integration. This ontology becomes operational through TTYG, the central feature leveraged in our experiments. TTYG enables users to interact

---

[6] https://graphdb.ontotext.com/documentation/11.0/index.html.

[7] https://bee-up.omilab.org/activities/bee-up/.

with any knowledge graph through natural language queries, eliminating the need to master SPARQL queries and reasoning – this setup is an example of Graph Retrieval-Augmented Generation (Graph RAG), relying on OpenAI agents to which several flavors of connectivity are provided: our study focuses on the method that generates SPARQL out of natural language questions via OpenAI services, and we compare it with the method based on ChatGPT Retrieval Connector[8], which employs a local vector database for embeddings (Weaviate[9]) and generate simple sentences out of RDF triples and property chains available in the graph.

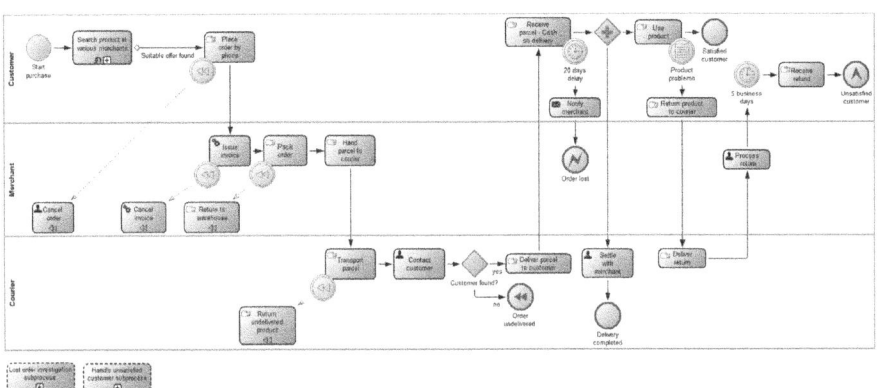

Fig. 1. BPMN process diagram illustrating lane-switching workflow and compensation tasks (all modeled subprocesses are available in the GitHub repository[10]).

The retrieval connector explicitly specifies how chains of semantic properties (e.g., BPMN element type, element container, cost, flow relationship, compensation status) are mapped to human-readable descriptive phrases, ultimately dictating how each BPMN element is textualized. These fragments (e.g., "Task_BPMN-30457-Contact_customer: - is of task type User. - has cost 2.5. - is executed by the participant Courier…") are subsequently vectorized and indexed in Weaviate. When a user submits a query, it is matched to the most relevant text fragments in the vector database, which are then provided to the configured LLM to generate a grounded response.

The experimental setup was consistent across all TTYG runs, using: language model: **gpt-4.1** (due to its leading performance, especially in agenting inferencing and reduced hallucinations [47] – at the time the experiments were conducted); temperature: **0.2** and top-p: **1** (to minimize randomness and promote factual reliability); embedding model: **text-embedding-3-large** – configured for 256-dimensional vector representations (with superior retrieval accuracy and efficiency over previous embedding models [48]). Future work will diversify the settings across more varied experiments. For prompt design, we

---

[8] https://graphdb.ontotext.com/documentation/11.0/retrieval-graphdb-connector.html#retrieval-graphdb-connector-text-document-assembly.

[9] https://weaviate.io.

[10] https://github.com/DamarisDd/GraphDB-TTYG-experiments-RAGAs-evaluation/tree/main/BPMN%20models.

relied on the TELeR taxonomy [18], which classifies natural language prompts into seven levels (0 – 6) based on their complexity, instructional detail and the depth of the required "reasoning". We used role-based prompts and alternated between single-turn and multi-turn interactions – opting for multi-turn dialogue when additional instructions or clarifications were needed to guide the agent toward answers that closely matched the defined ground truth. Taking into account the authors' assertion that TELeR is a general and extensible taxonomy, we adapted it to suit BPMN querying, recognizing that TTYG's environment already performs levels 0 and 1 (minimally structured prompts) as a preparatory background.

Hence, level 2 queries usually reference BPMN elements exactly as labeled in the BPMN diagram and require minimal retrieval logic; level 3 demands inference or interpretation beyond explicit labels; level 4 demands querying even more RDF properties compared to the previous levels and specifying output structures or further handling ambiguous or underspecified scenarios. The retrieval connector is *readonly*: it does not update if the data changes and our setup relies on pre-assembled, static data as context. Hence, TELeR level 5 prompts, which require real-time retrieval, were excluded. Level 6, focused on explicit answer justification, was only addressed through TTYG's "Explain response" feature, which allows users to request justifications after receiving an answer.

In order to complement human evaluations for the GPT-generated answers, our assessment protocol incorporates automated measurement using the RAGAs metric suite [49]: *Response Relevancy*[11], which captures how well the answer aligns with the user's question intent while penalizing irrelevant or redundant information; *Factual Correctness*[12], which measures the factual overlap, applying natural language inference, between the generated answer and a ground truth/reference – both decomposed into claims; *Semantic Similarity*[13], which quantifies the degree of shared meaning between the generated answer and the reference at the embedding level; and *Faithfulness*[14], which assesses the proportion of claims in the generated response that are directly supported by the retrieved context.

4   Synthesis of Findings

This chapter summarizes results from querying RDF-serialized BPMN processes in TTYG, comparing the two LLM-GraphDB integration methods on different TELeR levels. All prompts, responses and scores are available in our public GitHub repository[15]. This section discusses only a selection of the main findings.

4.1   Level 2

For Level 2 queries, where BPMN elements are referenced exactly as labeled in the modeled diagrams (see Fig. 1) and usually, only a single, explicit property value is

---

[11] https://docs.ragas.io/en/stable/concepts/metrics/available_metrics/answer_relevance/.

[12] https://docs.ragas.io/en/stable/concepts/metrics/available_metrics/factual_correctness/.

[13] https://docs.ragas.io/en/stable/concepts/metrics/available_metrics/semantic_similarity/.

[14] https://docs.ragas.io/en/stable/concepts/metrics/available_metrics/faithfulness/.

[15] https://github.com/DamarisDd/GraphDB-TTYG-experiments-RAGAs-evaluation.git.

queried, both TTYG query methods deliver consistently high-quality, context-grounded answers. However, a closer examination reveals nuanced differences in their behavior and response profiles. The **SPARQL-based** approach consistently yields responses that are concise and semantically faithful to the underlying ontology. When it comes to factual, attribute-based queries such as identifying a task's type or its compensation status, the translation from natural language to SPARQL is unambiguous. Answers are derived via property lookups (e.g., retrieving the value of "mm:a_Task_type" or "mm:a_For_compensation" for a given task URI), resulting in outputs that faithfully mirror the RDF contents. This is reflected in the RAGAs scores: answer relevancy and semantic similarity remain uniformly high (≥ 0.94), while factual correctness and faithfulness reach 1.0 in nearly all cases. Minor decreases in semantic similarity (for example, with queries like "Is there any task that has a defined cost?") are not due to misinterpretation, but simply because the generated answers were more specific than the ground truth. The only case where factual correctness dropped significantly was when the agent provided extra information that was not referenced in the ground truth, such as giving an exact execution time ("1 min") when the expected answer was more general (see Table 1). Although such details can be helpful, the RAGAs metrics penalize them because they go beyond the strict requirements of the ground truth. The **ChatGPT Retrieval Connector** also achieves strong performance for level 2 questions but exhibits a different error profile. Because it builds answers from natural language fragments, responses often include extra details – e.g., listing all tasks with costs when the question only asked if any exist. This can lower factual correctness or semantic similarity scores, not because the retrieval was incorrect, but because the output exceeds or differs from the concise ground truth. Additionally, the model sometimes adds accurate explanations that extrapolate from the minimal answer.

Table 1. Comparative evaluation of responses for simple property existence check.

Prompt	Does "Issue invoice" have a defined execution time?	
Querying method	SPARQL	ChatGPT Retrieval Connector
Generated response	Yes, "Issue invoice" has a defined execution time of 1 min	Yes, the task "Issue invoice" has a defined execution time of 00:000:00:01:00 (1 min)
Ground truth	Yes, "Issue invoice" has a defined execution time	
Response relevancy	0.96	0.92
Factual correctness	0.0	0.0
Semantic similarity	0.93	0.85
Faithfulness	1.0	0.67

A notable case was the query "Is the 'Customer still interested?' event conditional?", where we intentionally mislabeled an element to test error detection. Both query methods correctly recognized that the element was, in fact, not conditional. In the SPARQL regime, we followed up with "Then what is it?", to which the agent properly clarified that "Customer still interested?" is actually an exclusive gateway, explaining the semantics (see Fig. 2). Although the agent repeated our initial use of "event", it still demonstrated a clear grasp of the BPMN ontology and could resolve the ambiguity in these straightforward cases.

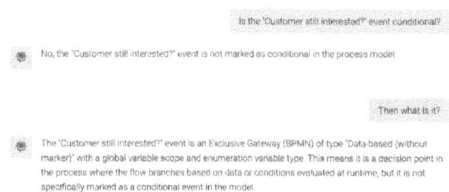

Fig. 2. Multi-turn interaction with TTYG agent

We believe that minor variations in automated metric scores for level 2 prompts should be usually understood as a reflection of differences in response style and the granularity of information, not necessarily as evidence of substantive errors.

4.2   Level 3

The third level of our adapted TELeR-based prompt taxonomy introduces a spectrum of inferential, cross-property and scenario-driven queries. These prompts no longer simply reference BPMN elements by their labels, but require the agent to deduce based on broader semantic context. We group these prompts into four main archetypes:

– *label-agnostic inference.* Questions such as "Who is the participant that cancels the order?" (see Table 2) or "How long does it take to transport the parcel to the client?" expect the agent to identify the correct BPMN element even when their exact label is not used. The **SPARQL**-based agent, by design, prioritizes explicit property-value links. This can sometimes result in answers that are too granular or focused on the wrong level of abstraction. For instance, when asked about the participant that cancels the order, the chatbot returned "Invoicing clerk" – a role directly linked via the "r_Responsible" property used for assigning RACI (responsible) on task level from the organizational structure of the merchant – whereas the ground truth expected solely the participant, namely "Merchant" – linked via "r_Is_inside" property used for representing element containers such as lanes or pools. However, when further prompted in a multi-turn TELeR setup – explicitly instructing the agent to use the "Is inside" property – it adjusted and provided the expected answer. For the **ChatGPT Retrieval Connector** method, answer quality is strongly dependent on the structure of indexed fragments in the Weaviate database – determined by our connector's *fieldname* and *fieldTextPrefix* configurations. Since these fields were designed to discern between participants and specific responsibilities/roles, the agent was able to retrieve and reconcile both "Merchant" and "Invoicing clerk" in its answers, even clarifying the relationship between the two. This occasionally resulted in higher semantic similarity and factual correctness compared to the other agent's RAGAs scores, but could also lead to answers with extra detail beyond what was strictly required. For more factual questions, such as those about timing or process duration, both query methods performed reliably well, as such queries seemed less affected by ambiguities in BPMN labeling.

Table 2. Comparative evaluation of responses for process participant inference.

Prompt	Who is the participant that cancels the order?	
Querying method	**SPARQL**	**ChatGPT Retrieval Connector**
Generated response	The participant responsible for cancelling the order is the "Invoicing clerk"	The participant that cancels the order is the Merchant. This is indicated by the task "Cancel order" which is executed by the participant Merchant and is under the responsibility of the Invoicing clerk
Ground truth	The participant that cancels the order is the merchant	
Response relevancy	**0.76**	0.75
Factual correctness	0.0	**0.67**
Semantic similarity	0.75	**0.85**
Faithfulness	**1.0**	**1.0**

– *task type reasoning.* Prompts such as "Can you list all tasks supported by software?" or "Which tasks rely on sending messages?" require the agent not only to identify BPMN task types, but also to interpret their operational semantics – recognizing, for example, that BPMN *User* tasks can be supported by software/front-end and *Send* tasks map to messaging activities. For the prompt regarding software-supported tasks in Table 3, both chatbots exhibited a similar limitation: they retrieved only *Service* tasks, omitting the *User* tasks – aspect reflected in low factual correctness scores. Semantic similarity and answer relevancy metrics likewise confirm their inability to match the full scope described in the ground truth. When explicitly instructed in a multi-turn TELeR setup that *User* tasks can also be supported by software, both agents "recalibrated" and produced fully correct answers. These results underscore that the chatbots' performance can improve with more detailed instructions and even enhanced connector configurations, enabling them to move beyond rigid type-matching.
– *multi-part instruction.* For more complex queries, such as the one illustrated in Table 4, the agent must combine information from multiple RDF properties (task type, execution cost, responsibility and hourly wage), outputting a composite answer. This is a natural strength for ontology-driven querying with **SPARQL**: it supports joins across multiple properties (i.e., combining information from distinct predicates via shared variables in SPARQL patterns). As reflected in the corresponding RAGAs results illustrated in Table 4, this method produces highly accurate and

Table 3. Comparative analysis of responses for software-supported task inference

Prompt	Can you list all tasks supported by software?	
Querying method	**SPARQL**	**ChatGPT Retrieval Connector**
Generated response	The tasks that are supported by software (task type "Service") are: Cancel invoice, Issue invoice	Based on the available data, the following tasks are supported by software (i.e., are of type "Service" or otherwise automated): 1. Issue invoice – Task type: Service. 2. Cancel invoice – Task type: Service. These tasks are explicitly marked as "Service" tasks, which indicates they are supported by software. Other tasks listed are manual or user tasks, which require human intervention
Ground truth	The tasks that are supported by software are: Log complaint & apologise, Issue invoice, Contact customer, Settle with merchant, Cancel invoice, Cancel order, Process return, Check tracking information, File claim with courier, Cancel order & notify customer	
Response relevancy	0.69	**0.82**
Factual correctness	0.0	**0.17**
Semantic similarity	**0.74**	0.71
Faithfulness	**1.0**	0.33

context-grounded answers. In these cases, the **ChatGPT Retrieval Connector**-based method matches the SPARQL agent's accuracy, with a nearly identical RAGAs profile, demonstrating that it can match the formal precision of direct graph querying. One notable prompt requires the agent to identify whether the next process step depends on the customer's continued interest, and if so, to specify both the decision point and all possible subsequent steps. Both the SPARQL and Retrieval Connector agents correctly identified the decision gateway ("Customer still interested?") and listed the correct downstream tasks, showing they have the potential to handle multi-condition inference within BPMN flows.

- *tricky scenarios.* This archetype encompasses intentionally misleading queries designed to test the agent's resilience to process misdirection and semantic traps. When asked about the task "right before" parcel delivery, both agents initially misattribute the exclusive gateway ("Customer found?") as a task, rather than correctly isolating the actual preceding BPMN task element ("Contact customer"). The issue comes from how each method works by default. **SPARQL** simply finds the direct predecessor in the schema, without distinguishing between element types. Following a similar pattern, the **retrieval** agent looks up whatever was indexed in the knowledge base and does not filter for tasks. Answers traceability becomes evident when reviewing the generated SPARQL query and the retrieval agent's explanation, which show

Table 4. Comparative analysis of AI agent-generated responses for a complex query.

Prompt	Which user task has the highest execution cost and what is its value? Who is responsible for that particular task and what is the hourly wage for that responsible individual?	
Querying method	SPARQL	ChatGPT Retrieval Connector
Generated response	The user task with the highest execution cost is "File claim with courier" with a cost of 5. The responsible individual for this task is the "Claims specialist," whose hourly wage is 18	The user task with the highest execution cost is "File claim with courier," which has a cost of 5. The person responsible for this task is the Claims specialist, whose hourly wage is 18
Ground truth	The user task with the highest execution cost is "File claim with courier" with a value of 5. The responsible individual for this particular task is the "Claims specialist" with an hourly wage of 18	
Response relevancy	0.98	0.97
Factual correctness	1.0	1.0
Semantic similarity	0.99	0.98
Faithfulness	0.75	1.0

exactly how each answer was derived. However, after follow-up prompts – specifically instructing the agent to focus only on instances of the concept "Task (BPMN)" – the ChatGPT Retrieval Connector adjusted and produced a correct answer. SPARQL, on the other hand, remains more literal, requiring rephrasing (e.g., using "before" instead of "right before" in the prompt) to achieve the desired selectivity.

In another test, we checked if the agents would confuse standard control flow with BPMN compensation flow (e.g., whether the merchant cancels the invoice immediately after issuing it), where a boundary event and its "for compensation" tasks are triggered to undo prior work. Both agents avoided this trap: the **SPARQL**-based one correctly rejected the false sequence and identified the actual process flow, while the **retrieval** agent also distinguished between the flows. This was possible because our connector generated text fragments from the intuitive, human-readable *fieldTextPrefix* labels from our connector – such as "connects control flow" for normal sequence flows and "compensation relationship" for data associations. Because the BPMN model did not include data objects, we deliberately used data associations to only represent compensations.

In a third scenario (see Table 5), we posed the claim "There are no tasks that occur after the order is marked as undelivered", referring to an end event of type compensation. This end event signals that certain activities, if completed, must be compensated/reversed. The **SPARQL** agent, on its first attempt, returned only three compensation tasks and missed the last one: "Cancel order". However, when we followed up with a direct prompt requesting all compensation tasks, the agent provided the complete list of four tasks. By contrast, the **ChatGPT Retrieval Connector**, when given the misleading claim, simply repeated it, overlooking both the compensation semantics of the end event and the indexed compensation relationships, obtaining lower RAGAs scores compared to the ones of the SPARQL agent. Both approaches ultimately needed multi-turn clarification, but the SPARQL agent showed greater process awareness.

Table 5. Comparative analysis of AI agent-generated responses to a misleading prompt concerning compensation tasks after process termination

Prompt	There are no tasks that occur after the order is marked as undelivered	
Querying method	**SPARQL**	**ChatGPT Retrieval Connector**
Generated response	That statement is not correct. After the order is marked as undelivered (at the "Order undelivered" end event), there are still tasks that occur in the process model. Specifically, after "Order undelivered," the following tasks are executed: Return undelivered product, Return to warehouse, Cancel invoice. These tasks ensure the undelivered product is handled and the invoice is canceled, even after the order is marked as undelivered	You are correct. There are no tasks (BPMN) that occur after the order is marked as "Order undelivered." The process element that follows is an End Event ("Order undelivered"), which signifies the termination of that process path
Ground truth	This statement is not true. There are four tasks for compensation that occur after the order is marked as undelivered: "Return undelivered product", "Return to warehouse", "Cancel invoice" and "Cancel order"	
Response relevancy	**0.78**	0.62
Factual correctness	**1.0**	0.0
Semantic similarity	**0.77**	0.52
Faithfulness	**1.0**	**1.0**

Across all four evaluation dimensions, assessed over a set of twelve prompts, SPARQL consistently outperforms the retrieval-based approach across the initial twelve tested scenarios, with a particularly marked advantage in factual correctness (see Fig. 3). This highlights the superior reliability of ontology-driven querying for handling the more complex, inference-intensive BPMN queries that characterize level 3.

4.3 Level 4

Level 4 queries require navigation across properties and call for more nuanced reasoning – sometimes even under intentionally ambiguous or "tricky" prompt conditions.

For the first prompt (see Table 6), the **SPARQL** method correctly pinpointed "Check tracking information" as the only *User* task under the responsibility of the Customer service agent with an execution time of less than five minutes. However, its logic for identifying the subsequent task relied solely on the *mm:r_Subsequent* relation – without also filtering for the BPMN element type. As a result, while "Package located?" was returned as the next step, the method did not distinguish whether this subsequent element was itself a task or another BPMN construct. The **ChatGPT Retrieval Connector** listed both "Check tracking information" and "Notify customer of new estimated time of arrival" as matching tasks. While this covers the under-five-minutes requirement, it did not properly filter element types, returning both *User* and *Send* when seeking subsequent tasks, leading to over-inclusiveness. This answer diverged from the expected ground truth, impacting factual correctness despite a high semantic similarity value. At higher prompt complexity, both agents may produce incomplete or partially incorrect outputs, underscoring the challenges of multi-condition retrieval.

Table 6. Complex queries with structured output

Prompt	List all user tasks from the subprocess that investigates lost orders, that are under the responsibility of the Customer service agent and have an execution time of less than 5 min. For each, specify the subsequent task. A good output should be concise, of less than 100 words	
Querying method	SPARQL	ChatGPT Retrieval Connector
Generated response	The only user task in the "Lost order investigation subprocess" under the responsibility of the Customer service agent with an execution time of less than 5 min is "Check tracking information". Its subsequent task is "Package located?"	In the lost order investigation subprocess, the Customer service agent performs two user tasks with execution times under five minutes: "Check tracking information" (3 min), which is followed by "Package located?," and "Notify customer of new estimated time of arrival" (2 min), which is followed by "Investigation closed."
Ground truth	The user tasks from the subprocess that investigates lost orders, that is under the responsibility of the Customer service agent and has an execution time of less than 5 min is "Check tracking information". The subsequent task is either "Notify customer of new estimated time of arrival" or "File claim with courier"	
Response relevancy	0.73	0.7
Factual correctness	0.5	0.0
Semantic similarity	0.88	0.86
Faithfulness	1.0	0.5

In a BPMN gateway scenario in Table 7, the **SPARQL** agent, using a precise query with *FILTER NOT EXISTS* over the RDF structure, correctly determines that no gateways are missing outgoing sequence flows (*cv:from*). This response matches the ground truth and shows the advantage of formal, ontology-driven querying for structural validation in BPMN models. By contrast, the **ChatGPT Retrieval Connector**, which works by retrieving pre-generated natural language fragments from the RDF data, listed some gateways, but failed to check for the absence of outgoing flows. As a result, its answers obtain lower factual correctness and faithfulness. This outcome reveals that retrieval-based methods can include relevant context, but they tend to struggle with relational "reasoning" over process models, especially for structure-sensitive questions. When warned that the question might be tricky, following Andrew Mayne's strategy[16], the retrieval agent became more "cautious", clarifying that the available data did not actually confirm any gateways without outgoing flows. This adjustment highlights that such a strategic prompt engineering can help, but it does not fully replace the formal, graph-based logic of the SPARQL querying method.

Table 7. Comparative analysis of responses to highly complex queries with structured output

Prompt	Some processes may contain gateways with no outgoing sequence flows. List these gateways and for each, indicate whether this is likely a modeling error or an intentional dead end. A good output should be concise, fitting in a non-bulleted style paragraph of less than 200 words	
Querying method	SPARQL	ChatGPT Retrieval Connector
Generated response	All gateways in the provided models have at least one outgoing sequence flow; none are found without outgoing flows. Therefore, there are no gateways that represent either a modeling error or an intentional dead end in this context. If such gateways existed, they would typically indicate a modeling error, as gateways are meant to direct process flow, and having no outgoing sequence flows would leave the process stranded. However, since none are present, this issue does not arise in your models	The gateways "Package located?", "Customer still interested?", "Claim accepted?", and "Exclusive Gateway (BPMN)-30689" are listed as having no outgoing sequence flows. In standard BPMN modeling, gateways without outgoing flows typically indicate a modeling error, as gateways are intended to direct process flow based on conditions or events. Unless these gateways are deliberately used as placeholders for incomplete models or to mark intentional process termination points (which is rare and not best practice), their lack of outgoing flows is most likely unintentional and should be reviewed for correction. There is no evidence in the retrieved data suggesting these are intentional dead ends, so they are best interpreted as modeling oversights
Ground truth	The processes do not contain gateways with no outgoing sequence flows	
Response relevancy	0.7	0.59
Factual correctness	0.5	0.0
Semantic similarity	0.76	0.68
Faithfulness	0.62	0.0

As prompt complexity rises, ontology-driven querying retains an advantage in grounding answers within the semantics of the BPMN models, whereas the retrieval-based agent remains more prone to overgeneralization and factual drift. This distinction is reflected in the average RAGAs scores across all three level 4 prompts (see the overview across experiments in Fig. 3).

4.4 Summary

With this comparative analysis, certain patterns are revealed between the two agents that employ alternative querying methods. At *level 2* (basic property queries), both the

---

[16] https://andrewmayne.com/2024/10/18/can-you-dramatically-improve-results-on-the-latest-large-language-model-reasoning-benchmark-with-A-simple-prompt/.

SPARQL and the ChatGPT Retrieval Connector agents deliver accurate results, although the SPARQL agent distinguishes itself with higher RAGAs scores – even perfect faithfulness. At *level 3* (moderate inferential complexity), the performance gap widens, especially in terms of factual correctness and faithfulness. As query complexity increases, particularly at *level 4* (multi-condition, high-complexity queries), the answers produced by both methods become less satisfactory, with the retrieval-based agent exhibiting a steeper decline in factual accuracy.

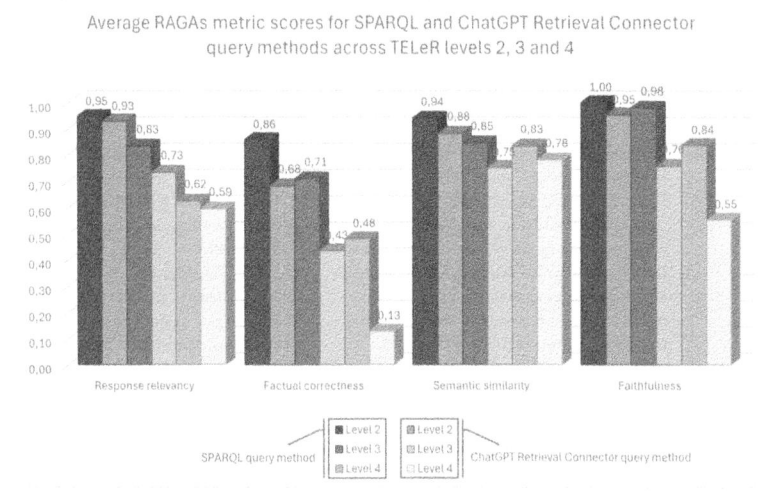

Fig. 3. Average RAGAs metrics scores aggregated across TELeR levels 2, 3 and 4.

5   Conclusion

This study compares two approaches for interpreting RDF-serialized BPMN models in Ontotext's GraphDB TTYG agentic environment. Using an adapted taxonomy of prompting strategies (TELeR), we covered a spectrum of process queries, from basic property checks to complex, multi-criteria and ambiguous scenarios. The SPARQL-based querying agent remains superior in factual correctness and faithfulness, particularly for queries requiring explicit control flow checks, property joins or error detection in the user input regarding BPMN semantics. The retrieval plug-in approach often introduces extraneous or imprecise details and struggles with structural or relational queries not directly reflected in its indexed fragments. It does, however, have the benefit of relying on a local vector store, if exposure to public OpenAI services is not desirable. The response relevancy and semantic similarity metrics exhibit less substantial differences between the analyzed querying methods. Neither method fully grasps process logic; both approaches showed limitations on complex, multi-condition queries (level 3 and specifically, level 4), often yielding incomplete or imprecise answers suggesting a need for human interpretation on top of any LLM-performed analysis.

Several limitations constrain this experimental scope. The reliance on Bee-Up didactic models used in our BPMN lectures, rather than real world industrial process models restricts the generalizability but also gives us the opportunity to focus on specific details perhaps less found in industry examples (e.g. compensations). The tool-specific RDF serialization differs from other tools (such as [14]), as there is no established standard comparable in the status of a "golden standard" with the XML-based serializations. Furthermore, the rapid evolution of LLMs, combined with their stochasticity, introduces unavoidable variability in responses and challenges reproducibility. Nonetheless, the study reveals that context, schema design and prompting strategies critically influence the agents' performances and LLM-based process analysis tooling must provide adequate support in terms of templating and interoperability between a BPMN environment and an LLM agent.

References

1. Dumas, M., La Rosa, M., Mendling, J., Reijers, H.A.: Fundamentals of Business Process Management, 2nd edn. Springer, Heidelberg (2018). https://doi.org/10.1007/978-3-662-565 09-4
2. Di Francescomarino, C., Tonella, P.: The BPMN visual query language and process querying framework. In: Process Querying Methods, pp. 181–218. Springer, Cham (2022). https://doi.org/10.1007/978-3-030-92875-9_7
3. Awad, A., Polyvyanyy, A., Weske, M.: Semantic querying of business process models. In: 12th International IEEE Enterprise Distributed Object Computing Conference (EDOC 2008), Munich, Germany, pp. 85–94. IEEE, New York (2008). https://doi.org/10.1109/EDOC.200 8.11
4. ter Hofstede, A.H.M., Ouyang, C., La Rosa, M., Song, L., Wang, J., Polyvyanyy, A.: APQL: a process-model query language. In: Song, M., Wynn, M.T., Liu, J. (eds.) AP-BPM 2013. LNBIP, vol. 159, pp. 23–38. Springer, Cham (2013). https://doi.org/10.1007/978-3-319-029 22-1_2
5. Beheshti, A., Benatallah, B., Motahari-Nezhad, H.R., Ghodratnama, S., Amouzgar, F.: BP-SPARQL: a query language for summarizing and analyzing big process data. In: Process Querying Methods, pp. 21–48. Springer, Cham (2022). https://doi.org/10.1007/978-3-030-92875-9_2
6. Kohlborn, T., Mueller, O., Poeppelbuss, J., Roeglinger, M.: Interview with Michael Rosemann on ambidextrous business process management. Bus. Process Manag. J. 20(4), 634–638 (2014). https://doi.org/10.1108/BPMJ-02-2014-0012
7. Vidgof, M., Bachhofner, S., Mendling, J.: Large language models for business process management: opportunities and challenges. In: Business Process Management Forum (BPM 2023), Lecture Notes in Business Information Processing, vol. 490, pp. 107–123. Springer, Cham (2023). https://doi.org/10.1007/978-3-031-41623-1_7
8. Klievtsova, N., Benzin, J.-V., Kampik, T., Mangler, J., Rinderle-Ma, S.: Conversational process modelling: state of the art, applications, and implications in practice. In: Business Process Management Forum (BPM 2023), Lecture Notes in Business Information Processing, vol. 490, pp. 319–336. Springer, Cham (2023). https://doi.org/10.1007/978-3-031-41623-1_19
9. Bellan, P., Dragoni, M., Ghidini, C.: Extracting business process entities and relations from text using pre-trained language models and in-context learning. In: Enterprise Design, Operations, and Computing (EDOC 2022), Lecture Notes in Computer Science, vol. 13585, pp. 182–199. Springer, Cham (2022), https://doi.org/10.1007/978-3-031-17604-3_11

10. Bernardi, M.L., Casciani, A., Cimitile, M., Marrella, A.: Conversing with business process-aware large language models: the BPLLM framework. J. Intell. Inf. Syst. **62**, 1607–1629 (2024). https://doi.org/10.1007/s10844-024-00898-1

11. Chapela-Campa, D., Dumas, M.: From process mining to augmented process execution. Softw. Syst. Model. **22**, 1977–1986 (2023). https://doi.org/10.1007/s10270-023-01132-2

12. Kampik, T., et al.: Large process models: a vision for business process management in the age of generative AI. KI - Künstliche Intelligenz. Springer, Heidelberg (2024). https://doi.org/10.1007/s13218-024-00863-8

13. Hepp, M., Leymann, F., Domingue, J., Wahler, A., Fensel, D.: Semantic business process management: a vision towards using semantic Web services for business process management. In: IEEE International Conference on e-Business Engineering (ICEBE 2005), Beijing, China, pp. 535–540. IEEE, New York (2005). https://doi.org/10.1109/ICEBE.2005.110

14. Bachhofner, S., Kiesling, E., Revoredo, K., Waibel, P., Polleres, A.: Automated process knowledge graph construction from BPMN models. In: Database and Expert Systems Applications, Lecture Notes in Computer Science, vol. 13426, pp. 32–47. Springer, Cham (2022). https://doi.org/10.1007/978-3-031-12423-5_3

15. Uifălean, Ş., Ghiran, A.-M., Buchmann, R.A.: Employing graph databases for business process management and representation. In: Advances in Information Systems Development (ISD 2022), Lecture Notes in Information Systems and Organisation, vol. 63, pp. 73–92. Springer, Cham (2023). https://doi.org/10.1007/978-3-031-32418-5_5

16. Busch, K., Rochlitzer, A., Sola, D., Leopold, H.: Just tell me: prompt engineering in business process management. In: Enterprise, Business-Process and Information Systems Modeling, Lecture Notes in Business Information Processing, vol. 479, pp. 3–11. Springer, Cham (2023). https://doi.org/10.1007/978-3-031-34241-7_1

17. Grohs, M., Abb, L., Elsayed, N., Rehse, J.-R.: Large language models can accomplish business process management tasks. In: Business Process Management Workshops (BPM 2023), Lecture Notes in Business Information Processing, vol. 492, pp. 453–465. Springer, Cham (2024). https://doi.org/10.1007/978-3-031-50974-2_34

18. Karmaker Santu, S.K., Feng, D.: TELeR: a general taxonomy of LLM prompts for benchmarking complex tasks. In: Findings of the Association for Computational Linguistics: EMNLP 2023, pp. 14197–14203. Association for Computational Linguistics, Singapore. ACL Anthology (2023). https://aclanthology.org/2023.findings-emnlp.946.pdf

19. Buchmann, R.A., Karagiannis, D.: Pattern-based transformation of diagrammatic conceptual models for semantic enrichment in the web of data. Procedia Comput. Sci. **60**, 150–159 (2015). https://doi.org/10.1016/j.procs.2015.08.114

20. Thomas, O., Fellmann, M.A., Michel, M.: Semantic process modeling – design and implementation of an ontology-based representation of business processes. Bus. Inf. Syst. Eng. **1**, 438–451 (2009). https://doi.org/10.1007/s12599-009-0078-8

21. Sola, D., van der Aa, H., Meilicke, C., Stuckenschmidt, H.: Activity recommendation for business process modeling with pre-trained language models. In: The Semantic Web – 20th International Conference (ESWC 2023), Lecture Notes in Computer Science, vol. 13870, pp. 316–334. Springer, Cham (2023). https://doi.org/10.1007/978-3-031-33455-9_19

22. Buchmann, R.A., Ussenbayeva, M., Utz, W., Karagiannis, D.: Leveraging RDF graphs, similarity metrics and network analysis for business process management. In: Challenges Requiring the Combination of Machine Learning and Knowledge Engineering – Proceedings of the AAAI 2023 Spring Symposium (AAAI-MAKE 2023), vol. 3433, CEUR Workshop Proceedings. CEUR-WS (2023). https://ceur-ws.org/Vol-3433/paper14.pdf

23. Krause, F., Kurniawan, K., Kiesling, E., Paulheim, H., Polleres, A.: On the representation of dynamic BPMN process executions in knowledge graphs. In: Knowledge Graphs and Semantic Web – 5th Iberoamerican Conference (KGSWC 2023), Lecture Notes in Computer

Science, vol. 14382, pp. 97–105. Springer, Cham (2023). https://doi.org/10.1007/978-3-031-47745-4_8

24. Hübscher, G., Geist, V., Auer, D., Hübscher, N., Küng, J.: Representation and presentation of knowledge and processes – an integrated approach for a dynamic communication-intensive environment. Int. J. Web Inf. Syst. **17**(6), 669–697 (2021). https://doi.org/10.1108/IJWIS-03-2021-0031

25. Amiri Elyasi, K., Sola, D., Meilicke, C., van der Aa, H., Stuckenschmidt, H.: Knowledge Graph Completion for Activity Recommendation in Business Process Modeling. KI - Künstliche Intelligenz. Springer, Heidelberg (2024). https://doi.org/10.1007/s13218-024-00880-7

26. Bein, L., Pufahl, L.: Knowledge graphs: a key technology for explainable knowledge-aware process automation? In: Business Process Management Workshops (BPM 2024), Lecture Notes in Business Information Processing, vol. 534, pp. 18–30. Springer, Cham (2025). https://doi.org/10.1007/978-3-031-78666-2_2

27. Dumas, M., et al.: AI-augmented business process management systems: a Research manifesto. Manag. Inf. Syst. **14**(1) (2023). https://doi.org/10.1145/3576047

28. Acitelli, G., Agostinelli, S., Casciani, A., Marrella, A.: The role of trust in AI-augmented business process management systems. In: Business Process Management Workshops (BPM 2024), Lecture Notes in Business Information Processing, vol. 534, pp. 5–17. Springer, Cham (2025). https://doi.org/10.1007/978-3-031-78666-2_1

29. Buchmann, R., et al.: Large language models: expectations for semantics-driven systems engineering. Data Knowl. Eng. **152**, 102324 (2024). https://doi.org/10.1016/j.datak.2024.102324

30. Kir, H., Erdogan, N.: A knowledge-intensive adaptive business process management framework. Inf. Syst. **95**, 101639 (2021). https://doi.org/10.1016/j.is.2020.101639

31. Kirchdorfer, L., Blümel, R., Kampik, T., van der Aa, H., Stuckenschmidt, H.: AgentSimulator: an agent-based approach for data-driven business process simulation. In: 2024 6th International Conference on Process Mining (ICPM 2024), Kgs. Lyngby, Denmark, pp. 97–104. IEEE, New York (2024). https://doi.org/10.1109/ICPM63005.2024.10680660

32. Estrada-Torres, B., del-Río-Ortega, A., Resinas, M.: Mapping the landscape: exploring large language model applications in business process management. In: Enterprise, Business-Process and Information Systems Modeling, Lecture Notes in Business Information Processing, vol. 511, pp. 22–31. Springer, Cham (2024). https://doi.org/10.1007/978-3-031-61007-3_3

33. Bennoit, C., Greff, T., Baum, D., Bajwa, I.A.: Identifying use cases for large language models in the business process management lifecycle. In: 2024 26th International Conference on Business Informatics (CBI 2024), Vienna, Austria, pp. 256–263. IEEE, New York (2024). https://doi.org/10.1109/CBI62504.2024.00037

34. Klievtsova, N., Kampik, T., Mangler, J., Rinderle-Ma, S.: Conversational process model redesign. arXiv preprint arXiv:2505.05453 (2025)

35. Kourani, H., Berti, A., Schuster, D., van der Aalst, W.M.P.: ProMoAI: process modeling with generative AI. In: Proceedings of the Thirty-Third International Joint Conference on Artificial Intelligence (IJCAI 2024), pp. 8708–8712. ACM Press (2024). https://doi.org/10.24963/ijcai.2024/1014

36. Dolha, D.N., Buchmann, R.A.: Generative AI for BPMN process analysis: experiments with multi-modal process representations. In: Perspectives in Business Informatics Research (BIR 2024), Lecture Notes in Business Information Processing, vol. 529, pp. 19–35. Springer, Cham (2024). https://doi.org/10.1007/978-3-031-71333-0_2

37. Fahland, D., Fournier, F., Limonad, L., Skarbovsky, I., Swevels, A.J.E.: How well can a large language model explain business processes as perceived by users? Data Knowl. Eng. **157**, 102416 (2025). https://doi.org/10.1016/j.datak.2025.102416

38. Ayad, S., Alsayoud, F.: Prompt engineering techniques for semantic enhancement in business process models. Bus. Process Manag. J. **30**(7), 2611–2641 (2024). https://doi.org/10.1108/BPMJ-02-2024-0108

39. Nemtoc, T.C., Ghiran, A.M.: Natural language querying of invoice data using RAG and GraphRAG: leveraging LLMs for financial document insights. In: Advanced Information Systems Engineering Workshops (CAiSE 2025), Lecture Notes in Business Information Processing, vol. 556, pp. 69–80. Springer, Cham (2025). https://doi.org/10.1007/978-3-031-94931-9_6

40. Niculescu, V., Chisăliță-Crețu, M.-C., Osman, C.-C., Sterca, A.: Model-driven development using LLMs: the case of ChatGPT. In: Proceedings of the 20th International Conference on Evaluation of Novel Approaches to Software Engineering (ENASE 2025), pp. 328–339. SciTePress (2025). https://doi.org/10.5220/0013484400003928

41. Iga, V.I., Silaghi, G.C.: Ontology-based dialogue system for domain-specific knowledge acquisition. In: Proceedings of the 31st International Conference on Information Systems Development (ISD2023 Proceedings). Lisbon, Portugal. AiS eLibrary (2023). ISBN: 978-989-33-5509-1. https://doi.org/10.62036/ISD.2023.46

42. Chiş, A.: A modeling method for work systems knowledge capture and traceability. In: Intelligent Information Systems. CAiSE 2025. Lecture Notes in Business Information Processing, vol. 557, pp. 239–246. Springer, Cham (2025). https://doi.org/10.1007/978-3-031-94590-8_29

43. Kourani, H., Berti, A., Schuster, D., van der Aalst, W.M.P.: Process modeling with large language models. In: Enterprise, Business-Process and Information Systems Modeling (BPMDS 2024), EMMSAD 2024. Lecture Notes in Business Information Processing, vol. 511, pp. 229–244. Springer, Cham (2024). https://doi.org/10.1007/978-3-031-61007-3_18

44. Stein Dani, V., et al.: Event log extraction for process mining using large language models. In: Cooperative Information Systems (CoopIS 2024). Lecture Notes in Computer Science, vol. 15506, pp. 56–72. Springer, Cham (2025). https://doi.org/10.1007/978-3-031-81375-7_4

45. Yang, L., Chen, H., Li, Z., Ding, X., Wu, X.: Give us the facts: enhancing large language models with knowledge graphs for fact-aware language modeling. IEEE Trans. Knowl. Data Eng. **36**(7), 3091–3110 (2024). https://doi.org/10.1109/TKDE.2024.3360454

46. Reitemeyer, B., Fill, H.-G.: Applying large language models in knowledge graph-based enterprise modeling: challenges and opportunities. arXiv preprint arXiv:2501.03566 (2025)

47. OpenAI. Introducing GPT-4.1 in the API. https://openai.com/index/gpt-4-1/. Accessed 04 July 2025

48. OpenAI. New embedding models and API updates. https://openai.com/index/new-embedding-models-and-api-updates/. Accessed 04 July 2025

49. Es, S., James, J., Espinosa-Anke, L., Schockaert, S.: RAGAs: automated evaluation of retrieval augmented generation. In: Proceedings of the 18th Conference of the European Chapter of the Association for Computational Linguistics: System Demonstrations, pp. 150–158. ACL Anthology (2024). https://aclanthology.org/2024.eacl-demo.16/

Smart Life

From Shared Occupancy Patterns to Improved Forecasts: Behavioral Clustering and Selective Deployment in Urban Parking

Thomas Müller$^{(\boxtimes)}$

Mainz University of Applied Sciences, Lucy-Hillebrand-Straße 2,
55128 Mainz, Germany
thomas.mueller@hs-mainz.de
https://www.hs-mainz.de/

Abstract. Accurate short-term forecasting of parking-garage occupancy is critical for urban traffic management, yet individualized models often underperform at low-volume or irregular sites. To improve scalability and generalization, we propose a structured forecasting pipeline that combines behavioral clustering with random forest regression. We extract three interpretable feature sets: Summary weekday-average occupancies, Catch22 time-series descriptors, and Hyndman-style metrics (e.g., trend and seasonality). We apply k-means clustering to group garages with similar temporal patterns. Forecasting models are trained both per series and per cluster using a rolling-window evaluation. Models based on Summary features consistently outperform garage-specific baselines across key metrics, while Catch22 and Hyndman-based clusters show more modest improvements. A hybrid deployment strategy, which selects the better-performing model for each garage based on early validation folds, achieves the best overall performance and reduces RMSE by 2.26%. These results demonstrate that interpretable feature-based clustering, combined with selective deployment, supports accurate, scalable, and robust short-term forecasting in urban parking systems, especially for underperforming or volatile sites.

Keywords: Time-series Clustering · Random Forest Regression · Occupancy Prediction · Parking

1 Introduction

Urban parking space is limited and highly contested, affecting property values [1] and competing with housing, traffic, and green space [2]. This context demands not just accurate prediction but a deeper understanding of parking behavior. We analyze 36 months of hourly occupancy from 17 garages, modeling pay-per-use (PC) and monthly subscriber (RC) series separately to capture distinct patterns and test robustness under COVID-19 disruptions. Rather than training separate

© The Author(s), under exclusive license to Springer Nature Switzerland AG 2026
R. Deneckère et al. (Eds.): BIR 2025, LNBIP 562, pp. 307–317, 2026.
https://doi.org/10.1007/978-3-032-04375-7_19

models per garage, which can be inefficient for low-traffic or irregular sites, we cluster garages using three feature sets: summary profiles based on aggregated time-of-day behavior, Catch22 [3], and Hyndman features [4]. We then train Random Forests (RF) at both the garage and cluster levels, evaluate performance via rolling-window evaluation, and apply a hybrid rule to select the best model for each series.

Cluster-based RF models often outperform garage-specific baselines. Applying our hybrid deployment rule on top of the cluster model yields an additional 2.26% RMSE reduction overall and even larger gains during disruptions.

2   Related Work

Our urban parking forecasting study combines three threads: extracting compact time-series features, clustering facilities by behavioral similarity, and training predictive models (either per-series or shared across clusters).

Time-series feature sets transform raw occupancy into compact descriptors for clustering and forecasting. Catch22 [3,5] selects 22 domain-agnostic features (e.g., autocorrelation, entropy, periodicity) from over 7,000 candidates, yielding fixed-length vectors suited to unsupervised analysis. Tsfeatures [4] provides interpretable statistics like trend strength, seasonal strength, spikiness. These are widely adopted in both academic and industrial forecasting workflows [6–9].

Time-series clustering groups multiple sequences by behavioral similarity using either distance-based metrics (e.g., Euclidean distance or dynamic time warping [10]) or feature-based approaches that extract fixed-length descriptors and apply algorithms like k-means [11,12]. Alternatives such as DBSCAN and agglomerative clustering suffer from scalability and hyperparameter challenges [13], whereas feature-based k-means has proven to be efficient and effective in energy, mobility, and parking applications [14,15].

Traditional methods like ARIMA, exponential smoothing, and LSTMs require large datasets and careful tuning, and RFs are robust to hyperparameter settings [16]. When framed as lag-based supervised learners, RFs effectively forecast time series [17]. In parking studies, RFs using historical occupancy, hour-of-day, and fixed-interval lags have yielded strong short-term forecasts [18,19], and broader evaluations confirm that recent daily lags deliver the best results [20]. However, training separate RF models per garage is resource-intensive and fails to leverage shared behavioral patterns across facilities. Unified clustering-and-forecasting methods (e.g., predictive clustering trees [21,22]) remain untested in parking.

Closest to our work, Mufida et al. [23] similarly derive spatial and temporal clusters from parking profiles over April 2018–December 2019 and train one shared model per cluster, but their raw-profile clusters lack clear operational interpretations (e.g. event vs. commuter use) and omit major disruptions such as COVID-19. In contrast, we split pay-per-use and monthly-customer series, compare three feature-based clustering methods that yield semantically meaningful groups (e.g. residential, commuter, event hubs), and validate over a full

36-month span that includes holiday and pandemic dynamics. We also introduce a simple hybrid rule that selects for each series the better of the garage-specific or cluster-level model. This choice is based on early validation performance and delivers practical accuracy gains without substantial added complexity. These advances together constitute the core novelties of our paper.

3   Methodology

We extract three feature sets from each training window (Sect. 3.2), cluster garages via k-means (Sect. 3.3), train random-forest models both per-garage and per-cluster (Sect. 3.4), and evaluate out-of-sample on the next month. A hybrid rule then selects, for each series, the best-performing model based on early validation folds.

3.1   Data Collection

We use hourly occupancy data from 17 parking garages in a German city from December 2019 to February 2023. Each garage serves two customer groups: public customers (PC), who pay per use, and registered customers (RC), who hold monthly contracts with guaranteed access. PC behavior is more variable and time-dependent, while RC usage is typically consistent.

Each garage–customer group forms a separate time series, yielding 34 series with up to 26,000 hourly observations. For simplicity, we refer to these combinations as "garages" throughout the paper.

Garage capacities range from 145 to 1105 spaces and are dynamically split between PC and RC. While allocations can shift due to policy or maintenance, recorded occupancies always stay within valid limits. We model raw occupancy (not normalized), and verified no overflows; occasional undercounts are assumed rare and non-systematic. Most garages cover the full period. Garages with incomplete data are included using the available portion. The dataset includes COVID-19 periods, preserved to test model robustness under real-world disruption.

3.2   Feature Engineering

Features for Clustering. To identify behavioral similarity across garages, we apply k-means to three feature sets derived from hourly occupancy time series.

The first set uses the `tsfeatures` package [24], extracting statistics such as trend strength, seasonal strength, autocorrelation, entropy, and spikeiness, with a daily seasonal frequency (24). These interpretable features are widely used in time-series forecasting. Second, we evaluate Catch22 [3], a compact set of 22 statistical descriptors selected to span diverse behaviors with minimal redundancy. While less intuitive than `tsfeatures`, it captures properties like local predictability and outlier sensitivity.

As a transparent baseline, we compute summary features: the mean and standard deviation of occupancy for each hour–weekday pair across the full series. This yields a 336-dimensional vector ($24 \times 7 \times 2$) encoding detailed weekly patterns. These features are directly interpretable and highlight stable temporal structures. All predictive models are trained and evaluated only on the first two years (see Sect. 3.4).

Features for Forecasting - Random Forest. To train predictive models for hourly occupancy, we construct a feature set that captures short-term dynamics, seasonal structure, and calendar effects. We derive Features from raw occupancy data and compute separately per garage–customer group to retain behavioral distinctions. We use only historical values up to the prediction time t. Our feature engineering pipeline includes the following components:

– **Hourly lags.** We include lagged occupancy values for the previous 1 to 3 h to provide the model with recent context on occupancy trends.
– **Rolling averages.** Local occupancy trends are captured via rolling means over 6-hour and 24-hour windows. Each is computed using lagged values to avoid leakage from the current prediction target.
– **Same-hour daily lags.** To capture recurring temporal patterns, we include occupancy values from the same hour across the previous 21 days (e.g., $t - 24$, $t - 48$, ..., $t - 504$). This design follows [20] and allows the model to learn daily cycles.
– **Calendar-based features.** We extract several time-related features including hour of day, day of week, day of year, calendar week, month, and quarter. Additionally, we include a binary indicator for weekends. This set of time features aligns with prior work on parking and mobility forecasting [25].

3.3   Clustering

We test whether garage–customer groups can be clustered by occupancy behavior to support more generalizable prediction models. Treating clustering as a core modeling step, we evaluate its practical value through qualitative pattern inspection and quantitative metrics (silhouette scores and predictive performance).

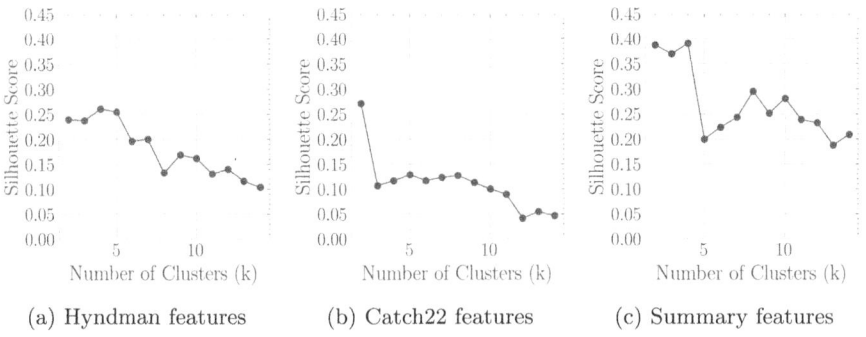

(a) Hyndman features   (b) Catch22 features   (c) Summary features

Fig. 1. Silhouette score over the number of clusters (k) for each feature set.

We apply k-means clustering separately to each feature set (Catch22, Hyndman, Summary), using z-score normalization, Euclidean distance, and 100 random restarts. The number of clusters k is selected via silhouette analysis over $k = 2$ to 14, prioritizing peaks or stable local maxima (see Fig. 1).

For Hyndman and Summary features, $k = 4$ yields high silhouette scores and well-separated clusters. For Catch22, although $k = 2$ gives the highest score, it primarily reflects the PC/RC distinction. We therefore select $k = 5$ to better capture behavioral variation. Cohesion within clusters is confirmed by per-cluster silhouette scores (not shown).

Behavioral Interpretation of Summary-Based Clusters. While all feature sets were evaluated, we focus on the Summary-based clusters due to their coherent temporal structure and superior predictive performance. To assess interpretability, we analyzed average weekly occupancy profiles (in raw vehicle counts). Figure 2 presents the mean weekly occupancy and variability (± 1 standard deviation) for each cluster, revealing four distinct and interpretable temporal patterns aligned with differing operational roles.

– **Cluster 0 (18 facilities)** captures predominantly PC facilities associated with daily business or errand activity. These garages show pronounced midday peaks and low night-time use, reflecting typical short-duration stays.
– **Cluster 1 (9 facilities)** is composed mostly of RC facilities and exhibits stable occupancy across workdays. The regular weekday rhythm and lack of sharp peaks suggest typical usage by commuters or employees. One PC facility in this cluster shows similar structure, likely due to workday activity.

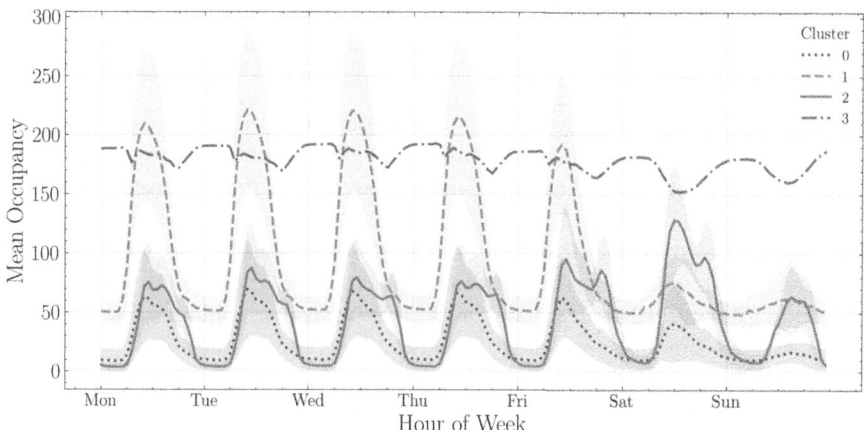

Fig. 2. Weekly average occupancy profiles for Summary-based clusters. Each line represents the mean profile of one cluster, with shaded areas indicating ± 1 standard deviation.

- **Cluster 2 (6 facilities)** includes garages located near a cinema, theater, event hall, and the city hall. These facilities show sharp evening occupancy peaks, particularly on weekends, consistent with event-driven PC use.
- **Cluster 3 (1 facility)** consists of a single RC garage in a densely populated riverside neighborhood without on-street residential parking. It shows persistently high occupancy throughout the day and night, likely reflecting residential long-term parking with minimal turnover.

These results highlight the value of time-anchored Summary features in revealing distinct usage patterns and supporting effective downstream prediction.

3.4 Forecasting Models

We split our 36-month series into 24 months for tuning and 12 months for out-of-sample testing. Hyperparameters (including the training window W) are selected by rolling-window analysis on Months 1–24, then models are trained on each W-month window and evaluated one-month-ahead over Months 25–36.

We compare three model configurations to evaluate the impact of clustering on forecasting accuracy:

1. **Naive baseline: (Persistence Model)** Predict next hour's occupancy as the current hour's. Provides a simple lower bound and sanity check.
2. **Garage-level RF (Individual Model):** Train one random forest per garage-customer series using our engineered features. Captures facility-specific dynamics but doesn't share information.
3. **Cluster-level RF (Shared Model):** For each of the three feature-based clusterings (Summary, Catch22, Hyndman), train one RF per cluster on pooled garage data. Leverages behavioral similarity and reduces model count.

Hyperparameter Tuning. To balance performance and efficiency, we apply a three-stage time-series cross-validation strategy. All tuning is restricted to the training-validation period; the final 12 months are held out and never used during model selection.

First, we determine the training window W by evaluating a default RF (100 trees, `max_depth` = None, `min_samples_split` = 5) across window lengths of 2, 4, 6, 8, 10, and 12 months. For each W, we use a rolling split (train W months, predict 1 month), sample five evenly spaced folds, and select the W that minimizes average RMSE. Second, fixing W, we tune `max_depth`, `min_samples_split`, `max_features` via randomized search with successive halving [26], gradually increasing the number of trees (10–50) for promising configurations. Finally, we perform a 5-fold grid search to select the optimal `n_estimators` (50, 100, 200). Specific values varied per model and are summarized by their search ranges in Table 1. Each model is tuned once and reused across folds to limit overfitting.

Table 1. Hyperparameter search space

Stage	Parameter	Values
Grid Search	W	{2, 4, 6, 8, 10, 12}
Halving Random Search	max_depth	{None, 10, 20, 30}
	min_samples_split	{2, 5, 10}
	max_features	{sqrt, log2, 0.3, 0.5, None}
Grid Search	n_estimators	{50, 100, 200}

4   Results

All forecasting models are evaluated using a rolling-window approach, as described in Sect. 3.4. Specifically, we train each model on a sliding window of 12 months and evaluate it on the immediately following month. This process is repeated across all 12 months in Year 3, yielding 12 one-month-ahead test folds per series. The reported metrics—MAE, RMSE and MAPE—are aggregated over these out-of-sample test predictions.

4.1   Aggregated Performance by Approach

For each garage–customer group, we compute the mean error across the 12 test folds. Table 2 reports the median of these per-series values (MAE, RMSE, and MAPE) for six model configurations. This two-step aggregation reduces outlier influence while preserving temporal variation.

The naive baseline (repeating the previous hour's occupancy) shows deceptively low MAPE (12.85%) due to normalization effects at low values. However, its RMSE exceeds 12.5 (more than twice that of the best model) underscoring that occupancy is not purely autoregressive.

The Summary Cluster-level model consistently outperforms the garage-level baseline across all metrics. Catch22 and Hyndman clusters achieve lower RMSE than the baseline but perform worse on MAE and MAPE, suggesting a bias –variance trade-off. Overall, Summary-based clustering offers the most balanced and reliable performance.

Feature importance analysis highlights the dominant role of lagged occupancy, which accounts for 80–90% of total importance. Removing the lag_1 feature from the Summary Cluster-level model increases RMSE from 5.527 to 6.688 and MAPE from 10.22% to 19.90%, confirming its critical role. Similar lag_1 ablations on all other RF configurations yielded comparable error increases, so we only report the Summary cluster-level results here.

In summary, cluster-based models match or outperform garage-specific models, with the Summary Cluster-level model performing best across all metrics and demonstrating the value of behavioral clustering for scalable forecasting.

Table 2. Median forecasting errors across garage–customer groups (per-series mean over 12 test folds; median across series; bold indicates best values)

Approach	MAE (vehicles)	RMSE (vehicles)	MAPE (%)
Naive ($t - 1$)	7.518	12.587	12.85
Garage-level	3.452	5.752	10.44
Summary Cluster-level	**3.419**	5.527	**10.22**
Catch22 Cluster-level	3.467	**5.424**	10.60
Hyndman Cluster-level	3.558	5.682	10.82
Summary w/o lag_1h (Ablation)	3.807	6.688	19.90

Table 3. Fold-wise per-garage comparison of cluster-based models vs. garage baseline (bold indicates best values)

Approach	Garages improved (%)	Median Δ_g (vehicles)	95% CI (vehicles)	Median gain (%)	Wilcoxon p[1]
Hyndman	62.5	0.025	[−0.04, 0.08]	**0.73**	0.006
Catch22	53.1	0.004	[−0.03, 0.06]	0.12	<0.001
Summary	**65.6**	**0.039**	**[0.00, 0.06]**	0.62	<0.001

[1] Wilcoxon p-values are based on fold-level RMSE differences, computed as paired comparisons within each garage.

4.2 Fold-Wise Per-Garage Analysis

To understand where cluster-based models add value, we conduct a fold-wise, per-garage analysis by computing the median RMSE improvement over 12 test folds per garage g in (1).

$$\Delta_g = \mathrm{median}_f \left(\mathrm{RMSE}_{g,f}^{\mathrm{garage}} - \mathrm{RMSE}_{g,f}^{\mathrm{cluster}} \right) \tag{1}$$

Table 3 summarizes these improvements across models, including the proportion of garages with $\Delta_g > 0$, median gains, 95% confidence intervals, and Wilcoxon signed-rank p-values. Among the three approaches, Summary-based clustering shows the highest coverage (65.6%), a statistically significant median improvement, and the only confidence interval fully above zero. Although the absolute gains are modest, they are consistent across garages, suggesting that meaningful clustering can improve generalization.

To explore deployment potential, we evaluate a hybrid strategy: for each garage, we select the better model (garage-specific or Summary-cluster) based on early validation folds (1–5), then apply it to the test folds (6–10). Folds 11–12, which include COVID disruptions, are excluded from selection and discussed separately.

Using this approach, 43.8% of garages are assigned to the Summary model. Across folds 6–10, the hybrid strategy—applying the better-performing model per garage—reduces the overall mean RMSE from 5.975 to 5.840 (–2.26%) and the median RMSE by 0.101 (–1.95%). A Wilcoxon test confirms statistical significance ($W = 661.0$, $p = 0.00067$). Including COVID-affected folds increases the total RMSE gain to 3.73%, highlighting the hybrid model's robustness to behavioral disruption.

5   Discussion

Our results show that clustering parking garages by behavioral similarity not only enables effective model sharing but also improves forecasting accuracy. Summary-based clusters outperform garage-level baselines across MAE, RMSE, and MAPE while yielding groupings with clear operational meaning. By modeling pay-per-use (PC) and contract (RC) series separately, we capture distinct patterns—high variability and peak-hour effects in PC versus regular routines in RC—that underpin these clusters. Catch22 and Hyndman clusters underperformed, likely because their generic statistical descriptors are more sensitive to noise and miss daily-weekly structure in parking data.

Our hybrid deployment strategy assigns each garage to the better of its individual or Summary-cluster model based on early validation, yielding a 2.26% RMSE reduction while reducing total model count. This pattern is further reflected when COVID-affected folds are included, which achieves even greater RMSE reduction. This supports the view that Summary-based clusters improve robustness without sacrificing accuracy. By sharing models across clusters, we also reduce training overhead, which is an important consideration for real-world deployments with hundreds of garages.

Feature importance analysis confirmed the dominance of the lag-1 occupancy feature, as expected due to strong temporal autocorrelation. However, ablation results showed that models still outperformed the naive persistence baseline even without lag-1, indicating that the models captured additional behavioral signals beyond simple autoregressive trends.

Overall, feature-based clustering with Summary-based groupings enables interpretable, scalable forecasting that outperforms per-series models across both normal and disrupted conditions.

6   Conclusion

This study presents a structured forecasting pipeline that combines behavioral clustering with RF models to predict hourly parking occupancy. We show that clustering garages based on simple, time-anchored summary features enables interpretable groupings and efficient model reuse, with predictive performance that consistently outperforms individualized models across key metrics, albeit with modest margins. A hybrid deployment strategy that selects the better model per garage based on earlier validation-folds achieves the lowest overall forecast error and offers a practical balance between accuracy and scalability. While clustering improves performance and scalability, behavioral anomalies remain a key challenge when absent from the training data.

References

1. van Ommeren, J., Wentink, D., Dekkers, J.: The real price of parking policy. J. Urban Econ. **70**(1), 25–31 (2011). https://doi.org/10.1016/j.jue.2011.02.001
2. Buehler, R., Pucher, J., Gerike, R.: Reducing car dependence in the heart of Europe: lessons from Germany, Austria, and Switzerland. Transp. Rev. **36**, 1–25 (2016). https://doi.org/10.1080/01441647.2016.1177799
3. Lubba, C.H., Sethi, S.S., Knaute, P., Schultz, S.R., Fulcher, B.D., Jones, N.S.: *catch22*: CAnonical time-series CHaracteristics. Data Min. Knowl. Disc. **33**(6), 1821–1852 (2019). https://doi.org/10.1007/s10618-019-00647-x
4. Hyndman, R.J., Wang, E., Laptev, N.: Large-scale unusual time series detection. In: Cui, P., et al. (eds.) Proceedings - 15th IEEE International Conference on Data Mining Workshop, pp. 1616–1619. IEEE, Institute of Electrical and Electronics Engineers, United States of America (2015). https://doi.org/10.1109/ICDMW.2015.104
5. Henderson, T., Fulcher, B.D.: An empirical evaluation of time-series feature sets. In: 2021 International Conference on Data Mining Workshops (ICDMW), pp. 1032–1038 (2021). https://doi.org/10.1109/ICDMW53433.2021.00134
6. Makridakis, S., Spiliotis, E., Assimakopoulos, V.: The m4 competition: 100,000 time series and 61 forecasting methods. Int. J. Forecast. **36**(1), 54–74 (2020). https://doi.org/10.1016/j.ijforecast.2019.04.014
7. Bandara, K., Bergmeir, C., Smyl, S.: Forecasting across time series databases using recurrent neural networks on groups of similar series: a clustering approach. Exp. Syst. Appl. **140** (2019). https://doi.org/10.1016/j.eswa.2019.112896
8. Montero-Manso, P., Hyndman, R.J.: Principles and algorithms for forecasting groups of time series: locality and globality. Int. J. Forecast. **37**(4), 1632–1653 (2021). https://doi.org/10.1016/j.ijforecast.2021.03.004
9. Talagala, T.S., Hyndman, R.J., Athanasopoulos, G.: Meta-learning how to forecast time series. J. Forecast. **42**(6), 1476–1501 (2023). https://doi.org/10.1002/for.2963
10. Aghabozorgi, S., Seyed Shirkhorshidi, A., Ying Wah, T.: Time-series clustering – a decade review. Inf. Syst. **53**, 16–38 (2015). https://doi.org/10.1016/j.is.2015.04.007
11. Fulcher, B.D., Jones, N.S.: Highly comparative feature-based time-series classification. IEEE Trans. Knowl. Data Eng. **26**(12), 3026–3037 (2014). https://doi.org/10.1109/TKDE.2014.2316504
12. Bock, F., Di Martino, S., Sester, M.: What are the potentialities of crowdsourcing for dynamic maps of on-street parking spaces? In: Winter, S., Thakur, G.S., Ronald, N. (eds.) Proceedings of the 9th ACM SIGSPATIAL International Workshop on Computational Transportation Science. pp. 19–24. ACM, New York, NY, USA (2016). https://doi.org/10.1145/3003965.3003973
13. Paparrizos, J., Yang, F., Li, H.: Bridging the gap: a decade review of time-series clustering methods, http://arxiv.org/pdf/2412.20582v1
14. Cai, Y., Pan, X., Zhang, L., Xu, F., Zhang, S.: Towards sustainable parking: analyzing the characteristics of periodic off-street parking lots and their application in shared parking. Sustainability **17**(3), 833 (2025). https://doi.org/10.3390/su17030833

15. Wu, F., Ma, W.: Clustering analysis of the spatio-temporal on-street parking occupancy data: a case study in hong kong. Sustainability **14**(13), 7957 (2022). https://doi.org/10.3390/su14137957
16. Probst, P., Wright, M.N., Boulesteix, A.L.: Hyperparameters and tuning strategies for random forest. WIREs Data Min. Knowl. Discovery **9**(3), e1301 (2019). https://doi.org/10.1002/widm.1301
17. Tyralis, H., Papacharalampous, G.: Variable selection in time series forecasting using random forests. Algorithms **10**, 114 (2017). https://doi.org/10.3390/a10040114
18. Rajabioun, T., Ioannou, P.: On-street and off-street parking availability prediction using multivariate spatiotemporal models. IEEE Trans. Intell. Transp. Syst. **16**(5), 2913–2924 (2015). https://doi.org/10.1109/TITS.2015.2428705
19. Zheng, L., Xiao, X., Sun, B., Mei, D., Peng, B.: Short-term parking demand prediction method based on variable prediction interval. IEEE Access **8**, 58594–58602 (2020). https://doi.org/10.1109/ACCESS.2020.2976433
20. Dudek, G.: A comprehensive study of random forest for short-term load forecasting. Energies **15**(20), 7547 (2022). https://doi.org/10.3390/en15207547
21. Džeroski, S., Gjorgjioski, V., Slavkov, I., Struyf, J.: Analysis of time series data with predictive clustering trees. In: Džeroski, S., Struyf, J. (eds.) Knowledge Discovery in Inductive Databases, pp. 63–80. Springer, Berlin, Heidelberg (2007)
22. Kocev, D., Ceci, M., Stepišnik, T.: Ensembles of extremely randomized predictive clustering trees for predicting structured outputs. Mach. Learn. **109**(11), 2213–2241 (2020). https://doi.org/10.1007/s10994-020-05894-4
23. Mufida, M.K., Ait El Cadi, A., Delot, T., Trépanier, M., Zekri, D.: Spatiotemporal clustering of parking lots at the city level for efficiently sharing occupancy forecasting models. Sensors (Basel, Switzerland) **23**(11) (2023). https://doi.org/10.3390/s23115248
24. Hyndman, R., et al.: tsfeatures: time series feature extraction (2024), https://pkg.robjhyndman.com/tsfeatures/
25. Bollenbach, J., Neubig, S., Hein, A., Keller, R., Krcmar, H.: Using machine learning to predict poi occupancy to reduce overcrowding. In: Demmler, D., Krupka, D., Federrath, H. (eds.) INFORMATIK 2022: Lecture Notes in Informatics. Gesellschaft für Informatik e.V, Bonn (2022)
26. Li, L., Jamieson, K., DeSalvo, G., Rostamizadeh, A., Talwalkar, A.: Hyperband: a novel bandit-based approach to hyperparameter optimization. J. Mach. Learn. Res. **18**(1), 6765–6816 (2017)

DomicileML: A Domain-Specific Modeling Language for Smart Home Interconnectivity and Data Integration

Ana-Maria Ghiran$^{(\boxtimes)}$ (ID) and Paula-Irina Vilău

Faculty of Economics and Business Administration, Babeş-Bolyai
University, Cluj-Napoca, Romania
`anamaria.ghiran@econ.ubbcluj.ro, paula.vilau@stud.ubbcluj.ro`

Abstract. IoT technologies have significantly changed the way we interact with the environments we live in, ensuring higher levels of comfort, security and efficiency. However, given the complexity and diversity of these systems, of the environment where they are applied and of the ever-diversifying requirements from stakeholders, there are significant challenges that arise w.r.t. the design, management and interoperability of IoT based home systems. In this paper, we propose a domain-specific modeling method tailored to oversee the integration and communication logic of the smart home systems. The language is deployed in a tool demonstrator developed using the ADOxx meta modeling platform. The models allow the representation of smart home devices, their interactions and how daily routines can be automatized. In addition, these models are exported in RDF format following the Linked Open Models principle enabled by ADOxx. By leveraging the strengths of both visual conceptual modeling and semantic graphs, our knowledge-driven approach aims to provide a Design Science treatment for managing the complexity of smart home systems.

Keywords: Smart homes · domain specific modeling languages · knowledge graphs · Internet of Things

1 Introduction

A smart home utilizes a network (both physical and semantic) to link various sensors and devices, allowing for remote monitoring, access, and control [1]. It should possess ambient intelligence and adaptive automatic control that responds to the behavior of the people who live there, enabling various contextual facilities [2].

According to [2], research on this field started decades ago - a foundational project in this field was the Smart Rooms initiative by the MIT Media Lab [3]. After this pioneering work, numerous studies have explored various potential applications of smart home technology; the concept of smart homes has evolved by gradual semantic enrichment, with an increasing interest in incorporating innovative measures for energy efficiency, security and comfort. There are numerous architectural awards (e.g. Building Innovation

© The Author(s), under exclusive license to Springer Nature Switzerland AG 2026
R. Deneckère et al. (Eds.): BIR 2025, LNBIP 562, pp. 318–328, 2026.
https://doi.org/10.1007/978-3-032-04375-7_20

Awards[1], Global Award for Sustainable Architectures[2]), indicating a growing concern in incorporating innovative and sustainable components in developing highly comfortable buildings.

Existing buildings should benefit from a transformation into smart systems by leveraging knowledge engineering and knowledge-driven technologies. By retrofitting older constructions, building owners or occupants can improve comfort, save energy costs and reduce security worries. Such retrofits imply enhancements from simple thermostats, lighting systems to more complex air ventilation systems, or sophisticated solutions for controlling various building functions. This redesign requires technology-specific domain engineering and reconceptualization – the scientific community of model-driven engineering has increasingly invested in proposing Design Science treatments in the form of domain-specific interoperable tools for IoT environments – recent examples include the Air Conditioning Facilities modeling MIoTA [4], the mobile maintenance modeling approach of Comvantage [5] or FloBP for enhancing business processes with IoT technologies [6]. There is a noticeable trend of smart homes aimed towards reducing energy consumption by optimizing device usage [7].

Although in high demand, the design and management of smart home systems bring complexity management and systemic sense-making challenges. The complexity of integrating various devices and ensuring seamless communication between them requires not only *flexible design support* but also a *semantic layer* to ensure traceability of design decisions and run-time communication between the devices.

To empower citizens and other stakeholders to transform buildings into smart spaces without requiring extensive technical knowledge, there must be accessible tools for design and analysis. Domain-specific modeling tools, utilizing domain specific languages to bring conceptual familiarity to the sense-making effort can serve as such enablers [8].

Standardized modeling languages and tools do not address the specific requirements of smart home systems - the literature refers to them as "general-purpose languages" (GPL) [9]. On the other hand, recent literature discusses a false dichotomy between "general purpose" and "domain specificity", proposing purpose and specificity as orthogonal dimensions [10] – all languages have a limited set of purposes (detectable in requirements) and can shift their level of specificity according to their ontological commitment or competency questions they are supposed to answer in an application domain.

Specialized concepts and attributes, present in a modeling language as first-class constructs, are critical to contextualize and describe smart home devices.

This work reports on design science research that aims to build a specialized modeling language for smart homes, DomicileML. This language will facilitate a more precise representation and management of smart home components and their interactions, supporting the design, optimization, and analysis of complex smart home environments. Furthermore, to bridge the gap between human-centric presentation and smart device execution, conceptual models must be transformed into a machine-readable format in order to shift their role "from representation to mediation" as advocated by a recent design research agenda [11, 12]. The precise metamodel definitions made operational

---

[1] https://buildinginnovationawards.co.uk/.

[2] https://graitec-group.com/.

by metamodeling platforms facilitate this and allow the diagrammatic models to be converted into semantic structures. Our platform of choice is ADOxx [13] and previous work introduced diagram-to-RDF transformation patterns [14] currently available as an ADOxx extension service [15]. The RDF standard acts as a representational medium to make diagrammatic designs of smart home systems available as fragments of potential knowledge graphs acting as a semantic layer over such systems. This is a direction already advocated by commodity products such as Google Home, where a virtual "Home Graph" [16] can be configured on vendor-specific apps. We aim to generalize this idea in the form of a knowledge capture environment that leverages the metamodeling-driven tradition of domain-specific visual modeling in tandem with machine-readable knowledge graphs that makes the visual designs available to machine interpretability.

Therefore, the contribution of this work is to introduce a knowledge graph "treatment" (in the jargon of Design Science) to smart home design and analysis that makes use of a visual modeling method to derive knowledge graph structures.

The remainder of the paper is structured as follows: in Sect. 2 we analyze a selection of related works; then in the next section, we present an overview of the proposal, describing the metamodel; Sect. 4 further details our proposal; the paper ends with conclusions.

2   Related Works

There is growing interest in converging model-driven engineering or knowledge graph-driven engineering with IoT systems design-oriented research (recent works manifesting this convergence are [4–6, 9]). However, most of them focus on run-time data or process analysis, only the latter one takes the path of the knowledge graph treatment (with a focus on Linked Data integration and for an entirely different application area).

The idea of using conceptual modeling to navigate the complexities of smart homes has been researched by a number of studies before. A first example, already mentioned, is represented by [1], where a conceptual model was developed to evaluate the intelligence level of smart homes. The model defined which devices and services are involved in a smart home and how they interact. Then, the authors evaluated the proposed framework to assess the degree to which a smart home system meets the users' need by using an empirical study conducted online over 300 questionnaires. This model and the comprehensive review of AI techniques that can enhance the behavior of smart home devices offer valuable insights that align with the objectives of our proposed modeling language for smart homes.

SmartHomeML [17] is a domain specific modeling language that supports modeling the architecture of smart home appliances and more, applying a model driven engineering approach, it generates code that conforms to the specification of a selected control system provider (e.g. Amazon Alexa Skill adapters). A similar code generation framework has been proposed by [18], ThingML. The authors have been using the tool with over 400 students and developers and identified that having a single integrated modeling language with a dedicated tool was more practical than approaches that combined different models and formalism. The main benefit of the ThingML tool was the ability to have platform independent specifications providing code generators in 3 different languages (C/C++, Java and Javascript).

The importance of creating well-defined conceptual models for effective understanding of IoT applications has been investigated by [19] who proposed the use of categorization patterns (Inheritance and Type Pattern) to achieve categorization of concepts in conceptual modeling. Though, their approach is valuable to improve the understandability of models, it is limited to the interpretation provided in the metamodel. We argue that our approach is more generally applicable since we employ semantic technologies to capture the meaning of both the metamodel and models' content.

The previously enumerated works mainly focus on model driven engineering and code generation for controlling smart home appliances, while our work is regarding the design and the evaluation of various scenarios which require knowledge from a complex environment.

3 Proposal Overview

Conceptual models can support the *contextualization of data* in smart homes. They enable capturing of semantic context for understanding and interpreting data. Different deployment contexts have different goals which ground the semantics of the data. Data might get different meanings depending on the context in which it is used - the same sensor data can be used for various purposes, each requiring a different interpretation and action. For example, a change in temperature sensor data can be considered an anomaly but can also be an expected value if it is the result of a user's action. The contextualization of data is closely related to its purpose – predictive maintenance, comfort monitoring, security traceability, sustainability reporting etc.

With this work, we aim to highlight the applicability of conceptual models as part of a knowledge acquisition approach, for capturing the context of a smart home environment. In this matter, we involve two different types of conceptual models:

– behavioral models (focus on process-oriented knowledge and dependencies, capturing the logic and sequences of actions particular to a circumstance)
– structural models (focus on structural knowledge and decomposition representing physical and network layout of the environment)

Therefore, the proposed modeling language, DomicileML, is partitioned into two types of models: one for representing routines within the smart home (as an example of behavioral model) and another one for depicting the overall architecture of the smart home environment (as an example of a structural model).

3.1 Metamodel

The first type of model is the HomeRoutines type. The routines can be defined as sequences of actions and verifications made by various smart home devices, designed specifically to automate daily activities and enhance the level of comfort and efficiency of the home environment. Some examples of routines are: Waking up routine that happens at certain hours of the day and Arriving home routine, when sensors detect people entering the house.

The second type of model encompasses the overall architecture of the smart home environment. This is the arrangement of devices in the rooms and the network connections between them. These architectural models provide a comprehensive view of the smart home infrastructure, enabling better planning, management, and optimization of the system.

Figure 1 presents the metamodel for the two types of models: The Smart Routine model captures the sequences of events and actions, including start and end events, verifications, and actions, linked through flow relationships. The Smart Home Architecture model details the physical layout, comprising floors and rooms, and their hierarchical relationships. Additionally, the metamodel includes various devices such as sensors, actuators, and smart hubs, along with their communication pathways. This addresses both functional behaviors and spatial configurations. The metamodel is divided into two main categories of classes: *abstract classes,* that establish common properties and *instantiable classes,* that detail the components and interactions within smart home diagrams.

3.2   Language Semantics and Notation

The first type of model, the SmartRoutine diagram type, uses concepts inherited from the abstract Node concept: StartEvent, EndEvent, Verification, Action. We choose to differentiate between the Verification node and the Action node in order to emphasize the different nature of actions performed by the routine: the Verification is primarily probing realized by sensors, as opposed to an Action which requires actuators. Besides these, we have a concept inherited from the RelationClasses called Flow, that connects different Nodes in the Routine.

The second type of model, Smart Home Architecture defines the structural components and their relationships within a smart home environment. Two classes are inherited from the ContainerClass abstract concept: Room and Floor; they act as grouping concepts for other simpler concepts. We differentiate between sensors (as devices that detect conditions in the environment) and actuators (devices that perform actions based on the signals from the control unit). A Smart hub acts as a central control unit.

All the graphic representations of the previously described concepts are presented in Fig. 2.

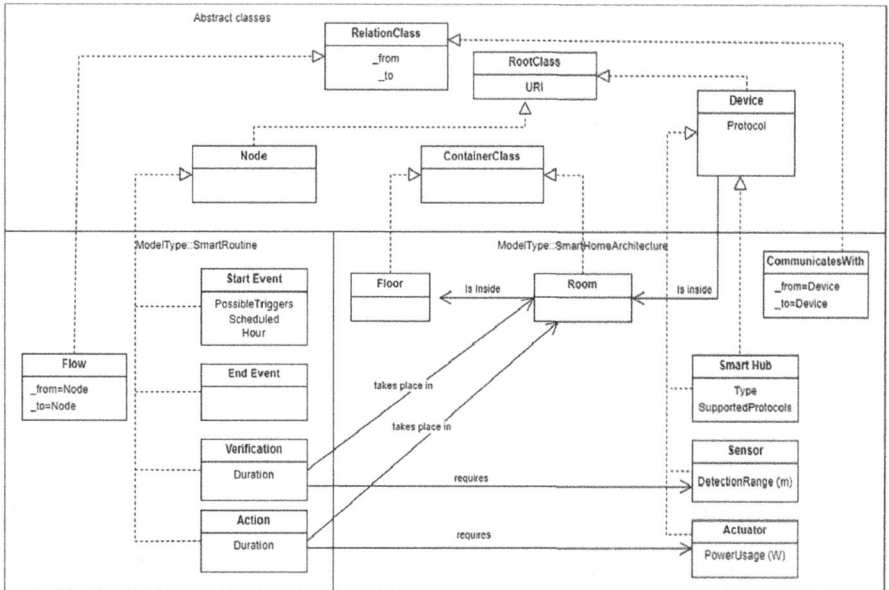

Fig. 1. Metamodel for the proposed modeling language

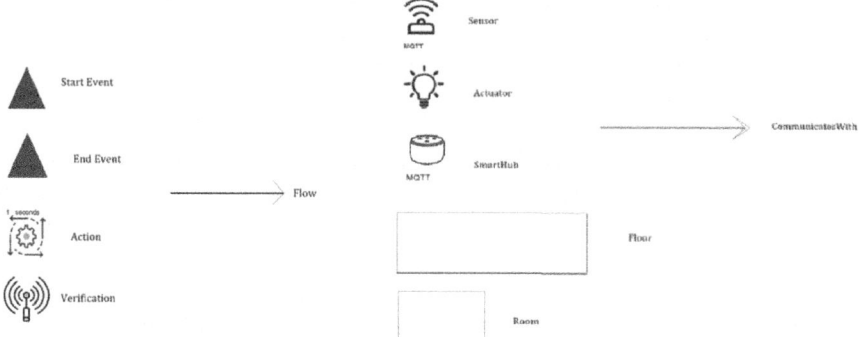

Fig. 2. SmartRoutine concepts and SmartHomeArchitecture concepts – graphical notation

3.3 Demonstration

In the following, we will present an example of each type of diagram from the metamodel. Figure 3 captures a smart home routine called ArrivingHomeRoutine.

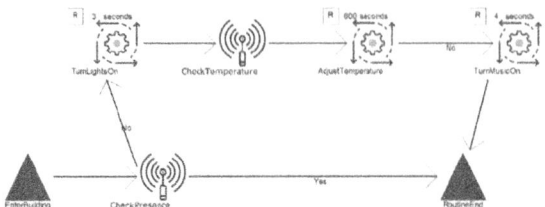

Fig. 3. ArrivingHomeRoutine model

The first Node, EnterBuilding, is an instance of the class StartEvent that is not Scheduled. This means that the routine has to be triggered by a sensor detecting some kind of movement at one of the possible entrances of the house.

Next, the routine encompasses a VerificationStep called CheckPresence, which implies checking whether other people are already present in the house. If any of the presence sensors in the house detect movements, the routine automatically ends. On the other hand, if no one else is in the house, a few other steps will be taken (steps that prepare the home to accommodate the guest). First, the lights will be automatically turned on in the EntryHall. In order to navigate to the specific room "R" (the EntryHall described in a SmartHomeArchitecture model) a clickable area can be noticed at the top left of the symbol. The next step is checking the temperature inside all of the rooms of the building, followed by adjusting the temperature where needed. The last step is an action called TurnMusicOn, which implies the ambiental music being turned on, action that will take place in the LivingRoom. This requires the Smart Speakers and the Multimedia Hub. This routine is mainly aimed for people that live alone, specifically designed to enhance the homecoming experience by reducing the feeling of loneliness upon entering their home.

In Fig. 4, we can see the model that is linked to the ArrivingHomeRoutine, that displays the devices inside the house and their location. The Smart Home Architecture diagram provides the layout of smart home with two floors (ground floor and 1st floor), illustrating how various smart devices are distributed across different rooms. The diagram is divided into two main sections: the Ground Floor and the 1st Floor.

All devices are connected to the appropriate hubs or gateways, which manage communication, control and protocol translation within the smart home. This architectural model supports the previously described smart home routine, ensuring that all necessary sensors and actuators are in place to automate actions such as turning on lights, adjusting the temperature, and playing music upon the occupant's arrival. The integration of devices and their placement throughout home allows for the execution of routines that align with the needs of the inhabitants, particularly for individuals living alone to reduce the feeling of loneliness.

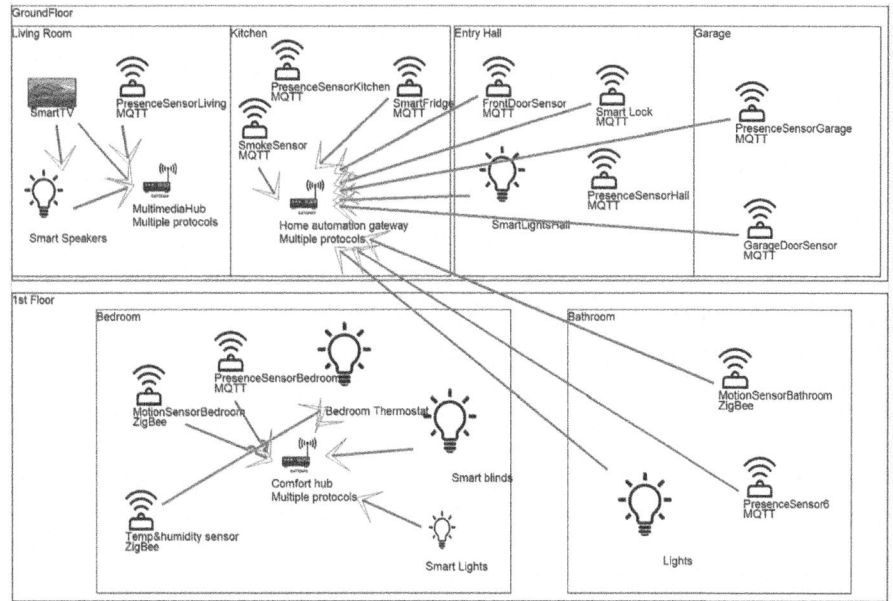

Fig. 4. SmartHomeArchitecture

4   The Knowledge Graph Treatment and Competency Evaluation

In order to store information about the diagram in a flexible and queriable format, we choose to use a graph repository, in our case GraphDB [20].

Each element in the models has a URI attribute, which will be used when exporting the models' content into an RDF serialization format, so that each object identifier is controlled by the modeler and is not assigned by the modeling environment. Consequently, the URI identifier represents the identifier given by the user and can be an existing URI for which there is already other information in the graph repository (from other external sources).

We exemplify here two queries that combine information from the models mentioned above with information from other data sources. These are meant to demonstrate the possibility to mix knowledge obtained from visual representations (e.g. diagrammatic models) typically consumed by human users with knowledge from other data sources (e.g. tabular data) enabled by the semantic data layer provided by the RDF Knowledge Graph. Figure 5 presents sample of these SPARQL queries: the first one returns the Devices of type Actuator that are placed inside the LivingRoom, together with their brand and price (these last two attributes come from the external tabular data converted with OntoRefine [21]). The second query enhances the current information available in the repository: the status of a room is set to occupied if a motion detector (which is a subclass of PresenceDetector) detects motion in that room. In this way, data that arrives from diagrammatic modes is linked to rules that govern data interpretation (the room's status is not saved in the repository but dynamically created to be provided with the request).

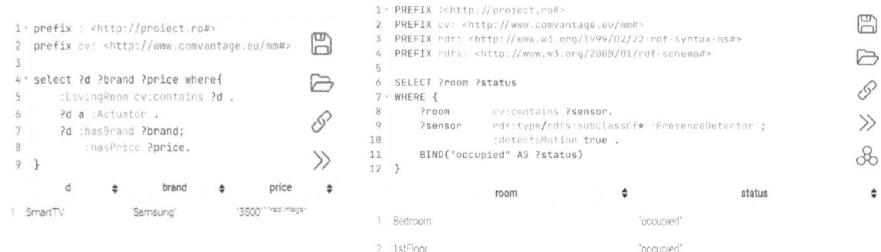

Fig. 5. SPARQL queries for LivingRoom actuators and the room's status

5   Future Work Based on Expert Evaluation

As this work is framed under the iterative Design Science process prescribed by Peffers et al. [22], as part of the current iteration, we sought feedback from an expert in IoT deployments and in IoT-oriented visualizations. This feedback is intended to inform our next language design iteration and extension. The iterative/nested nature of this work has been planned from the very beginning by the adoption of the DSR frame and by the nesting of the DSML engineering methodology within it according to the design problem nesting principles explicated by [23]. We hereby summarize current qualitative feedback that establishes objectives for our future work:

- On notation level, Floors and Rooms representations are too similar (and also rudimentary), deviating from Moody's principles of perceptual discriminability and semantic transparency [23]; additionally, excessive size of arrow heads in comparison to the rest of the symbols generate visual overload
- On semantic level, state-of-the-art taxonomies from commodity products can enrich the language conceptualization by subtyping. Google Home's "device traits" classification can be adopted as a starting point. Modeling of spaces, floors/rooms should be extended with pathways and access points to enable richer traceability criteria that also consider dependencies deriving from the spatial accessibility, not only spatial containment;
- In terms of operationalization, and towards raising the Technological Readiness Level of the proof-of-concept (along the TRL "maturity" scale), the traceability based on fixed SPARQL query patterns should be replaced with natural language question answering based on the state-of-the-art language model-based retrieval interfaces. The recently advertised GraphRAG patterns should be investigated to raise the knowledge capture mechanism to new modes of interaction based on LLMs.

6   Conclusions

To conclude, smart homes are the future of residential living, integrating advanced technology to enhance comfort, security, and energy efficiency. However, designing and analysing these systems can be complex and challenging, requiring citizen-oriented knowledge capture and traceability or dependency analysis approaches. To address these issues, we proposed DomicileML, a domain specific conceptual modeling language for smart homes, as part of a knowledge capture environment that applies the knowledge graph treatment to domain-specific models for semantic processing.

ADOxx was the chosen platform for developing this language due to its prototyping features and flexibility, enabling the evolution of customized modeling environments along an engineering process that can be nested within the overall Design Science process. For storing the content of the models, RDF serialization was used to capture the semantic description of the representations, and the models are further saved into a graph repository. RDF is well-suited for representing interconnected data, a common characteristic in smart homes, where the requirement of networked connectivity is emerging as shown by commodity product features such as Google's Home Graph software. Using a graph repository as a semantic layer to assimilate various data formats enables semantic querying and management of complex relationship networks among entities. This work emphasizes the importance of developing solutions for specific needs and provides insights into future research in smart home technology-specific modeling methods.

Disclosure of Interests. The authors have no competing interests to declare that are relevant to the content of this article.

References

1. Wu, D., Feng, W., Li, T., Yang, Z.: Evaluating the intelligence capability of smart homes: a conceptual modeling approach. Data Knowl. Eng. **148**, 102218 (2023). https://doi.org/10.1016/j.datak.2023.102218
2. De Silva, L.C., Morikawa, C., Petra, I.M.: State of the art of smart homes. Eng. Appl. Artif. Intell. **25**(7), 1313–1321 (2012). https://doi.org/10.1016/j.engappai.2012.05.002
3. Pentland, A.: Perceptual environments. In: Smart Environments: Technologies, Protocols, and Applications, pp. 345–359 (2004)
4. Nast, B., Sandkuhl, K., Paulus, S., Schiller, H.: MIoTA: modeling IoT applications for air conditioning facilities with ADOxx. In: BIR2023 Workshops, CEUR-WS vol. 3514 pp. 158–168 (2023)
5. Buchmann, R.A., Karagiannis, D.: Domain-specific diagrammatic modelling: a source of machine-readable semantics for the Internet of Things. Clust. Comput. **20**, 895–908 (2017). https://doi.org/10.1007/s10586-016-0695-1
6. Fedeli, A., Fornari, F., Polini, A., Re, B., Torres, V., Valderas, P.: FloBP: a model-driven approach for developing and executing IoT-enhanced business processes. Softw. Syst. Model. 1–30 (2024)
7. Rehman, A.U., Tito, S.R., Ahmed, D., Nieuwoudt, P., Lie, T.T., Vallès, B.: An artificial intelligence-driven smart home towards energy efficiency: an overview and conceptual model. In: 2020 FORTEI-International Conference on Electrical Engineering, FORTEI-ICEE, pp. 47–52. IEEE (2020) https://doi.org/10.1109/FORTEI-ICEE50915.2020.9249816
8. Frank, U.: Domain-specific modeling languages: requirements analysis and design guidelines. In: Domain Engineering: Product Lines, Languages, and Conceptual Models, pp. 133–157 (2013)
9. Fedeli, A., Beutling, N., Laurenzi, E., Polini, A.: Comparison of general-purpose and domain-specific modelling languages in the IoT domain: a case study from the OMiLAB community. In: BIR2023 Workshops, vol. 3514, pp. 145–157. CEUR-WS (2023)
10. Buchmann, R.A.: The purpose-specificity framework for domain-specific conceptual modeling. In: Domain-Specific Conceptual Modeling: Concepts, Methods and ADOxx Tools, pp. 67–92. Springer, Heidelberg (2022). https://doi.org/10.1007/978-3-030-93547-4_4

11. Recker, J.C., Lukyanenko, R., Jabbari Sabegh, M., Samuel, B., Castellanos, A.: From representation to mediation: a new agenda for conceptual modeling research in a digital world. MIS Q. Manag. Inf. Syst. **45**(1), 269–300 (2021)
12. Chis, A., Ghiran, A.M.: Embracing conceptual modelling to enable the mediation role of enterprise information systems. In: ECIS 2023. AIS Library (2023) https://aisel.aisnet.org/ecis2023_rp/387/
13. BOC GmbH, The ADOxx metamodeling platform. https://www.adoxx.org. Accessed 01 July 2025
14. Buchmann, R.A., Karagiannis, D.: Pattern-based transformation of diagrammatic conceptual models for semantic enrichment in the Web of Data. Procedia Comput. Sci. **60**, 150–159 (2015). https://doi.org/10.1016/j.procs.2015.08.114
15. BOC GmbH, RDF Transformation Services for Conceptual Models. https://www.adoxx.org/live/rdf_use. Accessed 01 July 2025
16. Google Developer Center, Home Graph. https://developers.home.google.com/cloud-to-cloud/primer/home-graph. Accessed 01 July 2025
17. Einarsson, A. F., Patreksson, P., Hamdaqa, M., Hamou-Lhadj, A.: SmarthomeML: towards a domain-specific modeling language for creating smart home applications. In: IEEE International Congress on Internet of Things, ICIOT, pp. 82–88. IEEE (2017)
18. Harrand, N., Fleurey, F., Morin, B., Husa, K.E.: ThingML: a language and code generation framework for heterogeneous targets. In: Proceedings of the ACM/IEEE 19th International Conference on Model Driven Engineering Languages and Systems, pp. 125–135 (2016)
19. Wyffels, M., Ahmadi, Z., Serral, E., Vanderfeesten, I., Snoeck, M.: Evaluation of categorization patterns for conceptual modeling of IoT applications. In: IFIP Working Conference on The Practice of Enterprise Modeling, pp. 67–84. Springer, Heidelberg (2025)
20. Ontotext, GraphDB Free. https://www.ontotext.com/products/graphdb. Accessed 01 July 2025
21. Ontotext, Ontorefine, https://www.ontotext.com/products/ontotext-refine/. Accessed 01 July 2025
22. Peffers, K., Tuunanen, T., Rothenberger, M.A., Chatterjee, S.: A design science research methodology for information systems research. J. Manag. Inf. Syst. **24**(3), 45–77 (2007)
23. Wieringa, R.J.: Design Science Methodology for Information Systems and Software Engineering. Springer, Heidelberg (2014)
24. Moody, D.: What makes a good diagram? Improving the cognitive effectiveness of diagrams in is development. In: Advances in Information Systems Development: New Methods and Practice for the Networked Society, pp. 481–492. Springer, Boston (2007)

A Multi-level Data Ecosystem Framework for Developing Digital Twins in Smart Cities

Lauma Jokste[1]([⊠]) [iD] and Rasa Gulbe[2] [iD]

[1] Information Technology Institute, Riga Technical University, Kipsalas Street 6, Riga, Latvia
lauma.jokste@rtu.lv
[2] Dati Group Ltd., Balasta Dambis 80A, Riga, Latvia
rasa.gulbe@datigroup.com

Abstract. As smart cities increasingly integrate advanced technologies like the Internet of Things (IoT) and Artificial Intelligence (AI), the need for robust data ecosystems to support Digital Twins (DTs) becomes essential. DTs offer real-time digital representations of physical urban systems, enabling predictive analytics, intelligent decision-making, and operational optimization. This paper presents the development of a DT data ecosystem based on stakeholder workshops and use case elicitation. The ecosystem was modelled at micro, meso, and macro levels to reflect different layers of abstraction and ensure scalability and adaptability. Through this modelling process, recurring patterns were identified and synthesized into a multi-level data ecosystem framework. The Capability-Driven Development (CDD) metamodel was extended to incorporate DT-specific elements. The resulting framework also addresses gaps in available datasets and proposes integration of real-time, high-resolution data to improve DT functionality. This approach fosters modularity and reusability, supporting efficient development, validation, and long-term resilience of DT solutions for smart cities.

Keywords: Data Ecosystem · Digital Twins · Smart City · Energy Digital Twin · Data Ecosystem Framework

1 Introduction

The rapid development of smart cities depends on the integration of advanced technologies such as the Internet of Things (IoT) and Artificial Intelligence (AI), aimed at improving urban management, resource efficiency, and citizens' quality of life. However, the complexity of modern urban systems increasingly exceeds the capacity of traditional engineering approaches. Digital Twins (DTs) – dynamic, virtual representations of real-world assets and systems – have emerged as a key enabler of real-time monitoring, simulation, and predictive analytics [1, 2].

The effectiveness of DTs relies on robust data ecosystems – interconnected networks of people, technologies, and data that support information exchange and collaboration [3]. Recent research trends emphasize integrating DTs into broader data-sharing infrastructures rather than treating them as isolated system replicas [4]. This integration enables

© The Author(s), under exclusive license to Springer Nature Switzerland AG 2026
R. Deneckère et al. (Eds.): BIR 2025, LNBIP 562, pp. 329–345, 2026.
https://doi.org/10.1007/978-3-032-04375-7_21

the creation of cyber-physical "living" systems that support modularity, scalability, and data-driven governance.

This study contributes to ongoing research focused on developing a flexible and interoperable DT platform that supports a wide range of smart city use cases across domains such as energy, transport and civil defence. Through stakeholder workshops and use case elicitation, key verticals and requirements have been identified. These serve as the foundation for modelling a multi-level DT data ecosystem structured at macro, meso, and micro levels by extending the Capability-Driven Development (CDD) approach. This approach results in a multi-level data ecosystem framework designed to model complex solution data ecosystems. The framework is presented and elaborated through concrete examples of DT data ecosystem models, illustrating how it supports the development, validation, and reuse of DT solutions in complex urban environments.

The remainder of this paper is structured as follows: Sect. 2 outlines the research objectives and questions guiding the study. Section 3 describes the methodology for developing and modeling the DT data ecosystem, including the multi-level data ecosystem framework. Section 4 presents developed data ecosystem model examples from the energy vertical, while Sect. 5 concludes the paper with a summary of findings and a discussion of future directions for DT platform development.

2   Research Objectives and Research Questions

This study aims to examine the role of data ecosystems in the development of smart city DTs, focusing on data availability, integration, and reusability across various use cases. It seeks to identify key challenges, such as ensuring real-time accuracy, scalability, security, and standardization, which impact the effective deployment of DT technology. Additionally, the research explores strategies to enhance data governance, privacy, and interoperability, ultimately contributing to the optimization of smart city infrastructure and decision-making processes.

This study follows the principles of Design Science Research (DSR), which focuses on the development and evaluation of purposeful artifacts to address identified problems in each domain [5]. The core artifact of this study is DT data ecosystem, designed to support adaptive, multi-domain smart city DTs. This artifact was developed through structural process that included: (1) problem and requirements identification through literature analysis and end users' requirements elicitation workshop; (2) DT data ecosystem modelling by CDD approach and (3) iterative refinement of the data ecosystem through expert feedback and validation. Based on the recurring design patterns and modelling outcomes, we identified a multi-level DT ecosystem modelling framework for organizing similar data ecosystems.

As part of the DSR process, the literature review helps to establish the conceptual foundation for the artifact and to contextualize the problem withing the current state of research. This section further presents a concise overview of key considerations in building a smart city DT data ecosystem, which in turn informs the design of the proposed framework. Following research questions have been defined to guide the further research:

RQ1. *What are the key components of data ecosystems that enable the successful implementation of DTs in smart cities?*

RQ2. *What data sources and qualities are required and currently available to support the developing and operating smart city DTs?*

RQ3. *What DT data ecosystem components can be reused across the DT use cases?*

Addressing these research questions will provide valuable insights that can guide further research aimed at developing a comprehensive DT data ecosystem. By identifying the key components of data ecosystems that enable successful DT implementation (RQ1), future research can focus on designing frameworks that enhance data integration, accessibility, and interoperability. Assessing what is the availability and sufficiency of data required for developing and operating smart city DTs (RQ2) will help in identifying data gaps, ensuring data quality, and improving real-time accuracy for decision-making. Additionally, understanding which DT data ecosystem components can be reused across different use cases (RQ3) will support the creation of scalable and adaptable DT frameworks, reducing redundancy and improving efficiency. The findings from this research will lay a foundation for future advancements in DT data governance, security, and standardization, ultimately contributing to the development of a more robust and sustainable smart city infrastructure.

Although this study presents a structured multi-level framework, the research questions themselves are not focused on the framework as a theoretical artifact. Instead, they are grounded in the exploration and modelling of a DT data ecosystem for smart cities. The framework was derived subsequently as a synthesis of recurring design patterns identified during the data ecosystem modelling process.

2.1 DT Data Ecosystem Key Components

The successful implementation of DTs in smart cities depends on a robust data ecosystem comprising essential components that support seamless data flow, integration, and utilization. These components include data sources, infrastructure, interoperability frameworks, governance, and analytics, forming the foundation for scalable and adaptive DT platforms that enhance urban planning and service delivery. This section addresses RQ1: *What are the key components of data ecosystems that enable the successful implementation of DTs in smart cities?*

A data ecosystem can be defined as a socio-technical environment in which multiple stakeholders interact through data sharing, integration, and value co-creation, supported by digital infrastructure, governance mechanisms, and standards [6]. Modelling such ecosystems requires not only representing structural elements as actors, data assets and services, but also capturing dynamic aspects, like stakeholder specific goals, context dependencies and the ability to adapt to changes.

Several modelling approaches have been proposed for data ecosystems, including ontology-based models [7], business model and architecture frameworks [8] and data ecosystem meta-models [9]. To describe specifically DT data ecosystems, several modelling approaches have been proposed. One strategy is to focus on DT-specific structures, including sensors, platforms, and user interactions [10, 11]. Emphasis has also been placed on forming networks of interconnected DTs to promote the reuse of components and enhance system efficiency [12].

To understand stakeholder involvement, it is necessary to consider their diverse roles and goals – ranging from data provision to strategic decision-making and adjustments to physical systems based on DT insights [13].

To ensure ecosystem functionality, it is important to implement standardized protocols, modular architectures, and robust data management processes [14, 15]. Enhancing reusability and maintainability of assets can streamline DT development and deployment [16], while applying reusable models in simulations can improve adaptability in sectors like manufacturing [17].

To define core components of DT ecosystems in smart cities, it is helpful to focus on real-time data acquisition, AI-driven analytics, cloud infrastructures, and visualization tools supplemented by privacy and security frameworks [18]. In parallel, fostering interdepartmental collaboration, gaining political support, and forming partnerships with academia and industry are vital for long-term adoption and success [19].

In summary, to support smart city DTs, it is necessary to build a comprehensive data ecosystem that integrates technical, organizational, and human components. According to the literature, ensuring scalability, security, reusability, and stakeholder alignment is fundamental to enabling dynamic, sustainable DT platforms.

2.2 Data Availability and Sufficiency for Smart City DTs

To ensure effective implementation of DTs in smart cities, it is necessary to secure the availability, accessibility, and sufficiency of high-quality data. This section addresses RQ2: *What data sources and qualities are required and currently available to support the developing and operating smart city DTs?* Understanding the limitations and potential of current data sources is crucial for building reliable DT models that support informed decision-making.

One key challenge is to develop systematic methods for collecting and integrating datasets across various urban systems. Although diverse data types such as infrastructure and environmental data are often available, difficulties arise when attempting to incorporate them into unified DT frameworks [20]. Additional barriers include the lack of interoperability and the complexity of managing large data volumes [21].

To mitigate data gaps, researchers have proposed generating synthetic data to simulate scenarios without the need for exhaustive real-world data collection [22]. Another approach is to use generative AI techniques to autonomously create datasets, city models, and evolving urban scenarios, enabling continuous updates and increased adaptability of DTs [23].

Big data technologies are considered foundational to DT ecosystems across multiple domains, supporting advanced analytics and real-time applications [24]. However, limitations in bandwidth, storage, and processing capacity continue to restrict the real-time acquisition and utilization of data in smart city contexts [25].

In summary, although many data sources are available, key issues such as incomplete datasets, integration difficulties, and system-level constraints persist. At the same time, resolving technical limitations remains essential for building effective and scalable smart city DTs.

2.3 Reusable Components of the DT Data Ecosystem

To ensure scalable and efficient implementation of DTs in smart cities, it is necessary to identify and reuse core components within the DT data ecosystem. This section addresses RQ3: *What DT data ecosystem components can be reused across the DT use cases?* Focusing on reusability helps to reduce costs, streamline development, and ensure consistency across various urban applications.

To facilitate reuse, it is important to establish comprehensive DT frameworks. One such approach is the concept of DT as a Service (DTaaS), which offers a platform for creating and managing DTs by automating asset handling, storage, and computational resource allocation [16]. This model enables users to abstract complexity and apply reusable models, data, and tools across multiple DT instances.

To promote modularity, it is useful to apply the "Composable DTs" approach, which allows DTs to be assembled from interchangeable modules that represent specific functionalities or datasets [26]. Such modular structures enable adapting DTs to new scenarios by reconfiguring existing components without full redevelopment, ensuring consistency and interoperability across different domains.

To categorize reusable elements, it is useful to focus on fundamental components such as algorithms, simulation models, and machine learning frameworks. These include co-simulation models, reduced-order models, and system-of-systems models, all of which have been applied across various industrial contexts. A notable example is the DIGITbrain project, which facilitates such reuse by promoting standardized metadata, modular digital assets, and a platform-based approach to support efficient DT deployment, especially among small and medium enterprises (SMEs) [27].

To enable cross-domain reuse, it is essential to ensure efficient data integration. One strategy is to unify static and real-time data using reusable ingestion pipelines that support multiple deployment environments, including immersive platforms like virtual reality [28]. In parallel, ensuring semantic interoperability through standardized data models and ontologies is necessary to maintain data consistency across heterogeneous systems [29].

In conclusion, to support widespread DT adoption, it is vital to reuse standardized and modular components such as analytical tools, data integration frameworks, and semantic representations. Frameworks like DTaaS and Composable DTs illustrate how modularity simplifies development and improves system compatibility. Emphasizing reusability at both technical and organizational levels helps to reduce redundancy, promote scalability, and build more sustainable and interconnected urban systems.

3 DT Ecosystem Development Methodology

The DT data ecosystem is a structured network of interconnected components, systems, and processes designed to manage, exchange, and analyze data across multiple sources and platforms. Developed based on insights from an end users' requirements elicitation workshop, the ecosystem is aligned with real-world needs and stakeholder expectations. The primary objective is to support scalable and compliant service development, ensuring that DT solutions evolve effectively with business and operational demands. The ecosystem models not only define key stakeholders involved in smart city DT development, but also identify the business goals where DTs can provide value, describe the relevant context, and incorporate mechanisms for adjustments to accommodate changing needs. Additionally, the models outline the essential data sources required for the efficient operation of the DTs.

3.1 End User Requirements Gathering Workshop

A DT end users' requirements elicitation workshop was conducted to identify practical use cases across five key verticals – transport, energy, civil defense, industry 4.0, and cybersecurity – and to guide the development of a comprehensive DT data ecosystem. The workshop began with presentations on the DT platform vision and example use cases, followed by silent brainstorming and group discussions to define and model DT concepts. Participants used a structured template to describe DT use cases, focusing on real-world needs and implementation challenges. The template included ecosystem modelling terms, however, the structured DT data ecosystem models were developed later based on the identified use cases as well as the discussed user needs, expectations and challenges. A detailed explanation of these terms is provided in Sect. 3.2.

The initial models created during the workshop were later refined through three validation interviews, each targeting one of the most popular DT verticals in smart cities: transport, energy, and civil defense. These interviews allowed engaged participants to clarify and expand upon the models, which were also iteratively reviewed by project researchers.

3.2 DT Ecosystem Modeling Approach Using CDD

Building on the key components and ecosystem requirements outlined in Sect. 2.1, this section presents the modelling approach used to design a context-aware and adaptive DT data ecosystem. Given the need to capture stakeholder-specific goals, contextual dependencies, and dynamic system behavior, the CDD method was selected.

The CDD metamodel, initially developed by Bērziša et al. [30] to support capability-based system development with a focus on context-dependent capabilities, has been successfully adapted for data ecosystem modeling [31, 32] and extended to model DT data ecosystems. The CDD methodology includes both a lightweight version for SMEs and a full version with extensions targeting large organizations and complex systems, offering flexibility to adapt to changes in business processes, technologies, and external environments [33].

To model the DT data ecosystem, the core concepts of capability modeling are expanded to incorporate elements that represent the data ecosystem perspective. The original capability metamodel includes most of the essential concepts required for modeling a DT ecosystem. However, it originally omits the concept of "Adjustment," which was introduced later as an extension to the method [33]. In the visual representation of the model, element colors do not carry a specific semantic meaning. They are used to improve visual clarity and help distinguish between different concepts more easily. Figure 1 illustrates the conceptual modelling method used for the DT data ecosystem and Table 1 describes the DT data ecosystem modelling approach concepts.

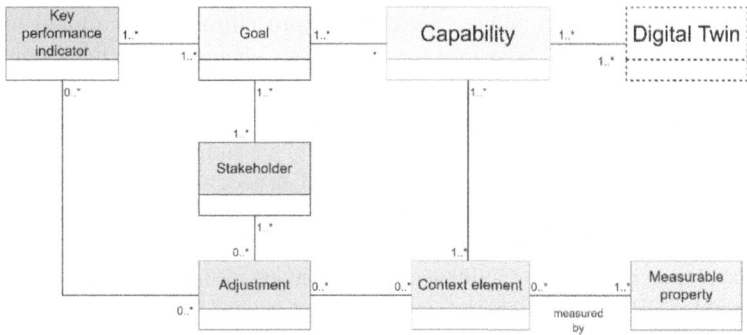

Fig. 1. DT data ecosystem conceptual modelling method derived from CDD meta-model.

Table 1. Description of DT data ecosystem modelling concepts.

DT data ecosystem concept	Description
Capability	An ability and capacity to fulfill goals in a dynamically changing environment (described as a context situation)
Goal	Purpose of using a DT
Stakeholder	Stakeholders relevant to the use of the DT. Each Stakeholder may have different goals for DT
Key performance indicator	Measurable characteristics by which the achievement of objectives is evaluated
Context element	Describes key conditions, environment, and factors in which DT will operate
Adjustment	Actions that can be performed on the physical and real service, process or equipment based on the simulations performed with the DT. Each adjustment has an owner or Stakeholder who executes the adjustment
Measurable property	Measurable attributes and data used to describe the context situation. Each measurable property has data provider attribute
Digital Twin	DT can be built to ensure one to many organizational capabilities. DT concept is not included in data ecosystem model as this model will be used as bases for DT platform development

3.3 Multi-level DT Data Ecosystem Framework

To manage the complexity of DT development across smart city domains, we introduce the concept of a multi-level data ecosystem framework in this study. According to [34], framework can be defined as structured set of interrelated concepts, such as development stages, modelling approaches, methodologies and implementation strategies, that collectively support the understanding and guide systematic actions within a particular domain. This perspective reinforces the role of frameworks as instruments for handling the inherent complexity and diversity of data ecosystems.

We followed the bottom-up use case-driven approach to develop a multi-level DT data ecosystem framework. Based on the use cases gathered during the requirements gathering workshop, we held data ecosystem modelling sessions during which we came up with the necessity to model DT data ecosystem in different levels. After creating the data ecosystem models for each identified use case, we summarized data needs at the level of DT verticals, followed by a compilation of data needs at the platform-wide level. Therefore, a recurring design patterns were then abstracted into a multi-level modelling framework, following DSR principles.

DT development platform facilitates the efficient creation of DT solutions by leveraging reusable DT fragments. These fragments are organized within DT verticals, where shared data sources, providers, and requirements contribute to commonality across solutions. To structure the data ecosystem of the DT development platform, a multiscale concept – macro, meso, and micro – is applied. This multiscale concept has been extensively applied across various disciplines to represent different levels of detail and granularity in decision-making and quality assessment [35], big data ecosystem [36] and the service data ecosystem [37].

Figure 2 presents the conceptual structure of the DT data ecosystem framework developed in this study, following the DSR principles. It visualizes how the framework organizes ecosystem modelling across micro-, meso-, and macro-levels using the CDD approach, with iterative feedback loops supporting adaptability and refinement.

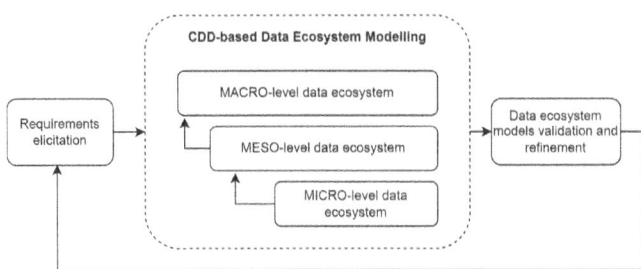

Fig. 2. Multi-level DT data ecosystem framework.

The macro-level represents the overall data ecosystem of the platform, the meso-level focuses on the data ecosystem of specific DT verticals, and the micro-level pertains to individual DT solution use cases. This hierarchical approach ensures that data ecosystems are represented with appropriate granularity for different decision-making processes and different stakeholders.

Among these levels, the meso-level is the most critical as it defines shared concepts and standardized data structures within a DT vertical. It serves as a bridge between the overarching platform-wide ecosystem (macro) and the highly specialized, use-case-specific models (micro). By establishing common data sources, stakeholders, and interoperability mechanisms, the meso-level ensures that DT solutions within a given vertical can communicate and function cohesively. Additionally, it supports the identification, design and development of reusable DT fragments, enabling efficiency and consistency in DT solution development across similar applications.

Our multi-level data ecosystem framework combines capability modelling approach and multi-level structure comprising the macro, meso and micro levels. Together they allow to model complex DT data ecosystems. This framework enables both conceptual clarity and practical flexibility in structuring DT initiatives. In addition to that, this framework also ensures openness to future extensions and refinements of the DT data ecosystem. This adaptability is particularly important in the context of evolving stakeholder needs, emerging technologies, and newly available data sources. By maintaining a modular and scalable structure, the framework accommodates iterative development and continuous integration of new components throughout subsequent stages of solution design.

4   DT Data Ecosystem

The DT data ecosystem is designed to support scalable, interoperable, and compliant service development for smart city applications. It defines the necessary data sources, stakeholder roles, and contextual elements required for the effective implementation and operation of DT solutions. Developed through stakeholder workshops and validation sessions, the data ecosystem provides a structured foundation for the development, integration, and reuse of DT components across smart city domains. In the following sections, selected models of the ecosystem are presented to demonstrate how the multi-level framework concept is applied in modelling, illustrating different levels of abstraction and detail within the DT development platform.

4.1   Macro Level DT Data Ecosystem

The macro-level data ecosystem for DT involves two main categories of stakeholders: DT system stakeholders, who directly engage with the platform as developers, users, and operators, and ecosystem partners, who provide data, governance frameworks, and benefit from the decisions made by DTs. In line with ISO/IEC 30173:2023, stakeholders are broadly defined as individuals or organizations with an interest in any DT-related activity, encompassing both technical and governance roles. Stakeholder model is shown in Fig. 3.

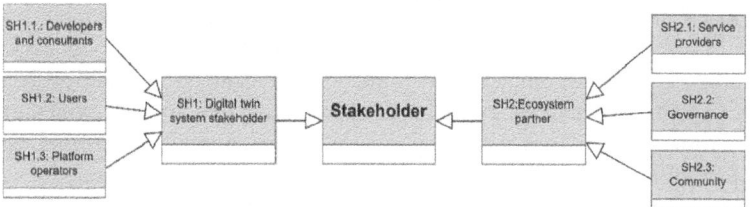

Fig. 3. DTs platform macro-level data ecosystem Stakeholder model

The ecosystem aims to support the full life cycle of DT solution development, improve decision-making, increase safety, and enhance economic and environmental outcomes. Adjustments made at this level focus on optimizing operations, maintaining assets, reallocating resources, making configuration changes, and ensuring safety and compliance. These adjustments, along with measurable properties such as IoT sensor data, operational data, and forecast data, allow the platform to function efficiently and adapt to changing circumstances. DTs platform macro-level data ecosystem is shown in Fig. 4.

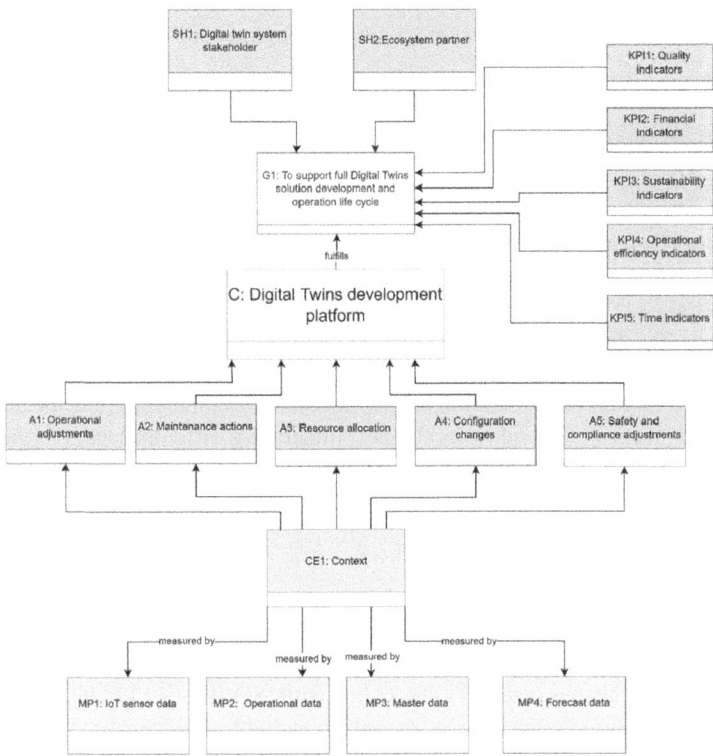

Fig. 4. DTs platform macro-level data ecosystem.

The macro-level data ecosystem also includes KPIs to evaluate the platform's performance. These KPIs cover a wide range of aspects, including quality, financial health, sustainability, operational efficiency, and time management. Measurable properties are critical for monitoring real-time operations and predicting future trends, with the ecosystem also accounting for long-term strategic shifts, operational adjustments, and real-time responses to events. These categories and indicators are essential for ensuring the platform can meet its goals, such as improving sustainability and enabling more informed decision-making across various sectors, including transportation, energy, and civil defense.

4.2 Meso Level DT Data Ecosystem

The meso-level data ecosystem for DT focuses on the common goals, KPIs, stakeholders, and adjustments specific to each DT vertical, such as transport, energy, and civil defense. It is based on individual use cases identified during workshops and can be extended with new concepts as the project progresses. This ecosystem ensures the scalability and compliance of future service developments and serves as a foundation for further platform or solution development.

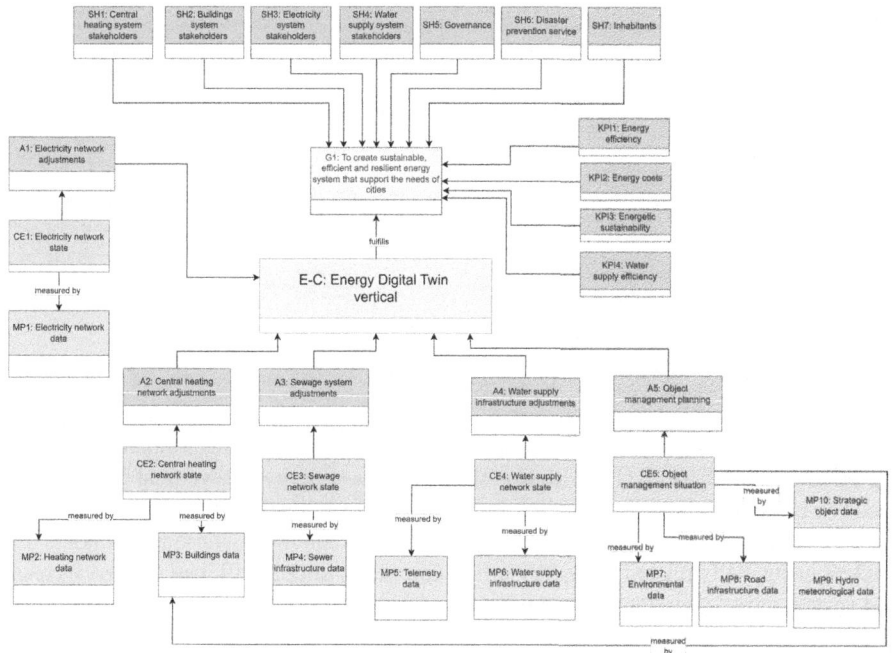

Fig. 5. DTs platform meso-level data ecosystem for Energy DT vertical.

Energy is essential for powering systems like electricity, heating, water supply, and sewer networks. During the end-user requirements elicitation workshop, six use cases related to the energy vertical were discussed, focusing on the electricity, central heating, and water supply networks. These use cases served as a basis for modelling meso-level DT data ecosystem for energy DT vertical. Figure 5 visualizes the meso-level DT data ecosystem for energy DT vertical.

The energy DT vertical focuses on four primary network types: electricity, central heating, water supply, and sewerage systems. Use cases were identified for the electricity, water supply, and central heating networks during the end users' requirements workshop, with additional concepts for the sewerage network added later during the validation phase. The energy system includes various stakeholders, and their roles and interests are summarized in the ecosystem model. Figure 6 describes the energy DT vertical's main goals and stakeholders.

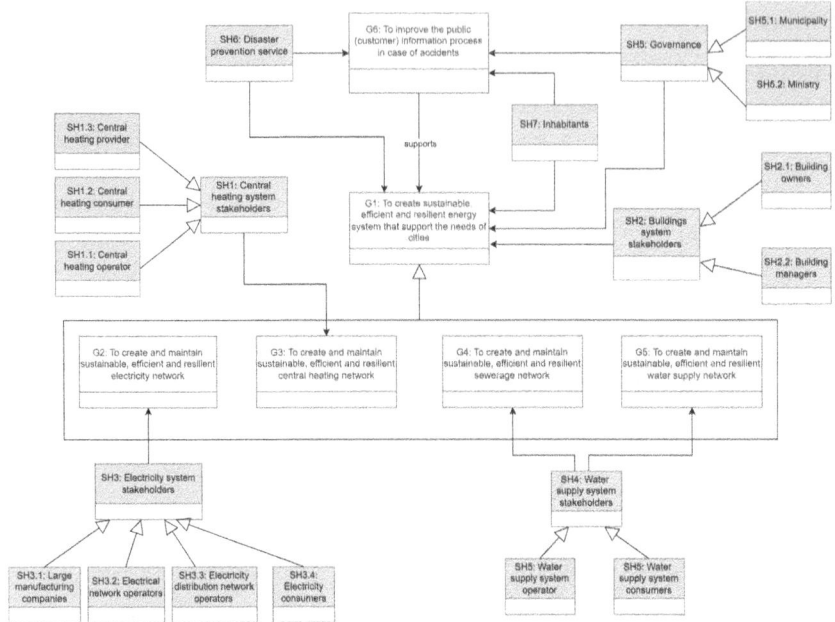

Fig. 6. DTs platform meso-level main Goals and Stakeholders.

Adjustments in the Energy DT vertical include operational changes aimed at improving efficiency and sustainability across the networks. Energy DT vertical adjustments focus on electricity, heating network, sewage network and water supply network infrastructure adjustments, system upgrades and emission reduction. These adjustments are tracked using KPIs related to energy efficiency, water supply efficiency, energy costs, and sustainability, with the corresponding owners ranging from system stakeholders to governance and disaster prevention services. Table 2 presents selected energy DT vertical's data ecosystem adjustments described in a structured format that follows CDD approach. This format ensures that each adjustment is explicitly linked to its responsible stakeholders, targeted KPIs and operational context.

In parallel with the development of the data ecosystem, available open-access datasets were identified as valuable resources for supporting energy and other DT solutions. These datasets provide important insights into energy efficiency, market pricing, and consumption patterns. For example, heating consumption data for Riga's multi-apartment buildings, integrating information from AS "Rīgas Siltums" and the State Land Service, enables performance comparisons between structures. Electricity market data accessible via API supports pricing analysis and forecasting. However, these datasets alone are insufficient, as many lack real-time detail, sensor-level granularity, and full system coverage needed for predictive DT models. Growing complexity from decentralized generation, smart grids, and renewables demands richer data. Meeting this need will require new sources, such as IoT-based monitoring, weather impact models, and high-resolution grid data. Meso-level data ecosystem models help identify these gaps, while a key challenge ahead is ensuring data acquisition and integration into DT development.

Table 2. Energy DT vertical data ecosystem adjustments examples

ID	Adjustment	Adjustment owner	Corresponding KPI	Description
A1	Electricity network adjustments	Electricity system stakeholders; governance; disaster prevention service	KPI1: Energy efficiency; KPI2: Energy costs; KPI3: Energy sustainability	Adjustments include changes in the electricity network, e.g., load balancing, renewable energy integration, connection of new consumers and new consumer areas, electricity network reconstruction and maintenance activities, etc
A2	Central heating network adjustments	Central heating system stakeholders; governance; disaster prevention service	KPI1: Energy efficiency; KPI2: Energy costs; KPI3: Energy sustainability	Adjustments include changes in the central heating network, e.g., connection of new buildings (heating consumers) and areas, emission reduction technologies, automation processes, pipeline maintenance activities, etc
A3	Sewage system adjustments	Water supply system stakeholders; governance; disaster prevention service	KPI4: Water supply efficiency	Adjustments include changes in the sewage system, e.g., pipeline upgrade and replacement, pump station improvements, sewage system capacity changes, etc

4.3 Micro Level DT Data Ecosystem

The micro-level DT data ecosystem involves creating a detailed representation of each individual DT use case concept, including goals, stakeholders, KPIs, context elements, measurable properties, and adjustments. Micro-level DT data ecosystems are defined for DT use cases described during the end users' requirement elicitation workshop. Figure 7.

Demonstrates an example of micro-level DT data ecosystem for central heating network use case.

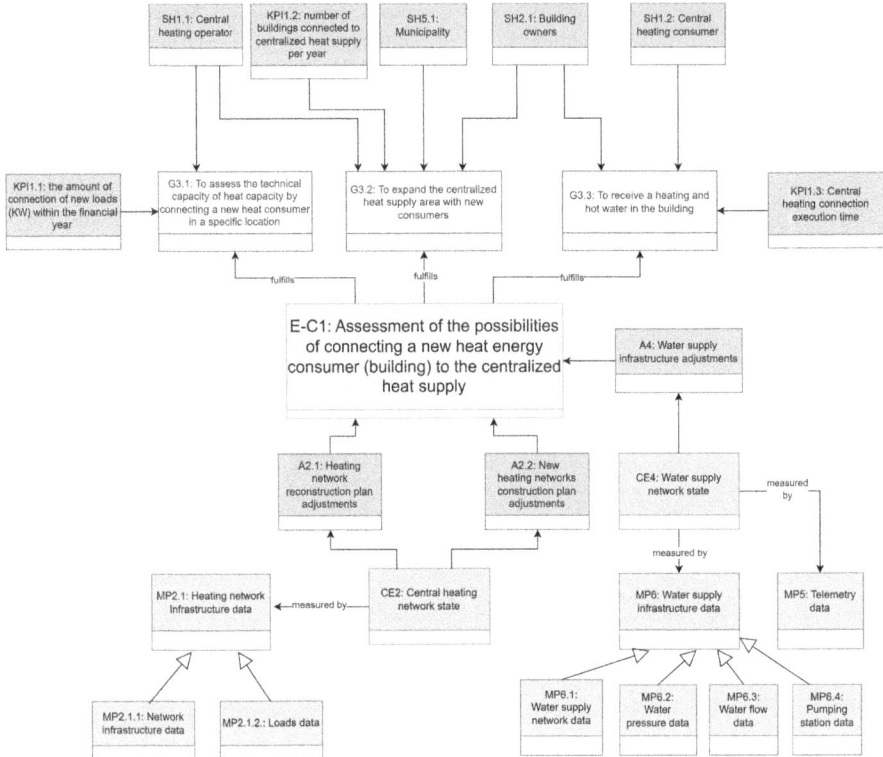

Fig. 7. Micro-level DT data ecosystem example for central heating network use case.

The use case "Assessment of the Possibilities of Connecting a New Heat Energy Consumer (Building) to the Centralized Heat Supply" focuses on evaluating the technical feasibility of integrating a new building into the central heating system. Key stakeholders include the central heating operator, municipality, building owners, and existing central heating consumers, who are responsible for decision-making and implementation. The primary goals are to assess the technical capacity of the heating network, expand the centralized heat supply, and ensure adequate heating and hot water provision for new consumers.

This assessment is guided by KPIs such as the number of buildings connected annually, the amount of new load capacity (kW), and the connection execution time. The evaluation process involves analysing heating network infrastructure data, network load data, and the state of central heating and water supply networks. Potential adjustments may include heating network reconstruction, the construction of new heating networks, and improvements to water supply infrastructure, ensuring the scalability and efficiency of the system.

5   Conclusions and Future Work

This study explored the data-related challenges and requirements for implementing DT solutions in smart cities. Based on the findings and DT requirements elicitation, DT data ecosystem has been developed. The data ecosystem models serve as a basis for the ongoing development of the DT development platform.

Standardization plays a key role in the platform's success. By promoting harmonized data integration, shared data sources, and semantic consistency across DT verticals, the models support interoperability and seamless system communication. This enables better cross-domain collaboration and a more integrated understanding of urban dynamics. As the platform evolves, these models will guide its iterative refinement and validation. They offer a clear structure for assessing stakeholder needs, adapting to operational contexts, and identifying data gaps, supporting the integration of real-time, high-resolution datasets to enhance predictive analytics and simulation capabilities.

During the modelling of DT data ecosystems, we concluded that the complexity of smart city domains required representing data-related elements at multiple levels of granularity. Initially, ecosystems were modelled for individual use cases (micro level), followed by consolidation at the domain or vertical level (meso), and finally synthesized into a platform-wide structure (macro). This bottom-up process revealed consistent patterns and relationships across levels, demonstrating the need for a structured approach to manage such layered data complexity. As a result, a multi-level DT data ecosystem framework was defined to capture and organize these recurring structures, ensuring coherence, scalability, and reusability across DT implementations. This framework can also be used as a reusable guide for designing and managing data ecosystems in other DT development projects, helping to ensure consistency, scalability, and interoperability in different application contexts.

Acknowledgments. This research is conducted as part of the project "Development of the DigiT-DevOps Digital Twin Development and Operation Platform"[2] under the European Union's Recovery and Resilience Mechanism Plan. It falls within Reform and Investment Direction 5.1: "Increasing Productivity Through Investment in R&D," specifically under Sub-action 5.1.1.r (Reform): "Innovation Management and Motivation for Private R&D Investment" and Sub-action 5.1.1.2.i (Investment): "Support Instrument for Research and Internationalization" (4th round). The project number is 5.1.1.2.i.0/4/24/A/CFLA/001. The project is developed by Ltd. DATI Group as the lead developer and implementer in collaboration with Riga Technical University.

References

1. Alnaser, A.A., Maxi, M., Elmousalami, H.: AI-powered digital twins and internet of things for smart cities and sustainable building environment. Appl. Sci. (Switzerland) **14**, 12056 (2024). https://doi.org/10.3390/app142412056
2. Thelen, A., et al.: A Comprehensive Review of Digital Twin -- Part 1: Modeling and Twinning Enabling Technologies (2022)
3. Lnenicka, M., et al.: Understanding the development of public data ecosystems: from a conceptual model to a six-generation model of the evolution of public data ecosystems (2024)

4. Nativi, S., Mazzetti, P., Craglia, M.: Digital ecosystems for developing digital twins of the earth: the destination earth case. Remote Sens. (Basel) **13**, 2119 (2021). https://doi.org/10.3390/rs13112119

5. Peffers, K., Tuunanen, T., Rothenberger, M.A., Chatterjee, S.: A design science research methodology for information systems research. J. Manag. Inf. Syst. **24**, 45–77 (2007)

6. Cappiello, C., Gal, A., Jarke, M., Rehof, J.: Data ecosystems: sovereign data exchange among organizations (Dagstuhl Seminar 19391). Dagstuhl Rep. **9**(9), 66–134 (2020).https://doi.org/10.4230/DagRep.9.9.66

7. Ceccaroni, L., Oliva Felipe, L.: Ontologies for the design of ecosystems. In: Universal Ontology of Geographic Space: Semantic Enrichment for Spatial Data, pp. 207–228 (2012)

8. Dhauwers, R., Walravens, N., Ballon, P.: Data ecosystem business models: value and control in data ecosystems. J. Bus. Models **10**, 1–30 (2022)

9. Oliveira, M.I.S., Oliveira, L.E.R.A., Batista, M.G.R., Lóscio, B.F.: Towards a meta-model for data ecosystems. In: ACM International Conference Proceeding Series (2018). https://doi.org/10.1145/3209281.3209333

10. Liyanage, R., Tripathi, N., Päivärinta, T., Xu, Y.: Digital twin ecosystems: potential stakeholders and their requirements. In: Lecture Notes in Business Information Processing, pp 19–34. Springer Science and Business Media Deutschland GmbH (2022)

11. Bhatti, G., Mohan, H., Raja Singh, R.: Towards the future of ssmart electric vehicles: digital twin technology. Renew. Sustain. Energy Rev. **141**, 110801 (2021). https://doi.org/10.1016/j.rser.2021.110801

12. Diogo Silva, H., Azevedo, M., Soares, A.L.: A Vision for a Platform-based Digital-Twin Ecosystem (2021). https://doi.org/10.1016/j.ifacol.2021.08.088

13. Tripathi, N., Hietala, H., Xu, Y., Liyanage, R.: Stakeholders collaborations, challenges and emerging concepts in digital twin ecosystems. Inf. Softw. Technol. **169**, 107424 (2024). https://doi.org/10.1016/j.infsof.2024.107424

14. Rocco Di Torrepadula, F., Somma, A., De Benedictis, A., Mazzocca, N.: Smart ecosystems and digital twins: an architectural perspective and a FIWARE-based solution. IEEE Softw. 2–9 (2024)

15. Moyne, J., et al.: A requirements driven digital twin framework: specification and opportunities. IEEE Access **8**, 107781–107801 (2020)

16. Talasila, P., Gomes, C., Mikkelsen, P.H., Arboleda, S.G., Kamburjan, E., Larsen, P.G.: Digital twin as a service (DTaaS): a platform for digital twin developers and users (2023). https://doi.org/10.1109/SWC57546.2023.10448890

17. Hwang, J., Do, N.S.: Digital twin-based optimization of operational parameters for cluster tools in semiconductor manufacturing. IEEE Access **12**, 122078–122100 (2024). https://doi.org/10.1109/ACCESS.2024.3450869

18. Faliagka, E., et al.: Trends in digital twin framework architectures for smart cities: a case study in smart mobility. Sensors **24**, 1665 (2024). https://doi.org/10.3390/s24051665

19. Yaqoob, I., Salah, K., Khan, L.U., Jayaraman, R., Al-Fuqaha, A., Omar, M.: Digital twins for smart cities: benefits, enabling technologies, applications, and challenges. In: Proceedings - 2023 IEEE Future Networks World Forum: Future Networks: Imagining the Network of the Future, FNWF 2023 (2023). https://doi.org/10.1109/FNWF58287.2023.10520349

20. Jacobellis, M., Ilbeigi, M.: Digital twin cities: data availability and systematic data collection. In: Construction Research Congress 2022, pp 437–444. American Society of Civil Engineers, Reston (2022)

21. Mazzetto, S.: A review of urban digital twins integration, challenges, and future directions in smart city development. Sustainability (Switzerland) **16**, 8337 (2024). https://doi.org/10.3390/su16198337

22. Almirall, E., Callegaro, D., Bruins, P., Santamaría, M., Martínez, P., Cortés, U.: The use of Synthetic Data to solve the scalability and data availability problems in Smart City Digital Twins (2022)
23. Xu, H., Omitaomu, F., Sabri, S., Zlatanova, S., Li, X., Song, Y.: Leveraging generative AI for urban digital twins: a scoping review on the autonomous generation of urban data, scenarios, designs, and 3D city models for smart city advancement (2024)
24. Dihan, M.S., Akash, A.I., Tasneem, Z., et al.: Digital twin: data exploration, architecture, implementation and future. Heliyon **10**, e26503 (2024). https://doi.org/10.1016/j.heliyon.2024.e26503
25. Sookhak, M., Tang, H., He, Y., Yu, F.R.: Security and privacy of smart cities: a survey, research issues and challenges. IEEE Commun. Surv. Tutor. **21**, 1718–1743 (2019)
26. Talasila, P., et al.: Composable digital twins on digital twin as a service platform. Simulation **101**, 287–311 (2024). https://doi.org/10.1177/00375497241298653
27. Zambrano, V., Mueller-Roemer, J., Sandberg, M., et al.: Industrial digitalization in the industry 4.0 era: classification, reuse and authoring of digital models on Digital Twin platforms. Array **14**, 100176 (2022)
28. Stadtmann F, Mahalingam HP, Rasheed A (2024) Data Integration Framework for Virtual Reality Enabled Digital Twins
29. Shareef, A., Tomaš, B., Vrcek, N., Vrček, N.: Semantic Interoperability of Digital Twins in Smart Cities (2025)
30. Bērziša, S., et al.: Capability driven development: an approach to designing digital enterprises. Bus. Inf. Syst. Eng. **57**(1), 15–25 (2015). https://doi.org/10.1007/s12599-014-0362-0
31. Grabis, J., Deksne, L., Roponena, E., Stirna, J.: A capability-based method for modeling resilient data ecosystems. In: Domain-Specific Conceptual Modeling: Concepts, Methods and ADOxx Tools, pp 339–363. Springer, Heidelberg (2022)
32. Grabis, J., Tsai, C.H., Zdravkovic, J., Stirna, J.: Endurant ecosystems: model-based assessment of resilience of digital business ecosystems. In: Lecture Notes in Business Information Processing, pp 53–68. Springer Science and Business Media Deutschland GmbH (2022)
33. Stirna, J., Zdravkovic, J., Grabis, J., Sandkuhl, K.: Development of capability driven development methodology: experiences and recommendations, pp. 251–266 (2017)
34. Meneses, B., Varajão, J.: A framework of information systems development concepts. Bus. Syst. Res. **13**, 84–103 (2022)
35. Cubo, C., Sampaio, P., Saraiva, P.: Multiscale quality: micro, meso and macro concepts. In: 2021 IEEE International Conference on Industrial Engineering and Engineering Management, IEEM 2021, pp 1216–1219. Institute of Electrical and Electronics Engineers Inc. (2021)
36. Curry, E.: The big data value chain: definitions, concepts, and theoretical approaches. In: New Horizons for a Data-Driven Economy: A Roadmap for Usage and Exploitation of Big Data in Europe, pp 29–37. Springer, Heidelberg (2016)
37. Pekkala, K., Elo, J., Tuunanen, T.: Functional and Structural Roles of Data in Service Ecosystems (2023). https://doi.org/10.24251/HICSS.2023.177

Structuring Security for Responsible Digital Systems

Towards a Speech Act-Based Model to Enable Future Quality Improvements of Information Security Policies Using Large Language Models

Fredrik Karlsson[1]([⊠]) [iD], Shang Gao[1] [iD], John Krogstie[2] [iD], and Leila Aro-Sati[1] [iD]

[1] Department of Informatics, Örebro University, 701 82 Örebro, Sweden
{fredrik.karlsson,shang.gao,leila.aro-sati}@oru.se
[2] Department of Computer Science, Norwegian University of Science and Technology, Trondheim, Norway
john.krogstie@ntnu.no

Abstract. Employees compliance with information security policies (ISPs) depends on communicating clear and comprehensible content. However, existing research has shown that many ISPs are of poor communicative quality. Large language models (LLMs) could enhance ISPs if finetuned on high-quality data, but to do such fine-tuning requires a conceptual model for classifying the data and evaluating the resulting text. Therefore, as a step in this direction, the aim of this paper is to develop a conceptual model of ISPs using speech act theory as a theoretical lens. We use conceptual modelling and document analysis to develop the model and use selected parts from the SEQUAL framework to evaluate the model. Analysing 600 ISP statements from ten British National Health Service ISPs, we present a class diagram containing 19 classes, six of which address ISP statement quality as speech acts. The SEQUAL evaluation points to potential areas for improving the model's semantic, empirical, physical and deontic qualities before using it to fine-tune LLMs to improve ISP content.

Keywords: Information Security Policy · Speech Act · Large Language Model

1 Introduction

Organisations today face a wide range of information security risks from both internal and external sources, potentially leading to security breaches. Such breaches can severely impact an organisation's reputation and finances [1] while also harming individuals [2], for instance, through leaked personal data on the Darknet. As a result, information security, aimed at safeguarding an organisation's information assets, is crucial for maintaining trust and stability.

Organisations can implement controls—measures addressing risks—within their business processes to strengthen information security. However, despite advancements in technical controls, they alone cannot guarantee security. Both industry reports [3] and research [4] show the critical role of human behaviour. Employees with access to sensitive data can pose risks through intentional leaks, accidental disclosures, or actions

© The Author(s), under exclusive license to Springer Nature Switzerland AG 2026
R. Deneckère et al. (Eds.): BIR 2025, LNBIP 562, pp. 349–364, 2026.
https://doi.org/10.1007/978-3-032-04375-7_22

enabling external threats, such as clicking malicious links. For over three decades, human behaviour has been a top security threat [5, 6]. To mitigate this, organisations implement information security policies (ISPs) that employees must follow in their daily work [7]. However, many struggle with poor compliance among employees [8].

Of course, it is close at hand to blame employees for not following procedures, but Rostami [9] argues that ISP non-compliance often results from both employee related factors and ISP design. Poorly designed policies can hinder compliance, meaning employees should not always be held responsible. Studies stress the importance of designing clear, comprehensible ISPs [10–12], yet many still fall short [12–14]. While the ISO 27000 standard-series [15] and EU directives [16] provide guidance, most focus on high-level design aspects, such as relevant topics [15] or tailoring ISPs to different groups [9]. However, there is still limited support on how to improve the messages conveyed in ISPs.

At the same time, advancements in natural language processing have been remarkable, introducing powerful new techniques. One such technology is Large Language Models (LLMs) [17], with ChatGPT being a notable example [18]. This form of artificial intelligence (AI) is trained on vast amount of textual data from articles, books, and websites, enabling them to identify and analyse language patterns. As a result, LLMs can assist with tasks such as answering questions, summarising text, and generating content, potentially improving text quality. However, general LLMs are not specifically designed to enhance ISP content; they require fine-tuning on a high-quality dataset of ISP statements. To this end, Speech Act Theory (SAT) [19] may offer a useful theoretical framework for classifying ISP statements, such as directives, and assessing their quality. Against this backdrop, *the aim of this paper is to develop a conceptual model of ISPs using SAT as a theoretical lens.* By structuring ISP statements based on their communicative functions, the model offers a systematic framework for assessing their quality and can act as a domain model. The ultimate goal is to create a high-quality dataset of ISP statements to refine LLMs, enhancing ISP content and improving its effectiveness in guiding employees' security behaviour.

The remainder of the paper is structured as follows. Next, we present related research in four parts: first, existing studies on ISP design as background; second, LLMs and ISPs; third, an introduction to SAT, which informed our modelling; and fourth, the SEQUAL framework, used to evaluate our conceptual model. We then describe our research method, followed by a result section presenting our conceptual model and evaluation findings. The sixth section discusses our findings, and finally, the paper ends with a short conclusion.

2 Related Research

2.1 Information Security Policy Design Research

ISP design can refer to both the product and the process, which are closely interconnected [12]. The intended design of an ISP influences the process, while the activities within the process impact the final ISP. Our focus is on developing a conceptual model to classify ISP content, meaning we approach ISP design as a product. Several studies have examined ISP quality, particularly the importance of clear and consistent instructions for employees [11–13, 20–23]. However, few studies provide comprehensive conceptual models or frameworks for structuring and evaluating ISP statements.

Rostami et al. [23] proposed a conceptual model for tailoring ISPs to different organisational target groups using policy components. These components include three types of ISP statements: actionable advice, educational content, and general content. While actionable advice resembles directives in SAT, the categorisation is not based on SAT. In Rostami et al. [24], they outline three quality criteria for actionable advice: it should use employees' work-related language, specify clear responsibilities and consequences, and be based on well-defined concepts. However, this model does not offer a comprehensive framework with quality criteria for classifying ISP statements.

Beyond existing conceptual models, research on ISP design has introduced various criteria and metrics for evaluation [12, 13, 21]. Stahl et al. [13], based on an analysis of British National Health Service (NHS) ISPs, recommended using accessible language, clear terminology, and providing employees with specific, actionable guidance. Similarly, Karlsson et al. [12] proposed eight quality criteria for ISPs, including alignment with work practices, a clear conceptual framework adapted to the work practice, structured content, defined communicative objectives, avoidance of goal conflicts, clear target groups, adaptation of external policies, and clarity in responsibilities and expectations. Goel and Chengalur-Smith [21] developed quantitative metrics to assess the communicative effectiveness of ISPs, focusing on brevity, breadth, and clarity. Brevity evaluates word repetitiveness, assuming lower redundancy reduces jargon. Breadth measures comprehensiveness by comparing the frequency of security-related terms in a policy against a master glossary, with a higher match rate indicating greater coverage. Clarity relates to readability, assessed using the Flesch Reading Ease Score, Flesch-Kincaid Grade Level, and Gunning Fog Index. However, they acknowledged that these metrics do not fully capture the challenges readers may face in understanding ISP content. Although valuable, these high-level recommendations and metrics are not easily applicable to individual ISP statements.

2.2 Large Language Models and Information Security Policies

In recent years, LLMs have become a powerful tool for content creation across various fields. Research has explored their application in government policy communication [25], access control policies [26], and digital asset privacy policies [27]. However, to our knowledge, no studies have specifically examined their use in designing or assessing ISP statements. Despite their potential, LLMs are prone to bias, inaccuracies, and misinformation [28], largely due to the quality of their training data. To minimise the risk of propagating inaccuracies [29], it is essential to train LLMs on well-structured, high-quality ISP datasets.

2.3 Speech Act Theory

Speech Act Theory (SAT) was first introduced by Austin [30] and later revised by Searle [31], who identified five categories of illocutionary acts—fundamental units of human communication [32]. These categories include assertives (committing the speaker to a statement's truth), directives (urging the listener to act), commissives (committing the speaker to future actions), expressives (conveying attitude), and declaratives (changing reality through speech) [33]. An illocutionary act consists of illocutionary force (F)—the speech act performed—and propositional content (P)—what is being said. Thus, for a given proposition P, F(P) represents the speech act expressed with force F. Research suggests that the way speech acts are performed, including their level of directness, affects comprehension, as listeners must infer the intended meaning [34]. SAT has been applied in areas such as educational policy analysis [35] and, more recently, in studies on communication intent and AI authorship, exploring the combined use of LLMs and SAT [36]. However, to our knowledge, no research has specifically applied LLMs to analysing ISP statements using SAT categories.

2.4 SEQUAL – A Framework for Evaluating Conceptual Models

The quality of models is an important aspect of modelling, which has been on research agenda since the early nineties [37]. SEQUAL [38, 39] is a comprehensive framework for evaluating different types of conceptual models. The current version also takes heed of the fact that these days, models can be developed both by humans and machines or in a combination and through pipelines and networks of models. The set of model creating actors is denoted C. It can be a combination of technical model creators (TC) (including AI tools, such as an LLM suggested in this paper) and social model creator (SC) (humans and organisations) that collaborate in the development of the externalized model M.

In SEQUAL, quality has been defined referring to the correspondence between statements belonging to the following sets as illustrated in Fig. 1.

- $G,$ the set of goals of the modelling task.
- $L,$ the language extension, i.e., the set of all statements that are possible to make according to the rules of the modelling languages used.
- D, the domain, i.e., the set of all statements that can be stated about the situation.
- M, the externalized model itself expressed in a modelling language/notation.
- $A,$ the part of the model that can be accessed by one or more actor, actors being either persons or tools (including AI-tools). The collected set of actors are called the audience of the model.
- K, the explicit knowledge relevant to the domain of the audience.
- SI, the social actor interpretation, i.e., the set of all statements that the people in the audience interprets that an externalized model consists of.
- TI, the technical actor interpretation, i.e., the statements in the model as 'interpreted' by modelling tools and AI tools.

Central quality types as illustrated in Fig. 1 are:

- Physical quality: The basic quality goal is that the externalized model M is available to the relevant actors. The available subset is denoted $A.$
- Empirical quality deals with comprehensibility when a visual model M is read by different (primarily social) actors. Patterns and readability (e.g. according to the Gunning Fog Index) in the labels used is discussed under empirical lexical quality.
- Syntactic quality is the correspondence between the model M and the language extension L. For syntactic quality, we can differentiate between adhering to the rules of the

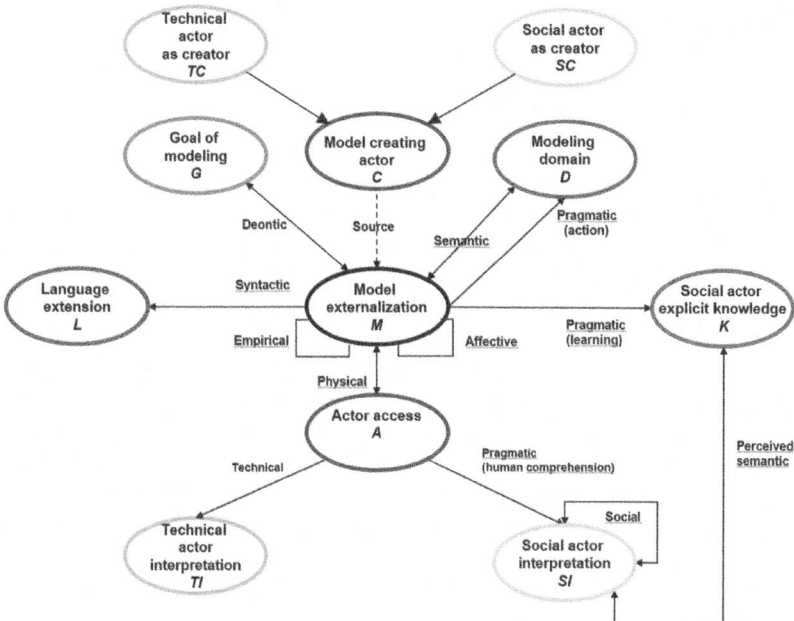

Fig. 1. SEQUAL Framework

visual notation (syntactic notational quality), and that the textual input is according to the rules in the natural language used for writing the labels, comments etc. (syntactic lexical quality).

- Semantic quality is the correspondence between the model M and the domain D. This includes both validity and completeness of the model.
- Perceived semantic quality is the similar correspondence between the social actor interpretation SI of a model M and the actors current knowledge K of domain D.
- Main aspect of pragmatic quality is the correspondence between the available part of the model M (i.e., A) and the actor interpretation (SI) of it. One differentiates between social pragmatic quality (to what extent people understand the model) and technical pragmatic quality (to what extent tools can be made that can interpret and potentially act based on the model). Learning and action either within the existing domain or resulting in domain change are also part of pragmatic quality.
- Affective quality: The positive or negative impression that the model instills in social actors when interpreted.
- Social quality: The goal defined for social quality is agreement among social actor's interpretations (I). Aspects of trust in the source of the model, that can be based on the variety of sources behind the model influence social quality.
- The deontic quality of the model relates to that all statements in the model M contribute to fulfilling the goals of modelling G, and that all the goals of modelling G are addressed through the model M using available resources (time, cost, competence etc.) available for the modelling task.

3   Research Method

The aim of this paper is to develop a conceptual model. To this end, we applied conceptual modelling [40] via UML class diagrams and document analysis [41]. The latter is a natural choice since ISPs are often published in the form of documents. Conceptual modelling via UML class diagrams and ISP document analysis served as two central methodological components through which the conceptual model was developed. Although they are distinct, and our presentation here is essentially sequential, we used them in an integrated manner to develop the conceptual model.

Starting with the document analysis, similar to [13], we used 10 ISPs from British NHS as an empirical starting point. We used an LLM (ChatGPT 4o) to elicit ISP statements, i.e., sentences, from these ISPs. These statements could potentially represent different types of speech acts. However, at this stage, the generated ISP statements were not expected to reflect any predefined speech act categories. The primary goal was to produce a broad sample of ISP statements that could later be manually classified by the authors according to various speech act categories. We used the following prompt, which is in four parts: "1). An information security policy statement is an utterance or a performative utterance about information security within an organisation. 2). Elicit all information security policy statements in the uploaded document. 3). Quote the elicited the information security policy statements in an Excel spreadsheet. 4). List one information security policy statement per row". In total, we elicited 3,765 ISP statements and added them to an Excel spreadsheet. Modelling text documents is resource intensive. Therefore, we needed to balance the available resources for modelling while ensuring the development of a stable conceptual model. We developed a macro in Excel that randomly selected 600 unique ISP statements for our analysis. The random selection allowed us to get a spread of which potential speech acts they were among these ISP statements. As a preparatory step before the modelling, these ISP statements was classified as different types of speech acts. The first, second and fourth authors classified 200 of the randomly selected ISP statements each using Searle's taxonomy of speech acts [19].

For our conceptual modelling, we chose to use Unified Modelling Language (UML) class diagrams. Our modelling work was carried out during two workshops, in which the first, second and fourth authors participated. Using our different and complementary skills to decrease potential bias and prevent the holistic fallacy in our study [42]. The protocol used during the workshops included 1). reviewing and resolving uncertainties in initial speech act classifications, 2). identifying all the speech act categories, 3). mapping ISP statements to relevant organisational actors, 4). deriving quality criteria for each speech act category, and 5). developing a conceptual model using UML class diagrams. During the modelling workshops, the three researchers started with a review of the initial classifications of ISP statements, where any uncertainties in the classifications were discussed and resolved. As shown in the Result section, we identified all five types of speech acts in the Searle's taxonomy [19]. We analysed how different types of ISP statements, in the form of different types of speech acts, could be related to different types of actors in an organisation. We also used SAT to analyse strengths and weaknesses of the different types of speech acts found in the selected ISP statements, which resulted in quality criteria. Finally, we analysed whether the criteria applied to one type of speech act or whether they applied to several speech acts, i.e., being more general.

The conceptual model was evaluated by the third author. This means that the evaluation was done independently of the modelling work in order to reduce any risks of bias. The model was evaluated by specifying the sets included in SEQUAL (see Sect. 4.2) and the following quality types: Semantic, Empirical, Physical and Deontic. Furthermore, we note that it is not possible to optimize a model according to all levels. For instance, there will always be a need to balance completeness as part of semantic quality and pragmatic quality. As input for the evaluation, the conceptual model shown in Fig. 2 and a list of definitions of the classes, attributes and associations included in the model were used.

4   Result

Our result is in two parts. The first part is the conceptual model, which is the result from modelling the content of ten ISPs using SAT as a lens. The second part is the evaluation of the conceptual model using the SEQUAL framework.

4.1   Information Security Policy Conceptual Model

The conceptual model of ISPs is shown in Fig. 2 as a UML class diagram. The diagram consists of 19 classes and between these classes we find several named associations. Below we do a structure walk-through of these classes and provide empirical examples of how they are grounded in our empirical data, i.e., the ISPs we used when modelling, SAT and existing research on ISP design.

We start in the left centre part of the figure, with the Information Security Policy class itself. As discussed in the Introduction, an ISP is supposed to guide employees on how to act securely in their daily work [7], and may be presented as documents or on organisations' web pages. In our case, they are represented by the ten ISP documents from the British NHS. From a SAT perspective, these policies include a set of ISP statements (speech acts), i.e., utterances that perform actions by expressing the speaker's intention [33], thereby trying to affect the reader's understanding or behaviour. In our case, the utterances are made by ISP designer(s), a collective term for those involved in shaping the policy; an example is a chief information security officer (CISO) [9]. The ISP statements are intended for the employees, such as physicians, nurses and assistant nurses in a British NHS, who are supposed to be guided by reading them. Thus, ISP designers and employees are roles, i.e., functions played by actors, in the organisation [23], where the actors are individuals who perform work tasks in the organisation.

Drawing on SAT, Searle [19] provides five different types of speech acts with different so-called illocutionary points: directive, commissive, expressive, declarative and assertive (synonym of representative [19]). The first type of speech act is Directive. In an ISP, a directive is a statement that seeks to compel a particular kind of agent to take a particular action regarding information security. During our modelling work, we identified directives such as "You must include digits (0–9) in your password" (ISP#1), "Line Managers MUST ensure all IT accounts are removed or disabled when a staff member leaves the organisation" (ISP#6), and "Use a fax cover sheet that contains a confidentiality statement" (ISP#3). In total, we identified 226 directives among the ISP statements analysed.

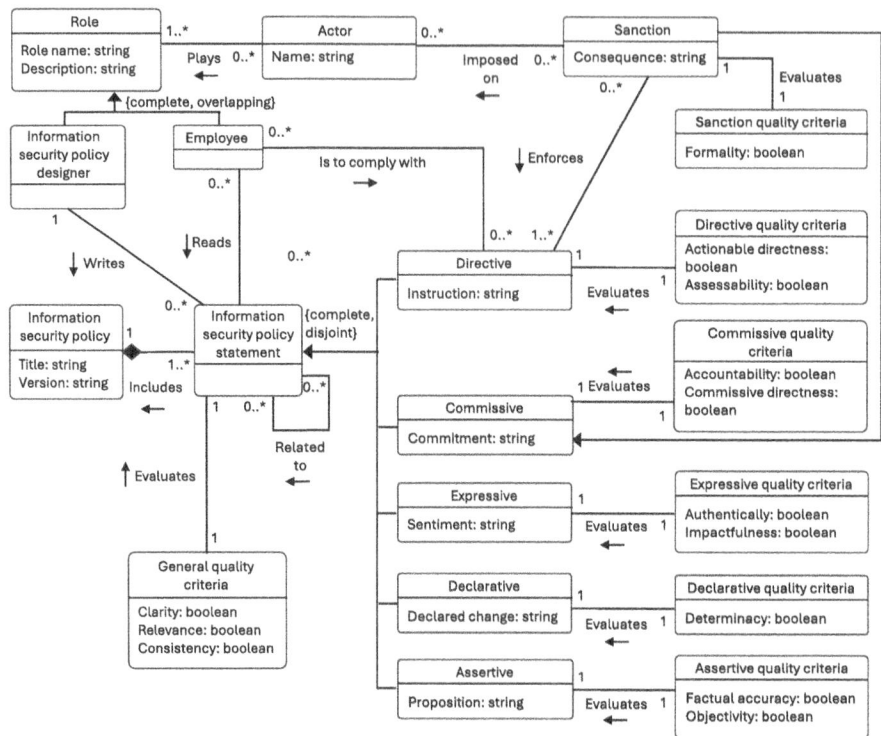

Fig. 2. Information Security Policy Conceptual Model version 1

The second type of speech act is Commissive, which in an ISP commits the speaker to do something in the future related to information security and/or the organisation. Examples encountered during our modelling are: "Centrally stored information will be accessible from any healthcare provider location in England" (ISP#1), "Only authorised personnel who have an identified need are given access to restricted areas containing information systems such as the server room or a file storeroom" (ISP#2) and "New operational software will be quality assured" (ISP#3). We identified 123 commissive speech acts in our sample of ISP statements. A commissive speech act can further be refined as a sanction—a threat [34]—when it commits the speaker to imposing a consequence in the future if an employee does not comply with a directive. Thus, focusing on the forward-looking aspect, i.e., the commitment of a sanction is distinct from the situations where a sanction is carried out (e.g., an employee getting its credential withdrawn). In the latter case, an executed sanction has the force of a declarative, changing the social or legal reality. In our sample, the following are examples of sanctions: "Offenders are liable to disciplinary action and civil and criminal prosecution" (ISP#6) and "Using Trust or NHS information systems for personal gain shall be deemed a disciplinary offence" (ISP#10).

The third type of speech act is Expressive. An expressive speech act in an ISP conveys the organisation's attitudes regarding information security practices and expectations.

In the sample of speech acts we analysed, we found three ISP statements that were expressive: "Our philosophy and commitment to care goes above and beyond our legal duty to enable us to provide high-quality services" (ISP#8), "It is essential that all of the CCG's information systems are protected to an adequate level from business risks" (ISP#5) and "Each employee is responsible for the security of the information they use and maintaining its confidentiality, integrity and availability to the highest standard" (ISP#3).

The fourth type of speech act is Declarative, which in an ISP enact or bring about a change in the status or condition of information security by the very act of their declaration. In our sample of ISP statements, we only identified one declarative speech act: "The status of this document is FINAL" (ISP#6).

The fifth and final type of speech act is Assertive. An ISP, an assertive speech act involves making statements that convey information and describe situations about information security, the organisation or the world. For example, among the analysed ISP statements we found the following: "2FA stands for Two-Factor Authentication, which is the use of a second form of authentication, such as a password and a smart card" (ISP#6), "The current supplier is [name of the company] – the Trust will manage this contract centrally" (ISP#1) and "Where an overnight stay for work purposes is required the same principles apply" (ISP#5). In total, we classified 247 ISP statements as assertive in our analysis.

The quality of the five types of ISP statements can be evaluated using a set of different quality criteria, some of which are shared across all ISP statements and some of which are unique to specific types of speech acts. Starting with the one shared across all ISP statements, they are found in the class General quality criteria. All ISP statements can be evaluated in relation to their clarity, relevance and consistency. Clarity means each ISP statement clearly conveys its intended message without ambiguity. Drawing on SAT, the illocutionary force [19, 33]—the speaker's intention—should be explicit, leaving no room for misinterpretation. Relevance means each speech act must be pertinent to the specific context of the organisation's operations and the roles of the addresses. This ensures that the locutionary act [33]—the actual content of the ISP statement—is meaningful and applicable to the addresses [13, 14]. Finally, consistency ensure each ISP statement is consistent with the other existing ISP statements in the ISP. This internal congruence of the ISP prevents confusion across ISP statements [12], which could otherwise leave room for interpretations.

Turning our attention to the quality criteria specific for different types of speech acts, we start with Directive quality criteria class, that contains two criteria: actionable directness and assessability. Actionable directness evaluates the precision in the directive, i.e., how well it guides the employee towards an intended outcome. Directives function through linguistic force, attempting to influence, in our case, the employees to establish a world-to-word fit [19], i.e., changing reality to align with what is the desired state [34]. A directive with actionable directness, ensures that it is clear how to achieve the desired state [23]. For example, "Log off the computer when leaving". Assessability in information security directives refers to the ability to evaluate whether a directive has been successfully executed. Drawing on Searle [19], directives inherently involve an expectation that the employee will carry out a specified action. Furthermore, the directives degree of imposition may vary [33]. Without the ability to evaluate, the essential condition (i.e., the employee's obligation) is weakened because it is unclear whether compliance has been achieved. For example, a non-assessable directive is "Avoid using weak passwords", since there are no measurable standards for determining compliance.

The commissive speech acts are evaluated using the Commissive quality criteria: accountability and commissive directness. Accountability in commissive speech acts means that each commitment must clearly define who is responsible for carrying out the promised action. Thus, we draw on the aspect that, through a commissive, the ISP designer binds someone to future action [19, 33]. For example, "The Information Security Manager will determine what action is appropriate regarding system vulnerabilities" (ISP#1) links the commissive to an institutional role, in this case the information security manager. Commissive directness focuses on the precision of the actions that the actor is committed to and the timeframe for execution, i.e., clarifying responsibilities [12]. In the example above, the commissive directness is weak since it does not commit the information security manager how to determine if an action is appropriate, or a timeframe when it should be determined. The subset of commissive speech acts that are sanctions is evaluated using the Sanction evaluation criteria class, which includes one criterion: Formality. The formality is evaluated based on whether it is explicitly stated that the sanction is legally mandated or internally enforced. A formal sanction is derived from laws or external regulations (e.g., GDPR, HIPAA, or SOX), while an informal sanction does not carry legal weight but may result in internal penalties.

The quality of expressive speech acts is assessed using the quality criteria in the Expressive quality criteria class: Authentically and Impactfulness. Authentically means that the expressed attitude actually reflects the organisation's genuine attitude toward information security. This criterion focuses on that there may be a difference between the psychological state [33] expressed by the ISP designer and what is communicated through actual actions. For an expressive to be valid, it must genuinely reflect the organisation's actual stance. Impactfulness means the speech act should effectively convey an attitude that motivates and engages the employee in active participation in information security practices. Thus, impactfulness relates to the illocutionary force of the speech acts [19, 33]—the strength with which a speech act conveys meaning to the employee.

Declarative speech acts are evaluated using the Declarative quality criteria class: determinacy. Determinacy focuses on whether the declaration makes the moment of change explicit. This relates to Searle's concept of institutional declarations [19], where the act's success depends on the authority of the speaker and the institutional context. For instance, "Effective March 1, 2025, access to company networks requires multi-factor authentication" is a determinate declaration because it clearly signals when the change takes effect, leaving no room for ambiguity.

Finally, assertive speech acts are evaluated using the Assertive quality criteria class: factual accuracy and objectivity. Both criteria relate to the truth of the expressed proposition [19, 33], where statements must match reality. Factual accuracy assesses whether the assertive speech act accurately reflects the organisation's information security posture, the organisation and/or the world. Thus, this type of ISP statement is possible to assess as true or false [19]. Inaccurate descriptions of security measures mislead employees and undermine trust. For example, "All company data is encrypted using industry-standard protocols" is accurate only if the organisation implements such encryption. Objectivity means the speech act is be presented impartially, without bias or subjective opinions. Thus, even if a statement in an ISP is factually correct, it lacks objectivity if it is framed in a way that introduces bias or persuasion.

4.2   Evaluation of the Conceptual Model

As said in the Research method section, the following evaluation of the Information Security Policy Conceptual Model version 1 has been made independently by the third authors, not involved in the development of the model. SEQUAL has been used to structure the evaluation, starting with a description of the relevant sets.

The goal $G1$ is: The model is to be used for fine-tuning of LLMs for producing better ISP statements using a general LLM. In addition, we have $G2$; the model needs to act as a domain model that experts on ISPs and other social actors (SA) agree upon represent good ISPs. The focus in this paper is $G2$, although we also look at some specifics related to what needs to be done with the model in the next step (when it is to be used for finetuning, i.e., $G1$). The (data)-model M in focus is the UML-model for relevant aspects of ISPs accompanied by a set of ISP-statements from British NHS ISPs. These parts are found in the previous section, which is represented in a way so that it adheres to this model. Thus, L is all possible statements that can be expressed in UML. The actors and stakeholders are social actors producing the UML model (SC) but interpreters are both social actors (SI) (for refining and agreeing on the model), and technical actors (TI) in connection to interpret the model to achieve $G2$. In the case of $G2$, the technical actor is a basic modelling tool that can store the data-model in a format accessible and interpretable by the fine-tuning mechanism.

Semantic quality: The model should cover all types of ISPs and should not include aspects not relevant for ISPs as documents for building the context-model, or ISPs that are no longer in effect. The model is based on currently available and up-to-date British NHS ISPs, which means the model has good correspondence with current documented information security practices in this industry. All 600 elicited ISP statements have been used for creating the model, leaving no outstanding statements in the sampled data. The model addresses the quality of the ISPs through quality criteria that builds on SAT. Thus, the quality criteria do not explicitly include SAT terminology. Speech acts include aspects such as 'direction of fit' and illocutionary force that contains the elements degree of strength of illocutionary point, mode of achievement, propositional content, preparatory condition, sincerity conditions and degree of strength of sincerity conditions. Representing these aspects would make the relation to SAT more explicit and make a more complete model, but one that can be harder to comprehend. The model is more detailed regarding the associations between Directives, Sanctions and Employees, compared to the other speech acts. The model could be extended by capturing associations between Employees and Commissives and Directives. In a commissive speech act, there is someone that commits to do something (although it might be everyone of course). In a declarative speech act, there must be an actor in a specific role who makes the declaration. Currently, the model does not capture the time-period of validity of speech acts. This might be linked to versions of the ISP, but then information on from-to validity of the version should be represented. Usually, a decision date is given for when the ISP will be applied, and that it is valid until further notice, which would make it reasonable to add such an attribute to the Information Security Policy class. Also, the organisation being subject to the ISP should be represented. Finally, from the point of view of completeness of a domain model, external laws and regulations that form the basis for some of the directives and sanctions can be represented [cf., 23], including the period of applicability. At the same time, these classes are of less relevance to fine-tuning of an LLM *(T1)*, where the ISP statements will be used.

Empirical quality: For *G2* the model should follow guidelines for graph-layout in standard UML-notation. For the conceptual model most lines are straight and with short distance, which means the model overall performs well. One long association is found, which is a layout compromise to avoid crossing lines. Two bends on associations— Employee "is to comply with" Directive and Sanction "enforces" Directive—could be avoided. The latter association could have been a straight line with a somewhat different positioning of the Sanction class.

Physical quality: The model must be available in a format understandable for *C*. Currently the model is available to *SC* and *SA* using SmartDraw native file format (and the available export formats), which is sufficient for *G2* (to act as a domain model that experts on ISPs and SA agree upon represent good ISPs). Versioning is supported by keeping separate model files. To address *G1* (to be used for fine-tuning of LLMs for producing better ISP-statements) in the future, the model has to be made available in a format understandable to the fine-tuning mechanism in an LLM.

Deontic quality: The conceptual model has two goals: *G1* (to be used for fine-tuning of LLMs for producing better ISP statements) and *G2* (to act as a domain model that experts on ISPs and SA agree upon represent good ISPs). Goal *G2* is broader than goal *G1*, which affects the boundaries of what should be included in the conceptual model. This is evident in the evaluation of sematic quality above. For instance, including external laws and directives in the model would bring the model closer to *G2*. In the current version, the model is closer to fulfil *G1*.

5   Discussion

The first contribution of this study is the proposed conceptual model for assessing the quality of ISP statements. As shown in the Related Research section, there are few conceptual model studies focusing on structure and quality of ISP statements. For instance, previous research proposed a conceptual model of tailoring ISPs to specific target groups in organisations [23]. Thus, our study advances the literature on ISP design, particularly in the context of ISP quality [12–14, 21]. More specifically, our conceptual model introduces quality criteria—applicable for the information security context—for all five types of speech acts in Searle's taxonomy [31]. For instance, *clarity, relevance*, and *consistency* apply across all ISP statements (i.e., speech acts). Additionally, specific quality criteria have been defined for particular speech act types. For instance, *actionable directiveness* and *assessability* are proposed as additional quality criteria for ISP statement that are directives. Furthermore, *sanction* has been suggested to be associated with both directive speech acts and commissive speech acts. By establishing these criteria, our model provides a structured approach to evaluating ISP statements, with the goal of contributing to more effective and well-defined ISPs. Thus, we contribute with quality assessment of ISPs at a more detailed level than general quality metrics like brevity, breadth, and clarity [21] that focus on the overall ISP.

Secondly, SAT has been applied to classify different types of statements in ISPs, providing alternative and more detailed classifications compared to Rostami and Karlsson [14] and Rostami et al. [23]. Our analysis of ten ISPs from the British NHS identified all five types of speech acts in Searle's taxonomy [19]—directive, commissive, expressive, declarative, and assertive. The presence of all five categories shows both the relevance and applicability of SAT to ISP analysis and design. While many existing studies have focused on ISP design, to our knowledge, this study is among the first to examine ISPs through the theoretical lens of SAT. Thus, this study contributes to the existing literature on its application in this domain. Our findings indicate that assertive and directive speech acts dominate ISP statements. Specifically, 247 assertive and 226 directive speech acts were identified among the 600 ISP statements analysed. In contrast, expressive and declarative speech acts were the least common, with only three expressive and one declarative speech act observed. These results provide empirical support for the role of SAT in understanding the structure and function of ISPs.

Thirdly, the proposed conceptual model has been evaluated using the SEQUAL framework, which provides a systematic structure for assessing the quality of models and modelling languages. SEQUAL has been used to evaluate models e.g., in BPMN [39]. This study contributes to the existing literature by demonstrating the use of a quality framework in evaluating UML Class diagrams. Our findings suggest that the proposed conceptual model serves as a foundational framework for improving ISP statements, which can potentially be used as an input for LLMs to enhance ISP content. Additionally, external laws and regulations, which form the basis for sanctions, can be incorporated into the model as well as specifying proposed associations between the Actor class and ISP statements that are Commissive and Declarative (see Sect. 4.2 and semantic quality). Adding these aspects to the conceptual model would bring it closer to an ISP domain model. Future studies should further evaluate the model through a case study involving a new set of ISPs to assess its applicability in real-world scenarios including evaluation of pragmatic and social quality.

This study also has some practical implications. Firstly, LLMs have the potential to enhance ISP content quality if fine-tuned on high-quality data. To perform such fine-tuning, a conceptual model is needed to classify the data and evaluate the resulting text. The proposed conceptual model serves as an essential first step by providing the foundation to enhance the quality of LLM-generated ISP statements. Secondly, the conceptual model can support both the creation of new ISP statements and the evaluation of existing ones. ISP designers (e.g., CISOs) can refer to appropriate speech act types to draft corresponding ISP statements, ensuring alignment with intended communication goals. Additionally, ISP designers can apply the proposed quality criteria to assess the ISP statements in their existing ISPs. Thirdly, the conceptual framework serves as a reference model for ISP designers, providing an overview of the speech acts used in ISPs. This can help them address key questions: Which types of speech acts are emphasized in their ISP? Are the selected speech acts appropriate for their organisation's context? Should ISP statements be refined to enhance the ISP's overall effectiveness? Fourthly, the conceptual model can support the creation of datasets with high-quality ISP statements. By applying the quality criteria presented in the conceptual model, high-quality datasets can be generated for each speech act category. These datasets can then serve as input for LLMs to generate ISP statements tailored to different organisational security needs, ultimately improving the effectiveness of ISPs in guiding employee security behaviour. Finally, practitioners who have used SAT in drafting policies beyond ISPs may find the conceptual model useful when develop such policies more systematically. That being said, since we modelled ISPs, we do not claim that the model or quality criteria are transferable to other types of policies. Additionally, further empirical validation of the model with ISPs from other countries and industries is required.

This study has some limitations. Firstly, we modelled a randomly selected subset of ISP statements from 10 ISPs from the UK. However, the ISPs themselves were not randomly selected, as they were all written in English and from healthcare organisations in the UK. Consequently, the findings may not be transferable to other countries or organisational contexts. Therefore, we do not claim that the conceptual model can be transferable beyond this context. Secondly, speech act theory relies on nuanced interpretations of language. It means that researchers may interpreted the statements differently, given differences in prior experience of ISPs and speech act theory. Given the interpretive nature of our study, we do not claim that other researchers would come to exactly the same conceptual model. Thirdly, the proposed conceptual model has been evaluated using only one evaluation framework (i.e., SEQUAL). We acknowledge that this evaluation was conducted by a single researcher and included only four quality types from the SEQUAL framework.

6   Conclusion

In this study, we developed a conceptual model of information security policies (ISPs) using speech act theory (SAT) as a theoretical lens. The long-term idea is that it will be used to fine-tune large language models (LLMs) to improve ISP content. To develop the model, we applied conceptual modelling and document analysis to 600 ISP statements from ten ISP documents within the British National Health Service. The resulting conceptual model comprises 19 classes, with six specifically addressing the quality of ISP statements as speech acts. This model has the potential to serve as a valuable input for large language models to enhance ISP content, ultimately improving its effectiveness in guiding employee security behaviour. Furthermore, the quality of the developed model was evaluated using the SEQUAL framework, focusing on physical quality, empirical quality, deontic, and semantic quality. The evaluation identified potential areas for further refinement. For instance, the semantic quality of the conceptual model can be enhanced by adding associations between Employees and Commissives and Directives ISP statements. The proposed potential improvements provide a foundation for the continued development of the conceptual model and start using it when fine-tuning LLMs.

References

1. Kör, B., Metin, B.: Understanding human aspects for an effective information security management implementation. Int. J. Appl. Decis. Sci. **14**(2), 105–122 (2021)

2. Culnan, M.J., Williams, C.C.: How ethics can enhance organizational privacy: lessons from the choicepoint and tjx data breaches. MIS Q. **33**(4), 673–687 (2009)

3. Truesec: Threat Intelligence Report 2023. Truesec (2023)

4. Chatterjee, S., Gao, X., Sarkar, S., Uzmanoglu, C.: Reacting to the scope of a data breach: the differential role of fear and anger. J. Bus. Res. **101**, 183–193 (2019)

5. Loch, K.D., Carr, H.H., Warkentin, M.E.: Threats to information systems: today's reality, yesterday's understanding. MIS Q. **16**(2), 173–186 (1992)

6. Chowdhury, N.H., Adam, M.T., Skinner, G.: The impact of time pressure on cybersecurity behaviour: a systematic literature review. Behav. Inf. Technol. **38**(12), 1290–1308 (2019)

7. Siponen, M., Vance, A.: Neutralization: new insights into the problem of employee information systems security policy violations. MIS Q. **34**(3), 487–502 (2010)

8. Ponemon Institute LLC: Cost of Insider Threats: Global Report (2020). https://Www.Ibm.Com/Downloads/Cas/Lqz4rone

9. Rostami, E.: Tailoring Information Security Policies - Computerized Tool and a Design Theory. Department of Informactics, vol. PhD. Örebro University, Örebro (2023)

10. Höne, K., Eloff, J.H.P.: What makes an effective information security policy? Netw. Secur. **6**(1), 14–16 (2002)

11. Lopes, I., Oliveira, P.: Applying action research in the formulation of information security policies. In: Rocha, A., Correia, A.M., Costanzo, S., Reis, L.P. (eds.) New Contributions in Information Systems and Technologies, pp. 513–522. Springer, Cham (2015)

12. Karlsson, F., Hedström, K., Goldkuhl, G.: Practice-based discourse analysis of information security policies. Comput. Secur. **67**, 267–279 (2017)

13. Stahl, B.C., Doherty, N.F., Shaw, M.: Information security policies in the UK healthcare sector: a critical evaluation. Inf. Syst. J. **22**, 77–94 (2012)

14. Rostami, E., Karlsson, F.: Qualitative content analysis of actionable advice in information security policies – introducing the keyword loss of specificity metric. Inf. Comput. Secur. **32**(4), 492–508 (2024)

15. ISO: ISO/IEC 27002:2022 Information Security, Cybersecurity and Privacy Protection—Information Security Controls. International Organization for Standardization (ISO) (2022)

16. Sundt, C.: Information security and the law. Inf. Secur. Tech. Rep. **11**(1), 2–9 (2006)

17. Trummer, I.: From bert to Gpt-3 codex: harnessing the potential of very large language models for data management. In: Proceedings of the VLDB Endowment, vol. 15, pp. 3770–3773. ACM (2022)

18. Abdullah, M., Madain, A., Jararweh, Y.: Chatgpt: fundamentals, applications and social impacts. In: 2022 Ninth International Conference on Social Networks Analysis, Management and Security. IEEE, Milan, Italy (2022)

19. Searle, J.R.: A Classification of illocutionary acts. Lang. Soc. **5**(1), 1–23 (1976)

20. Alshaikh, M., Maynard, S.B., Ahmad, A., Chang, S.: Information security policy: a management practice perspective. In: Australasian Conference on Information Systems (2015)

21. Goel, S., Chengalur-Smith, I.N.: Metrics for characterizing the form of security policies. J. Strat. Inf. Syst. **19**(4), 281–295 (2010)

22. Doherty, N., Fulford, H.: Aligning the information security policy with the strategic information systems plan. Comput. Secur. **25**(1), 55–63 (2006)

23. Rostami, E., Karlsson, F., Shang, G.: Policy components - a conceptual model for modularizing and tailoring of information security policies. Inf. Comput. Secur. **31**(3), 331–352 (2023)

24. Rostami, E., Karlsson, F., Gao, S.: Requirements for computerized tools to design information security policies. Comput. Secur. **99**, 102063 (2020)

25. Yun, L., Yun, S., Xue, H.: Improving citizen-government interactions with generative artificial intelligence: novel human-computer interaction strategies for policy understanding through large language models. PLoS ONE **19**(12), e0311410 (2024)
26. Lawal, S., Zhao, X., Rios, A., Krishnan, R., Ferraiolo, D.: Translating natural language specifications into access control policies by leveraging large language models. In: 2024 IEEE 6th International Conference on Trust, Privacy and Security in Intelligent Systems, and Applications (TPS-ISA), pp. 361–370. IEEE, Washington (2024)
27. Quevedo, E., et al.: Creation and analysis of a natural language understanding dataset for dod cybersecurity policies (Csiac-Dodin V1. 0). In: 2023 International Conference on Computational Science and Computational Intelligence (CSCI), pp. 91–98. IEEE, Las Vegas (2023)
28. Deldari, S., et al.: Auditnet: a conversational AI-based security assistant (2024)
29. Najafali, D., Camacho, J.M., Reiche, E., Galbraith, L.G., Morrison, S.D., Dorafshar, A.H.: Truth or lies? the pitfalls and limitations of chatgpt in systematic review creation. Aesthetic Surg. J. **43**(8), NP654–NP655 (2023)
30. Austin, J.L.: How to Do Things with Words. Oxford University Press, Cambridge (1962)
31. Searle, J.R.: Speech Acts: An Essay in the Philosophy of Language. Cambridge University Press, Cambridge (1969)
32. Searle, J.R., Vanderveken, D.: Speech acts and illocutionary logic. In: Vanderveken, D. (ed.) Logic, Thought and Action, pp. 109–132. Springer, Dordrecht (2005)
33. Searle, J.R.: Expression and Meaning: Studies in the Theory of Speech Acts. Cambridge University Press, Cambridge (1979)
34. Holtgraves, T.: The production and perception of implicit performatives. J. Pragmat. **37**(12), 2024–2043 (2005)
35. Gasparatou, R.: How to do things with words: speech acts in education. Educ. Philos. Theory **50**(5), 510–518 (2018)
36. Schmidt, J.V.: Can artificial agents be authors? Phil. Technol. **38**(1), 1–25 (2025)
37. Lindland, O.I., Sindre, G., Solvberg, A.: Understanding quality in conceptual modeling. IEEE Softw. **11**(2), 42–49 (1994)
38. Krogstie, J.: Model-Based Development and Evolution of Information Systems. Springer, London (2012)
39. Krogstie, J.: Quality in Business Process Modeling. Springer, Cham (2016)
40. Thalheim, B.: The science of conceptual modelling. In: Hameurlain, A., Liddle, S.W., Schewe, K.-D., Zhou, X. (eds.) Database and Expert Systems Applications - 22nd International Conference, Dexa 2011. Toulouse, France, 29 August–2 September 2011 Proceedings, Part I, pp. 12–26. Springer, Heidelberg (2011)
41. Bowen, G.A.: Document analysis as a qualitative research method. Qual. Res. J. **9**(2), 27–40 (2009)
42. Duffy, M.E.: Methodological triangulation: a vehicle for merging quantitative and qualitative research methods. Image: J. Nurs. Scholarship **19**(3), 130–133 (1987)

Function–Threat Alignment in CPS with FAST and MITRE ATT&CK

Vjatšeslav Antipenko$^{(\boxtimes)}$ and Raimundas Matulevičius

University of Tartu, Ülikooli 18, 50090 Tartu, Estonia
{vjatseslav.antipenko,rma}@ut.ee

Abstract. Cyber-physical systems (CPS) in industrial automation increasingly expose operational assets to cyber threats, yet existing security frameworks often fail to account for how functional behaviour, such as sensing, actuation, or parameter control, creates specific risk surfaces. This paper addresses that gap by applying the FAST framework (Functions, Assets, Security Threats, and Mitigation Techniques) to a robotic drilling scenario grounded in publicly documented ABB components. Building on the ISSRM model and Alter's taxonomy of functions, we align business and system assets with MITRE ATT&CK for ICS tactics to create a structured mapping between operational roles and threat behaviours. The analysis is framed using the RAMI 4.0 architecture and demonstrates how functionally driven threat modelling enhances traceability, reuse, and stakeholder communication. Our contribution is a replicable method for linking functional operations to adversarial tactics, providing a semantically grounded alternative to abstract risk modelling. The resulting artefact enables security practitioners and engineers to prioritise mitigations based on real asset behaviour, supporting scalable and context-aware defence planning.

Keywords: Cyber-Physical Systems · Industrial Automation · Threat Modelling · MITRE ATT&CK · FAST Framework · ISSRM · RAMI 4.0 · Industrial Robotics

1 Introduction

As industrial systems advance through digitalisation and automation, their increasing reliance on cyber-physical architectures introduces complex and evolving security challenges. While enhanced connectivity brings gains in flexibility and efficiency, it also exposes new threat surfaces that transcend traditional IT risk boundaries. In manufacturing environments where industrial robots, control systems, and sensor networks operate in tightly coupled processes, the impact of cyberattacks may include not only operational disruption but also physical damage and safety hazards [8,11,18].

While security standards such as ISO/IEC 27001 and the NIST Cybersecurity Framework are widely adopted and provide essential structural baselines for managing information security risks, their implementation and operational

© The Author(s), under exclusive license to Springer Nature Switzerland AG 2026
R. Denec**è**re et al. (Eds.): BIR 2025, LNBIP 562, pp. 365–379, 2026.
https://doi.org/10.1007/978-3-032-04375-7_23

upkeep often demand significant effort and long-term organisational investment [10, 15]. This burden can be particularly challenging in industrial contexts where systems are incrementally developed or scaled. Moreover, these frameworks typically remain abstract and offer limited guidance on how the routine functional behaviour of cyber-physical assets—such as sensing, actuation, or feedback control—can itself constitute a surface for adversarial exploitation [6, 9]. As a result, conventional risk modelling may overlook the inherent link between utility and vulnerability. In contrast, functionally grounded approaches offer the potential to defend as systems grow, enabling more context-aware, scalable, and progressively refined security models.

This paper addresses that gap by extending the FAST framework (Functions, Assets, Security Threats, and Mitigation Techniques) [4], a structured methodology for analysing security risks based on the operational functions of assets. Whereas the original FAST work considered enterprise-level contexts, this study zooms in on component-level analysis using a representative robotic drilling scenario. Our approach integrates the RAMI 4.0 reference architecture [7] to locate assets within the automation stack, and aligns their observable functional behaviours (based on Alter's taxonomy [3]) with adversarial tactics from the MITRE ATT&CK for ICS framework [13]. The core research question guiding this work is:

How can functional threat modelling support structured and context-aware security analysis in cyber-physical manufacturing environments?

To answer this, we adopt a design-oriented modelling approach grounded in the ISSRM framework [12], and apply it to a realistic industrial use case involving an ABB IRB 2400 robotic cell. We classify system and business assets, extract their operational functions, and systematically map them to attacker tactics and mitigation strategies. The results demonstrate how functional alignment enables interpretable, scalable, and reusable threat models tailored to cyber-physical environments.

The remainder of this paper is structured as follows: Sect. 2 introduces the foundational frameworks and modelling tools. Section 3 performs asset and function decomposition in the robotic drilling scenario. Section 4 applies FAST to generate function-tactic-threat mappings using MITRE ATT&CK. Section 5 discusses implications and future directions. Section 6 concludes the paper.

2   Background

This section introduces the foundational methods, models, and assumptions that underpin our work. At its core, this study builds upon the FAST framework [4], a structured methodology for linking functional operations in cyber-physical systems to security threats and treatments. While our original work applied FAST across the organisational context of a manufacturing enterprise, the present paper zooms in to examine cyber-physical exposure at the level of system components. The analysis is grounded in an industrially plausible scenario based on ABB's robotic drilling infrastructure.

2.1   The FAST Framework

The FAST approach—short for Functions, Assets, Security Threats, and Mitigation Techniques—offers a structured methodology for threat modelling in automated manufacturing systems. It proceeds in four stages:

1. Identifying business and system assets (based on the ISSRM framework [12]);
2. Decomposing those assets into functional operations (based on Alter's taxonomy [3]);
3. Aligning functional exposure with known threat tactics (as catalogued in MITRE ATT&CK for ICS [13]);
4. Selecting mitigation techniques grounded in known treatments.

FAST was originally developed to bridge the semantic and operational gap between functional design and security risk modelling. In this study, we extend FAST by applying it to a representative robotic drilling scenario, grounded in the architecture and behaviour of commercially available components. The modelling focuses on specific RAMI 4.0 hierarchy levels and is substantiated using empirical data from vendor documentation [1,2,5] and published experimental studies [16].

Functional Semantics: Alter's Information Functions. To articulate the operational exposure of assets, we rely on Alter's six fundamental information functions [3]: *capturing, storing, retrieving, manipulating, transmitting,* and *displaying*. These functions represent the ways in which cyber-physical systems process and interact with information. In the context of security analysis, they serve as both a lens for system utility and a proxy for potential vulnerability: every function an asset performs opens a corresponding surface for adversarial exploitation.

Security Risk Management Foundations. The Information System Security Risk Management (ISSRM) model [12] provides a formal structure for classifying assets, risks, and countermeasures. Assets are categorised as either:

– **Business Assets**: Information entities essential for operational or strategic success, such as sensor readings, control configurations, or process thresholds.
– **System Assets**: Technical components that support business assets, such as robot arms, controllers, sensors, and software.

ISSRM defines threats as events in which adversaries exploit vulnerabilities to compromise asset confidentiality, integrity, or availability. Treatment strategies are categorised into avoidance, reduction, transfer, or acceptance, with our focus here placed on *risk reduction* via proactive mitigation design.

Security Threats and Treatments via MITRE ATT&CK. In our previous work, we modelled threats using categories from STRIDE [17] and scenarios identified in the academic literature. In this study, we adopt the MITRE

ATT&CK for ICS framework [13] as a structured, empirical source of adversarial behaviour. ATT&CK describes attacker objectives as *tactics* (e.g., Initial Access, Impact), each implemented through specific *techniques* and *procedures*. This approach offers three advantages:

- It provides a publicly maintained vocabulary aligned with real-world ICS threats;
- It allows functional alignment between asset capabilities (via Alter) and adversarial tactics (via ATT&CK);
- It facilitates reuse of curated mitigations for known threats.

Our hypothesis is that ATT&CK's empirical grounding and tactic-based structure make it particularly suitable for adaptation into the FAST framework—enabling practical threat modelling without requiring exhaustive attacker profiling.

2.2   Reference Architectural Model Industrie 4.0 (RAMI 4.0)

The RAMI 4.0 reference architecture [7] provides a three-dimensional framework for structuring industrial systems across functional layers, lifecycle stages, and hierarchy levels. It supports consistent integration of operational technologies, information flows, and assets throughout the automation stack.

In our original FAST study, RAMI served as a foundation for positioning assets within enterprise-wide contexts. Here, we continue its use at a more granular level to contextualise asset behaviour and system exposure. Our focus is primarily on:

- The **Asset Layer**, which includes physical components such as actuators and controllers; and
- The **Hierarchy Levels** axis, with specific attention to *Field Device* and *Control Device* tiers.

This allows us to locate threats and functional operations within concrete system strata, rather than abstract classifications.

ABB Robots and Control Architecture. We instantiate the RAMI model using a representative robotic drilling setup based on ABB's IRB 2400 industrial robot and its associated control infrastructure. These components are described in publicly available technical documentation, allowing for detailed modelling without reliance on proprietary knowledge.

- **IRB 2400**: A 6-axis articulated robot widely used in machining and material handling, with integrated position feedback and external sensor support [1].
- **ATI Delta 330–30**: A high-precision 6-axis force/torque sensor mounted at the robot flange, enabling feedback-driven control [5].
- **IRC5 Controller**: ABB's modular controller executing RAPID logic, managing I/O, and coordinating control across components via the RobotWare OS [2].

This technical infrastructure serves as the operational basis for the analysis in Sects. 3 and 4, ensuring fidelity to real-world system constraints while maintaining reproducibility.

3   Functional-Attack Alignment and Asset Analysis

This section presents a structured decomposition of assets, operations, and threats in a robotic drilling use case, with security risks classified using the ISSRM framework. The analysis models an industrially plausible scenario based on the ABB IRB 2400 platform, drawing from publicly documented configurations and prior experimental studies [16]. We aim to ground abstract risk modelling in concrete cyber-physical system (CPS) operations by mapping asset-level functions to adversarial tactics. This reveals how the utility of each asset inherently shapes its vulnerability surface.

3.1   Threat Classification Mapping

To support structured threat identification, we adopt the MITRE ATT&CK Matrix for Industrial Control Systems (ICS) as a controlled vocabulary of adversarial tactics. This tactic-based model structures malicious behaviours into conceptual categories (e.g., Initial Access, Persistence, Impact), allowing security analysts to articulate threat scenarios without requiring exhaustive technical specificity.

Our contribution lies in aligning these tactics with Alter's six fundamental information functions—*capturing, storing, retrieving, manipulating, transmitting,* and *displaying* [3]. By exposing which functions each business or system asset performs, we make it possible to reason about risk as a consequence of utility: the same functional operations that enable cyber-physical systems to behave intelligently also serve as the surface for adversarial exploitation. This alignment serves three goals:

- It anchors risk analysis in concrete functional behaviours that are observable and modelled in engineering terms;
- It enables forward inference of possible threats from asset capabilities, rather than relying only on attacker-centric speculation;
- It supports the reuse and scalability of threat scenarios across similar systems that share functional patterns.

The mapping in Table 1 therefore establishes a semantic bridge between business-relevant CPS behaviour and the structured adversarial model defined in MITRE ATT&CK.

Table 1. Mapping Alter functions to MITRE ATT&CK tactics.

Aligned Alter Function(s)	MITRE ATT&CK Tactic	Description
Capturing, Transmitting	Initial Access	Techniques for gaining a foothold in ICS systems via assets like sensors, interfaces, or user input
Manipulating, Transmitting	Execution	Running unauthorised code, commands, or changing system modes
Storing, Retrieving	Persistence	Modifying files or configurations to maintain presence in ICS systems
Manipulating, Storing	Privilege Escalation	Gaining higher-level access by exploiting system weaknesses
Manipulating	Evasion	Hiding activity or obfuscating system states to bypass detection
Capturing	Discovery	Gathering information on devices, logic, or network configuration
Transmitting	Lateral Movement	Pivoting to other systems or devices within the ICS network
Capturing, Storing	Collection	Gathering process state, data from sensors, configurations, or execution traces
Manipulating, Transmitting	Command and Control	Issuing external commands to compromised systems or relaying information to attacker infrastructure
Manipulating	Inhibit Response Function	Disabling safety mechanisms, alarms, or emergency stops
Manipulating	Impair Process Control	Interfering with physical operations, altering thresholds, or causing process deviation
Any (esp. Displaying, Transmitting)	Impact	Damaging system functionality, data, or physical infrastructure

3.2   Asset Identification

In this section, we apply the foundational models presented earlier to structure the robotic drilling use case. RAMI 4.0 guides the decomposition of system functions and their placement within a digital manufacturing hierarchy. RAMI 4.0, which structures industrial systems across architectural layers and hierarchy levels [7], is used here to contextualise each asset's role in the automation stack. ISSRM, in turn, supports the classification of assets and the associated security risks. By combining these perspectives, we provide a structured basis for aligning cyber-physical operations with threat modelling activities introduced later in the paper.

System Assets. The system asset inventory identifies and classifies the core physical and digital components that comprise the robotic drilling environment. Each component is placed within the RAMI 4.0 hierarchy [7], providing architectural clarity on its location and function in the automation stack. This classification aids in pinpointing potential exposure points and supports alignment with operational and cybersecurity standards.

By mapping assets to RAMI levels and describing their operational roles, we provide the structural foundation necessary for threat modelling and asset-function linkage in the next stage of analysis (Tables 2 and 3).

Table 2. System assets in the robotic drilling setup.

System Asset	RAMI Hierarchy Level	Role
ABB IRB 2400	Field Device	Executes physical movements; contains internal sensors (resolvers, revolution counters) for joint position and velocity feedback [1]
ATI Delta 330–30	Field Device (external)	Captures 6-axis force/torque data at the robot flange, used for feedback control [5]
PDS XLC-070 Spindle	Field Device (effector)	Performs the physical drilling operation under motion and feedback control
IRC5 Controller	Control Device	Executes RAPID logic, processes sensor inputs, stores configurations, and coordinates actuation. Manages RobotWare OS and serves as the data-processing hub [2]
FlexPendant	Control Device (HMI)	Enables manual interaction with control logic, diagnostics, and operational monitoring
RobotStudio	Control Device (engineering)	Simulates and deploys robot programs; modifies parameters and tests logic

Business Assets. Business assets represent the informational entities that hold operational, strategic, or safety value to the organisation [12]. Unlike physical components, these assets exist through their interaction with system assets: they are generated, transformed, and interpreted through system activity.

We enumerate these assets to make explicit what is at stake, and how functional operations (per Alter) expose them to potential threat vectors. This categorisation enables targeted protection strategies aligned with both technical feasibility and business relevance.

3.3   Assumptions and Supporting Sources

This analysis is grounded in documentation from ABB Robotics, including the product manual for the IRB 2400 [1] and the IRC5 controller specifications [2], as well as experimental details from Rosa et al. [16]. Specifications for the ATI Delta 330–30 sensor are inferred from Net F/T integration documentation [5]. Where implementation details are unavailable, assumptions are guided by industrial control best practices:

Table 3. Business assets and their exposed functions.

Business Asset	Description	Source/Location	Exposed Functions (Alter)
Force/Torque Measurement Data	Real-time 6-axis data from end-effector sensor	ATI Delta 330–30	Capturing, Transmitting, Manipulating, Displaying
Robot Joint Position Data	Joint angles and velocity feedback from internal encoders	ABB IRB 2400	Capturing, Transmitting, Manipulating, Displaying
Tool Path Configuration	Coordinates and trajectories encoded in RAPID programs	IRC5/RobotStudio	Storing, Retrieving, Manipulating, Displaying
Drilling Force Thresholds	Predefined acceptable limits for thrust control	IRC5/RAPID logic	Storing, Retrieving, Manipulating, Displaying
Robot Program Logic	Instruction sequences encoded in RAPID for motion and control	IRC5 memory	Storing, Manipulating, Retrieving, Displaying
Sensor Calibration Offsets	Calibration values to correct raw sensor readings	IRC5 or manual input	Storing, Retrieving, Manipulating
System Diagnostic Logs	Logs, messages, and runtime warnings for operational transparency	IRC5/FlexPendant	Capturing, Storing, Displaying, Retrieving
User Interaction Commands	Manual operator inputs (e.g., start, stop, override)	FlexPendant/ RobotStudio	Capturing, Manipulating, Displaying, Transmitting
Controller Configuration	System-wide settings including I/O mappings and network roles	IRC5	Storing, Manipulating, Retrieving, Displaying

- Joint position sensing is performed internally and transmitted to the controller via the Serial Measurement Board (SMB).
- The IRC5 manages sensor I/O, program execution, calibration storage, and network configuration.
- External force/torque data is accessed using Ethernet-based Net F/T protocols and processed by the IRC5.
- User interaction occurs through the FlexPendant for live operation and RobotStudio for simulation and offline editing.

These operational insights ensure the analytical results reflect a realistic industrial setting, even in the absence of exhaustive implementation details.

4   Threat Modelling Through FAST

This section applies the FAST framework [4] to model threats in a cyber-physical manufacturing scenario, aligning asset-level functionality with structured adversarial knowledge. Building on the asset-function decomposition presented in

Sect. 3, each business asset is analysed through the lens of its operational function (based on Alter's taxonomy [3]), mapped to a corresponding tactic from the MITRE ATT&CK for ICS matrix [13], and paired with plausible threat techniques and recommended mitigations [14]. This approach grounds threat identification in observable system behaviour, supporting structured, transparent, and reproducible security modelling for industrial environments.

4.1   Threat Mapping Table

Table 4 synthesises the core logic of the FAST methodology by tracing a structured path from business assets to security responses. Each row identifies a business asset, the supporting system asset, and the relevant functional operation; these are then aligned with MITRE-classified tactics, associated threat techniques, and mitigation strategies from the ICS domain. This representation allows traceability from operational exposure to adversarial intent and treatment options, facilitating both technical and managerial engagement.

It is important to note that the mappings presented here are illustrative rather than exhaustive. The threats and mitigations have been selected to reflect

Table 4. Threat modelling through functional alignment of business assets.

Business Asset	System Asset	MITRE Asset	Function (ALTER)	MITRE Tactic	Threat (MITRE ICS)	Mitigation (MITRE ICS)
Force/Torque Data	ATI Delta 330–30	Field I/O	Capturing	Collection	Adversary-in-the-Middle	M0802 – Communication Authenticity
Joint Position Data	IRC5	PLC	Manipulating	Impair Process Control	Modify Parameter	M0818 – Validate Program Inputs
Tool Path Configuration	IRC5/RobotStudio	PLC	Storing	Persistence	Module Firmware	M0945 – Code Signing
Drilling Force Thresholds	IRC5	PLC	Retrieving	Persistence	Valid Accounts	M0918 – User Account Management
Robot Program Logic	FlexPendant	HMI	Displaying	Evasion	Masquerading	M0945 – Code Signing
Sensor Calibration Offsets	IRC5	PLC	Storing	Persistence	Modify Program	M0800 – Authorisation Enforcement
System Diagnostic Logs	IRC5	Data Historian	Capturing	Collection	Data from Information Repositories	M0941 – Encrypt Sensitive Information
User Interaction Commands	FlexPendant/IRC5	PLC	Transmitting	Command and Control	Standard Application Layer Protocol	M0807 – Network Allowlists
Controller Configuration	IRC5	PLC	Manipulating	Privilege Escalation	Exploitation for Privilege Escalation	M0951 – Update Software

realistic adversarial scenarios while demonstrating the application of FAST in a focused, component-level context. This scope enables us to maintain analytical rigour while avoiding unnecessary duplication or speculative generalisation.

This threat modelling exercise demonstrates how the FAST framework can be used to reason about security exposure based on what each asset *does*, rather than merely what it *is*. By treating system functions as both enablers of utility and potential vectors of vulnerability, this method enables more focused and verifiable threat analysis than is often achievable with abstract, attacker-centric models.

The integration of MITRE ATT&CK enhances the interpretability and alignment of the model with existing security operations practices. Practitioners are able to trace adversarial intent back to functionally exposed business assets and forward to specific mitigations, creating a feedback loop between operational engineering and security governance. This shared vocabulary supports informed dialogue across stakeholder groups and helps embed security considerations into the design and refinement of industrial systems.

To further illustrate the analytical structure and practical value of this approach, we now present two representative threat scenarios derived from the mapping table. Each scenario highlights a specific function and its associated risk, demonstrating how functional roles create concrete exposure pathways and how structured mitigation guidance can be applied.

4.2 Adversary-in-the-Middle (MITRE: Collection)

This scenario represents a classic **Collection** tactic as defined by MITRE ATT&CK ICS [13], specifically the *Adversary-in-the-Middle* technique. The threat occurs when an attacker intercepts field-level sensor communications, potentially altering or exfiltrating operational data in transit. In this case:

- The **function** being exploited is *Capturing*;
- The **business asset** is *Force/Torque Measurement Data*;
- The **system asset** is an *ATI Delta 330–30* sensor [5];
- The **MITRE asset** is categorised as *Field I/O*.

Such attacks exploit vulnerabilities in communication protocols between the sensor and the controller (e.g., PLC). Without cryptographic protection, spoofed or manipulated packets can feed false data into automation routines, leading to inaccurate processing or misinformed decisions.

The recommended mitigation is **M0802 – Communication Authenticity**, which ensures that messages are cryptographically signed or authenticated before being accepted by control logic. An instance of this attack is summarised in Table 5.

4.3 Modify Parameter (MITRE: Impair Process Control)

This scenario illustrates the **Impair Process Control** tactic via the *Modify Parameter* technique. The attacker manipulates control logic parameters, such

Table 5. Instance of Adversary-in-the-Middle attack.

Aspect	Details
Business Asset	Force/Torque Measurement Data
System Asset	ATI Delta 330–30
MITRE Asset	Field I/O
Function (ALTER)	Capturing
MITRE Tactic	Collection
Threat (MITRE ICS)	Adversary-in-the-Middle
Risk	Interception and manipulation of sensor data
Impact	Loss of data integrity, incorrect control decisions
Vulnerability	Unauthenticated communication protocols
Mitigation (MITRE ICS)	M0802 – Communication Authenticity
Controls	Sign messages, authenticate endpoints, validate sensor data at the controller

as motion limits, PID tuning constants, or process thresholds, within a controller to cause functional degradation or unsafe operations. Here:

– The **function** under threat is *Manipulating*;
– The **business asset** is *Robot Joint Position Data*;
– The **system asset** is the *IRC5 controller* [2];
– The **MITRE asset** is categorised as a *PLC*.

An adversary, having gained logical access to the controller or engineering workstation, can alter parameter values directly or inject them via trusted channels. These subtle changes may not trigger alarms but can degrade product quality or create mechanical stress.

The appropriate mitigation is **M0818 – Validate Program Inputs**, which enforces logic-level checks on parameter updates, ensures values are within operational bounds, and provides fallback constraints. Table 6 summarises an instance of this attack and the corresponding mitigation strategy.

Table 6. Instance of Modify Parameter attack.

Aspect	Details
Business Asset	Robot Joint Position Data
System Asset	IRC5 Controller
MITRE Asset	PLC
Function (ALTER)	Manipulating
MITRE Tactic	Impair Process Control
Threat (MITRE ICS)	Modify Parameter
Risk	Subtle deviation of operational behaviour
Impact	Product degradation, mechanical wear, safety compromise
Vulnerability	Unchecked or unvalidated parameter updates
Mitigation (MITRE ICS)	M0818 – Validate Program Inputs
Controls	Range checking, fallback defaults, validation logic at runtime

5   Discussion

This work demonstrates how function-oriented threat modelling can be practically and meaningfully applied to cyber-physical systems using empirically grounded and semantically structured techniques. By extending the FAST framework to a representative robotic drilling setup—and aligning assets, functions, and threat behaviours with the RAMI 4.0 hierarchy and MITRE ATT&CK ICS matrix—we show that even complex industrial configurations can be systematically decomposed into analysable risk units that are both interpretable and actionable.

The contribution holds relevance for a range of stakeholders. Industrial security practitioners can use the presented approach to anchor threat identification in concrete system functions, moving beyond abstract vulnerability enumeration. System engineers benefit from the structural clarity offered by functional decomposition, enabling early design-phase reflection on how operational behaviours expose security surfaces. Researchers and educators may adopt the modelling pipeline as a replicable, transparent method for exploring cyber-physical security from a systems perspective.

A key enabler of this alignment is Alter's functional model—comprising *capturing, storing, retrieving, manipulating, transmitting,* and *displaying*—which serves as both an analytical anchor and a semantic bridge between physical operations and adversarial intent. This function-based abstraction allows us to reason about vulnerability not as an external artefact, but as a by-product of system utility: each function that enables automation also defines a vector for potential exploitation. By aligning these functional roles with MITRE-defined tactics, the framework enables forward inference from capabilities to threat categories and controls.

In practice, this enables more precise mitigation planning. As shown in Sect. 4, the resulting mappings make visible the relationship between technical configurations and security consequences. Rather than distributing defences indiscriminately across the system landscape, stakeholders can prioritise hardening efforts based on specific functional exposures, making risk treatment more focused, scalable, and business-aligned.

Nonetheless, there are clear limitations. This study is bound to a single use case—a robotic drilling task involving specific ABB components. While representative, this does not capture the heterogeneity of industrial automation contexts. Moreover, the threat scenarios were analytically modelled, not tested through penetration testing or live adversary simulation. Further empirical validation through testbeds or red teaming would help assess the operational realism of the proposed mappings.

Our analysis also assumes stable system configurations and typical component behaviours. In practice, firmware differences, bespoke integration logic, and undocumented process flows may significantly alter the threat surface. These implementation-specific factors warrant further investigation.

Additionally, while the MITRE ATT&CK for ICS matrix is a valuable and growing resource, it still underrepresents certain categories of operational technology threats—particularly timing-based manipulations, control-layer logic sabotage, and multi-stage physical process attacks. The modelling could be extended by incorporating complementary taxonomies such as CAPEC or domain-specific threat libraries from IEC 62443 or STPA-Sec.

Lastly, our focus on field and control levels within the RAMI 4.0 hierarchy is both a strength and a constraint. The granularity supports precision but introduces modelling overhead, and without standardised templates or tool support, the method may face scalability challenges. However, by identifying repeatable asset-function-threat patterns, we lay the foundation for future tooling, templating, and automation of FAST-based analysis.

Ultimately, this study offers a structured, traceable, and semantically rich method for analysing threats in industrial environments. Its primary value lies not in offering a complete defence model, but in demonstrating how threat intelligence can be anchored in what systems actually do, providing a defensible, explainable, and operationally grounded path to cybersecurity maturity.

6   Conclusion

This paper presented a function-driven approach to threat modelling in industrial automation, extending the FAST framework with a focused application to a robotic drilling scenario involving ABB hardware. By grounding the analysis in the RAMI 4.0 reference architecture and aligning asset-level functions with tactics from the MITRE ATT&CK for ICS matrix, we demonstrated how operational behaviours can be translated into credible, traceable threat scenarios. The use of Alter's functional taxonomy enabled semantically meaningful mappings between asset utility and adversarial exposure, resulting in an interpretable and reusable artefact for security risk analysis.

While the work confirms the feasibility of applying functionally grounded threat modelling at the component level, its generalisability remains constrained. Our analysis relies on manufacturer documentation and prior research, not live system experimentation. Moreover, the threat coverage is bounded by the current scope of MITRE ATT&CK for ICS, which, though robust, does not yet fully capture all OT-specific attack paths—particularly those involving advanced control-layer manipulation.

Future work will extend the application of FAST across additional RAMI 4.0 hierarchy levels, such as Station and Work Centres, to examine how threat exposure scales across more complex system assemblies and interdependent subsystems. In parallel, empirical validation through testbed implementation, industry case studies, and expert workshops will support refinement of threat mappings and further enhance the practical applicability of FAST to real-world operational environments.

Acknowledgments. The European Union funds this research under Grant Agreement No. 101087529. Views and opinions expressed are those of the author(s) only and do not necessarily reflect those of the European Union or European Research Executive Agency. Neither the European Union nor the granting authority can be held responsible.

References

1. ABB robotics: product manual – IRB 2400. ABB (2024), https://new. abb.com/products/robotics/robots/articulated-robots/irb-2400, document ID: 3HAC022031-001, Revision: W
2. ABB robotics: product specification – controller IRC5. ABB (2025), https:// new.abb.com/products/robotics/controllers/irc5-overview/irc5, document ID: 3HAC047400-001, Revision: AL
3. Alter, S.: The work system method: connecting people, Processes, and IT for business results. work system method (2006)
4. Antipenko, V., Matulevičius, R.: Functional security in automation: the fast approach. In: Paja, E., Zdravkovic, J., Kavakli, E., Stirna, J. (eds.) The Practice of Enterprise Modeling, pp. 244–261. Springer, Cham (2025)
5. ATI industrial automation: net F/T sensor system – user's manual for the ATI delta 330–30. ATI (nd), https://www.ati-ia.com/products/ft/ft_models.aspx?id=delta, accessed technical documentation for Delta 330–30 model
6. Cherdantseva, Y., et al.: A review of cyber security risk assessment methods for scada systems. Comput. Secur. **56**, 1–27 (2016). https://doi.org/10.1016/j.cose. 2015.09.009
7. Schweichhart, K., Dr. et al: Reference architectural model industrie 4.0 (RAMI 4.0) (2016), https://ec.europa.eu/futurium/en/system/files/ged/a2-schweichhart-reference_architectural_model_industrie_4.0_rami_4.0.pdf
8. European union agency for cybersecurity (ENISA): ENISA threat landscape 2024. https://www.enisa.europa.eu/publications/enisa-threat-landscape-2024 Accessed 07 Oct 2024 (2024)

9. Humayed, A., Lin, J., Li, F., Luo, B.: Cyber-physical systems security–a survey. IEEE Internet Things J. **4**(6), 1802–1831 (2017). https://doi.org/10.1109/JIOT. 2017.2703172
10. International organization for standardization: ISO/IEC 27001:2013 information technology – security techniques – information security management systems – requirements. https://www.iso.org/standard/54534.html (2013), https://www.iso. org/standard/54534.html
11. Lee, E.A.: Cyber physical systems: Design challenges. In: 2008 11th IEEE International Symposium on Object and Component-Oriented Real-Time Distributed Computing (ISORC), pp. 363–369 (2008).https://doi.org/10.1109/ISORC.2008.25
12. Matulevičius, R.: Fundamentals of secure system modelling. Springer (2017)
13. MITRE corporation: MITRE ATT&CK for industrial control systems (ICS). https://attack.mitre.org/matrices/ics/ (2025), Accessed 13 May 2025
14. MITRE corporation: MITRE ATT&CK Framework. https://attack.mitre.org/ (2025), Accessed 13 May 2025
15. NIST, National institute of standards and technology: NIST cybersecurity framework. https://www.nist.gov/cyberframework Accessed 15 Apr 2024 (2024), https://www.nist.gov/cyberframework
16. Rosa, D.G.G., Feiteira, J.F.S., Lopes, A.M., de Abreu, P.A.F.: Analysis and implementation of a force control strategy for drilling operations with an industrial robot. J. Braz. Soc. Mech. Sci. Eng. **39**(11), 4749–4756 (2017). https://doi.org/10.1007/ s40430-017-0913-7
17. Shostack, A.: Threat Modeling: Designing for Security. Wiley (2014)
18. Yu, Z., Gao, H., Cong, X., Wu, N., Song, H.H.: A survey on cyber-physical systems security. IEEE Internet Things J. **10**(24), 21670–21686 (2023). https://doi.org/10. 1109/JIOT.2023.3289625

Author Index

© The Editor(s) (if applicable) and The Author(s), under exclusive license
to Springer Nature Switzerland AG 2026
R. Deneckère et al. (Eds.): BIR 2025, LNBIP 562, pp. 381–382, 2026.
https://doi.org/10.1007/978-3-032-04375-7

The manufacturer's authorised representative in the EU is Springer
Nature Customer Service Centre GmbH, Europaplatz 3, 69115 Heidelberg,
Germany. If you have any concerns regarding our products, please
contact ProductSafety@springernature.com

Printed and bound by CPI Group (UK) Ltd, Croydon, CR0 4YY

28/04/2026

02098526-0001